ARTHUR J MARDER was a   ,
teacher and writer who, born in 1910, was to become
perhaps the most distinguished historian of the modern
Royal Navy. He held a number of teaching posts in
American universities and was to receive countless
honours, as well as publish some fifteen major works on
British naval history. He died in 1980.

BARRY GOUGH, the distinguished Canadian maritime
and naval historian, is the author of *Historical Dreadnoughts:
Arthur Marder, Stephen Roskill and the Battles for Naval History*,
recently published by Seaforth Publishing.

ADMIRAL SIR DAVID BEATTY

Commander in Chief, Grand Fleet, 1916–19

Portrait by Sir Arthur Cope : National Maritime Museum

FROM THE
DREADNOUGHT
TO
SCAPA FLOW

The Royal Navy in the Fisher Era 1904–1919

VOLUME V
VICTORY AND AFTERMATH: JANUARY 1918–JUNE 1919

ARTHUR J MARDER
INTRODUCTION BY BARRY GOUGH

Naval Institute Press

Annapolis

Seaforth
PUBLISHING

THE MAPS
Large-scale versions of the maps located at the back
can be downloaded from the book's page
on the publishers' websites.

Copyright © Arthur J Marder 1970
Introduction copyright © Barry Gough 2014

This edition first published in Great Britain in 2014 by
Seaforth Publishing,
Pen & Sword Books Ltd,
47 Church Street,
Barnsley S70 2AS

www.seaforthpublishing.com

Published and distributed in the
United States of America and Canada by the
Naval Institute Press,
291 Wood Road, Annapolis,
Maryland 21402-5034

www.nip.org

British Library Cataloguing in Publication Data
A catalogue record for this book is available from the British Library

Library of Congress Control Number: 2013937405

ISBN 978 1 84832 203 5

Printed and bound in Great Britain by CPI Group (UK) Ltd, Croydon, CR0 4YY

Introduction

WHEN ARTHUR MARDER came to write the fifth and concluding instalment of *From the Dreadnought to Scapa Flow*, he faced a number of challenges. By that time so many books on the subject of the naval history of the First World War had come to breezy, even flattering, conclusions that helped to sustain the mystique of the Royal Navy. Marder's analytical propensities could not countenance a similar perspective. To date he had examined the great Anglo-German naval race and the lead up to the War in 1914. Then, he had probed the complications of the *Goeben* and *Breslau*'s escape to Istanbul and described the faltering purposes of the naval and military campaign to seize the Dardanelles and Gallipoli. Moreover, giving the most convincing account of what went wrong at Jutland while the British nevertheless retained command of the sea had been no mean feat. And getting to the root of the 'crisis of the naval war,' the U-boat peril and the prodigious loss of Allied shipping before convoy was instituted, had been an historical triumph. Many a writer in the historical line had tackled these, and related, subjects before. In his previous instalments, Marder, by contrast, had linked them, one after another, in one remarkable epic narrative. He could see the larger and far horizons. Each of the smaller perspectives seemed to meld into the larger view. Without the use of purple prose, but with the employment of the most sober judgments, he had taken his grand theme and brought it to its penultimate state or phase.

Yet the problem, or problems, remained: how to draw all the strands together, and how to make sense of the whole. Marder might well have taken the easy route and avoided the burning issues. He faced many a difficulty, and not the least of these was that from the naval standpoint the war at sea finished with a whimper rather than a bang.

There are other reasons why winding up the epic posed difficulties for Marder. The first of these was largely of his own making. Not only had his indulgent publisher already stretched out the pages in print to unimaginable length. We need reminding here that the book was originally planned as one large volume; then it became two. Before long a third and then a fourth volume appeared, and truth to tell Volume IV was to have been the final volume. However, enough material existed that it was split in two: thus a fifth volume could be published. Given the universally glowing reviews of all the volumes to date, the publisher had no difficulty in granting the fifth and final volume. Marder was thus under no duress to write a short conclusion. As before, he grasped the advantage accorded to him by his publisher.

In addition, Marder still had many loose ends to tie up. These included the following, in general chronological form: a new order had come to the Admiralty at the beginning of 1918; the *Goeben* (ever a thorn in the British side) had sortied but the British naval units in the eastern Mediterranean could not end the career of this trouble-maker; in the Black Sea the Italians proved obstructionist to British aims; and barrage operations were instituted in the Adriatic. Meanwhile, on the broader seas, the convoy system had brought due rewards at last and helped bring Germany to the peace table; the US Navy had arrived in force in European waters; the Dover Strait barrage and the problematic raids on Zeebrugge and Ostend needed to be described and discussed as did the Northern barrage, to close a gap eastward of the Orkneys. Of all these subcomponents of the British and Allied war at sea that of 'beating the U-boats' was the most critical (worthy of five chapters) to which needed to be added discussion of the Queenstown Command – essentially US naval units under British command – and how the US battle squadron would be integrated into the Grand Fleet, given there were US Navy Department-Admiralty differences. Many another difficulty had presented itself, and the Naval Staff searched for offensive possibilities without success. At last came the Armistice.

In November 1918 Admiral Sir David Beatty received the surrender of the German fleet under terms of the Armistice. How was this painful episode (with British naval frustrations boiling beneath the surface) to be told? And if that were not all, for eight frustrating months many quarrels in Paris had ensued before the Peace Treaty was signed in June 1919. The naval settlement with Germany needed addressing, as did the differences of opinion and policy between the Admiralty and the US Naval Department. A bibliography, comprehensive of the whole work, had to be included. A retrospective on the performance of the Royal Navy – more particularly its admirals – needed to be made. Put differently, this final volume was not just a tidying up of various points and loose ends: it was intended to be the grand finale of the whole events of the Fisher era, dating back to the years when the reform-minded Jacky Fisher had come to the Admiralty as First Sea Lord in 1904.

Of a lesser difficulty was the intemperate demand made in private correspondence by Captain Stephen Roskill, author of the official *War at Sea*, that Marder halt his book with year-end 1918. That was when, so Roskill announced peremptorily, his own intended two-volume work *Naval Policy Between the Wars*, intended to pick up the story. Perhaps the matter would have passed without public comment. Here, for our understanding, the timing is critical: Volume I of Roskill's book appeared in 1968 while Volume V of *From the Dreadnought to Scapa Flow* was still in the making (it came into print in 1970). Marder, perhaps foolishly and certainly in forthright fashion, wrote this of Roskill's initial offering (below, p393): 'Badly organized and something of a jungle of facts in places, yet an indispensable work for its extensive use of British and American source material and its shrewd judgments. The Armistice period is dealt with in the first seven chapters, *passim.*' Any slur on Roskill's fine reputation as an historian, made after all that Roskill had done for Marder in the working up of his volumes II, III and IV, was bound to make sparks. Roskill was easily offended. The quarrel between the two became the subject of high drama and reached the pages of the press. Hidden deep in the background (and unknown to the public at the time) was a spat between the historian-gladiators concerning the use of Colonel Maurice Hankey's diaries. In this Marder had been disadvantaged, for Hankey's son, in error, had given Roskill exclusive use of the diaries. From this time forward the quarrel had continued in the pages of the *Times Literary Supplement*, in footnotes of respective works, even in appendixes. The details are found in my *Historical Dreadnoughts: Arthur Marder, Stephen Roskill and Battles for Naval History* (Seaforth, 2010), and they need no further recapitulation here. Volume V disclosed the first public indication of a quarrel previously unknown in naval history circles, though in English and American university circles such 'spats' were more common then than nowadays. Roskill had also told Marder privately that he thought Marder was rather allowing the subject to grow beyond its dimensions, in other words that he was giving greater length to the topics when he should be winding them up. Marder would not like to have been charged with 'exceeding his remit,' and he carried on, riding his own star.

Yet another matter called Marder to an enlarged finale. His publisher wanted him to give the finale full weight and treatment. 'The higher direction of naval affairs in the concluding months of the War and during the Armistice, the personalities involved, the state of inter-allied relations, and the dawn of postwar problems. . . concluding with a retrospective of the whole period,' as the publisher's description at the time proclaimed handsomely, needed to be treated 'with all Professor Marder's authority and skill.' Marder did not disappoint.

In the concluding segment of Volume V, 'Reflections on an Era,' Marder returned to the task of the anatomist. He had concluded, and here he restated the fact, that the influence of sea power had brought the War to a successful conclusion for the Allies. This was in keeping with the Admiralty's intentions. In a 1917 document the Admiralty had drawn up a list of the 'ultimate objects' of British naval policy. These may be listed: 1. protecting the sea communications of the Allied armies, 2. preventing enemy trade thereby handicapping his military operations and similarly exerting pressure on the mass of his people, 3. protecting British and Allied trade, essential to the supply of munitions and foodstuffs to Allied armies and peoples, and 4. providing resistance to invasion and raids. Far from these being the 'sharp end' of war so urgently expected by the public and press, this formed the slow and steady work of a dominant power at sea. The Trafalgars of naval history were few and far between, Marder knew. Even so, the course of the naval war had shown many faults in British naval practice. Conservatism in strategy had a parallel in conservatism in tactics, and this led to centralisation in command. Taking the initiative was frowned upon. Naval aviation was slow to develop. The cult of the battleship continued. The submarine in enemy hands posed a danger not yet fully realised through experience, and mines and minesweeping had unforeseen dangers. When Jellicoe's *The Grand Fleet* appeared in 1919, disclosure of the inadequacies of the technical and materiel means of fighting a new war at sea provided a great shock. The fact of the matter was that the nature of technological change was outstripping the means of countering the same. Thus ASW was in its infancy, and all sorts of hair-brained schemes were tried to defeat the U-boat. Convoy proved to be the only workable solution in the end. The unity of the air command was always in doubt. Naval planning was uncertain; communications between departments in the Admiralty was appallingly bad; sea-officers were not listened to in Whitehall; frustration reigned. Naval education was in short supply, and history was not read for any applicable value for the present. Marder turned to admirals, their types and their qualities.

Some were brilliant, most mediocre. Character, leadership, and unlimited physical and moral courage existed among the top commanders. But mastery of strategy, an understanding of the nature of war, and problem-solving were sadly absent. It is true that excessive centralisation dominated naval methods of command. The man on the spot, who ought to have been trusted, was curtailed. The Admiralty's detailed orders deterred innovation and invention at the sharp end.

Marder always liked to discuss the human factor as a source of strength or weakness. This proved a good topic for his conclusion. He found in British naval officers and men an admirable force. Against them he contrasted the Germans. Marder liked to think that British naval tradition had been a factor in the decisive outcome, and it is hard to quarrel with this perspective. But the aspects of the British naval tradition that he displays show many examples of lack of judgement, failure to take risk, absence of teamwork, poor inter-service cooperation, and much more. He never could leave his hero Jacky Fisher to the fates of history. Rather, in winding up his book, this Volume V, he reasserted his argument that Fisher's name would live forevermore.

* * *

From our perspective nearly half a century later when we continue to evaluate British naval strategic thinking in the years up to the opening of the War, when we seek to match intended naval tactics with materiel available, and when we discuss blockade possibilities of a long war against what the British officers and men of the Royal Navy of that age intended – a knockout blow against the German fleet along the lines of a hoped-for Trafalgar – we are on different courses than was Marder. When scholars discuss range finding and gunnery effectiveness and efficiency, re-examine the nature of the naval staff, or try to rewrite the battle of Jutland they are necessarily reverting to topics that Marder had covered. That is the nature of the world that the practitioners of Clio, the muse of history, inhabit. Modern naval historians invariably find that Marder had preceded them. This is undeniable, and for the obvious reason that at the time he was compiling his five-volume tour of the horizon, no such analysis had been undertaken by a private scholar. Naturally, then, the scholarly tactic is to point out Marder's errors or negligence. But they will never rewrite Marder, as some preposterously claimed in public that they intended to do. Only vanity and false pride would allow any contenders to make such a claim. What has set Marder apart from the rest, and what makes him an historian for all time, is his ability to put the whole remarkably complicated story together in one grand narrative, but a narrative not without the sharp and well founded criticisms of the subjects of his story. His progressive instincts always clamoured for an examination of his topics, giving a certain edge or bite to his narrative.

Marder never had the advantage of specialised studies concerning the war at sea, as Alan Pearsall of the National Maritime Museum, Greenwich, reminded me on more than one occasion. For instance, studies of anti-submarine warfare were not available or in the public realm. The account of the philosophy and conduct of maritime war (that is, the protection of trade) was privileged information, though Marder through his connections with the learned authority on this subject, Lieutenant-Commander W D Waters, had been tutored in that subject through an exchange of correspondence. Naval Staff Studies and Histories completed at the Admiralty did not cover every subject and were invariably of an uncritical tone. Moreover, they were intended for internal consumption, and designed so that a staff history of the War might later be compiled. Sir Julian Corbett and Sir Henry Newbolt's *History of the Great War, Naval Operations* (five volumes, 1920–31, two later revised,) never dealt with what Marder loved best – 'the war behind the war' – though it covered material in a detailed and authoritative manner, as Marder said, and with restrained judgments. 'It was intended to be an interim semi-popular treatment of the subject for the public, as opposed to the Staff History which was being written by the Historical Section of the Naval Staff.' (below, this volume, p362). Marder's preference as an historian's technique was to exploit existing, living sources; his correspondence files, now in the University of California, Irvine, Archives attest to how he was in touch with mainly officer informants. Pressing them for answers to this and that he would at last get to what he thought could be an informed judgement. He built up a vast network of naval informants, and by doing so had an enlarged sphere of information to draw on. Even so, his knowledge of the secondary literature and the periodical sources was extensive. Thus, when he came to compile his bibliography for the five-volume work (included below in this volume, pp346–403) he was able to provide the reader, and not least the interested student and future writer, with a guide to the literature. Many of the entries contain pithy annotations, as this for Rear-Admiral J E T Harper, *The*

Truth about Jutland (John Murray, 1927): 'A popular volume marred by excessive pro-Jellicoe bias.'

Many students, then as now, have found his list of 'Unpublished Papers' of immense help (pp346-56). Marder had thought the Admiralty haphazard in the way its papers, now held in The National Archives, Kew, were arranged, but this is an unwarranted criticism, for they were arranged for essentially operational uses not historical retrospection. Under the changing statutory public access by various Acts of Parliament documents were moved from the Admiralty at an unprecedented speed, though many were still withheld from use for reasons of 'public policy.' Court-martial proceedings were embargoed for 100 years. At the time that Marder was writing *From the Dreadnought to Scapa Flow* many of the documents collections were still held in family and private hands, or otherwise embargoed. Many have now found themselves into the public realm, but his listing of these always provided a treasure for first-time researchers. The list is now out of date, but in its time it served its purpose.

Volume V, like its predecessors, proved a publishing triumph. 'British admirals and British historians alike bow down before Arthur Marder,' trumpeted A J P Taylor in *The Observer*, 'His five volumes on the Royal Navy before and during the First World War rank high among the historical masterpieces of our age.' *The Times Literary Supplement* noted that future students of the Navy in the Fisher era would find the whole indispensable. 'Professor Marder sees Fisher as the founding-father of the Navy which triumphed in 1918; he himself can claim a similar role in its history.' *The Spectator* commented on the compulsive readability of the history and the unlocking of sources hitherto ignored that gave freshness to what had been a twice-told tale. To this was added Marder's remarkable gift of organising his material and maintaining the reader's interest through such a long period of time. As *The Economist* commented, Marder had 'produced a rarity – and indispensable piece of naval history that will influence all those that come after it.' 'We in Great Britain,' wrote Admiral of the Fleet the Early Mountbatten of Burma in the Foreword of the *festschrift* to Marder, *Naval Warfare in the Twentieth Century*, edited by Professor Gerald Jordan (Croom Helm, 1977), 'regard this work as the classic naval history of the years 1906 to 1919, and I am convinced that it will stand as a permanent monument to Arthur Marder's skill, industry and integrity as a historian of the highest class.' The Admiralty Board on 1 July 1970 commanded the Secretary to write to Marder to say that the Board had noted with pleasure the recent publication of the fifth and final volume. The letter concludes: 'You have thus brought to a successful conclusion a work of outstanding scholarship, illuminated by both judgement and humanity and a deep understanding of this important period in the Navy's history; and the Board wish to take this opportunity both of offering their congratulations on the completion of your task and also of expressing their warm appreciation of the service which in their view your have thereby rendered to the Royal Navy.'

Nowadays the five-volume set is confirmed as 'core history' among naval historians. And it is the beginning point of analysis and critique. Marder was always definite in his opinions, and he could argue from his point of view as strongly as any other scholar. On the other hand, he never contended that he had written the last word. In discussions with many who knew him I have learned that modesty was one of his characteristics. His rise to Olympian heights as an historian had been on the basis of solid commitment and extensive training under some of the very best of the profession, mainly at Harvard University, where he took all his degrees. He had never been trained or educated in naval or military history; rather, international relations and the histories of France, Russia and Japan has been subjects of special interest. He approached British naval history from the point of view of British statecraft and security in the last years of the nineteenth century. He followed the general tendency right through to his last book *Old Friends, New Enemies*, a study in Anglo-Japanese relations and war. Volume I of this work, with dates 1936-1941, was published by Oxford University Press in 1981, the year after his death.

Marder delighted in the telling of history as the interrelationships of personalities and character. He explored the human dimension. In this way he stood aside from the prevailing academic proclivities. At a basic level the dictates of historical method require a review of existing literature for the subject in question, thereby identifying its main themes, attacking its databases or lack thereof, probing weaknesses, spotting biases and the like. Then the proposal of a new or at least revised theme and an indication of new evidence used or old evidence re-evaluated. This forms a long-established method, though it enjoyed a more formalised acceptance under what is called Social Science, which rose to prominence in the mid-twentieth century in American academic circles. Marder was not a devotee of this line of scholarship. Rather he aimed at the telling of history as a human story, seeking to weave his underlying argument or arguments through the episodes of the grander narrative. The golden thread that wove through the whole was what he sought to follow. On the other hand, he had mastered the documentation, and in pursuit of evidence he liked to think that he had left no stone unturned. Readers will observe a note of self-satisfaction (below, this volume, px) when, as a distant echo of what the naval journalist Archibald Hurd had written years before, Marder wrote of having been able to use 'the true distillate' that fifty or sixty years since the events described and analysed had been allowed to come to the surface.

Natural it is therefore for recent, some of them well established as well as newer or contemporary naval historians to set Marder up as *primus inter pares* of the 'core histories.' By identifying Marder's themes, coverage of certain points, limitations in documentation, even blind spots (for all historians have them), the newer practitioners have then moved on to their own positions, discussion of evidence, and conclusions. This is the world that historians inhabit; it is the world that many types of scholars inhabit. The irony is that in so setting up Marder for a gigantic fall, his critics may well find themselves at the brink of a precipice of their own making. Revisionist history often leads to a reappraisal of the original works under review. Fair enough. The undeniable consequence of which is that those who have attacked Marder have themselves now come under review.

The progress of naval history since Marder's *From the Dreadnought to Scapa Flow* has witnessed some remarkable contributions, not all of them in disagreement with Marder but rather generally in line with his arguments and points of view. At the risk of excluding the works of many fine historians, the following are two works that are particularly noteworthy. In 1996 a book with the engaging title *The Rules of the Game: Jutland and British Naval Command* (John Murray) made its welcome appearance. Written by Dr Andrew Gordon, the work explored a conflict in command structures existing in armed services. In his book Gordon portrayed how doctrines and attitudes of the Victorian age rose in the age of Jutland with suffocating effect. Some evaluators comment that this work had acquired 'cult status,' which may well be the case. Certainly it is the most widely read naval history since Marder. The other important work is that of Paul Halpern, *A Naval History of World War I* (Naval Institute Press and UCL Press, 1994), a survey of all the navies in that war, an even-handed work deserving far more attention than it has received; Halpern's related tomes on the Mediterranean explore many of the themes in depth. Neither Gordon nor Halpern intended to rewrite Marder and it is clear that both used Marder with effect. Not to be forgotten, though standing on its own, is Paul Kennedy's *The Rise and Fall of British Naval Mastery*, launched in 1976 (Charles Scribner; second edition 2006) which though having but two chapters on the Fisher era, in its totality gave credence to the necessity of placing naval history against the large canvas of economic history. It was the first examination of British seapower since Admiral Mahan's influential classic of 1890, showing how the Navy's fortunes rested on prevailing political and economic conditions, both national and international. It opened new horizons. The first biography of Fisher to appear in the wake of Marder's studies was Ruddock Mackay's *Fisher of Kilverstone* (Oxford University Press, 1973), which had the advantage of Marder's advice in its draft stage. Marder was never afraid that some other scholar would counter his views, but in this work Marder and Mackay were essentially on parallel courses, with the latter having had the benefit of access to the full run of the Fisher papers.

In later years the world of naval historiography has become both more complex and more disputatious. The literature may be broken usefully into three broad schools: first, the orthodox which accepts and builds on Marder's ground-breaking work; second, the revisionists, headed up by Jon Tetsuro Sumida and Nicholas Lambert; and third, the emerging post-revisionist school, which includes, among others, Matthew Seligmann, John Brooks and Christopher M Bell. It has been observed by many that the notable thing about the revisionists is that they openly disparage Marder and seem to think that they have to demolish his work and reputation in order to promote their own. Interestingly, too, the revisionists sometimes imply that those who are in disagreement to their views are simply longing for a return to the old Marder orthodoxy. The post-revisionists have taken care to lay out a new path that builds on and diverges from both Marder and the revisionists.

The plot runs along these lines. The specific re-examination of Marder was a different and narrower task than that which Gordon, Kennedy or Mackay had, in their divergent ways, undertaken. The origins are identifiable. Sumida, of the University of Maryland, in a work entitled *In Defence of Naval Supremacy* (Unwin Hyman, 1989; paperback 2014) looked at finance and technology in the making of British naval policy, 1889–1914. The general focus was on 'the *Dreadnought* revolution,' so called. This work explored many themes of the Fisher era, but the reader's attention was specifically drawn to Arthur Pollen's system of fire control, which if it had been adopted by the Navy would have given, 'a monopoly of long-range hitting.' In 1984, the Navy Records Society published a collection of the privately-circulated works of Pollen, edited by Sumida, and this enlarged the view that the procurement process of the Navy had been flawed. We will never know if the Grand Fleet would have done better at Jutland with different range-finding equipment but that is the nature of the argument.

At this time the world of historical scholarship dealing with British naval matters of the twentieth century was expanding quickly and in many directions. Marder was less under assault than being outflanked as the historical profession went in new directions as it always does. In the year 1990, for instance, the centenary of the publication of Admiral Mahan's first 'Influence' book gave a chance for naval historians (under the auspices of a conference arranged at the US Naval War College under John Hattendorff) to re-examine and re-interpret a number of themes, and by this time Barry Hunt's *Sailor-Scholar* (Wilfrid Laurier University Press, 1982) ,the biography of Admiral Sir Herbert Richmond, and Donald Schurman's *Julian S. Corbett* (Royal Historical Society, 1981) had made their appearance. Roskill had completed *Churchill and the Admirals* (Collins, 1977) and *Admiral of the Fleet Earl Beatty: The Last Naval Hero, an Intimate Biography* (Collins, 1980), all of these in one way or another touching on Marder's work.

In short, naval history was enlarging its bounds, opening up new horizons, and, in some cases, examining more specific points. Sumida's work was just one example of the new case studies in naval history. Nicholas Lambert's *Sir John Fisher's Naval Revolution* (University of South Carolina Press, 1999) and James Goldrick's *The King's Ships Were at Sea* (Naval Institute Press, 1984) were others. Malcolm Murfett's multi-authored *The First Sea Lords: From Fisher to Mountbatten* (Praeger, 1995) examined all manner of aspects of 'the war behind the war,' a favourite theme of Marder's.

British gunnery effectiveness at Jutland was always a bone of contention, though Marder had been more interested in tactics at Jutland and the failure of communications (matters that Andrew Gordon had handsomely re-examined). Sumida's work on Pollen, already noted, stood for some considerable years uncontested. In 2005, however, a computer engineer, John Brooks of Kings College,

London, produced a counter: *Dreadnought Gunnery and the Battle of Jutland: the Question of Fire Control* (Routledge, 2005). Brooks revealed that in 1913 the Admiralty rejected Pollen's Argo system for the Dreyer fire control tables. Brooks shows that contrary to what Sumida had argued the Dreyer tables – said to be inferior – were in fact better suited. It was deficient tactics and training that were the cause of the problem. Brooks said that the battlecruisers would have performed worse with the Pollen system. (See, further, William McBride 'Dreadnought Gunnery and the Battle of Jutland: The Question of Fire Control' in *Technology and Culture*, July 2007). In a number of articles, Sumida looked at other aspects of British gunnery, exploring influence on tactics. One such, 'A Matter of Timing: the Royal Navy and the Tactics of Decisive Battle, 1912-1916' (*Journal of Military History*, January 2003) challenged Marder's statement that the Navy lacked 'a generally accepted, comprehensive, authoritative tactical doctrine in 1914.' By contrast, in 1912 the Admiralty adopted a secret tactical system. In five minutes at medium range a British battlefleet would destroy a German opponent with effective gunnery. This having been effected, the British would simultaneously turn away, thus countering the threat of enemy torpedoes. Misleading in its conceptualisation and development, this set the stage for what went wrong for the British at Jutland.

Marder, and doubtless others including Winston Churchill himself (reflecting on the Admiralty during the First World War) hammered away at the lack of staff development and planning at the Admiralty. In his book *The British Naval Staff in the First World War* (Boydell & Bewer, 2009), Nicholas Black challenged Marder and also the prominent naval figures of the age, Captains Herbert Richmond and Kenneth Dewar, pointing out that their views were unhealthy and misinformed. By re-evaluating the connection of operations and staff work in a broad sweep from 1912 to 1919 new insights are provided. Jacky Fisher had always been disdainful about staffs: 'So far as the Navy is concerned, the tendency about these "Thinking Establishments" on shore is to convert splendid Sea Officers into very indifferent clerks.' But that, too, was one of Fisher's exaggerations.

Recently, too, the study of British naval preparations and planning in the years leading up to 1914 had brought a further re-evaluation of Marder's work, not only his Volume I of *From the Dreadnought to Scapa Flow* but his earlier work *Anatomy of British Sea Power: A History of British Naval Policy in the Pre-Dreadnought Era, 1880-1905* (Alfred A Knopf,

1940, English edition Putnam 1941). Among various works recently appearing the following are notable: Nicholas Lambert, *Planning Armageddon: British Economic Warfare and the First World War* (Harvard, 2012), and Matthew S Seligmann, *The Royal Navy and the German Threat 1901-1914: Admiralty Plans to Protect British Trade in a War Against Germany* (Oxford, 2012). Broad perspectives are advanced in Shawn T Grimes, *Strategy and War Planning in the British Navy* (Boydell & Brewer, 2012), an essential work. Churchill will always attract attention, perhaps, given all that has been written about him, more than he deserves. Even so, Christopher M Bell's essential treatment, *Churchill and Sea Power* (Oxford University Press, 2013), offers a fine survey based on the best sources (some unavailable to Marder), and is likely to remain the standard source for years even to come. Of note, it follows the general tendencies of Marder and reinforces his positions. A long historiographical essay could and deserves to be written on the recent state of British naval history, but the above must suffice to indicate the nature or tendencies of current scholarship and critique.

It is worth noting that Marder went on to many more historical projects after finishing *From the Dreadnought to Scapa Flow*. The highlights are as follows. 'The Influence of History on Sea Power: the Royal Navy and the Lessons of 1914-18,' 1972, showed how little interest the Navy had in learning lessons, most having to be relearned in the next war. A study of 'The Royal Navy and the Ethiopian Crisis of 1935–1936,' 1970, broke new ground, 'The Dardanelles Revisited,' 1973, attempted to show just how close the British had come to success. And 'Winston is Back,' 1972, defended Churchill against charges of influence in the operations of the Navy in the early years of the Second World War. These essays and studies were conveniently gathered together in *From the Dardanelles to Oran: Studies of the Royal Navy in War and Peace, 1915-1940* (Oxford, 1974). The followed: *Operation 'Menace': the Dakar Expedition and the Dudley North Affair* (Oxford, 1976), which shows him at his detective best. But Marder was not done with big projects. *Old Friends, New Enemies: the Royal Navy and the Imperial Japanese Navy, Volume I: Strategic Illusions, 1936-1941* (Clarendon, 1981) was published posthumously. Dr Mark Jacobsen and Dr John Horsfield, two PhD students who had been tutored by the master, completed *Old Friends, New Enemies: the Royal Navy and the Imperial Japanese Navy, Volume II: the Pacific War, 1942-1945* (Clarendon, 1990), a work that is finer than many a critic has claimed. Naturally it could not contain the Marder touch throughout, but it completed the larger story on the basis of Marder's research materials and outlines. Incidentally, when Marder went to Japan on research (he did so on three different occasions), he visited the Japanese Naval Academy at Etajima and was surprised to find that the Japanese were reading the British lessons of the First World War, and that Marder's 'The Influence of History on Sea Power' was required reading among the cadets and future officers.

Before closing, it is useful to remind ourselves that at the time of his death Marder's contemporaries and critics accorded him the highest professional praise. Ronald Lewin, reviewing (*The Times*, 9 March 1981) the first volume of *Old Friends, New Enemies*, wrote that the pre-eminence of an American professor as a master historian of the Royal Navy in the twentieth century would seem anomalous, save for the fact that a fellow-countryman, Admiral Mahan, had preceded him. 'Marder, however, sparkled with a constellation of qualities many of which are lacking in Mahan and some, at least, in his British rivals, among whom Captain Stephen Roskill is – in every sense – outstanding. He shovelled up facts and formed them into intelligible patterns like those engineers of the US Marines who, almost overnight, bulldozed airstrips out of the Pacific coastal islands. His relentless intellectual energy was expressed in a buoyant, athletic style. He was a nonpareil in the use of oral history for legitimately academic purposes; and a predisposition to praise never prevented him from identifying the occasions when, in the conduct of war, man... "like an angry ape/Plays such fantastic tricks before heaven/As make the angels weep."' A J P Taylor wrote in *The Observer* (30 August 1981): 'Arthur Marder wrote in the preface of his book [*Old Friends, New Enemies, Volume I*]: "I bring no theories of history to my research and writing, nor do I arrive at any startling conclusions. I am essentially a narrative historian. I want to tell a story and to tell it well, with a liberal infusion of the personal, the human component." Let these words stand as the epitaph of a great historian who was also my dear friend.'

And last, this tribute, published as a personal memorial tribute in *Old Friends, New Enemies, Volume I*, by the one who knew him best in the line of the historian's trade, Peter Kemp, former Admiralty Librarian: ' "To look at yesterday with the eyes of yesterday, that is the historian's real task." I cannot remember how many time Arthur said this to me but it was frequent enough to make a deep impression. And it is, I think, the reason why he made himself the supreme historian, for he made it a rigid rule in all of history he wrote and taught. "It's unfair to criticize a man because you know something he didn't know" was another of his rules....' He towered above his contemporaries in his knowledge of history. He had a prodigious appetite for research. To this was matched his own energy and his powers of meticulous organisation of materials collected. 'His industry, his dedication, his knowledge, his judgement, his integrity, his happy facility with words, made him one of the giants of his profession.' Marder had been devastated by the loss of the materials for the balance of his work (these had been incinerated by a janitor). This was a blow from which he could hardly recover. And yet he returned to England to start the research all over again. 'That was his courage, indomitable, undismayed. His love of life, of his children, of his friends, above all, his constant devotion to Jan, his wife, was his happiness, which is reflected in his work.'

BARRY GOUGH
Victoria, BC, Canada

Preface

This, the final volume of a quintuplet ('five children born in the same labour') that began with the pre-war decade, is the story of the Royal Navy from January 1918 until the summer of 1919: essentially from the New Order established at the Admiralty after Jellicoe's dismissal through the scuttling of the High Seas Fleet at Scapa Flow. Between these terminal events we have such highlights as the *Goeben* sortie, the stirring blocking expeditions against Zeebrugge and Ostend, the High Seas Fleet sortie, the laying of the Northern Barrage, the naval Armistice and the surrender of the High Seas Fleet, and the negotiation of the naval terms of the peace settlement with Germany. As an epilogue I have attempted, in a chapter of 'Reflections', to distil some of the larger meanings of the war and of the whole 'Fisher Era.'

The following officers did me the great kindness of answering countless queries and of reading the manuscript and offering valuable criticism: Admirals Sir Angus Cunninghame Graham and Sir William James, Vice-Admiral Sir Peter Gretton, Rear-Admiral W. S. Chalmers, Captains John Creswell and Stephen Roskill, Commander W. M. Phipps Hornby, and Lieutenant-Commanders P. K. Kemp and D. W. Waters. I, of course, accept full responsibility for any and all errors of fact or interpretation.

I wish to thank Captain Creswell for overseeing with his usual care and skill the preparation of the maps and charts, and Mr. N. Atherton for the cartographic work itself.

In addition to those whose permission to examine collections of papers was acknowledged in previous volumes, I am grateful to the Hon. Mrs. Frances Cunnack for the use of the Wemyss Papers and the late Mrs. Gertrude Dewar for the Dewar Papers. Warm thanks go to these gentlemen for their assistance of various sorts: Admiral J. H. Godfrey, Vice-Admirals Sir Aubrey Mansergh, Sir James Pipon, and B. C. Watson, Rear-Admiral P. N. Buckley, Captains Lennox Boswell, E. W. Thring, and Andrew Yates, Kapitän zur See Gerhard Bidlingmaier, Group Captain H. A. Williamson, Commanders R. B. Mitchell, the late W. B. Rowbotham, and I. C. M. Sanderson, Fregattenkapitän Friedrich

Forstmeier, Squadron Leader L. A. Jackets, Professor Robert M. Grant, Dr. E. K. Timings, and Messrs. J. D. Lawson and A. W. H. Pearsall. The staffs of the Naval Historical Branch and Naval Library, Ministry of Defence, and of the Public Record Office and National Maritime Museum performed, as always, well above the call of duty. My special thanks are once more due to Miss Cathy Smith for transforming a nearly illegible manuscript into an elegant typescript—a feat of magic.

This is a good time to acknowledge my profound indebtedness to two friends for their unfailing support: William L. Langer, Professor Emeritus of History at Harvard University, who was directly responsible for my initial interest in British naval history, and Dr. Henry Allen Moe, onetime Secretary General of the John Simon Guggenheim Memorial Foundation and benefactor of scholars without peer, who made certain at various critical times that my work would not suffer from financial anaemia. My gratitude also goes out to my good friends in Ely House: the Publisher, Mr. John Brown, the late Mr. John White, Promotion Manager, my Job-like Editor, Mr. Geoffrey Hunt (who will now begin to live), for counsel, guidance—and extraordinary patience, and his able Assistants, successively, Miss Nesta Coxeter and Miss Joyce Horn, for helping me over many an obstacle. I would like again to acknowledge the splendid support I have received at one time or another from the John Simon Guggenheim Memorial Foundation, the American Philosophical Society, the University of California, and the University of Hawaii.

It gives me pleasure to thank the following publishers and individuals for their kind permission to quote from the copyright material indicated: Beaverbrook Newspapers Ltd., from the *War Memoirs of David Lloyd George*; Cambridge University Press, from Norman Rich and M. H. Fisher (eds.), *The Holstein Papers*; Cassell & Co. Ltd., and Lord Jellicoe, from Admiral of the Fleet Earl Jellicoe's *The Submarine Peril*; Peter Davies Ltd., and Stein and Day Publishers, from Vice-Admiral Sir Arthur Hezlet's *The Submarine and Sea Power*; Eyre & Spottiswoode Ltd. and, for the first title, E. P. Dutton & Co., Inc., from *The Naval Memoirs of Admiral of the Fleet Sir Roger Keyes* and Lady Wester Wemyss's *The Life and Letters of Lord Wester Wemyss*; William Heinemann Ltd., from Admiral of the Fleet Lord Chatfield's *The Navy and Defence*; Dr. Ives Hendrick, from Rear-Admiral W. S. Sims's *The Victory at*

Sea; Her Majesty's Stationery Office, from Sir Julian Corbett and Sir Henry Newbolt's *History of the Great War. Naval Operations*, C. Ernest Fayle's *History of the Great War. Seaborne Trade*, and Sir Walter Raleigh and H. A. Jones's *History of the Great War. The War in the Air*; Hodder & Stoughton Ltd. and Rear-Admiral W. S. Chalmers, from the latter's *The Life and Letters of David, Earl Beatty*; The Hogarth Press Ltd. and Mr. Denys Oglander, from Brigadier Cecil Aspinall-Oglander's *Roger Keyes*; Houghton Mifflin Company, from Elting E. Morison's *Admiral Sims and the Modern American Navy*; Hutchinson Publishing Group Ltd., and for the first two titles the executors of the estate of Admiral Sir Reginald Bacon, from Admiral Bacon's *The Concise Story of the Dover Patrol* and *From 1900 Onward*, Admiral Sir Sydney R. Fremantle's *My Naval Career, 1880–1928*, and Lieutenant-Commander J. M. Kenworthy's (Lord Strabolgi) *Sailors, Statesmen —and Others*; Little, Brown and Company, from Rear-Admiral Alfred T. Mahan's *Naval Strategy*; E. S. Mittler & Sohn, from the Official German History *Der Krieg zur See*: Captain Otto Groos and Admiral Walther Gladisch's *Der Krieg in der Nordsee*; Frederick Muller Ltd., from Geoffrey Cousins's *The Story of Scapa Flow*; Princeton University Press, from Seth P. Tillman's *Anglo-American Relations at the Paris Peace Conference*; Putnam & Company, from Robert M. Grant's *U-Boats Destroyed*; Sampson Low, Marston & Co. Ltd., from Captain D. J. Munro's *Scapa Flow: a Naval Retrospect*; Warner R. Schilling, from his unpublished Ph.D. dissertation, *Admirals and Foreign Policy, 1913–1919*; the University of North Carolina Press, from Josephus Daniels's *The Wilson Era: Years of War and After*; George Weidenfeld & Nicolson Ltd., from Admiral Karl Doenitz's *Memoirs: Ten Years and Twenty Days*. I would like to repeat my sincere thanks to Lieutenant-Commander D. W. Waters for the privilege of quoting from certain of his restricted writings. Unpublished Crown copyright material is published by permission of the Controller of Her Majesty's Stationery Office. As in the previous volumes I have made good use of the pertinent articles in the *Naval Review*, but without citing this restricted journal, in accordance with its long-established policy.

Fifty years ago the naval journalist Archibald Hurd (afterwards the author of the official study of the merchant navy in the war) wrote:

Who would not give a king's ransom, if he possessed it, to be in a position to examine this country's recent naval effort with the eyes of the historian of fifty or sixty years hence, when all that remains secret to-day will be known of all men? It may be that even then there will be wide differences of opinion, but the froth of contemporary controversy will have been blown away and there will remain only the pure distillate, on which the historian will feed his mind with the complete assurance that nothing remains of prejudice, personal animosity, or party strife, for the struggles of politicians, even in time of war, react on naval policy, as indeed upon every aspect of the life of the nation.*

It has been my privilege and pleasure to have chronicled the story of the Royal Navy in 1914–18, as well as the crucially important pre-war decade and the immediate aftermath of the war, out of the 'pure distillate'.

Gibbon commemorated the completion of the last volume of his *Decline and Fall of Rome* in a famous passage in his autobiography: '. . . I will not dissemble the first emotions of joy on the recovery of freedom . . . But my pride was soon humbled, and a sober melancholy was spread over my mind by the idea that I had taken my everlasting leave of an old and agreeable companion . . .' I am no Gibbon; but for this remark I confess a fellow feeling.

ARTHUR J. MARDER

Oxford
September 1969

* 'The Confessions of the Admirals', *Fortnightly Review*, December 1919.

Abbreviations Used in the Text

(whether official or in common Service usage)

A.C.N.S.	:	Assistant Chief of Naval Staff
A.D.O.D.	:	Assistant Director of the Operations Division
A.P. shell	:	Armour-piercing shell
A/S	:	Anti-Submarine
A.S.D.	:	Anti-Submarine Division
B.C.	:	Battle Cruiser
B.S.	:	Battle Squadron
C.I.G.S.	:	Chief of the Imperial General Staff
C.M.B.	:	Coastal Motor Boat
C.N.S.	:	Chief of the Naval Staff
C.O.S.	:	Chief of Staff to a Flag Officer Commanding*
D.A.S.D.	:	Director of the Anti-Submarine Division
D.C.I.G.S.	:	Deputy Chief of the Imperial General Staff
D.C.N.S.	:	Deputy Chief of Naval Staff
D.M.I.	:	Director of Military Intelligence, War Office
D.N.C.	:	Director of Naval Construction
D.N.I.	:	Director of Naval Intelligence†
D.N.O.	:	Director of Naval Ordnance
D.O.D.	:	Director of the Operations Division
D. of P.	:	Director of the Plans Division
D.T.S.D.	:	Director of the Training and Staff Duties Division
D.1S.L.	:	Deputy First Sea Lord
G.F.	:	Grand Fleet
H.S.F.	:	High Seas Fleet
I.W.C.	:	Imperial War Cabinet
L.C.	:	Light Cruiser
M.L.	:	Motor Launch

* Also, prior to May 1917, Chief of the Admiralty War Staff.
† The pre-war title, revived in 1918. 'D.I.D.' (Director of the Intelligence Division) was the official title, 1912–18.

N.I.D.	:	Naval Intelligence Division
R.A.F.	:	Royal Air Force
R.F.C.	:	Royal Flying Corps
R.N.A.S.	:	Royal Naval Air Service
S.N.O.	:	Senior Naval Officer
S.O.	:	Senior Officer
T.B.D.	:	Destroyer
T.S.D.	:	Training and Staff Duties Division
W.C.	:	War Cabinet
W/T	:	Wireless telegraphy

Contents

page

PREFACE   vii

PART I. THE WEMYSS–GEDDES RÉGIME
January 1918–November 1918

CHAPTER I. THE NAVAL DECISION MAKERS

1. BOARD AND NAVAL STAFF CHANGES   3

Wemyss becomes First Sea Lord—His background, assets, and methods—The other naval members of the Board—Alterations in Naval Staff organization—Distribution of duties between naval members belonging to the Staff—The most significant result of the new organization—Clarification of Board responsibility for operations.

2. RESULTS   9

The New Order is a great success—Richmond's appointment as D.T.S.D.—Harmony at the Admiralty—Relations between Wemyss and Beatty—Geddes on the improved efficiency of the Navy.

CHAPTER II. MEDITERRANEAN PROBLEMS

1. THE *GOEBEN* SORTIE   12

The possible objectives of a sortie—Precautions against a sortie—Hayes-Sadler separates the two battleships at Mudros —Distribution of the Aegean Squadron—Fremantle's orders —The German plan—The sortie—The *Breslau* is mined— The *Goeben* turns back—She is stuck fast at Nagara—The submarine and air attempts to sink her—Her subsequent career —The fiasco disgusts Wemyss—Public reaction.

2. THE BLACK SEA FLEET   20

The command situation in the Mediterranean—Establishment of an Allied Naval Council—The threat of a German seizure of the Russian Black Sea Fleet—The problem posed by the Austrian Fleet in the Adriatic—The Aegean problem— The French solution to both strategic problems—British opinion of the Italian Fleet—The Allied Naval Council proposes a solution to both problems, 26–27 April—The Italians will not play—The battle is continued at the Supreme War Council, Abbeville, 1 May—The Italians continue to drag their feet—Wemyss suggests an 'Admiralissimo' for the Mediterranean—The heated discussion at the Supreme War Council, Versailles, 1–2 June—Italian obstructionism worsens —Allied complaints—Revival in September of the Admiralissimo scheme.

3. THE OFFENSIVE IN THE ADRIATIC   30

Gough-Calthorpe's views on convoy—Institution of 'barrage operations' in the Adriatic—Analysis of the system—The basic weakness of the barrage—Evaluations of the barrage operations—The brunt of the A/S effort falls on the Royal Navy—The puny Italian contribution—The Mediterranean Fleet feels neglected.

CHAPTER III. HOME WATERS: BARRAGES AND BLOCKING OPERATIONS

1. THE DOVER STRAITS BARRAGE   39

Keyes assumes the Dover command—His limitations and assets—Keyes infuses life into the command—He introduces massed patrols and brilliant illumination of the deep minefields—Results—The German destroyer sortie, 14–15 February —The incredible denouement—The findings of the Court of Inquiry—German elation—Keyes strengthens British control of the Straits—The raid disturbs the War Cabinet.

2. THE ZEEBRUGGE OPERATION   45

The Zeebrugge–Ostend situation—Bayly and Tyrwhitt suggest plans for Zeebrugge–Ostend blocking and combined operations—Plans Division work out a blocking scheme— Bacon rips it to shreds—He puts forward his own plan— —Jellicoe combines it with a blocking operation—Keyes's plan is accepted—Its objectives—The main features of the Zeebrugge plan—Requirements of the Zeebrugge plan— False starts in April—Keyes decides to go ahead—The Zeebrugge–Ostend operations, 22–23 April—The comment of the German Official History—Bacon's criticisms—Zeebrugge's great boost to morale—A hard look at the practical results— The revelations in the German Official History—Other evidence—Keyes presses for a bomber offensive against the Flanders bases—Keyes succeeds in closing the Straits to the Flanders U-boats.

3. THE NORTHERN BARRAGE   66

Laying the barrage—Beatty insists on a gap eastward of the Orkneys—The American mines are a tremendous disappointment—Beatty is critical of the barrage—The problem of Norwegian territorial waters—Withdrawal of the barrage force—How effective was the barrage?—British minelaying in the Heligoland Bight.

CHAPTER IV. BEATING THE U-BOATS

1. THE SHIPPING SITUATION   77

The position early in 1918—Improvement—Falling off in losses by mine—The turning-point.

2. THE U-BOATS IN THE FINAL PHASE   81

U-boat construction in 1918—War losses in 1918—The Admiralty is heartened by the falling off in U-boat morale—Scheer's reasons for the decline in U-boat successes—An analysis of Scheer's statement.

3. CONVOY IN FULL BLOOM   85

Development and results of the various convoy systems—Analysis of the final convoy statistics—Explanation of the success of convoy—German assessment of convoy—The U-boats' respect for destroyer escorts—The role of aircraft in A/S warfare and the convoy system—The practical results of convoy air escorts—Night attacks by surfaced U-boats—A note on U-boat wolf-pack tactics—Convoy alters U-boat strategy—German post-mortems on the submarine campaign.

4. THE CONVOY SYSTEM: EVALUATIONS   97

The attitude of the Admiralty remains ambivalent—Reasons for and analysis of the mixed feelings on convoy—Why more U-boats were destroyed in 1918—Weak links in the convoy system—Handicaps under which the system operated.

5. GROWING ANXIETIES   105

High Authority is increasingly optimistic about the A/S campaign—Public opinion remains sceptical—The Admiralty begin to have doubts—The Germans admit failure of the U-boat campaign—The Admiralty nearly panic: the naval mission to Washington in October—Statistics on shipping losses, shipbuilding output, the convoy system, and U-boats.

CHAPTER V. ANGLO-AMERICAN NAVAL RELATIONS
(April 1917–November 1918)

1. THE QUEENSTOWN COMMAND   121

Bayly proves an ideal choice for the command—His relations with Sims and Pringle—The general harmony between the two Navies at Queenstown—Sims's relations with the Admiralty.

2. THE GRAND FLEET   124

The U.S. battle squadron is integrated into the Grand Fleet—British estimates of the Americans—The co-operation between the two Navies—U.S. Navy Department–Admiralty differences.

CHAPTER VI. THE GRAND FLEET: UNCERTAINTIES AND A MISSED OPPORTUNITY (January 1918–June 1918)

1. MORALE   128

Sturdee leaves the Grand Fleet—War weariness and boredom are pronounced—Yet morale remains very high—An explanation of the paradox.

2. THE 'NEW' STRATEGY   131

The strain on Grand Fleet resources—Beatty's 'momentous report' of 9 January on Grand Fleet strategy—The Board lays down a programme to meet the situation—Jellicoe's criticism of the new departure—Similarity of his and Beatty's strategy.

3. THE NUMBERS GAME AND OFFENSIVE IDEAS   138

The Grand Fleet preponderance in ships—The problem of the Russian Baltic Fleet—An extraordinary plan to destroy this fleet—The battle-cruiser position causes concern—Richmond's offensive schemes—Beatty urges an air offensive—The Admiralty stress the difficulties—The Naval Staff searches for offensive measures.

4. THE HIGH SEAS FLEET SORTIE   143

British expectations and plans *re* a sortie—Anxiety over the Scandinavian convoy—The intervals between sailings are increased—Discussion of changing the convoy routes—The Intelligence factor—Scheer's decision to attempt a bold stroke—His plan—The Fleet passes out of the Bight—The *Moltke* suffers a breakdown—The operation continues, then turns back—Admiralty–Grand Fleet response—Missed opportunities—Observations on the sortie—Disappointment of the Navy—Room 40 holds an inquiry.

5. INVASION AND OTHER BOGIES   156

Plans Division envisages a battle-cruiser raid into the Atlantic —The possibility of a German raid on Ireland—The serious threat to the French Channel ports—The invasion problem is re-examined in August 1916—And again in March 1917—Grand Fleet invasion strategy—Still another joint Service conference on invasion, December 1917—Jellicoe is unhappy with its main result—The Admiralty–War Office report—The last flurry of invasion jitters, 1918 spring—A note on the Dutch problem—A final word on the invasion question.

CHAPTER VII. THE FINAL RECKONING
(July 1918–November 1919)

1. THE BEGINNING OF THE END   165

Beatty's mood in the summer of 1918—The air of expectancy in naval circles—Wemyss and Beatty exchange views on the enemy's intentions—An armistice is signed with Turkey—The Allied fleets anchor off Constantinople—Scheer orders the recall of the U-boats—Hipper's plan for a bold operation—The Admiralty are alerted—Mutiny in the High Seas Fleet—What lay behind it.

2. THE NAVAL ARMISTICE   175

The Allied draft conditions of 8 October—The mood of the
Navy—Wemyss's attitude—The Admiralty present their views
on a naval armistice—Beatty's position—The War Cabinet
considers the Navy's proposals—The Allied Naval Council's
terms—The Supreme Council debates these—The Allied
Naval Council will not heed the politicians—The die is cast
by the Supreme War Council, 4 November—The naval terms
—Later alterations—The Admiralty do not immediately
appreciate the full import of the mutiny in the German Fleet
—Beatty's unhappiness over the naval terms—11 November:
contrasting moods of the public and the Navy.

3. DER TAG   188

Admiral Meurer arrives to arrange internment details—The
scene in the *Queen Elizabeth*—The High Seas Fleet surrenders,
21 November—How the Grand Fleet viewed it—Press reaction—A note on Baltic operations and Imperial naval problems.

PART II. AFTERMATH
November 1918—June 1919

CHAPTER VIII. RIFTS AND REFORMS

1. THE CHANGING OF THE GUARD   199

Geddes leaves the Admiralty—Long succeeds him—How the
press and the Service viewed the appointment—Other changes
in the Board—Browning, the new Second Sea Lord—The
inexplicable appointment of Fergusson as D.C.N.S.—Sinclair
replaces Hall as D.N.I.—Shrinkage of the Fleet—The Grand
Fleet ceases to exist.

2. WEMYSS AND BEATTY   203

Beatty complains that he is ignored—Friction over appoint-
ments—The misunderstanding over Wemyss's retirement and
Beatty's succession—*The Times* announces a change in First
Sea Lord—Beatty proposes to hold the two offices of First Sea
Lord and C.-in-C.—Wemyss and Beatty go over their
differences—Long is distressed—The press campaign against
Wemyss—Long becomes his champion—Long on the Beattys
—Wemyss promotes an earldom for Beatty—Wemyss resigns.

3. PERSONNEL AND NAVAL STAFF REFORMS   212

Causes of lower-deck unrest—The situation moves towards a
climax late in the war—The near-flash point is reached after
the war—The status of officers' pay—The Jerram and Halsey
Committees—Most of their recommendations are accepted—
Wemyss reorganizes the Naval Staff.

CHAPTER IX. NAVAL POLICY: UNCERTAINTIES AND NEW RIVALRIES

1. THE NAVY ESTIMATES 221

The First Lord introduces the 1919-20 Estimates—Press reaction to the speech—The Estimates are revised in July—The initial uncertainty over the future of the capital ship—The Admiralty reaffirm their faith in capital ships.

2. THE 'SEA BATTLE OF PARIS' 224

The U.S. naval challenge—The whys of the ambitious American naval plans—British opinion is not unsympathetic—But the Admiralty are suspicious of American naval expansion—Plans Division analyses U.S. motivations—The First Lord expresses his concern—Anglo-American naval discussions in Paris—Daniels and Lloyd George square off—An informal agreement is reached—Daniels gives assurances in his London visit—Long is prepared to accept them—The significance of the naval imbroglio—The Admiralty's views on the likelihood of war with the U.S. and Japan—Admiralty strategic plans for a war with Japan.

3. THE 'FREEDOM OF THE SEAS' 238

Point 2 of Wilson's Fourteen Points—What did the U.S. mean by it?—The Admiralty state their views—Lloyd George stoutly opposes the doctrine of the Freedom of the Seas—A compromise is reached with the U.S.—The question is not discussed at the Peace Conference.

4. THE LEAGUE OF NATIONS AND ARMAMENTS LIMITATION 242

The U.S. Navy and the idea of a League Navy—The Admiralty have no faith in a League of Nations or an international navy—They oppose any limitation of armaments—The League Covenant does not provide for an international force—The Versailles Treaty provisions for international armaments limitation—The U.S. Navy opposes a liquidation of German sea power—A note on relative naval strength.

CHAPTER X. THE NAVAL SETTLEMENT WITH GERMANY

1. COLONIES, KIEL CANAL, HELIGOLAND, BALTIC, AND SUBMARINES 249

Admiralty policy on the German colonies—The Versailles colonial settlement—The Admiralty and the Kiel Canal—The Council of Ten discussion of the problem—The Peace Treaty provision on the Canal—Wartime views on Heligoland—Post-war consideration of alternatives—The problem comes before the Council of Ten—The Peace Treaty provision on Heligoland—On Germany's Baltic defences—Inter-Allied controversy over the abolition of submarines—The wrangle over the disposition of the U-boats—U-boat provisions of the Peace Treaty.

CONTENTS

2. DISPOSAL OF THE HIGH SEAS FLEET   262

The Admiralty decide on a policy—Its essentials are accepted
by the Allied Admirals and Council of Ten—The French
advocate partition of the German Fleet—Lloyd George and
House reach a compromise—The U.S. and Britain prefer
destruction—Opposition to destruction within the Navy—
Support for the Admiralty's position—The French are not to
be put off—Deadlock.

CHAPTER XI. GÖTTERDÄMMERUNG (21 June 1919)

1. INTERNMENT   270

Arrival of the interned ships—The demoralization of the
German Fleet—Communication among the ships and with the
British—The guardships—Von Reuter is an ideal prisoner—
British plans to prevent scuttling.

2. THE SCUTTLING   275

Fremantle takes his squadron to sea—Von Reuter's preparations to scuttle his ships—He signals the order—His message
that morning to Fremantle—Fremantle hurries back to Scapa
—The results of the scuttling—Fremantle's attitude—He
rebukes von Reuter—Could the scuttling have been prevented?
—Madden recommends a severe punishment of the Germans
—The Council of Four discusses the scuttling and warns the
Germans—British reaction to the scuttling—Long's statement
in the Commons—The French and Italians hint at British col-
lusion in the scuttling—Lieutenant-Commander Kenworthy's
blatant assertion—'Pertinent questions which have never been
satisfactorily answered'—An attempt to answer them—
Wemyss's reaction to the scuttling—Lloyd George pins the
ultimate responsibility on the Americans—Wemyss spells out
the essentials—He overlooks Lloyd George's role.

3. EPILOGUE   293

The eventual fate of the scuttled ships—Naval terms of the
Versailles Treaty—The problem of the disposition of the surrendered ships—A settlement is finally reached—Admiralty
satisfaction with the peace terms.

CHAPTER XII. REFLECTIONS ON AN ERA

1. THE PERFORMANCE OF THE NAVY, 1914–18   297

Conflicting interpretations of the role of sea power—The
'ultimate objects' of British naval policy—The Navy is successful in achieving them—Critics of the naval war effort—
Criticism of the failure to bring on a general fleet action—The
benefits that would have followed a crushing victory—
Factors working against an aggressive strategy and tactics—
The naval authorities feel the game is not worth the candle—

CONTENTS

The general expectation of Trafalgars—Misinterpretation of the 'Nelson Tradition'—Other sources of the primacy-of-battle fetish—The 'Young Turks' are critical of the 'passive strategy' —Jellicoe's *The Grand Fleet* exposes the *matériel* shortcomings— Reasons for the unsatisfactory *matériel* position—Comparisons between German and British *matériel*—But British self-depreciation went too far—A partial catalogue of errors of commission—A gentle word of understanding.

2. FUNDAMENTAL WEAKNESSES 313

The lack of a well-organized and efficient Naval Staff—Staff officers—'Round and round go the dockets'—The poor intra-Staff co-operation—The work of the Plans Division—The officer educational system—Richmond's ideas for educational reform—He pinpoints the failures of the system—Naval officers and naval history—The pre-war immersion in *matériel* concerns—Outstanding senior officers—Why were there so many square pegs in round holes?—Richmond, a case history of dominant attitudes *re* intellect and independent thinking—Others of the same stamp—Senior officer veneration—Over-centralization in the Admiralty and Fleet—Methods of work and training in ships and fleets—Four principles of human relations.

3. THE HUMAN FACTOR 330

How is the British victory to be explained?—The personnel factor in the Royal Navy—In the German Navy—The Germans lack a maritime tradition—How they handled their surface fleet—Observations on the Anglo-German naval rivalry—A discussion of leadership—Mahan on practical experience and a knowledge of history—Wartime relations between the two Services—And between the seamen and the politicians—Some final thoughts on 'Jacky.'

BIBLIOGRAPHY

i. Unpublished Papers   346

ii. British Official Works—Unpublished   356

iii. Official Works—Published   361

iv. Published Works   364

v. Newspapers and Periodicals   401

vi. Miscellaneous   402

vii. Addenda   403

INDEX   405

List of Illustrations

(The rank and title at the end of the war are the ones given)

Admiral Sir David Beatty, Commander-in-Chief, Grand Fleet, 1916–19 *Frontispiece*
(*From the 1920 portrait by Sir Arthur Cope, by permission of the Trustees of the National Maritime Museum*)

Facing page

I. Sir Eric Geddes, First Lord of the Admiralty, 1917–18   8
(*Photograph: by permission of Sir Reay Geddes*)

II. Walter Long, First Lord of the Admiralty, 1919–21   9
(*From the portrait by A. H. Collins, 1918, by permission of the 4th Viscount Long*)

III. Admiral Sir Rosslyn Wemyss, First Sea Lord, 1917–19   24
(*From the portrait-drawing by Francis Dodd, by permission of the Trustees of the Imperial War Museum*)

IV. 1. Rear-Admiral George P. W. Hope, Deputy First Sea Lord, 1918–19   25
(*From the portrait-drawing by Francis Dodd, by permission of the Trustees of the Imperial War Museum*)

2. Acting Vice-Admiral Sydney R. Fremantle, Deputy Chief of Naval Staff, 1918–19   25
(*Photograph taken on the Northern Patrol, 1917, from My Naval Career, by permission of Messrs. Hutchinson (Publishers) Ltd.*)

V. Acting Vice-Admiral Sir Roger Keyes, Commanding Dover Patrol, 1918   264
(*From the portrait by Glyn Philpot, by permission of the Trustees of the Imperial War Museum*)

VI. 1. Vice-Admiral the Hon. Sir Somerset Gough-Calthorpe, Commander-in-Chief, Mediterranean, 1917–19   265
(*From the portrait by Philip Connard, by permission of the Trustees of the Imperial War Museum*)

xxi

VI. 2. Admiral Sir Lewis Bayly, Commanding Coast of
Ireland Station, 1915–19   265
(Photograph: Lafayette Ltd.)

VII. 1. Admiral Sir David Beatty at the surrender of the
High Seas Fleet, 21 November 1918   280
(Photograph: Graphic Photo Union)

2. British seamen watching the surrender   280
(Photograph: The Sphere, 7 December 1918)

VIII. 1. Scuttled German battleship *Bayern* at Scapa Flow   281
*(Photograph: by permission of the Trustees of the Imperial War
Museum)*

2. German destroyer sinking at Scapa Flow. One of
the 'G 101–104' Series, still moored to her buoy   281
(Photograph: by permission of V.-Adm. Friedrich Ruge)

3. H.M. Whaler *Ramna* perched on the armoured
belt of the scuttled battle cruiser *Moltke* at Scapa
Flow*   281
*(Photograph: by permission of the Trustees of the Imperial War
Museum)*

* The *Ramna* was classed at the time as a guard trawler, though she was in fact a whaler. The *Moltke* had turned on her side as she sank. The following day, at about high tide, the *Ramna* slid on to the *Moltke*'s side before anyone on board realized what was happening. When the tide fell, she was of course left high and dry!

List of Maps and Charts

at end of book

1. Home Waters, including the Northern Barrage.
1A. The Baltic.
2. The Mediterranean.
3. Sortie of the *Goeben*, 20 January 1918.
4. The Dover Straits, including Destroyer Raid of 14–15 February 1918.
5. The Zeebrugge Operation, 22–23 April 1918.
6. Shipping Losses in 1918.
7. Sortie of the High Seas Fleet, 23–25 April 1918.

Plans in text:

A. Otranto Straits Barrage.   31
B. The Scuttling, Scapa Flow, 21 June 1919.   276

PART I

The Wemyss–Geddes Régime

January 1918 – November 1918

I

The Naval Decision Makers

I fear as you do, that Wemyss is not the man for it [directing Allied naval strategy] and I am full of fear for the future. . . . The Grand Fleet is all right, as Beatty is strong enough to refuse to throw it away on wild cat schemes, but the wider field of operations are not in such able hands.

ADMIRAL SIR CHARLES MADDEN to
Jellicoe, 27 December 1917.

I think Wemyss will do well and he has some first rate young brains to help him, he is full of sound common sense and does not go into details as much as J. did. I am sure there will be much more sympathy between the Admiralty and Grand Fleet than there was formerly.

KING GEORGE V to Beatty, 10 February 1918.

It is fair to say that the Geddes-Wemyss combination exactly suited the Navy's mood of the moment.

LORD GEDDES, *The Forging of a Family.*

1. BOARD AND NAVAL STAFF CHANGES

THE new Board of Admiralty was 'read in' on 10 January 1918. Wemyss was off to a rocky start. He was almost unknown to the press and the general public, and his appointment scandalized many senior officers who believed that Jellicoe's Deputy had 'slyly' moved into the vacated position. Terms like 'dirty work' and 'betrayal' were bandied about. This appraisal of the situation was unfair, since there is no reason to doubt Wemyss's denial that he had had anything to do with Jellicoe's going or the sincerity of his regret, expressed to Jellicoe, over the turn events had taken. Indeed, he seems to have accepted Geddes's offer only after the First Lord had insisted. His feelings are indicated in a letter to the King: 'I am fully aware of my limitations and I do not think that I have left the First Lord in any doubt about them; at the same time I do think that I have certain qualities which should prove useful . . . On personal grounds I am more sorry than I can say about Jellicoe. He is a splendid fellow, and I am afraid will feel the wrench terribly, and I wish to heaven that I could have been relieving him under more auspicious circumstances.'[1]

The appointment also aroused surprise in the Navy: Wemyss was, at least until 1914, regarded as a Court sailor—an officer without exceptional ability, let alone the ability to conceive brilliant strategic surprises. He was, moreover, a non-specialist, which was not in his favour. (Wemyss was one of the only four First Sea Lords between 1905 and 1945 not chosen from a small section of ex-gunnery and torpedo specialists. The others were Prince Louis of Battenberg, Beatty, and A. B. Cunningham.) He had never held either of the principal naval commands afloat, and until he became Deputy First Sea Lord in the summer of 1917, he had never filled any important administrative post. In these respects, the appointment was unique in the history of the Navy in modern times. But war creates its own precedents. Beatty, who was personally well disposed to Wemyss, expressed the general feeling in the Service: 'What experience Wemyss has to run the complex and great machine I do not know but I fear for the future.'[2]

There was another side to Wemyss. 'Rosy' Wemyss (as everybody knew him) possessed many valuable assets for the post of First Sea Lord—apart from 'a fighting face with a monocle set in it.' He was, to begin with, one of the most popular senior officers in the Navy. This he owed to his buoyancy, charm, invariable courtesy, incomparable tact, and talents for story-telling and mixing. The same attributes enabled him to get the best out of subordinates. He was also an officer of good judgement and common sense, and one who in times of crisis never got rattled or even worried. For all his jolly casual manner, he had clear ideas as well as a will of his own. His great moral courage was well known: he would take risks and never hesitate to assume full responsibility for everything that was done. He made every possible use of the brains of the Naval Staff, instituting regular and formal morning Staff meetings for a discussion of the general situation and

---

1 Wemyss to King George V, 25 December 1917; Windsor MSS.
2 Beatty to Jellicoe, 27 December 1917; Jellicoe MSS. Jellicoe was afraid that Wemyss would not 'stand up to' Geddes, 'as he seems to be imbued with the idea that it is his duty to carry out the 1st Lord's wishes and not what he considers is best for the Service.' Jellicoe to Admiral the Hon. Sir Alexander Bethell (C.-in-C., Plymouth), 28 December 1917; Bethell MSS.

the planning in outline of schemes and operations. He allocated considerable responsibility to the Deputy First Sea Lord, D.C.N.S., and A.C.N.S. Even when commanding afloat, he never became involved in technical details—he knew little about that side of the Navy, anyway—and he would not deal with trifles, whether, for example, a certain class of trawler should be armed with 4-inch or 12-pounders: the kind of problem Jellicoe, who was a real centralizer, had dealt with. (Even as a fleet commander, Wemyss had been a decentralizer. He was quite exceptional in this respect.) By decentralizing and trusting his colleagues on the Board he was able to concentrate on the essentials and the larger issues. Yet he maintained control. Even Jellicoe's keenest supporters later admitted that they welcomed their greater freedom. They knew that the First Sea Lord was on call if they needed his support and authority to overcome any obstruction. Wemyss understood the importance of 'that greatest of modern requirements, organized co-operation —the welding together into an harmonious whole of the humblest as well as the greatest effort, i.e. what is commonly called team work.'[3]

Wemyss was much more a man of the world, of larger vision, than most of his contemporaries. Brought up in Wemyss Castle, Fife, he had spent far more of his life in the 'houses of the great' than other naval officers. Thus, he was one of King George's oldest and most trusted friends. (His maternal grandmother, by the way, was an illegitimate daughter of King William IV.) His wide knowledge of men and affairs enabled him to deal on equal terms with the politicians (for whom he had no love) and military chiefs, British and foreign, and to expound Admiralty views clearly to them. Most First Sea Lords were simple sailors with no understanding of how the political mind worked. Wemyss spoke French fluently, had many French friends, and had got on well with their officers in the Mediterranean. For these reasons he was *persona grata* to the French, and to the Italians as well. This made him the ideal First Sea Lord at a time when naval collaboration with Britain's Allies was increasing and later, when the naval terms of the Armistice and Peace Treaty were discussed with them. He was, in short, a naval statesman.

Vice-Admiral Sir Herbert Heath, who had performed ade-

---

3 Admiral of the Fleet Lord Wester Wemyss, *The Navy in the Dardanelles Campaign* (London, 1924), p. 277.

quately as Second Sea Lord since September 1917, continued in
this post. Rear-Admiral Lionel Halsey, the Third Sea Lord since
December 1916, and a 'blue-water sailor' in every sense of the
word, had long been anxious to get back to the sea. When he left
the Board in June 1918, and the civilian Controller Sir Alan
Anderson quit at the same time, on Halsey's advice a naval officer
once more became Controller and Third Sea Lord.[4] He was the
competent, Napoleonic-looking Commodore Charles M. de
Bartolomé. (The office of Controller was officially merged with
that of Third Sea Lord in November 1918.) Halsey assumed
command of the 2nd Battle Cruiser Squadron of the Grand Fleet.
Rear-Admiral Hugh Tothill, the Fourth Sea Lord since May
1917, stayed on, as did the A.C.N.S., Vice-Admiral Sir Alexander
Duff. Rear-Admiral George Hope, D.O.D. since the spring of
1917, became Deputy First Sea Lord, *vice* Wemyss, but with
changed functions.[5] The reorganization announced on 14 January
gave him responsibility for operations in foreign waters (transferred from the D.C.N.S.), with a D.O.D. (Foreign) under him.
He also rid the First Sea Lord, as well as the D.C.N.S. and
A.C.N.S., of a great deal of administrative detail. Under the old
system the First Sea Lord began his day's work by answering
hundreds of letters and telegrams, most of which had only the
remotest connection with operations. The Deputy First Sea Lord
now dealt with this paper work, leaving his Chief free to concentrate on 'the general direction of operations'. Wemyss thus became
the C.N.S. in fact as well as in name. The dapper Rear-Admiral
Sydney Fremantle, a man of considerable presence and some force
of character, replaced Oliver as D.C.N.S. 'My boy Syd', as he
was known throughout his career (his father, Admiral Sir E. R.
Fremantle, had once so referred to him), was a great-grandson of
Nelson's friend and follower, Admiral Sir Thomas Fremantle.
Though wanting to do everybody's job, he was not an absolute

---

[4] In March 1918 Lord Pirrie, head of Harland and Wolff, shipbuilders, was put in
charge of merchant shipbuilding (Controller-General of Merchant Shipbuilding),
directly responsible to the First Lord. Merchant shipbuilding had been under a
civilian Controller (Geddes, then Anderson since May 1917.

[5] Richmond's opinion of the unassertive, yet able, Hope was too harsh: 'a very
undecided person—the sort of man who would call for councils of war in any serious
matter rather than decide on a courageous course.' Diary, 1 June 1918. Arthur J.
Marder, *Portrait of an Admiral: the Life and Papers of Sir Herbert Richmond* (London,
1952), p. 312. (Hereafter cited by title only.)

ass, being of somewhat better-than-average ability.[6] The new Director of Plans, *vice* Keyes, was Captain Cyril Fuller, a live wire, clever, charming, and always ready to listen to others. (Commander Kenneth Dewar became Assistant Director of Plans in March 1918.)

Alterations in Naval Staff organization were announced on 14 January 1918. They amounted to this (in addition to the change noted above for the Deputy First Sea Lord): the Operations Division was separated into two parts (Home and Foreign), with a Director for each: Captains Dudley Pound and Charles Coode, respectively. Formerly, there had been a Deputy Director for home and an Assistant Director for foreign work, both coming under the D.O.D. The D.N.I. and the D.T.S.D. (Director of Training and Staff Duties) were shown as working directly under the First Sea Lord–C.N.S. The second major change was a new division, Training and Staff Duties, that had been established on 7 December 1917 (in accordance with Geddes's memorandum of 10 September 1917) under Rear-Admiral James C. Ley. Many difficulties arose in the definition of the Division's duties, and it was not until June 1918 that they were finally announced. 'They were very different from those of its counterpart on the General Staff [described as: 'to examine and promote every measure necessary to ensure the fighting efficiency of the forces'] and, speaking generally, embraced only the organization of Staff Duties, and responsibility to the C.N.S. for the principles governing the system of entry and training of officers and men.'[7] A Director of the Air Division was introduced (under the D.C.N.S.) early in 1918: Wing-Captain F. R. Scarlett, an officer of progressive ideas and broad experience in naval aviation. He dealt with naval air operations and all questions of air policy and organization from

---

6 Richmond was ungenerous, if not too wide of the mark, in his estimate of Fremantle: 'Fremantle tries to run his division of the Staff like an old-fashioned Commander ran a ship—hoisting out the dinghy, getting up to scrub decks & seeing the hammocks down himself. He does not understand the A.B.C. of staff work.' 'Fremantle is a doctrinaire, unable to take "the other man's point of view," never consults anyone, is, in fact, the antithesis of a Staff officer.' Diary, 1 June 1918, 12 February 1919; *Portrait of an Admiral*, pp. 312, 333. Wemyss, on the other hand, was too generous in rating Fremantle 'a decided success' as D.C.N.S. Wemyss's unpublished memoirs; Wemyss MSS.

7 Naval Staff Monograph, *The Naval Staff of the Admiralty. Its Work and Development* (1929), p. 93. The original intention had been that the T.S.D. should perform duties analogous to those of the Staff Duties Division of the General Staff.

the point of view of the Naval Staff and served as a liaison officer between the Admiralty and the Air Ministry.

To sum up, the Naval Staff now, and for the duration of the war, consisted of these divisions and with the general distribution of duties between members of the Board belonging to the Naval Staff as shown: *under the C.N.S.* (responsible for naval policy and general direction of operations): Intelligence, Training and Staff Duties (and in June 1918, a new division, Gunnery and Torpedo, under a Director of Naval Artillery and Torpedo—Captain F. C. Dreyer[8]); *under the D.C.N.S.* (responsible for Home waters operations): Operations (Home), Air, Signals, Plans (the last-named was transferred to the C.N.S. some time in 1918); *under the A.C.N.S.* (responsible for trade protection and A/S operations): Anti-Submarine, Mercantile Movements, Minesweeping, Trade; *under the D.1S.L.* (responsible for general policy questions and operations outside Home waters): Operations (Foreign). (In March 1918, operations in the White Sea and Baltic were transferred to the D.C.N.S.)

The Admiralty's statement pointed to the most significant result of the new organization: 'The principle of isolating the work of planning and directing naval war operations from all other work, in order that it may receive the entire attention of the officers selected for its performance, is now being carried a stage further and applied systematically to the organisation of the operations side of the Board and that of the Naval Staff.'

A memorandum of 14 January 1918, initiated by Geddes and Wemyss, tried to clarify the troublesome problem of Board responsibility for operations. It stated:

The D.C.N.S., A.C.N.S. and D.1S.L. will in the name of the C.N.S. issue operation orders in their own spheres on their own responsibility, subject always to their reference of important matters to the C.N.S. and in accordance with his instructions from time to time, and the responsibility for these orders is not Board responsibility unless the question at issue is referred to the Board. In the absence of the C.N.S. the responsibility for operations in their respective spheres falls auto-

---

8 Admiral Sir Percy Scott and other authorities interested in naval gunnery had long advocated a differentiation in the functions of the D.N.O. Design and supply of gunnery material remained in the hands of the D.N.O. (Captain H. R. Crooke, *vice* Dreyer), whereas Dreyer ('a most exceptional man,' in Wemyss's judgement) in his new post served as an adviser to the Naval Staff on the best employment of guns and torpedoes.

PLATE I

SIR ERIC GEDDES

First Lord of the Admiralty, 1917–18

Photograph: by permission of Sir Reay Geddes

WALTER LONG

First Lord of the Admiralty, 1919–21

Portrait by A. H. Collins: by permission of the 4th Viscount Long

matically on to those officers who will, it is hoped, be in close and constant communication with each other. In questions of gravity they were in the absence of the C.N.S. to consult the First Lord and the Second Sea Lord, the responsibility for doing so being theirs. Unless operation orders result from Board decision the responsibility of issuing them remains under Order-in-Council [23 October 1917] on the shoulders of the C.N.S. and of the First Sea Lord.[9]

2. RESULTS

The New Order was overall a smashing success. Wemyss summed up the results of his methods and of the Staff reorganization fairly: 'The results were better and quicker even than I had hoped for, and decisions were now reached quickly and with everybody's knowledge, whereas before the rage for secrecy had resulted in confusion, overlapping and clumsy work. Confidence and cheerfulness now took the place of uncertainty and gloom at the Admiralty, and I had not been seated many weeks in the First Sea Lord's chair before I had the pleasure of knowing that the machine was running more smoothly and efficiently than before.'[10]

Richmond's appointment as D.T.S.D. in April 1918 (he had been in command of the *Conqueror*, 2nd Battle Squadron, Grand Fleet) gives us the measure of Wemyss's tolerance and breadth of mind. Richmond's independent character, outspokenness, and reputation for being a visionary and an intellectual had blocked his getting to the Admiralty before, despite Beatty's support. Wemyss was aware of Richmond's drawbacks and of the doubts of senior Grand Fleet officers about the soundness of his views on education: Richmond held strong opinions against the early entry and training of officers. Everett, the Naval Secretary, was among those dead against Richmond coming to the Admiralty, and the Secretary, Oswyn Murray, advised Wemyss against the appointment of Richmond because the Fleet 'would be against it'. Wemyss finally overcame his doubts and brought this officer of outstanding talents to the Admiralty. 'I am', he wrote to the C.-in-C., 'in entire agreement with Evan-Thomas, Napier, Goodenough, Sinclair, Bentinck and Brand on the subject of his disqualifications as regards education; and as I know something

[9] Naval Staff Monograph, *The Naval Staff of the Admiralty*, p. 91.
[10] Lady Wester Wemyss, *The Life and Letters of Lord Wester Wemyss* (London, 1935), p. 370, quoting from the Admiral's unpublished memoirs. (Hereafter cited as *Wester Wemyss*.)

about it and have strong opinions myself, I shall be on the look out and shall not let him run off the rails. This will be all the easier as I intend him to work directly under me. Now that I have withdrawn all opposition and got him here, I realise that there are things in which he will be of the greatest value in helping us.'[11] Such was the spirit of the new régime.

For the first time in the war there was harmony in the High Command at the Admiralty and as between the Admiralty and the Grand Fleet. 'The mutual relations established between the First Lord and the new First Sea Lord were almost ideal,' Geddes's brother tells us, 'and they worked together with unmistakable cordiality. The First Lord protected the sailors from political interference, and the sailors saw to it that their whole service responded heartily to the lead given by the reconstituted Board of Admiralty.'[12] Their relations may not have been quite ideal— Wemyss and Geddes did have their differences, especially on *matériel* matters—but they did like and trust each other and were able to work together with a considerable degree of amicability.

The relations between Wemyss and Beatty were, if anything, even more satisfactory, and a vast improvement over the 1917 situation. 'The relations between Beatty and Jellicoe,' Wemyss reflected after the war, 'had never been cordial—the former always considered that the latter had thrown away the Battle of Jutland and had no opinion of him generally, and it is certain that the relations between Admiralty and Grand Fleet became very much closer and more cordial with my advent.'[13] Wemyss and Beatty were on a 'My dear Rosy'—'My dear David' footing. There was a free exchange of ideas and points of view and no serious differences until practically the end of the war. As Beatty told the First Lord, 'Everything works smoothly between the Admiralty and the Grand Fleet as you say on the operational side and I feel that we are in much closer touch with each other than we ever were before.'[14] Wemyss echoed the sentiment. 'I was very glad to have had that meeting with you on Monday last. I came away with a very clear conception of your ideas, and believe that the co-operation between the Grand Fleet and the Admiralty is excellent . . . there is no doubt that the communications are improving as

[11] Wemyss to Beatty, 26 March 1918; Wemyss MSS. But see below, p. 326.
[12] Baron Geddes, *The Forging of a Family* (London, 1952), p. 243.
[13] Wemyss, memoirs.
[14] Beatty to Geddes, 9 April 1918; Geddes MSS.

we realise your mind and what it is you want to know.'[15] Not that controversial subjects did not arise. Thus, Beatty was insistent on the Grand Fleet receiving more destroyers: its needs were declared to be paramount. 'When an impasse was evident,' Admiral Fremantle writes, 'Wemyss used to send me up to Rosyth to do my best with the C.-in-C., and provided I sat quiet for the first hour of an interview, and gave him the full chance of declaiming against Admiralty iniquities, he was ready to hear and to give full weight to our case, and I was usually able to return having arrived at an understanding.'[16]

In response to a request from the Prime Minister to know in what ways there had been an improvement in the efficiency of the Navy 'since the changes which you effected were made,' Geddes responded on the same day:

. . . I am far more than satisfied with the division between the 'Operations' and the 'Maintenance' side which was carried out. . . . It has strengthened the control of the Board, fixed responsibility, and quickened decisions, ensuring at the same time that decisions in important matters are taken with a full knowledge of the facts. The reorganisation of the staff since Sir Rosslyn Wemyss became First Sea Lord has resulted, in my opinion, in great benefit. The staff is no longer overworked and has time to plan ahead and to devise operations. There is hardly a day now when the Navy is not doing something. . . .

There is now an agreed policy on most matters between ourselves and the Commander-in-Chief, Grand Fleet, and the relationship is undoubtedly very good indeed. . . .

There are new plans to be brought into operation as soon as circumstances and material permit. There is a policy in all matters of importance. . . . To an increasing extent men are being judged on their merits rather than upon their seniority, and there is a determination, which I think is growing, to search out and deal with inefficiency.[17]

There was some substance in this rather idyllic picture.

After the chronic U-boat migraine in the Atlantic and Home waters, it was in the Mediterranean that the new Board found most of their urgent problems in the first months of the New Year. It all began with an encore of the *Goeben* fiasco of 1914.

15 Wemyss to Beatty, 4 May 1918; Wemyss MSS.
16 Admiral Sir Sydney Fremantle, *My Naval Career, 1880–1928* (London, 1949), p. 244.
17 Geddes to Lloyd George, 24 April 1918; Geddes MSS. On the first sentence, see *From the Dreadnought to Scapa Flow*, iv. 219–21. The division of the Board into Operations and Maintenance was not entirely a success, as it caused some overlapping and duplication. The *matériel* departments disliked it.

II

Mediterranean Problems

Our dear allies the French and Italians are really almost more difficult to deal with than is the enemy, and to get them in accord to move their ships to the proper places in the Mediterranean is the great difficulty.

WEMYSS to Beatty, 29 May 1918.

So few people at home seem to bother much about this part of the world. The problems that arise from time to time in the Mediterranean appear to be looked upon as being so many nuisances, having no connection with the home problems, and are brushed aside, or settled by the Allied Council, which means that, our representative being more or less indifferent, the French and Italian opinions are those that govern the decisions.

COMMANDER GERALD C. DICKENS (Flag-Commander to C.-in-C., Mediterranean) to Acting Captain K. G. B. Dewar, 9 May 1918.

I. THE *GOEBEN* SORTIE

(*Charts 2, 3*)

AN EVENT in the first month of the new régime at Whitehall acutely reminded the Navy and the country of the fiasco which had ushered in the war at sea. The possibility of a sortie from the Dardanelles by the battle cruiser *Goeben* and light cruiser *Breslau* (under German command, though flying the Turkish flag and renamed the *Yavuz Sultan Selim* and the *Medilli*, respectively) had been in Allied thoughts for a long time. It was expected that an attempt to leave the Dardanelles would coincide with a breaking out of the Austrian Fleet from the Adriatic. Fremantle, Rear-Admiral Commanding Aegean Squadron since August 1917, had listed three possible objectives of a German sortie alone:

(1) To effect a junction with the Austrians in the Adriatic.

(2) A raid on our transport routes, returning to the Dardanelles or to Smyrna.

(3) Attack on our bases at Mudros, or Salonika, or possibly Port Said or Alexandria.

Of these alternatives:—

(1) is considered to be the least unlikely, and to have a fair prospect of success.

(2) Is possible, but the chances of success would seem to be insufficient to warrant the risk incurred.

(3) Would be a desperate venture, which could only end in the eventual destruction of the enemy, and is conceivable only as a last resort, which might be decided upon in the event of Turkey determining upon a separate peace.[1]

In the event, it was the third possibility which the Germans adopted.

Precautions had been taken against a sortie. Look-out stations had been established on the islands of Tenedos and Mavro, and at Cape Kephalo on Imbros, and there was a naval air base in Imbros from which daily reconnaissance flights were carried out over the Dardanelles. From four to six destroyers, also, were normally on patrol in these waters. The two best pre-dreadnoughts, the *Lord Nelson* and *Agamemnon*, were at an hour's notice at Mudros. Too slow (18 knots at best) to overtake the German ships (the *Breslau*, nominally 27·5 knots, was still able to do 20 knots and the *Goeben* could do 22), but armed with four 12-inch and ten 9·2-inch each, they could protect the base and bar a line of retreat to the Dardanelles. (The *Goeben* mounted ten 11-inch, twelve 5·9-inch, the *Breslau*, twelve 4·1-inch). Finally, mines had been laid in 1916–17 between Gallipoli and Imbros. The British were confident that this would ensure the receipt of some warning of the exit of the German cruisers, since they would attempt to sweep a channel first.

Unfortunately, Rear-Admiral Hayes-Sadler, that 'good average officer of no outstanding qualities' (as an officer on the staff of the C.-in-C., Mediterranean, Gough-Calthorpe, described him), had succeeded Fremantle on 12 January. Hayes-Sadler had left Mudros for Salonika, where he had business, on 16 January. He would normally have used the *Triad*, a yacht kept at Mudros for the purpose; but since she was away, though due back in a few days, he elected to go in the *Lord Nelson*, thus separating her from her sister ship. He could, of course, have postponed his visit until the *Triad* arrived or have taken a destroyer or other craft. Hayes-Sadler afterwards confessed to an error of judgement; but he had

---

[1] Fremantle's memorandum of 31 December 1917; Admiralty MSS.

not known there was a definite understanding that the two battleships were to be kept together. Gough-Calthorpe was critical of
this separation of the two battleships, although it had not affected
the action of the raiders (had the two battleships been together,
and left Mudros at the first enemy report, they could not have
caught the *Goeben*), 'except that possibly it may have influenced
them in deciding to come out.' The Germans were aware through
air reconnaissance that there was only one battleship at Mudros.

The Aegean Squadron on 20 January were spread over that
sea. In Mudros harbour, Lemnos, were the *Agamemnon*, three light
cruisers, a sloop, a monitor and an auxiliary minesweeper (both
under repair), and four destroyers (with a fifth en route), only two
of which were ready for action. Additionally, there were 24 vessels
(including the *Lord Nelson*, 2 cruisers, 4 light cruisers, 6 destroyers,
and 8 monitors) divided among six 'detached squadrons': at Suda
Bay (Crete), Salonika, Kusu Bay (Imbros), etc. The organization
of the Aegean into a large number of areas, each under a Senior
Officer, was a relic of the earlier days when a very large force was
based there. Fremantle's orders, to which Hayes-Sadler fell heir,
read: 'The primary consideration is to destroy the enemy.'
Aware, however, that the *Goeben* could mop up the British
squadron, except perhaps for the two old battleships, he went on
to say: 'This is best attained not by attack regardless of circumstances, but by leading him in a direction in which support may
be obtained, and where he can be brought to action by superior
force.' 'This very sensible caution,' Newbolt observes, 'was, however, somewhat weakened by the wording of the general signal
which was to be made if the Germans were known to be out. The
signal ran: "Take all necessary action to engage the enemy," and
this was an order which British naval officers could only interpret
in one way.'[2]

After the armistice with Russia (15 December 1917), which
signalled the end of hostilities in the Black Sea, the German Vice-
Admiral von Rebeur-Paschwitz had begun to plan an operation
in the Aegean. It was for him intolerable that his two ships should
simply lay up in the Bosphorus for the duration. There was also

---

[2] Sir Julian S. Corbett and Sir Henry Newbolt, *History of the Great War. Naval Operations* (London, 1920–31, 5 vols., iv and v by Newbolt), v. 84.

the thought that a naval success might raise Turkish morale, following their loss of Jerusalem on 10 December. The plan that emerged called for a sortie to destroy the patrol craft off the Dardanelles, and, if this went well, a thrust towards Mudros for a bombardment of the harbour by the *Goeben*, while the *Breslau* swept along the south-east corner of Lemnos on the lookout for any large enemy warships that might put out. A submarine was to lay mines off Mudros and to remain off the Bay.

The *Goeben* and *Breslau*, with four destroyers in company, sailed at 4 p.m. on 19 January, passing through the exit from the Dardanelles towards 6 a.m. on the 20th. As planned, the destroyers were sent back at the exit. The British destroyers *Tigress* and *Lizard* (reduced to two by A/S requirements) did not sight the enemy force. They could patrol only well to the westward of the minefield off the Straits; at the time they were patrolling to the north-east of Imbros. Nor did the look-out station at Mavro Island sight the enemy. Gough-Calthorpe afterwards criticized this lapse; subsequent inquiry showed that nothing was visible from Mavro until 7.40 a.m., owing to the thick mist that morning and the early hour at which the sortie was made.

The *Goeben* and *Breslau* turned to the south-west. The Admiral had an imperfect knowledge of the minefields and had not made a careful reconnaissance of them. At 6.10 the *Goeben* struck a mine, which caused only slight damage. She altered course towards Imbros at 6.32, while ordering the *Breslau* to speed on and pin down any shipping lying in Kusu Bay at the north-east corner of Imbros, about four miles north of Cape Kephalo. The *Goeben* destroyed the wireless and signal station at Cape Kephalo with her fourth salvo at a range of two miles. She now joined the *Breslau*, which had chased off the *Tigress* and *Lizard*, in quickly dispatching with accurate gunfire at 10,000 yards the two monitors (*Raglan*, *M28*) lying at anchor in Kusu Bay. It was a little after 8 a.m., and there being no more targets, the Admiral ordered a turnabout. He intended to follow the same course initially, which he believed to be mine-free, towards the south of Imbros and then to head for Mudros Bay, 40 miles away, to execute the more dangerous part of his plan. Hauling wide to port of the flagship, so that the *Goeben* could bring her anti-aircraft guns to bear on bombers that had arrived from Imbros and were attacking, the *Breslau* struck a mine in the western extremity of the minefields

(8.31).[3] The serious damage to her steering and to the starboard turbine put her out of control. As the *Goeben* manœuvred to take the *Breslau* in tow, she, too, ploughed into a mine (8.55). The situation was desperate. There were mines all around the German ships, plainly visible in the clear water; aeroplanes were repeatedly attacking with bombs (the *Breslau* received a direct hit); it was thought that an enemy submarine had been sighted; the *Tigress* and *Lizard*, which had maintained touch with the enemy force, were clawing away at the *Breslau*; and four more mines struck her between 9 and 9.05, whereupon she heeled over to port, righted herself for a moment, and slipped under, her bows high in the air.

Rebeur-Paschwitz, realizing that he could not save the *Breslau* and that his own ship was in mortal danger, abandoned the Mudros operation and ordered a return to harbour. He was in no danger from enemy warships, since the forces at Mudros did not leave harbour until too late to intercept him. Mudros had known of the sortie by 7.35 through a signal from the *Raglan*; but Hayes-Sadler, at Salonika, did not know what had happened until just before 8. And when he did, he busied himself with making preparations against a raid that he expected would last for many days: he had the detached squadrons steaming to the patrol stations allocated to them in Fremantle's orders, and so on.

The German Admiral's course was to the south-west, skirting the mines, and then south-eastwards and eastwards towards the Straits by the track followed on the outward journey. The troubles of the *Goeben* were not over. At 9.48 she struck a mine at just about the position where she had exploded her first mine. Again damage was slight, though by now she had a 15-degree list to port. Approaching the Dardanelles, the *Goeben* was subjected to attack by British aircraft, none of whose bombs came close. She passed into the Dardanelles at 10.30. As she steamed through the German minefields, she once more escaped a shower of bombs from aircraft. At 11.32, when she had negotiated the minefields and the worst seemed over, she ran on to a sandbank at Nagara. For the

---

[3] This was the one tactical manoeuvre of which the German Official History was critical. 'Even with *Breslau* astern, *Goeben*'s guns should have been capable of action. . . . In the mine-infested area, any manoeuvre that was not absolutely essential should have been avoided, and all the more so, since the failure of *Goeben*'s compass [due to the mine damage] meant that accurate navigation could no longer be guaranteed.' Rear-Admiral Hermann Lorey, *Der Krieg zur See, 1914–1918. Der Krieg in den türkischen Gewässern* (1928–38, 2 vols.), i (*Die Mittelmeer-Division*), 341.

next six days she was stuck fast while bombed vigorously by R.F.C. and R.N.A.S. aircraft operating from Mudros and Imbros, and from the carriers *Ark Royal* and *Empress*: 270 flights were made and fifteen tons of bombs were dropped. Strong winds, low clouds, and fierce and accurate anti-aircraft fire, which kept the planes at a great height, rendered the attacks ineffective. Two small bombs hit, doing little damage. Even had the bombing accuracy been greater, the 65-lb. and 112-lb. bombs available could not have done much damage to a ship of the *Goeben*'s construction. The small carrier *Manxman* arrived at Mudros at 7 a.m. on the 25th; with her were two seaplanes fitted with 18-inch torpedoes. By the time they were ready for action, on the 26th, wind and sea conditions prevented the seaplanes getting away. It was too late, anyway. Of course none of these 'carriers' were carriers as understood today.

An attempt to get at the *Goeben* through indirect fire by a monitor was no more successful than the air bombing. Submarine attack offered the only hope. The one submarine immediately available was *E-12*, at Mudros, and she had a fractured shaft (not uncommon in the 'E'-class) on the port side between the diesel engine and the electric motor. This, if disconnected from the motor, in no way affected her underwater speed or endurance, but it reduced her surface speed; and if she had to recharge her batteries, she could have done so only when lying stopped on the surface or moving very slowly. The Lieutenant in command, F. Williams-Freeman, was furious because the S.N.O. on the spot, subsequently backed up by Hayes-Sadler (he had steamed into Mudros in the early afternoon of 21 January), would not allow him to have a go at the *Goeben* as soon as it was known that she was aground. Williams-Freeman reported that his boat was ready with a surface speed of 7 knots (she was normally capable of 12 knots) and a submerged speed of 6 knots. The Rear-Admiral, however, persisted in the belief that she was too crippled to do the job, and 'decided, after full consideration, not to send him up the Straits, in view of the additional risk he would have had to take with only one engine available for [battery] recharging purposes.'[4] *E-2* (Lieutenant P. H. Bonham-Carter) and *E-14* (Lieutenant-Commander G. S. White) were by now (22 January) at Mudros,

---

[4] Hayes-Sadler's final report, 17 February 1918; Admiralty MSS. Another factor in his decision was the clear nights and smoothness of the sea, which reduced the chances of success. Geddes to Gough-Calthorpe, 21 February 1918; Geddes MSS.

having been ordered from Malta and Corfu, respectively, as soon as the news about the *Goeben* came through. A junior officer in *E-2* 'remembers vividly Bonham-Carter's air of contempt and exasperation when he returned from discussing with Hayes-Sadler whether we should have a shot at the *Goeben*—refusing to take any responsibility or allow it to others, and with a pipe in his mouth all the time down which he dribbled! It seems that he was waiting for the arrival of [Gough-]Calthorpe to make the decision.'[5] The Admiralty, upon receiving the news of the sortie, had wired the British C.-in-C., Mediterranean, to go to the Aegean. Gough-Calthorpe reached Mudros on 25 January. Later that day (it may have been the next day), at a conference which Hayes-Sadler, White, and others attended, it was decided that *E-14* should go in. 'Lieutenant-Commander White was the senior and most experienced Commanding Officer of the submarines present; he had previously reconnoitred the *Goeben* from an aeroplane [22 January—Bonham-Carter with him, in case he might subsequently get the call]; and his boat was clearly the one to be selected, as *E-12* had defects and *E-2* had an inexperienced Commanding Officer, a new crew, and only one stem tube [*E-14* had two bow tubes].'[6] *E-14* sailed late on the 27th and managed to penetrate to Nagara on the 28th, only to find her quarry gone: the *Goeben* had been floated off and towed to Constantinople two days earlier. *E-14* turned back, but was detected by Turkish hydrophones. Depth-charged, she was blown to the surface and sunk off Kum Kale by shore batteries.

The minefields off the Dardanelles were greatly strengthened, and the C.-in-C. gave definite orders that the two battleships were not in future to be separated. But the damage to the *Goeben*

---

5 Captain John Creswell's letter to the author, 24 February 1967. Captain Creswell describes Bonham-Carter as 'the only man I have ever known who absolutely and literally did not know what fear was. Such men are few. It was mainly because he was deeply religious as well as physically tough. He was known as "Bonham the Good" and had a cousin of about the same age who was known as "Bonham the Bad" [now Admiral, ret., Sir Stuart Bonham-Carter], who was a bit of a rip in his younger days but commanded a blockship at Zeebrugge and was a very successful leader of men.' Letter to the author, 31 December 1968.

6 Gough-Calthorpe to Admiralty, 1 February 1918; Admiralty MSS. Captain Creswell writes: 'By that time nearly a week had elapsed, and with the idea that the enemy must have been doing everything possible to strengthen their anti-submarine defences, the exhilaration of the exploit was not what it had been. *E-14* was lying alongside us until she sailed, and I don't think my opposite number there expected to come back, and didn't, of course.' Letter of 24 February 1967.

was too extensive to be repaired at Constantinople, and, unknown to the Allies, she was through for the war. (The Naval Staff and Gough-Calthorpe had the idea for a time that she might try to get out of the Dardanelles and proceed to block the Suez Canal. The latter even thought she might 'sweep up the convoy routes' in the Mediterranean and take refuge in a Spanish port.) After the war, the *Goeben* served with the Turkish Fleet for a number of years (as the *Yavuz*, the most powerful unit in the Fleet), then became a training ship, and was laid up in 1954. In 1965 the Turkish Government had the idea of selling her for scrap. When none of the foreign companies bidding came close to the minimum price of about £1,000,000, and no doubt also influenced by the public outcry against the sale of so distinguished an historical monument, the Turks reprieved her from the ship-breaker's yard. They planned to anchor her off Dolmabahce Palace as a naval museum —the last capital ship afloat which had fought in the First War. That idea, too, was given up when they calculated the cost of converting her. A few German firms wanted to purchase the ship, but the sum offered was not satisfactory. Today the *Goeben-Yavuz* is docked at Golcuk, the headquarters of the Turkish Navy. At last report (late 1969) she was headed for the scrap heap.

The outcome of the sortie disgusted Wemyss. 'The *Goeben* getting away is perfectly damnable and has considerably upset me, since we at the Admiralty were under the happy delusion that there were sufficient brains and sufficient means out there to prevent it: of the latter there were; of the former, apparently not.' Beatty called the affair 'truly a tragedy'.[7] The Admiralty unshipped the dithering and indecisive Hayes-Sadler from the Aegean Command for his mismanagement of the business. There was an extenuating factor: he was a sick man. The onetime Fourth Sea Lord, the formidable Rear-Admiral Cecil F. Lambert (he had been commanding the 2nd Light Cruiser Squadron, Grand Fleet, 1917–18), relieved Hayes-Sadler on 23 February and was himself relieved by Rear-Admiral Michael Culme-Seymour in the summer.

It was less the bungled operation itself that was criticized in the British press than the 1914 escape of the two German vessels to the Dardanelles. The 1918 sortie was a poignant reminder of the might-have-beens and the wherefores of August 1914. This was the line taken by *The Observer* and *The Times*, the latter remarking

[7] Wemyss to Beatty, 7 February; Beatty to Wemyss, 13 February 1918; Wemyss MSS.

(22 January) that 'no two warships have had such an important effect upon the war . . . They will always be remembered in naval history. The story of their escape from Messina represents one of the greatest of our blunders. . . . A long train of disastrous events was set in motion when these two vessels entered the Dardanelles.'

The escape of the *Goeben*, the Russo-German Peace Treaty of Brest-Litovsk on 3 March, and the threat of a German takeover of the Russian Black Sea Fleet in April transformed the naval strategic situation in the Mediterranean.

2. THE BLACK SEA FLEET

The command situation in the Mediterranean had never been satisfactory. The responsibility for holding the enemy in that sea was, except for the Adriatic, French; the Italians were responsible in the Adriatic; the British played a subordinate role with subsidiary responsibility only throughout the Mediterranean. The British C.-in-C., at Malta, had a particular responsibility for A/S and escort work, but everything he did was under the nominal command of the French Admiral at Corfu, Gauchet, 'a dour, hard-working little Norman.' It had long been apparent that there was a pressing need for a co-ordination of the Allied naval effort in the Mediterranean. As a step, at least, in that direction an Allied naval conference in Paris on 29–30 November 1917 decided to create an Allied Naval Council (the Ministers of Marine and Chiefs of the Naval Staffs) 'in order to ensure the closest touch and complete co-operation between the Allied Fleets.' Its constitution stated that it had 'no responsibility for the command and direction of the respective Naval forces,' but that to it would be referred, *inter alia*, 'all important questions of principle regarding joint Naval operations.' The first meeting of the new body, 22–23 January 1918 in London, was enough to disillusion the Admiralty. Reported the A.C.N.S.: 'I have been very busy with that most unsatisfactory body known as Allied Naval Council. The cry of the Italian is "Give, Give", and to obtain real disinterested co-operation appears an ideal impossible of attainment.'[8]

---

[8] Duff to Bethell, 28 January 1918; Duff MSS. Geddes, who attended the second Allied Naval Council meeting, in Rome on 8–9 February, reported: 'I do not think that we are going to get any more destroyers out of the Italians for use in anti-submarine work, but I think at any rate that we have scotched their reiterated

A regular topic on the agendas of the Council into June was the Russian Black Sea Fleet: how its seizure by the Germans would affect the naval situation in the Mediterranean and what should be done about that contingency. The third Council meeting, held in London on 12–13 March, would not panic, concluding that: 'If Germany so desires she will have no great difficulty in obtaining possession of the Russian Black Sea Fleet, and also that Germany will be able to man at least the most modern units of this Fleet if she obtains possession, though she will have difficulty in so doing, using either Russian or Turkish personnel or personnel transferred from Germany, and that time will be required to train the personnel.' The Germans would need two to six months to restore the ships to seagoing fighting efficiency once they got them. It was considered 'probable' that the exit of this force from the Dardanelles would be signalled to the Allies by the clearing in advance of a passage through the minefields at the entrance. (Apparently, nothing had been learned from the *Goeben* sortie!) The Council felt no need to rearrange Allied forces in the Eastern Mediterranean for an eventuality so far in the future—if, indeed, it came to pass at all.

The Admiralty considered the maximum number of Russian ships likely to be used by the Germans as 2 dreadnoughts (*Volya* and *Svobodnaya Rossiya*), 3 pre-dreadnoughts, 2 old cruisers, 1 light cruiser, 16 destroyers, and 6 submarines. The Allies had to guard against two related situations. To contain the Austrian force in the Adriatic, whose backbone was 4 dreadnoughts (one of them, the *Szent-Istvan*, was sunk by an Italian coastal motor-boat on 10 June during an attempted raid on Allied light forces in the southern Adriatic), they had an overwhelming force in the French and Italian Fleets, which included 7 French and 5 Italian dreadnoughts. This enormous preponderance, as Gough-Calthorpe pointed out, was 'of course, a serious waste of energy, of fighting ships and of men; and, what is still more serious, a waste of mercantile tonnage in providing them with coal and stores. It is difficult to propose any remedy, because the situation no doubt results from the desire of both the French and Italians each to

demand for more destroyers from us. The mentality of the Italian Naval authorities is most extraordinary . . .' Geddes to Lloyd George, 9 February 1918; Geddes MSS. The Cab. 28 class (I.C. series) at the P.R.O. includes the minutes (proceedings and conclusions) of the Allied Naval Council.

keep a force sufficient to defeat the enemy single-handed.'[9] On the other hand, this superiority was to some extent dissipated by the division of the two fleets between Corfu and Taranto and the fact that the inner harbour at Taranto, where the Italian battleships lay, was separated by a very narrow passage from the outer harbour. In case of damage to the bridge which crossed the passage, the Italian fleet might not effect a junction with the French until too late. (On one occasion, when the mechanism for opening the bridge had broken down—not for the first time—over thirty hours passed before it could be opened.) Gough-Calthorpe's 'ideal solution' for the Adriatic problem, if the difficult question of command could be overcome, was to place the best units of the two fleets under one C.-in-C. at Corfu. The other potential danger lay in the insufficiency of force in the Aegean to ensure the containment of the enemy's force in the Dardanelles: the 2 British and 2 French pre-dreadnoughts, at Mudros and Salonika, respectively, all of inferior speed, were no match for the *Goeben* and the two Russian dreadnoughts. Some time in late March or early April the Admiralty concurred in a French proposal to solve both strategic problems: the Italian Fleet would join the French Fleet and a French battleship force would reinforce the squadron in the Aegean.

One consideration that underlay the British acceptance was their low opinion—contempt might not be too strong a word—of the fighting efficiency and morale of the Italian Fleet. As an illustration, we have these impressions of Geddes after a visit to Taranto and other naval bases in southern Italy:

> The Italian battlefleet at Taranto lies in the inner harbour and seldom or never goes to sea, and the only exercise or practice the ships obtain is that, occasionally, one ship at a time goes into the outer harbour for gunnery practice with sub-calibre ammunition. Under these conditions it is impossible for these five ships to be really efficient, and the opinion I formed, which is fully confirmed by the expert Naval Officers who accompanied me, was that they never would become efficient and a source of strength to the Allied Naval forces in the Mediterranean until they were got away to another base and exercised as a fleet and put through a rigorous course of gunnery and torpedo practice.[10]

9 Gough-Calthorpe's memorandum for the First Lord, 'Brief Review of the Present Situation in the Adriatic,' 20 February 1918; Geddes MSS.
10 Geddes to Lloyd George, 6 April 1918; Lloyd George MSS.

Nothing was done, however, until a grave turn in the Black Sea situation compelled the Allies to strengthen their forces in the Aegean. On 19 April the Germans entered the Crimea, which was part of the Ukrainian state whose independence the Germans had recognized. They had already taken over the warships building at Nikolaiev on the Black Sea (occupied on 15 March), and the capture of the Black Sea Fleet, or as much of it as they wanted, seemed imminent.[11] The Allied Naval Council met in Paris on 26–27 April as the Germans were approaching the main naval base at Sevastopol. It agreed that it was 'possible, and even probable, that in the near future Germany may acquire, man, and utilise for operations in the Mediterranean at least the more modern and efficient units of the Russian Black Sea Fleet.' There was also agreement that the Allies had ample strength in the Mediterranean to meet and defeat both the *Goeben* and the Black Sea Fleet on the one hand and the Austrian Fleet on the other, if only the Allied forces were regrouped. This would take the form of reinforcing the British squadron at Mudros with six French battleships. To compensate for this reduction in French strength at Corfu, and with an eye to a possible Austrian attempt to leave the Adriatic to effect a junction with the Black Sea Fleet, Italy should dispatch a dreadnought squadron (four ships) to Corfu. These ships would be 'permanently attached to and incorporated in the Fleet under the Allied Commander-in-Chief at Corfu.' This would, as Wemyss expressed it to the War Cabinet, 'ensure effective co-operation, strategic dispositions, and tactical efficiency.'

The Italian representatives balked at this proposal: 'The principle of subordinating the sending to the Aegean of some of the French units now at Corfu to the arrival at Corfu of the Italian Dreadnoughts is not acceptable; the advisability of such

---

11 For a long time the Allies were without exact knowledge as to which ships, built and building, had fallen into German hands. They had to assume and prepare for the worst. The facts were that on 30 April Russian naval officers loyal to the Allied cause and the old régime had sailed the two dreadnoughts and about fifteen destroyers from Sevastopol to Novorossisk on the eastern coast of the Black Sea. All the Germans acquired upon entering Sevastopol on 2 May were the three old battleships and two cruisers, together with an old Turkish cruiser, and under the Treaty of Brest-Litovsk the Germans had the right to disarm them, no more. Later, in June, the Russian sailors destroyed the *Svobodnaya Rossiya*; the other dreadnought, the *Volya*, and six destroyers were brought back to Sevastopol and put under the control of the German disarmament commission. The Germans made no attempt to transform the collection of Russian ships into a fighting squadron.

a movement is exclusively dependent upon events in the Adriatic, which cannot be foreseen and may not be related to those in the Aegean.' What lay behind the Italian *non possumus* was the hoary problem of the command situation in the Mediterranean. Behind that lay 'the jealousies of our two dear Allies,' as Wemyss declared. Put in the baldest terms, Italian *amour propre* prevented their agreeing to come under the command of the French. The same *amour propre* would even more strongly have prevented the French, who had the larger force in the Mediterranean, to say nothing of a French Admiral as C.-in-C., Mediterranean, from coming under the Italian command. This, however, was more understandable. There were also political reasons behind the Italian unwillingness to commit their Fleet outside the Adriatic. They conceived of their role in the war as being confined to the defeat of Austria-Hungary and the reaping of the territorial rewards that had been promised in the Treaty of London (26 April 1915).

The Allied Supreme War Council,[12] meeting at Abbeville on 1 May, took up the problem. The Italian Prime Minister, Orlando, at first would not discuss the matter, on the ground that, as Admiral Thaon di Revel, the Chief of the Italian Naval Staff, was not present, he did not know enough to give an opinion. Having just received a telegram that the situation in the Black Sea was critical, Wemyss was able to press the point and insist that delay was not permissible. The Council then passed a resolution urging the Italian Government to accept the Allied Naval Council redistribution scheme. Orlando in a somewhat flowery speech accepted the resolution, while pointing out that he understood from di Revel that there were technical difficulties. The battle was not over. The British information was that the Italian Naval Staff favoured the redistribution. This was, for Wemyss, not enough.

---

[12] The Supreme War Council, which had been established on 7 November 1917, had as its missions the co-ordination of military action on the Western Front and 'to watch over the general conduct of the war.' It originally consisted of the Prime Ministers (or their deputies) of Britain, France, and Italy, a second representative from each country, and, acting as technical advisers, a Permanent Military Representative from each. The United States soon became a member of the Council when it appointed General Tasker H. Bliss as its Military Representative. But, to maintain its political independence, it avoided political representation on the Council, except for two of the eight wartime sessions. Other important soldiers, sailors, and statesmen often attended and participated in the discussions. Although the Allied Naval Council was not directly affiliated with the Supreme War Council, the latter occasionally functioned as a clearing house for recommendations from the Naval Council.

PLATE III

ADMIRAL SIR ROSSLYN WEMYSS

First Sea Lord, 1917–19

Drawing by Francis Dodd: Imperial War Museum

PLATE IV

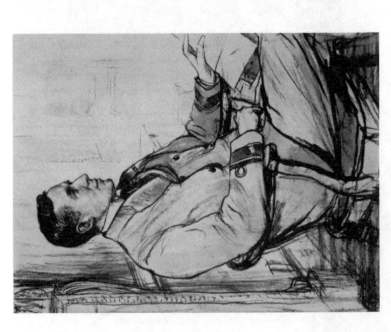

ACTING VICE-ADMIRAL
SYDNEY R. FREMANTLE
Deputy Chief of Naval Staff, 1918–19

Photograph: from My Naval Career, by permission of Messrs.

REAR-ADMIRAL GEORGE P. W. HOPE
Deputy First Sea Lord, 1918–19

Drawing by Francis Dodd: Imperial War Museum

But for the position to be truly satisfactory [he wrote to the Naval Attaché, Rome], we must gain our point with more than the sullen acquiescence of the Italians. We should have their enthusiastic support. . . .

You can, if you think fit, point out to them the very great success which has accrued from the American battleships being incorporated in the Grand Fleet; how excellently they work; on what excellent terms are Admirals, Officers and men with each other; and how, far from any friction arising, the two elements have mingled together and produced nothing but good results. . . .

Now, my dear fellow, this matter has not only got to be put through, but it has got to be put through with the least possible delay, for, if it is not, I do not disguise from you that there is a chance of a very disagreeable debacle in the Eastern Mediterranean.

Di Revel's ideas that more ships than already exist in the Mediterranean should be sent out are perfectly ridiculous. I should hardly point out to you that every extra ship which enters the Mediterranean is an increased difficulty in the matter of supply. Moreover, throwing in the Black Sea Fleet and anything else that the enemy may lay his hands on, we have sufficient heavy forces out there to eat them up over and over again, if only they are properly disposed of and the dispositions put up are the only ones possible. Of this there can be no doubt.[13]

On 11 May, 'as a way out of the difficulty, and as an improvement also on the present proposal,' Wemyss suggested to the War Cabinet the appointment of an 'Inter-Allied Admiralissimo in general command of all Allied Naval Forces in the Mediterranean, Adriatic and Aegean.' He would serve under the Allied Naval Council and be bound by its decisions (to be approved by the Supreme War Council) on the general disposition of the forces under him. Under such an arrangement 'it would perhaps be unnecessary, strategically, for Italian battleships to leave Taranto, as they would all be under an Admiralissimo, and their cooperation and co-ordination with the Corfu Forces would thus be secured'. The British would be prepared to nominate a British Admiral 'if it would ease matters and be acceptable to the Allies.'[14]

13 Wemyss to Acting Captain Dennis Larking, 3 May 1918: Wemyss MSS.
14 Wemyss's memorandum, 'Note upon the Naval Situation in the Mediterranean, Adriatic, and Aegean,' read to the War Cabinet (409A). Wemyss had drawn up his scheme after consulting Lord Milner and the Italian Ambassador. The minutes of the War Cabinet and Imperial War Cabinet meetings will be found in the Cab. 23 class at the P.R.O. Material from this source will be identified merely by 'W.C.' or 'I.W.C.' number of the meeting. The 'A' and 'B' minutes of the War Cabinet were of the more secret meetings.

The War Cabinet approved the plan and instructed the Prime Minister to submit it to the French Premier, Clemenceau; Jellicoe would serve as Admiralissimo 'if [the] Allies wished it.' (The Admiralty had sounded Jellicoe out early in May and secured his acceptance.) The French agreed, though they preferred the original proposal of a reorganization of the commands.

The Supreme War Council had 'a prolonged and heated' discussion of the Admiralissimo question, as well as of the concentration of the French and Italian dreadnoughts at Corfu, at Versailles on 1–2 June. The Italians alone would not accept either solution, Admiral di Revel refusing to contemplate the possibility that an Admiralissimo might order the Italian battle fleet away from Taranto and into the riskier waters of the Mediterranean. He alluded to the difficulty of supplying these ships, then stated this major consideration: 'At present every big ship ran risks at sea. Big ships must therefore move as little as possible.' He contended that battleships must be kept at their bases, safe from submarine and, so far as possible, air attack, emerging only to meet the enemy's battleships. 'If urgent reasons required the despatch of Italian battleships to Corfu, he would accept them, but he did not wish to run unnecessary risks . . . the Allied situation [in the eastern Mediterranean] was strong, and he saw no necessity for sending Italian ships to Corfu.'15 Haig summed up the feelings of all the non-Italians present at the meeting: 'Their objective seemed to be to stay in port and keep their fleet safe. I was disgusted with their attitude.'16

The Eastern Mediterranean situation could not wait, and a few days later the French sent reinforcements to the Aegean: 4 old battleships, 4 submarines, and 6 destroyers were sent to Mudros under Vice-Admiral Darrieus. Being senior to the British Rear-Admiral in command of the British Aegean Squadron (Lambert), he assumed command of the combined Allied Aegean Squadron with British approval. As a further protection against a sortie, more minefields were laid off the Dardanelles.17 Lambert, of

---

15 Minutes of the 1 June meeting; I.C.-64. The I.C. class (Cab. 28 class, P.R.O.) contained the minutes and conclusions of the Allied conferences of 1915–19.

16 Diary, 1 June 1918; Robert Blake (ed.), *The Private Papers of Douglas Haig, 1914–1919* (London, 1952), p. 313.

17 The Naval Staff judgement after the war was that 'it would have been better for the Allies to have kept a squadron of ships in the Aegean numerically, and if possible individually, superior to that of the enemy . . . and that instead of laying down

course, did not care for the new command arrangement; but Wemyss had more important things on his mind.

As long as the whole French Fleet was at Corfu its excess of strength over the Austrian Fleet was sufficiently great to enable it to act without the efficient co-operation of the Italian Fleet, but now that it has become necessary to detach a French Battle Squadron to the Aegean, the efficient co-operation of at least one Italian Battle Squadron is under the circumstances essential, and this efficient co-operation cannot be obtained without combined training under one Command.

It is certain that the only way in which unity of action of the Allied Fleets in the Mediterranean, Aegean and Adriatic, and the most economical and efficient use of those Forces can be obtained, is by uniting them under the strategic Command of one Admiralissimo. . . .

Wemyss recommended that the War Cabinet renew their efforts to win Italian acceptance of the Admiralissimo concept.[18]

Italian obstructionism became, if anything, worse. At the fourth Allied Naval Council, which met in London on 11–12 June, their naval representative, the Deputy Chief of Naval Staff, said No to everything. 'It was apparent . . . that Admiral Triangi had come with instructions to agree to no co-operation which he could avoid, and that the whole attitude of the Italian Navy, as represented by him, was that it should be kept in a water-tight compartment, prepared to seek all the help that the Allies could give, but not prepared to share or co-operate in any way.'[19] On the question of having an inter-Allied survey made of warship-repairing facilities in the Mediterranean, with a view to their more effective use, the Italians, though willing to attend a conference on the subject, refused to bring their own repairing facilities within its purview! The French proposed that (in the words of the Admiralty memorandum of 13 June) 'since apparently the Italians do not

---

many mines it would have been wiser to have left a clear channel by which the enemy could have come out, thus giving themselves (the Allies) a chance of gaining a most important victory; the destruction of the enemy's fleet was of far greater importance than the containing of it.' Naval Staff Monograph, *Mediterranean Staff Papers relating to Naval Operations from August 1917 to December 1918* (1920), p. 24. (Hereafter cited as *Mediterranean Staff Papers*.)

18 Admiralty Memorandum for the War Cabinet, 'Command in the Mediterranean' (G.T.-4788), 8 June 1918. All cited memoranda for the War Cabinet (G. and G.T. series), where a source is not given, are from the Cabinet Office Papers in the Public Record Office (Cab. 24).

19 Admiralty Memorandum for the War Cabinet, 'Command in the Mediterranean' (G.T.-4808), 13 June 1918.

propose to exercise or use their Battle Squadron, and as they were looking only to the Adriatic, it was essential that the British and French Light Forces at present based on Brindisi for the maintenance and protection of the Barrage in the Straits of Otranto, should be placed under the Command of the French Admiral at Corfu [in an emergency], so that in the event of his Battle Squadron having to engage the Austrian Fleet he would have light forces to screen his Battleships.' The Italians were again in a minority of one: there was no need for it, and they pleaded the London Naval Convention with Britain of 10 May 1915 as justification for the retention under their command of the 4 British light cruisers at Brindisi. The Convention did not apply to the 27 British destroyers, which the Italian Admiral was graciously prepared to allow to be put under the Allied C.-in-C., Admiral Gauchet, 'provided that Italy were convinced that the menace from the Russian Black Sea Fleet was serious and imminent, which they did not agree was the case at the present time.' The Council was able to agree on one thing: in view of the 18 or so efficient Russian destroyers the Germans had acquired, the 10 French destroyers would by agreement with the Italians be shifted as soon as practicable from the Adriatic to the Aegean for service with the Allied Fleet there.

The Council meetings also revealed that the Italians were not disposed to increase their effort in the Mediterranean A/S campaign. They preferred as always to hold back their A/S craft for the protection of their ports and coasts, and would not even, an irate Geddes told the War Cabinet (17 June), furnish escorts for the convoys bringing supplies from Britain.

Italian intransigence had reached the point where, on the advice of the Admiralty, 'judicious pressure' on the Italian Government was approved by the War Cabinet on 17 June: the Foreign Office was to communicate with the French and American Governments with a view to the presentation of separate memoranda to the Italian Government, 'urging upon that Government the need for efficient co-operation in the Mediterranean, with combined training, under one command'; and a joint representation was to be made to the Italian Government by Wemyss, Sims, and de Bon (the Chief of the French Naval Staff), 'setting out in specific terms the alterations proposed to improve the Allied naval situation in the Mediterranean.'[20] One of the 'specific terms' apparently

[20] W.C. 431.

called for the ouster of di Revel, who was held responsible for the existing state of affairs: the non-cooperative attitude in general and the inactivity of the Italian light forces in the A/S campaign in particular. The Allied complaints did not produce any tangible results. Di Revel was not toppled.

To the end of the war the naval situation in the Eastern Mediterranean remained unsatisfactory to the Admiralty. On 25 September the First Lord warned: 'If the enemy made a determined effort he could after the end of November come out of the Dardanelles in excessive force at his selected moment, do great damage, and then return to his bases. . . . This state of affairs need not and should not exist if the Allied Naval Forces already in the Mediterranean were used to the best and most economical advantage.' This was possible only through the appointment of a British Admiral as Admiralissimo, which proposal should be resurrected 'as one of urgency and of great importance.'[21]

There had been a momentary break in the clouds in the middle of September. In response to Geddes's continuing conversations with the Italian Government (through the British Ambassador at Rome), the Italians had had second thoughts. They were now ready to accept Jellicoe as Admiralissimo, provided he was in exactly the same position *vis-à-vis* the Supreme War Council at Versailles as General Foch, who had been appointed Generalissimo in the spring: that is, he would be subject to the Council. The

---

[21] Admiralty Memorandum for the War Cabinet (G.T.-5775), 'Naval Situation in the Black Sea and Command in the Mediterranean.' Attached was a memorandum showing the naval position. In efficient fighting ships the Allied Aegean Squadron numbered 8 pre-dreadnoughts (6 French, 2 British), 1 cruiser (Greek), 5 light cruisers (4 British, 1 Greek), 17 destroyers (4 British, 9 French, 4 Greek), and 11 submarines (2 British, 9 French). Besides 5 submarines of their own and 9 efficient Turkish warships (the *Goeben*, 2 cruisers, 6 destroyers), the Germans had these modern Russian ships: 1 dreadnought with another building and nearly completed, 4 pre-dreadnoughts, 2 cruisers, 1 light cruiser nearly completed, 21 destroyers, 12 submarines and 6 more building, of which 3 were nearly completed. A number of the Russian warships were in a bad state of repair, but most would, it was believed, be ready by the end of November; the ships building would probably be ready within two months. The Germans would be able to man all the ships—with German, Russian, and allied crews. At the enemy's *selected moment* after the end of November, and making allowance for the normal number of Allied ships absent refitting, a force superior to the Aegean Squadron could emerge from the Dardanelles: 1 or 2 dreadnoughts *v.* none in the Allied Aegean Squadron, 1 battle cruiser *v.* none, 4 pre-dreadnoughts *v.* 7, 4 cruisers *v.* 1, 1 light cruiser *v.* 4, 23 destroyers *v.* 13, and 20 submarines *v.* 8. To help right the balance the Admiralty sent out the dreadnoughts *Superb* and *Temeraire* in October.

objections of Geddes and Wemyss quashed the Italian plan. They did not relish the thought of a British Admiralissimo being responsible to a body of Allied politicians and its military advisers, which had no technical expertise in naval matters. They wanted Jellicoe to be under the Allied Naval Council, which had the technical knowledge and staff. As Geddes explained to the Prime Minister, 'The First Sea Lord and I therefore feel very strongly that while we could accept the appointment of Lord Jellicoe as a Supreme War Council appointment, if that is of importance, the procedure should provide that he should deal regularly with the Chiefs of Staff of the various Ministries of Marine or Commanders of the various Allied forces, and that the Allied Naval Council should be able from time to time to lay down on broad lines the dispositions and operations which he is to undertake.'[22] The whole subject was about to become an academic one.

Despite the potential threat of the *Goeben* and the Black Sea Fleet and the tedious problems of command, the main source of anxiety in the Mediterranean remained for the British the U-boat warfare against trade.

3. THE OFFENSIVE IN THE ADRIATIC

A convoy system had been operating in the Mediterranean since November 1917; but it was Gough-Calthorpe's view, upon receiving instructions to start convoy, that 'the true solution is to be found in an increased and unceasing offensive which should in time enable us to dispense with the convoys and these methods of defence.' He was the leader of the school of thought which believed

that without a vigorous offensive, the enemy's morale would never be sufficiently shaken so as to seriously deter him from a continued and successful war on seaborne commerce and lines of communication. It was evident that shipping had to be protected, but it was felt that *no lasting success against submarines would be achieved if the enemy knew he was only running risks at the moments chosen by him for attack.* The necessity for seeking him out and engaging him on a ground not of his own choosing and robbing him of the entire initiative of attack was recognised.[23]

22 Geddes to Lloyd George, 17 September 1918; Lloyd George MSS.
23 *Mediterranean Staff Papers*, p. 99. The C.-in-C. had powerful support at the Admiralty. As Geddes informed the Allied Naval Council on 9 February 1918: the convoy system in the Mediterranean had so far been 'only a moderate success. At present we are short of craft and we doubt that even if full practicable escorts are given, it

OTRANTO STRAITS BARRAGE

Cattaro

MONTENEGRO

ALLIED SUBMARINE

DIVING PATROL AREA

Adriatic Sea

A L B A N I A

Advanced Destroyer Force
Northern day limit

Brindisi

Advanced Destroyer Force
Night Patrol

Taranto

C. Linguetta

Otranto
Deep Minefield

Main Trawler line
3 Destroyers in Support

Gulf
of
Taranto

Motor
Launches

Fixed Barrage Patrol
Drifters and 2 Sloops
With Kite Balloons

Deep Minefield

U.S.
Submarine Chasers

Faro

Corfu I.

The italics are mine. This extraordinary aberration calls for comment. Of course, in war this is exactly what happens: when the enemy knows he is running risks at the moments chosen by him for attack, he ceases to attack or he gets destroyed or, if not destroyed, driven off, usually without achieving anything. This is precisely what can be achieved only by a convoy system, as proven in the two World Wars.

At an Allied Naval Council meeting in Rome, 8–9 February 1918, Gough-Calthorpe's idea of a sustained vigorous offensive in the Straits of Otranto was combined with the old Franco-Italian scheme for a permanent net barrage across the Straits. In its developed form the offensive took the shape of 'barrage operations' in the Adriatic: four interrelated operations or devices to destroy the U-boats before they could penetrate the Mediterranean proper and attack shipping.

(1) *The fixed barrage*. The Allied naval conference in Paris on 24–26 July 1917 had decided to establish a fixed barrage of mined nets across the Straits of Otranto. Bad weather broke up the British barrage started in October 1917. The Allied Naval Council meeting at Rome approved a fresh start with a new design. The nets were British, the mines French, and the Italians had the responsibility for laying and maintaining the barrage. It was in operation from 15 April, though not completed until 30 September. The barrage extended from the end of a deep minefield, seven miles east of Otranto, to Fano Island, a distance of 45 miles, and consisted of 150-ft. nets carrying mines with the top of the net submerged 33 feet from the surface.

(2) *The Otranto Mobile Barrage Force*. Since 1915 the British had maintained in the Straits of Otranto drifters, working with nets, and M.L.s (both with hydrophones since 1917), with destroyers for protection, and the assistance of a few seaplanes at Otranto and an intermittent Allied submarine diving patrol. The Rome conference decided to strengthen this force with craft already in the Mediterranean and by reinforcements from Britain. The total force was well over 200 ships: 27–31 destroyers (British and French), 1–6

---

would be efficient. It is not to-day having the effect of destroying submarines, and submarines are increasing, and we think it desirable to devote more of our limited resources to attack submarines in the Straits even if that means to a certain extent reducing the number of craft on escort duty . . .' See further, below, p. 86.

sloops (kite balloons), 3–4 torpedo-boats, 30–36 American submarine chasers, 18–38 hydrophone trawlers, 14–20 trawlers, 101–
109 drifters, 40–41 M.L.s, and a yacht. In addition at Taranto and
Otranto, under Captain Arthur Longmore, were 72 bombers,
fighters, and seaplanes, which was an imposing air force in those
days. The Barrage Force was under the general direction of the
British C.-in-C., Mediterranean, but under the direct command
of the Commodore Commanding British Adriatic Force, Howard
Kelly, of *Goeben* (1914) fame. This was a new departure in the
Adriatic, where the Italians had always been jealous of any other
power working independently. (However, the 8th Light Cruiser
Squadron, based on Brindisi, which Kelly also commanded,
nominally came under the Italian C.-in-C.) Kelly was a good
choice. He was a gifted officer of imposing presence and sound
judgement who but for his cynicism and sarcasm to all and sundry
might have gone much further. It was this attitude which made
him such a poor leader, and he was the last man to make use of the
brains of his juniors. He was the right man for the Adriatic job,
being at his best with foreigners. He got on well with both the
French (he had served as Naval Liaison Officer in Paris) and the
Italians.

The barrage craft were planned to be used in three ways: to
force submarines to dive into the fixed net barrage (the special
responsibility of the drifters on the Fixed Barrage Patrol), to keep
the submarines down, and to hunt them. The saturation coverage
of the entrance to the Adriatic was intended to ensure that a submarine could not surface by day without being sighted. That meant
that she must do a slow submerged passage during daylight, and
must recharge her batteries with one engine after dark while
making the best speed she could with the other engine. It was
hoped that the hydrophones of the several lines of drifters and
trawlers would ensure that U-boats could be heard and hunted by
these craft, which were fitted with depth charges, and by 'Killer'
destroyers, which sacrificed part of their gun and torpedo armament for a large depth-charge armament. The destroyers also
protected trawlers and drifters from U-boat gunfire attack. (There
were also 'Fritz-hunting' patrols in the Aegean and elsewhere in
the Mediterranean.) South of the last line of trawlers was a line of
American sub-chasers working from Corfu, and south of them two
sloops flying kite balloons. Working above the drifters and

trawlers was an advanced destroyer patrol based on Brindisi. It was maintained principally to guard against a surprise enemy raid on the barrage with surface forces, though useful, too, in forcing submarines to dive.

(3) *The Allied submarine patrol* (under the orders of the Italian C.-in-C.) *in the lower Adriatic* constituted an additional hazard for the U-boats. It carried out diving patrols in various patrol areas between the parallels of 41° N. and 42° 30 ' N., watching the various routes which the U-boats were believed to follow between Cattaro and the Otranto Straits. It could also give notice of the movements of any enemy heavy ships. Until the end of April, part of the British, French, and Italian flotillas patrolled together. On 16 April the British submarine *H-2* torpedoed and sank a submarine on the surface. Unfortunately, she proved to be an Italian boat, and thereafter it was thought best to rotate the Allied flotillas, each patrol period to be the affair of one nation only. At the start the British flotilla could generally supply 5 boats, the French 5, and the Italians 2. By the end it was 7 British, 5 French, and 4 Italian.

(4) *Air offensive against the two main submarine bases, Pola and Cattaro.* There were constant and vigorous attacks by British planes with Italian participation. This was in addition to the carrying out of patrols in the Straits of Otranto and working with surface craft in attacks on submarines.

In addition to all this, lines of fixed hydrophones were laid out from all the salient points, and the inshore waters on both sides of the Straits were patrolled by M.L.s, and seaplanes and flying boats carried out a continuous daylight patrol.

The whole system, from the lines of submarines and destroyers in the north to the hydrophone drifters, trawlers, and sub-chasers, had a north–south breadth of 180 miles, and lay between the 39th and 43rd parallels. Admiral Usborne sums up the general picture:

The aims of the barrage were:— Firstly, to secure depth: that is, a band of patrolled waters so broad that a submarine must proceed part of the way on the surface; secondly, to ensure that in this band the submarine should be hunted from one end to the other and, if possible, destroyed; (it was so disposed as to give a clear field for hunting to the fish trawlers, and to the submarine chasers); to use the kite balloons to extend the horizon of the southernmost hunting units; to watch the fixed barrage; to have killer destroyers supporting the hunting units;

and to guard the barrage from raiding by an advanced line of destroyers, which, in turn, were supported by light cruisers from Brindisi.[24]

The basic weakness of the barrage was that, whereas in the Dover Straits the Barrage Patrol was supplemented by a deep minefield, which was the main destructive agency, this was not possible in the waters of the Straits of Otranto (mostly between 300 and 500 fathoms). The Patrol by itself could not do the job. The Allied Naval Council, at its meetings on 13–14 September 1918, decided to reinforce the mine-net barrage by successive lines of deep mines to catch U-boats that dived under the nets, and to lay a shallow minefield barrage between Otranto and Cape Linguetta. The United States was to lay both minefields. The war ended before the programme could materialize. The Naval Staff judgement is that 'the American officers were perhaps over sanguine as to the capabilities of their mines, and there is no proof that any satisfactory mines existed that could be moored in 500 fathoms . . .'[25]

Now what of the effectiveness of the Otranto barrage operations? Judged by the frequency with which the Mobile Barrage Force heard or sighted enemy submarines (198 times from April through August), the operations were a huge success. Judged by whether the barrage offensive stopped the regular passage of U-boats to and from the Adriatic, it was an out-and-out failure, despite the resources lavished on it: nearly 300 warships, squadrons of aircraft, submarine flotillas, minefields, A/S nets. In the same April–August period there were 121 U-boat passages through the Straits, or a monthly average of 24. The monthly average for the two months previous to the institution of the mobile barrage was 23. There was small compensation in the number of U-boat kills. Barrage forces attacked 58 times (mostly with depth charges), yet total definite kills were *two*. The fixed barrage registered its first and last success on 3 August 1918, when *UB-53* fouled the mined nets, was badly damaged by the explosion of two mines, and surfaced. Her Captain ordered her to be sunk. For this meagre result Mediterranean convoys had been drastically cut to meet the patrol requirements of the barrage. The Allied submarine patrol in the lower Adriatic also accounted for one U-boat: on 23 May

---

[24] Captain C. V. Usborne, 'The Anti-Submarine Campaign in the Mediterranean Subsequent to 1916,' *Royal United Service Institution Journal*, August 1924.
[25] *Mediterranean Staff Papers*, p. 23.

the British submarine *H-4* sank *UB-52* with two torpedoes fired at 250 yards.

The C.-in-C., Mediterranean, afterwards found fault with Newbolt's Mediterranean chapters in his Volume v. 'Throughout the whole narrative, in these two Chapters, there runs a thread of criticism directed against the Otranto barrage operations, which, I suggest, is one-sided, and does not sufficiently take account of the moral effect on the enemy submarines, both outgoing and returning, of having to run the gauntlet of a wide space of dangerous waters, in which it is admitted they were frequently sighted and chased, and attacked with depth charges.'[26] Gough-Calthorpe was hardly a disinterested witness, and his main concern was that history judge his stewardship favourably. Much more convincing is the evaluation of a then Lieutenant-Commander on his staff: 'In the light of our after knowledge it is now clear that we were wrong in placing reliance in the Otranto mobile barrage. As we had not weapons or detecting devices to make the barrage effective, we should have put everything into perfecting the convoy-escort system. That, in fact, would have been a true offensive for the place to find and engage the U-boats was where the convoys were. Nevertheless, craft not suitable for escort work, e.g. submarines, were rightly used in the Otranto narrows.'[27]

As in the Adriatic, so elsewhere in the Mediterranean the brunt of the A/S effort fell on the Royal Navy, whether for hunting operations or the supply of escort craft for the convoy system. The Greek and Japanese ships were efficient but few. The dozen Japanese destroyers spent 72 per cent of their time at sea. compared with 60 per cent for the British and about 45 for the French and Italian. Admiral Sato was always very co-operative. His

---

[26] Gough-Calthorpe to Admiral of the Fleet Sir Charles Madden (First Sea Lord), 11 May 1929; Newbolt MSS. The Naval Staff Monograph on the Mediterranean in 1917–18, whose principal author was Gerald Dickens, Gough-Calthorpe's Flag-Commander (he would be called 'Staff Officer Operations' today), reached a similar conclusion: 'By the summer of 1918 the Otranto Mobile Barrage was doing excellent work, the number of submarines hunted and attacked being high, and the lower *morale* of the enemy submarine personnel in the Mediterranean began to show itself very markedly.' *Mediterranean Staff Papers*, p. 10. So, too, Vice-Admiral Usborne, then a Captain, who had established a base for the Barrage Force at Corfu in 1918: 'That the Otranto Barrage was hated and feared by the Germans is known.' 'The Anti-Submarine Campaign in the Mediterranean Subsequent to 1916.'

[27] *The Naval Memoirs of Admiral J. H. Godfrey* (privately printed, 1964–6, 7 vols. in 10), ii. 108.

flotilla (based on Malta) worked in consultation with the British senior officers. The British officers 'thought the "Japs" very good when they knew exactly what they had got to do and all went according to plan—but inferior to our men when unforeseen awkward situations cropped up.'[28] So impregnated with a sense of duty were the Japanese that some of their destroyer captains committed hara-kiri when a U-boat sank a ship they were escorting! The Americans had no seagoing forces in the Mediterranean proper: they worked from Gibraltar out into the Atlantic. The French were eager to do all they could with their modest A/S force. But common British opinion, as expressed by Gough-Calthorpe's Flag-Commander, was that the French 'are on the whole incapable of running a sound naval campaign. Their organisation is not practical, and they somehow think on unsound lines, and no sooner do you imagine you've roped them in to a concentrated effort, than off they go diffusing their forces in every possible way.'[29] As regards convoy, both the French and the Italians operated virtually independently of the main system.

It was the Italians, though, with their parochial view of the war, who really were not pulling their weight in the A/S campaign. They kept an unnecessarily strong destroyer force in the Adriatic and were stubborn on this point, resisting all attempts to draw their light forces into the general A/S pool. 'Italy's share,' Dickens asserted, 'except in certain narrow circumstances is infinitesimal. Bar the protection of traffic creeping round her shores, and the protection is of poor standard, Italy will offer nothing towards any sort of anti-submarine warfare we like to wage, defensive or offensive. If she did, her Navy is so inefficient that her assistance would be of little value.'[30] The Admiralty view was that

the Mediterranean is infested with submarines, all of which are based on Austrian ports; that the Italians have light forces which any other Navy would use for hunting and harassing these submarines; that they do nothing to prevent the exit of submarines from Austrian ports; that they do not co-operate in the Otranto Barrage; that they do not even provide sufficient escort craft for their own sea-borne supplies; and that

[28] Vice-Admiral Sir James Pipon's letter to the author, 25 March 1968. He served on the staffs of Gough-Calthorpe and Kelly in 1917–18.
[29] Commander Gerald C. Dickens to Acting Captain K. G. B. Dewar (Assistant Director of Plans), 9 May 1918; Dewar MSS.
[30] *Ibid.*

our Light Forces under great difficulties and with no help from the Italians have to hunt the submarines which come out of the Adriatic simply because the Italians will not agree to 'team play.'[31]

When Napoleon was once asked against whom he would prefer to wage war, he replied without hesitation, 'Allies.' To the end of the war the Allied sea campaign was never properly co-ordinated anywhere, least of all in the Mediterranean. The immense naval resources in that sea were never distributed with a view to making the best use of them. Thus, it made no strategic sense to have the entire French and Italian battle fleets (except for the few old French battleships in the Aegean) employed in bottling up the little navy of Austria-Hungary in the Adriatic.

With the British having to carry a disproportionate share of the A/S campaign in the Mediterranean, and with so much of their naval strength committed to the barrage operations, the stream of complaints from Malta is understandable: that the Mediterranean Fleet was getting nothing like its fair share of A/S craft and *matériel*. There was not a single destroyer later than the 'I' class, a sixth of the destroyer total were 'River' boats, which were in dockyard hands much of the time, there were no P-boats and few torpedo-boats, more aircraft were needed, and so forth and so on. The fleet in the inland sea resented what they felt was their neglect by the authorities at Whitehall. 'A submarine sunk out here is as great a loss to the enemy as a submarine sunk at home. A cargo vessel sunk out here is as great a loss to us as one sunk at home.'[32] True enough; but the Admiralty looked upon the Mediterranean as a backwater, a strictly secondary theatre of operations. In the idiom of today, the 'action' was in Home waters.

---

[31] Admiralty Memorandum for the War Cabinet, 'Command in the Mediterranean' (G.T.-4808), 13 June 1918.
[32] Dickens to Dewar, 9 May 1918.

III

Home Waters: Barrages and Blocking Operations

The only fresh offensive action taken in 1918 over that in operation during 1917, were the attacks on Zeebrugge and Ostend, which had been planned and approved of in 1917, and which it was intended to carry out early in 1918.

JELLICOE, *The Submarine Peril.*

Every child knows the story of Zeebrugge, the one Naval exploit of the war that moved and still moves the imagination of the Nation. Sir Roger Keyes, the Admiral who directed the attack, had the unmistakable Nelson Touch.

LLOYD GEORGE, *War Memoirs.*

The U-boat war has suffered no restriction or delays whatsoever as a result of the British attack. In other words, the real object of the enemy's attack has not been achieved.

ADMIRAL LUDWIG VON SCHRÖDER
(Commanding the Marine Corps at Zeebrugge), 25 April 1918.

It [the Northern Barrage] is the keystone of our offensive Anti-Submarine policy.

WEMYSS to Beatty,
23 August 1918.

I. THE DOVER STRAITS BARRAGE

(*Chart 4*)

WEMYSS had sent for Keyes on 28 December 1917 and, the moment Keyes entered the room, said: 'Well, Roger, you have talked a hell of a lot about what ought to be done in the Dover area, and now you must go and do it.' Keyes claims 'this was rather a shock' and that it 'seemed hardly decent' that Bacon's leading critic should supersede him.[1] But he agreed, assuming the Dover command on 1 January 1918.

Keyes was 45 and his rank acting vice-admiral, though he had been a rear-admiral only nine months. Elsewhere I have summed him up as one of the most attractive of men, warm-hearted and

[1] *The Naval Memoirs of Admiral of the Fleet Sir Roger Keyes* (London, 1934–5, 2 vols.), ii. 151.

39

full of boyish enthusiasm—a born leader with few brains, as even his friends Richmond and Beatty admitted. Captain A. C. Dewar described Keyes as 'a very limited man absolutely obsessed with the idea of doing something striking and brilliant.' Keyes knew his limitations. 'I am so very conscious of being thick headed, but I do believe I have the knack of getting the right people about me and making good use of them.'[2] This is an important as well as self-revealing point, for, in addition to putting a heavy premium on gallantry and leadership of the highest order, the Zeebrugge operation that was uppermost in Keyes's thinking required for its mounting the most meticulous staff work; and this called for the ability to select a first-class staff and make the best use of it. The 'right people' included Wilfred Tomkinson as Captain of the Dover destroyers, Commodore the Hon. A. D. E. H. Boyle as C.O.S., and Commander A. F. B. Carpenter as a Staff Officer.

Keyes was in his element at Dover. Bacon had more brains in his little finger than Keyes in his head, but Keyes brought the Dover command to life when it was flagging. He had the gift of drawing loyal service from his subordinates and firing them with his enthusiasm. (Bacon was a cold fish.) 'How he shook us all up when he got there!' reminisced an old bluejacket after the war. 'We always used to be able to count on Sundays in port. But all that was changed as soon as Sir Roger came!' On 2 January he called together the principal officers of the Patrol, explained the inefficiency of the existing A/S measures, and pointed to the urgency of immediate improvement. 'At the outset of the meeting he was conscious of an atmosphere of coolness which amounted almost to hostility. The assembled officers had all held Admiral Bacon in high respect, and had obviously resented his sudden supersession, a supersession, moreover, for which, if rumour could be believed, this new Admiral had been to some extent responsible. . . . By the end of the meeting, however, Keyes's earnestness, his obvious sincerity, and his quiet simplicity of manner had gained his hearers' confidence. He had fully persuaded them that the situation was critical and that a far more active policy must be pursued in the Dover area.'[3]

Bacon's Cross-Channel mine-net barrage,[4] having proved

---

[2] Keyes to Beatty, 19 February 1918; Beatty MSS.

[3] Brigadier-General C. F. Aspinall-Oglander, *Roger Keyes* (London, 1951), pp. 220–1.

[4] See *From the Dreadnought to Scapa Flow*, iv. 73–4.

utterly ineffective in stopping the U-boats, was abandoned early in 1918. The buoys and nets were simply not replaced when they broke adrift. This decision released a large number of small craft for more constructive work.

Keyes introduced massed patrols and brilliant illumination of the deep minefields between Folkestone and Cape Gris Nez, which Bacon had not favoured. There were always eighty to a hundred vessels patrolling above the Straits during the day and the night —ships of low fighting value (trawlers, drifters, etc.), covered to the north by the destroyers of what were called the East and West Barrage Patrols. These patrolled to the south of the old net barrage (no longer being maintained) on two parallel lines. (There were also destroyer forces in the Downs and at Dunkirk.) Wing-Commander F. A. Brock, an authority on pyrotechnics (he was a son of the founder of Brock's fireworks), was brought to Dover to improve the illumination of the Channel barrage. Thanks to his skill, the Straits at night were 'from end to end as bright as Piccadilly.' Flares burned by trawlers were used, also searchlights worked by old 30-knot destroyers, P-boats, and paddle mine-sweepers. The object was to make it impossible for submarines to pass through the Straits on the surface at night. The illumination and the concentration of patrolling craft above the deep minefields would force the U-boats to dive.

Results were marked, if not sensational. Three submarines were destroyed by Dover Barrage mines between 19 January and 8 February, or a total of four if we include *UB-56*, destroyed on 19 December 1917, that is, since the institution of the new patrol system. A fifth (*UB-35*) was destroyed in the Dover area on 26 January by depth charges from the destroyer *Leven*. Contrast this figure with the two U-boats accounted for in the Straits during the entire war up till 19 December. More significant than these figures, the growing deadliness of the barrage was making the Straits too risky for U-boat transit. The intensive patrolling by air and sea, and the illumination, were compelling the U-boats to dive into the deep minefield day and night. The availability of *efficient* mines was an important factor here.

The High Seas Fleet boats (they operated from the Heligoland Bight, mainly Brunsbüttel, Wilhelmshaven, Emden, and Heligo-land) had the choice in the period March–October 1917 of reaching their operation areas off the west coast of England or the Western

Approaches to the Channel by the long north-about route (round Scotland) or the shorter Channel route. Most of them, larger than the Flanders boats, which were used to the Channel, preferred the longer route. On 1 November 1917, Michelsen, the Senior Officer U-boats, ordered the use of the Channel route, except when such conditions as fog, full moon, etc. made it an unacceptable risk. Subsequent unexplained losses in the Channel, notably the failure of *U-109* to return to base (we know that she was destroyed in the barrage on 26 January 1918), caused Michelsen at the beginning of February to again leave the choice of route to the commanding officer of a High Seas Fleet boat proceeding to or from his operation area. In practice, the Channel route was now given up. This added about five days to the passage each way and reduced the time in the operation area accordingly. N.I.D. became aware of this during the second week in February. (*U-55*, the last North German boat to pass through the Straits, left Heligoland on 18 February.)

The massed patrolling of the illuminated minefields was a 'constant anxiety' to Keyes, who, like Bacon before him, expected that it would invite attack by surface ships, 'particularly on dark and misty nights.' And this came about: the first flotilla raid on the Dover Straits since April 1917. The effective light-barrier was making it very difficult for the Flanders U-boats to pass through the Straits, and the German Naval Command decided in February to do as much damage as possible to this barrier. Conditions on the night of 14–15 February were favourable to a surprise destroyer sortie. It was very dark—the moon set before 10 p.m.—the weather was overcast, the sea remarkably calm for that time of year, and the visibility varied considerably, with patches of haze present. On this night the powerful 2nd Destroyer Flotilla of the High Seas Fleet proceeded undetected as far as the entrance to the English Channel, north-east of Sandettie Bank. They then separated (11.30), one group (Heinecke Group, 4 boats) attacking the minefield patrols west of Varne Bank and Le Colbart Bank (the Ridge), the other (Kolbe Group, 3 boats) attacking the barrage patrols to the east. The whole affair lasted an hour, from about 12.30 till about 1.30 a.m., and was devastatingly successful. The raiding force sank by close-range gunfire 7 drifters and a trawler and severely damaged 5 drifters, a trawler, and a minesweeper. (They thought they had done even better: some 30 craft sunk.)

They were not molested by the six destroyers on the barrage patrol, nor by any other vessel in the Straits. They all heard the gunfire (it was audible to Keyes at Dover), but attributed it to the wrong causes: the fighting in Flanders or an engagement with a U-boat that had been reported. Nobody suspected an enemy destroyer raid; the tocsin was not sounded even by the few ships that got a glimpse of the raiders. The denouement is almost incredible, even when one allows for the fact that a patrol maintained for months on end without an encounter tends to be less alert than it should be.

The homeward-bound Kolbe Group was sighted by the Eastern Barrage Patrol: *Termagant* (Commander, M. R. Bernard), *Melpomene*, *Zubian*, *Amazon*, in single line ahead in that order.

At 0221 [quoting the Naval Staff account, which is based on the Court of Inquiry proceedings] the *Termagant*, then about one mile S.W. of No. 11A buoy, commenced to alter course to starboard from N. 60° E. to S. 60° W. Hardly had she started to turn when the *Amazon*, the last ship in the line, and somewhat astern of station, sighted three destroyers coming up astern, steering approximately east. They passed within two cables astern of the *Amazon*, steaming at moderate speed, and when on the starboard quarter were challenged. No reply was received to this challenge, but the commanding officer of the *Amazon* formed the opinion from their general appearance, the fact that they were showing dim stern lights, and from their not opening fire, that they were some of our own destroyers on the way to Dunkirk. He therefore, in reporting the matter to the *Termagant* [2.25 a.m.], only stated that 'three of our destroyers had passed.' None of the other vessels sighted them, although they cannot have passed far ahead of the *Termagant*.

The Senior Officer was apparently not satisfied that they were friendly, and asked the *Amazon* how it was known that they were ours, but owing to the delay in passing the signal down the line* it was not till 0250, when the division had been steering S. 60° W. for half an hour, that it was known in the leader that the challenge had not been answered. It was then considered too late to proceed in chase, and the ordinary patrol was continued.[5]

* 'This signal was delayed in passing down the line as *Termagant* did not make it clear to *Zubian* that *Amazon* was addressed.'

[5] Naval Staff Monograph No. 18 (1922), *The Dover Command*, pp. 108–9. The German commander had thought it wise to avoid an action: he believed there were *six* British destroyers, and one of his boats had condenser trouble, which reduced his group's speed. Captain Otto Groos and Admiral Walther Gladisch, *Der Krieg zur See, 1914–1918. Der Krieg in der Nordsee* (Berlin, 1920–65, 7 vols., vi and vii by Gladisch), vii. 194. (Hereafter cited as *Der Krieg in der Nordsee*.)

Keyes was 'consumed with cold fury against those whose failure had let the patrol down so badly.' The Court of Inquiry which he convened (16 February) brought out the faulty functioning of the challenging, reporting, and signalling arrangements for a surface-craft raid in the Dover Straits. For instance, the commanding officer of the *Amazon*, Lieutenant Adam Ferguson, testified that he had challenged *three times* with hand flashing lamp. (The three times 'has always been understood since I have been here.') He was supposed to shoot if he got no answer; but the enemy was practically out of sight by then. Anyway, he was 'certain' they were British.[6] The more important consideration was pithily summed up by Richmond: 'If a force can't be blocked in a port, it's always precious hard to lay hands on them once they're out.'[7]

The Germans were, naturally, elated over both the determined and skilful execution and the results of the operation. The raid 'had not only inflicted direct damage on the enemy, but also opened up a gap in the Straits of Dover–Calais. It was confirmed that on the very next night the Dover barrage was no longer illuminated. [This is questionable.] The S.O. of the Flanders U-boats stated on 3 March that "the operation of the 2nd

6 A Court-Martial on 8 March sentenced Ferguson to be severely reprimanded. Keyes and the Admiralty were not impressed by the thrust of the defence—that enemy vessels had often passed through the patrols without previous warnings. They agreed that the case had 'disclosed an extraordinary and regrettable laxity which has grown up in regard to vessels passing unchallenged through the Dover Patrol,' and that the sentence inflicted by the Court was unduly lenient. Ferguson was relieved, as was the Captain of the *Termagant*, though not tried by Court-Martial.

7 Diary, 18 February 1918; *Portrait of an Admiral*, p. 298. This, too, was Newbolt's judgement. 'As far as can be judged by experience, it was inevitable that the drifters and trawlers in the Straits should suffer loss if the Germans managed to pass the barrage patrols without being sighted. The trawlers burning flares were exceptionally vulnerable; and it is most doubtful whether any system of reporting, or any distribution of forces could have prevented the Germans from entering or leaving the Straits if they determined to do so. Admiral Keyes admitted this at the Court of Inquiry, and said that all he could do in the circumstances was to station his available destroyers on the barrage and hope they would get news of an attack upon the mine-field patrol and intercept the enemy upon their return. Experience showed, however, that although this might be the best that could be attempted, the chances of executing it successfully were not good. . . . If the chances of defeating the enemy decisively by intercepting him during a night raid were slight [the *Broke* and *Swift* action on 20 April 1917 was the one exception in the six previous raids], the chance of bringing him to action at all was slighter still.' *Naval Operations*, v. 218–19. Jellicoe was not so kind. 'The heavy losses sustained were due to the system of patrols adopted by Keyes against the advice of Bacon.' Jellicoe, 'Errors in *Naval Operations*, Vols. IV & V' (c. 1927–9); Jellicoe MSS. On Bacon's ideas, see *From the Dreadnought to Scapa Flow*, iv. 318.

Torpedo-Boat Flotilla . . . and the destruction of most of the patrol vessels providing the illumination of the Channel, had eased matters considerably for the U-boats".'[8] Not for long, however: the damage done by the raid was evanescent and the British control of the Straits was not shaken. Keyes abbreviated and clarified the patrol orders (11 March). Thus, 'Suspicious vessels are to be regarded as enemy, unnecessary challenges are to be avoided; if the V.B.S. challenge is made and not immediately answered offensive action is to be taken without further delay.' (The 'V.B.S.' stood for 'Very Brock Signal,' a challenge made by firing a sequence of coloured Very lights from a 'Very pistol'; the reply was a different combination of colours.) Also, in Keyes's words, 'Fresh lines of mines were laid, the patrols were strengthened, and continued to invite attack in a blaze of light.' The 14–15 February destroyer raid on the Straits, the seventh in the war, turned out to be the last.

The raid, coming less than a month after the *Goeben* episode, was upsetting to the War Cabinet. The minutes of its 6 March meeting record: 'Some misgivings were expressed at the War Cabinet in regard to the bad results which had attended so many naval actions during the last year or two. It was pointed out that, since the Battle of the Falkland Islands, there had been no clear cut and complete naval success. On the other hand, there had been a good many mishaps to convoys and in minor operations of various kinds. Special allusion was made to the *Goeben* incident and to the recent German raid on the Channel. In many cases explanations had to be made as to why the failure had occurred, and in the aggregate these produced an unsatisfactory impression.'[9] It needed St. George's Day to convince the politicians as well as the country that the Navy was at last performing according to expectations.

2. THE ZEEBRUGGE OPERATION

(*Chart 5*)

The heavy increase in the hazards of the Dover Straits under the new régime reduced the effectiveness of the Flanders U-boats. But it was obvious that despite mounting casualties some were getting through into the Channel and others were fully employed in the

---

8 *Der Krieg in der Nordsee*, vii. 194.
9 W.C. 360A.

North Sea. From this it was obvious that the only certain way of putting an end to the threats they posed was to block Zeebrugge and Ostend.[10] The situation, put concisely, was as follows. The interior base at Bruges was an advanced submarine and destroyer base some 300 miles nearer to Dover than the German home ports in the North Sea. The craft at Bruges could reach the sea at Zeebrugge through an eight-mile-long ship canal which was navigable by the largest submarines and destroyers, or at Ostend through an eleven-mile-long canal that was too shallow for use except by the smaller U-boats. Bruges was, then, the apex of a triangle whose base, the heavily fortified Ostend–Zeebrugge coastline, was twelve miles long and whose sides were the two canals. Zeebrugge lay 72 miles from Dover. It had a dockyard and bombproof submarine shelters.

Vice-Admiral Bayly, when commanding the 1st Battle Squadron, had suggested a Zeebrugge blocking operation in the autumn of 1914, and renewed the proposal, this time as a combined operation against Zeebrugge and Ostend, on 13 November 1916. Authority showed no interest in either. The first scheme discussed at all seriously was Tyrwhitt's of 25 November 1916. His idea was to make the lock at Zeebrugge (about 1,100 yards inland from the canal mouth) unusable by sinking a ship of slightly less than the width of the lock in the lock itself, under cover of a smoke-screen, a gas attack, and gunfire. Tyrwhitt explained the scheme at a meeting attended by Jellicoe (First Sea Lord), Oliver, and Bacon. Chiefly due to Bacon (according to Tyrwhitt), 'the scheme was considered impossible and too dangerous! Bacon referred to it as a scheme for the self-glorification of aspiring young Naval officers. It was turned down, greatly to my annoyance.'[11] In May 1917 Tyrwhitt put forward a more ambitious proposal: an amphibious

10 For the period January 1917–October 1918 the High Seas Fleet flotillas sank 3,940,805 tons, compared with 2,166,149 tons for the Flanders flotillas. But this is an unfair comparison, since over the period the number of High Seas Fleet operational boats was constantly greater than that of Flanders. The average number of boats at sea on the 10th of each month over this period was in the region of 22 High Seas Fleet to 9 Flanders. The only true comparison would be that of tonnage sunk by each boat. The outcome of such an analysis would undoubtedly show in favour of Flanders. The 1918 figures for tonnage sunk per boat per day at sea (January–September) indicates as much: Fleet, 192 tons; Flanders, 258; Mediterranean, 289.

11 Tyrwhitt to his sister 'Polly' (Miss Frances Mary Tyrwhitt), 6 May 1918; Tyrwhitt MSS. There is a copy of this paper (and the one of 7 May 1917) in the Keyes MSS., attached to a Keyes note of 15 February 1919.

operation (a thousand men would be needed) to capture the Zeebrugge mole and to occupy the town with the object of making Zeebrugge a base for an advance by the Army on Antwerp, with the ultimate intention of turning the flank of the German Army. This *coup de main*, to be covered by smoke-and-gas screens, was killed by Bacon, whose opinion was called for and who convinced Jellicoe that the chances of success appeared small. More to the point, Bacon strongly opposed the operation being attempted at that particular time, on the eve of the Third Battle of Ypres. The necessity of keeping the Belgian ports unblocked was a paramount consideration, he believed, since Haig's offensive was to include a large-scale landing on the Belgian coast, in the vicinity of Ostend. Blocking Ostend or Zeebrugge with blockships would close these harbours for four to six months against large ships, *'which the enemy did not want to pass,* but which we ourselves confidently hoped to pass during an advance in Belgium.'[12]

There the matter rested for a period, while the military scheme for driving the Germans from the Belgian coast ports held sway. In the last months of 1917, when it was clear that the Third Ypres offensive would not drive the enemy out of Belgium, the idea of naval operations pure and simple against the Belgian ports came to the front again. Beatty now lent the weight of his prestige to the operation. 'The port of Zeebrugge is so narrow that blocking it is practicable. A blockship built of concrete, fitted with a crinoline with mine-mooring cutters to take it through the minefields, and directed by wireless from aircraft, would have many chances in her favour of reaching the entrance to the locks.'[13] Realizing that a blocking operation had wide support in the Navy, Jellicoe in September directed the Plans Division to prepare an appreciation and a scheme for blocking Zeebrugge and Ostend. Keyes and Pound, who had been discussing such a scheme and had faith in its practicability, needed little encouragement. The scheme they worked out, basically an elaboration of Tyrwhitt's plan of November 1916, was submitted to the Admiralty on 3 December. Keyes's covering minute admitted that the blocking operation

12 Admiral Sir Reginald Bacon, *The Concise Story of the Dover Patrol* (London, 1932), p. 213. The initial progress of the main offensive in Third Ypres, which began on 31 July, was disappointing, and on 23 September the decision was taken to postpone the coastal operation. Bacon was completely involved in the Ostend plan.
13 Beatty's paper, 'Mining Policy,' forwarded to Jellicoe on 26 August 1917; Jellicoe MSS.

would be a hazardous enterprise, especially at Zeebrugge, 'but I feel very strongly that we shall not be asking the personnel engaged to be taking any greater risks than the infantry and tank personnel are subjected to on every occasion on which an attack is delivered on shore.'[14] The plan called for a simultaneous attack on both canals and the sinking of three blockships (old cruisers) in the entrance to each, these ships to be escorted by destroyers and further protected by a dense smoke-screen produced by a C.M.B. flotilla.

Bacon, to whom the Admiralty had sent the scheme for evaluation, ripped it to shreds:

It was marred by the very mistakes that might have been expected from men who had had no experience of operations off the Belgian coast. The attack was to be in daylight, from which it was evident that the originators knew nothing of the accuracy of fire of the batteries. Merchant ships with slow speed were to be employed to block; when at least sixteen-knot ships were necessary to give any chance of success. There was to be no gunfire attack on the lock-gates. The mole was left unattacked, and consequently the batteries were left undisturbed to fire on the blocking ships. . . .

I was very busy at the time; and, like St. Paul, I did not endure gladly those who produced unworkable schemes. My strictures on the proposals were therefore much to the point. However, the scheme did include one good suggestion, and that was to block Ostend at the same time as Zeebrugge, not that dumping down ships could block either port . . .[15]

Besides, Bacon had worked out a Zeebrugge scheme which he believed far superior to one 'that had been evolved in a back room in London.' It was a revival of a 1915 plan which had gathered dust chiefly because of the difficulty of making a good smoke-screen early in the war. It had as its main features an assault on the mole by landing parties from monitors run alongside the outside of the mole, and a short-range bombardment of the lock-gates by the 12-inch guns of other monitors, the whole to be carried out under cover of a smoke-screen.

It may be asked with some reason if blocking was so undesirable why did we bombard the lock-gates at Zeebrugge? The answer is a simple one. If a lock-gate were hit when shut, the chances were that the canal would be efficiently blocked for some weeks, for a caisson must be dead

14 Keyes, *Naval Memoirs*, ii. 132.
15 Bacon, *From 1900 Onward* (London, 1940), p. 283.

true to slide in and out of its housing position. Should, however, we require to use the canal it was not so long a job to repair the caisson as to remove a blocking-ship, especially as we had accurate plans, and, in case of necessity, could have built a new one in England. Damage to the caisson blocked the canal efficiently against small craft for some weeks; blocking-ships did not do so.[16]

Jellicoe approved the plan 'generally,' when it was put before him on 4 December 1917; but, perhaps because of the strong case made out for a blocking operation by the Plans Division, he wanted Bacon's plan to be combined with a blocking operation, as the landing would divert attention from such an operation and improve the chances of the blockships. Bacon pointed out (as he had done repeatedly) that blocking was a farce: it could not cause more than temporary inconvenience (it would be effective for not more than three weeks) to the exit of vessels of the small beam of destroyers and submarines. 'To put the matter quite bluntly,' as Bacon later summarized his position, 'it was an absolute physical impossibility to close either Ostend or Zeebrugge to the passage of submarines short of building a stone barrage across the entrance piers in the case of Ostend, or across the canal in the case of Zeebrugge. . . . It may be accepted as a maxim that *any blocking operation must be ineffective unless the rise of the tide above low water is appreciably less than the draught of water of the vessels which it is intended to block in or out.*'[17] The rise and fall of the tide was 14 feet at Ostend and 13 feet at Zeebrugge (for about half the days in the month), which was about what destroyers and submarines drew. It would therefore not be difficult for the Germans to cut a passage through a portion of a blockship (through removal of the portions above low water) sufficient for submarines, as well as destroyers, to use for a few hours on each side of high water. Jellicoe agreed that under the circumstances a block could only be temporary, but that 'it would undoubtedly be a source of considerable inconvenience. At the same time . . . *the moral effect alone of such an operation would be of great value.*'[18] Bacon agreed to enlarge his

16 Bacon, *The Concise Story of the Dover Patrol*, p. 213.
17 *Ibid.*, pp. 209, 211.
18 Jellicoe, *The Crisis of the Naval War* (London, 1920), p. 199. Oliver (then in his last days as D.C.N.S.) had remarked: 'Blocking the ports is only a temporary measure which can be got over very soon owing to the range of the tide.' Minute of 10 January 1918 on Beatty's memorandum, 'Situation in the North Sea' (9 January 1918); Admiralty MSS.

scheme: the blocking 'would prove an exhilarating addition to the proposed exploit for the Patrol. At the same time it would *inconvenience* the enemy *in case the gates were not destroyed by gun-fire.*'[19] Bacon's conversion to blocking was no doubt influenced by the strong support it mustered at the Admiralty following the submission of the Plans Division memorandum. It was Bacon's modified plan that won Jellicoe's final approval, and on 18 December the approval of the Operations Committee of the Admiralty (Jellicoe, Oliver, Wemyss, Keyes, *et al.*), which gave Bacon a directive to commence the necessary preparations. The scheme did not come off, since within two weeks both Jellicoe and Bacon had lost their jobs and Wemyss and Keyes were at the controls.

On 24 February 1918 Keyes brought his own detailed plan to the Admiralty, where he was questioned for over two hours. A few days later he received the official go-ahead. His zest for and confidence in the success of the operation never deserted him. 'If it fails,' he wrote in January, 'it will be better to have tried and failed than never to have tried at all. Success will mean so much and release torpedo craft from here if we make a proper job of it. At present it is an awful strain on my flotilla to keep up this constant watch on the Z. destroyers who have so many and such easy objectives within a short steam. But we won't fail . . . [I] am full of fire over this . . .' And a few weeks later: the enterprise, 'if it fails even, and it is not going to, can only bring credit to the Service. Anyhow I'd much rather go under, or be superseded having tried it, than sit here content to act on the defensive.'[20]

The immediate objects of the enterprise were (1) to block the Bruges ship canal by sinking blockships at its entrance into the harbour at Zeebrugge; (2) to block the entrance to Ostend harbour from the sea, in order to seal up the Bruges canal, by sinking blockships in the entrance channel to Ostend harbour; (3) to do as much damage as possible to the ports of Zeebrugge and Ostend. The ulterior objects were, first of all, to strike a heavy blow at the U-boat offensive by denying to the Germans for an indefinite period the use of the two ports, at the same time immobilising the 40-odd submarines that were usually there; and, secondly, to reduce the threat of destroyer raids in the Channel.

The main features in the Zeebrugge plan, the thrust of the

19 Bacon, *The Concise Story of the Dover Patrol*, p. 218.
20 Keyes to Beatty, 18 January, 7 February 1918; Beatty MSS.

operation, were four in number. (1) The old cruiser *Vindictive* (Acting Captain A. F. B. Carpenter) was to lay herself alongside the massive stone mole (1,850 yards long, 80 yards wide) which covered the entrance to the Bruges canal at Zeebrugge. It swept north and east from the shore and formed the harbour. The position was to be as close as possible to the fortified zone. This was about 150 yards from the end of the mole. Since any minefields protecting the harbour would constitute a grave danger to the *Vindictive* with her 19-foot draught, the shallow-draught Mersey ferry-steamers *Iris* and *Daffodil* were to attend her and, if necessary, push her alongside the mole and keep her there. Keyes could not know that minefields had not been laid off Zeebrugge or Ostend, 'in order,' the German Official History informs us, 'not to add to the already very difficult navigational conditions the U-boats had to contend with.' Note in Chart 5 the narrow mole extension, 260 yards long, with a lighthouse at the end, whose battery of five 4·1-inch and 3·5-inch guns commanded the sea approaches.

(2) Once in position, the *Vindictive* would put ashore the bluejackets and marines, with the former storming the guns and the latter attacking the fortified zone from inside. The all-important object was to put the mole batteries out of action before the blockships arrived, then go on to blow up the installations on the mole —the submarine shelters, seaplane base, etc. All the commotion connected with (1) and (2) was also supposed to divert attention from the approaching blockships. Keyes had derived this 'brilliant' idea of landing troops on the outer (seaward) wall of the mole from Bacon's sheme. He departed from Bacon's plan in two respects, however. The latter had only contemplated the use of a battalion of troops borrowed from the Army, since bluejackets and marines lacked experience in this type of warfare. For Keyes this was nonsense. The Navy could do the job and would be insulted if not given this opportunity to emulate the heroic deeds of the soldiers. In his plan the assault was to be carried out by 200 bluejackets and 700-odd marines—all volunteers, the former from the Grand Fleet, at Beatty's suggestion. Keyes did not care for Bacon's method of putting the men ashore, which involved building a collapsible bow on the monitor that would carry the storming party, strong enough to stand a 1,000-ton shock; rigging up an enormous gangway on the forecastle; and having the monitor ram the mole and drop the gangway over the parapet on to the main mole. The

scheme was impracticable, Keyes thought, particularly because speed was of the essence. If the whole operation were to be beyond range of the coastal batteries by daylight, the attack on the mole must be finished within an hour. He would, therefore, have the landing party carried in a vessel faster than a 4-knot monitor (its maximum speed when burdened with an artificial bow and special fittings), and this ship would be equipped on its port side with a number of narrow gangways. 'The troops would dash ashore (or so it was hoped, but in practice this scheme also unhappily proved impossible) from all the gangways simultaneously and launch their attack on a comparatively broad front.'[21]

(3) The three old cruisers that were to serve as blockships (*Thetis*, *Intrepid*, and *Iphigenia*), loaded with cement, were to approach the harbour entrance. This was to be at high water and the lock gates of the canal would probably have been drawn back into their concrete shelters. It was for this reason that Keyes had rejected Bacon's original plan to bombard them. The *Thetis* was therefore to sink herself in the lock, but if either gate was shut, she was to ram it before settling down. The other two ships were to sink themselves across the mouth of the canal, between the lock and the pierheads.[22]

(4) Two old submarines, with five tons of high explosives in each, were to be jammed under the railway viaduct (about 580 yards long and 40 feet wide) linking the mole proper to the shore, and left to blow a breach in it. This would isolate the scene of action from any chance of reinforcement from the town. There were provisions for the escape of the crews before their boats crashed into the viaduct. This operation had the secondary purpose of augmenting the main diversion—the activity of the *Vindictive* and her landing party. The destruction of the viaduct had the further purpose of reducing the efficiency of the mole as an air and naval base and depriving the enemy of an embarkation port for military purposes.

The German defences were so formidable that, as Aspinall-

---

21 Aspinall-Oglander, *Keyes*, pp. 225–6.
22 The Commodore at Dunkirk, Hubert Lynes, had in the planning stages several times asked Keyes not to rely on placing the blockships sideways, but to fill the stems with explosives and aim to blow up the lock gates. This would be more effective, he argued, because the sides of the canal itself between the northern lock gate and the outer harbour were sloping, which fact meant there would inevitably be a gap. His

Oglander says, 'Truly the intended operation would call not only for supreme professional skill, but also for courage, faith, and self-confidence of the highest possible order.' The Zeebrugge plan also required for successful execution a moonless night and high water within an hour and a half of either side of midnight. The block-ships could enter the canal only during this time interval on either side of high water, and the midnight factor was due to the need for the armada to approach and to leave the Belgian coast in darkness. These prerequisites restricted the date of the operation to four or five nights in each lunar month. Even then weather conditions had to be right: needed were a calm sea and a gentle on-shore wind. The latter consideration stemmed from the need to blow the smoke-screen like a sea fog towards the shore, the idea being, as Keyes tells us, 'to get the blockships and assaulting ships quite close to their objective before they were discovered.' A calm sea was required for the motor launches, which were to lay the smoke-screen across the line of approach of the armada. The brilliant scientific brain of Wing-Commander Brock had perfected a means of producing a smoke-screen of unheard-of density.

By early April the preparations and training for the operation were complete. The first attempt to carry out the scheme was made on the night of 11–12 April, the third day of the 'possible' period that lunar month. When the expedition was launched that day, conditions were ideal. '. . . everything depended on the direction of the wind,' Keyes has written. 'My thoughts constantly turned to the assault on Santa Cruz in the Island of Teneriffe in July, 1797, when Nelson's impatient ardour impelled him to undertake a hazard, which was foredoomed by the state of the weather.' Then the wind suddenly turned unfavourable, blowing off shore, 90 minutes before the 2.05 a.m. arrival time. 'The conditions were otherwise ideal, they might not be better during the two days left to us, and then the moon and tide conditions would not recur until the 9th of May. I went through a pretty difficult time during the next few moments. I knew that every man in the expedition felt, as I did, keyed up for the ordeal. . . . However, with a last thought of the shades of Nelson and Troubridge at Teneriffe, I made the

---

advice was not taken. Commander G. A. Titterton's memorandum for the author, 6 July 1966. In the Second World War the British proved they had learned this lesson of Zeebrugge: at St. Nazaire the *Campbeltown* went bows first into the caisson and put the dock out for good.

fateful signal—one word on the wireless—which cancelled the proceedings for the night.'[23] The time was 1.10 a.m.

On the 13th, the last possible day in April, Keyes assembled his forces again. The vessels raised steam, but two hours later it came to blow very hard. It was too rough for the small craft, so once more the expedition returned to port. On the 14th Wemyss brought sad tidings to Dover. After commiserating with Keyes on his bad luck and commending him for his prudence in turning back, he informed him of the Admiralty decision to cancel the operation on the ground that it could no longer be a surprise. The armada had been sighted by a score of ships, neutrals among them; the enemy would be certain to have this intelligence in the three weeks before the operation could be attempted again.[24] Keyes persuaded Wemyss to let him try again in about ten days' time (22–26 April), when there would be high water about midnight. The moon would be full, which would pose risks, but he was ready to sacrifice what he had till now considered an essential requirement for success rather than wait till the second week in May for ideal tide and moon conditions.

On 22 April, the first possible day of the full-moon period, the weather report being favourable, Keyes made the decision to go ahead. Early that afternoon, as he tells the story, 'My wife walked down to the pier [at Dover] with me to see me off, apparently quite unperturbed. She alone knew what a hell of a time I had been going through and her last words were, that the next day was St. George's Day (which I had not realised), and that it was sure to be the best day for our enterprise, as St. George would bring good fortune to England, and she begged me to use "St. George for England" as our battle-cry.'[25] As soon as the expedition set out that evening, Keyes made a general signal by semaphore: 'St. George for England.' Carpenter, in the *Vindictive*, signalled back: 'May we give the dragon's tail a damned good twist.' This

---

23 Keyes, *Naval Memoirs*, ii. 252–3.

24 As a matter of fact, the Germans had captured the operation order on 12 April, when a British C.M.B. had run aground outside the entrance to Zeebrugge in the 11–12 April effort and the plans of the Zeebrugge–Ostend operations had been found in her. The element of surprise was only slightly impaired, however. 'It was fortunate for the British that German foreknowledge of the operation order resulted in nothing more extensive than a somewhat ineffectual order for a higher degree of alert for some, and not even the most essential, sections of the coastal defence.' *Der Krieg in der Nordsee*, vii. 267.

25 Keyes, *Naval Memoirs*, ii. 261.

epitomized the prevailing spirit of supreme confidence in the outcome of the adventure just ahead. Setting off for Zeebrugge from a rendezvous off the Goodwin Sands (it lies on the eastern side of the Downs), with Keyes flying his flag in the destroyer *Warwick*, were 76 vessels.

The Zeebrugge armada approached its objective in bright moonlight (it was, says Keyes, 'almost as bright as day'), with a visibility of at least eight to ten miles. Then, soon after 11 p.m., an hour before arrival time, it suddenly became misty, clouds hid the moon, it began to drizzle, and visibility was reduced to less than a mile. This, with the 'pea-soup fog' of a smoke-screen created by the motor launches, enabled the *Vindictive* to approach within 300 yards of the mole extension before coming under fire. It was now four minutes before midnight. Unfortunately, the wind now changed to an off-shore direction, quickly dissipating the smoke-screen and suddenly revealing the *Vindictive* to the enemy in the full glare of their star-shell and searchlights. The mole extension guns could hardly fail to hit their hapless target as they poured shell into it, doing considerable damage to the upper works and upper deck and, worse still, to the personnel. Among those killed in the approach to the mole were the officer in command of the marines' landing party, his second-in-command, and the officer in command of the seamen's landing party. By increasing to full speed the *Vindictive* escaped destruction: she reached a position at 12.01 alongside the outer mole, where only her superstructure was exposed to the mole-end battery. However, the increase in speed carried the *Vindictive* 340 yards beyond her allotted position, from where she was unable to bring her guns to bear on the mole-extension battery or on the troops protecting those guns. As a consequence the storming and demolition parties were without support. Pinned down and badly punished by a hail of fire, they were unable to accomplish much.

In the meantime the three blockships, shepherded by Keyes in the *Warwick*, were groping their way through the enemy fire to carry out the most vital part of the whole operation—indeed, its *raison d'être*. The *Thetis*, which was in the lead, was supposed to steam up the canal and sink herself in the lock. The *Intrepid* and *Iphigenia* were then supposed to sink themselves 'in interlocking positions one behind the other athwart the narrowest part of the tidal channel between the lock and the sea' (Aspinall-Oglander).

The *Thetis*, subjected to a withering fire from the mole-extension battery, ran aground before she reached the canal entrance. In fact, none of the blockships was sunk in her allotted position, though the *Intrepid* and *Iphigenia* managed to settle down well inside the canal entrance.

There was, finally, the story of the two submarines charged with blowing up the viaduct. One of them parted her tow on the way out and failed to arrive in time. The crew of the other, *C-3* (Lieutenant R. D. Sandford), disregarding Keyes's advice to abandon their craft short of the objective and let her proceed by gyro steering, rammed her into the viaduct, then pushed off in their skiff. There was a deafening roar as the explosive-laden boat blew up, a shower of debris and bodies—and a 100-foot gap in the viaduct. The skiff, holed by intense rifle and machine-gun fire, managed to stay afloat until her crew of six was rescued, as planned, by a picket boat.

At about 1.10 a.m., with the *Vindictive* taken in tow by the *Daffodil*, and protected by a smoke-screen laid by the motor launches, the battered armada drew off and sailed home. The losses were a destroyer and two M.L.s; the casualties, 170 killed, 400 wounded, 45 missing.

The simultaneous attempt to block Ostend was an out-and-out fiasco. The plan was similar to the Zeebrugge one, except for the absence of a diversionary attack. A grand total of 146 ships and craft participated. Ostend had no protecting mole; coast artillery and machine guns guarded the harbour entrance. Just prior to the arrival of the blockships *Brilliant* and *Sirius*, a sudden change of wind rolled back from the shore the smoke-screen that had been laid by the M.L.s. This led to the obscuration of the harbour entrance, which, along with the sinking by German gunfire of the now visible calcium buoys used by the M.L.s and C.M.B.s to mark the entrance to the harbour, necessitated reliance on a light-buoy. Unknown to the British, the Germans had shifted this buoy overnight over a mile to the eastwards. Taken in by this elementary piece of deception, the blockships missed the harbour entrance and ran aground a mile to the eastwards. The ships were blown up and their crews taken off by three M.L.s. The attempt on Ostend was repeated without success on 10 May. One of the blockships, the old cruiser *Sappho*, broke down; the other, the *Vindictive*, was sunk in a position that blocked only a third of the channel.

The 'ifs' and 'might-have-beens' of Zeebrugge are still being debated. The German Official History makes this comment:

Daring and bravery, great as it was, could not compensate for such things as the partial failure of the smoke-screen in the latter stages of the approach until *Vindictive* was alongside, going alongside at the wrong spot, the destruction of *Vindictive*'s landing gear, and the loss of leading men. These and other divergencies from the minutely worked-out and exercised plan, were bound to have such a strong influence on the total success that all the great daring displayed was in vain and the aim not achieved. Furthermore, even if one of the two harbours had been completely blocked, this would not have meant the immobilisation of Flanders. The operation would have achieved its object only if both harbours, Zeebrugge and Ostend, had been simultaneously and completely blocked.[26]

These mishaps could, of course, have been neither foreseen nor prevented.

Quite different are the criticisms made by Bacon in comparing Keyes's plan with his own. (1) A monitor would have provided greater protection for the men against shell-fire than did the *Vindictive*. (2) A division of destroyers should have attacked the mole batteries: their 4-inch would have done more to occupy the battery than the three M.L.s, with their light guns, who fired on the battery from their position along the western side of the mole. (3) The movable gangways fitted in the *Vindictive* instead of Bacon's collapsible bow were 'more or less useless, since, at the best, they only landed the men on to the parapet, from this they had to drop fourteen feet on to the Mole, with only a couple of iron-rung ladders to help them down and back again. These gangways were mostly shot away or broken up by the *Vindictive* rolling . . . so that men could only be dribbled ashore over two narrow gangways.' (4) The 'fatal mistake of taking the *Vindictive* *alongside* of the Mole instead of *bows on* prevented rapid contact being made with the Mole, and the necessary element of surprise [from being] ensured. . . . In fact, the *Vindictive*, as I had foreseen, was unmanageable off the Mole owing to tide and swell. . . . I would never have sanctioned taking any ships alongside the Mole . . . experience had taught me there was bound to be a considerable sea alongside raised by our destroyers and other vessels steaming in

[26] *Der Krieg in der Nordsee*, vii. 267.

the offing . . .' (5) Bacon also criticized the deletion of his idea of destroying the lock-gates with gunfire at almost point-blank range.[27] These charges are not without substance, yet, as an astute reviewer of his book remarked: 'There is scarcely any naval operation which would not have been carried out more effectively if it could be tried out first as an experiment and modified in the light of experience. Admiral Bacon makes a great point of "experience", but neither he nor anyone who actually took part in the Zeebrugge-Ostend operations had any experience of this particular form of attack under modern conditions.'[28]

The thrilling Zeebrugge exploit, as revealed to the press in a sensational account that stated the channel had been blocked, came when the Allied cause desperately needed something to cheer. The operation gave a tremendous boost to morale both in the Army in France, then reeling from the blows of the Hindenburg spring offensive, and in the Navy, where the strategy of leaving the initiative to the enemy was putting a severe strain upon morale. 'It's done more for the honour and reputation of the Navy than anything in this war,' Walter Cowan thought. For Churchill Zeebrugge had given the Navy back 'the *panache* that was lost at Jutland.' Indeed, the whole Allied cause received a lift. No incident in the war, on sea or land, had more deeply touched the popular imagination in Britain. It restored faith in the Navy. The country enthused over the magnificent skill and audacity of the exploit and hailed it as the rebirth of the spirit of Nelson and Drake. A *Punch* cartoon (1 May), 'Drake's Way,' depicted Drake's ghost addressing a saluting Keyes: 'Bravo, Sir! Tradition Holds. My men singed a King's beard, and yours have singed a Kaiser's moustaches.' 'Instead of being only magnificent and not war,' declared *The Observer* (28 April), 'it was magnificent and the soul of war.' 'An immortal deed,' shouted the *Daily Mail* (24 April). 'Our High Command to-day believes in using our sea-power to strike, and not merely to fend off blows.' The Prime Minister congratulated the Admiralty 'most heartily' upon an achievement that was 'worthy of the greatest traditions of the British Navy, both in conception and execution.' 'Never,' said Lord Milner, 'has the banner of St. George floated over more magnificent fighting men.' Eleven V.C.s were awarded—eight of

---

[27] Bacon, *The Concise Story of the Dover Patrol*, pp. 221–4.
[28] *Royal United Service Institution Journal*, November 1932.

them for Zeebrugge—and Keyes was immediately awarded the K.C.B. His exercise of the command had been superb. Barrie Pitt puts his finger on the essential point: 'But although it was frequently noticed that Keyes was eyeing the crucial areas rather wistfully, he never lost sight of the conception as a whole—and indeed there seems to have been a strange feeling in all units, that his was the guiding hand which steered not only the expedition but also each separate individual and craft as well . . .'[29] Not that Keyes and H.M.S. *Warwick* had not been in the thick of it.

Public opinion accepted Admiralty claims at face value, believing that at long last the prime hornets' nest for the submarine warfare had been sealed up and rendered useless to the enemy, at least for a considerable period. What were the facts? Was Zeebrugge more than a naval Balaclava? Wemyss's appraisal a day after the operation was: 'It happened just as I thought it would *not*. I expected *complete* success and few casualties, or absolute failure with appalling casualties. Neither the one nor the other.'[30] On 17 May the D.C.N.S. told the War Cabinet that 'he did not think that any submarines had yet passed down the canal from Bruges to Zeebrugge and that aircraft still reported congestion of submarines and destroyers at Bruges.' At Ostend 'the Germans had had some success in clearing the channel, having let water through with a rush, and slewed the *Vindictive* round, so that the obstruction she now afforded was only that of her own breadth.'[31] On 23 May Wemyss informed the same body that 'air reconnaissances indicated that there were twenty-four destroyers or torpedo-boats and twelve submarines locked up in the Bruges Docks. The view was now held that the Bruges–Ostend canal contained less water than had previously been thought, and consequently, although Ostend Harbour was now partially clear, that port could not be used for the ingress and egress of destroyers and submarines now at Zeebrugge.'[32] On 15 June the Admiralty stated that the blocking operations 'were attended with a high measure of success, and have proved of great value in restricting the use of

[29] Pitt, *Zeebrugge* (London, 1958), pp. 144–5.
[30] Wemyss to Beatty, 24 April 1918; Beatty MSS. Geddes judged that the Zeebrugge operation 'appears to have met with even more measure of success than we could have reasonably hoped for, having regard to the delicacy of the undertaking.' Geddes to King George V, 23 April 1918; Geddes MSS.
[31] W.C. 413.
[32] W.C. 415.

those ports as bases for enemy craft.'[33] Keyes himself saw these as the results:

> . . . our operations were completely successful in attaining their first and most important object. The entrance to the Bruges ship-canal was blocked. . . .
> The main results achieved have, however, proved greater than I expected when the fleet returned to port on the morning of the 23rd April. Aerial observation and photographs up to the present day (9th May)* show clearly that even the lighter craft in the Bruges ship-canal and docks have so far been unable to find an exit through the smaller waterways to Ostend harbour. At least 23 torpedo craft [destroyers and torpedo boats] have remained sealed up at Bruges ever since the operations on St. George's Day, and so far as can be seen not less than 12 submarines would likewise appear to be still imprisoned. As yet no effective steps seem to have been taken to clear the Zeebrugge entrance to the Bruges ship-canal, where the silt is shown to be collecting; and although doubtless in time the enemy will succeed in opening a way out, it seems likely that this important section of his raiding- and commerce-destroying forces must inevitably be seriously hampered for a considerable period.[34]

This was not the true picture. The psychological effect was considerable; the strategic, almost nil, since nothing material was in fact achieved. It is a myth that the Zeebrugge channel had been blocked and the submarine menace abated. Admiral Sir William James, who was Head of 'Room 40,' N.I.D., at the time, tells us: 'At the Admiralty we knew five hours after the attempt from an intercepted signal that the canal had not been blocked, but no good purpose would be served by publishing this.' Within days the Germans were, with some inconvenience, to be sure, passing their submarines and destroyers out from Bruges as before 22–23 April. The inconvenience was removed when, after three weeks, the Germans dredged a channel, usable in all conditions of tide, past the blockships. A few authoritative details may be useful.

The publication of the last volume in the *Nordsee* series of the

---

* 'On the 19th May, photographs established that the same vessels were still immobilized.'

33 Admiralty memorandum for the Imperial War Cabinet, 'General Review of the Naval Situation (April, 1917, to June, 1918)' (G.T.-4861).

34 Keyes, 'Reports on Zeebrugge and Ostend Operations, 22–23 April 1918, and Ostend Operations, 10 May 1918,' July 1918; Admiralty MSS. This was a revised edition of his 9 May report on the former and his 15 June report on the latter. The report was not published but was issued to the Fleet for their information.

German Official History in 1965 once and for all revealed that Zeebrugge, though 'the perfect example of a well-planned, excellently prepared and bravely executed attempt to eliminate a strongly defended enemy base by approaching from the sea and blocking it,' had been a failure.

It is understandable that the British at first regarded the attack on Zeebrugge as having achieved complete success. The entrance was blocked at low water, so that the Marine Corps instructed those U-boats which were at sea that when returning they should enter by Ostend. This order, passed by W/T and intercepted by the enemy, strengthened the British impression that Zeebrugge had been successfully blocked. The Germans themselves at first had a similar impression. On the morning after the attack, when the German Flag Officer, Admiral von Schröder, inspected the mole and locks, and saw the blockships lying in the narrow entrance, he naturally felt anything but happy about the situation; it looked as if the enemy had succeeded in delivering a grievous blow to the prosecution of the U-boat war. Yet the true situation very soon proved to be entirely different. . . .

Closer examination of the situation very soon showed that the conduct of the war from Zeebrugge had suffered only minor and temporary restrictions.[35]

At noon on 24 April four torpedo-boats (each displacing 240 tons and drawing 7½ feet), and at noon on 25 April five torpedo-boats (375 tons, a little over 7 feet), had left the Zeebrugge locks at high water for routine minesweeping duties. They experienced no difficulty in negotiating the narrow gap to the east of the blockships. On the 25th *UB-16* (127 tons, nearly 10 feet) left the same way and returned, and again on the 26th, when she sailed on operation. 'It was only the larger U-boats and the destroyers that had to be diverted for a short period to Ostend for entering or leaving. For this purpose, starting on 24th April, the locks of the Ostend-Bruges Canal were maintained at high level.' As regards the blockships, after considering the possibility of raising them or blowing them up, the Germans decided on 1 May to use dredgers to deepen and widen the channels to the east and west of the sunken ships. By 14 May the channel leading west past the stern of the two ships had been restored to a depth of 11½ feet at low water and could now be used by all the U-boats and destroyers of

[35] *Der Krieg in der Nordsee*, vii. 265. What follows is from *ibid.*, pp. 265–9.

the Marine Corps Command. Since none of these exceeded a draught of just under 13 feet (3·9 metres), they could leave Zeebrugge at almost any state of the tide. On 14 May four destroyers (950 tons, roughly 11–13 feet) left Zeebrugge, and thereafter all the Flanders vessels entering or leaving Bruges were again using Zeebrugge without difficulty. 'At no time had the freedom of movement of the Marine Corps' naval forces been substantially [*wesentlich*] restricted by the blockships, let alone interrupted.' The breach in the Zeebrugge mole was soon repaired. By noon of 24 April a narrow suspension bridge over the gap had been completed and opened for pedestrian traffic. To prevent any possibility of British success, should they repeat the attack against Zeebrugge and Ostend, various defensive measures were adopted, including the distribution of twenty-four large-calibre guns along the coast.

Keyes remained serenely confident that his exploit had done the job. Commander Titterton, who went out to Dunkirk (actually, Spica, eleven miles inland) at this time as Naval Liaison Officer to the 5th Group, R.A.F., which worked under Keyes's orders, recalls how:

On arrival there [about 1 June] I was immediately summoned to the presence of the Brigadier commanding the 5th Group, Brig. Charles Lambe, ex-Captain, R.N. He said, 'Titterton, I am glad you have come here, we are in trouble; the V.A. Dover still does not accept that enemy destroyers and submarines can pass the blockships at Zeebrugge. Air recce's show a width of at least 45 feet of water at L.W.O.S. [Low Water of Ordinary Spring Tides] between the nearest part of either blockship and the dockside. This means, with an average rise of tide of 14 feet, that both destroyers and submarines can pass certainly within two hours of high water, and possibly at longer intervals. Apart from air recce's, agents reported destroyers passing the blockships within 24 hours of the operation. Now something has got to be done about this, or one of these fine days there'll be an enemy destroyer raid as before and I shall be told that my information should have been pressed more strongly. What do you propose? Go and talk to the R.A.F. Intelligence boys here, and then report to me tomorrow.'

The next day I reported to the Brigadier that after talking to his very experienced Intelligence Staff, particularly the Photographic expert, it seemed to me that nothing less than a periodical mosaic of the whole Canal area could prove adequate to provide irrefutable evidence of changes in the numbers of ships inside the lock gates from Zeebrugge to Bruges. I added that Group Captain Cheshire recommended that the

Canal from Bruges to Ostend should be included, though it was thought to be too shallow for destroyers or submarines.

This plan was carried out. At the end of the third mosaic no possible doubt could be expressed on the feasibility or not of passing the block-ships.[36]

Ten months after the operations N.I.D. admitted that they had accomplished nothing practical. 'Ostend was never blocked and submarines from Bruges could always go to sea that way. Zeebrugge was only blocked to submarines for a few days.'[37] The truth was published in the Official History in 1931: 'Previous to the operation about two submarines were entering or leaving the Flanders bases every day . . . the average figure . . . was maintained during the five weeks immediately subsequent to the operation. It was not, in fact, until June that there was any falling off, and then the decline was sharp, for only thirty-three submarines entered and left the Flanders bases during the month.'[38] This, as will be pointed out, was not a consequence of the blocking operations. But the fiction that the Zeebrugge canal was blocked has so far not been overtaken by the truth.

Keyes himself never altered his conviction that Zeebrugge had been a strategic success. '. . . week after week, our aerial photographs of Bruges clearly showed large destroyers lying in the Bruges basin and in the canal system . . . Until the middle of June, large submarines could also be clearly distinguished in the open, so we were justified in supposing that the huge submarine shelters were occupied by as many submarines as they would hold. Such photographs cannot lie . . .'[39] In the authorized life of Keyes, his biographer made the claim: 'The Zeebrugge canal was to be useless to the enemy for many critical weeks, and for most of that period forty German destroyers and submarines, tightly imprisoned at Bruges, could take no part in the war. . . . The blocking of the Zeebrugge canal had halved at one blow the deadly menace of the submarine campaign.'[40] Admiral James, who knew Aspinall-Oglander, wrote and asked him why he had made this grossly exaggerated statement, since he must know quite well that the

36 Titterton's memorandum of 6 July 1966.
37 Minute by the D.N.I., 19 February 1919, on a draft of a report for the War Cabinet, 'Work of the Navy in 1918'; Admiralty MSS.
38 Newbolt, Naval Operations, v. 274–5.
39 Keyes, Naval Memoirs, ii. 319.
40 Aspinall-Oglander, Keyes, pp. 247–8.

channel had not beeen blocked, and that, in any case, it was the large U-boats, operating from German bases, not the Flanders flotillas, which had been doing the heavy damage on the Atlantic trade routes since February 1917. 'He replied that he had had no option, and I judged from his letter that he felt a little ashamed of surrendering to pressure.'[41] The 'pressure' had presumably come from the redoubtable Lady Keyes, who never ceased extolling and magnifying her husband's achievements.

Keyes wanted badly to follow up the Zeebrugge operation with a sustained bomber offensive against the large number of U-boats and destroyers which aerial photographs showed to be crowded in the harbour at Bruges. The opportunity seemed too good to be missed. But he ran into serious difficulties, since the former R.N.A.S. bombers stationed at Dunkirk were no longer under his control.[42] He pleaded with the Air Ministry (through a letter of 1 May to the Admiralty) that four bomber squadrons be placed under his direct orders. The Air Ministry replied on 16 May that No. 214 Squadron would be asked to help, but that was all that was possible 'in view of the extreme urgency of the demands for long-distance bombing squadrons elsewhere . . .'[43] In the end some bombers were made available to Keyes. He used them to attack Bruges, Zeebrugge, and Ostend, though with unimpressive results so far as material damage is concerned. More important for the future was the revelation that naval needs were being neglected. This harbinger of what was to come stemmed, basically, from the

---

41 Admiral James's letter to the author, 28 September 1962.

42 On 1 April 1918 the R.N.A.S. had turned over to the R.A.F. 103 airships, 2,949 aircraft, 126 air stations, and 67,000 officers and men. The Admiralty retained responsibility for the construction and maintenance of airships (until May 1919) as well as for the design, construction, administration, and operation of aircraft carriers, while the evolution of the carrier aircraft took place in other hands. The office of Fifth Sea Lord and Chief of Naval Air Service lapsed, and the Air Department of the Admiralty was absorbed by the Air Ministry, which had been established in January 1918. Two Navy men sat on the Air Council of eight: Godfrey Paine and Mark Kerr (the former only by the end of the war). The R.A.F. officers all received military titles. In time Jellicoe's doubts (see *From the Dreadnought to Scapa Flow*, iv. 332) proved all too real, to which we must add the deplorable inter-Service rivalries and bickerings that were an inevitable, and foreseeable, consequence of 1 April 1918. Immediately, 'it is plain that the most serious result was the loss to the Royal Navy of nearly all its officers who were experienced in and enthusiastic advocates of naval aviation.' Captain Stephen Roskill, *Naval Policy between the Wars*, Vol. i, *The Period of Anglo-American Antagonism, 1919–1929* (London, 1968), p. 241.

43 Walter Raleigh and H. A. Jones, *History of the Great War. The War in the Air* (London, 1922–37, 6 vols. and a volume of appendices, all but Vol. i by Jones), vi. 389.

R.A.F.–Air Ministry concentration on strategic bombing plans, although Haig's inflexible and over-cautious approach was a factor in the denial to Keyes of the additional squadrons he needed. The Zeebrugge–Ostend operations were not successful in any practical sense. Keyes did, however, succeed in closing the Dover Straits to the Flanders U-boats by increasing the effectiveness of the barrage, by incessant air attacks on the Flanders bases, and by re-energizing the whole command. The Flanders boats used the Straits less and less after March. From the beginning of June, the flotillas displayed little interest in attempting the increasingly hazardous passage through the Straits and concentrated their efforts against the independent shipping off the East coast of the United Kingdom, north of the Humber. During June only five submarines left Flanders for the Channel; during July, nine. Early in September the Germans finally gave up the Dover route, and thereafter the Flanders boats sailing for the west used the long route north of Scotland. The last U-boat had sailed for the Straits on 14 August, and the last one to attempt to return that way was blown up on the barrage on 16 September.

On 3 September the Admiralty reported to the Prime Minister that 'Although the influence of the enemy submarines operating from Zeebrugge was not entirely negligible, nevertheless, even if these ports were not entirely blocked it would no longer make any great difference to us.' The reason given was that submarines from Zeebrugge and Ostend were hardly attempting the passage of the Straits. Since March, 24 of the 43 U-boats based on Flanders had been destroyed.[44] This, the heavy losses, is the key to 'the downfall of the Flanders Flotillas,' as Professor Grant has brought out.

At the beginning of 1918 the flotillas included 25 U-boats; by early September, 19 had been added, but of the total of 44, 33 had been or were about to be sunk or interned, three had been damaged and were not fit for war cruises, and one had been retired from service. During the first quarter of the year, 8 per cent of the cruises ended in a loss; in the second quarter this percentage increased to 33, and in the third to

---

[44] 'Notes of a Conversation at 10 Downing Street, S.W., on Tuesday, September 3, 1918, at 11 a.m.'; X-28. 'X' minutes (Cab. 23, P.R.O.) are notes of conversations, mostly between the Prime Minister, War Secretary, and C.I.G.S., on secret military matters, etc.

40. With a steadily diminishing number of submarines, these rates of loss could not be supported.

The Dover Barrage was responsible for about a dozen of the sinkings and, in addition, for the damage to *UB-59* and *UC-71* which put both out of commission and encouraged the view that the Straits could not be crossed.[45]

The Dover Straits Barrage had practically denied the English Channel to the U-boats. Concurrently, an heroic attempt was being made to block the northern exit of the North Sea.

3. THE NORTHERN BARRAGE

(*Chart 1*)

The Allies had reached the decision in principle in September 1917 to limit the submarine campaign by closing the North Sea exits through a mine barrage between the Orkneys and the Norwegian coast. The lack of British minelayers and the delay in the collection of British patrol craft and production of American mines set back the original date for commencing to lay the minefield. Laying operations began on 3 March (Area B) and 8 June 1918 (Areas A and C). The barrage had been substantially completed when the war ended.

In its final wartime form the barrage stretched for 240 miles between the parallels of 59° and 60° N., from the Orkneys to the approaches to Hardanger Fjord; 15,093 British mines (including 1,441 swept up after the mining of the sloop *Gaillardia* in Area B) and 56,033 American mines were laid. (The original requirements were 200,000 mines.) The central section (Area A) was laid by the American Navy and extended for 130-odd miles. The two wing sections were laid by the two Navies: Area B to the west, about 50 miles long, and Area C, about 70 miles, to Norwegian territorial waters. The American section was mined to the surface (from a depth of 200 feet). In view of the shallow minefield, Area A was regarded as not requiring patrols. Area B was to consist of deep minefields, and the plan called for strong surface patrols to force the U-boats to dive into the mines or attack them when they appeared on the surface. In fact, the only patrols were hydrophone flotillas in the Fair Island Channel above the western end

---

[45] Robert M. Grant, *U-Boats Destroyed* (London, 1964), p. 94.

of the barrage. Each unit consisted of a destroyer or sloop working with three trawlers equipped with fish hydrophones. Area C was to be mined with British mines both deep and shallow, as it was too far away for patrolling.

One facet of the mine-laying led to a first-class row in August. It was evident by this date that the U-boats were avoiding the central and eastern areas and were passing through Norwegian territorial waters or across Area B in the west. Consequently, it was decided to mine Area B with shallow as well as deep mines. Enter Beatty, who insisted that a 10-mile gap be left to the eastward of the Orkneys, in order to allow a clear passage for supporting forces to the Scandinavian convoys. This demand, wrote Wemyss,

has raised a very serious and critical position between ourselves and the Americans. Admiral Sims holds very strong views on the subject [Beatty's marginal note: 'So do I and I have to command the sea, not Admiral Sims.'], which may be summarised as follows:

The American Government desire to complete the Northern Barrage from land to land, and nothing short of this will satisfy them; their views being that any gate in the Barrage, however small, renders it ineffectual. If it is ineffectual, they consider that the whole of their great efforts and large expenditure is thrown away, and Admiral Sims would, under these circumstances, recommend his Government to stop work on the whole business.

Now such a state of affairs will have a much more disastrous effect on our relations with the United States than it would have on the actual material position. [Beatty: 'Cannot believe this.'] It would inevitably lead to the recall of Admiral Sims. . . . For us to lose Admiral Sims would be a very serious matter. His loyalty and co-operation with us has been extraordinary. . . .

It would indeed be a calamity if the Americans were now to chuck their hand in over the Northern Barrage. The enemy would know it, and, moreover, it would surely lead to that friction and want of sympathy between the United States and ourselves which has hitherto been so conspicuous by its absence.[46]

Beatty was not to be budged, claiming that 'In the original schemes it was provided that a 60 mile area would be available for passage of surface craft, whereas I now agree to a passage of only ten miles.'[47] He had his way (though a passage of only three miles

46 Wemyss to Beatty, 23 August 1918; Beatty MSS.
47 Beatty to Wemyss, 26 August 1918; Beatty MSS.

wide was left) and Anglo-American relations withstood the shock nicely.

Several factors worked against an effective barrage. For one thing, the antenna mines (see below) were set too deep to catch the surfaced U-boats, which were merely shaken up and reached their bases with only slight damage. Then again, the American mines were a tremendous disappointment. They were of a new and unproved type which in theory would be actuated by the U-boat making contact either with an upper antenna, which was flexible with a float on it to bring the upper end to the surface, or with a lower antenna which formed part of the mooring rope, or with horns on the mine itself. They therefore covered a greater area in the vertical plane than did the orthodox contact mines and should have rendered dangerous an area from the surface to 200 feet. One line of antenna mines could do the work of five contact-mine lines. These mines, unfortunately, had an alarming way of going off prematurely; many of them exploded in a series of spectacular countermining 'ripples.' Beatty, who was annoyed that the American mines had not been carefully tested in advance, was a regular critic of them. Writing of Area A, where the mines were entirely American and were being laid by their Navy: 'The latest fiasco is such that the Americans themselves gave up and went home after laying one line, which apparently blew up as it was laid. The mines that are still remaining are of no value against enemy submarines on the surface and there is no reason for them to dive in those waters. So all we have done is to waste valuable vessels, time and material, in planting the North Sea with stuff which debars us from using it and can do no harm to the enemy. When the winter's gales come along they will turn the North Sea into a place in which it will be extraordinarily dangerous to cruise at all.'[48] Wemyss sympathized with Beatty's feelings about the mines, but asked him to remember 'that the decision was arrived at at a time when the Submarine Campaign overshadowed every-thing, and that drastic measures necessitating the whole-hearted operations of the Americans were required, and this, I believe, it was only possible to obtain by agreeing to the use of their mines. In spite of all their faults, the American mines have caused the

[48] Beatty to Wemyss, 10 August 1918; Wemyss MSS. Beatty had raised 'the question of the durability of their mooring aparatus and whether they would become safe when they break adrift' at an Admiralty conference on 2–3 January 1918.

submarines to avoid the notified area and pass through waters through which our Patrols might have dealt effectively with them had the Fish Hydrophone done all that we expected of them.'[49]

Beatty had never cared for the idea of a barrage. He impressed on Balfour in a conversation on 21 August that 'he disliked the whole business, and had the gravest misgivings as to its results. . . . The whole scheme of the barrage is American, and the Admiralty have allowed themselves to be rushed into it without sufficient experimental knowledge.'[50] More particularly, he was critical because the barrage hampered Grand Fleet movements. An increase in the mining effort in the Heligoland Bight and the Kattegat and the mining of the Fair Island Channel and the northern and southern ends of the Irish Sea would be more productive, he always insisted, and therefore should receive a higher priority. His main argument was that Germany could always use Norwegian territorial waters to circumvent the barrage and (with Plans Division support) that it was extremely difficult to maintain an effective patrol at the eastern end of the North Sea with forces based on the Orkneys. The deep minefield was not of much value without an efficient patrol force that could force the U-boats to dive into it. Needed was a naval and air base on the adjacent Norwegian coast.

There was some discussion when the minefields were first laid down whether to ask Norway to mine her territorial waters, or to go ahead anyway and lay mines up to the Norwegian coast. The decision was to mine only up to territorial waters and depend on Norwegian insistence on respect for her neutrality. This did not work out, and throughout 1918 the British were much exercised over the illegal German use of Norwegian waters. There was some support at the Admiralty, notably in the Plans Division, for solving the problem by persuading Norway to throw her lot in with the Allies or, under plea of yielding to *force majeure*, to allow the British to seize a base on her coast. A fleet based there would be in an excellent strategical position relative to the barrage: its small craft could patrol the eastern end of the barrage. Beatty raised the question of obtaining a Norwegian port in connection with the Northern Barrage at conferences with the First Lord in January

[49] Wemyss to Beatty, 15 August 1918; Wemyss MSS.
[50] Balfour's memorandum of 22 August 1918: copy enclosed in Balfour to Beatty, 3 September 1918; Beatty MSS.

and the D.C.N.S. on 25 February. It could not be contemplated, the C.-in-C. was told. A different approach to the problem came to the fore during the summer, by which time British submarine patrols were securing 'definite ocular evidence' of the U-boats' use of Norwegian territorial waters in order to get around the barrage minefields. On 2 August Geddes made the position of the Admiralty clear to the Imperial War Cabinet:

> In view of the evidence which we had now secured, he thought Norway should be definitely asked whether she would immediately put a stop to the passage of submarines through her waters or leave us to do it. If she was willing to take the former course, we could supply her with the necessary mines. He reminded the Imperial War Cabinet that both Sweden and Norway had laid minefields in their territorial waters at the instance of Germany, in order to prevent our submarines getting into the Baltic through the Kogrund Channel. He considered a week sufficient time to give Norway to come to a decision in the matter. We could lay the mines ourselves in 48 hours.[51]

The Imperial War Cabinet agreed that the passage of U-boats in territorial waters must be stopped and authorized the First Lord and the Foreign Secretary to consult as to how best to deal with the Norwegian Government in the matter. On 7 August the British Minister at Kristiania handed a memorandum to the Norwegian Foreign Minister in the sense of the Admiralty recommendation. The American, French, and Italian Ambassadors in Kristiania supported the British position. The Norwegian Government, much perturbed, replied on 13 August that they could not accept the mining proposal—the use of Norwegian territorial waters by German submarines was not confirmed by any reports in their possession; nor could they allow the Allies to carry out the mining operation themselves, as this would be a clear breach of neutrality. They had, however, at once taken measures to render the protection of their waters more effective through an increase of patrols. On 19 August the British Ambassador informed the Norwegian Government that their reply was unsatisfactory, cited details of the infringement of Norwegian waters by U-boats, and again impressed on the Norwegians that mining was the only effectual means of preventing infringement of neutrality. The

51 I.W.C. 29.

Norwegian Government confirmed the British reports of violation of territorial waters (20 August) but would go no further than to take certain steps, such as putting out lights on the coast. 'We, however, continue to press upon them that nothing short of mining will be efficacious, and that mining we intend to get.'[52]

Beatty received orders to mine Norwegian territorial waters that implied that the Norwegian Government would not be informed and resistance might be expected. He was emphatically opposed to any high-handed policy. He was, as Balfour reported in his memorandum of 22 August,

evidently most anxious not to drive things to an extremity with Norway. His main reasons are:

(a) That, however striking was our show of superior force, an untoward incident might easily occur—a Norwegian Destroyer might fire a shot in defence of the integrity of Norwegian waters, she might be sunk, and irreparable injury thus be done to the good relations of two friendly navies and two friendly countries.

(b) The operation of forcibly laying mines within the three mile limit could only be carried out by daylight and in clear weather: it would therefore be provocative on the face of it;

(c) The lead between the islands and the Norwegian coast would of course be left open to merchant ships. But what, in these circumstances, is to prevent the German submarines using it for their own purposes? Are we to patrol it, and fight the submarines when we find them? If so, the insult to Norway's independence is flagrant and continuous. On the other hand, it is unreasonable to think that the Norwegians would patrol it, after we had flagrantly forced their hand;

(d) If we violate Norwegian neutrality, Germany will certainly do the same. In that event all the coastwise traffic which now goes round the South of Norway and gets made up into convoys at Bergen would be interrupted. The Commander-in-Chief thought this might prove most serious to our interests. . . .

The Commander-in-Chief begged us not to be precipitate.

Here is Beatty at his statesmanlike best, looking beyond immediate strategic advantages to larger issues, strategic, economic, political —and humanitarian. Balfour 'told him in reply that, from a Foreign Office point of view, the whole operation of violating the rights (even if they were but technical rights) of a small and friendly

Power was odious: but that the strongly pressed policy of the Admiralty might drive the Government to take this course in the interests not merely of the Associated belligerents, but of Neutrals themselves.' The C.-in-C. saw to it that this did not happen. (Sobering second thoughts of Britain's Allies were also a factor.) At a conference late in August on board the *Queen Elizabeth*, Beatty stated that 'it would be most repugnant to the officers and men in the Grand Fleet to steam in overwhelming strength into the waters of a small, but high-spirited people and coerce them. If the Norwegians resisted, as they very probably would, blood would be shed; this, said the Commander-in-Chief, "would constitute a crime as bad as any the Germans had committed elsewhere".'[53] The withdrawal of the Northern Patrol to Buncrana in August (see below) made it all the more imperative that something be done quickly about the gap at the eastern end of the barrage.

On 23 August the Government decided to confine their efforts to *persuading* the Norwegians to mine their territorial waters. Persuasion and patience were rewarded. On 29 September the Norwegian Government proclaimed that from 7 October they would close their territorial waters through an extension of the Northern Barrage near Utsire. The mines were not actually laid, as by then the war was nearly over.

It only remains to note another handicap to the efficient working of the Northern Barrage. In August (3rd Sloop Flotilla on the 3rd, the trawlers about the 20th) the Admiralty withdrew the barrage force (Northern Patrol under Admiral Tupper, now turned over to Captain H. T. Walwyn) to Buncrana (Lough Swilly) to counteract U-boat activity in the North Western Approaches to the Irish Sea and generally to keep the U-boats harrying Atlantic convoys on the defensive. This move, Newbolt remarks, 'restricted the scope and purpose of the Northern barrage. The plan as conceived and originally executed was a project for forcing submarines into deep minefields by harrying them whilst they were on the surface. When the patrol craft were withdrawn, one-half of the plan was virtually abandoned, and from then onwards the mine barrage was more a dangerous obstacle than a death-trap into which our surface forces were to drive the German submarines.'[54]

---

[53] Newbolt, *Naval Operations*, v. 349.
[54] *Ibid.*, p. 344.

The Northern Barrage was a great technical achievement, largely the product of American ingenuity, drive, and resources. How effective was it, though? The Secretary of the United States Navy, naturally, saw the barrage as a grand success. He accepted the estimate of Captain Dudley Knox, U.S.N. (*A History of the United States Navy*) that 'possibly as many as eight submarines were destroyed, and probably more than this were damaged in the maze of mines,' rates the barrage as 'the most daring and original naval conception of the war,' and approvingly quotes the post-war statement of the American Admiral Joseph Strauss, who had been in command of the mining operations, that the barrage 'would have ended the submarine menace.'[55] Now, all this sounds fine; but what were the facts? Leith, the official historian of British minefields in the war, who claimed the barrage had proved 'a serious hazard' to the U-boats, Fremantle, and Sims all believe that the barrage accounted for at least six U-boats. Gibson and Prendergast give six; Newbolt writes that five were 'sunk in September alone'; Admiral Gladisch says 'probably' six; the Official Historian of the U-boat warfare, Spindler, cites four as certain losses: *U-92, U-102, U-156, UB-127*. The Admiralty's final post-war list of U-boats sunk had three for certain: *U-92, U-156, UB-123* (and three more 'probables': *U-102, UB-104, UB-127*). Grant, in his newest book, concludes after a most careful study of all the evidence that 'six submarines certainly or almost certainly perished in the Northern Barrage, and one more may have done so.'[56] And so it goes. It would be reasonably safe to conclude that anywhere from four to six boats were blown up in the barrage; two or three others were damaged. This was a meagre result for an enormous expenditure of mines; these might have been employed with better results elsewhere, in accordance with Beatty's ideas, or in implementing Naval Staff pleas for small patrolled deep minefields and patrolled mine-net areas laid across the tracks of outward- and homeward-bound U-boats.[57]

---

55 Josephus Daniels, *The Wilson Era: Years of War and After* (Chapel Hill, North Carolina, 1946), p. 91.
56 Robert M. Grant, *U-Boat Intelligence, 1914–1918* (London, 1969), p. 109.
57 Late in September 1917 the Admiralty planned an operation against U-boats which N.I.D. had discovered were proceeding up the North Sea on a regular route. A force of submarines, destroyers, and trawlers was used to keep the U-boats down and drive them on to a mine-net trap laid on their path in a zone east of the Dogger Bank. Despite abominable weather, as many as three submarines were claimed as

A post-war German naval manual states: 'The cardinal error of this Barrage was that it went counter to the fundamental principle of mine-warfare, in that it was taken through the deepest spot to be found in the North Sea . . . the closure of such great depths as in the Northern Barrage is irrational as well as completely impracticable.'[58] The Senior Officer U-boats at the end of the war summarized the effectiveness of the barrage this way: 'For some unknown reason many of the mines detonated spontaneously. This tendency was well known to our U-boats . . . Considering the number of mines lost in this way, one will readily appreciate that this barrage was far from being a complete seal to the North Sea's northern exit, and could have no more than a limited effectiveness. . . . In fact, it might be said that the Barrage was more of a danger to the minelayers and minesweepers (post-war) than to the U-boats.'[59]

But did the barrage have a major deterrent effect, which is a better indicator of its success than number of U-boats destroyed? Wemyss had argued with Beatty: 'Admiral Sims believes [the mines of the barrage] to be more materially efficient than we do. I, on the other hand, believe them to be more morally effective than, probably, you do. . . . If the Barrage is completed, the situation will be that the enemy will have to order his submarines to pass twice over a minefield, however effectual or ineffectual it actually may be, and the moral consequences on the crews of such procedure should not be left out of account when balancing the pros and cons.'[60] The German authority Gayer admits, 'It is not to be denied, however, that the threat of this barrage was extremely unpleasant.'[61] The German Official Historian of North Sea operations implies the same: 'In the North the Northern Barrage made

---

certainties by N.I.D. in this operation in the first ten days of October. (Newbolt and Gibson and Prendergast list *U-50*, *U-66*, and *U-106* as the victims. But the official German list, also Grant, accept only *U-106* as destroyed on this occasion.) This pilot project was never followed up, because the Admiralty would not, or could not, find the necessary patrols or, after the Northern Barrage was started, the mines.

[58] M.Dv. 352, *Mine und Seestrategie* (1935), p. 20, by Korvettenkapitän Hagen.

[59] Vice-Admiral Andreas Michelsen, *Der U-Bootskrieg, 1914–1918* (Leipzig, 1925), p. 85. Spindler's last volume makes no mention of the effectiveness of the Northern Barrage.

[60] Wemyss to Beatty, 23 August 1918; Beatty MSS.

[61] Captain Albert Gayer, 'Summary of German Submarine Operations in the Various Theatres of War from 1914 to 1918,' *United States Naval Institute Proceedings*, April 1925. And see below, p. 84.

its presence felt. The main reason for this was that it lay too far from the German bases, ruling out all minesweeping possibilities and also the provision of escorts for U-boats. Just how effective the Northern Barrage would have been against the U-boat war in the long term remains an open question.'[62] The barrage was not so unpleasant or so risky as to force the U-boats to abandon transits to the trade routes via Area B and the Fair Island passage (Area A in October, after the Fair Island passage had become quite dangerous), or through Norwegian territorial waters until October. Grant states that transits, which averaged 30 a month in the first half of 1918, increased to 42 during July–September, as the barrage was being laid.[63] The last known transit northward through the barrage was *UB-86*, which sailed on 15 October. Returning boats crossed the barrage (Area C) through October.

There was a second, older mine barrage in the North Sea, a southern one extending across the Heligoland Bight. The endeavour in 1917 to close the Bight to enemy submarines with a quadrant of mines had not succeeded in its primary purpose. The Germans had countered this strategy by marking, buoying, and regularly sweeping a number of channels through British minefields. By the end of 1917 the barrage was worrying the Germans and keeping a vast force of sweepers and auxiliaries busy. The Admiralty intensified the minelaying in the Bight during 1918: over 21,000 mines in 129 minefields were laid, compared with 15,686 and 76, respectively, in 1917. (The total number of British mines laid in the Bight through 1917 was about 23,000.) There was a new emphasis on blocking the swept channels instead of maintaining a complete barrier across the Bight. Only one U-boat for certain was destroyed in the Bight minefields: *UB-22* on 19 January. Yet the Heligoland barrage achieved a success by forcing most, if not all, of the U-boats from German bases to be routed via the Kattegat from February 1918. 'This had shortened the productive period of each submarine cruise by something like four days,' Newbolt points out, 'and had been partly responsible for the fall in the sinkings in Home waters.'[64] Early in 1918 (February,

[62] *Der Krieg in der Nordsee*, vii. 317–18.
[63] Grant, *U-Boats Destroyed*, p. 107. The transits served one useful purpose for the Admiralty. 'The U-boats had orders to report when they had passed the barrage and that helped us [in Room 40] to track them.' Admiral Sir William James's letter to the author, 7 February 1966.
[64] *Naval Operations*, v. 337.

April) about 1,400 deep mines were laid in two minefields in the Kattegat. Since they were not patrolled by surface craft (quite apart from the many premature explosions soon after laying), they had little influence on the U-boats. The policy of mining the Bight never achieved complete success because of the difficulties of attacking the German minesweepers and the inability to patrol the Kattegat minefield.

What of the convoy system all this time? Captain Roskill has got to the heart of the matter: 'Even if the ready acceptance of the original proposal [for the Northern Barrage] can, at any rate, be explained by the fact that, at the time, the convoy strategy had not yet fully proved itself, its execution was continued long after the success of the ancient principle was beyond all doubt. Indeed the whole idea of the Northern Barrage underlines the lack of the Admiralty's faith in the strategy of convoy and escort . . . '[65] This judgement applies equally to the Otranto Straits Barrage, to say nothing of 'offensive' A/S warfare generally during 1918.

[65] Roskill, *The Strategy of Sea Power* (London, 1962), p. 135.

IV

Beating the U-Boats[1]

(*Chart 6*)

In the First World War the German U-boat arm achieved great successes; but the introduction of the convoy system in 1917 robbed it of its opportunity to become a decisive factor.

ADMIRAL KARL DOENITZ, *Memoirs : Ten Years and Twenty Days.*

Although we never discovered a complete answer to the S/m menace, there is no doubt that the cumulative effect of all our measures was sufficient to defeat it.

DUFF to Admiral Sir Alexander Bethell, 21 December 1918.

I. THE SHIPPING SITUATION

THE position at the end of the first year of the unrestricted U-boat campaign, that is, from February 1917 to January 1918 inclusive, is summed up by Fayle. In that period war losses had reduced the world's shipping by nearly 6,200,000 tons. Of this figure 3,750,000 tons were British (all but 250,000, of ocean-going shipping), or over 20 per cent of the tonnage available in January 1917. Enemy action had damaged 1,175,000 tons of shipping in the same twelve-month period, 925,000 tons of which were British. Most of this tonnage was out of service for four to six months. With marine casualties (collisions, running ashore), the total British tonnage under repair at the end of January 1918 was 1,500,000, a third of it undergoing major repairs. 'With such losses the programme of new construction was utterly unable to cope . . . it was unable even to keep up with the current rate of loss, greatly as that rate had been reduced since the summer of 1917.'[2]

The shipping situation improved greatly in the course of 1918, particularly from the spring. The average daily sinkings of world

[1] The reader is referred to the various tables appended to this chapter dealing with shipping losses, shipbuilding output, the convoy system, and U-boats.

[2] C. Ernest Fayle, *History of the Great War. Seaborne Trade* (London, 1920–4, 3 vols.), iii. 255. All mercantile tonnage figures cited in the chapter are in gross tons.

tonnage in the second quarter were little more than a third of the corresponding quarter of 1917. The following tables show the steady reduction in British and world losses:

BRITISH MERCHANT SHIPPING LOSSES BY ENEMY ACTION IN 1918[3]

(Gross tonnage with number of ships in parentheses)

	By Surface Craft	By Mines		By Submarines		Total	
January	—	—		179,973	(57)	179,973	(57)
February	—	2,395	(1)	224,501	(68)	226,896	(69)
March	—	4,619	(3)	194,839	(79)	199,458	(82)
April	4,211 (3)	1,863	(2)	209,379	(66)	215,453	(71)
May	—	3,707	(1)	188,729	(59)	192,436	(60)
June	—	4,330	(2)	158,660	(49)	162,990	(51)
July	—	—		165,449	(37)	165,449	(37)
August	—	—		145,721	(41)	145,721	(41)
September	—	—		136,864	(48)	136,864	(48)
October	—	3,030	(1)	54,577	(23)	57,607	(24)
November	1,622 (1)	1,721	(1)	10,315	(2)	13,658	(4)
TOTAL	5,833 (4)	21,665	(11)	1,669,007	(529)	1,696,505	(544)

ALLIED AND NEUTRAL TONNAGE SUNK IN 1918 BY ALL ENEMY CAUSES

	Allied	Neutral	Total British, Allied, Neutral
January	87,078 (45)	35,037 (21)	302,088 (123)
February	54,904 (27)	36,374 (19)	318,174 (115)
March	94,321 (61)	51,035 (26)	344,814 (169)
April	50,879 (32)	11,361 (13)	277,693 (116)
May	80,826 (33)	20,757 (19)	294,019 (112)
June	51,173 (26)	38,474 (24)	252,637 (101)
July	70,900 (34)	23,552 (24)	259,901 (95)
August	91,209 (32)	41,946 (31)	278,876 (104)
September	39,343 (22)	10,393 (9)	186,600 (79)
October	41,308 (19)	13,512 (9)	112,427 (52)
November	7,319	5,880	26,857 (15)
TOTAL	669,260	288,321	2,654,086 (1,081)

[3] Director of Statistics, Admiralty, 'Statistical Review of the War against Merchant Shipping' (December 1918), Appendices A and D, for this and the following table. There is a copy of this valuable paper in the Naval Library, Ministry of Defence. The November figures in the two tables are suspect. June 1919 figures of the Trade Division, Naval Staff, are: U.K., 10,220 (3), Allies, 5,303 (2), Neutrals, 2,159 (2), total, 17,682 (7).

World's Daily Average Loss[4]

Quarter	Number of Vessels	Gross Tonnage
1st quarter 1917	7·60	16,530
2nd quarter 1917	10·43	23,550
3rd quarter 1917	6·22	15,270
4th quarter 1917	5·04	12,500
1st quarter 1918	4·50	10,740
2nd quarter 1918	3·37	8,600
3rd quarter 1918	2·91	7,813

Noteworthy is the falling off in losses by mine. The Germans laid some 11,000 mines in 1,360 groups in British Home waters during the war. Only two groups remained undetected at war's end, which is a testimonial to the remarkable work done by the British minesweepers. British merchant shipping losses due to enemy minelaying were reduced substantially in 1918: to 21,000 tons from the 296,000 tons of 1917. The total figure (British, Allied, neutral) dropped from 404,000 in 1917 to 60,000-odd in 1918. 'In 1918 the total number of vessels lost by mining in waters, both at home and abroad, in which the responsibility for sweeping rested upon Great Britain was 12. The average of ships lost per mine swept being one in 85, a remarkable improvement.'[5]

Convoy was in itself almost a complete antidote to the German mining operations (from the summer of 1917 160 independent ships were mined as against five of the nearly 84,000 convoyed ships in ocean and Home waters convoys) for the simple reason that ships were under continuous operational control of naval vessels with the latest information as to where mines had been discovered or were suspected. As a consequence, ships in convoy could be diverted around minefields or stopped from entering minefields. Furthermore, whereas independently sailed ships were often held up for days because of a threat of a minefield in the vicinity, no convoys are known to have been held up because of a threat of a minefield (or of a U-boat) in the offing. In other words, the delivery rate of shipping under risk of mine attack was greatly expedited by the convoy system.

Though it was not until June, and not again until September,

---

[4] Technical History Monograph TH 14, *The Atlantic Convoy System, 1917–1918*, p. 35.
[5] Naval Staff, *History of British Minesweeping in the War* (1920), p. 70. In the first year of the war 10½ mines were swept for each vessel mined in Home waters, in 1918, 35: 'probably a good indication of the improvement in dealing with new minefields.' Admiralty, 'Statistical Review of the War against Merchant Shipping,' p. 16.

that total British mercantile shipping construction surpassed the tonnage destroyed by direct war causes, and not until September that new construction exceeded war losses and marine risk losses combined, the turning point appears to have come in May. The shortage of steel and labour had kept shipbuilding down. But the spurt in new construction, beginning in May and averaging over 150,000 tons monthly through October (though Geddes had hoped for 250,000 by the end of the year), coupled with the acceleration in the repair of damaged ships[6] and the reduction in losses, resulted in more tonnage being available at the end of June than at the beginning of the month. Even more significant was the total world output of new ships, whose upward curve, due mostly to the American effort, crossed the downward graph of sinkings (all causes) in March and continued upwards.

The worst was definitely over by June, and the U-boat campaign as good as defeated, even if world losses continued to average more than 200,000 tons a month during the remainder of the war. 'This great victory at sea,' as Newbolt remarks, 'had passed almost unrecognised. Public attention was still divided between the battles in Flanders, where the Allied armies were still staggering and reeling under the German onslaught, and operations at Zeebrugge and Ostend, which had just been announced as far-reaching successes. The columns of figures that recorded the victory were not suitable for issue as bulletin news: even if they had been published, few persons would have grasped their immense significance.'[7] Certain it was, as will be noted elsewhere, that the public mood did not match the growing optimism in high naval quarters.

In the first months of the unrestricted campaign the average U-boat commander was sinking 700 tons of shipping a day; by the summer of 1918, the figure was about 275 and still declining. 'Twelve months previously, therefore, the German submarine

6 The proportion of British ships under repair increased in 1918. The average of 100,000 tons damaged by enemy action was at the same level, but marine casualties, as a result of convoy conditions (sailing without lights and postponement of repairs), were on the rise: a monthly average (January–October) of 378,000 tons. (The Allied and neutral figure was 226,000 tons.) In July 1918 over 8 per cent of British steam tonnage was undergoing serious repairs.

7 *Naval Operations*, v. 337. I must point out that the losses still being suffered were almost entirely incurred by ships which were passing through areas which were known to be infested by U-boats and through which ships in convoy passed virtually unscathed.

commanders had been a danger to the Empire and to the Alliance: they were now only a danger to unescorted ships and their crews.'[8] How are we to explain the virtual defeat of the U-boats, or, to put it another way, their declining effectiveness?

2. THE U-BOATS IN THE FINAL PHASE

During the final phase of the unrestricted submarine campaign, the first ten months of 1918, the Germans made extraordinary efforts to get more submarines on the trade routes. The average monthly total of U-boats available for operations was 123, six fewer than in 1917; the average monthly total of operational boats at sea was 45, one more than in 1917, with a maximum of 60 at any one time, as compared with 70 in 1917. The Germans were no more successful in accelerating construction of U-boats. Admiral Capelle (Tirpitz's successor at the Ministry of Marine) had stated in the Reichstag in July 1917 that the output of submarines was expected to be between 8 and 12 a month. This figure, if realized, would have added between 80 and 120 submarines during 1918 by the end of October. The actual figure was 80, or a monthly commissioning rate of 8. The prohibitive factor all along had been the allocation of workers, the High Command refusing to heed the pleas of the naval authorities to release skilled workmen from the Army. At the Armistice Germany's total submarine strength (the number of boats in commission) was scarcely greater than when the year began: 180 in October (monthly average), 167 in January (monthly average). On the other hand, the number of operational boats had declined from the monthly average of 130 in January to 115 in October.

At first glance the decreasing effectiveness of the U-boat campaign would appear to have been due to the number of war losses in 1918 (69), which, with the boats scuttled between 1 October and 1 November (14), exceeded the number of boats built in this period (80). The monthly breakdown of war losses in 1918 was: January: 9; February: 3; March: 5; April: 7; May: 14; June: 3; July: 6; August: 7; September: 9; October: 5; November: 1. (The Admiralty were careful not to overestimate their successes.

[8] *Ibid.*, p. 339. 'In March 1917 the H.S.F. U-boats had been destroying an average of rather more than one ship every two days on patrol . . . In June 1918 the average had fallen to one ship every *fourteen* days . . .' Rear-Admiral Sir William Jameson, *The Most Formidable Thing* (London, 1965), p. 243.

The number of kills they registered was close to the actual figures.) Captain W. W. Fisher, the D.A.S.D., afterwards called May the 'glorious month'. 'May 1918 was the knock-out blow and there was little heart in the U-boat Commanders after that.' The monthly average in 1918 (through October) was 6·8, the highest in the war; 1914: 1; 1915: 1·59; 1916: 1·83; 1917: 5·17; for the whole war: 3·42. Note, however, that the 6·8 figure for 1918 was *below* the monthly commissioning rate of eight. If the improvement in the rate of destruction of U-boats did not go far enough, the difficulty was that the Allies lacked effective means of locating submerged submarines. The important thing is that the declining effectiveness of the U-boats was not due to any significant decrease in their total number or in their operational strength, and certainly not in the number of boats at sea, which in October actually rose to 54. We must look elsewhere for the key to the problem.

The Admiralty was much heartened by evidence of the falling off in U-boat morale.

From recent interrogations of submarine prisoners of war, it can definitely be stated that the morale of submarine crews is steadily declining.

This, no doubt, is partly due to the heavy losses of submarines in general, which arouse in the minds of officers and men the presentiment that each cruise they make will be their last one (several instances have occurred in which these sentiments were expressed in letters to relatives of prisoners of war), but largely also to the increasing number of attacks to which they are subjected.

Prisoners from Submarine *U-110* (sunk 15.3.18) stated that the old and experienced ratings were becoming very 'nervy,' and that any sudden shock affected them in an abnormal degree.

The Commanding Officer of *UB-55* (sunk 22.4.18), a very experienced officer, remarked that the crews of new submarines could not be relied upon. He also added that both officers and men frequently require rest and nerve cures. Recently several Officers of the Flanders Flotilla had to be given leave for that purpose.

The Navigation Warrant Officer of *U-103* (sunk 11.5.18), who is a powerfully built man, admitted that his nerves were 'going all to pieces' as the result of our anti-submarine measures. His most anxious time was during the boat's fourth cruise in March last, when they were harried from place to place in the Irish Sea, and on one occasion over 20 depth charges exploded uncomfortably close within a quarter of an hour. Though no damage was done to the boat, the crew were badly rattled, and more than one had a presentiment that, if they got home then, the next cruise would probably be their last. This Warrant Officer stated further that depth charges are much more feared now than a few months ago, as they are set deeper and produce a more violent explosion.

He attributed the low state of his nerves partly to the 'jumpiness' of his commanding officer, who had been in the Mediterranean before commissioning *U-103* in July 1917. On one occasion, after a hot pursuit, this officer flung down his chart and exclaimed: 'Es ist alles Mist', which might be rendered: 'This is a dog's life.' The other officers did their best to calm him, but his outbreaks of temper were frequent and violent.

The Commanding Officer and sole survivor of *UB-16* (sunk 10.5.18) repeatedly let slip in general conversation the fact that a great many submarine officers had nervous breakdowns.[9]

The morale of the U-boat personnel had, undoubtedly, been shaken; yet it would not be wise to make too much of it. On the whole, morale remained high (above all in the Flanders Flotilla), as proven in the last days of the war, when the U-boats were not affected by the revolutionary agitation that eventually resulted in mutiny in the surface vessels of the High Seas Fleet.

A report by Admiral Scheer (he was then Chief of the Admiralty Staff) to the Emperor on 21 September 1918 singled these out as the factors in 'the steady decline in the successes of the individual U-boats': (1) 'improved and strengthened enemy defensive measures' were the 'primary' cause; (2) 'the loss of old seasoned commanders'; (3) the steady increase in enemy mercantile construction, which would in the foreseeable future exceed shipping losses. 'This will reduce the effect of U-boat warfare considerably.'[10] The last calls for no comment. As regards the second, which is a fact, out of the 400 commanders a scant 20 or so were responsible for approximately 60 per cent of all Allied sinkings from submarine action. These remarkable figures show how important were the ability and enterprise of the individual commanding officer. U-boat commanders (of *both* World Wars) varied greatly in their capacity for boldness and initiative in attack, in which respect they did not, as a class, differ substantially from other categories of professional military commanders in any nation. There was great scope in the First War for enterprising

9 Admiralty to Beatty, 4 June 1918; Admiralty MSS.
10 Appendix V to the War Diary; Levetzow Papers, German Ministry of Marine MSS.

U-boat commanders, especially, but far from entirely, in the early years. The point I am making is that there were fewer outstanding commanders by 1918—so many of them had been killed. 'Not all the officers now being given command possessed the combination of guts and instinctive good judgment for the lone and difficult task of attacking well-protected, moving targets glimpsed through a periscope or dimly seen when on the surface at night. There had always been a great difference between the results obtained by the best and run-of-the-mill commanding officers.'[11] A related consideration is the decline in the efficiency of the U-boat crews. The rapid increase in submarine construction, coupled with the heavier submarine personnel losses, led to a reduction in the training time for the men and to a dilution of crews to commission new boats.

This brings us to Scheer's first point, 'improved and strengthened enemy defensive measures'. One facet of these is mentioned by the Official Historian of the North Sea operations: 'Towards the end of the war the U-boats experienced considerable difficulty in breaking through the North Sea to and from their operation areas west of England. The closure of the Dover Strait had become more or less effective. It was difficult to break through the Pentland Firth, because the patrols forced the U-boats to submerge, where the current made navigation extremely difficult. In the north the Northern Barrage made its presence felt.'[12] The Official Historian of the U-boat warfare fills out the picture: 'In spite of a considerable increase in the number of U-boats employed [in 1918], the Allied defences had succeeded in reducing the shipping losses. This had been brought about not only by the convoy system and the anti-submarine measures, but also because of the long and time-consuming passage through the mine-infested North Sea and the consequent shortening of the U-boat's time in the operation area. The war diaries of the U-boats provide adequate evidence of the difficulties the U-boat crews had to contend with before getting into a suitable position for an attack.'[13]

Returning to Scheer's first point, he undoubtedly had the convoy system in mind above all other 'enemy defensive measures'. There is not a shadow of a doubt that convoy proved to be the greatest

---

[11] Jameson, *The Most Formidable Thing*, p. 242.
[12] *Der Krieg in der Nordsee*, vii. 317–18.
[13] Rear-Admiral Arno Spindler, *Der Handelskrieg mit U-Booten* (Berlin, 1932–66, 5 vols.), v. 341. I query his 'considerable increase in the number of U-boats employed'.

single factor in overcoming the submarine menace—far greater than any other technical or tactical antidote.

3. CONVOY IN FULL BLOOM

During the last months of 1917 just over half the total traffic in the United Kingdom's overseas trade was in convoy, whether ocean or short-sea convoy. The proportion had risen to 90 per cent by the end of the war.

The Dover Straits Barrage deflected the Flanders U-boats from the Channel to the East Coast. There, until May 1918, only a proportion of the shipping was in convoy and shipping losses were high. From June the proportion of ships sailed in convoy increased until practically the whole of the trade between the Humber and the north was covered. (The convoys did not operate south of the Humber because the submarines rarely moved into the shoal waters off East Anglia and the Thames.) Aircraft were concentrated on the protection of convoys, and the surface patrols operated additionally as support groups to convoys during their passage through their area. Evasion of submarines was not possible. Because of the danger from surface raiders and mines, shipping had to proceed along a clearly marked swept channel. The submarines, therefore, knew the route and course of the convoy. Shipping losses on the East Coast were, nevertheless, reduced to a very low figure, except among the few ships still sailed independently. During 1918 (from 16 January), 16,102 ships were sailed in East Coast convoys; a trifling 35 were sunk, thus the loss rate was a mere 0·2 per cent.[14] And whereas in the first five months of the year no U-boats were destroyed off the East Coast, from June (more accurately, from 31 May) six were disposed of. The development of the coastal convoy system forced the U-boats back to the Western Approaches in the last months of the war.

[14] I define 'loss rate' as the percentage of ships sunk of those sailed over a given period of time and, if appropriate, in a given area. My convoy statistics are derived from Technical History Monographs TH 8 (*Scandinavian and East Coast Convoy Systems, 1917–1918*), TH 14 (*The Atlantic Convoy System, 1917–1918*), and TH 15 (*Convoy Statistics and Diagrams*), various papers in the Barley–Waters MSS. in the Naval Historical Branch, Ministry of Defence (especially No. 37, 'Analysis of Statistics of Shipping Losses, 1917–1918'), and Lieutenant-Commander D. W. Waters's published writings, some of them in restricted journals. Discrepancies abound in the statistics, though they are not of a really substantive kind.

The efficiency of the Scandinavian convoy system remained high. During 1918 (from 19 January) 4,230 ships were sailed; 15 were sunk, for a 0·35 per cent loss rate. For the whole of 1917–18 the figures are 7,653, 55, and 0·72 per cent.

A new regular outward convoy, the Irish Sea Convoy, was started from Liverpool late in March 1918.

In the Mediterranean convoys were denuded of escorts by the voracious appetite of the Otranto Straits Barrage for small craft, once it got going in April 1918. The aim was to have at least a destroyer or sloop assisted by two trawlers, but often the escort amounted to the two trawlers—and this for convoys of up to 30 ships, though 7·5 ships was the average size. Indeed, the escorts were reduced to below the minimum considered necessary to ensure immunity against attack. They were so weak that when a U-boat attacked, only one or two of the escorts could be detached for a short time to counter-attack. In October 1918 the Director of Mercantile Movements at the Admiralty, Captain F. A. Whitehead, who was responsible for the smooth functioning of convoy in the Mediterranean, reported that 'the escort which can now be given to each convoy is so small that it has ceased to be an efficient protection, and is now little more than a means of keeping the convoy in order, standing by any casualty which may occur, and endeavouring to destroy the submarine after an attack.'[15] Yet these weak and slow escorts did the job, despite Gough-Calthorpe's prophecy (28 November 1917) that, since convoy was 'at best, a deterrent, and not a reliable safeguard,' its effectiveness would decrease as its novelty wore off.

Convoy losses in the Mediterranean, (November) 1917–18, totalled 136 ships of 11,509 convoyed, or a loss rate of 1·19 per cent, and the escorts destroyed 8 of the 12 U-boats sunk in the Mediterranean from mid-1917 till the end of the war. (The commander of one of these boats was the future Admiral Doenitz, who was captured when attacking a convoy.) The convoy statistics show:

15 Waters, 'Notes on the Convoy System of Naval Warfare, Thirteenth to Twentieth Centuries.' Part 2. 'First World War, 1914–18,' Historical Section, Admiralty (1960). The escort forces in the Mediterranean when the war ended totalled approximately 92 destroyers (10 of them British), 105 sloops, gunboats, armed boarding vessels, and yachts (63), 224 trawlers (95); grand total, 421 craft, which did not include a large number of Italian vessels used for escort purposes along the Italian coastal routes. *Mediterranean Staff Papers*, p. 31.

Total through convoys: 627 vessels
Sunk by enemy action: 9
Loss rate: 1·43%
Total local convoys: 10,882 vessels
Sunk by enemy action: 127
Loss rate: 1·17%

As Mediterranean convoy was developed and extended (on the average 35 per cent of the shipping was in organized convoys and 27 per cent was under escort for a part of their voyage), there was a progressive drop in sinkings, beginning in June 1918 (except for July). The monthly loss of British, Allied, and neutral ships (500 gross tons and upwards) due to submarines in 1918 was: January: 30; February: 20; March: 27 (plus one through mines); April: 20 (1); May: 28; June: 13 (2); July: 20; August: 13; September: 10; October: 10 (1). At the time this was attributed to the Otranto Straits Barrage. The barrage and the bombing of the submarine bases in the Adriatic may have helped somewhat; but the credit must chiefly go to the convoy system.

The final and complete statistics of the convoy system are startling. Of the 16,070 ships sailed in ocean convoys (including through Mediterranean), U-boats sank 96, or 0·60 per cent. The effect of ocean convoy was to reduce the percentage of losses to sailings in the United Kingdom overseas trade from nearly 5 per cent in April 1917 to approximately one-half per cent at war's end, when, as stated, 90 per cent of this trade was in convoy. Of the 67,888 ships sailed in Home water convoys (coastal, Dutch, French Coal Trade, Scandinavian), U-boats sank 161, or 0·24 per cent. If we add Mediterranean local convoys, the grand total of ships convoyed is nearly 95,000, with total losses of 393, or a loss rate of 0·41 per cent.

Equally revealing is a comparison between the number of ships convoyed in the Atlantic and Home waters in the February 1917–October 1918 period (83,958, of which 16,070 were in ocean convoys) and the number of independent sailings (48,861 for November 1917–October 1918: figures are not available for February–October 1917), on the one hand, and the losses inflicted on both types of shipping (260 and 1,497, respectively), on the other hand. Total losses were, then, 1,757, *with independent losses accounting for 85 per cent.*

Commander Waters sums up the effectiveness of convoy as contrasted with independent sailings in this terse statement: 'The available statistics and a variety of comments in contemporary reports indicate that the loss rate of independent shipping was consistently in the order of ten (10) times or more that of ships in convoy in Home Waters and the Atlantic throughout the period that convoy was operated.'[16]

Wherein lay the strength of the convoy system? I cannot improve on this précis in a recent study by a submarine officer:

The first effect of the convoy system was that the ocean suddenly seemed to the U-boats to be devoid of shipping. This was because, strange as it may seem, a convoy of ships was not much more likely to be sighted than a single vessel. A single ship will probably be seen by a U-boat lurking within ten miles of its track. A convoy of twenty ships is only two miles wide and so would be seen by a U-boat lying within eleven miles of the centre of the track of the convoy. Five convoys of twenty ships each were not, therefore, very much more likely to be seen than five single ships and were obviously much harder to find than a hundred independents. The result was that the vast majority of ships when in convoy were never seen, and the greatest advantage of the system was the difficulty the U-boats had in finding the convoys at all.

It is also true that the British intelligence of U-boat movements at this period was surprisingly good. The U-boats used their radio a great deal and their positions could be fixed by direction-finding stations on shore. The distress calls of merchant ships also gave information which enabled the U-boats to be tracked with considerable accuracy. With ships in convoy and the better control it gave over them, this information could be used to divert them into safer waters.

When all shipping sailed independently, U-boats were presented with a long succession of targets at which to fire, and they had time to take deliberate aim and then reload before the next victim appeared. With convoy there would be only one chance to fire as the enemy swept by *en masse*. Whilst the selected ship was being attacked, the rest of the convoy would slip by unscathed and a second shot was seldom possible even if

16 'Notes on the Convoy System of Naval Warfare.' A large part of his proof is the figures in the 'Statistical Review,' p. 14. This source adds 'A' (0·53: percentage of losses in convoy) and 'B' (0·68: percentage of losses before joining and after dispersal) together and calls this the convoy loss rate: 1·21 per cent. The non-convoy loss rate is 4·79 per cent. Of course, the actual figures should be 'A' = 0·53—compared to 'B' and non-convoy, i.e., 0·68 + 4·79 = 5·47. Thus, the convoy loss rate was one-tenth that of the non-convoyed ship loss rate, and not one-quarter. Quite a difference!

the escorts permitted it. With only two, or sometimes four, torpedo tubes, only one ship, or at most two, would generally be hit. Moreover the attack was complicated by the presence of the escorts and the anticipation of the heavy counter attack which was likely to descend on the U-boat after firing. Convoy brought the escorts into the vicinity of the U-boats at a time when they had to reveal their position by firing. When the anti-submarine vessels patrolled at random they could never find the U-boats, but with a convoy system, the U-boats, when they did find the convoys, could not help bringing themselves into contact with the anti-submarine vessels. . . .

Convoys therefore achieved their great success not so much because the escorts protected them, but because they were much harder to find, gave only a fleeting chance of attack as they swept by and then offered the escorts a better chance to destroy the U-boats than they had ever had before.[17]

These are the very factors stressed by the Germans in assessing the effectiveness of the convoy system. Thus, Admiral Doenitz writes that with the introduction of convoy:

The oceans at once became bare and empty; for long periods at a time the U-boats, operating individually, would see nothing at all; and then suddenly up would loom a huge concourse of ships, thirty or fifty or more of them, surrounded by a strong escort of warships of all types. The solitary U-boat, which most probably had sighted the convoy purely by chance, would then attack, thrusting again and again and persisting, if the commander had strong nerves, for perhaps several days and nights, until the physical exhaustion of both commander and crew called a halt. The lone U-boat might well sink one or two of the ships, or even several; but that was but a poor percentage of the whole. The convoy would steam on. In most cases no other German U-boat would catch sight of it, and it would reach Britain, bringing a rich cargo of foodstuffs and raw materials safely to port.[18]

Michelsen describes the repeated attacks, despite a rain of depth charges, by two U-boats (*UB-64, U-54*) on the huge White Star liner *Justicia* (32,334 tons), which was in a heavily escorted convoy in the North Channel (19–20 July 1918). They finally sank her after a 24-hour fight. He states (and he is right) that this kind of success by U-boats against escorted convoys was by no means

[17] Vice-Admiral Sir Arthur Hezlet, *The Submarine and Sea Power* (London, 1967), pp. 94–5. And see *From the Dreadnought to Scapa Flow*, iv. 285–6.
[18] Karl Doenitz, *Memoirs: Ten Years and Twenty Days* (London, 1959), p. 4.

uncommon.[19] But it does not tell the whole story. The U-boats had a healthy respect for destroyer escorts. Sims's remark of 15 June 1917, 'It is possible that for every submarine sighted by a destroyer there are many submarines that sight destroyers and avoid them,' is accurate and points up the deterrent effect of the convoy escort. When a U-boat found a convoy, she had to be careful not to expose herself to instant counterattacks from the escorting destroyers, which by this time had a vast arsenal of depth charges. (The original equipment of an escort ship, four depth charges, had been increased to 30 by 1918.) As one commander testified, 'Never as long as I live shall I forget those convoy attacks . . . I do not know if I possess the power to convey the maddening nervous strain which an attack like this [by a destroyer escort] imposed.'[20] The U-boat commander had, therefore, if he decided to press home an attack, to make a submerged approach to the target. His low endurance if he used his full submerged speed made it impracticable for a U-boat to attack a convoy unless he was well before its beam on first sighting it. In any other position his only chance lay in coming to the surface and working round ahead of the convoy—at the risk, of course, of being sighted. If the U-boat commander got into an attack position, his problems were only beginning, as Commander Waters brings out:

. . . attacking a ship in convoy is one of the most difficult and most dangerous operations of war; it always has been. . . . This is because a submarine can sink a ship only by attacking her within a peripheral attack area whose radii are determined largely by the submarine's weapon performance and relative speed of attack. If a surface antisubmarine escort is disposed around a convoy at the probable submarine attack range and an air escort is present, in order to sink a ship the submarine commander must penetrate the defence perimeter; concentrate on attacking a ship and not on evading the escorting surface and aircraft; must remain in the attack area long enough to identify, aim and fire at a target successfully; yet, when attacking must avoid betraying his presence to the surface and air escorts although they are trained and disposed to anticipate attack; must betray his presence by a successful attack, and will probably betray it by an abortive one; yet, if not sunk before, must withdraw from the scene of the attack in the

19 Michelsen, *Der U-Bootskrieg, 1914–1918*, pp. 111–14. Spindler, however, says there was a third U-boat present, *UB-124*, which was sunk by depth charges.
20 Commander Ernst Hashagen, *The Log of a U-boat Commander* (London, 1931), pp. 227–8.

presence of alerted surface and air escorts operating within the probable range of detection and of counter-attack.

Attacking unescorted ships—even anti-submarine vessels on anti-submarine patrol—particularly in the absence of escort aircraft is a much less hazardous operation, the submarine commander has fewer diverse problems to attempt to solve concurrently and fewer distractions.

Attacks, when made, were from about 700 yards, yet in few convoys that were attacked was more than a single merchant ship sunk: the risks of the U-boat lingering in the vicinity for a second shot were too great. Statistics of ocean convoys attacked and ships sunk in ocean convoy by U-boat action reveal that of the 84 convoys successfully attacked (average size of convoys, 15 ships), in 69 of these instances only one ship was sunk; in each of 12 convoys two ships were sunk; in each of three convoys, three ships were sunk. These statistics are highly significant in another way. Note that the average size of the ocean convoys was 15 ships. The Mediterranean convoys of 1918 were on the average half this size (7·5 ships). But their loss rate was, as stated above, twice as high: 1·19 per cent, compared to 0·6 per cent. These statistics bear out a fundamental law of convoy: that if you double the number of ships in a convoy, you halve the risk; if you halve the number of ships in a convoy, you double the risk. However, until 1943, when Professor P. M. S. Blackett, as Director of Naval Operational Research, produced some interesting statistics about ocean convoys and analysed them, it was Admiralty gospel that 'the larger the convoy the greater the risk.' See further, below, pp. 99–100, n. 33.

The role of aircraft in the fully developed convoy system and in A/S warfare generally merits further discussion. They were increasingly used on coastal A/S patrol, working with surface vessels, and on convoy escort, especially from June 1918 onwards. During the last six months of the war, the daily strength of A/S aircraft in Home waters alone averaged 189 aeroplanes, 300 seaplanes and flying boats, and 75 airships. Of these 564 aircraft an average of 310 were available daily for operations. The monthly averages in the last six months were: 28 U-boats sighted, 19 attacked; nearly 14,000 hours flown on A/S escort, support, and patrol. Aircraft did not sink any U-boats in 1918 (they may have got one in 1917), despite the Official Air Historian's claim that six were so destroyed.

As patrols they proved ineffective. Their 100- and 230-lb. A/S bombs, fitted with unsatisfactory 2½-seconds delay-action fuses, were not lethal. Needed was a missile at least two-and-a-half times as heavy, to detonate close to the surface, or a weapon capable of penetrating the pressure hull. As convoys were increased in numbers in coastal waters, aircraft were switched from patrol duties and used more and more as integral parts of the convoy escort (generally, one aircraft), whether in close escort or distant escort (support). In 1918, seaplanes and aeroplanes carried out nearly 5,000 escort sorties; airships, over 2,000; kite balloons, 131—for a total of over 7,000 escort sorties. The results are given below.

Since the middle of 1917, kite balloons, towed from a destroyer or sloop and carrying an observer, had been used on A/S operations and frequently to provide air escort to convoys. They had the great advantage of being able to operate in weather conditions which rendered other forms of air escort impossible. It was particularly in the Mediterranean (beginning in May 1918) that kite balloons became an important element in the convoy system. The Official Air Historian makes the point that the common objection to kite balloons in convoy, that they advertised the approach of merchant ships,

did not have much force in the Mediterranean where the air was usually so clear that the smoke from vessels in company could be seen from great distances, with the result that the presence of a convoy was betrayed whether or not a balloon was flown. . . .

There is little doubt that a balloon, no matter where it was flown [ahead of the ships or close to them: both methods were used], added to the security of the ships. It is fairly certain also that this result was achieved mainly by moral effect. To the U-boat commander the balloon represented a large all-seeing eye which it was the part of wisdom to avoid. . . . those convoys in the Mediterranean which had a kite balloon in company were almost immune from attack.[21]

It was as convoy escorts that aircraft had their greatest naval value. The usefulness of aircraft in the convoy system lay in these advantages: (1) When the air escort preceded a convoy at a distance, it caused U-boats to submerge, which reduced their power of manœuvring into a good attack position. (2) The U-boat feared an air escort in the immediate vicinity of a convoy because

21 Jones, *The War in the Air*, vi. 316–17. Seaplanes, airships, and flying boats, even if long range, were at the mercy of weather conditions at their base. This was not so important in the Mediterranean, where kite balloons were available and could be used effectively.

it could locate with precision the position of an attack by following the torpedo track back to its source. 'In other words, although we had not solved the problem of destroying U-boats by aircraft, by employing our aircraft as convoy escorts and supports we had largely solved the tactical problems of sighting and attacking U-boats, and of preserving convoys from attack.'[22] In short, air escorts deprived U-boats of their chief advantage—surprise attack after unobserved approach. The surfaced U-boat (of both World Wars), with lookouts using excellent Zeiss glasses, could usually spot a victim long before the latter realized the danger, whether in daylight or at night. This is one of the chief reasons why the U-boats never liked the air escorts that increasingly covered the coastal convoys towards the end of the war.

The practical results of convoy air escorts are seen, first of all, in the *deterrent* effect they had upon the submarines. In 1918 the U-boats pressed home only six attacks against convoys with air escort, of which only two were successful, sinking three ships. During the whole war only five ships were sunk in convoy when an air escort was present, as well as a surface A/S escort, and these, it seems pretty clear, were sunk because the U-boat concerned on each occasion did not realize an aircraft was present. The U-boats' greater wariness of aircraft helps to explain why the hours flown per sighting and attack in 1918 were so much greater than in 1917. In 1917 sightings and attacks by A/S aircraft in Home waters, exclusive of those of the Fleet, were 169 and 106, respectively; in 1918, 192 and 131, respectively, though the flying effort in 1918 was three times greater than in 1917: 4,801,000 hours *v.* 1,526,000 hours. There is the further consideration that the extension of convoy to most of the shipping in coastal waters meant that U-boats did not reveal themselves so often by a successful attack; they usually preferred to wait for an independent ship.

---

[22] Historical Section, Admiralty, *History of the Second World War. The Defeat of the Enemy Attack on Shipping, 1939–1945* (1957, 2 vols., of which the second, 1B, consists of plans and tables), p. 9. This is a restricted publication. The Naval Staff in 1918 laid down these principles for the correct use of air escorts: 'A single escorting machine should keep close to the convoy, as, for fear of being betrayed by their torpedo track, the U-boats' Commanders "refrain from attack on convoys with aerial escort." On the other hand the ideal was "that a convoy should be escorted by at least two aircraft, one keeping close, and one cruising wide to prevent a submarine on the surface from getting into a position to attack." The rear of the convoy should not be omitted, for a submarine may be following on the chance of getting in an attack after dark.' *Ibid.*, p. 10.

In the second place, air escorts affected U-boat *strategy*. As more and more of the coastal shipping came into the convoy system, the submarines tended to shift their activities to the Western Approaches, that is, beyond the range of existing naval aircraft. In the third place, air escorts had a *restrictive* effect on U-boat tactics. In the last eighteen months of the war the submarines increasingly operated against shipping, independent as well as convoyed, at night, so as to escape air attack. (The only form of air escort the submarine was likely to meet at night was kite balloons or airships.) They were at the same time tending to attack *on the surface*, 'to exploit their high surfaced speed and for ease of identifying and firing at targets in darkness.' In 1918 half the U-boat attacks were made at night surfaced, and in the closing months of the war the percentage was nearing two-thirds. Night attacks by surfaced U-boats were the predominant form of attack in 1918.

The Technical Histories [wrote the Head of the Historical Section, Admiralty, after the war] are also quite firm on the point that during 1918 the U-boats were attacking independent ships in coastal waters chiefly at night and usually surfaced. . . .

Night attacks were the initial, and perhaps logical, reaction to the introduction and expansion of air escort and support for convoys in 1918. Night surface attacks, while usually freeing the U-boats from the attentions of air escorts, also enabled them to exploit their relatively high surface speed, and to make the most of the difficulty the surface escorts always experienced in sighting the low silhouette of a U-boat in the darkness near a convoy. Moreover the U-boats' own powers for observation in a night attack were increased by using the surface tactics.

When these night attacks proved to be unrewarding the U-boats tended to resume daylight attacks on Convoys (when they *did* attack convoys) outside the range of aircraft. . . .

All the U-boat night attacks were made by boats operating singly; necessarily so in coastal waters, but in the Western Approaches partly because there were too few boats but mainly owing to the fact that radio communications were at that time not sufficiently developed for reliable Homing and pack control by a shore headquarters, the method effectively developed in the Second World War for co-ordinating the efforts of a number of boats.[23]

23 Rear-Admiral Roger M. Bellairs to Captain John Creswell, 20 October 1954; reproduced with minor editorial changes in the *Royal United Service Institution Journal*, August 1966. The last paragraph of Bellairs's letter reminds us that in the First

By the summer of 1918 the U-boat, which in 1917 could be and often was surprised on the surface by aircraft, had been fitted with an altiscope, a periscope with a top prism that could be elevated. With this instrument, and without surfacing, the U-boat could see whether aircraft were in the vicinity. (It did nothing to prevent a submarine on the surface being surprised.)

There is not much doubt [the Official Air Historian records] that the Germans made greater progress in tactics and appliances, aimed at avoiding attack from the air, than the air service did in making attacks more effective. . . . but it is right to say that the value of the anti-submarine aircraft patrols in the war is to be judged in the light of the limitations they imposed on the activities of the U-boat commanders, and not by the number of submarines destroyed. Time and again the underwater craft were scared away from convoys by escorting aircraft, and that no more than six attacks were made in 1918 on convoyed ships during more than 7,000 air escort journeys is perhaps the best index to the efficacy of the air patrol work.[24]

War the Germans did not use the wolf-pack tactics (U-boats operating in groups on the surface, and diving only when they had to) that proved so dangerous in the Second War. In April 1917 Captain Bauer, the Senior Officer U-boats, submitted a proposal that foreshadowed the wolf-pack tactics of World War II. The U-boats were to be co-ordinated and concentrated on homeward-bound convoys by a large radio-equipped submarine operating in the South Western Approaches as a kind of radio command centre. It would monitor the Allied radio signals and U-boat sighting reports to deduce the movements of the convoys. Fortunately for the Allies (to say nothing of the neutrals), the German Admiralty Staff turned down this imaginative and perfectly sound idea. Hermann Bauer, *Als Führer der U-Boote im Weltkriege* (2nd ed., Leipzig, 1941), p. 457. Bauer's suggestion is proof that he realized convoys would make it more difficult for scattered and undirected U-boats to find targets. The only effort to concentrate tactically against a convoy was made towards the very end of the war. Two U-boat commanders at Pola arranged a rendezvous on 3 October 50 miles off the south-east corner of Sicily to deliver a night surface attack on a large through convoy from the East. One of the boats did not turn up, her sailing delayed by the need for repairs. The other, commanded by the future Admiral Doenitz, got into a muddle with a convoy at night and was sunk. The experience taught him 'a lesson as regards basic principles. A U-boat attacking a convoy on the surface and under cover of darkness, I realized, stood very good prospects of success. The greater the number of U-boats that could be brought simultaneously into the attack, the more favourable would become the opportunities offered to each individual attacker. In the darkness of the night sudden violent explosions and sinking ships cause such confusion that the escorting destroyers find their liberty of action impeded and are themselves compelled by the accumulation of events to split up. In addition to all these practical considerations, however, it was obvious that, on strategic and general tactical grounds, attacks on convoys must be carried out by a number of U-boats acting in unison.' Doenitz, *Memoirs*, p. 4. Here is the true birth of the wolf-pack tactics of the Second War.

[24] Jones, *The War in the Air*, vi. 344–5.

It all boils down to this: the convoy system severely restricted the activities, and hence the usefulness, of the submarines. This is best seen in the altered strategy of the U-boat campaign. In the first place, the convoy system forced the U-boats to attack nearer to shore; the proportion of losses more than 50 miles from land dropped from a maximum of 62·1 per cent in pre-convoy days (May–July 1917) to a minimum of 1·7 per cent (November 1917–January 1918). In other words, the U-boats concentrated their attacks upon small ships, hitherto neglected for the larger ships, because it was the small ships which constituted most of the independent sailings and were now the easiest quarry, and these could be mostly found in coastal waters, where little or no convoy, but an extensive patrolling system and numerous hunting forces, were in existence. Throughout 1918 the heaviest losses occurred close to the coast, but as coastal convoy was instituted, until practically the whole of the traffic was included, sinkings decreased steadily. This was accompanied by a tendency at the end of the war for U-boat operations to be extended once again into the Atlantic, and right across it to the American coast, while continuing to concentrate on coastal areas without the convoy system. The statistics tell the story. The February–April, May–July, and August–October quarters saw an increase in the attacks more than 50 miles from shore: to 11·6, 26·8, and 21·7 per cent, revealing that the U-boats preferred to operate under less hazardous conditions, away from the risk of attack by air escorts, even if it meant finding fewer targets.

In their post-mortems on the submarine campaign, German authorities, Spindler among them, claimed that the sinkings might well have remained at the peak 1917 level and won them the war had the number of operational submarines been increased substantially by a timely decision in the early part of the war to start a large U-boat construction programme. The argument does not impress me. The expansion of the U-boat fleet in 1917–18 would have made no fundamental change in the situation *unless the Germans could at the same time have found a counter to the convoy system.* This they did not succeed in doing. Indeed, Newbolt finds it 'truly surprising' that the German Admiralty Staff made only one attempt to disrupt the convoy system, and that not until May 1918; even then the attempt was 'feeble.' Between 10 May and 25 May the Germans concentrated as many as 10 boats in or near the convoy routes in the Western Approaches. They succeeded in destroying only two and damaging three merchant ships while 183 convoyed ships reached harbour safely, and 110 others passed outwards safely. Two of the U-boats were destroyed. That only one attempt to disrupt the convoy system was made is comprehensible in the light of this result. No U-boat fleet could afford to destroy two ships at the price of losing two U-boats.

4. THE CONVOY SYSTEM: EVALUATIONS

The attitude of the Admiralty towards convoy remained ambivalent to the end of the war. On the one hand, there was the admission at the beginning of 1918 that 'the convoy has so far proved eminently successful,'[25] and, five months later, that 'the principal factor in reducing losses from enemy submarine attack has undoubtedly been the introduction of the Convoy system.'[26] Two months later the A.C.N.S. declared that the steady reduction in losses since June 1917 was 'undoubtedly in a large measure due to Ocean Convoy.' Only 99 ships out of 12,008 which had sailed in ocean convoys through 27 July 1918 had been lost, a loss rate of about 1 in 120 or 0·83 per cent.[27]

On the other hand, the Admiralty representatives at a conference with American naval authorities late in the war stated that

[25] Wemyss's minute of 11 January 1918 on Beatty's paper, 'Situation in the North Sea,' 9 January 1918. The Plans Division at this time recommended against the reversion to independent sailings, which Beatty had recommended in the Scandinavian trade 'as being at least during the winter months, with the short days, some measure towards solving the problem of providing Escorts (substantial and adequate) and thereby permit the vessels to be freed to carry out more offensive form of sweeps and so deny the initiative to the Enemy which he most certainly holds at the present time.' Plans would not have the convoy system tampered with: it 'has on the whole proved remarkably successful; and from previous experience of individual sailings it is certain (assuming that neutral vessels could be induced to sail) that a return to that system would inevitably lead to greatly increased losses due to submarine action.' Beatty to Wemyss, 15 January 1918, Wemyss MSS., and Plans Division minute, 20 January 1918, Admiralty MSS. But see below on the Plans Division's change of heart.

[26] Admiralty paper for the Imperial War Cabinet, 'A General View of the Naval Situation (April, 1917, to June, 1918)' (G.T.-4861), 15 June 1918.

[27] Duff, 'Ocean Mercantile Convoys,' 19 August 1918; Admiralty MSS. An interesting thing about the A.C.N.S.'s report is that, probably through ignorance, he falsified the statistics of losses of ships actually in convoy by including ships which were sunk out of convoy, that is, ships which had sailed in convoy or which were going to sail in convoy but were attacked, respectively, after being dispersed from a convoy or before joining a convoy.

convoys, 'although affording a great measure of safety to the mercantile marine and resulting in the destruction of some submarines, were quite inadequate by themselves to counter the submarine menace. The British Admiralty had therefore decided to add to the other measures some purely offensive units for hunting submarines.'[28]

'The Naval Staff,' in Commander Waters's opinion, 'was untrained in the work, and by training was antipathetic to the whole concept of mercantile convoy which, to the end of the war, it regarded as a palliative and not as a system of war.'[29] Illustrative is the attitude of the Plans Division. A joint appreciation of A/S policy by the British and American Plans Divisions expressed doubts about the efficacy of convoy.[30] 'Convoy escorts have the great advantage of getting in touch with the submarines, but their tactics are generally defensive, and they seldom kill.' They stressed the desirability of more intensive patrolling and attack of U-boats through a concentration of A/S forces in Home waters. This was to be accomplished by a strengthening and consolidation of the coastal Auxiliary Patrol commands (P-boats, 30-knot destroyers, trawlers, and motor launches, which hunted submarines in their own localities). As matters stood, the vast majority of A/S forces in Home waters were spread over a wide area and were not concentrated to attack submarines. There was no concentrated attack on U-boats except in the Dover area. To get the required force, it was argued, they should reduce the escort destroyers, sloops, and P-boats by approximately 30 per cent, and the coastal trawler patrols by about 50 per cent, and the Grand Fleet should abandon 'the idea of inveigling the High Sea Fleet into a fleet action' and relinquish 'a small proportion of its destroyers.' Fremantle did not agree with the reduction of convoy escorts but was in agreement with the general policy advocated in the paper. Beatty was 'exceedingly impressed' with the appreciation. Authority did not approve because the central point, that affecting Grand Fleet strategy, conflicted with the policy of instantly reacting to the movements of the High Seas Fleet. This was of special importance at a time when there was a good possibility that

28 'Memorandum of a Conference Held at the Navy Department on 8th October, 1918, to Discuss the Naval Situation'; Admiralty MSS.
29 Waters, 'Notes on the Convoy System of Naval Warfare.'
30 'Anti-Submarine Policy in the Immediate Future,' 29 March 1918; Admiralty MSS.

the High Seas Fleet would move; it was, therefore, not the moment to weaken the Grand Fleet.

Later in the year, a Joint Plans memorandum urged that more destroyers be made available (taken from convoy duty or the Grand Fleet, when conditions permitted) to strengthen the recently instituted policy of attacking U-boats on the north-about route.[31] Plans Division papers in the last weeks of the war suggested two measures to meet the submarine situation in addition to the convoy system: completion and strengthening of the Northern Barrage and the provision of strong hydrophone hunting flotillas in the North Sea. As between these flotillas and convoy, the requirements for the former were to receive a higher priority.[32]

Finally, we should note that Admiral Sims, too, though originally an ardent advocate of convoy, had reservations by 1918. He felt 'very strongly that the only promising effective solution of the submarine problem lies in the field of listening devices. Escort vessels with convoys are effective in direct proportion to their numbers. It is apparent, however, that we cannot hope to have sufficient escort vessels for adequate protection for some time. Escort, regardless of its *temporary effectiveness* in protecting shipping, is not a solution of the problem . . .'[33]

It is not difficult to ascertain the reasons for the mixed feelings on convoy. Basic was the idea that convoy was a 'defensive' measure (or sometimes a 'defensive-offensive' measure). As such it was grouped with the arming of merchant ships, the use of smoke apparatus, the Otter defence gear against mines, and other measures and devices. Convoy was contrasted, to its disadvantage,

---

[31] 'Joint Memorandum by the British and American Planning Sections on the Occasional Use of Grand Fleet Destroyers on the Northern Patrol,' 13 June 1918; Dewar MSS. It was not desirable 'at present' to reduce convoy escorts, owing to the large number of American troop convoys (there is no mention of protection of trade!), and using Grand Fleet destroyers was 'impracticable' so long as the Grand Fleet expected to be called on to meet the High Seas Fleet at short notice. But opportunities would arise.

[32] 'Measures Required to Meet the Submarine Situation in the Future,' 28 August 1918, Dewar MSS., 'Future Anti-Submarine Policy with Special Reference to Hunting Tactics,' 30 October 1918, Admiralty MSS.

[33] Sims to Daniels, 5 April 1918; U.S. Navy Dept. MSS. Italics mine. Sims was absolutely wrong in his last statement. Escort was precisely the one effective solution. As the war showed, as the following war showed, and as all previous wars had shown, escort was not *temporarily* effective; it was *permanently* effective. He was, of course, quite wrong also in stating that 'escort vessels with convoys are effective in direct proportion to their numbers.' The fact is that the bigger you make your convoy, the

99

with the 'offensive' side of the A/S war, which featured the 'blocking' of Zeebrugge and Ostend, the Dover and Otranto Straits Barrages, the fitting of all hunting and patrol vessels to carry many more depth charges, and, not least important, the activities of the hunting destroyer flotillas.

The contrasting schools of thought were described this way in 1920:

One school basing their opinion on the old maxim that 'attack is the best defence' was in favour of 'Hunting Patrols' of all descriptions which should continually harass the enemy submarines, both in their areas of operations and on passage to and from their bases. Unfortunately, the enthusiasm of the many inventors of devices for finding and hunting the submarines, and the confidence of the officers in the various hunting flotillas responsible for obtaining results with these devices, kept all concerned buoyed up with the hope that success was just within reach. . . . The other school, whilst admitting the general truth of the principle, qualified it with the proviso that attack must be effective to justify the employment of craft for this purpose. In other words, the offensive patrols must either drive submarines out of their operating areas or, when operating on the submarine routes, bring about the destruction of a reasonable number of submarines. Until hunting devices were

---

fewer escorts do you require to provide the same defence to the ships in convoy. Had the convoy statistics of 1917-18 been analysed after the war, and the printed results of the mathematical research on comparative escort strength by an Acting Commander, R.N.V.R. (Rollo Appleyard) early in 1918 been studied, the Admiralty would have been aware of 'the law of convoy size': 'The escort strength requires to be measured, not in terms of the number of vessels in convoy, but in terms of the total area comprised within the boundary formed by lines connecting all outer vessels.' Appleyard went on to prove mathematically that the ratio of the torpedo track area around the convoy perimeter to the number of escorts directly watching it is 'a more correct numerical measure of the escort strength of a convoy than is the ratio of the number of ships in convoy to the number of close escorts.' Commander Waters, who rescued Appleyard's work from oblivion, sums up the essence of the matter: '. . . as the escorts of a convoy protect the perimeter of that convoy and not the individual ships in the convoy, for the purpose of assessing comparative escort strength the number of ships within the perimeter of the convoy is irrelevant . . . The investigator had almost, but not quite, formulated the explanation of why the larger convoys sailed in 1918 did not incur heavy losses, or why their escorts proved as intimidating as a like number escorting numerically smaller convoys, that is to say, that the perimeter of a large convoy is only slightly larger than that of a small convoy, because the area occupied by the ships increases as the square, while the perimeter is directly proportional to the length of the radius.' Waters, 'Notes on the Convoy System of Naval Warfare, Thirteenth to Twentieth Centuries.' Part 2. 'First World War, 1914-18'.

sufficiently advanced to ensure this, it was maintained that the best places to attack submarines were at the points of departure from their home waters, in narrow channels through which they had to pass, for example, the Dover Strait and Straits of Otranto, or at their objective, by a system of convoys and grouped sailings with offensive-defensive escorts.[34]

The 'hunting patrol' or offensive school misunderstood the nature of convoy. It was, in reality, as Admiral Sims once phrased it, 'a purely *offensive* measure.' This was because a convoy attracted the submarine and the latter could attack only at the high risk of destruction by the concentrated escort craft. There is, however, evidence that the escorts themselves were defensive-minded. Richmond noted:

Plans, finding that escorts adopt a wholly defensive attitude, suggest broad instructions for an offensive one. The convoy, they point out, attracts the S.M. That then is the place to destroy her. Merely to drive her off is not enough. Duff contemptuously says that this is a matter for 'practical experts' . . .
The matter was referred to 'practical experts'—the p.e.'s being the R.N.R. men and R.N.V.R.s—wholly unacquainted with the principles of war, who are engaged in the escort work. It was found that all of them, or very nearly all, had only the defensive in view. They had never looked at it in the military light of destroying the submarine. Quite natural. They were not to blame. Those who are to blame are Duff and his like who in their jealous passion refuse to listen to suggestions from their colleagues on other Divisions.[35]

Even so, a comparison shows that during the period between August 1917 and October 1918, that is, during the period of fully developed ocean and developing coastal and Mediterranean convoy, 'the convoys brought about more actions between the contending forces than any other cause,'[36] and they sank more U-boats than did the hunting groups and the patrols. The Naval Staff monograph on the A/S war concludes:

Despite the functional disabilities of escorts they succeeded in sinking

---

[34] Quoted in Naval Staff Monograph, *The Defeat of the Enemy Attack on Shipping, 1939–1945*, p. 11.
[35] Diary, 3 July 1918; *Portrait of an Admiral*, pp. 313–14.
[36] Technical History Monograph TH 14, *The Atlantic Convoy System, 1917–1918*, p. 33.

24 [20] out of the 40 U-boats destroyed by surface vessels in the last fifteen months of the war when much of the shipping was in convoy. In addition, they safeguarded all but a few of the ships placed in their charge. On the other hand, the numerous hunting forces accounted altogether for one U-boat and made no contribution to the defence of shipping. Patrols off headlands on shipping routes, off ports and in the Strait of Dover in conjunction with the mine barrage were more successful in sinking U-boats than hunting forces, but as preservers of shipping they failed. This was eventually recognised and in mid-1918 comprehensive convoy between the Tyne and Humber and in the Irish Sea and Channel was instituted and losses almost ceased.[37]

The same study credits hunting forces and patrols with 20 kills for the entire 21 months of unrestricted submarine warfare, February 1917–October 1918. We should add one to the patrol figure: *U-34*, sunk on 9 November 1918.

The Navy was not aware of these statistics at the time, since contemporary A.S.D. reports analysed the destruction of submarines by types of vessels involved, not by the operational task in which the craft were engaged. The Admiralty did not understand that an increase in convoys meant an increase in opportunities to attack U-boats, and therefore more U-boats destroyed; nor that if it was a fine thing to dispose of a U-boat, it was even better to keep them down and thus bring the convoy to harbour without loss. In other words, the merits of convoy can be argued cogently

---

[37] *The Defeat of the Enemy Attack on Shipping, 1939–1945*, p. 10. However, Lieutenant-Commander Waters, a co-author of this study, has amended the escort figure: the correct number of U-boats sunk by escorts to single ships (4) or convoys (16) during the fifteen months of the convoy period (August 1917 through October 1918) totalled 20, or 21 (crediting one kill to convoy escort in February 1917) for the entire period of unrestricted submarine warfare. D. W. Waters's letters to the author, 17 May, 16 June 1968. His revised figures are identical with those in the final approved Admiralty list of U-boats destroyed, 'Chronological List of German U-Boats Sunk in First World War, 1914–1918' (copy in the Naval Historical Branch, Ministry of Defence). Grant's figure for U-boats credited to escort action in 1917–18 is 15. He admits that 'in many instances, however, it is not clear whether the losses should be ascribed to patrols or to convoy escorts; the same ships often acted in both capacities. Moreover, because of the geographical situation of the war, and the tendency of the rather primitive submarines to operate close to shore, the areas in which patrols and convoy escorts operated were often the same.' *U-Boats Destroyed*, p. 143. It might be helpful before proceeding to clarify the distinction between hunting forces and patrols. The former operated in U-boat transit areas and on hunches and D/F bearings—*not where shipping was!* Patrols were on definite beats in areas shipping passed through. Note that Grant's '15' is a revised figure. See below, p. 119.

without the question of sinking submarines ever coming into it. *Sinking submarines is a bonus, not a necessity.* The only necessity in war is to stop submarines sinking ships. Or let me put it this way: it is immaterial whether the submarine gets sunk or not in the process, because what matters is that the ships deliver cargoes regularly and adequately, and this, the First World War proved, can be assured by a system of convoy. Indeed, one can safely go a step further: it really did not matter how many U-boats the Germans had, if they were forced to keep out of the way and the British and their Allies got their ships with their literally vital cargoes through and without being delayed by fear of attack.

Any question about the comparative effectiveness of convoy is dispelled by the analysis that Commander Waters has made, using his revised figures, of the exchange rate of ships sunk in convoy per U-boat sunk by convoy escorts as compared with independent ships sunk by U-boat per U-boat sunk by hunting forces and patrols.

	Total Ships Sunk by U-boat	*U-boats Sunk by*
February 1917– November 1918	3,329	
Sunk in Convoy		
Home waters	257	
Mediterranean	136	
	393	21 Escorts
Independent ships	2,936	21 Hunting Forces and Patrols

Exchange rate—Convoy $\dfrac{21}{393}$ = 1 : 18·75, i.e., one U-boat sunk per 19 ships sunk.

Exchange rate—Independent $\dfrac{21}{2936}$ = 1 : 140, i.e., one U-boat sunk per 140 ships sunk, or a convoy exchange rate more favourable by a factor of 7·5.

(A ratio of 10 : 1 prevailed in the Second World War.)

* * *

The increased number of U-boats sunk in the last year of the war was mainly due to a large-scale use of depth charges, counter-attacks by convoy escorts (they relied on depth charges), more efficient mines (the horned mine, which did not become available in large numbers until the autumn of 1917), and an intensification of mining in the Dover Straits and Heligoland Bight areas, the former in conjunction with air and surface patrols. Looking at the statistics for the whole war, although the various authorities differ on the figures allocated to each cause, there is agreement that mines (including mine nets) and depth charges, in that order, sank the most U-boats. It is possible that many of the 'unknown' losses were due to mines. And they did much to shake the morale of U-boat crews.

* * *

The continuation of sizeable shipping losses through October overshadowed the effectiveness of convoy. Sinkings (British, Allied, neutral) averaged 230,000 tons a month during the last six months (the British figure alone was more than 140,000). Yet, nobody ever claimed that convoy was an absolute protection against submarines, but only that it was the most effective antidote yet devised. Moreover, there was a weak link in the convoy armour to the end of the war. It was the portion of the route from a ship's port to the convoy assembly ports and from the convoy dispersal point to the point where it picked up the coast. There were, in consequence, a number of ships going up and down the coast— under P-boat escort if valuable, under trawler escort if not so valuable, sometimes with no escort at all. These and stragglers were prime targets for the submarine. Also, had convoys been organized for East Coast shipping more extensively, and protected more strongly, earlier, the probability is that more U-boats would have been destroyed—and earlier. The fact is that, because of one or other of these two factors, most of the shipping losses in 1918 were suffered in coastal waters, where convoy was either imperfectly, tardily, or never organized. It was among the independent ships that the losses mainly occurred to the end; the losses of ships in convoy were extraordinarily small.

The achievements of convoy are all the more remarkable when we consider the handicaps under which the system operated.

There was, first of all, a relatively small number of British warships directly engaged on convoy escort: in October 1918, 257 ships, or 5·1 per cent of the 5,018 British warships in commission. The total is still a mere 15 per cent, if we add some 500 ships which served as escorts or in support from time to time. Moreover, the bulk of the escort forces were over-age destroyers, sloops, and other craft which had been designed for other work, and obsolescent aircraft manned by inadequately trained crews, who had, moreover, to rely upon their own eyesight to pick up U-boats. The destroyers and aircraft best suited for convoy work were used chiefly on A/S patrol and hunting: these operations were, after all, 'offensive'. There were hunting patrols in the Irish Sea and the North Western Approaches. In the spring of 1918 the Admiralty weakened convoy escorts to form the vessels so released into a hunting patrol (part of the Northern Patrol Force) to cover the Fair Island Channel. The purpose was to waylay submarines on the North-about passage. The result as regards U-boats destroyed was nil. We should also note that the hydrophone, for all its imperfections not without usefulness, was not fitted to convoy escorts. It could not function successfully in a convoy situation: submarine noises were not readily distinguished from those of merchant ships. The escorts had, therefore, no means of locating a U-boat and, like all surface craft, no way of judging her depth. And from April 1918, when the newly created Air Ministry assumed the task of providing and allocating aircraft (though not the operation of naval aircraft), long-range aircraft, which would have been so useful in ocean convoy, were concentrated on strategic bombing operations.

5. GROWING ANXIETIES

Aware of Capelle's estimate that the German monthly output had averaged about 9, and that the rate of destruction for September–December 1917 was also nine (it was a little over 8), the Admiralty hoped to crush U-boat warfare by sinking in 1918 'more than 9 enemy submarines per month, and the greater the number over this figure accounted for, the quicker will be our ultimate victory.'[38] There was a cautious note of optimism at the

[38] Admiralty to Beatty, 14 January 1918; Admiralty MSS.

Admiralty after February. Hankey reported Geddes on 1 March as 'very cheerful about submarines and says that the Admiralty have absolutely certain, but very secret, information that they are destroying ten a month and he believes they will master this terrible menace in six months.'[39] Geddes undoubtedly had the January figure in mind, as the February total could not have been available on 1 March. But the First Lord was still wearing rose-tinted spectacles when he addressed Parliament on 5 and 20 March. The 'statistical curve' was continuing in their favour: they were now sinking U-boats as fast as they were built. The dark spot in the picture was the shipyards, which were not turning out new tonnage to anything like their full capacity. May was distinctly encouraging to the Admiralty: both streams, the shipbuilding and the destruction of submarines, were flowing, for the moment at any rate, strongly in the right direction. On the 24th the Prime Minister spoke confidently about the submarine: it was still a nuisance, but no longer a danger, and he ruled it out as a factor that could cause the war to be won or lost; and the output of British and American shipbuilding yards now exceeded the tonnage lost. The press greeted the official view with the hope that it might prove better justified than some of its predecessors. A few weeks later the Admiralty assured the Imperial War Cabinet: 'Though the enemy's submarine campaign is still the most important factor in the Naval situation, the position is steadily improving; the shipping losses are gradually decreasing, and it can be claimed that since January 1st enemy submarines have been destroyed at least at the same rate as the enemy has built them.'[40] On 11 July Geddes, in a speech at the Prince's Galleries, related striking stories of how the U-boat was being circumvented and driven from the seas. There was a vein of cheerful optimism in his remarks, as also in his address to a thin and listless Commons on 30 July on the progress of shipbuilding.

Unfortunately, public opinion had been so frequently disappointed in the past—it had seen the shipbuilding rate go up one month, only to go down the next month, and had heard so often that the U-boat had been beaten, only to learn subsequently,

[39] Diary, 2 March 1918; Lord Hankey, *The Supreme Command* (London, 1961, 2 vols.), ii. 656.
[40] 'A General Review of the Naval Situation (April, 1917 to June, 1918)' (G.T.-4861), 15 June 1918.

on the evidence of the Admiralty's own figures, that it was as lively as ever—that it had become allergic to all official optimism. The press warned against premature rejoicing: they were a long way from the turn of the corner. This was the mood of the country as late as September, there being nothing in the U-boat and ship-building statistics for August that suggested that the submarine problem had been solved. In the latter part of the month Admiralty optimism gave way to deep concern: there was a realization that the submarine menace had not been mastered.

Geddes expressed one aspect of the gravity of the U-boat problem in these words: 'I am getting very concerned, as are we all, at the reduction in killing power of our anti-submarine methods. We are not getting them as we should, and although we know, to a great extent, the reason, there is no doubt that the submarine fleet is growing on us.'[41] The 'reason,' as explained to the War Cabinet, was that their 'destructive forces' (i.e., hunting forces) had been diverted from the A/S war during the German military offensive, when the Navy had been called upon to make 'a tremendous effort' in the escorting of American supply ships and troop convoys. Consequently, their 'plans for hunting the sub-marine, which had matured during the preceding months, were scrapped, and our craft and trained personnel used in other ways.'[42] The other, and graver, aspect of the problem was intelligence that the Germans were preparing for a renewed submarine offensive on a great scale. Some 160 U-boats were believed to be available, and there would be 180 by the end of the year—the largest number so far. 'The situation is not one free from anxiety. . . . A great enemy submarine offensive is not only threatened but is mate-rialising.'[43]

The Germans were, indeed, up to something. On 21 September, Scheer, in a paper already mentioned, had proposed to the Emperor the following 'great U-boat programme' to guarantee that they would be able to sink more shipping tonnage than the

[41] Geddes to Beatty, 27 September 1918; Geddes MSS.
[42] 'Some Important Aspects of the Naval Situation and Submarine Campaign,' 27 September 1918; Admiralty MSS.
[43] *Ibid.* The point of the paper was to protest the recent serious cuts in manpower the Cabinet had imposed upon the Admiralty—a few thousand skilled workers had been taken by the Army—and which delayed the production of gun mountings for the new destroyers and the programme of mounting at least one large modern gun in each ocean–going merchant ship.

Allies could build: 16 boats per month in the last quarter of 1918; then 20, 25, 30, 36 monthly in the successive quarters of 1919, with 36 becoming the basic figure from the last quarter of 1919. The Marine Office did at last succeed in wresting several thousand shipyard workers from the military authorities for this crash programme. Scheer, however, in the same document admitted that U-boat successes against shipping had declined steadily and would continue to decline. The future of U-boat warfare was not bright: 'New construction will exceed the number of sunk ships in the foreseeable future.' What, then, did he hope the new programme would accomplish?

. . . the overall situation forces us to promote U-boat warfare by all means. The U-boat weapon is now the only offensive weapon at our disposal. With defence alone we will not obtain a satisfactory peace. It is therefore absolutely necessary that we build up our only offensive weapon with all the resources Germany has at her disposal, so that we may attain our goal—a satisfactory peace. It is also necessary for possible peace negotiations to hold a trump in our hands in the form of a strong U-boat weapon. In addition to this, the firm, determined will to expand our U-boat weapon vigorously will revive and stir up our own people and show our enemy that Germany's determination to win is unbroken and that we are determined to hold out.[44]

Here is a frank admission that the A/S campaign was succeeding —that the U-boats were being defeated. They had not succeeded in their two primary objectives of sinking the Allies', and in particular Britain's, merchant ships, so starving Britain into submission, and preventing the American troopships from reaching France. (Only one eastbound troopship was sunk, with the loss of under 100 men.) The future of the U-boat anti-shipping campaign looked none too bright: the Straits of Dover were, practically speaking, impassable; the Northern Barrage would probably become more effective; the convoy system, for which the Germans had no counter, was improving all the time; and the Allied shipbuilding effort was approaching formidable proportions. Ironically, it was at this very moment that the Admiralty nearly panicked. They knew that an intensified U-boat construction effort was being made; they did not know what lay behind it—

[44] Appendix V to War Diary; Levetzow Papers, German Ministry of Marine MSS.

that it was intended as a bargaining weapon in any peace negotiations.

Early in October a British naval mission, led by Geddes and Duff, appeared in Washington to discuss A/S measures after a cable to the American naval authorities had explained that the matter was so urgent that a personal meeting must be held. The British position was made clear at an evening conference with Daniels and his advisers that lasted well into the morning. The message was simple and cogent: 'Up to May of this year submarines were being satisfactorily dealt with. Since May, mainly on account of the diversion of the British hunting forces to American escort work, the submarine situation has steadily become more formidable, and we are faced with a tremendous submarine effort, on the enemy's part, whilst our hunting forces are inadequate . . . In fact it is doubtful whether the Allies can continue this policy of escort without incurring the grave risk of the submarines again becoming a serious menace.'[45] The Germans would mount a submarine campaign on the largest scale of the war as soon as their great submarine programme was completed in the spring. 'Unless we can have an adequate number of destroyers and weapons and devices to defeat them, the war will go against us.' 'They were scared stiff,' Daniels tells us, 'and believed that the fate of the war depended upon our ability to meet the grave situation. They answered every question and convinced our admirals that the situation was grave in the extreme. . . . This conference of greatly disturbed Naval leaders perfected every detail of a big program of construction of destroyers and submarine chasers and detective and destructive devices by our Navy. We were assured by Sir Eric that before leaving London a speed-up program had been begun by the British Navy.'[46] Late in October, after the mission had returned home, Geddes cited 181 as the enemy's U-boat strength, their highest figure in the war. 'Geddes does not view the prospect with alarm, but thinks that if the Germans begin the campaign against us in earnest we may have serious times! He believed the Germans had slowed down their U-boat campaign during October because of the peace negotiations.'[47] They had, and to this con-

---

[45] 'Notes for Guidance as to the Line to Be Adopted in Conferences with United States Navy Department and in Informal Conversations,' September 1918; Geddes MSS.

[46] Daniels, *The Wilson Era: Years of War and After*, p. 330.

[47] Diary, 25 October 1918; *Lord Riddell's War Diary, 1914–1918* (London 1933), p. 375. Riddell had seen Geddes that day.

cluding phase of the war at sea we must now turn as the last topic in a discussion of Grand Fleet strategy in 1918, following a brief digression on the relationship between the British and American Navies.

STATISTICS

A. MERCHANT SHIPPING LOSSES BY ENEMY ACTION THROUGH OCTOBER 1918[48]

World Total (excluding enemy countries)

No. of Ships	Gross Tonnage	Sunk by Submarine
5,516	12,741,781	11,135,460 or 87·4 per cent

(Plus 15 ships of 26,857 tons, 12,567 of them sunk by submarines, reported in November.) Including losses by marine risks, the total was just over 15,000,000 tons. Setting against this 10,850,000 tons of new construction and nearly 2,400,000 tons of enemy shipping captured, the net loss in world tonnage was 1,811,000, or about 5 per cent of the pre-war position (nearly 35,000,000).

British Total

No. of Ships	Gross Tonnage	Sunk by Submarine	By Surface Craft	By Mine	By Aircraft
2,475	7,747,935	6,673,998	441,080	624,945	7,912

(Plus 13,658 tons reported in November 1918: 10,315 sunk by submarine, 1,622 by surface craft, and 1,721 by mine.) The tonnage figure represented 60·8 per cent of the world tonnage figure lost by enemy action (72 per cent of Allied losses). Including losses by marine risks, internment in enemy ports, and transfers and sales, the total was 9,763,000 tons. Allowing for gains of 6,679,000 tons (new construction, tonnage captured, and gained by transfer and purchase), the tonnage position on 31 October 1918 was 15,272,000. This represented a net loss during the war of 3,084,000, or 16·8 per cent of the position in August 1914—18,356,000 tons for the United Kingdom and Colonies.[49]

---

[48] Admiralty, 'Statistical Review', pp. 6, 9, 23, 27.
[49] Using the same figures, except for a 'British Empire' tonnage figure of 21,045,000 in July 1914, Fayle comes up with a net loss of 14·6 per cent.

B. GROSS TONNAGE OF MERCHANT SHIPPING LOST THROUGH ENEMY ACTION, TO 11 NOVEMBER 1918[50]

N.B.—These figures exclude Commissioned Auxiliaries. The British figures include merchant vessels only; the world total includes British and foreign fishing vessels. The figures include steam and sailing vessels of all sizes.

	British	World Total		British	World Total
1914			**1917**		
August	40,254	62,767	January	153,666	368,521
September	88,219	98,378	February	313,486	540,006
October	77,805	87,917	March	353,478	593,841
November	8,888	19,413	April	545,282	881,027
December	26,035	44,197	May	352,289	596,629
			June	417,925	687,507
Total	241,201	312,672	July	364,858	557,988
			August	329,810	511,730
1915			September	196,212	351,748
January	32,054	47,981	October	276,132	458,558
February	36,372	59,921	November	173,560	289,212
March	71,479	80,775	December	253,087	399,111
April	22,453	55,725			
May	84,025	120,058	Total	3,729,785	6,235,878
June	83,198	131,428			
July	52,847	109,640			
August	148,464	185,866			
September	101,690	151,884			
October	54,156	88,534			
November	94,493	153,043	**1918**		
December	74,490	123,141	January	179,973	306,658
			February	226,896	318,957
Total	855,721	1,307,996	March	199,458	342,597
			April	215,543	278,719
1916			May	192,436	295,520
January	62,288	81,259	June	162,990	255,587
February	75,860	117,547	July	165,449	260,967
March	99,089	167,097	August	145,721	283,815
April	141,193	191,667	September	136,859	187,881
May	64,521	129,175	October	59,229	118,559
June	36,976	108,855	November	10,195	17,682
July	82,432	118,215			
August	43,354	162,744	Total	1,694,749	2,666,942
September	104,572	230,460			
October	176,248	353,660	Grand Total	7,759,090	12,850,814
November	168,809	311,508			
December	182,292	355,139			
Total	1,237,634	2,327,326			

[50] Fayle, *Seaborne Trade*, iii. 465. The figures are based on Admiralty, 'Statistical Review', Appendix A, with figures for November 1918 added. (The 'Statistical Review' world totals are for merchant ships only.)

C. CAUSE OF SHIPPING LOSSES[51]

	By Cruisers, TBDs., etc. (tons gross)	By Submarines (tons gross)	By Mines (tons gross)	By Aircraft (tons gross)	Total (tons gross)
British, 1914	203,139	2,950	35,112	—	241,201
1915	29,685	748,914	77,122	—	855,721
1916	103,352	888,689	244,623	970	1,237,634
1917	100,693	3,325,534	296,616	6,942	3,729,785
1918	5,833	1,668,972	19,944	—	1,694,749
	442,702	6,635,059	673,417	7,912	7,759,090
British fishing vessels	5,637	57,583	8,545	—	71,765
Total British	448,339	6,692,642	681,962	7,912	7,830,855
World Total (British, Allied, Neutral)	568,537	11,153,506	1,120,732	8,039	12,850,814

[51] Fayle, *Seaborne Trade*, iii. 466.

D. COMPARISON OF LOSSES AND SHIPBUILDING OUTPUT TO 31 OCTOBER 1918 (in 1,000 tons gross)[52]

Preiod	British Empire		U.K.	World (excluding Enemy Countries)		
	Losses, War and Marine	New Ships brought on to Register	Output	Losses, War and Marine	Output	Enemy Tonnage brought into Service
1914						
Aug.–Sept.	342*	154	253	428*	—	705
4th Quarter	155	330	422	281	—	28
	497	*484*	*675*	*709*	*1,013*	*733*
1915						
1st Quarter	216	246	266	320	—	9
2nd ,,	224	244	147	380	—	89
3rd ,,	356	156	145	530	—	5
4th ,,	307	176	93	494	—	2
	1,103	*822*	*651*	*1,724*	*1,202*	*105*
1916						
1st Quarter	325	93	96	524	—	245
2nd ,,	271	113	108	522	—	3
3rd ,,	284	118	125	592	—	194
4th ,,	618	220	213	1,159	—	—
	1,498	*544*	*542*	*2,797*	*1,688*	*442*
1917						
1st Quarter	912	326	246	1,619	587	—
2nd ,,	1,362	305	249	2,237	685	656
3rd ,,	953	287	248	1,494	675	339
4th ,,	783	389	420	1,273	991	116
	4,010	*1,307*	*1,163*	*6,623*	*2,938*	*1,111*
1918						
1st Quarter	697	329	320	1,143	870	1
2nd ,,	631	423	443	962	1,243	—
3rd ,,	512	477	411	916	1,384	—
Oct.	84	144	136	178	511	—
	1,924	*1,373*	*1,310*	*3,199*	*4,008*	*1*
Total	9,032	4,530	4,342	15,053	10,894	2,392

[52] *Ibid.* p. 467.   * Includes ships interned in enemy ports.

N.B.—In the above table the second column, which represents new ships actually brought on to the Register in the United Kingdom and the Overseas Dominions and Colonies, is taken from a table in *Allied Shipping Control*, by Sir J. A. Salter. The remaining figures are from Cmd. 9221, *Merchant Tonnage and the Submarine*. 'Enemy tonnage brought into service' is credited in the table to the quarter during which the ships were seized.

(Ships of 500 G.R.T. and above)

	Feb.–Apr. 1917 convoyed	sunk	loss rate	May–July 1917 convoyed	sunk	loss rate	Aug.–Oct. 1917 convoyed	sunk	loss rate	Nov. 1917–Jan. 1918 convoyed	sunk	loss rate	Feb.–Apr. 1918 convoyed	sunk	loss rate	May–July 1918 convoyed	sunk	loss rate	Aug.–Oct. 1918 convoyed	sunk	loss rate	Feb. 1917–Oct. 1918 convoyed	sunk	loss rate	
Dutch and Scandinavian Convoys, and U.K. Coastal Convoys	3,223	18	0·55%	8,540	25	0·29%	9,317	33	0·35%	8,596	24	0·28%	9,384	19	0·20%	13,516	35	0·26%	15,312	7	0·05%	67,888	161	0·24%	
Ocean Convoys	0	—		167	2	0·84%	2,495	16	0·64%	2,663	19	0·71%	3,036	18	0·59%	3,647	22	0·60%	4,062	19	0·47%	16,070	96	0·60%	
Total Convoy	3,223	18	0·55%	8,707	27	0·31%	11,812	49	0·41%	11,259	43	0·38%	12,420	37	0·30%	17,163	57	0·33%	19,374	26	0·13%	83,958	257	0·30%	Only 5 ships were sunk which had AIR as well as SURFACE escort
Independent Losses		410			356			221			156			169			85			103			1,500		
Loss rate in U.K. overseas trade sailed independently		not less than 10% (Apr. 20%)			10%			8·8%			4·44%			5·41%			5·61%			3·14%			5·93%		

	428	383	270	199	206	142	129	1,757
Total of Independent and Convoy Losses	428	383	270	199	206	142	129	1,757
% of total Losses that were 'Independent'	95·5%	93%	83%	78·4%	82%	60%	80%	85·5%
Remarks	Dutch and French Coal Trade (cross-Channel) and Scottish N.E. Coast Convoys started Feb. Scandinavian and East Coast Convoys started end of Apr.	Homeward Ocean Convoys started July	Outward Ocean Convoys started mid-Aug. Through Gibraltar and Mediterranean Convoys started Oct.	Ocean Convoy system fully developed by Nov.	Irish Sea offensive by U-boats. Ocean Convoys extended to terminal ports in England. East Coast Convoy system reorganised Feb.	Irish Sea Convoy developed in June	East Coast Convoy reorganised and extended Aug. North Cornish Coast Convoy started Oct.	Sources:— *Statistical Review of The War against Merchant Shipping.* Admiralty, 1918 and *Technical History Series* of the First World War. Admiralty, 1918-20
Distance from Land								
% Within 10 miles	20·4	17·7	42·6	62·8	47·6	53·5	57·4	Av. 43
% Between 10 and 50 miles	29·6	20·2	31·6	35·5	40·8	19·7	20·9	Av. 29
% More than 50 miles	50·0	62·1	25·8	1·7	11·6	26·8	21·7	Av. 28

Exact statistics of the loss rate of Independent Coastal Shipping are not available. It was however considerably greater than that of Coastal shipping in Convoy

53 Historical Section, Naval Staff, *The Defeat of the Enemy Attack on Shipping, 1939-1945*, Vol. 1B, Tables 1, 2, with a revision by Commander Waters (August 1958) of the figure in the last column of p. 114, above.

E. (CONT.) NUMBERS AND PERCENTAGES OF LOSSES OF SHIPS SUNK IN EACH QUARTER OF THE UNRESTRICTED U-BOAT CAMPAIGN 1917–18 IN THE NORTH SEA, OFF THE EAST, SOUTH, AND WEST COASTS OF THE U.K., IN THE WESTERN APPROACHES, AND IN THE ATLANTIC (INCLUDING THE BAY AND U.S. COASTS), OTHER AREAS, AND UNKNOWN

(Ships of 500 G.R.T. and above)

Area	Feb.–Apr. '17	May–July '17	Aug.–Oct. '17	Nov. '17–Jan. '18	Feb.–Apr. '18	May–July '18	Aug.–Oct. '18
North Sea and East Coast	62 (12%)	47 (14%)	48 (14%)	32 (11%)	22 (8%)	42 (21%)	15 (9%)
U.K. South and West Coastal Waters	127 (24%)	86 (18%)	89 (27%)	128 (45%)	141 (51%)	48 (23%)	64 (40%)
Western Approaches (including West Coast)	135 (26%)	137 (30%)	43 (12%)	6 (2%)	13 (6%)	18 (9%)	8 (5%)
Atlantic and Bay (and U.S. Coast)	67 (22%)	90 (19%)	66 (19%)	31 (11%)	26 (9%)	33 (16%)	41 (26%)
Other areas and Unknown*	37 (7%)	23 (5%)	24 (7%)	2 (1%)	4 (1%)	11 (5%)	15 (9%)
	French coal trade convoys started early *Feb.* (night sailings). End of April Scandinavian and E. Coast Convoys started	*Mid-July* home N. Atlantic convoys start. Convoy assembly ports: Buncrana Lamlash Queenstown Milford Devonport Falmouth	*Aug.* Outward ocean convoys. Gibraltar home convoys start *Aug.* Home S. Atlantic convoys start *Sept.*	Through Mediterranean convoys start *Nov.* Queenstown given up as convoy assembly port *Jan.*	Very slow N. and S. Atlantic ships included in Gibraltar convoys in *Mar.* Ocean-going ships in Irish Sea start using Liverpool late *Mar.*	F.C.T. daylight sailings start *Mid-June*. Special south coast Inshore Route started *June* More ocean-going ships in convoy in Irish Sea in *June*	North Cornish coast convoys started *end Oct.*

Mid-Oct. Gibraltar out convoys made 'Through'	Dover barrage effective from *Apr.*	Southend used as convoy assembly port (till *Oct.*) from *June*
Through Mediterranean convoys start *Oct.*	Large U-boats N. about Scotland from *Feb.*	Milford–Rosslare convoy started in *June.*
		Offensive off U.S. east coast started *June*

* Not including the Mediterranean. The 'Other Areas and Unknown' are included in order to show an important effect of the ocean convoy system, that is the marked decrease in 'unknown' losses, following upon its introduction. In fact they virtually disappear.

It will be noticed that the percentage of Atlantic losses is highest in the last quarter—41 ships, 26% of the world's losses.

It will also be noticed that a drop in losses occurs in the U.K. South and West Coastal Waters in the May–July '18 quarter (48 ships, 23%) upon the effective blocking of the Strait of Dover and a consequent U-boat offensive in the North Sea and off the East Coast. Losses in S. and W. coastal waters, Aug.–Oct. 1918, rise again—64 ships, 40% losses when comprehensive East Coast Convoy system instituted.

Air escort and support (day only) was provided to all ocean convoys when within aircraft range and weather conditions permitted. In June 1918 aircraft provided air escort and support to coastal convoys when within aircraft range and weather conditions permitted. In June 1918 aircraft provided air escort and support to coastal convoys so escorted.

Convoys with air escort were virtually immune from attack. In June 1918 aircraft provided air escort and support to coastal convoys also, in lieu of area patrol. No successful attacks were made on coastal convoys so escorted.

(a) Average monthly totals of U-boats in commission (not including boats paid off because of lengthy repairs).
(b) Average monthly totals of *Frontboote* (i.e., operational boats).
(c) Average number of *Frontboote* at sea daily.
(d) Greatest number of boats at sea on any one day during month.
(e) Number of U-boats built in each year of the war.

	1914	1915	1916	1917	1918 (Jan.–Oct.)
(a)	32	52	103	163	172
(b)	26	38	71	129	123
(c)	4	7	19	44	45
(d)	13 (Sept.)	19 (Aug.)	49 (Oct.)	70 (Oct.)	60 (Mar., May)
(e)	10	52	108	93	80

U-Boat Statistics—2. Construction and Losses, etc.[55]

Construction
28 boats built before war
344 boats built during war
226 boats building, November 1918
<u>212</u> boats projected[56]
810

Destruction, Surrenders, etc.
178 lost in war (1914:5; 1915:19; 1916:22; 1917:63; 1918:69)
14 scuttled (between 1 October and November 1918 on the evacuation of the Flanders and Adriatic bases)
5 ceded to Austria and Bulgaria

[54] The (a) through (d) figures are from statistical data compiled by or for Spindler from the daily *Admiralstab* lists 'Standort und Bereitschaft der Kriegs- und Hilfsschiffe' for the whole war period. (Referred to below as Spindler, 'Hand-Material'. There is a copy in the Naval Historical Branch, Ministry of Defence.) This material was probably intended for the final volume (v) of *Der Handelskrieg mit U-Booten*, which Spindler never lived to complete properly. The Michelsen figures for (b) and (c) (R. H. Gibson and Maurice Prendergast, *The German Submarine War, 1914–1918*, 2nd ed., London, 1931, Appendix III, pp. 354–5) are for the 10th of each month and are very similar to the figures in Spindler's 'Hand-Material'. The (e) figures are from Erich Gröner, *Die deutschen Kriegsschiffe, 1815–1936* (Munich, 1937), which is less complex than the '1815–1945' second edition (Munich, 1966–7, 2 vols.) and is reliable.
[55] Gibson and Prendergast, *The German Submarine War, 1914–1918*, p. 364.
[56] The 'building and projected' figure of 438 is by other official figures given as 453: the official lists at the end of the war (probably prepared for the Armistice Commission), amended by data in Gröner, *Die deutschen Kriegsschiffe, 1815–1945*, Vol. i.

1 internee purchased by Holland
1 internee scuttled before surrender
7 foundered en route to surrender
176 surrendered to Allies (including 18 finished for delivery)
8 old craft broken up in Germany
208 incomplete boats broken up on stocks or dismantled
212 projected
___
810

Of the 178 war losses, British action was responsible for 133 definitely; the Russians, 6; the French, 1; the others were lost through accident or unknown causes.

U-Boat Statistics—3. Causes of War Losses[57]

	1914–16	1917	1918	Total
Man-of-war (ram)	2	0	1	3
Patrols/hunters				
(1) Ram	1	4	1	6
(2) Gunfire	5	1	1	7
(3) Sweep	2	0	0	2
(4) Depth charge	2	4	16	22
(5) Aircraft (bomb)	0	1	0	1
(6) Torpedo [submarine torpedo]	5	7	6	18
Decoy gunfire	5	6	0	11
Merchant vessels/transports				
(1) Ram	0	2	3	5
(2) Gunfire	0	0	1	1
(3) Explosion [sweep]	0	1	0	1
Escorts				
(1) Ram	0	3	1	4
(2) Gunfire	0	1	2	3
(3) Sweep	0	0	1	1
(4) Depth charge	0	2	5	7

[57] Grant, *U-Boats Destroyed*, p. 159, as revised by Professor Grant in letters to the author, 23 September, 4 October 1969. I have chosen this analysis of U-boat war losses, as now up-dated, because it is the most recent one and based on careful study of all the data of consequence, including Spindler's Vol. V. (The latter does not have a breakdown of the 178 losses.) But one must take heed of Gibson and Prendergast (p. 367): 'It is only possible to hazard a guess as to the totals, for the destruction of a submarine sometimes involved the simultaneous use of several methods. Many boats were sunk by gunfire after being forced to the surface by depth-charges.' The complexities of this type of analysis may be observed by comparing Grant's table

	1914–16	*1917*	*1918*	*Total*
Mines	10	20	22	52
Accidents				
(1) German mines	3	5	1	9
(2) German torpedoes	1	0	1	2
(3) Stranded	3	2	0	5
(4) Other	0	2	0	2
Unknown	7	2	7	16
Totals	46	63	69	178
Ramming	3	9	6	18
Gunfire	10	8	4	22
Sweep	2	0	1	3
Depth charge	2	6	21	29
Torpedo (inc. German)	6	7	7	20
Mine (inc. German)	13	25	23	61

with Gibson and Prendergast, p. 367, Technical History Monograph No. 7, *The Anti-Submarine Division of the Naval Staff. December 1916-November 1918*, p. 69, and *Brassey's Annual*, 1950, p. 119. Grant, *U-Boat Intelligence, 1914-1918*, contains a revised list of U-boats sunk (pp. 182-90), which has incorporated findings from Spindler's last volume and the second edition of Gröner, *Die deutschen Kriegsschiffe*

V

Anglo-American Naval Relations

(April 1917–November 1918)

The relations between our men and those of the British Service are excellent
and in fact are all that possibly could be desired.

Sims to Josephus Daniels, 11 September 1917.

They [U.S. Navy] are really heart and soul in the business, and they are not
influenced by the national jealousies which apparently must always exist
between European nations.

Jellicoe to Beatty, 30 November 1917.

Co-operation is as complete as it can be, and the relationship in every way is
equally satisfactory.

Geddes, at a luncheon given by the Board of Admiralty
to the members of the Committee of Naval Affairs
of the U.S. House of Representatives, 2 August 1918.

1. THE QUEENSTOWN COMMAND

NO HAPPIER choice could have been made than Bayly for
the Queenstown command, which was the one chiefly concerned with the Western Approaches. (Queenstown is now
Cobh, of course.) Indeed, it was during the latter part of his
command that 'Luigi' Bayly earned his claim to fame. He was an
outstanding success, working in remarkable amity with the
Americans. He proved the ideal commander of this mixed Anglo-
American force, being tactful, flexible, and friendly, though a hard
taskmaster and firm when he had to be. There was little of the
rudeness and unpleasantness that had distinguished his earlier
career.[1] The generous, kindly side of his nature came to the fore.
The American Navy discovered a human side in Bayly which led
him to be known to all their sailors as 'Uncle Lewis'. (His other

---

[1] See *From the Dreadnought to Scapa Flow*, ii, especially 12–13, 98–100, 363. He had
been appointed to the Queenstown Command in July 1915: Vice-Admiral Commanding on the Coast of Ireland; from May 1917, C.-in-C., Coast of Ireland.

American nickname, 'Old Frozen Face'—he looked more like an undertaker than an Admiral—suited him perfectly.) He turned his smoking-room at Admiralty House, Queenstown, 'into a sort of students' gallery. Here he hung big maps of the War areas. Daily he was to be seen explaining to a crowd of young American naval officers the progress of the struggle on the Western Front. And his anecdotes. He had nearly half a century's naval service to his credit: had sailed the Seven Seas—small wonder that he was laden with "yarns", and how those clean, straight-limbed youths from "over the way" loved him for his talking!'[2] He mixed the ships of the two navies in his flotillas and squadrons so that within a few months they were all in effect a single navy under his operational control. The Americans, however, had their own organization for ship maintenance and discipline. 'The remark is frequently heard in our forces at Queenstown,' Sims wrote home, 'that they look upon Vice-Admiral Bayly . . . as one of their own Admirals . . .'[3] Again, Sims on Bayly:

He always referred to his command as 'my destroyers' and 'my Americans,' and woe to any one who attempted to interfere with them or do them the slightest injustice! Admiral Bayly would fight for them, against the combined forces of the whole British navy, like a tigress for her cubs. . . . Relations between the young Americans and the experienced Admiral became so close that they would sometimes go to him with their personal troubles; he became not only their commander, but their confidant and adviser. . . .

Admiralty House was always open to our officers; they spent many a delightful evening there around the Admiral's fire; they were constantly entertained at lunch and at dinner, and they were expected to drop in for tea whenever they were in port.[4]

Sims, who first met Bayly in London late in April, had been forewarned that this officer was 'a peculiarly difficult one to get along with'; Bayly lived up to his reputation. 'He was as rude to me as one man can well be to another,' Sims reported. Jellicoe told Carson that Bayly would have to go unless he improved his manners. Matters did improve when Sims visited Queenstown early in May. By June the two men had developed such a tremendous mutual respect and affection that when Bayly went on leave

2 'English Ties with America,' *The Times*, 11 February 1921.
3 Sims to Daniels, 15 June 1917; U.S. Navy Dept. MSS.
4 Rear-Admiral William S. Sims, *The Victory at Sea* (London, 1920), pp. 65–6, 68.

that month, he had Sims take over the command for five days. The idea had originated with Sims, who saw in it 'an imaginative gesture designed to publicize American and British co-operation, and to head off any criticism from home that American interests are being subordinated to England's.'[5] For the first time in history an American was in command of a detachment of the Royal Navy. (It was not the last time: *vide* World War II experience, when in 1945 the British Pacific Fleet worked with the U.S. Pacific Fleet.) 'We never had a difference of opinion,' Bayly wrote after the war.

Sims, who had the title of Commander of the United States Naval Forces Operating in European Waters, was the nominal commander of the American force under Bayly (mainly destroyers and sub-chasers), but since he had to spend so much time in London, his C.O.S. at Queenstown, Pringle, was its real commander. Bayly hit it off nearly as well with the sophisticated, highly competent Pringle.

Sims's biographer writes of the general harmony between the two Navies at Queenstown:

> For the men of both nations who served there, the base has become a precious memory. . . . The splendor of its success has hidden many of the difficulties that lay in the way of that success. To a few officers, Admiral Bayly remained 'Old Frozen Face.' At times, in his pride in the men under him, he exceeded his authority and reprimanded American officers to their chagrin and mortification. . . . The enlisted men of both countries, upon occasion, irritated one another. . . . Inevitable difficulties and frictions frequently could not be solved by the ordinary salvation of command, an appeal to rules and regulations. Adjustments had to be made by instinct, tact, and intuition. Upon the leaders, Admiral Bayly, Admiral Sims, and Captain Pringle, fell the heavy burden of the command. To all of them belongs the credit for a great achievement. With this triumvirate quite properly belongs another, Miss Violet Voysey [Bayly's niece and hostess]. Each man appealed and not in vain to this young woman. 'Petticoat influence' has seldom been used by woman with such wise restraint.[6]

As must be apparent by now, Sims was an equally happy choice for his position. This Anglophile officer of great sea experience, broad views, quickness of mind, and easy manner was accepted

[5] Elting E. Morison, *Admiral Sims and the Modern American Navy* (Boston, 1942), p. 382.
[6] *Ibid.*, p. 386.

in Royal Naval circles practically as one of their own. Within a few weeks of his arrival in England, Sims was having daily conferences with Jellicoe and was given complete freedom of the Admiralty and access to all Government officials, from the Prime Minister down. He attended many meetings of the Board of Admiralty when naval operations were under discussion.[7] In November 1917 the Admiralty began to furnish Sims with their very secret 'Weekly Appreciation,' which was prepared for the War Cabinet. There was 'frank and cordial co-operation,' in Dewar's words, between the Plans Division and the American Planning Section formed in London at the turn of the year. By the end of 1917, co-operation was, as Jellicoe writes, 'absolutely complete.' Sims did nothing to disturb the cordial relations when he instructed American officers not to criticize what they did not approve in the British (also the French) Navy. Wemyss paid Sims this supreme tribute: 'His loyalty and co-operation with us has been extraordinary, and I very much doubt whether any other United States Naval Officer would have achieved the same result as he has. He has suppressed himself and a good deal of American "amour propre" to obtain this satisfactory state of affairs, and has shown himself to be very broad-minded and thoroughly loyal to the Allies. The manner in which the United States Naval Forces co-operate with ours, the way in which their Officers consider themselves part of our forces, are facts which I believe to be mainly due to him . . .' Beatty noted on this: 'As regards those with the G.F. it is mainly due to Admiral Rodman.'[8]

2. THE GRAND FLEET

The United States had 10 coal-burning and 5 powerful oil-burning dreadnoughts, of which 4 of the former (and 1 more later) joined the Grand Fleet early in December 1917 as one of the two fast wings of the battle fleet: the 6th Battle Squadron. 'Nothing

[7] The British in December 1917 offered to make Sims an honorary member of the Board and allow him to participate in their deliberations. President Wilson and Daniels emphatically rejected this invitation. 'While appreciative of the unprecedented honour, both Daniels and Wilson felt that it would tie Sims, a strong Anglophile, too closely to the Admiralty point of view. Undoubtedly one factor in Sims's subsequent enmity and criticism of Daniels was his refusal to let him accept this honor.' E. David Cronon (ed.), *The Cabinet Diaries of Josephus Daniels, 1913–1921* (Lincoln, Nebraska, 1963), p. 242.

[8] Wemyss to Beatty, 23 August 1918; Beatty MSS.

would have been easier,' as Chatfield remarked in his memoirs, 'than a clash of ideas, of principles of fighting, of routine methods between two Services which had never been at sea together and had been trained in completely different environments.' It did not work out that way. The American squadron was completely integrated into the Grand Fleet in every way: tactics, gunnery methods, signals, etc. 'Within three days of their arrival they were taking part in a full-scale Fleet operation, apparently having no difficulty in conforming to British tactical manœuvres. It is a tribute to American naval training that the British signal codes and methods were so quickly assimilated. There were certain aspects, however, where skill could only be acquired by long experience of war conditions, such as keeping accurate station at night with no lights showing.'[9] Their gunnery was in the beginning 'distinctly poor and disappointing,' Beatty judged, and he gave no higher marks to their signalling. Yet the Americans made an excellent impression on him. 'They are desperately keen and are all out to make a success of the co-operation. But we must not hurry them too much. . . . They are making every use of the [British] officers appointed to them and are quick to learn.'[10] In June 1918 the Plans Division estimated, on the basis of the experience of the 6th Battle Squadron, that about four months' combined work was necessary for efficient co-operation. However, as late as June 1918, Beatty was cited by the D.C.N.S. as considering the American battleships with the Grand Fleet 'rather as an incubus to the Grand Fleet than otherwise. They have not even yet been assimilated to a sufficient degree to be considered equivalent to British Dreadnoughts, yet for political reasons he does not care that the Grand Fleet should go to sea without them.'[11]

At first the British Fleet could not understand why the American ships had come: they felt they could handle the German Fleet by themselves. This mood passed, and the spirit of co-operation at Scapa Flow and Rosyth became as admirable as that at Queenstown. 'As time wore on, our friendship ripened into a fellowship and comradeship, which, in turn, became a brotherhood . . .' So

[9] Rear-Admiral W. S. Chalmers, *The Life and Letters of David, Earl Beatty* (London, 1951), p. 300.
[10] Beatty to Jellicoe, 10 December 1917; Jellicoe MSS.
[11] Fremantle's minute of 12 June 1918 on a Plans Division paper, 'Concentration of the U.S.A. Battle-Fleet in the North Sea,' 5 June 1918; Admiralty MSS.

spoke the Commander of the American squadron, Rear-Admiral Rodman, himself an important reason for the harmony between the two fleets and the smooth integration of his squadron into the Grand Fleet. 'I realized that the British fleet had had three years of actual warfare and knew the game from the ground floor up; that while we might know it theoretically, there would be a great deal to learn practically. There could not be two independent commands in one force if our work was to be harmonious, and the only logical course was to amalgamate our ships and serve under the command of the British commander-in-chief.'[12] The co-operation went as far as the American adoption of the British system of signals and methods of fire control and concentration of fire. Beatty gave Rodman many opportunities to carry out independent operations in support of North Sea convoys where British escort forces automatically came under his command. The two Admirals became as good friends as had Sims and Bayly, and Rodman and his officers were frequent visitors to Aberdour, Beatty's home near Rosyth.

Relations between the two Navies were of 'the happiest nature' (Jellicoe) at Gibraltar, where the American detachment of patrol and escort vessels was under the British S.N.O., Rear-Admiral Heathcote Grant.

The two Navies had their differences: that over the Northern Barrage was the most serious, and even here it was only Beatty, not the Admiralty, who was involved in the disagreement. And at the top level in Washington—President Wilson, Secretary of the Navy Daniels, and the Chief of Naval Operations (equivalent to First Sea Lord) Benson—there was a continual carping at the British for not using the substantial Allied naval superiority more aggressively. One example must suffice. Daniels had Northcliffe come and see him. Northcliffe reported: 'He says that whole-hearted co-operation of America in naval matters could not be obtained while we were on continual defensive. . . . Said that he could appreciate difficulties of some of the projects discussed [at Allied Naval Conference in London, September 1917], *but he urged*

12 Admiral Hugh Rodman, *Yarns of a Kentucky Admiral* (Indianapolis, 1928), pp. 267, 268. Worth recording is this story about Rodman, who was never at a loss for an answer. He was having his leg pulled about the tendency of the American antenna mines to fire prematurely. With a perfectly straight face he denied that such was the case. The noise being heard, he explained, was not of the mines firing before they should, but of the sinkers hitting the bottom!

action. Spoke strongly of the failure to prevent growth of Zee-brugge, and in general is dissatisfied. . . . I send you this because on Reading's [British Ambassador] arrival he was at once tackled by Roosevelt, Assistant Secretary of the Navy, on the same lines and also because I know the President holds the same views.'[13]

At the same level in London there was the complaint in the closing months of the war that the American share in the naval war was disappointing. The British were frank about their feelings. Geddes told a luncheon meeting in Washington that the British bore the main responsibility of combating the U-boat menace. 'Per month the British ocean escort for the Allied sea communi-cations is, roughly, a million and a half vessel miles. The American corresponding mileage may be put, I think, at not more than 150,000 miles per month. Possibly the other Allies do an approxi-mate 200,000 to 250,000 miles.' Similarly, as compared with the patrolling effort, the work done by the American Navy was 'very small, as also the contribution of our Allies.' In European waters, the British Navy had 5,360 craft against the 223 of the U.S. Navy (down to but exclusive of M.L.s and sub-chasers, respectively). In the first five months of 1918 the Americans completed 11 war vessels, the British, 203. Battle cruisers sent to European waters would be useful. However: 'What is essential is the quick, fast craft and the patrol craft, light cruisers and destroyers, and a good, simple, comparatively slow seagoing escort ship.' Geddes closed his speech with a strong plea for a greater American naval effort.[14]

Having said all this, the fact remains that the general harmony of the Anglo-American naval effort, above all as between the two Fleets directly, is a rare exception in the annals of wartime relations between Allies.

[13] Northcliffe's telegram to Geddes, 1 November 1917, quoted in Geddes to Balfour, 5 November 1917; Admiralty MSS. The italics are Geddes's underlining, and with three exclamation marks in the margin. Lloyd George had sent Northcliffe, 'that turbulent spirit', to the United States in June as Head of a British War Mission, whose functions were to maintain liaison with the American Government and co-ordinate the work of the British agencies in the United States concerned with the war effort.

[14] 'Transcript of a Speech Made by the First Lord of the Admiralty at a Luncheon given by the Board of Admiralty to the Members of the Committee on Naval Affairs of the House of Representatives, Washington,' 2 August 1918; Lloyd George MSS. Geddes headed up a naval mission that included Duff and Admiral Everett, the Naval Secretary, and whose purpose was to reach an understanding with the United States as to the division and co-ordination of naval effort in the future.

VI

The Grand Fleet: Uncertainties and a Missed Opportunity

(January 1918–June 1918)

(*Chart 1*)

> The main thought in 1918 was, would the German Fleet come out? Beatty
> was sure it would and said so. It was the real line to take.
>
> CHATFIELD, *The Navy and Defence.*

> The only change in Naval War Policy during 1918 was the decision come to
> by the War Cabinet that the Grand Fleet was no longer to do its utmost to
> force an action on the High Sea Fleet. I find it difficult to reconcile the decision
> thus arrived at with the views expressed to me by Mr. Lloyd George in 1917.
> In that year he pressed for more offensive action on the part of the Navy in
> general, and the Grand Fleet in particular, pointing out the superior Naval
> strength possessed by us as compared to the Germans.
>
> The proper offensive action for the Grand Fleet was to seek engagement with
> the High Sea Fleet if an opportunity should arise, or if by any means the High
> Sea Fleet could be induced to put to sea. The 1918 decision cancelled this.
>
> JELLICOE, *The Submarine Peril.*

1. MORALE

THERE was only one Grand Fleet personnel change of
importance during the last ten months of the war. Sturdee
left to become C.-in-C., the Nore, and was succeeded by
Vice-Admiral Sir Montague Browning. The C.-in-C. penned this
valedictory: 'Old Sturdee departed yesterday for good. I gave him
a farewell banquet and an eulogistic speech which pleased him and
did no harm. Between you and me, I am glad he has gone. He was
becoming very tiresome and is obsessed with the idea that every
man's hand is against him and he has been badly treated, when in
reality he is the luckiest man in the Service. He has made many
mistakes, big ones, and has suffered for them not at all.'[1]

War weariness and annoyance over the lack of action were, if

1 Beatty to Lady Beatty (1 February 1918); Beatty MSS.

anything, even more pronounced than in 1917. This entry in the diary of a young officer, though written in 1917, reflects the dominant mood of the Grand Fleet in 1918 as well: 'The fact is that I *am* "weary, in the uttermost part of the Sea"—War-weary, Scapa-weary, weary of seeing the same old damned agony of grey grey grey, grey sky, grey sea, grey ships.'[2] The C.-in-C. himself was thoroughly irked by his inability to get at the enemy, as witness these extracts from letters to his wife: 'Is Mrs. Dubois in Edinburgh? You must . . . tell her if she does not produce something good for us soon, I shall have to dismiss her from my staff' (7 February). 'It frets me terribly that with all this terrible fighting going on [the Western Front] that we cannot help' (31 March). 'Weather just awful, tinges everything with depression. Truly this is the most damnable place on earth. For four days it has been the same without respite. Even the Midshipmen are becoming depressed . . .' (26 June).[3]

Despite the war-weariness, Grand Fleet morale remained extraordinarily high during 1918. A young American officer in the battleship *Arkansas* afterwards wrote: 'To the officers and enlisted men attached to the American Sixth Battle Squadron of the British Grand Fleet . . . the outstanding characteristic of British Sea Power was its extraordinarily high morale in the face of great handicaps. At a moment when Allied military morale was at the breaking point, and the refusal of the German High Seas Fleet to come out and fight imposed heavy burdens on [Beatty] . . . Grand Fleet morale was at such a peak that it was a joy to serve in it.'[4]

How are we to explain this seeming paradox? Beatty himself is a most important factor. The fleet had complete confidence in him. His Flag-Captain brings out that 'The mainspring of the Fleet's spirit was that of its leader. It had confidence in him, that he was a fighter; that he would take the Fleet out whatever the circum-

---

[2] Lieutenant Oswald Frewen, 17 January 1917; Frewen MSS. For the record it should be stated that grey skies are largely confined to the winter, as in most of Great Britain. In June the Orkneys are lovely: primroses, yellow iris, and water lilies come late and join up with heather and fuschia in hedges.

[3] The first two extracts are from the Beatty MSS.; the last, from Chalmers, *Beatty*, pp. 325–6. Mrs. Dubois was the celebrated fortune-teller! See *From the Dreadnought to Scapa Flow*, ii. 12.

[4] Eugene E. Wilson, 'Grand Fleet Morale,' *Shipmate* (organ of the U.S. Naval Academy Alumni Association), January 1964.

stances of weather or other dangers, and that he would not let the enemy go once he was in contact. . . . It is to David Beatty's everlasting credit that during these monotonous and testing two years he maintained the spirit of the Grand Fleet, its efficiency, harmony and cheerfulness at the highest possible level and enthusiasm.'[5]

Confidence was another component in the superb fleet morale. The Grand Fleet was supremely confident that it would administer to the High Seas Fleet an almighty drubbing, if it would come out for a final battle *à outrance*. And it was the general expectation, particularly in the closing months of the war, that the Germans would have to come out and fight them if they wanted to avert final defeat.

Morale received a boost when the main fleet moved to Rosyth, hitherto the battle-cruiser base, on 12 April 1918. Rosyth was thereafter the new permanent base of the combined Grand Fleet. Its advantages over Scapa were considerable from the morale point of view, to say nothing of the strategic. Rosyth and the Firth of Forth were a much more civilized place than remote, isolated, grim, and depressing Scapa Flow. Short visits to Edinburgh were possible, and Rosyth had much better sports grounds and canteens for the men. Whether at Scapa or Rosyth, every effort was made to keep the men physically fit (as through football and annual squadron regattas: racing in ship's boats like cutters, gigs, and whalers) and to provide diversions for them on board ship as well as ashore such as deck hockey, boxing, and theatricals. The store ship *Gourko* had a prominent role; she was used as a theatre with great success.

The services of the *Gourko* [writes Admiral Chalmers] were much in demand, ships vying with one another to put on the best show. There was plenty of talent in the Fleet, and as time went on a very high standard was achieved. Costumes and wigs were hired from London. Lighting effects, equal to the best London theatres, were devised by the ship's torpedo party . . . An augmented orchestra from the Royal Marine band was ensconced in the orchestral pit below the stage . . .

As no women were available, the female parts were usually taken by young midshipmen, beautifully bewigged and frocked, among whom was Lord Louis Mountbatten, then serving in Beatty's flagship.

There was plenty of variety in the type of entertainment. The

5 Admiral of the Fleet Lord Chatfield, *The Navy and Defence* (London, 1942), p. 172.

Warspite won a high reputation by presenting a complete light opera based on Edward German's 'Merrie England.' The *Queen Elizabeth*, being Fleet Flagship, feeling she must outclass them all, astonished the Fleet by putting on a Russian ballet to the music of Liszt. . . .

Beatty was an ardent theatre-goer, and seldom missed a show. These entertainments, usually attended by over two thousand officers and men, made it possible for his personality to become known outside his own Flagship. At the end of the performance he would address the men, always on the same theme: 'Soon they [the High Seas Fleet] will have to come out, and there is only one thing for us to do. Annihilate them.' His optimism was infectious and could be felt throughout the Fleet. . . . In their preparation and presentation, the theatrical entertainments refreshed the minds of many men, recalling nostalgic memories of the last leave, and bringing to them the latest song hits, such as, 'If you were the only girl in the world,' 'Roses of Picardy,' 'Pack up your troubles,' and 'Keep the home fires burning.' The theatre ship played no small part in upholding the morale of the Fleet during these weary months of waiting.[6]

One officer 'does not remember a dull moment at Scapa, and at Rosyth, of course, there was all manner of things to do ashore.' As an index to the high morale in the fleet, discipline was very good. Few defaulters had to be dealt with, though at all times ships were on four hours' notice to go to sea, so nobody could get very far away from his ship. Once a year the ship went into dry-dock for ten days; everybody then went on leave.

2. THE 'NEW' STRATEGY

The outlook was not entirely cheerful as the New Year opened. The submarine was being mastered; but the campaign was imposing a considerable strain on Grand Fleet resources. This took three forms: (1) the call for destroyers for convoy escort and other A/S work; (2) the maintenance and efficiency of the mined area in the Heligoland Bight involved a constant activity by the light forces, which meant that the destroyers and light cruisers of the Grand Fleet might not always be available for fleet operations; (3) the attacks by the surface raiders on the Scandinavian convoys in the autumn of 1917 made it evident that in future heavy ships must cover the convoys, and for all practical purposes this detachment must be regarded as a permanent reduction in Grand Fleet

6 Chalmers, *Beatty*, pp. 306–8.

capital-ship strength. The weaknesses of protection and shell continued, as the C.-in-C. saw it, to represent a further discount in the real strength of the battle fleet.[7] It was the third factor above that operated as the catalytic agent.

These were the views which Beatty laid before a startled Admiralty in the first day of a highly important conference early in January. His conclusion was that it was 'to our general interest to adopt measures which would tend to postpone a Fleet action.'[8] He was asked to draft a letter on the subject. This memorandum, dated 9 January and hailed by Geddes as 'an important and momentous report,' ranks with Jellicoe's memorandum of 30 October 1914[9] as one of the two most important British naval documents of the war. The key passages follow:

The Grand Fleet has two duties to perform—
(i) To defeat the enemy's Fleet.
(ii) To control communications in the North Sea.
If the first is achieved, the second follows—the important point to consider is whether the Grand Fleet is in a position to achieve the first. . . .

The possibility of an encounter with the High Sea Fleet resulting in an indecisive engagement, or one in which the British losses are greater than those of the enemy, cannot be disregarded, and I am desirous that my views should be on record in case of any subsequent enquiry. . . .

It is recognised universally, I believe, that it is not in our power to force the enemy to sea at a moment of our choosing. We are faced therefore, with the problem of how to concentrate at the moment he may select, a force sufficiently superior to his to achieve his destruction. So long as he remains in his harbours he is in a position to operate, on interior lines and with such forces as he may choose, against our vitally important mercantile traffic with the Scandinavian countries.

His interior position, and the presence of his agents in the neutral ports from which convoys sail, facilitate the execution of surprise attacks with forces stronger than our covering forces. To take an extreme case, it is obviously impossible to have the whole Grand Fleet covering the convoy, whereas it is practicable for the whole High Sea Fleet to effect a surprise attack with reasonable prospect of escape to their bases during dark hours.

---

[7] See *From the Dreadnought to Scapa Flow*, iv. 44–5.
[8] 'Discussion at Admiralty on Occasion of Visit of Commander-in-Chief, Grand Fleet, on 2nd–3rd January 1918'; Admiralty MSS.
[9] See *From the Dreadnought to Scapa Flow*, ii. 75–6.

The forces which we employ to cover these convoys would almost certainly be unavailable to effect a junction with the main Fleet, should the enemy come out and offer battle. They must therefore be deducted from the strength of the force with which we can meet the enemy. The larger the forces which we detach for convoy protection, the smaller will be our fighting Fleet, and the enemy's appreciation of this fact will doubtless lead him to carry out operations and demonstrations against convoys accordingly. Frequent employment of heavy ships in our covering forces will afford the enemy good opportunity of submarine attack by day and possibly of destroyer attack by night. Such chances of effecting the desired attrition will be welcomed by him. . . .

The Russian debacle has released all the German forces in the Baltic, and the latter are now in a position to concentrate all their Fleet to meet us.

So far as battleships are concerned the Grand Fleet is considerably superior to the enemy . . .[10] In contemplating this superiority, however, the fact that the enemy has the power of selecting the moment for inviting a Fleet action must be borne in mind. He has therefore the advantage of being able to dispose submarines and lay mines on the lines of approach of the British Fleet, and it has long been recognised by the Flag Officers of the Fleet and by himself that casualties must be anticipated from this cause before battle is joined. . . .

In Battle Cruisers we have nine to the German six: *Mackensen, Seydlitz, Moltke, Hindenburg, Derfflinger, Von der Tann*. A considerable superiority on paper, but of the British vessels only three, viz. *Lion, Princess Royal*, and *Tiger* are fit to be in the line against the German five [*sic*]. The 'Renown' class are insufficiently armoured, they cannot stand a hammering. The 'New Zealand' and 'Invincible' classes are deficient in speed, protection and armament. . . .

Beatty next pointed to the dangerously slim margin in light cruisers—'The calls on this class of ships for convoy work may render us inferior'—the great inferiority in submarines, and the desperate destroyer situation.[11] The Grand Fleet could not count

10 The C.-in-C. had qualified this on 29 December 1917: 'As regards Battleships, though superior in numbers, the British ships are inferior in construction and protection. The latter has to some extent been improved by alterations made since 31st May, 1916, but these, at best, are a makeshift and do not compensate for radical defects in design, more particularly as regards magazine protection.' 'The situation in the North Sea'; Admiralty MSS. The relative dreadnought strength at the time of Beatty's paper was 34–19.

11 Beatty did not cite figures; but the light-cruiser figures were 27 British *v.* 20 German, 115 Grand Fleet destroyers *v.* 88 attached to the High Seas Fleet with many more available to the latter.

on its nominal destroyer complement in an action because so many were dispersed and employed in extraneous duties caused by A/S warfare. (As many as 15 were detached on 1 January, and 3 to 9 at the beginning of each month thereafter through August.) The C.-in-C. then stressed the inefficiency of the shell with which the fleet was supplied: improved shell would not be available until the summer. 'Until then the Grand Fleet could only meet the enemy under a most serious handicap. I wish to lay emphatic stress on this point . . .'

Beatty's deduction from the foregoing was that

the correct strategy of the Grand Fleet is no longer to endeavour to bring the enemy to action at any cost, but rather to contain him in his bases until the general situation becomes more favourable to us.

This does not mean that action should be avoided if conditions favour us, or that our role should be passive and purely defensive.

Offensive minelaying in the vicinity of his bases would give us a measure of initiative, and the sweeping operations necessary before his fleet could put to sea would afford us warning and enable detached units to be collected in readiness to meet him. . . .

Offensive operations should also be undertaken against the enemy's bases on the Flemish coast. Pressed with determination to a successful issue, these operations together with the closing of the Straits of Dover may alter the whole situation in our favour, releasing some needed light craft and confining enemy activity to more restricted areas.

The policy advocated would exert steady pressure, harass the enemy and weaken his morale, until the advent of additional destroyers and the replacement of our projectiles alter the situation in our favour.[12]

In short, the C.-in-C. recognized that circumstances had driven the fleet back from a 'seek out and destroy' policy to a policy of almost passive defence. The correct strategy was no longer to bring the enemy to action at any cost, but rather to contain him in his bases until the general situation became more favourable. Fundamentally, Beatty's position was not the radical departure that it appeared to be. It had, in effect, been his strategy through-

12 'Situation in the North Sea'; Admiralty MSS. The italics are mine. Beatty's 29 December paper, which is quite similar (even to the language), concluded that 'the situation is a dangerous one, and, while I have the fullest confidence in the courage and determination of the Officers and Men under my command, I feel that there may be a rude awakening for the Country if the Grand Fleet should have to meet the High Sea Fleet under the present conditions.'

out 1917. What was new was, first, the clear spelling out of the whys and wherefores of Grand Fleet strategy, and, second, the formal Admiralty and War Cabinet approval of the C.-in-C.'s strategy.

Oliver concurred with Beatty, 'who puts his case very clearly except in Para. 19 [re the Flemish coast and Dover Straits] which is rather indefinite.' Wemyss went further: 'The very weighty paper by the C.-in-C. . . . entirely confirms the opinion that I have formed since my advent to the Admiralty. . . . Although, as the C.-in-C. points out, there is no cause for alarm, the facts as they exist do call for a certain alteration in policy [on] which, after close consultation with the C.-in-C., I have already taken steps which it is hoped will effectually delay and keep on delaying the exodus of the High Seas Fleet, and this policy I propose to pursue until such time as the facts pointed out by the C.-in-C. have been remedied.'[13] On 17 January the Board discussed Beatty's memorandum and drew up their own, which closely followed its main arguments and laid down this concrete programme to meet the situation:

The policy which the Board of Admiralty consider should be pursued to an increased extent in the future is to take all possible steps to confine the German naval forces within the limits of the German naval bases. . . .

It is particularly desired to point out that the adoption of this policy is rendered necessary only by the exigencies of the present situation, and should be regarded as a purely temporary measure. . . . a deficiency in destroyers exists, reflecting upon the fighting efficiency of the Grand Fleet, and necessitating the adoption of temporary measures, such as those indicated, in order to meet the situation created. In a few months time it is anticipated that the strength of both the British and United States Navies in light craft will be considerably increased by the output of destroyers now in course of construction—and when that time arrives, the temporary protective measures which are outlined in this memorandum can be abandoned, and the mining policy in the Heligoland Bight can be altered in order to give greater scope to the prosecution of offensive schemes against the enemy fleet and bases.

The schemes to secure the end in view, which the Board of Admiralty have had under consideration for some time, and which are now well in hand, are—

[13] Minutes of 10 and 11 January 1918, respectively, on Beatty's paper.

(1) The laying of a minefield to form a complete Northern Barrage from the North of Scotland to the Norwegian coast.

(2) The laying of additional minefields in the Heligoland Bight.

(3) The laying of a minefield in the Straits of Dover to form a complete barrage and prevent the passage of both surface and submarine craft in the Channel.

The protection afforded by the laying of these minefields will, in the opinion of the Board, very materially hamper the movements of enemy submarines and surface craft, and result in damaging or destroying some, at any rate, of the enemy vessels attempting to pass through them. . . . At the same time, the consequent release of destroyers and auxiliary craft at present employed in protective work in the Dover Channel, will enable minor offensive operations to be undertaken, will release forces for submarine hunting, will ease the strain on the destroyer forces of the Grand Fleet, and will materially improve the shipping situation between England and France. The release of German forces in the Baltic, consequent upon the Russian debacle, renders it all the more necessary to strengthen, as far as possible, our Grand Fleet by the addition of destroyers. This can be done by building and by reducing the demands upon the Commander-in-Chief for escort and other duties. . . .

The situation, whilst giving no cause for alarm, renders it desirable, in the opinion of the Board of Admiralty, that the protective measures outlined in this memorandum should be made effective at the earliest possible date . . .[14]

On 18 January the War Cabinet discussed this paper and Beatty's. They 'looked very glum' during this session, Madden heard. But they accepted the situation and approved the policy of the Board as expressed in its document. This Admiralty statement of policy was the blueprint of British naval policy in Home waters during much of 1918. Its implementation has already been discussed in Chapter III.

As one of the introductory quotes to this chapter indicates, Jellicoe was highly critical of the new departure. 'The change of view was presumably due to a somewhat tardy realization by the War Cabinet of some of the dangers attendant upon a system of convoy for mercantile trade. The danger of surface attack on the Scandinavian Convoy brought about this change of view.'[15]

14 'Naval Situation in the North Sea,' 17 January 1918, over Geddes's signature and marked 'VERY SECRET'; Admiralty MSS.

15 Jellicoe, The Submarine Peril (London, 1934), p. 185.

Elsewhere he wrote: 'I should never have accepted this view had I been at the Admiralty.' His reason was that the Grand Fleet was considerably stronger than at Jutland. There were 34 battleships as against 28, 25 light cruisers as against 23, and at least 100 destroyers as against about 70. 'As regards Battle Cruisers, even if the *Mackensen* and *Hindenburg* were added to the High Sea Fleet the disparity in force was not very serious, nor was it very important in a real *fleet action*, although no doubt adding somewhat to our scouting difficulties.' As for the Scandinavian convoy factor,

Even if Beatty detached a complete Battle Squadron (which he never did) to protect the convoy, there was no reason why this squadron should not join the Grand Fleet if it went to sea; the squadron would obviously have plenty of fuel, and it could reach a position say in Lat. 56, 30 N. Long. 3 E. at least as soon as the Grand Fleet from Rosyth could do so, the distance in each case being about the same and the squadron on convoy duty having the advantage of having steam ready. The only disadvantage would be a slight shortage of fuel on the part of the escorting destroyers, but this shortage could not be very serious unless the Battle Squadron had been on escort duty for 2 or 3 days. It is obvious that if the High Sea Fleet was expected by the Admiralty to move, there was no danger to the convoy in withdrawing the protecting Battle Squadron and the C. in C. Grand Fleet would not be 'seeking action' unless the High Sea Fleet was on the move. The actual attempt by the High Sea Fleet on April 23rd 1918 on the convoy did not co-incide with an attempt on our part to seek a fleet action.[16]

Jellicoe's reasoning is incontrovertible, yet it does not alter the fact that the new strategy was basically identical to his own, and, like his, based on a wise and prudent restraint. As Madden reported, almost gleefully, when Beatty's ideas were officially approved:

B. also [has] written a letter to the Board to go on to the War Council [Cabinet], pointing out that the deficiencies in Lt. Crs., Destroyers and Subs *available* to go to sea with G.F. renders caution necessary in accepting action with H.S.F. at their own time and place and that considerable losses may be incurred in reaching their prepared place. Also pointed out disadvantages until new A.P. shell are available. . . . The Admiralty of course wrote a covering minute. When History is

---

[16] Jellicoe, 'Errors in *Naval Operations*.' As regards the first clause, Jellicoe was wrong. Beatty on at least one occasion sent the 4th Battle Squadron on convoy support.

written these papers will be a complete vindication of your policy, as Commander-in-Chief and as 1st Sea Lord.[17]

But whereas Jellicoe's strategy was based mainly on the mine and torpedo menace, Beatty's resulted from doubts about the sufficiency of the Grand Fleet in capital ships and, above all, in destroyers.

3. THE NUMBERS GAME AND OFFENSIVE IDEAS
(Chart 1A)

The Grand Fleet preponderance over the High Seas Fleet remained, on paper anyway, a healthy one. Plans Division figures for July showed (the German figures are in parentheses): 34 dreadnoughts (19), 9 battle cruisers (5), 37 light cruisers (32), 13 flotilla leaders (0), 134 destroyers (200), 35 submarines (100). The dreadnought position could not be considered safe so long as there existed the possibility that the Germans would acquire the large Russian fleet in the Baltic. This contingency, which had come up in the strategy discussions during January, caused increasing concern.

The Germans occupied Reval on 26 February, Hangö on 3 April, and Helsingfors (Helsinki of today) on 13 April. The Russians evacuated the ships at these bases to Kronstadt, where they had all been concentrated by the end of April. This force included 4 dreadnoughts, 3 pre-dreadnoughts, 9 cruisers, 70 destroyers, and 26 submarines. The Admiralty hoped that if the Germans advanced and occupied Petrograd, the Russians would destroy the more valuable ships at Kronstadt. Lockhart, the British agent in Moscow, had on 3 April reported Trotsky's statement that the Fleet, in the Black Sea as well as the Baltic, would be destroyed if necessary to prevent it falling into German hands. A telegram, whose substance the War Cabinet had approved on 26 April, went out to Lockhart on 7 May: 'Great importance is attached by Admiralty to destruction of Baltic Fleet in case of need. You should take any action you may think necessary to remind Trotsky of his undertaking.' When the Germans were reported on 11 May as being 150 kilometres, only three or four days' march, from Petrograd, and Trotsky showed no disposition to take action, something had to be done quickly.

The War Cabinets of 10 and 11 May[18] had under consideration

---

[17] Madden to Jellicoe, 28 January 1918; Jellicoe MSS.
[18] W.C. 408A and 409A.

an extraordinary plan for the destruction of the Baltic Fleet as outlined in an Admiralty memorandum of 9 May. The plan, as worked out by the Naval Attaché in Petrograd, Captain Cromie, involved secret service officers and other Russians, who would block Kronstadt harbour with three British steamers and blow up the 4 dreadnoughts and 14 'Novik'-class destroyers. It was a business deal. The Russians were asking nearly £300,000 for the job: £48,758 for the blocking, £107,420 for the destruction of the dreadnoughts, £135,900 to dispose of the destroyers, and £9,677 for 'agitation propaganda to complete scheme.' The terms were 5 per cent to be paid on the engaging of the personnel; 10 per cent on the attempt being made; 85 per cent if the scheme was a success. Cromie urgently wanted a reply on whether he was to proceed and whether the scheme was to be enlarged on a similar basis to cover the older warships and vessels under construction. The central question debated at the War Cabinet was the wisdom of taking an action that would antagonize Russia, since British instigation would become known or would be assumed. As the Prime Minister pointed out, the Admiralty proposal 'necessitated an important decision on the part of the War Cabinet as to future policy in Russia. The question which had to be decided was whether there was hope of any material assistance from Russia in the future, or whether anything was to be gained by not driving Russia into the arms of Germany.' Balfour, the Foreign Secretary, was dismayed over the prospect of driving Russia into the German camp, which was pretty certain if they blew up the Baltic Fleet. Geddes took the position that, while it was important not to antagonize the Russians, they should urge Trotsky to have the Baltic Fleet destroyed, and at the same time instruct the Naval Attaché to continue with his preparations and be ready to execute the plan, if necessary, and with or without Russian acquiescence. The First Lord was particularly alarmed that the Germans might acquire the 70 destroyers, a class of warship in which the Grand Fleet was 'somewhat short.' The War Cabinet approved the continuation of Cromie's preparations for the destruction of the Baltic Fleet, including ships under construction; but he was to take action only if the Germans advanced on Petrograd and the Fleet was in 'imminent danger' of seizure. Cromie was authorized 'to initiate any expenditure to carry out the above, but care should be taken not to alienate unnecessarily the Russian Government'. On 27

May the War Cabinet authorized him 'to take whatever steps he thought necessary' to avoid the ships falling into German possession, 'deferring his action as long as possible.'[19]

Nothing was done, as the Germans did not advance on Petrograd and it was understood that Trotsky was making his own arrangements for blowing up the Fleet if it came to that. The Baltic Fleet problem was thereafter, for the duration of the war, no longer an Admiralty–War Cabinet preoccupation.

As during 1917, it was the battle-cruiser position that most vexed the Admiralty and the C.-in-C. The War Cabinet of 4 September[20] had before it an Admiralty paper that gave these figures: 9 British v. 6 German; in mid-1919: 10 v. 6 or 7; 1920: 10 v. 9. As before, the Admiralty credited the Germans with ships that were never completed, and with an advantage in a more complete armour protection, particularly as compared with the *Repulse* and *Renown*, which were 'dangerously liable to destruction by a single hit.' The new A.P. shell, however, was declared to be capable of penetrating German armour and putting their ships out of action. The British position was 'consequently much improved as the vulnerability of both sides is now more equal.'[21] In the War Cabinet discussion of this paper, Geddes indicated that in 1919 the Germans would be practically equal in battle cruisers, and superior in 1920. He asked for authorization to continue the construction of the three 'Hoods', to be completed in 1919. They had long been in a state of suspension. That the ships would not be ready till 1921 weighed heavily in the minds of the politicians, as did the shortages of manpower for the Army and, most important, Lord Pirrie's estimate that 450,000 tons of merchant shipping could be built with the manpower needed to complete the two battle cruisers. Lloyd George made the telling point that they 'had to bear in mind, from a *post*-War point of view, the extensions that were being made to the American mercantile marine, and the effect on our welfare of the loss of nearly half a million tons of shipping on our part.' The War Cabinet's decision was to defer the question of the construction of the two battle cruisers till December.

The uncertainties and misgivings about the strength of the Grand Fleet that had so disturbed Beatty in January, and had

---

[19] W.C. 418A. [20] W.C. 469A.
[21] 'Battle Cruiser Position and Shipbuilding Programme' (G.T.-5575), 31 August 1918.

caused the adoption, with Admiralty and War Cabinet approval, of a defensive strategy, did not discourage the emergence of offensive schemes in the Grand Fleet and at the Admiralty. Richmond, Captain of the *Conqueror* (2nd B.S.), continued his espousal of an offensive naval strategy in the Mediterranean. He would secure effective command in the Adriatic through the destruction or immobilization of the Austrian Fleet at Pola with torpedo-carrying planes and through the neutralization of Pola as a fleet and submarine base with bombardments, mines, and mine nets, if it could not be taken by a combined operation. With sea command in the Adriatic established, the U-boat campaign in the Mediterranean would be crippled and the way opened for Allied troop landings to make the Austrian campaign in the Alps difficult. Richmond also promoted his pet offensive scheme since 1916, his Syrian coast project: amphibious raids to disrupt Turkish communications.[22] Richmond's ideas, though supported by Beatty, were vetoed at the Admiralty as too risky, or too expensive in *matériel*, or both. Richmond was disgusted. 'What a timid lot they are! . . . Any risk is vetoed, as if you could make war without risk! . . . They are as timid as kittens when they can smell danger . . . '[23]

Offensive schemes in the Grand Fleet centred in an air offensive conducted from aircraft carriers. Unlike the multifarious schemes mulled over at the Admiralty, which never led anywhere, the C.-in-C. saw great possibilities in a naval air offensive against enemy naval bases and ships in harbour in the spring of 1918, using Grand Fleet aircraft. Apart from the material damage that such raids would inflict and the moral effects, the enemy's pre-occupation with defensive measures would tend to limit his offensive movements such as coast raids and attacks on convoys. Beatty's optimism stemmed from his faith in the 'Cuckoo' torpedo plane, a weapon which must be rapidly developed, as it 'might profoundly influence the whole campaign and especially our ability to carry out an active offensive on the High Seas Fleet.'[24] Beatty pressed his views on the Admiralty in a stream of letters

22 See *From the Dreadnought to Scapa Flow*, iv. 171, 236 n.
23 Diary, 11 January 1918; *Portrait of an Admiral*, p. 294. Richmond held Fremantle principally to blame. He was 'the block to every scheme in the Admiralty.'
24 'Notes on [Beatty's] Conversation with Captain Dewar, Assistant Director of Plans,' 7 March 1918; Bellairs MSS. On the wartime history of the torpedo-bomber and Beatty's hopes for it in 1917, see *From the Dreadnought to Scapa Flow*, iv. 22-3, 237-40.

and in conferences, such as those at the Admiralty on 2–3 January and with the D.C.N.S. (25 February) and First Sea Lord (5 March).

The cool response of the Admiralty (the Plans Division excepted) dashed Beatty's hopes. Geddes opined, on the basis of his observation in France and an analysis of the damage done by many tons of explosives dropped in bombing raids, that 'no such operation carried out from the sea was likely to be successful owing to lack of "Carriers" and the consequent impossibility of carrying out operations with an adequate number of 'planes to achieve material results.' Fremantle and Duff supported this view. Wemyss explained that the main difficulty lay in estimating the *matériel* that would be available.[25] Beatty's hopes for a spring naval air offensive were dashed late in February when Fremantle, after consulting with Captain Lambe, commanding the naval air units at Dunkirk, concluded that bombing, unless it could be carried out continuously, had little destructive effect. 'It had therefore been decided to turn down for the present the question of bombing offensives, the carrier situation not admitting of continuous attacks.' Beatty concurred that, to be effective, bombing had to be continuous; but he did not see how this prejudiced the question of the development and use of torpedo planes, which had great possibilities for fleet purposes. Fremantle agreed and stated that this decision would not affect the torpedo plane.[26] In the end, the Admiralty decided not to pursue Beatty's idea of an air offensive on German bases and ships. As matters developed, the first 'Cuckoos' were not supplied to the Grand Fleet until the war was in its last days. This, together with the insufficiency of aircraft carriers, throttled any hope of an air offensive before the spring of 1919.

The Naval Staff was active in the search for a naval offensive. Their schemes were afterwards summarized by the D.C.N.S.:

The Naval Staff wearied their brains in the search for offensive measures which offered a prospect of success, but with little result. Any attempt to enter the Baltic in force was ruled out by the undoubted presence of minefields whose positions were unknown, by the distance

---

[25] 'Discussion at Admiralty on Occasion of Visit of Commander-in-Chief, Grand Fleet, on 2nd–3rd January 1918'; Admiralty MSS.

[26] Beatty to Admiralty, 7 March 1918, with enclosure, 'Notes of Conference with the Deputy Chief of the Naval Staff,' 25 February 1918; Fremantle MSS.

which disabled ships would find themselves from our own bases, and by the strategical advantage possessed by the enemy in the existence of the Kiel Canal, which enabled him to move his Battle Fleet at will, in a comparatively short time, through the Canal, to the North Sea or the Baltic. A project for attacking one or other of the German naval bases was considered impracticable for similar reasons and on account of their heavy coast defences. The Grand Fleet made occasional sweeps of the North Sea as a deterrent to enemy movements and as an exercise for their own crews. The Harwich force carried out some useful operations, when the weather permitted, in attacking German minesweepers with the small 40-ft. coastal motor-boats which the light cruisers carried at their davits, and Sir Roger Keyes had attacked the port of Zeebrugge, and succeeded, after a gallant action, in blocking, temporarily, the canal leading from that port to the submarine base at Bruges. But much as we at the Admiralty, and the officers and men of the Grand Fleet and the Harwich and Dover forces, desired them, neither they nor we could devise any further practical measures and we had to content ourselves with following the practice of our predecessors in the fleets of Earl St. Vincent, Nelson, Cornwallis, and Collingwood by retaining our principal naval strength in the best strategical positions available and in a state of continuous readiness for action, always hoping that the effect of our blockade might be to tempt the enemy to come out and try conclusions with us, as it did at the Battle of Trafalgar, and, in the meanwhile, resting assured that the control of the sea communications was in our hands.[27]

4. THE HIGH SEAS FLEET SORTIE
(Chart 7)

Generally speaking, the dominant mood of the Admiralty and the Grand Fleet was one of *waiting*—waiting to see what the High Seas Fleet would do, but prepared to give it a sound drubbing if it, or detached units, dared venture far from their bases. The possibility of a battle-cruiser raid, or a raid by light forces backed by heavy ships, or, conceivably, one by the entire High Seas Fleet, against the Dover forces and into the Channel worried the Admiralty. The enemy's objects, it was thought, would be one or more of these: to assist his military offensive by disturbing British cross-Channel lines of communication; to break down the Dover barrage; and to inflict losses on the Grand Fleet by drawing it

[27] Fremantle, *My Naval Career*, pp. 245–6.

down across a submarine and mined zone. The Harwich Force and the weak 3rd Battle Squadron in the Swin (the *Dreadnought* and two 'King Edward' pre-dreadnoughts) were not believed to be sufficient to counter a raid in force. The solution proposed at the end of January was to form a strong southern battle squadron: three dreadnoughts ('Superbs') from the Grand Fleet would join the *Dreadnought* at the mouth of the Thames and the two old battleships would be paid off. The discussions continued through March. Beatty was hostile to the idea of weakening the battle fleet at a time when, on top of the four battleships constantly undergoing refit, it was often without a battleship division, off in support of a convoy. A reduction of possibly as many as 11 battleships on the critical day 'would militate against decisive results.' He also advanced the argument that if the Germans supported their military offensive with a naval offensive, 'it would surely be with a force sufficiently strong to render our force of 4 BS's [battleships] in the Swin innocuous and I do not like this policy of dispersion.' If it was considered that the danger from enemy heavy ships was great, the Grand Fleet as a whole should be brought to Rosyth.[28] On the main point the First Sea Lord was entirely in agreement with him: any disposition which would leave the Grand Fleet without that superiority which the C.-in-C. considered necessary would be unsound, and, under any circumstances, the matter would have to stand over until he considered the American battleships (6th Squadron) efficient.

Meanwhile, the battle fleet was shifted to Rosyth on 12 April. The lesson had finally sunk home that four good opportunities to cut off and destroy a raiding force (Scarborough in 1914, the Dogger Bank in 1915, Lowestoft in 1916, and possibly the sortie of nearly the whole High Seas Fleet in August 1916) might have turned out better if the main fleet at Scapa—that portion of the intercepting forces—had not been so far to the north. Scapa Flow continued to be used for full-calibre gunnery and other exercises, one squadron at a time going there, because the waters at the mouth of the Forth inside May Island were too restricted for full-calibre firing with heavy guns. (Sub-calibre practices—3-lb. or 6-lb. guns fitted inside the bores of 12-inch and bigger guns— were carried out in the Flow, full-calibre firings with A/S cover in the Pentland Firth and to the west of Hoy.)

[28] Beatty to Wemyss, 31 January 1918; Wemyss MSS.

The German offensive on the Western Front, which commenced on 21 March, led to speculation in the Grand Fleet that if this battle, on which the enemy were staking everything to achieve a decisive success, went against them, the German General Staff might order the High Seas Fleet to sea, 'as the last throw of all,' in Bellairs's words; 'for ultimately of course if the German High Sea Fleet could engage and defeat the Grand Fleet, the whole allied cause would fail automatically. . . . We may get a situation such as when Napoleon ordered Villeneuve to sea, and the German General Staff will order the High Sea Fleet similarly to sea.'[29] This reflected Beatty's views. The enemy was, the C.-in-C. believed,

> ruled by a great Military Party who count risks and losses as nothing, who make the same mistake as Napoleon did, and gamble upon obtaining a Naval victory. With such in my mind one cannot afford to run the shadow of a risk, as an indecisive action on the sea with the Main Fleet would amount to a German victory. Therefore, at all costs we must aim at annihilation. To obtain that is indeed a difficult problem, the North Sea is so small and the spread of ships so great that in a few hours the beggars can retire behind minefields and submarine screens in their own waters. I often wonder what Nelson would have thought of it. His high spirit would have chafed him to death by this time.[30]

By this date, however, the C.-in-C. and the Naval Staff were predicting that the Scandinavian convoy and its covering force would be the most tempting and therefore the most probable objective of an overpowering surprise enemy attack. This possibility had been causing Beatty and Whitehall much anxiety for some time. The Germans could estimate the routes and dates of this convoy with reasonable accuracy. Under the old system Scandinavian convoys had sailed daily, with a destroyer escort. Under the new system that came into force on 19 January convoys sailed every three days, though during the winter months occasionally at four- or five-day intervals on account of the weather. Even then the enemy could estimate that the sailing would be postponed 24 hours and know where to place an

[29] Bellairs to Dewar, 2 April 1918; Dewar MSS. Commander Roger M. Bellairs was Beatty's War Staff Officer throughout his time as C.-in-C.
[30] Beatty to Lady Beatty, 7 April 1918; Chalmers, *Beatty*, p. 324.

attacking force. It seemed reasonable also to assume that the enemy could ascertain that the strength of the covering force was pretty constant, a light-cruiser squadron and a battleship division or battle-cruiser squadron, and therefore send out a superior force. Beatty was extremely reluctant to employ larger forces: it meant more dispersion of force, should the enemy undertake any larger effort than a raid on a convoy.

Correspondence between Beatty and Wemyss and conferences between Beatty and Fremantle (25 February), Wemyss (5 March), Dewar (7 March), and probably the D.N.I., defined the problems and discussed solutions. There appeared to be two ways of making an attack more difficult for the Germans. One was by changing the intervals of time between sailings; the other was by changing the convoy routes. With regard to the former, Beatty's view was that 'it was necessary to avoid two covering forces being out at the same time; and it would be a great advantage if a system whereby the normal interval was 4 days was adopted, and this could be altered as required either speeding it up to a 3-day interval, or retarding it to a 5-day interval as circumstances demanded. This would mean that the enemy would not be able to forecast in the same way since occasionally sailings would be delayed 24 hours and occasionally they would be accelerated 24 hours. With the present 3-day system, owing to the difficulties of supporting forces, it was impossible to accelerate the sailing 24 hours bringing it down to a 2-day system.'[31] The Admiralty's position was that three-day intervals were necessary in order to keep up with the traffic. It was decided, however, at the beginning of March to give a trial to the four-day system as the standard interval, although the Naval Staff did not consider that it would work so satisfactorily as the three-day system and that, to carry out their contracts with Scandinavia, it would be necessary to revert to the three-day system.

As for changing the routes, this was being carried out by the end of February. The Plans Division wanted to go further. They worked out a plan early in April for routeing the convoys farther north, which would lessen the risk to which the covering force was exposed and make it easier for the Grand Fleet to cut off a raiding force. The Admiralty vetoed the plan: it would reduce the volume

---

[31] 'Notes of Conference with the Deputy Chief of the Naval Staff,' 25 February 1918, enclosed with Beatty to Admiralty, 7 March 1918; Fremantle MSS.

of trade. It was the considered opinion of the Naval Staff that it was imperative to route the convoys straight across the North Sea in order to save time, and this was why the C.-in-C., who thought the direct routeing undesirable, had accepted it. But the heretics in the Plans Division, Dewar and Fuller, 'continued to work out the details with the Mercantile Division and found that by careful organisation it would only reduce the annual carrying capacity of the convoys by 2 per cent and require only four additional destroyers as escorts.'[32] At a mid-April conference between Beatty and Fuller it was decided that once the Northern Barrage was laid, the Scandinavian convoy would be taken behind its protection and the battleship supporting force withdrawn. Beatty, it must be remembered, had full responsibility for safeguarding the convoy.

So much depended on the efficiency of Intelligence. If they received information in good time indicating a raid on a convoy and in what force, it would be easy to send out ample force, even the whole of the Grand Fleet, to cover the convoy. The difficulty here was that by 1918 the Admiralty could no longer rely on warnings of enemy movements through intercepts and Room 40 deciphering that had stood them and the Grand Fleet in such good stead practically since the beginning of the war. The Germans, with a suspicion of what was happening, were severely restricting their W/T signalling, to say nothing of changing their signal book from time to time. To some extent look-out submarines in the Heligoland Bight, now equipped with transmitters powerful enough to reach England, compensated for this falling-off in secret intelligence. But they could not be relied on with certainty to detect any important enemy fleet movement. There were two other possible ways to obtain a warning that the High Seas Fleet was coming out. Extensive minesweeping operations in the Heligoland Bight must precede a fleet sortie, it was thought. Also, it was hoped that any unusual dispositions of Zeppelins for reconnaissance would give warning of intended movements. In

---

[32] Vice-Admiral K. G. B. Dewar, *The Navy from Within* (London, 1939), p. 245. On 25 April Plans Division proposed that the route should be carried up to 63° 30'— altered to 62° N. on 27 April, after the A.C.N.S. had approved moving the route to the northward but thought the Plans proposal was not practicable. Although Beatty was in agreement with Plans, the D.C.N.S. (27 April) turned down the proposed alteration of route: the present system gave the best chance of securing the safety of the convoy.

this instance the Germans were prepared to do without advance minesweeping and airship reconnaissance. However, Beatty and the Admiralty saw the main insurance against surprise in the efficiency of Room 40. It came down to this, in Beatty's view: the Scandinavian convoy system would break down if Intelligence failed. Could he rely on sufficient warning of German movements? 'We are gambling upon obtaining accurate information and for the moment I cannot see that we can do otherwise.'[33] He was not hopeful, as he frankly told Dewar:

The Commander-in-Chief said that so far as possible he considered that all dispositions would be made on the supposition that Intelligence was not available, and he strongly deprecated the present system of relying on this. He felt that the Scandinavian supporting system was wrong, and he had represented that the volume of the traffic, and the importance of it was not sufficient to justify the possibility of strong enemy forces effecting a surprise and inflicting a defeat on the supporting force. He had, however, been informed by the Naval Staff that the vital question was the quick carrying on of trade across the North Sea to and from Scandinavia, and that this must take precedence, the risk to the supporting forces being accepted.[34]

What Beatty had so long feared was about to happen. During the early months of 1918 the German Naval Staff furnished Scheer with information, derived from U-boats, that the Scandinavian convoy was no longer running daily, but once or twice a week, mainly at the beginning or in the middle of the week. The number of merchantmen in each convoy had increased accordingly. Scheer also heard, via U-boat intelligence, that the recent convoys were being escorted by heavy ships, sometimes including American battleships. The information concerning sailing and arrival times was, as shown, not accurate. The convoys were sailing at regular four-day intervals, as far as weather permitted, not on fixed days of the week. This routine had been in force over a month. The misleading intelligence prompted Scheer's decision to attempt a bold stroke with his whole strength. His mistake had been to rely

---

33 Beatty to Wemyss, 22 February 1918; Wemyss MSS.
34 'Notes of Conversation with Captain Dewar, Assistant Director of Plans,' 7 March 1918; Bellairs MSS. Dewar speaks of a visit to the Grand Fleet at the end of March, when he warned Beatty that 'presumably the High Seas Fleet could go to sea without making any wireless signals and that perhaps insufficient attention had been paid to that possibility . . .' Dewar, *The Navy from Within*, p. 245.

on U-boat commanders' information, which could not possibly have given him the data to draw up a correct schedule of convoy movements. Newbolt finds it curious that Scheer had not obtained information of this sort from German consuls in Norway, who would surely have known of the four-day scheduled interval between convoys. For some unknown reason he failed to do so; it was to cost him dearly.

The German Official History explains the *raison d'être* of Scheer's plan:

An attack on a convoy protected by heavy naval forces promised an impressive military success, quite apart from the reward of merchant shipping; however, in view of the circumstances that could be expected, heavy forces would now have to be employed and these screened by the whole Fleet. A sortie towards the north conformed to the guiding principles agreed to with the Chief of the *Admiralstab* [Admiral Holtzendorff], which were, by means of sorties in force, to effectively ease the strain on the U-boats operating in the Channel and around England. This could also be expected to take some of the pressure from the Channel area, which had become the focal point of British interest during our Army's attack in the West.[35]

Scheer chose Wednesday, 24 April, as the day for the attack. The plan called for a one-day stay in the operation area west of Norway; the fuel capacity of most of the destroyer flotillas and of some of the cruisers did not permit of an operation of more than three days' duration. Hipper and the battle cruisers (1st Scouting Group), the light cruisers (2nd Scouting Group), and a destroyer flotilla were to attack the convoy and its covering force, with the rest of the High Seas Fleet, under Scheer, some 60 miles to the S.S.W., ready to support the attacking force. With Scheer were the 1st, 3rd (less the *Markgraf*), and 4th Squadrons (dreadnoughts), the 4th Scouting Group (light cruisers, less the *Stralsund*), and four destroyer flotillas. All available High Seas Fleet units were assembled in Schillig Roads on the evening of 22 April on the pretext of carrying out exercises and evolutions in the Bight the next day. All U-boats sailing on patrol on the day prior to the operation were instructed to search for targets off the Firth of Forth for a 24-hour period. There was no airship reconnaissance

---

[35] *Der Krieg in der Nordsee*, vii. 217–18.

on the 23rd or 24th owing to a stiff easterly wind. The Fleet sailed at 5 a.m. on 23 April.

The chances of a huge success were greatly enhanced by Scheer's ability to conceal his departure from the knowledge of Room 40 by restricting the use of wireless to an absolute minimum before as well as during the operation. This measure and an almost incredible mistake by a British submarine enabled the fleet to pass unobserved out of the Heligoland Bight. Four British look-out submarines were on patrol in the approaches to the Bight, stationed round the edge of the mined area, a rough quadrant from west to north: *V-4*, off the Texel, *E-42*, off the south-east side of, and *J-4*, to the north-east of, the Dogger Bank, and *J-6*, to the west of Horns Reef. *J-6* (Lieutenant-Commander G. Warburton), through whose area the High Seas Fleet was steaming, saw nothing, due to the thick and hazy weather, until she sighted destroyers and light cruisers at about 8 p.m. on the 23rd. It was the head of the German attack force. The Commanding Officer of *J-6* believed this was a British force providing cover for a minelaying operation and of whose presence in his patrol area he had been informed. Even the sighting of five battle cruisers escorted by destroyers about a half-hour later, followed soon after midnight by battleships, the van of the battle fleet, headed in a northerly direction, told *J-6* nothing. No signal was sent, the Commanding Officer being certain that these were British forces engaged in some operation! 'It was incredibly stupid and indeed heartbreaking' was Beatty's judgement at the time.[36] Captain Creswell is more charitable: 'It is easy enough to see now what a grave neglect of duty this was; but it is not so easy to judge to what extent it was the personal fault of the Captain of *J-6*, and how much may be attributed to the Higher Command failing to make it quite clear to subordinates—junior flag officers and captains of detached ships—what was required of them. One does not know, for instance, whether any officers had recently been rapped over the knuckles for reporting forces which were actually our own.'[37]

I cannot accept the statement in the German Official History that

36 Beatty to Wemyss, 5 May 1918; Wemyss MSS.
37 Commander (as he then was) John Creswell, 'The Grand Fleet, 1917–1918,' R.N. Staff College lecture, 1931; copy in Captain Creswell's possession. The lecture contains a useful table of the more important British signals and Room 40 intercepts during the sortie.

'Admiral Beatty's firm intention was to avoid a decisive battle, and the primary concern for the individual forces in the northern North Sea made it unlikely that even a timely report from *J-6* would have led to a Fleet battle.'[38] The reader should cast his eye over the italicized passages on page 134, above. Beatty would have regarded the opportunity to catch the High Seas Fleet so far from its bases as a 'favourable opportunity' and would not have been an onlooker while the enemy fleet roamed the North Sea. Certainly it was not a timid or reluctant Beatty who dashed out of the Forth. As for the reference to 'individual forces in the northern North Sea,' the Germans were, as will be brought out, 'steaming into a no-man's sea, abandoned alike by merchantmen and men-of-war' (Newbolt).

While Hipper and the attack force were searching towards Bergen, an unforeseen emergency threw the whole operation off. At 5.10 a.m. on the 24th, when about 40 miles W.S.W. of Stavanger, the battle cruiser *Moltke* suffered a grave mechanical breakdown. Her starboard inner propeller dropped off and before the turbine could be stopped racing, a gear wheel outside its casing (used for turning the engine at slow speed for maintenance work in harbour) flew to pieces. Some of the pieces pierced an auxiliary condenser. In a short time the engine-room flooded and the starboard and centre engines were soon out of action. When Hipper learned of this (through a visual signal), not wishing to be hampered by a cripple, he ordered the *Moltke* to join the battle fleet. The trouble got worse, with salt water in the boilers, and eventually she could barely crawl. At 6.43 a.m., the *Moltke* transmitted a signal by W/T to the C.-in-C., reporting 'breakdown serious, speed only 4 knots.' At 8.45 another W/T signal reported she was 'out of control.' The upshot was that Scheer closed the *Moltke*. At 10.50 a.m. (just as Beatty was preparing to put to sea), the battleship *Oldenburg* took the *Moltke* in tow and the main fleet set course for home through the Bight at 10 to 11 knots. (The port engines of the *Moltke* were able to function at half speed.) The unflappable Scheer had, in the meantime, ordered Hipper (he had turned back and at 9.40 a.m. was in sight of the main fleet) to continue the operation as planned, and at 10.23 a.m. the attack force was again steering N.N.W. at 18 knots. Hipper again crossed

[38] *Der Krieg in der Nordsee*, vii. 225.

and reconnoitred the area of the convoy routes as far as 60° N. At about 1 p.m., the *Admiralstab* reported through the W/T station at Neumünster that 30 ships were assembled at Flekkerö and should have sailed in convoy on the night of 23–24 April. Additional information soon afterwards stated that this convoy was to sail on the 24th. Visibility was good and there was a chance of intercepting the convoy. Acting on this report, the 2nd Scouting Group carried out a sweep to the eastwards to within sight of Utsire Lighthouse. At 2.10 p.m., having found no sign of a west-bound convoy, and knowing nothing about the eastbound convoy which had left Methil, in the Firth of Forth, at 6.30 that morning, Hipper turned for home. The 2nd Scouting Group joined him at about 4.30 p.m. Hipper had had no chance to intercept a convoy: there was none that day, the 24th. A Bergen convoy of 34 ships had sailed on 22 April, routed through Selbjorns Fjord, which it had cleared at 1.15 p.m., escorted by an armed boarding vessel and two destroyers, with the 7th Light Cruiser Squadron and the 2nd Battle Cruiser Squadron to the south as a covering force. By early morning of the 23rd, it was 140 miles east of the Orkneys; it arrived at Methil in the late morning of the 24th. By dawn of the 25th Hipper's forces had closed up the main fleet.

What were the Admiralty and Grand Fleet up to during the promenade of the High Seas Fleet? The Admiralty had two special reasons to keep a sharp watch on enemy fleet movements at this time. One was the Zeebrugge–Ostend blocking operation which had occurred on the night of 22–23 April. The other was indications that the High Seas Fleet was on the move. The 'especial and unusually comprehensive messages sent from Wilhelmshaven to the minesweepers in the Heligoland Bight'[39] and the airship patrol which was ordered (later countermanded owing to the wind) pointed to something extraordinary in the offing. There was an atmosphere of high suspense in the War Room, where the First Sea Lord, himself completely calm and master of the situation, personally took charge. The Admiralty, however, did not know where to expect the German thrust, since there was not one cheep from the Bight indicating that any ships were moving. It was only when the *Moltke* broke wireless silence to report her accident and position (6.43 a.m., 24 April), and the British directional stations

---

[39] Fremantle, *My Naval Career*, p. 253.

picked up this signal and others subsequently exchanged between Hipper and Scheer, that the Admiralty finally became aware that large German naval forces were operating well out in the North Sea. Beatty placed no reliance upon the first intercept (dispatched by Room 40 at 8.40 a.m. and received in the *Queen Elizabeth* at 8.58), for it put the *Moltke* in an obviously incorrect position: the middle of Norway. (The error was in the *Moltke*'s signal, not in Room 40.) At 9.55 a.m., however, he received a Room 40 report which convinced him that something important was in the wind: 'Enemy W/T procedure shows important operation in progress. "Neuminster" reports British unaware German forces are at sea.' Beatty now, at 9.58 and 10.26, made signals to the Battle Cruiser Force and the battle fleet, respectively, to raise steam. At 10.47 the Admiralty ordered the Grand Fleet to put to sea and concentrate east of the Long Forties. (It was at about this time that the convoy from Norway was arriving at Methil.) Early in the afternoon the Grand Fleet cleared the Firth of Forth through a pea-soup fog at top speed—31 battleships, 4 battle cruisers, 2 cruisers, 24 light cruisers, and 85 destroyers. It was the first time since 19 August 1916, and the last time in the war, that the full strength of the Grand Fleet was set in motion.

Beatty steered due east towards an intercepting position south of the Naze. He was too late. The High Seas Fleet had been retiring south all day, and during the night had crossed the Grand Fleet's line of advance over a hundred miles ahead of it. Had there been any real possibility of interception? From Captain Creswell's analysis: 'It appears that Scheer crossed ahead of the Grand Fleet about midnight 24th/25th, distant about 150 miles. [Beatty's light cruisers were considerably closer.] In order to intercept Scheer during daylight on the 24th it would have been necessary for our Fleet to have left harbour not later than the previous midnight, at which time there was a thick fog in the Firth of Forth. So it seems probable that even if *J-6* had reported promptly when he sighted heavy ships [see above, p. 150], and if immediate action had been taken on this report, Scheer would still have got safely back to harbour.'[40]

There were two last opportunities to inflict damage to the High Seas Fleet. About 4 a.m. on the 25th the luckless *J-6*, still in her

---

[40] Creswell, 'The Grand Fleet, 1917–1918.'

patrol position near Horns Reef, sighted light cruisers and destroyers to the northward on a southerly course. They were Hipper's advanced light forces, coming up astern of the main fleet. *J-6* submerged and about an hour and a half later saw a number of ships which her Captain took to be battle cruisers and light cruisers. He watched the parade of enemy ships pass south of his position and did not send out a report until he had lost sight of them. At 6.30 a.m. he reported by W/T: '5 B.C.s, 4 L.C.s and ['an unknown number of' in another version] destroyers bearing S. 60 E., course W.S.W. [*sic*]. My position Lat. 56° 10' N. Long. 5° 50' E.'

At 6.37 p.m. (25 April), an hour after casting off the tow of the *Oldenburg*, about 40 miles north of Heligoland, the *Moltke* came trudging along astern of *E-42* (Lieutenant C. H. Allen). The submarine got off an 18-inch torpedo which struck the *Moltke* in the region of her port engine-room; nearly 1,800 tons of water flooded in. She at first went out of control, but managed to reach the Jade under her own power. In the course of the night all forces had assembled in the Jade.

By the time *E-42* made her attack, the Grand Fleet was well on its way back to Rosyth. All night it had stood to the eastwards; by 10 a.m. on the 25th it was clear from *J-6*'s signal (received in the *Queen Elizabeth* at 7.56 a.m.) that they had missed the enemy. Beatty stood to the northwards till 11.30 a.m., then altered course for his base. Two hours later (1.41 p.m.), he received an Admiralty message, 'Return to base at your discretion.'

The sortie was the farthest yet undertaken by the High Seas Fleet and had been skilfully planned and executed; but the operation had not achieved its object, mainly owing to faulty intelligence, which had miscalculated the sailing date of the westbound convoy by 24 hours, and to the mechanical breakdown in the *Moltke*. Had Scheer sailed northwards a day earlier or a day later, he would probably have succeeded in destroying a convoy and its covering force: the convoy which left Bergen on the 22nd or the one that left Methil on the 24th. One can also argue that Scheer was lucky. He had taken a serious risk in visiting more northerly waters than ever before in ignorance of the fact that the concentrated Grand Fleet lay at Rosyth, on his flank, and not, as he supposed, at Scapa. Newbolt sums up the essence of the matter: 'The zone in which he desired to operate was, it is true, rather further from Rosyth than from Scapa; but it was well to the north of the new base, and eighteen hours' steaming, or even less, would always carry the bulk of our battle fleet to an intercepting position between Stavanger and the Horn Reefs channel.'[41]

The whole Navy was bitterly disappointed, no one more than the C.-in-C. 'We have just returned once again disappointed. It promised well but as on many other occasions was doomed to disappointment. . . . we must reconsider the outlook which permits apparently considerable Forces indeed *the High Seas Fleet* to get out without our knowledge—otherwise we might meet with a disaster of some magnitude over this cursed convoy supporting Force.'[42] Admiralty intelligence had failed, and there ensued a correspondence between Beatty and the authorities as to how far he could depend on it.

Many years later Admiral Sir William James recalled the situation in Room 40:

It was not possible at this time, or indeed at any time, to give a definite assurance. The one clear indication we had that something was afoot was the broadcasting by the submarine parent ship of what the Germans called a 'catchword.' The submarines carried a list of 'catchwords,' which usually consisted of only one word, and these indicated the general nature of surface vessel operations about to take place. It is an interesting point that the use of such a signal was forced on the Germans because their submarines were out as long as 28/30 days and there were always some returning to the North Sea who had to be warned that their own surface vessels would be operating. On this particular occasion the submarine depot ship sent out some groups (I think it was in the middle watch) which we could not make head or tail of. However, the Operations Division were told that an unusual message had been sent out. It was the policy to avoid as far as possible sending out our forces unless there was some *fairly certain information* that German surface vessels had left harbour, for we wished to guard against the Fleet going out on a wild goose chase and having to go back and refuel. It was, of course, a critical time in the War. Nothing else transpired until we picked up the *Moltke's* call sign off the Norwegian coast.

After it was all over we held a sort of informal Court of Enquiry in Room 40 to find out if any indication had been missed, other than this one signal from the submarine depot ship, which did prove afterwards to

---

[41] *Naval Operations*, v. 232.
[42] Beatty to Wemyss, 26 April 1918; Wemyss MSS.

be a 'catchword.'* A great volume of signals was always pouring in from all the stations and these were all overhauled. There was only one signal that had a connection with the German Fleet leaving. An outpost vessel reported aircraft and she was told 'They are our own.' It is true that their custom was to fly aircraft over the swept ways in front of surface vessels, but we never felt that this signal by itself justified any conclusions or even suspicions about surface vessels moving. It was only when read in conjunction with events, that we subsequently found to have happened, that the signal acquired any importance.

The lesson is true today. These wonderful modern inventions, the plane, wireless, cryptography, *may* assist, but *nothing* can give the same *assurance* as the 'frigate' off the enemy's coast.[43]

Spannkraft = full force. The S/M special cypher was not fully broken at the moment.

After the enquiry, Captain James wrote at once to Beatty's staff officers to tell them the whole story. It was after this that Beatty felt he could not count on Room 40 giving him warning before an attack on Scandinavian convoys.

The threat of a successful German raid in force against the Scandinavian convoys, and with it the possible mopping up of a covering squadron of heavy ships, remained, since intelligence could not be relied on absolutely and the naval authorities would not keep the whole battle fleet constantly at sea. The risks imposed by mines and torpedoes appeared to make such a strategy too dangerous. It was perhaps fortunate for the Navy that Scheer did not attempt another raid on the convoys.

Scheer's April sortie was the last time in which the two main fleets were engaged, even if no shots were exchanged. The next time the High Seas Fleet steamed into the North Sea was on 21 November 1918.

5. INVASION AND OTHER BOGIES

The failure of the High Seas Fleet sortie to achieve anything did not lessen Admiralty and Grand Fleet concern over other possible German naval moves. The Plans Division now thought a raid might take the form of an attempt to put one or more battle cruisers into the Atlantic. To counter this they proposed battleship escorts for the Atlantic convoys. The D.C.N.S. would not accept

43 Vice-Admiral James's letter (he was then D.C.N.S.) to Admiral of the Fleet Sir Ernle Chatfield (First Sea Lord), 12 March 1936; Chatfield MSS.

the solution. He did not regard the eventuality as a very probable one. He was, besides, 'strongly of the opinion that, (1) since the departure and return of a raiding battle cruiser will probably be supported by the High Seas Fleet, no diversion of strength from the Grand Fleet is permissible for the purpose of hunting a raider that is already out. (2) The way to reduce losses to the convoy is not by endeavouring to protect them all against heavy ships, but by measures which will prevent the enemy from finding them. (3) If a battle cruiser is at sea unlocated, after the maximum period her own fuel endurance permits of, it will be time to consider battleship escorts.' That is, the assumption would be that she was accompanied by a collier.[44]

For a time in May the Admiralty had to deal with a possible German landing of arms and men in Ireland—a small force in one or two fast transports. The originator of this fear appears to have been the Imperial General Staff. Again the D.C.N.S. refused to get worked up. 'The landing of such a force in England would constitute a raid, which the Navy cannot prevent, and which would be dealt with by the Army, but it is possible that in Ireland the effect of such a landing would be sufficiently important to justify the dispatch of a cruiser force to endeavour to intercept the transports, although it could never be guaranteed that such interception is possible.'[45]

At the end of April and into May, the Admiralty and Dover Command experienced a first-class scare when the German offensive in France for a while posed a threat to the French Channel ports. The General Staff claimed (23 April) that if the Allies were faced with the alternative of separation (of the British from the French Armies) or loss of the Channel ports, 'the loss of the ports is the lesser evil, and in the last resort must be accepted, preparation being made to destroy them and to press on with the construction of long range guns to keep them under fire from England.'[46] Acting on a directive from the General Staff, Haig began preparations for abandoning Dunkirk, Calais, and Boulogne, should this become necessary. The loss of the ports, as Wemyss and

[44] Plans Division, 'Proposals for Measures to be Taken If Enemy Battle Cruisers Enter the Atlantic,' and Fremantle's minute of 29 April 1918; Fremantle MSS.
[45] Fremantle, 'Possibility of a Landing in Ireland,' 11 May 1918; Fremantle MSS.
[46] Quoted in Lieutenant-Colonel L. S. T. Halliday, Plans Division, to Fuller, 24 April 1918; Admiralty MSS.

Keyes viewed the matter, would be a disaster, as it would then be impossible to maintain the Dover Barrage. The minefield would no longer be safe; it could be turned on the French coast, and enemy destroyers would play havoc with the patrol vessels. The larger consequence would be the inability to protect the cross-Channel traffic or the trade that passed through the Channel. The First Sea Lord warned the politicians that 'if Calais fell, he would be sorry to say what might happen to our anti-submarine campaign.'[47] He repeated his views before a very secret conference of the Supreme War Council at Abbeville on 2 May: 'In the event of the loss of Calais and Boulogne, it was certain for us that the war was lost at sea, because the whole of our strategy at sea depended on the Channel patrols. They were the key of our transport and of our anti-submarine warfare. But for the Channel patrols the enemy would be able to attack our transports in the Channel, and the trade of London could not be maintained as at present. If we lost the Channel ports the naval war would have to be fought under very bad conditions.' Admiral de Bon, the Chief of the French Naval Staff, supported him. Foch assured the Admirals that he realized the situation and did not contemplate the evacuation of the ports: 'it would never come to that.'[48] Beatty urged Wemyss to be firm. The 'uncovering of the Channel Ports would indeed be a disaster of the greatest magnitude.'[49] The pivotal Amiens position held and the dreaded contingency did not arise.

There was a renewed and final invasion scare in the spring. We must turn the calendar back. An extraordinary fear of invasion continuing to obsess many people, in August 1916 a joint Service committee had re-examined the invasion problem. Practically the same conclusions were reached as in January 1916[50] and were approved by the War Cabinet. Since it was agreed that the Germans had the transport to move 160,000 men, and that they might in future be able to spare that number (the Somme, Verdun, and Eastern Front operations made it impossible then to assemble sufficient troops for an invasion), and since the Navy would not, any more than before, guarantee to prevent this

[47] W.C. 401A, 30 April 1918.
[48] I.C.-56.
[49] Beatty to Wemyss, 5 May 1918; Wemyss MSS.
[50] See *From the Dreadnought to Scapa Flow*, ii. 409.

raiding force from crossing the sea, the Army had to be prepared to meet it.[51]

At the request of the War Cabinet the two Services reviewed the invasion problem once more on 16 March 1917. This was the result of an alarmist letter from Lord Fisher to Lloyd George, asserting it as his 'decided and considered opinion' that the Germans contemplated invasion in the near future with a half million troops, and that invasion was now feasible because of the great production of 'long-distance' submarines.[52] The review also stemmed from the desire of the War Office to strengthen the armies in France, which was possible only if the Admiralty could give assurances respecting the transport of enemy troops across the North Sea. At the joint meeting the Imperial General Staff estimated that the Germans had 160,000 men to spare for an invasion attempt; this force could be disembarked within thirty-six hours of arrival of the transports off the coast. The Admiralty believed that the Germans had sufficient tonnage to transport 160,000 men, but that the probability was remote, as the risks involved were very great. Again the admirals would make no guarantees.[53]

The Admiralty did not regard an invasion attempt as more probable or more practicable in 1917 than at any earlier time in the war. They would not admit, however, that, so long as the High Seas Fleet was undefeated, an attempt was out of the question or that its prospect of success was nil, because of the distance of the main portion of the Grand Fleet (Scapa Flow) from the region where an invasion force might land. Moreover, raids were always possible and difficult to defend against. *There* was the real problem.

The invasion discussion again raised the question of the way in which the Grand Fleet would be used in the event of a German attempt. The Admiralty did not clearly define that strategy. It appeared to Beatty that it was their intention to order the fleet south at full speed by the shortest route to interfere with the

---

[51] 'Report of a Conference between Representatives of the Admiralty War Staff and the General Staff Held to Consider the Possibilities of Attack on the United Kingdom,' 9 August 1916; Admiralty MSS.

[52] Letter of 14 March 1917; Arthur J. Marder, *Fear God and Dread Nought: the Correspondence of Admiral of the Fleet Lord Fisher of Kilverstone* (London, 1952–9, 3 vols.), iii. 438–9.

[53] 'Report of Joint Admiralty and War Office Conference on Invasion' (G.T.-217), 20 March 1917.

invasion. This would have been in accordance with the Admiralty decision of 23 September 1916, which stated that the Grand Fleet would not move south unless there was an attempt at invasion or a really good opportunity to bring the High Seas Fleet to action in daylight.[54] The prospect did not please the C.-in-C., as he informed the Admiralty.

This allows the enemy at any time to decide on a fleet action on the ground of his own choosing, in mined waters, and under conditions of the greatest disadvantage to the British Fleet; that is to say the policy gives the enemy the entire initiative. The experience of the 19th August, 1916 is an indication of the possible disastrous consequences of such strategy.

It is considered the Grand Fleet should move always with the object of cutting off and destroying the German High Sea Fleet the movement being such as to ensure as far as possible the action taking place in the northern half of the North Sea and in waters which the enemy will have been unable to prepare.

Any attempted invasion should be met by the Military Authorities, and it should be made clear at the earliest possible moment that the Grand Fleet does not deal with the actual operation of invasion.[55]

And once more round the course in December 1917, when a joint Service conference met to thrash out the invasion problem. It was held on Admiralty initiative after the Army had indicated a desire to take more men from Home defence for France. Having regard to such new and favourable factors as America's entry into the war, which had increased British naval resources, the extension of British minefields in the Heligoland Bight, the extension of submarine patrols, and the development of air reconnaissance, the Conference reached these conclusions (17 December): 'The difficulties of assembling and moving the number of ships required to transport 160,000 men within the time which would be at the enemy's disposal are so great as to be practically insuperable'; no absolute guarantee could be given against the arrival of *one* convoy —maximum size, 32 ships, carrying 30,000 troops. It would be impossible for subsequent convoys to reach British shores without a naval action such 'as would ensure the complete failure of the expedition.' The maximum force with which the Army might

54 See *From the Dreadnought to Scapa Flow*, iii. 252.
55 Bellairs (for Beatty), 'Notes for Conference,' 14 April 1917; Bellairs MSS. There is no record of the Admiralty's response.

have to deal was, therefore, 30,000. 'The experience at Gallipoli when the naval conditions were exceptionally favourable has shown the very limited effect of naval gunfire upon entrenchments, and demonstrated the impossibility of effecting a landing on an open beach, which is adequately protected with barbed wire and covered by fire from the land from well sited and suitably arranged entrenchments.'[56] The main result of the Conference, as concerns the Navy, was that it had undertaken to deal with any force larger than 30,000.

Wemyss (Deputy First Sea Lord) had been the principal Admiralty spokesman at the Conference. He outlined his position to the C.-in-C.:

Had we such a preponderance of force, and were matters all over the world going so smoothly with us that we could look with complacency upon the retention in England of four Divisions to meet an invasion, I would not be so insistent on my point of view as I am now; but the fact remains that the War Cabinet do wish to move troops from England to France, and they wish it very urgently; and I feel that, under these circumstances, the Admiralty should rise to the occasion and accept a risk which otherwise they need not take. But then, as I honestly believe, the risk is so small, I feel that it is not doing very much to rise to it and accept the views of the Committee, which would help the military authorities.[57]

Beatty agreed that the risk of invasion was 'extremely small,' indeed, 'incredible,' and he believed the War Cabinet would be justified in accepting it.

The effect of the Conference conclusions, if accepted by the War Cabinet, would have been to release a few divisions to reinforce the Army in France. But the First Sea Lord, Jellicoe, was unhappy with the 30,000 figure. It was too low; the Navy would not guarantee its ability to block a landing of up to 70,000 enemy troops. He did not see how they could calculate with precision the number of transports the Germans might bring over in a single convoy. The Grand Fleet could not be certain of preventing even *one* convoy of transports reaching British shores. Behind Jellicoe's

56 'Report of a Conference between Representatives of the Admiralty War Staff and the General Staff, Held to Consider the Possibilities of Attack on the United Kingdom, December, 1917'; Admiralty MSS.
57 Wemyss to Beatty, 21 December 1917; Beatty MSS.

calculations was this consideration: 'I do not minimise the difficulties of the operations to the Germans, but I am of the opinion that if we take upon ourselves the responsibility of saying that a force of not more than 30,000 can be landed in this country, we shall hamper our own operations, because we shall feel it necessary to make naval dispositions against invasion, at the expense of other naval operations, on the least hint of danger.' Better air defences, improved beach defences, more submarines for patrol, etc. made it possible to return to the pre-war figure of 70,000.[58]

Jellicoe left the Admiralty on Christmas Day. The Board of Admiralty recommended (27 December) that an Admiralty–War Office opinion on the Conference report be prepared and presented to the War Cabinet. This took the form of a joint report by the First Sea Lord and the C.I.G.S. that endorsed Jellicoe's essential point. The two Services were 'of opinion that though the Admiralty are unable to give an absolute guarantee that a force of 160,000 cannot be transported to these shores, still the risk of invasion by a force of 160,000 men, taking the naval and military difficulties of such an operation together into consideration, is so small as to justify them in advising the War Cabinet to accept it.' The report recognized that a raid, as distinct from invasion, was the danger to be guarded against, and here the Navy undertook to defeat any invasion attempt made by a force of 70,000 men, leaving the primary responsibility for coping with raids below that figure to the military.[59] The Admiralty approved the report on 10 January 1918, as did the War Office. Already the War Cabinet had decided 'to take the risk of reducing the forces allocated to Home Defence to such strength as would deter an enemy force up to 30,000 men from attempting a landing in this country,' and they authorized the reduction in the strength of the Home Defence force recommended in a memorandum by Robertson: a reduction from eight to five divisions, leaving a mobile force of 152,000 as compared with the existing 190,045.[60]

There was a last flurry of invasion jitters in the spring of 1918.

---

[58] Jellicoe's minute of 20 December 1917; Admiralty MSS. He enunciated the same position to the War Cabinet (W.C. 304, 21 December) as a 'provisional' decision of the Board of Admiralty.

[59] 'Possibilities of Attack on the United Kingdom,' signed by Wemyss on 31 December and by Robertson on 2 January; Appendix B to G.T.-3212 (see following footnote).

[60] W.C. 316A, 7 January 1918. Robertson's memorandum was 'Troops Required for Home Defence' (G.T.-3212), 3 January 1918.

One factor was the German diplomatic pressure on Holland which might 'be designed to place Germany in a position to pick a quarrel and so obtain possession of the Mouths of the Scheldt when it suited her. It was suggested that, if Germany had occupied both the Eastern side of the Channel and Holland, the question of invasion would require very careful consideration.'[61] The idea now was that the Germans might try to land 100,000 men on the East Coast as 'a last desperate venture.' For this reason the War Office continued to hold back the sizeable forces they still maintained for protection against invasion. The Admiralty saw no necessity for this. The D.C.N.S. has written of the episode: 'The

[61] W.C. 401A, 30 April 1918. The Naval Staff, as well as the Allied Naval Council, continued to weigh the pros and cons of Holland entering the war, invariably concluding that the continued neutrality of Holland was desirable. The necessity for supplying coal, artillery, munitions, men, and provisions to a fresh ally would cause a serious drain in tonnage; the possession by the enemy of bases on either side of the line of communication would lead to heavy losses of shipping; and unless the Dutch were prepared and able to hold Walcheren and Zeeland, one of the first results would be the German seizure of the Scheldt. These disadvantages, it was felt, more than counter-balanced the gain to the Allies of the use of the Helder and the Hook of Holland as naval bases for light forces operating in the Heligoland Bight and on the Belgian coast. It would be a different matter if Dutch neutrality were violated by Germany. The Admiralty and War Office were in agreement that the 'principal British interest was to maintain the Dutch possession of Walcheren, with a view to the denial to the enemy of the passage of the Scheldt,' but that no practical measures in the way of plans would be taken 'in the absence of information as to what prospect the Dutch themselves had of defending Walcheren against a surprise attack from the left bank.' Fremantle's minute of 17 May 1918 on a recent conference held with the D.C.I.G.S. and D.M.I.; Fremantle MSS. This, of course, involving as it did some co-ordination of the Allied and Dutch military effort, opened up a larger issue. Matters proceeded to the point where, on 6 August, a high-level inter-Service conference met with the Dutch Military Attaché at the Admiralty 'to consider a system of co-operation between the Dutch and British Navies in the Event of Great Britain coming to the assistance of Holland.' Apparently little more than the principle of co-operation was established. The final step was taken by the War Cabinet (W.C. 486) on 15 October, when it authorized the Naval and General Staffs to work out with the Dutch military authorities the details of a scheme of co-operation, in the event of a German attack, by means of which 'as many divisions as the military situation might require could be transported and landed in some port to be agreed upon in Holland.' These troops would be used to reinforce the Dutch Army, since the Dutch now considered they could deal with the question of Walcheren themselves. On 28 October representatives of the two Staffs met to consider the arrangements for placing troops in Holland if the Germans violated her neutrality. Briefly, two divisions in France would be embarked for a Dutch port, probably Rotterdam, at Dunkirk. They did not expect the Germans to move into Holland 'unless absolutely forced to do so, since it would eventually uncover the whole of their right flank.' The war ended two weeks later without the occasion for dispatching troops arising.

Admiralty and the War Office were called upon to report on this subject, and we informed the War Cabinet, after a joint Staff meeting, that, far from existing circumstances having rendered such a raid practicable and probable, the contrary was, in our opinion, the case, and that the worst that might be experienced was a small raid by a force of 5,000 men with some specific objective.'[62] The Army now released most of the men for France, keeping at home only a small mobile force sufficient to deal with a raid.

When the War Office, disturbed over the situation on the Western Front and anxious to strip Home defence further, tried to reopen the question on 12 June, the Admiralty showed no interest: no new factors from a naval point of view had arisen since the joint conference of December 1917 to justify another one.

The whole invasion question during the war was a mare's nest, and it is difficult to understand, let alone to try to justify, the countless precious hours invested in the discussion of invasion possibilities. As the C.I.G.S., Robertson, said long afterwards, the possibility was 'always much too remote to justify the attention which it received.' Yet it was the War Office, with frequent assistance from the press, which had been the chief fomenters of the scares.

[62] Fremantle, *My Naval Career*, p. 256.

VII

The Final Reckoning

(July 1918 – November 1918)

(*Chart 1*)

And we have got to have the H.S.F. either by surrender or as a result of Fleet Action. There are no two Naval opinions on this point in the Grand Fleet which opinions you will admit should carry weight.

BEATTY to Wemyss, 2 October 1918.

There was a marked disposition on the part of the Commander in Chief and his Staff to regard the climax [the Armistice] as unworthy. They had looked for a Trafalgar—for a defeat of the German Fleet in which they would have played a prominent and proud part. What they got was a victory far more crushing than any Trafalgar and with none of its attendant losses on our part— but also without any of the personal glory which would have been attached to the survivors. It was . . . a frame of mind which can readily be understood . . .

WEMYSS, unpublished memoirs.

The surrender of the German Fleet, was to many of us a highly painful if dramatic event. To see the great battleships come into sight, their guns trained fore and aft; the battle-cruisers, which we had twice met under such very different circumstances, creeping towards us as it were with their tails between their legs, gave one a real feeling of disgust. . . . Surely the spirit of all past seamen must be writhing in dismay over this tragedy, this disgrace to all maritime traditions.

CHATFIELD, *The Navy and Defence*.

I wish I had not been born a German. This despicable act will remain a blot on Germany's good name forever. . . . Although our army is still much respected by foreigners, the actions of our High Seas Fleet will live on with shame in history.

SEAMAN RICHARD STUMPF, of the dreadnought *Helgoland*, diary, 24 November 1918.

I. THE BEGINNING OF THE END

WITH the shell situation rectified by the summer, and the destroyer situation improved, Beatty was more disposed to seek out the enemy fleet. The old problem remained— how to get the German Fleet well out into the North Sea. A letter of the early summer captures his mood:

Our only role is to safeguard our weak points [see below] and harass him in his own waters all we can, and this we are doing. Tempt him, if possible, but at a considerable risk. Sooner or later he may make a false move. He has made two already and may make a third one. In the meantime we must exercise that patience which is so terribly hard and unsatisfactory. But we must remember that the same problem obtained in the old wars. There is a parallel for nearly every case, and they in the end reaped their reward [Trafalgar], and so I believe we shall reap ours . . . The submarine is still a thorn, a very unpleasant one too, but he is not the danger he was, and the Country is better off for food to-day than it has been for $1\frac{1}{2}$ years, and the American troops are pouring in uninterruptedly and in growing numbers. So on the whole we have much to be thankful for.[1]

It was thought that Scheer's relief of von Holtzendorff as Chief of the Admiralty Staff on 11 August indicated a change in German naval policy, since Scheer was supposed to favour a more active line of naval strategy. (Hipper succeeded Scheer as C.-in-C., High Seas Fleet.) There was an air of expectancy in British naval circles. The leading Service organ, the *Naval and Military Record* (21 August), expected another grand-scale tilt at the British Fleet: 'The eyes of many are now turned towards the North Sea, where, unless circumstantial evidence counts for nothing, we shall shortly witness the most thrilling events of the naval campaign.' Wemyss saw it this way in a letter that initiated an interesting exchange of views with the C.-in-C.:

It will be as well to presume that the changes of personnel at the German Admiralty will carry with them a change of policy. What that change of policy will be is difficult to foretell.

I have always maintained, and I see no reason for altering my opinion, that it is only psychology which will bring the German Fleet out with the idea of engaging our forces, and it is difficult to believe that Von Scheer would ever willingly seek an engagement. On the other hand, he may initiate more activity in surface raids, etc., and in combination with this, possibly more activity in mining. . . .

There is, of course, the possibility of their concentrating all their mining efforts in one area to be used in combination with a raid on the Coast. This, of course, is no new problem either to you or to me, and I do not think that there is any new move to be made by us in this direction.

[1] Beatty to Lady Beatty, 2 July 1918; Beatty MSS.

None of the foregoing really indicates any change of policy, though possibly it may indicate greater activity.[2]

Beatty replied that the 'Danger points' were unchanged: the Atlantic convoys (against which the enemy might think it worth while to send battleships or battle cruisers to assist the U-boats), the East Coast and Scandinavian convoys, an attack on the Dover Patrol or raid on the Channel ports, and raids on the East Coast. However, he considered the most probable activities to be mining by enemy surface vessels in the vicinity of the main British bases, especially as the nights got longer, an attempt to bring to action the light-cruiser squadrons when on distant sweeps, and interference with minelaying operations. The first was the most likely form of greater activity; but what exercised the C.-in-C. most was a raid on the Northern Barrage:

In the past we baited the trap with Forces varying from a Battle Squadron to a Light Cruiser Squadron, the trap being the Convoy. We took considerable risks with our eyes open in the hope of achieving a great success, and as you know, we all but brought it off on the 25th April 1918.

With the laying of the Barrage and the Convoy passing to the North of it, the same trap does not exist; but the laying of the Barrage itself provides the trap, and the supporting force the bait. You can realise therefore that the strength and composition of the Supporting Force provides me with plenty of anxious moments. The new German Command may deal more actively with the problem, and we have anxious times in front.

Anxiety will, however, be well repaid, if when a chance comes, our Intelligence Department can tell us a little more than last time, and our Outposts, i.e. the submarine on Patrol, do not again fail us.[3]

Wemyss did not think the enemy would try to intercept the minelayers working on the Northern Barrage, because he 'will have nothing like the same chances of obtaining information of their movements as he has in the case of the Scandinavian Convoys; the speed of the minelayers is much greater, and he will probably imagine that the laying of the fields commenced at the Southern limits and that to reach the minelayers he would have to pass over mines already laid. The question of Intelligence was carefully gone into after the events of the 28th [*sic*] April, and

2 Wemyss to Beatty, 6 August 1918; Wemyss MSS.
3 Beatty to Wemyss, 10 August 1918; Wemyss MSS.

though the organisation has been improved in minor respects since then, we must not anticipate that any greater degree of warning can be relied on.' He agreed with the C.-in-C. that mining by surface vessels was the most likely form of greater German naval activity, 'and unless we can get early information from our submarines, the chance of bringing vessels like the [fast mine-laying light cruisers] *Brummer* and *Bremse* to action is a very remote one.'⁴

Rumours of unrest in the German Navy at Kiel, so serious as to necessitate the Emperor's presence, raised Beatty's hopes. 'If here is real discontent, the best way to kill it is to send them to sea. On the other hand if there is no discontent, the advent of the Kaiser may be the preliminary to an undertaking by the Naval Forces . . .' He was realistic enough to admit that 'generally speaking the prospects are poor. It is terrible to think that after all these weary months of waiting we shall not have an opportunity of striking a blow.' Then, on a hopeful note, he reminded himself of the advance of the Allied forces in France. This might result in the clearing of the Flanders bases, which 'might cause Naval movement, hence I may return south at any moment.'⁵ Wemyss would not encourage Beatty's hopes: 'I wish I could think that these military successes are a prelude to naval action, but I cannot honestly believe that they are . . .'⁶ All that was happening, he believed, was that the Germans were beginning to move their Flanders destroyers to North Sea bases. Wemyss kept the Grand Fleet in the north: they had ample forces in the south to deal with

---

4 Wemyss to Beatty, 15 August 1918; Wemyss MSS. Wemyss considered that the laying of the Northern Barrage had reduced the danger to the Atlantic, as well as the Scandinavian, convoys of a raid by heavy ships. And the laying of the East Coast minefields was improving the situation as regards protection of those convoys. Nor did he think the enemy would attack the Dover Patrol or raid the Channel ports: they could hope for no more than 'a temporary dislocation of our communications.' Raids on the East coast to tie down troops in England were possible. On 19 September the Admiralty approved certain dispositions in Home waters for meeting a raid on the East or South coast with a stronger force than could be opposed to the enemy until the Grand Fleet had time to intervene. As a precaution against a battle-cruiser raid in the North Atlantic, the Admiralty and United States Navy Department worked out a plan of action in September. Its main feature was that an American dreadnought would be dispatched (from a pool of three established at Berehaven or from the four made available at an American Atlantic port) to reinforce each convoy upon receipt of intelligence that a raid was probable. The plan envisaged a raid on the American troop convoys in particular.

5 Beatty to Lady Beatty, (late) September 1918; Chalmers, *Beatty*, pp. 326–7.

6 Wemyss to Beatty, 2 October 1918; Wemyss MSS.

the destroyers—that is, attempt to intercept them; the principal objective of the Grand Fleet was the High Seas Fleet. Wemyss changed his tune when the Germans, on 5 October, asked for an armistice. 'Events are moving rapidly . . . we have arrived at a moment when either the war collapses or when the most likely psychological moment, if ever, has arrived for the High Sea Fleet to make some demonstration.'[7]

Events were indeed moving rapidly. The war in the East was in its last stages. Within days of the opening of an Allied offensive from Salonika on 15 September the Bulgarian Front collapsed; on the 30th the Bulgarians asked for an armistice. In the same month the British Army in Palestine advanced swiftly, and it looked as though Turkey would soon follow the Bulgarian example. The Admiralty, deeming the breakout of the *Goeben* and some of the Black Sea units quite possible, sent the dreadnoughts *Superb* and *Temeraire* out to the Aegean in October. On 20 October the Turks asked for an armistice. Negotiations were opened on the 27th. On the 30th Gough-Calthorpe (refusing to associate the French Admiral with him in this business) signed an Allied armistice with Turkish representatives on board the *Agamemnon* at Mudros. It was one of his finest moments. He displayed, as Admiral Godfrey writes, 'great firmness and diplomatic acumen' in his handling of the negotiations. The Armistice terms, whose essential points had been drawn up by the Supreme War Council, included a provision for the Allied occupation of the Dardanelles and Bosphorus forts. Clearance of the channels through the minefields began at once and was completed by 11 November. The French had wanted command of the naval force that would go up to Constantinople, but the Admiralty was adamant against 'a squadron going up the Dardanelles except under British command.' The argument was that the British naval force in the Aegean was much larger than the French force and had done all the spade work in connection with an attack on the Straits, should that have been necessary. Moreover, the British had borne the brunt of the war against the Turks. The French had to give way and Gough-Calthorpe was chosen for the honour. On 12 November the combined Allied fleet (*Superb*, flagship, *Temeraire*, *Lord Nelson*, *Agamemnon*, 2 French and an Italian battleship, the Greek

---

[7] Wemyss to Beatty, 12 October 1918; Wemyss MSS.

armoured cruiser *Averoff*, 6 British cruisers and 18 destroyers, the carrier *Empress*, and hundreds of auxiliary craft) triumphantly entered the Dardanelles, steamed past the memorable scenes and place names of 1915, and anchored off the Turkish capital the next day.

It is a pity that the plan of this volume does not permit us to go to the end of 1919 or mid-1920 and the evacuation of the Caspian Sea. The little C.-in-C., Gough-Calthorpe, the most modest of men, found himself C.-in-C. not only of the Mediterranean but of a bit of the Atlantic, as far west as Cape St. Vincent, of the Black Sea, Red Sea, Danube, Caspian, and all the rivers flowing into the Black Sea, and High Commissioner of Turkey, issuing orders to Allenby, etc. !

On 29 October the Italians signed an armistice with Austria-Hungary. October also saw the beginning of the end for Germany and the High Seas Fleet. The German lines in France had virtually collapsed by the latter part of September. On 17 October, Ostend, and on 19 October, Zeebrugge, were evacuated by the Germans after being in their occupation for four years. But already, when the Bulgarians quit, the German Military High Command saw the game was up and advised the Emperor to seek an armistice. On 5 October Germany asked President Wilson for the immediate conclusion of an armistice. On 20 October the new Chancellor, Prince Max of Baden, to speed up negotiations, accepted Wilson's demand of 14 October that submarines would no longer attack passenger ships. Scheer had fought hard against acceptance of this condition, as it was tantamount to a complete cessation of U-boat warfare. He would accept this only in return for an armistice, whereas Wilson promised only to start negotiations for an armistice if this preliminary condition were met. 'In so doing we should lay aside our chief weapon, while the enemy could continue hostilities and drag out the negotiations as long as he pleased.'[8] The Government having made the plunge, Scheer ordered (20 October) the recall of all U-boats at sea on operations against merchant shipping ; 17 were affected. The long years of being tied to the U-boat war against merchant shipping were at an end; the U-boats were now at the disposal of the C.-in-C., High Seas Fleet, for action against the Grand Fleet. With their return the High Seas Fleet had the

[8] Admiral Reinhard Scheer, *Germany's High Sea Fleet in the World War* (London, 1920), p. 349.

reconnaissance forces it needed for a bold operation. On the 22nd Captain von Levetzow, Chief of Staff of the Operations Department of the *Admiralstab*, met Hipper at Wilhelmshaven and verbally passed on Scheer's order: 'The Forces of the High Seas Fleet are to be employed to strike a blow against the English Fleet.' Levetzow added that there should be no delay in implementing the order.

Hipper's plan had these main features: (1) the entire High Seas Fleet would leave the Heligoland Bight out of sight of the Dutch coast by day; (2) a night sortie in the Hoofden (the southern part of the North Sea), with attacks on warships in the open sea, and on traffic off the Flanders coast and in the Thames estuary by destroyers and light cruisers, the battle fleet covering the Flanders group, and the battle cruisers, the Thames group; (3) this activity was intended to provoke the Grand Fleet to leave harbour immediately and steam in the direction of the Hoofden; (4) the 4th Scouting Group (light cruisers) and a destroyer flotilla would freely mine, and U-boats would patrol the British approach routes from the east coast of Scotland to Terschelling (the submarines had instructions to use every opportunity to fire torpedoes at battleships and battle cruisers); (5) Hipper intended to bring the enemy forces to action on the night of the second/third day: alternatively, should there be no encounter by that night, the destroyers would carry out an offensive sweep in the direction of the Firth of Forth.[9] Scheer approved the plan on 27 October, and the operation was set for the 30th.

The Admiralty had a pretty good idea of what was going on. Intercepts, reports from the D/F stations fixing the positions of many U-boats in the North Sea which had sailed to take up their assigned stations, the cessation of U-boat attacks on shipping, and extraordinary minesweeping ('more minesweeping has been done within the last 10 days than during the whole of the last 6 weeks,' the D.C.N.S. noted on the 27th) convinced the Admiralty by the 27th that something big was imminent. As early as the 23rd the Admiralty warned Beatty that the situation in the North Sea was abnormal. That day they ordered destroyers from Plymouth and Buncrana to reinforce Grand Fleet flotillas. Fremantle's opinion was that 'there is more likelihood of a Fleet movement of some

9 *Der Krieg in der Nordsee*, vii. 344–5.

description now than there has been at any time this year. . . . History impresses on us the tendency in the closing period of a war for public and Military opinion, uneducated in naval warfare, to force out an inferior Fleet (Villeneuve, Cervera, Rodjestvensky). The enemy must realise that some, at any rate, of his Fleet will be demanded of him in the armistice and peace terms and may think that they may as well try to inflict some losses on us before they lose the power altogether of doing so . . .'[10] On the eve of the operation the D.C.N.S. reported: '. . . it seems now absolutely clear that the enemy wishes you to come out to the Southward over a submarine trap.' He thought the High Seas Fleet would come outside their minefields, make W/T signals for a few hours, then return to their base.[11] On one point only was the Admiralty appreciation in error. They were sure that the enemy would not risk a fleet action while armistice negotiations were in progress. 'Actually,' as Newbolt says, 'Admirals von Hipper and Scheer were striving with the greatest energy to provoke a fleet action whilst the negotiations were proceeding; they were planning a stroke similar in its objects to the Dutch attack upon the Medway [1667], which so much affected the negotiations at Breda, at the end of the second Dutch war.' There is more to it.

The German plan miscarried and the fleet never left port. The assembly of the High Seas Fleet in Schillig Roads, outside Wilhelmshaven, was ordered for the afternoon of 29 October. As was usual, the operation was disguised under the pretext of manœuvres and evolutions, to be carried out on the 30th. The assembly of the fleet sparked off insubordination and considerable unrest on the 29th and during the night of the 29th–30th among the crews. The trouble was confined mainly to the larger ships, leaving the smaller ships—minesweepers, submarines, and destroyers—entirely unaffected. A large number of men, mainly stokers, from the battle cruisers *Derfflinger* and *Von der Tann* failed to report back from shore leave on the 29th and had to be rounded

[10] Fremantle to Beatty, 27 October 1918; Beatty MSS.
[11] Fremantle to Beatty, 29 October 1918; Beatty MSS. The D.N.I. thought an attack on Rosyth more likely—by net-breakers with submarines to follow them. *Ibid.* If the Germans had come out, what would the Grand Fleet have done? There is no record of Beatty's intentions, but I am certain he would have moved as soon as the High Seas Fleet was reported at sea. The reinforcement of Grand Fleet flotillas points in that direction. The prudent outlook of January was no longer operative by October.

up and brought back that evening. Mutiny in various forms and degrees occurred in the 3rd Squadron dreadnoughts *König, Kronprinz Wilhelm,* and *Markgraf* (where the crew assembled on the forecastle, creating a din, and shouting cheers for peace and for Wilson), and insubordination in the dreadnoughts *Thüringen, Kaiserin,* and *Helgoland*; a similar incident was reported in the light cruiser *Regensburg* in Cuxhaven, and there was confirmation that the mood of the dreadnought *Baden*'s crew was dangerous. 'The prevailing thought was that the fleet was putting to sea to seek a glorious end off the English coast.'[12] Or as Scheer phrased it afterwards, 'the idea had taken root in their minds that they were to be needlessly sacrificed.'

This fear was not without foundation. Note this entry by von Trotha in the war diary of the High Seas Fleet for 6 October, which, says the German Official History, 'vividly sets out the C.-in-C. Fleet's assessment of the situation at that critical time': 'If our people do not fail as a nation, an honourable battle by the fleet—even if it should be a fight to the death—will sow the seed of a new German fleet of the future. There can be no future for a fleet fettered by a dishonourable peace.'[13] Scheer himself stated on 16 October what he wanted to accomplish through an attack by the Fleet: 'It is impossible for the Fleet to remain inactive in any final battle that may sooner or later precede an armistice. The Fleet must be committed. Even if it is not to be expected that this would decisively influence the course of events, it is still, from the moral point of view, a question of the honour and existence of the Navy to have done its utmost in the last battle.'[14] This was the inner reason for the intended attack, now made possible by the recall of the submarines. But the operation was to be something more than a 'death ride' of the High Seas Fleet. There was the vague hope (one sees it expressed in the points formulated by Scheer as his views on the Wilson note of 14 October)[15] that a tactical success would bring about a reversal of the military position

12 From the report by Hipper's C.O.S., Rear-Admiral von Trotha, prepared for Hipper and delivered to him after the November Revolution; Levetzow MSS., in the German Ministry of Marine MSS.
13 *Der Krieg in der Nordsee,* vii. 341. Von Trotha expressed the same thought, this time his own, in a letter to Levetzow, 10 October 1918; Levetzow MSS.
14 *Der Krieg in der Nordsee,* vii. 336. Other authorities give the date as 25 October.
15 Commander Friedrich Fortsmeier, 'Zum Bild der Persönlichkeit des Admirals Reinhard Scheer (1863–1928),' *Marine-Rundschau,* April 1961.

and avert surrender. There was also the hope that a success would, at the least, exert a strong influence on the Armistice terms. The sailors, however, regarded the intended operation rather as a deliberate attempt to sabotage the negotiations for an end to a war already lost. A distinguished German historian writes:

> Could they possibly believe that the attack would have a favorable effect on the outcome of the war? Every German seaman knew the superiority of the British fleet and could reckon on the fingers of his hands that it would still be a grand fleet even if each German ship were to take an English vessel with it as it sunk. Did it not seem more likely that the officers were simply seeking that 'death with honor' which their naval code insisted upon? But did this code give the officers the right to drag to their death thousands of good sailors, men who for years had suffered the miserable life afloat and who now waited only for the day that was to mean freedom and home?[16]

Grasping the situation quickly, Hipper called off the operation on 30 October and detached the various squadrons, the 3rd Squadron being sent to the Baltic. It reached Kiel on 1 November; disturbances broke out there that evening and spread. By 4 November the red flag of revolution was flying at all the naval ports.

We may best conclude this sorry episode with the conclusions von Trotha reached at the time on 'how this collapse could occur and how such a rift could arise between officers and men':

> There appears to be ample proof that our armed forces were unable to withstand such a long war, as soon as the moral boost of success was missing and particularly when want and deprivation were presenting the home front with such a prodigious struggle. The unceasing depletion in the front-line ranks, of youthful enthusiasm and ability in officers and men; their replacement by older age groups already burdened by home worries, or by the very young and inexperienced age-groups, already influenced by the eroding effects of the struggle on the home-front—this endless and inevitable trend created an unsound foundation and provided the essential ingredients for discontent.
>
> In spite of its much lighter losses, this process wormed its way into the navy too. The creation of countless small units extended the officer corps to the very limit. Then the U-boat war with its enormous demands took away all the ablest officers and, as with the army, the considerable

---

16 Erich Eyck, *A History of the Weimar Republic* (Cambridge, Mass., 1962–3, 2 vols.), i. 41–2.

losses created an ever-widening gap in the middle ranks of the officer corps, which, in turn reacted adversely on the large ships. In fact, it might be said that on the battleships, one had difficulty in finding a really capable officer of middle rank who was still fit for U-boat service. Thus we were denuded of the type of officer with just those qualities essential for good relations between officers and men, and it was felt all the more acutely when even the senior officers were no longer available. We lacked the rising young officers from whom to select the right people for the top posts. It was this sort of foundation that had to bear the effects that the long war had had on the crews.

At the time of mobilisation, our reserves had enthusiastically put aside all their personal considerations in order to join up. At that time everything stemmed from patriotism. Later in the war other considerations crept in. Men became more and more sensitive to the change in the mode of living and loss of independence. Home worries, age, getting accustomed to service life, having to accept orders, etc., all weighed more and more heavily and had to be endured. Active service officers became ever scarcer and very often when such an officer was in command, his subordinates became younger and younger and lacked the proper training which would have enabled them to gain the trust of their commanding officer.

The same conditions prevailed in the N.C.O. corps too. Its influence on the older age-groups steadily declined until it was no longer dependable. Personal failings as well as blunders by individuals were very much to blame.

All these factors served to create the rift which now faces us. And it was natural that the chasm should open more fiercely at that point where there was no direct influence of the battle and where the antagonisms that arose were the most acute—that is, here in the battleships.[17]

It was not until about 6 or 7 November that the Admiralty knew of the extent of the mutiny and could be certain there would be no sortie of the Fleet. Meanwhile, the Allied naval authorities were working on the details of a naval armistice.

2. THE NAVAL ARMISTICE

Admiralty discussion of armistice terms slumbered until October 1918. They made it clear in the spring that 'from a naval point of

---

[17] See footnote 12, above. This is only half the story, and the lesser half at that. See below, p. 333.

view, an Armistice would be all to the advantage of the Central Powers.' 'The fundamental principle of the utilisation of superior sea power is the exercise of unremitting pressure, the suspension even for a week of this pressure would be to our disadvantage. Even if an armistice is forced by public opinion (which we should strive to prevent by every means in our power) it should not be allowed to affect sea warfare.'[18] This position was no longer realistic by October. Matters moved towards a climax from 8 October, the day the Allied Naval Council and the Military Representatives of the Supreme War Council met jointly at Versailles to draw up draft armistice conditions. The Admirals recommended that 60 submarines, 'of types to be specified,' proceed at once to specified Allied ports and remain there for the duration of the Armistice, and that 'all enemy surface ships' proceed to naval bases that would be specified and stay there during the Armistice. It was thought that 60 U-boats was the maximum number which could put to sea, since a large number were at any given moment refitting. Admiral Hope, the Deputy First Sea Lord, had attended without knowledge of the views of the Board.

The mood of the Royal Navy and the Admiralty as the war neared its end was grim. There was 'a feeling of incompleteness,' to quote the First Sea Lord. The Navy had, in a sense, won a victory greater than Trafalgar, but it was less spectacular—there had been no decisive sea battle—and therein lay the rub. Under the circumstances, Beatty and the Grand Fleet could muster little zeal for an armistice that preceded a Trafalgar. This was needful to salve British naval honour and to bring glory to the C.-in-C. and the whole Fleet. The Senior Service also felt aggrieved that the soldiers should have polished off the Kaiser without the Navy having its share of the fighting. If there *had to be* an armistice, the Navy insisted that the surrender of the fighting ships of the German Navy be a *sine qua non*. The D.C.N.S. afterwards put it this way: 'We at the Admiralty considered that, as the German Navy had never (except at Jutland) dealt with us in fair fight, it was reasonable that we should not be baulked of our prey and that we were entitled to claim the surrender of the whole of their

---

[18] Admiralty memorandum to Foreign Office, attached to D.N.I. (Rear-Admiral W. R. Hall) to Sir William Tyrrell (Head of the Political Intelligence Department of the Foreign Office), 15 April 1918; Admiralty MSS.

fighting ships.'[19] Keyes spoke for a not insignificant portion of naval opinion when he expressed the hope that the naval armistice terms 'will be so goading that the enemy's Army and Fleet will have no choice but to fight it out.'[20]

On the other hand, Wemyss could, no more than the politicians, or the generals in France, contemplate the prospect of a fifth winter of war. He was, in particular, disturbed by reports of the serious discontent among the British seamen.[21] In mid-October, as British naval terms of armistice were being drawn up, we hear of Wemyss 'endeavouring to moderate the zeal of violent Sea Lords.' Some of the Members of the Board thought the question of occupying Kiel and the Kiel Canal should be considered. On 14 and 16 October the Board considered the question of the surrender of the *whole* German Fleet, 'but it was turned down for various reasons, the principal one of which is that there would be so much contention about it'.[22]

The Navy's views on the naval conditions for an Armistice were made known to the War Cabinet on 19 and 21 October.[23] They differed from those of the Allied Naval Council, but were identical to Beatty's views, except in one important respect: the Admiralty also considered that the blockade should continue. The C.-in-C. had discussed them with the senior flag officers of the battle squadrons and had won their emphatic support. The conditions were these: the *surrender* to the Allies of two of Germany's three battle squadrons, the 3rd and 4th, containing the newest battleships (10), also the fleet flagship, the *Baden*, all six battle cruisers (the list included the *Mackensen*, which was thought to have been completed), 8 light cruisers, which were specified, 50 of the most modern destroyers, and *all* the submarines afloat. Wemyss explained the Admiralty position with regard to the submarines—that they were on a different plane from surface craft: 'The Submarine war has been carried on by the Enemy in contempt of the rules of International Law and of the dictates of humanity. In the interests, therefore, of International morality,

---

[19] Fremantle, *My Naval Career*, p. 259.
[20] Keyes to Beatty, 13 October 1918; Beatty MSS.
[21] See below, pp. 212–14.
[22] Wemyss to Beatty, 16 October 1918; Wemyss MSS.
[23] Admiralty Memorandum for the War Cabinet (signed by Wemyss), 'Naval Conditions of Armistice' (G. T.-6042), 19 October; X-29, 19 October; and W.C. 489A, 21 October. Wemyss spoke at both War Cabinets, Beatty at the second.

the first opportunity should be firmly taken of removing entirely out of his hand the weapon which he has so grossly misused.'[24]

Beatty based his case for the disposal of the German Fleet on two assumptions: (1) Their objective was to destroy Germany's naval and military power, otherwise war might be resumed as soon as the Germans had recovered sufficiently. Germany must be reduced to the status of a second-class naval power in order to secure Britain's position at sea. (2) Like Wemyss, he believed that the Armistice terms must closely approximate what they wanted to obtain in the peace terms, since a resumption of hostilities after an armistice had been declared was not likely.[25]

Beatty explained how he had arrived at the number of dreadnoughts to be handed over. 'If the Grand Fleet should encounter the High Sea Fleet, he hoped and expected to accomplish the entire destruction of the latter, but in achieving this he expected to have heavy losses which he estimated at 8 or 9 capital ships. His proposal was to leave the enemy the equivalent of what we should lose, and to take the remainder.' Furthermore, if they took all Germany's submarines, Germany still could, and probably would, replace them and soon be in a position to resume submarine warfare. Blocking in the U-boats would be out of the question if the enemy retained his 26 capital ships, since his battle fleet was the power behind the submarine warfare.

Only the C.I.G.S., Sir Henry Wilson, supported the Navy's hard line at the War Cabinets on the 19th and 21st. Lloyd George protested that the Navy's terms amounted to 'abject surrender.' They 'could only be accepted by a nation that was beaten to the dust,' and 'pride would overrule reason if the terms were too stiff.'

---

[24] The Board of Admiralty felt very strongly about the absolute necessity of requiring the Germans to surrender their entire submarine fleet as an essential condition of the Armistice terms, so that they would be incapable of resuming the U-boat campaign if the negotiations for a peace broke down. 'Naval Terms of Armistice,' 'Observations and Opinions' of the Second Sea Lord, D.C.N.S., A.C.N.S., Second Civil Lord, and D.N.I., 26 October 1918; Admiralty MSS.

[25] His written statement (see below) phrased the point differently: 'During the Armistice, and in arranging the Terms of Peace, assuming the best will in the world, friction was bound to arise between the Allies, which would be intensified by the action of Germany who would devote every effort to sowing dissension. These factors make it very desirable that the terms of the Armistice should be as nearly as possible the Terms of Peace.' Because the meeting was frequently interrupted, which had handicapped his presentation, Beatty stated his considered views in a memorandum prepared after the meeting and communicated to Hankey on 23 October: 'The Naval Terms of an Armistice' (G.T.-6107).

Haig, who was shocked by the apparent illogic of Beatty's dread-nought demands, reinforced the Prime Minister's fears. He thought 'the effect on the *moral* of the Army, of a very stiff demand on the part of the Allies resulting in a prolongation of the war, would be bad.' Wemyss admitted that the naval terms were so stiff that the Germans were not likely to accept them, but he did not see how they could be reduced, if the Armistice terms were to approximate the peace terms. He and Beatty countered the argument that the Navy was in no position to insist on terms equivalent to the Army's terms because the naval victories had in no way corresponded to the military victories. Declared Wemyss: 'This naval victory was no less real because it was not spectacular, for the Admiralty claimed by their strategy to have imposed their will upon the enemy.' 'It was true,' Beatty admitted, 'that we had obtained no decisive active victory, but we had achieved a passive victory. Because it was passive there was no reason why the nation should give up the object with which it had entered the War, namely, the destruction of German militarism.'[26]

The War Cabinet was anxious that none of the Armistice terms be of a character as to appear unnecessarily to humiliate the enemy. Their position strengthened by the disclosure that President Wilson opposed any excessive naval terms (he might agree to Germany's handing over all her submarines but not to her sur-rendering her large surface ships), the War Cabinet of 26 October would go no further than to approve of this formula as a guide to the Prime Minister and Foreign Secretary in their negotiations in Paris: 'The naval conditions of the armistice should represent the admission of German defeat by sea in the same degree as the military conditions recognise the corresponding admission of German defeat by land.'[27] A weary Wemyss reported to Beatty: 'As you can easily imagine, it has been most difficult to get any satisfactory conclusion out of the War Cabinet. They are always inclined not to come to any strong decision and leave matters in

---

[26] This fuller statement is found in Beatty's paper: 'The Military successes have been great and the Military Terms are commensurate with their achievements. The Navy made them possible and therefore shares in them. The Navy also has won a great Passive Victory, has swept the Enemy from the Seas, and rendered secure the vast lines of communications with our Allies, and permitted the trade of this country, necessary for existence, to continue. Because ours is a Passive Victory, it is no reason why the Empire should not reap the fruits of that victory.'
[27] W.C. 491B.

a nebulous state . . .'[28] In the event, one modification was made in the Beatty–Admiralty proposals: Lloyd George having objected to the word 'all,' Wemyss had fixed on 160 submarines, a number he was sure would give them just about what the Germans had.

The scene now shifted to the meetings (the Sixth Meetings) of the Allied Naval Council, held in Paris and Versailles from 28 October to 4 November, and which discussed the draft terms as proposed by the Admiralty, with the additions and amendments offered by the other Ministries of Marine. The basic decisions taken on 29 October included one substantive amendment of the British proposals: 160 German submarines were to be surrendered to the Allies, also the Beatty list of surface ships, *less the fleet flagship*, 'it not being considered essential to an Armistice to include this ship, while inclusion might be thought to be unduly humiliating to Germany.' All surrendered vessels were to be held in trust for final disposition at the peace conference. 'The existing Blockade conditions . . . are to remain unchanged, and all German merchant ships found at sea are to remain liable to capture.' A covering statement explained that the Armistice terms had been drawn up on the premise (*inter alia*) that the Allies were dealing with a beaten foe.

Geddes presented the Allied Naval Council terms to the Supreme War Council on the morning of 1 November.[29] The ships to be surrendered, he explained, were drawn up on these bases: that if the Grand Fleet and High Seas Fleet met in battle, the latter would lose the equivalent of these ships; that Germany must not be in a position to renew hostilities under better conditions than the existing ones; and that, given the German superiority to the Allies in battle cruisers, if they were not handed over, the Allies would have to build battle cruisers. Immediately there was trouble, since it was apparent that the politicians, with powerful assistance from Foch, wanted to whittle down the naval terms to make them more palatable to the Germans. They were afraid there was a point beyond which the Germans would not go. If the Allies pitched the terms too high, as through asking for the surrender of all the ships recommended by the Allied Naval Council, the

---

[28] Wemyss to Beatty, 26 October 1918; Wemyss MSS.
[29] I.C.-87. This was the eighth and last wartime meeting of the Supreme War Council (31 October–4 November) and the second attended by an American political representative—Colonel House, acting for President Wilson.

Germans would reject them and there would be another year of bloodshed. What lay at the heart of the problem was the paucity of information on how seriously Germany was defeated and how prepared she was to fight on, were the Armistice terms too harsh. The military terms were also stiff, 'so that,' as Wemyss reported, 'the politicians want a softening somewhere.' Foch was determined that this softening must be at the expense of the naval terms. Balfour, with his usual perspicacity, understood Foch's motives perfectly. 'I am,' he wrote, 'a little anxious about the naval side of the German armistice. Foch and the soldiers, naturally enough, care nothing about this. They want a Glorious Victory?—on *land*. No success by *Sea* will redound to their credit—or to the credit of any country but Great Britain. They are therefore—most naturally —indisposed to take the smallest—even the most infinitesimal— risk of any contre-temps which would delay their successes even for a day.'[30] That morning, at the Allied conference, Foch could understand why the submarines should be taken without questions —they had hurt the Allies the most—but he could not understand why the German surface fleet need be turned over. What was there to fear from it? It had given little trouble. He was not taken by Geddes's argument that the High Seas Fleet had posed a great danger which had been kept in check by the Grand Fleet. 'If these ships were not surrendered, the Grand Fleet during the Armistice would be in the same state of tension as that of two armies opposed to each other in battle array in the trenches.' Foch thought it would be enough to confine the German Fleet to the Baltic, with the Allies taking Heligoland and Cuxhaven 'as a gage.' Geddes replied that this would necessitate a close watch of the Belts, 'thus continuing for the navy all the strain of the war.'

At this point Lloyd George intervened. He thought the Allied Naval Council terms were 'rather excessive.' On the other hand, Foch went too far in the opposite direction. Lloyd George proposed that the submarines, battle cruisers (the Allies had none that could catch them), and some of the light cruisers be surrendered, but that the battleships be interned in a neutral port or ports. The conference accepted these proposals as a compromise.

The Allied Naval Council discussed the views of the Supreme War Council in the afternoon of 1 November. All the Admirals but one were strongly opposed to altering their recommendations.

[30] Balfour to Bonar Law, 1 November 1918; Balfour MSS. (F.O. 800 series, P.R.O.).

The great objection, as Wemyss put it, was that Germany 'would inevitably look upon these ships as pawns at the peace negotiations when these arrived, which they might perhaps get back at the Peace since they had not been taken at the Armistice.' Geddes added the warning: 'If Germany had a sufficiently strong fleet, war would always be possible. The war had primarily been caused by the relative strength which German armaments of all kinds had attained in respect to those of her neighbours—and the same situation might arise again if these ships were returned to her following their internment.' Admiral de Bon, the French Chief of Naval Staff, was even more outspoken. If the proposals of the politicians were adopted and Germany in consequence eventually got the return of the battleships, she would remain a first-class naval power. 'Eventual victory on our own terms was absolutely assured, and there was no reason whatever for timidity in fixing the terms of Armistice.' Only the American naval representative, Admiral Benson, supported the politicians, citing their reasons. His undeclared motive was his fear that the British Fleet would be the principal beneficiary of a distribution of the surrendered ships. Internment would ensure that the disposition of these ships would be left to the Peace Conference. This would, he hoped, frustrate any secret Allied agreements regarding the distribution of the ships. Beatty pleaded with Wemyss (whom he thought 'none too strong and hasn't very strong convictions, and so might easily be talked round') not to allow the Allied Naval Council to be overridden.

I am confident of the ability of the Grand Fleet to deal with the enemy Fleet both now and in the future.

Success, however, could only be expected at the cost of vast casualties, and my experience has shown me that, should the enemy be favoured with the best of the luck, fogs, fluctuating visibility, he will be compensated in a large measure for the inferiority of his forces.

Survival of the German Fleet in any strength will throw upon us the necessity for continuous increase of armaments.

We must not, therefore, in a short-sighted endeavour to accelerate the advent of peace, waive any of the conditions which we know to be essential for the safety of the Empire.

History will never acquit us if we miss the present opportunity of reducing effectively the menace to our sea power.[31]

31 Beatty to Wemyss, 5 November 1918; Chalmers, *Beatty*, pp. 338-9.

But already the die had been cast at the 4 November meeting of the Supreme War Council.[32] Admiral Hope, who was present, believed that a Benson memorandum read during the proceedings, and which had argued that internment of the 10 battleships and 6 battle cruisers would increase the probability of acceptance of the Armistice terms, had 'largely influenced' the decision in favour of the disarmament and internment under Allied surveillance of all the surface ships. (Lloyd George had quoted the Admiralty preference for the internment of *all* the surface ships, if they were going to intern any.) The politicians made it clear to the Admirals that the matter was already settled: they only wanted the support of the Allied Naval Council in demanding the internment and to draw up the conditions of internment. The Admirals succumbed that afternoon to the strong political pressures, particularly after the British naval respresentative, Hope, had urged that they should go along. The Admiralty had reluctantly acceded to Lloyd George's position only after he had given Wemyss an assurance in the presence of the War Cabinet that the Supreme War Council were determined that none of the interned ships would be returned to the Germans. It was on the same understanding that the Allied Naval Council accepted the decision reached at Versailles—'that this is an Armistice term only and that these Ships will not, under any circumstances, be returned to Germany on the conclusion of the Armistice, or at any other time.' The Supreme War Council did not contest this 'understanding.'

The naval terms now read, as regards the disposition of the German Fleet: *Article XXII*—surrender of 160 submarines; *XXIII* —internment in neutral ports, or failing them, in Allied ports, of 10 battleships, 6 battle cruisers, and so on, the ships to be designated by the Allies and with only (German) care and maintenance parties left on board. The reference to 'Allied ports' was a last-minute alteration in the draft conditions, after it was realized that the neutral governments in Europe might refuse to receive the German Fleet. *Article XXXI*—'No destruction of ships or of materials to be permitted before evacuation, delivery or restoration.' *Article XXVI* repeated the Allied Naval Council statement on the continuation of the blockade, and *Article XXIX* provided for the return of Russian warships in the Black Sea seized by

[32] I.C.-93.

Germany. The Armistice, signed on 11 November, incorporated these naval conditions.[33] The duration of the Armistice was to be 36 days; it could be extended, and was regularly: on 13 December for a month, on 16 January for a month, and on 12 February indefinitely. An Allied Naval Armistice Commission (under Vice-Admiral Sir Montague Browning) was set up after the Armistice to ensure the carrying out of the naval conditions.

During the Armistice negotiations with Germany at Compiègne, 8–11 November, the German naval delegate, Captain Vanselow, remarked that it was inadmissible that their Fleet should be interned, seeing that they had not been defeated. 'The reply to this,' Wemyss recorded, 'was obvious and it gave me a certain amount of pleasure to observe that they had only to come out!'[34] When Vanselow told Wemyss there were not nearly 160 submarines to be had, Wemyss saw an opportunity to get what he had always wanted: *all* the submarines, and Article XXII was so altered. It also transpired that the battle cruiser *Mackensen* was at least ten months from completion and in no state for towing, so only five battle cruisers could be interned. On 12 December, at the first renewal of the Armistice, the Admiralty demanded that the *Baden* be sent in lieu of the *Mackensen*, which was agreed to by the Germans. And so the Admiralty's conditions as regards the U-boats and the fleet flagship were secured in the end.

The full import of the mutiny in the High Seas Fleet that had started on 29 October was not appreciated at the Admiralty until too late to affect the final naval terms. By 4 November the German Fleet was definitely finished as a fighting force. Though news of the disorders had reached the Admiralty quickly enough, they had no means of judging how far the disintegration of the High Seas Fleet had gone. As late as 5 November the First Sea Lord was writing: 'The state of affairs in the High Seas Fleet is not very clear.' Had the true situation at Kiel and in the Elbe been known earlier, the British Admirals would have had the ammunition effectively to resist the demands of the politicians, Foch, and

---

33 The text of the Naval Armistice as signed is in Cd. 9212 (1918). The naval terms of the Armistice with Austria-Hungary (signed on 4 November) called for the surrender of 15 submarines, 3 battleships, 3 light cruisers, 9 destroyers, 12 torpedo-boats, a minelayer, and 6 Danube monitors. All other submarine and surface warships were to be paid off, completely disarmed, and placed under Allied supervision.

34 Diary notes, 'Armistice'; Wemyss MSS.

Benson for softening the naval terms of armistice, though possibly this would in the new conditions not have been necessary.

Geddes and Wemyss were not entirely satisfied with the naval terms, but they realized that, given the political circumstances, they were as good as could be expected. To Beatty, on the other hand, the decision to intern the ships came as a shock. He had repeatedly reiterated his belief that they had to have the High Seas Fleet, if not as the result of a fleet action, then by surrender. He much preferred the former solution:

Another question which weighs on my mind—are we in the Grand Fleet to be cheated of our reward of breaking the Sea Power of the Hun for ever? I do not think so if the talking gentlemen at Versailles don't let us down. If they are firm, the High Seas Fleet must have a run for its money, and it may happen at any moment, but it won't be until the very last thing, a forlorn hope to give him a better position from which to talk of Peace. It would be a very bad thing for our country if our great Fleet never has an opportunity of showing its power in a more demonstrative manner than it has. The public are very short-sighted, and would murmur at the necessity of expending large sums on the maintenance of the Sea Power if they had no *ocular* demonstration of its power to command the Seas.[35]

On 7 November he expressed the hope that 'the Enemy will not accept the Terms, but I fear that he will.'

The twin disappointments of no fleet action and no surrender were almost too much for the C.-in-C. He suffered a third great disappointment in the first part of November. He attached great importance to the inclusion of the surrender of Heligoland in the Armistice terms and had made his feelings known to the Admiralty several times in the weeks preceding the Armistice. He was, therefore, angry upon learning that the terms made no mention of Heligoland.

In pursuance of the policy outlined by the Prime Minister that the terms of armistice should approximate to the terms of peace, I consider that Heligoland should be handed over as one of the terms of armistice. It is difficult to conceive that the terms of Peace will be more stringent than those of the armistice, and a measure which is certain of popular support at the present time might well be considered oppressive when Germany's misdeeds are less fresh in the public mind.

[35] Beatty to a friend, 31 October 1918; Chalmers, *Beatty*, pp. 336–7.

It would be deplorable that Peace should find Germany with an advanced fortified naval base in the Bight still in her hands. Heligoland is an absolute bar to operations by the British Fleet in the vicinity of the principal German base. Its retention therefore as a fortified base will in the event of future hostilities prohibit efficient control being exercised over the exit of enemy vessels more especially submarines. That is to say the same strategic conditions will obtain as during the past four years.[36]

The First Lord could give him no satisfaction. It was too late to make any alterations in the Armistice terms, which had been handed to Germany; but his views would receive due weight in the consideration of the peace terms. 'We have to depart from the idea that Armistice Terms must include everything which we wish at the Peace, otherwise the conditions of Armistice would have been so stringent and so voluminous and so beyond what was necessary for an Armistice alone, that had Germany refused, we should have stood condemned before the world as being unreasonable in our terms of Armistice, but it is felt that the Naval and Military Terms put forward will make it possible to insist at the Peace Conference upon any Terms which . . . [the Allies may] see fit to impose.'[37]

There was a fourth reason for Beatty's unhappiness. He was as upset over the fact that the original decisions on the ships and Heligoland had been modified without reference to him as he was over the alterations themselves, since he had been led to believe that no alteration material to the Grand Fleet would be made in

36 Beatty to Geddes, 8 November 1918; Beatty MSS. A telegram on Heligoland also went out to Geddes that day. The original terms of the Allied Naval Council (8 October), as well as of the Admiralty (19 October), had included the surrender of Heligoland. This clause had been omitted at the 28 October meeting of the Council, when it was decided it 'was not an essential condition for an Armistice and little benefit would accrue to the Allied and Associated Powers from its occupation, while in various circumstances it might even be a source of embarrassment.'

37 Geddes to Beatty, 9 November 1918; Admiralty MSS. Wemyss, with whom the C.-in-C. had registered the same complaint, laid the blame at Lloyd George's door. 'As regards Heligoland, I was quite aware of your views. Unfortunately the Prime Minister, in spite of his original dictum that terms of Armistice should approach as nearly as possible the terms of peace, was as you know anxious to cut down the Naval terms. . . . Heligoland he objected to very much, and I was obliged to tell him when he asked me that I considered that as terms of Armistice, if we got those ships, the holding of Heligoland was not of such vital importance *now*, though eventually the enemy would have to give it up, and this is to be a matter for the peace conference.' Wemyss to Beatty, 10 November 1918; Wemyss MSS.

the terms without reference to him. Indeed, he charged Wemyss
with not taking him into his confidence and not consulting with
him at all, except for surface ships to be surrendered, during the
Armistice discussions. The First Sea Lord explained with gentle-
ness: 'As for consulting you—well, I seem to have lived the last
few days in motor-cars and trains . . . Conditions were perpetually
changing and it was physically impossible to keep you more *au
courant* than I did. . . . Whatever happens, do not ever let the
shadow of a misunderstanding come between you and me. We
both of us . . . have worked with too great a loyalty together for
the last ten months to let anything come between us, and moreover
my friendship for you is too great and too sincere to allow of
anything of the sort!'[38] Regrettably, internment, Heligoland, and
the non-consultation accusation resulted in the first serious rift
in the close and harmonious relations Beatty had enjoyed with
Wemyss since he became First Sea Lord. The denouement, we
shall see, was sad.

* * *

When the Armistice was declared, 11 November, a huge crowd
surged round the Admiralty clamouring for a speech from the
First Lord and calling for the members of the Board of Admiralty.
Hastily improvised platforms in front of the old building were
mounted and the crowd demanded a speech. Geddes replied,
calling for three cheers for Sir David Beatty. These having been
given in no uncertain voice, Geddes called for three cheers for the
British bluejackets. Other members of the Board appeared in
response to the acclamations of the crowd. When news of the
Armistice was received in the Grand Fleet, it was promptly
followed by a general signal from the C.-in-C. that 'the customary
method of celebrating an occasion by "splicing the main brace"
may be carried out at 1900.' That is, one tot of rum additional to
the daily tot would be issued, and, unlike the daily tot, to officers
as well as ratings. The last occasions were at the coronations of
Edward VII and George V.

Promptly at 7 p.m. Jack 'spliced the main brace' with rousing cheers
and mutual congratulations. Then followed a veritable pandemonium
of noise. The big ships started it with their deep-throated fog-horns.

[38] Wemyss to Beatty, 14 November 1918; *Wester Wemyss*, p. 399.

And quickly every ship, big and little . . . took up the tocsin. . . . a deafening din rose over the brightly moonlit waters. Steam whistles shrieked, syrens rent the air with shrill blasts, and fog-horns mingled their deeper hootings in the wild and tumultuous uproar. Alternately falling and then rising again to crashing crescendoes, the discordant but happy paeans of victory resounded over the water and far across the adjacent shores for three solid, uninterrupted hours from 7 till 10 p.m., only to break out afresh at midnight. On deck Jack danced and sang, shouted and cheered till hoarse and exhausted . . .[39]

Many of the officers did not share in this gaiety. 'The Fleet, my Fleet,' declared the Commander-in-Chief, 'is broken-hearted, but are still wonderful, the most wonderful thing in Creation, and although it would appear that they can never achieve their hearts' desire, they preserve a cheerfulness that is extraordinary. . . . All suffering from a feeling of something far greater than disappointment, depressed beyond measure.'[40] The mood at the Admiralty was no more joyous, Wemyss admitted. 'There can be no naval officer who does not see the end of this war without a feeling of incompleteness, and that that incompleteness does not arise from any sense of failure. We feel it strongly at the Admiralty and realise how much more it must be the case with you and the Grand Fleet. The Navy has won a victory greater than Trafalgar, though less spectacular . . .'[41] The feeling of 'incompleteness' was undoubtedly caused by the fact that the fruits of victory at sea had been won without any latter-day Trafalgar. The surrender of the flower of the High Seas Fleet did little to relieve the prevalent feeling of incompleteness and despondency.

3. DER TAG

When neutral governments showed little interest in undertaking the custody of the interned ships (Norway and Spain were ap-

---

39 *The Scotsman,* 13 November 1918.
40 Beatty to a friend, 12 November 1918; Chalmers, *Beatty,* p. 341. A Midshipman in the dreadnought *Malaya* expressed the feeling in a letter home: 'I'm afraid that the poor old Grand Fleet will never have the show of which we were so certain a short time ago. I suppose the GF will go down to history as the classic example of sea power which was so powerful that it was exercised without any fight worth mentioning. Which may be very jolly for historians but distinctly unsatisfying for the ships' companies.' Ian Sanderson to his father, 10 November 1918; letter in Commander Sanderson's possession, as are his other letters quoted below.
41 Wemyss to Beatty, 14 November 1918; *Wester Wemyss,* p. 398.

proached), an emergency meeting of the Allied Naval Council on 13 November in London accepted Wemyss's suggestion that the surface ships be interned in Scapa Flow under the supervision of the C.-in-C., Grand Fleet, with the submarines to proceed to British ports to be specified by the C.-in-C.

At about this time an angry Beatty concluded a speech with: 'I should like to go and fetch them now, and I don't care who knows it.' The Germans spared him the trouble. On the evening of 15 November, Hipper's representative, Admiral Meurer, anchored off May Island in the Firth of Forth in the light cruiser *Königsberg*. He had come to arrange the details of the internment. Meurer and his staff of four officers went on board the *Queen Elizabeth* and entered Beatty's cabin. With the C.-in-C. were Brock, Madden, Tyrwhitt, and several members of his staff. All stood up when the German officers entered. Beatty's Signal Officer, Commander Ralph Seymour, who was present, described the proceedings:

> The German Admiral was the most deathly ashy colour I have ever seen, and I thought he would fall down.
> Sir David looked straight at him and said, 'Who are you?'
> He pulled himself together and said, 'Rear-Admiral Hugo Meurer.'
> Sir David said, 'Have you been sent by Admiral von Hipper as his plenipotentiary to arrange the details for carrying out the terms of the armistice which refer to the surrender of the German Fleet?'
> Meurer said, 'Yes.'
> Sir David said, 'Where are your credentials?'
> These were produced and Sir David said, 'Sit down,' and they then proceeded to business . . .
> I have never seen him [Beatty] to better advantage. He was courteous in the extreme and as firm as a rock. He discussed details of the British and German Fleets without once referring to a paper, although British and German staffs were constantly looking up details.
> During the discussion he was only stern about twice, the intonation of his voice was low and clear, but it was effective in the extreme.[42]

Madden agreed that the C.-in-C. was in top form. 'B. carried it through very well and with dignity. The Germans were very quiet and tame . . .'[43] Three meetings were held on the 16th; all

---

[42] Seymour to his mother, 19 November 1918; Lady Seymour, *Commander Ralph Seymour, R.N.* (Glasgow, 1926), pp. 120–1.

[43] Madden to Jellicoe, 29 November 1918; Jellicoe MSS. Beatty's account of the meeting ('dramatic and tragic to a high degree') is contained in a letter of 26 November 1918; Chalmers, *Beatty*, pp. 344–5. After two hours of discussion, an

had been arranged by that evening for the submarines to surrender to Tyrwhitt at Harwich and the surface ships to Beatty in the Forth, from where they would be transferred to Scapa for internment until the peace treaty decided their disposal.

By daybreak on 21 November the whole Grand Fleet had put to sea from Rosyth—the operation was appropriately called 'ZZ' —to escort the High Seas Fleet to its anchorage in the Forth. As many a British officer of the First War maintained, the only sight finer than the Grand Fleet in harbour was the Grand Fleet at sea. Above all now. Such a force had never been collected before. Everyone was there—from Dover, from Harwich, from Scapa, from the Channel, they had all gathered together for the last great scene: 370 ships and 90,000 men. Additionally, an armoured cruiser and two destroyers represented the French Navy, and the 6th Battle Squadron, the American Navy. Every ship from dreadnought to submarine flew as many white ensigns as possible, as was the custom when going into action. This was the first occasion since Jutland that it had been done. The fleet steamed to a rendezvous 40 miles east of May Island: one immense line as far as open water, and then in two long columns, six miles apart, each column composed of over 30 battleships, battle cruisers, and cruisers, with a destroyer abreast each flagship. The British fleet arrived at the rendezvous at 8.30 a.m. Contact was made at about 9.30 a.m. The German Fleet was in single line ahead: 9 battleships, 5 battle cruisers, 7 light cruisers, and 49 destroyers—the flower of the German Fleet—in that order, under the command of Admiral von Reuter in the *Friedrich der Grosse*. One destroyer had struck a mine in the Bight and sank; the dreadnought *König* and light cruiser *Dresden* were in dock and came over early in December. Von Reuter's hope that fog would blot out his fleet and so diminish the impressiveness of the picture for the British was only partially realized, as it was a sunny, though misty, day. The light cruiser *Cardiff*, which had been sent ahead with the destroyer flotillas, led

---

adjournment was ordered and the Germans were given supper in one of the cabins leading off the Admiral's flat. When they resumed work, the Royal Marine sentry on the half deck, who was observing things through the bulkhead door, saw one of the German officers look round furtively and slip a package into his greatcoat, which was hanging on a hook. 'Were they secret papers he had pinched?' the sentry wondered, and he told Seymour, who promptly investigated and found a large piece of cheddar cheese, en route to the starving Fatherland!

the German warships down the line formed by the two columns, with the Germans 'looking for all the world like a school of levia-thans led by a minnow.' 'What a target!' murmured the Captain of the dreadnought *Monarch* (S. R. Drury-Lowe) regretfully, as he made a rapid calculation of how long it would take their 33 battle-ships to sink the German nine. Having gone to the end of the Ger-man line, the columns reversed course, retaining position on either side of the German line. Ships' companies were at action stations, guns loaded and kept trained fore and aft, although the Germans were supposed to have left behind all the breech blocks of their guns and all the ammunition. Nobody knew what to expect, and there was always the possibility of a last-minute defiant gesture. There was no untoward incident. In silence the two fleets pro-ceeded towards the Forth. Towards noon the German ships were at their prison anchorage at Inchkeith, surrounded by ships detailed to guard them. Boats of every description, steamers, row-boats, yachts, etc., packed with civilians, milled about, witnessing and savouring the triumph of British arms. (Lady Beatty, in her little yacht, went very close to the *Seydlitz*, which drew derisive laughter from the crew to her extreme annoyance!) As the *Queen Elizabeth* passed to her mooring (the Grand Fleet anchored above and below the Forth Bridge), the men of the Grand Fleet enthu-siastically cheered Beatty again and again. A well-known photo-graph shows him on the bridge, cap in hand, acknowledging the cheers. 'Otherwise,' as Ralph Seymour recorded, 'the whole thing silent and almost funereal.'

At about 11 a.m. Beatty made a general signal by flag: 'The German flag will be hauled down at sunset to-day, Thursday, and will not be hoisted again without permission.' Precisely at sunset (3.57 p.m.) the German ensigns were hauled down. All hands in the *Queen Elizabeth* had been piped aft. When the bugle rang out 'making sunset,' all turned to the flag and saluted. This was followed by deafening cheers for the C.-in-C. Beatty acknowledged the tribute and added, with a smile, 'I always told you they would have to come out.' Soon after the Admiral made a final signal reminiscent of Nelson's after the Nile: 'It is my intention to hold a service of thanksgiving at 18.00 [6 p.m.] to-day for the victory which Almighty God has vouchsafed to his Majesty's arms, and every ship is recommended to do the same.' It was accompanied by a message in which Beatty congratulated the officers and men of the Grand Fleet on 'the victory which has been gained over the sea power of our enemy. The greatness of this achievement is in no way lessened by the fact the final episode did not take the form of a fleet action. . . . Without joining us in action [the enemy] has given testimony to the prestige and efficiency of the Fleet without parallel in history . . .'

And so ended the dramatic and historic day. The surrender, if one may call it that, was one of the most decisive and dramatic events in the illustrious annals of British sea power. It would have been gracious and fitting had the authorities invited Jellicoe and Fisher, two of the prime architects of the British naval victory, to be present. They went unremembered, a slight that Fisher, at least, felt keenly.

' "How have the mighty fallen," ' the King entered in his diary on the 20th. The circumstances of the 'fall' were entirely unexpected. For four long years the Grand Fleet had expected a great and decisive sea battle would be fought before the war's end. To the last Wemyss doubted that the German Fleet would come over, believing they would scuttle themselves.

How did the Grand Fleet view the events of that memorable day? Contempt for the High Seas Fleet was the dominant feeling. 'The sailors,' reported a newspaper correspondent who had witnessed the scene on board the dreadnought *Royal Oak*, 'watch the phantom ships with an odd look of contempt and pity and mourning in their eyes, and they tell me that even now it all seems as though it could not be true, because it's against human nature.'[44] In addressing the officers and men of the *Lion* and the 1st Battle Cruiser Squadron on 24 November, just before it left the Forth to escort the High Seas Fleet to Scapa Flow, Beatty spoke with the utmost contempt for the manner in which the German ships had been surrendered without a fight:

I have always said in the past that the High Sea Fleet would have to come out and meet the Grand Fleet. I was not a false prophet; they are out (laughter), and they are now in. (Loud laughter.) They are in our pockets, and the 1st Battle Cruiser Squadron is going to look after them. The 1st Battle Cruiser Squadron, in fact the Battle Cruiser Force, has a more intimate acquaintance with the enemy than any other force of the Grand Fleet. It has been their great fortune to have cast their eye

44 Hugh Martin, ' "The Day" of the British Fleet,' *Daily News*, 22 November 1918.

upon them on several occasions, and generally with very good effect. But we never expected that the last time we should see them as a great force would be when they were being shepherded, like a flock of sheep, by the Grand Fleet. It was a pitiable sight, in fact I should say it was a horrible sight, to see these great ships that we have been looking forward so long to seeing, expecting them to have the same courage that we expect from men whose work lies upon great waters—we did expect them to do something for the honour of their country—and I think it was a pitiable sight to see them come in, led by a British light-cruiser, with their old antagonists, the battle-cruisers, gazing at them. I am sure that the sides of this gallant old ship, which have been well hammered in the past, must have ached—as I ached, as all ached—to give them another dose of what we had intended for them. But I will say this, that their humiliating end was a suitable end and a proper end for a foe so lacking in chivalry and in what we look for from an honourable foe. From the beginning his strategy, his tactics and his behaviour have been beneath contempt, and worthy of a nation which has waged war in the manner in which the enemy has waged war.

They are now going to be taken away and placed under the guardianship of the Grand Fleet at Scapa, where they will enjoy (laughter), as we have enjoyed, the pleasures of Scapa. (Laughter.) But they have nothing to look forward to as we had. That which kept up our spirits, kept up our efficiency. They have nothing to look forward to except degradation.

Seymour struck the same note: 'I must confess it was a pitiful and morbid sight which was somewhat distasteful. I felt rather as if I was one of a crowd such as used to assemble for the funeral of some very sordid person who had been murdered in pre-war days.'[45] Midshipman Yates in the *Malaya* found it incredible: 'That the second Naval power in the world should "pipe down" to the first, without striking a blow, is unparalleled . . . you would have thought that death would be preferable to the position in which the enemy sailors now find themselves.'[46] For Walter Cowan, who had hoped that the Germans would meet the Grand Fleet at the rendezvous with guns blazing rather than tamely

---

[45] Seymour to his sister, Margaret Walker, 30 November 1918; Seymour, *Seymour*, p. 129.
[46] Andrew V. S. Yates to his mother, 22 November 1918; letter in Captain Yates's possession. 'Andrew Yates and I thought it dreadful at the time that the High Seas Fleet should have such a tame "Der Tag," and all of us resented it that Waterloo should precede Trafalgar and that Trafalgar should never happen at all.' Commander Ian Sanderson's letter to the author, 11 March 1969.

submit to the ignominy of abject surrender, 'it was a sad business though really to see those splendid ships come on and accept such disgrace in silence.'[47] The reaction of the press to the tragic end of a once proud Navy was similar, it being widely remarked that this was the first time in the annals of naval warfare that a fleet had voluntarily, quietly, indeed ignominiously, surrendered. The *Naval and Military Record* was shocked. 'No really great nation would have tolerated such a degradation to its flag.' The *Manchester Guardian* spoke of 'so inglorious a surrender,' the *Daily Telegraph*, of 'the degradation and humiliation of a once great Power,' and the *Globe* declaimed: 'The German navy is not only defeated, it is dishonoured for all time, alike by the foulness of its fighting and by its cowardice in the day of its doom.' Reviewed in the press on this day of days was 'the catalogue of Germany's infractions of the chivalry of the sea': the bombardment of undefended towns, the firing on open boats, and so on.

The feelings in the German Navy were epitomized in the pathetic remark of an officer: 'If only in one of our actions a merciful British shell had spared us these last weeks and this wretched end!'

* * *

The period of the Armistice gave the Admiralty plenty to do. Post-war reorganization, the formulation of a new standard of naval strength, the incipient naval rivalry with the United States and Japan, and, above all, the naval aspects of the settlement with Germany: these were the problems that absorbed most of the energy and thought of the Navy and which constitute the principal themes of Part II.

I do not propose to say anything about the operations in the Baltic, partly because this is a subject which has been treated exhaustively and capably in works by Geoffrey Bennett (*Cowan's War*) and Stephen Roskill (*Naval Policy Between the Wars*, Vol. i), and partly because these operations were always peripheral to the main concerns of the Navy both before and after the Armistice. It is worth noting, however, that in the months following the Armistice many naval officers, not only junior ones, were eager to

47 Cowan to Commodore Rudolf Bentinck, 22 November 1918; Cowan MSS. Incidentally, Cowan's ship, the *Caledon*, leading the port column of the fleet, would probably have been blown out of the water at the first German salvo.

secure appointments to ships detailed for service in the Baltic—
the one theatre where the 'real thing' was still going on. British
naval forces were directly or indirectly involved in the operations
in North Russia (as well as elsewhere around the perimeter of
Russia) during 1918–20. This is a facet of the complicated story
of the Allied intervention in Russia whose initial objectives
included the tying down of as many German troops as possible in
the East and the prevention of the vast military stores at Archangel
from falling into German hands. After the Armistice, when Rear-
Admiral Sir Walter Cowan was sent to the Baltic with the 1st
Light Cruiser Squadron to relieve Alexander-Sinclair, the
objectives altered. They now were concerned with supporting the
anti-Bolshevik forces in Russia and assisting the nascent Baltic
nationalities to preserve their fledgeling independence against
Bolshevik attempts to re-establish Russian control. The former
policy was a failure, the latter a success. Cowan's reaction to the
briefing he got from Fremantle before going out to the Baltic is
an indication of the nearly hopelessly confusing situation. 'It
seemed to me that there was never such a tangle, and my brain
reeled with it. An unbeaten German Army, two kinds of belligerent
Russians, Letts, Finns, Esthonians, Lithuanians; ice, mines—
60,000 of them! Russian submarines, German small craft, Russian
battleships, cruisers and destroyers all only waiting for the ice to
melt to ravage the Baltic. I felt that I had better get out there as
soon as possible to get wise before the Gulf of Finland thawed out.'[48]

Nor do I propose to concern myself with post-war Imperial
naval problems, which transcend my terminal date. They are
intimately connected with the results of Jellicoe's Empire Mission
of 1919–20, whose purpose was to help the Dominions determine
their post-war naval policies and organizations. In May 1918 the
Admiralty had prepared a short memorandum on naval defence
for the Imperial War Cabinet. In order to obtain unity of direction and command, the memorandum suggested the creation of
a single Navy (with a single Imperial Naval Staff) in which
Dominion and British ships and personnel would be interchange-
able. The Dominion Prime Ministers rejected these proposals at
the Imperial Conference of June 1918. The immediate problem
after the war was the combination of independent Dominion

---

[48] Captain Lionel Dawson, *Sound of the Guns: Being an Account of the Wars and Service of Admiral Sir Walter Cowan* (Oxford, 1949), pp. 151–2.

Navies and a unified system of direction in wartime. In the end, late in 1919, the Admiralty, which had been pursuing the mirage of an Imperial Navy since 1909, saw it was impracticable and were prepared to accept the idea of individual Dominion navies co-operating with the Royal Navy.

PART II
Aftermath
November 1918 – June 1919

VIII

Rifts and Reforms

When Admiral Beatty's flag is hauled down to-day, there passes from its great stage that new Armada which, under Providence, has saved humanity. . . . To all ranks of that great Fleet every citizen of all free States owes homage, for the very battles that won the war rested ultimately for their issue on this Fleet's power to keep the seas.

DAILY EXPRESS, 7 April 1919.

Before the war the greater part of the nation was already ready to shout for ships and more ships; but it left officers and men to be sweated with all the indifference of ignorance. . . . But the war has brought the human element into proper proportion . . .

THE OBSERVER, 23 February 1919.

I. THE CHANGING OF THE GUARD

LLOYD GEORGE tried to persuade Geddes to stay on as First Lord during the demobilization of the Fleet and the reconstruction period that followed the Armistice. The Prime Minister later broadened his appeal, inviting Geddes to take over the co-ordination of the demobilization of the Fleet and the Army and industrial rehabilitation. Geddes preferred to concentrate on the transportation situation, which important work he could take on only if freed of responsibility for the Admiralty. He retired on 11 December and joined Lloyd George's new Coalition Government in January 1919 as Minister of Transport. The First Sea Lord acted in his stead until the appointment of a successor on 16 January 1919. Geddes had done an excellent job in his year and a half as First Lord, although his clumsy handling of Jellicoe's retirement and his direct and not always tactful methods had got under the skins of many senior officers.

The new First Lord (he held the post till February 1921), the 65-year-old Walter Long, had been Colonial Secretary in the second Coalition Government of 1916–19 and was making his first acquaintance with the Navy. (He had declined the post of

First Lord in 1905.) The amiable Long was a 'typical West country gentleman.' His greatest admirers could not call him clever, but he had horse sense in plenty and was a capable and painstaking administrator who worked in harmony with his professional advisers. The appointment, however, had a miserable press. *The Times* found it 'frankly inexplicable,' the *Daily Mail* called it a 'purely political appointment,' *The Observer* said Long was going to the Admiralty 'without any corresponding qualification whatever,' and *The Westminster Gazette* remarked that 'Of all the [Cabinet] selections, none is more obviously a concession to the "old gang," and none excites more doubt as to the possible consequences.'[1] The other newspapers were no kinder. The Service was prepared to give the new First Lord a chance. For instance, Beatty: 'I think we are lucky to get Long who is straight and a gentleman.'[2] The Service was, at least, relieved not to be saddled with Churchill, who had been rumoured as Geddes's successor. The *Naval and Military Record* (8 January) admitted that Churchill was 'undeniably sound on the naval question, as his election speeches at Dundee proved, but he does not possess the solid mental qualities requisite in a negotiator charged with the supremely important task of maintaining our sea rights at the coming Conference.' Wemyss would have resigned immediately 'on the grounds that I could not work with a man whose presence at the Admiralty I should consider a national danger.'[3] It was a near thing, for, as it happens, Lloyd George had asked Churchill to choose between the War Office and the Admiralty. He had accepted the latter. A day later the Prime Minister had a change of mind, induced by the need for a strong hand at the War Office to deal with the widespread unrest in the Army over the unfair demobilization procedures. And so Churchill had joined the Cabinet in charge of the War Office and also the Air Ministry.

Commodore Rudolf Bentinck relinquished his command of the 4th Light Cruiser Squadron to relieve Everett as Naval Secretary shortly after the Armistice. He was a sound all-round officer who had been Beatty's Chief of Staff in 1915–16. Wemyss, Duff, and

---

1 The dates of the leaders are 11 January 1919, except for *The Observer*'s, which was 12 January. On 14 March the *Daily Mail* made the unkind remark on Long that Lloyd George had 'pitchforked him into an office for which he has no apparent qualifications.'
2 Beatty to Wemyss, 11 February 1919; Wemyss MSS.
3 Wemyss to Beatty, 7 January 1919; Beatty MSS.

Bartolomé stayed on as First Sea Lord, A.C.N.S., and Third Sea Lord and Controller, respectively, and likewise Hope as Deputy First Sea Lord until August, when the office lapsed. The new Board appointments in the spring of 1919 were: Vice-Admiral Sir Montague Browning as Second Sea Lord (*vice* Heath, 31 March), Rear-Admiral James A. Fergusson as D.C.N.S. (*vice* Fremantle, 1 May), and Captain Sir Ernle Chatfield as Fourth Sea Lord (*vice* Tothill, 18 June).

Browning was the most important of the new appointments. He had been known as 'Hookey' since the hand he had lost in a gun accident early in his career was replaced by a substantial iron hook. Browning had the disconcerting habit of rapping the table with his hook! The story ran that if he was seen to be stroking his hook gently, it would be safe to meet him, but if he were rubbing it violently, it would be wiser to disappear. One of his maxims was: 'I trust nobody until I have tried him.' The story is told of the defaulter who thought he would be clever and, when asked if he had anything to say, replied, 'Nothing, Sir, except that to err is human, to forgive, divine. Shakespeare [Pope, of course].' 'Fourteen days cell. Browning' was the answer he got! Inflexible, unapproachable, and feared by his subordinates, Browning was, nevertheless, a very competent officer of sound judgement. Richmond thought he would be 'too reactionary.' 'His views are all for examinations & other crudities; though apart from that he is the best-read man in the upper ranks.'[4] If Browning, to say nothing of that brilliant all-rounder Chatfield, strengthened the Board, the appointment of the colourless Fergusson was inexplicable. Richmond's reaction was not untypical of the more progressive officers: 'And Jim Fergusson has been made Deputy C.O.S.!!!!!!!!!! Beatty nearly had a fit when he heard it. Poor old Jim, who knows nothing, quite one of the thickest-headed fellows in the Service, a very good Captain of a ship, having to decide matters of the kind that fall to a C.O.S. It is really too ridiculous for words & makes even the greatest optimist among us despair of improvement.'[5]

Commodore Hugh F. P. Sinclair, Hall's Assistant, relieved him as D.N.I. on 18 January 1919. He was a very strange and original

---

[4] Diary, 12 February 1919; *Portrait of an Admiral*, p. 333.
[5] Diary, 18 May 1919; *ibid.*, p. 343. O. de B. Brock, a really good choice, succeeded Fergusson on 4 August, the latter relieving Duff as A.C.N.S.!

character, a clever man who shone in command of men. (His nickname, 'Quex,' derived from a serious nasal drawl which suggested the quacking of a duck.)

* * *

The Admiralty recognized that the pre-war standard of naval strength, in which the rapidly increasing strength of the German Navy was the dominating factor, needed reconsideration. This was quite apart from the fact that the country naturally expected a major reduction in the Navy and naval expenditure as one of the immediate results of the war. The strength of the Navy at the date of the Armistice was 415,000 officers and men. By mid-June 1919, 13,600 and 202,000, respectively, had been demobilized. As regards the Fleet itself, the Auxiliary Patrol was broken up after the Armistice, the large forces which were employed on convoy duty were demobilized, and so forth and so on. Between the Armistice and the signing of the Versailles Peace Treaty in June 1919, 'it was necessary to keep the Fleet in Home waters at a very full strength, both on account of operational necessities, especially in the Baltic (the ships for which are provided from the Home organisation), and because active measures might have been necessary to induce the Germans to sign the peace treaty.'[6] But a massive battle fleet was no longer needed.

On 3 April, Beatty, as well as Jellicoe, was specially promoted to Admiral of the Fleet, there being no vacancies, three being the authorized maximum. The special promotion of the two Admirals was the first time for well over a century that this rank was conferred as a recognition of wartime service. At 48 Beatty was the youngest Admiral of the Fleet who ever adorned the Navy List. For four days the flagship *Queen Elizabeth* flew the Union Flag of an Admiral of the Fleet who was Commander-in-Chief—'a unique event in the annals of the service,' opined the *Naval and Military Record* (9 April), which 'formed an appropriate climax to a career of unexampled brilliance.' (As it happens, Norris did in 1744—at the age of 84!) On 7 April Beatty hauled down his flag for the last time and the Grand Fleet as such ceased to exist. Its task had been done. The like of this gigantic concentration of power, the

6 Cmd. 451 (1919), 'Statement of the First Lord of the Admiralty Explanatory of the Navy Estimates, 1919–1920' (1 December 1919), p. 10.

mightiest aggregate of floating armed force in world history (380 units, including the American ships), will never be seen again.

The main force was the new Atlantic Fleet (11 battleships, 5 battle cruisers). As a second line of defence in Home waters there was a Home Fleet (6 battleships). Both fleets were placed under Madden. There was also in European waters a Mediterranean Fleet (6 battleships).

The end of the Grand Fleet, whose approaching demise had been announced in January 1919, was accompanied by the emergence of a feud that cast a pall over the Navy in the first half of 1919.

2. WEMYSS AND BEATTY

The Long–Wemyss Board was utterly lacking in the harmony that had been a feature of the Geddes–Wemyss period. The trouble stemmed from the rapidly worsening relations between Wemyss and Beatty. Friction had developed before the end of the war over the differences and misunderstandings pertaining to the naval armistice with Germany. It was a *leitmotiv* in the C.-in-C.'s correspondence with the Admiralty that he was being ignored, and he continued to make this complaint during the Paris Peace negotiations. Wemyss could fairly plead Not Guilty.[7] Another ground for friction was over appointments. The First Sea Lord explained this difficulty:

My predecessor [Jellicoe] had very naturally and very rightly always consulted him on such matters, but the habit had so grown that the Commander in Chief almost had got into the way of looking upon such appointments as being his prerogative, and had more than once almost tried to use his veto. This had put me into difficulties more than once, but I had . . . made up my mind that if ever he should have to put to sea for a general engagement, he should do it with a mind perfectly at rest, with no lingering doubts as to the fitness of the personnel whom he had to lead . . . But now that the fighting was over I told the First Lord that I thought it was most necessary that the Admiralty should immediately resume its authority and prerogatives which it had gone perilously near to handing over altogether, and that no better way could

7 It is difficult to understand Beatty's position. The Admiralty had solicited his views on every naval issue, which views carried much weight, as, for instance, in the cases of Heligoland, the Kiel Canal, and the naval strength to be allowed Germany.

be found than by filling up the first admiral's appointment without consulting the C.-in-C.[8]

Geddes was in agreement. The showdown came early in the New Year, when the Admiralty, on Wemyss's recommendation, nominated Keyes to the command of the Battle Cruiser Squadron, and *then* informed Beatty of the forthcoming appointment. This was a reversal of the practice under which the Admiralty had asked the C.-in-C. if he concurred in a proposed appointment. 'Unfortunately,' Wemyss continues, 'the news reached Sir D. Beatty unofficially before he received the Naval Secretary's letter, and he chose to regard this as a slight upon himself.' Wemyss had no success in convincing Beatty that no offence had been intended; the latter could not be persuaded that he was being treated with the courtesy to which he was entitled.

The third source of friction was for Beatty the last straw. It derived from his ambition to relieve Wemyss in the near future. Now, Wemyss had no desire to stay on at the Admiralty with the war over and the vastly different problems of a post-war world. He planned to leave at the 'psychological moment': after the signing of the peace and by which time he hoped to have put through two reforms on which he had set his heart—improved naval pay and a Naval Staff reorganization. What did Beatty wish to do, now that hostilities were over?, Wemyss had asked him during a friendly conversation at the latter's London house, Hanover Lodge, in December 1918. The C.-in-C. made it plain that he wanted to become First Sea Lord. Wemyss had no objection and he left Beatty with the impression that the changeover would be made in the fairly near future: the Admiralty had no attraction for him and he hoped to go out as Governor of Malta and Naval Commander-in-Chief, when the business in Paris was finished, presumably in the spring. (Under the combined appointment Wemyss would not go afloat but have a Vice-Admiral commanding the fleet under him. He felt it was impossible to go out merely as naval C.-in-C., after having been First Sea Lord.) This project had fallen through by the end of February 1919 to Wemyss's profound disappoint-

8 Wemyss's unpublished memoirs, Wemyss MSS., also, with minor amendments, in *Wester Wemyss*, pp. 420–1. There was also a misunderstanding over Browning's appointment as Second Sea Lord. Beatty was under the impression that Wemyss had promised to consult him on Heath's successor. Wemyss had no recollection of any such promise. Wemyss to Beatty, 29 January 1919; Beatty MSS.

ment.[9] 'The situation, therefore,' as Wemyss wrote to Beatty, 'has quite altered since that day [of their conversation]; and I am quite sure you do not desire to appear to be trying to push me out.'[10] In fact, Wemyss was not at all sure.

On 6 January, shortly before Wemyss was supposed to leave for the Paris Peace Conference as the principal British naval representative (he did not set out till 24 January), *The Times* announced, in a story by its Parliamentary Correspondent: 'It is understood that Sir David Beatty will almost immediately come to the Admiralty—an appointment which will help to remove a very widespread anxiety about the control of the Navy during a difficult period of transition.' The Admiralty at once issued a categorical denial—it appeared in the press on 7 January—that 'a change in the office of First Sea Lord has been decided upon, and is about to take place'. Wemyss was upset by the story. 'I don't mean to be hustled out of here by a Press agitation, and when I do leave it will be at a time convenient to the Service and to myself and not to the Press.'[11] He at once sent a communiqué to *The Times* denying its statement. That evening he saw the Editor of *The Times*, Geoffrey Dawson, and asked him why he had published such a statement. Dawson replied that he had done so on the highest authority, which he refused to name. Long assured the Admiral he was not that authority. It was evident to Wemyss that a plot was afoot. 'An extremely disagreeable incident, and I could only infer that Beatty himself—either directly or indirectly could have been the source of his [Dawson's] information.'[12]

Beatty complicated matters by laying down terms for his going to the Admiralty. He would hold the two offices of First Sea Lord and C.-in-C., with the power to issue his own orders to the Navy under his signature independently of the Board. The proposal to merge the two positions, although novel for the Navy, was not a

9 The ostensible reason was Wemyss's indispensability at the Admiralty; the real reason was Churchill's opposition. 'This project was promptly knocked on the head by the Secy of State for War whose argument was that the Governorship of Malta had always been a military plum, and that now, when there were so many distinguished Generals who would be out of employment, was not the time to make such a change. The Prime Minister and the Cabinet were much too busy to pay attention to what they then considered such a trivial affair, and so my proposals got no hearing.' Wemyss's memoirs.

10 Wemyss to Beatty, 28 February 1919; Beatty MSS.

11 Wemyss to Beatty, 7 January 1919; Beatty MSS.

12 Wemyss's memoirs.

new one: such a system had been in force in varying forms in the Army until swept away by the Esher Committee in 1904. The Admiralty promptly shot down the idea. Such a constitutional innovation was out of the question, Wemyss asserted. 'It is fundamentally opposed to the present constitution of the Board of Admiralty who in their corporate capacity are responsible for the Navy according to their duties as allocated by the First Lord. Such an arrangement as the one under consideration would appear to upset this and to place in the hands of one man what had been deliberately decided should be in the hands of a Board capitulating [sic] to the old office of Lord High Admiral to carry out whose duties the members of the Board are Lords Commissioners.' The constitutional side of the question apart, the proposal was neither feasible nor desirable. 'The Office of Commander-in-Chief is an executive one and as such cannot be carried out by a member of the Board whose duty and responsibility it is to prepare and develop war plans.'[13] Long agreed with these views and informed Beatty that he could not assent to his proposal.

Throughout the developing controversy Wemyss kept his head, his good sense, and his courtesy. As he wrote the C.-in-C. in a letter of 28 February already quoted in which he went over their various differences,

I suppose it is more than can be humanly expected that two men, placed as you and I are, should see actually eye to eye on every subject that may arise, but that does not seem to be a reason for any personal feeling to be brought into the matter, and so far as I am concerned let me assure you that there is none. . . . However, we are I hope too old and firm friends to quarrel about anything, much less a comparatively minor question [the Keyes appointment], and I am certain you are as determined as I am that the Service shall not suffer as it must do if the C.-in-C. Grand Fleet and 1st Sea Lord are known to be at loggerheads. . . . Won't you come and see me and talk matters over?

Beatty's reply was unyielding. He was being 'generally ignored. This is a statement of fact which can be substantiated and therefore need not be enlarged upon in this letter.' As regards his coming to the Admiralty, he based his claim on Geddes's infor-

13 Wemyss's memorandum of 2 February 1919; Wemyss MSS. The Secretary of the Admiralty, Sir Oswyn Murray, demolished the proposal in a detailed, closely reasoned document, 'Question of Combining Offices of First Sea Lord and Commander-in-Chief', 6 February 1919; Wemyss MSS.

mation that Wemyss wanted to leave and his, Geddes's, offer of the post, the effective date to be the signing of the preliminary Peace. If this were delayed, Geddes planned to ask Beatty to come to the Admiralty 'in the first place in an additional capacity, in order to avoid delays in reconstruction problems.' Geddes had not remained in office long enough to confirm the appointment, but he had told Beatty he would inform his successor of his intention. Wemyss's visit to him that same day in December had 'confirmed what I had learned from the 1st Lord and that the invitation to me to come to the Admiralty was not putting your nose out of joint. There was therefore nothing speculative about it; it was a concrete proposal.' Long, when he came to office (to continue with Beatty's reply), told Beatty that he looked upon the appointment as a 'fait accompli'. On a visit to the *Queen Elizabeth* he had reconfirmed this, adding that the date was dependent upon the signing of the Peace, as Wemyss was needed until then.

Thus we have two First Lords inviting me to be 1st Sea Lord and the existing 1st Sea Lord informing me that he did not wish to remain. . . . The fact that you were off with the old love before you were on with the new does not alter the situation, and I think that some consideration is due to an officer of my position, and that I should not be kept 'backing and filling' indefinitely to suit your convenience, not to speak of the unfortunate effect it would have upon the Service a large number of which were acquainted with the contemplated change.

As regards appointments, Beatty's argument was that it was a matter for the First Lord alone, and that before he made an appointment he ought to 'consult those whom the appointment affects. In pre-war days this was invariably done, as has also been done during the war. During the latter period, however, the views of those who were affected by the appointment were given far greater consideration than in pre-war days. Nevertheless in pre-war days the C.-in-C. was consulted before and not after the appointment was made, although his wishes were not invariably accepted. I would remind you that I was Naval Secretary for a year [1911–12]. I know what I am talking about. It was a matter of common sense and common courtesy.' In the Keyes incident, it would have been 'futile' to consult him after the appointment had been officially settled. And it bothered him that the Admiralty had informed Pakenham that Keyes would relieve him before he, Beatty, ever saw Keyes. 'My complaint of lack of consideration and courtesy is therefore well founded. I of course accept your assurance that there is nothing personal in the matter, which makes my treatment appear all the more remarkable. As matters obviously cannot be left as they are, I will come and see you as you propose . . .'[14] We do not know if they met; if they did, nothing substantive was accomplished.

It was through this letter that Wemyss for the first time became aware that Geddes had given Beatty assurances, 'and I now perhaps understand more fully than I did before,' he wrote the First Lord, 'why it was that he looked upon my suggestions [in their December conversation] as being something concrete. It will thus be seen that from that date in December up till now, he and I have looked upon the matter from an entirely different standpoint.'[15]

A distraught and exasperated First Lord was anxious to bring Beatty to the Admiralty and end the uncertainty and the bickering. Nor could he see, any more than many officers, how Wemyss could manage the naval business in Paris and at the same time reconstitute the Navy on a peace basis. (For want of an effective Naval head, Madden charged, 'the Admiralty business is being muddled.') On 7 March he proposed to the Prime Minister that the time had come for 'the change in the position of First Sea Lord contemplated by Geddes.'[16] The Prime Minister was not prepared to discuss the matter until he was free from his duties in Paris. Long told the King's Private Secretary that Wemyss 'sticks his toes in the ground and I am sure you will agree he can't be "kicked out." So we must I think hold our hands for the present. . . . It is a most unfortunate legacy.'[17] Long was unable to interest Wemyss in going to the Mediterranean without the governorship, or to a Home port, nor would he resign: he could not carry on in Paris unless he occupied the position of First Sea Lord.

Long had no more luck with Beatty, whom he tried to appease with an offer on 13 March that he come to the Admiralty, bring his whole staff with him, and preside over an inquiry on warship designs and building programmes in the light of wartime experi-

[14] Beatty to Wemyss, 1 March 1919; Beatty MSS. Long's 5 May memorandum for the Prime Minister confirms the essential accuracy of Beatty's statements about the Geddes and Long promises.

[15] Wemyss to Long, 10 March 1919; Wemyss MSS.

[16] Long to Lloyd George, 7 March 1919; Lloyd George MSS.

[17] Long to Stamfordham, 9 March 1919; Windsor MSS.

ence with projectiles, torpedoes, and aircraft. Beatty replied (15 March) that he would not come to the Admiralty except 'in a position of responsibility rather than in one of a purely advisory capacity.'

Wemyss's position was hardened, and the situation worsened, by the press campaign against him and which Long had feared if he delayed his resignation. 'At first these attacks had bewildered, amazed him; he had believed himself to have some claim on the gratitude of his countrymen; he had not realized that to succeed there where others have failed is often in itself a crime.'[18] The opening salvo was fired in the *Evening Standard* of 15 March. The agitation quickly spread, the Northcliffe press leading the pack. The demand was openly and vigorously made that Wemyss give way to Beatty. On 7 April *The Times* came out with a strong leader. Beatty had just hauled down his flag. It was 'unthinkable' that he be unemployed when his leave expired. 'Beyond all doubt his presence at the Admiralty would strengthen its equipment immensely . . .' On 24 April *The Times* declared that 'there was, and is, no disposition anywhere to minimize his [Wemyss's] services; but at times it is felt universally that one man and one man only can fill a particular post to universal satisfaction . . .' The pro-Beatty press claimed that the Admiral had definitely been offered the post of First Sea Lord some months earlier and that it had not been consummated because of the difficulty of finding suitable employment for Wemyss. (On the assumption that Long had cancelled Geddes's offer, there was a demand for Long's resignation.) They drew (in the words of the pro-Wemyss *Naval and Military Record*) 'harrowing pictures of Sir David Beatty pining for work and eating his heart out amidst the ruins of Athens.' On 7 May a question in the House of Commons led to a public airing of the controversy which settled one thing: Long announced that there was no intention of changing the First Sea Lord. He could only wring his hands over the mischief that was being stirred up, 'bitterly' resenting 'the attempt to create a difference of opinion in the Navy to bring about the sort of trouble we had in the Fisher-Beresford controversy.'[19]

The press agitation had eased substantially by the middle of

---

[18] *Wester Wemyss*, p. 430.
[19] Long to Lloyd George, 29 April 1919; Sir Charles Petrie, *Walter Long and His Times* (London, 1936), pp. 221-2.

June. One factor in strengthening Wemyss's position, Long believed, was 'the dignified way in which he has borne these most undeserved attacks.' Indeed, Long had now become Wemyss's ardent champion. 'Whatever justification there may be for dissatisfaction in regard to the Peace terms, the Naval conditions are absolutely satisfactory, and for this we have to thank Wemyss more than anybody else; and, in addition I should like to say that I find him a most excellent First Sea Lord. I think it will be very difficult to improve upon him, very easy to have a worse one, and I, at all events, am not prepared to "put him on the beach" simply because it is thought in some quarters that Beatty ought to come to the Admiralty.' Beatty, on the other hand, had 'behaved very foolishly.'[20] This point he developed in an interesting letter to the Prime Minister.

Beatty has certainly played his cards very badly. I do not suggest for a moment that he has had any share in the Press agitation, but he is of course aware of it and he has not done anything to check it, while there is a very general impression that her Ladyship has been extremely active. But, as I have said, they have played their cards very badly. Beatty was prepared to go to the various functions [Guildhall and Mansion House, where he gave speeches which had 'fallen quite flat'] in plain clothes, on the ground that he is unemployed. It is difficult to imagine that he did not intend by so doing to call attention to his unemployment and give the signal for an attack upon the Government. We forestalled this at the Admiralty by giving him authority to wear uniform on these occasions and reminding him of an old Admiralty Order on the subject; but at St. Paul's Cathedral he objected to the place which had been assigned to him among the other Admirals of the Fleet, and insisted upon having a seat given to him further back, to quote his own words, 'as a private individual.' Of course this kind of conduct injures him with his best friends, the sailors, and his position to-day is certainly nothing like so strong as it was three months ago. Lady Beatty, on the other hand, has on two occasions openly cut me— about as silly a thing as a woman can do.[21]

We have some evidence here of the new Beatty. The supreme command afloat, which position he had exercised with little restraint from Whitehall, coupled with his strong belief that it was

[20] Long to Stamfordham, 14 June 1919; Windsor MSS.
[21] Long to Lloyd George, 15 June 1919; Lloyd George MSS. Sir Shane Leslie has remarked that Lady Beatty's 'hatred of all who failed or fought her David made her Homeric in her wrath.' Leslie, *Long Shadows* (London, 1966), p. 210.

through the Grand Fleet that the naval war had been won, had instilled in him more than a soupçon of arrogance and *folie de grandeur*. Beatty was probably not aware that he owed his earldom to Wemyss. Returning from a holiday cruise in the Mediterranean, he had honours heaped upon him: the Freedom of the City of London, the Order of Merit, honorary degrees from English universities, and, on 6 August, an earldom. The Prime Minister had originally had a viscountcy in mind. This was raised to an earldom on Wemyss's strong recommendation. The First Sea Lord was determined that nothing should be done that might create the impression that, because it had not won a notable naval victory, the Navy had played a subordinate role in the victory of the Allies. Therefore, since Haig was having an earldom bestowed upon him, Beatty must receive the same treatment. 'It was difficult to get the right balance, for certain it was that the latter's services could in no manner be individually compared to those of Sir Douglas Haig—but there is no doubt but that had Sir David Beatty merely been made a Viscount that the Navy would have considered it a slur on the Service as a whole.'[22] On 7 August Parliament voted Beatty £100,000; Jellicoe, £50,000; Sturdee, de Robeck, Madden, Keyes, and Tyrwhitt, £10,000 each, and they were created baronets as well (except for Sturdee, who already was one).

Wemyss resigned when the war honours list was published. Long had told him that he was to receive a viscountcy and a money grant. Yet, 'alone amongst the war leaders he was neither thanked, nor honoured, nor rewarded. It was the disavowal of his whole policy . . .' Within the hour Wemyss had sent a letter of resignation to the First Lord: '. . . What measures of success I achieved I leave to the Nation to judge; that I have not succeeded in pleasing the Government is evident. . . .' Long, for whatever reason, refused to accept his resignation. He must remain at his post. This, too, was the position of the Lords of the Admiralty and his friends. The argument was that 'his motives would be misconstrued and lay him open to the suspicion of acting from personal pique.' Wemyss would only consent to hold his resignation over for a couple of months. 'Besides, he had no desire to

22 Wemyss's memoirs. Wemyss adds: 'Had Sir David been less vain, or had been a man of more sound judgement, he would have realised the situation—but unfortunately the equality of his rewards to those of Haig gave him the idea that he was as big a man. He may have been—but he never showed it, for he never had the same opportunity.'

end his career on a scandal and become the subject of controversy, or more newspaper polemics.'[23] On 28 August he handed in his formal resignation, to take effect two months later. The 'psychological moment' had arrived for him to leave. 'The war has come to a successful end: Peace has been signed: the Naval Staff has been reorganized and placed on a sound basis, and the Naval pay has been put on a satisfactory footing, and I therefore consider that the tasks, for the carrying out of which I was called to the Admiralty, have been satisfactorily performed.'[24] The resignation took effect on 1 November—Beatty relieved him—on which day Wemyss was promoted to be an Admiral of the Fleet. He reluctantly accepted a peerage and was gazetted a Baron on 22 November. Though only 55 and 'still capable of much work,' it was obvious that his naval career had ended: there were no appointments in the Service for a former First Sea Lord.

3. PERSONNEL AND NAVAL STAFF REFORMS

There had been a growing disquiet among the lower-deck ratings from the latter part of 1917. Although there was no serious discontent, and no organized or concerted movement afloat to effect changes, nor any feelings against the officers, there was unrest among the ratings. During the war, until 1917, the basic pay of an able seaman was only twopence per day more than it had been in the middle of the nineteenth century (1852), when it had been fixed at 1s. 6d. per day. What now brought matters to a head was the invidious comparison with civilian pay scales. Other grievances included the Government's action in withholding the pensions of men who had completed their qualifying time before the war but had accepted an invitation to continue to serve, and the belief that a considerable sum of money had been accumulated in prize money: the men wanted part of it, at least, to be distributed. The key problem, in Beatty's view, was the pay, and he wrote to the Admiralty of 'the urgent necessity for an immediate increase of pay.'[25]

The few grudging concessions that were made on 1 October

23 *Wester Wemyss*, pp. 439–41.
24 Petrie, *Walter Long*, p. 223.
25 Beatty to Admiralty, 27 September 1917; Admiralty MSS. He had consulted the Flag Officers of the Grand Fleet squadrons in September 1917 on the sources and extent of the discontent.

1917 in pay, pensions, messing allowance, and kit upkeep allowance did not stem the tide of disaffection. Geddes had no success in his attempts to prod the Treasury into taking action. The situation moved towards a climax in the last months of the war. Lionel Yexley, Editor of the lower-deck organ *The Fleet*, submitted a confidential memorandum to Geddes on the causes of 'the present grave discontent.' The discontent had grown during the war until 'at the present moment the lower deck is one great combustible mass. Should an explosion point be touched . . . the whole Navy would burst into flame.' He detailed no fewer than sixteen causes of discontent over pay, pensions, leave arrangements, and so on—'many of them trivial in themselves, but in the aggregate forming a very dangerous combination of pinpricks.' The root evil was pay. 'There is universal discontent right throughout the Fleet at the pay. Men watch the strikes and threats of strikes amongst outside workers, all of which result in increase of pay or bonuses. Every rise of pay to civilian workers penalises the Service man and his wife because of the increased prices that follow.'

The leave arrangements at the Ports are the cause of great irritation. Take Portsmouth. At the commencement of hostilities a Port Order was issued stopping all week-end leave and night leave to every other night (this has recently been modified in the case of Chief P.O.'s [petty officers], to two nights out of three). This means that married men living at the Ports can only go home to their families every other night, whilst their Sundays are broken into by being forced to go on board for Church Parade. Men doing long service at sea and only very short periods at their Home Ports feel that they should be given every facility to spend time with their families, especially as the leave arrangements lead to very serious congestion in the Port Establishments.

Yexley pointed to the 'monster demonstrations' that were being planned for the three Home ports, and he concluded: 'This, then, is the situation as it stands. The men of the Navy are not disaffected in the way they were in 1797: *generally* speaking, the relationship between officers and men is good (but for that fact there would have been trouble long since), neither are the men "war weary" . . . from one cause and another the lower deck is a huge mass of combustible material and should some outward incident precipitate an explosion at a given point it would be almost impossible to localise it.'[26]

[26] Yexley to Geddes, 4 September 1918, and enclosed memorandum; Admiralty MSS.

What did the Admiralty do about these alarming statements? The Board 'tested the correctness' of Yexley's views on the feeling in the Navy. Their finding was that

although there is a certain amount of dissatisfaction on the Lower Deck, there is no probability of this assuming proportions that would impair the discipline of the Navy or lead to any serious incident. . . . So far as the dissatisfaction is due to minor causes, I can assure you that the Board have for some time past been giving much attention to questions of this kind. A considerable number of concessions have already been made, and others have been under consideration by Committees, etc.

Although, however, much will have been done in this way to remove the minor causes of complaint, the prime cause of dissatisfaction, namely, the apparent contrast between the advantages secured by civilian workers and those obtained by the Navy, will remain.[27]

What had been merely dissatisfaction while the war was on reached the near flash point after hostilities had ceased. A naval 'strike' was within measurable distance. The press got into the act, calling upon a niggardly Government to do justice to the men 'hidden in the northern mists' in the matter of wages and allowances, leave, improvement of chances of reaching the quarter-deck 'though the hawse-pipe,' and so on. 'Is this state of affairs to continue?' asked *The Observer* (22 December). 'Or are we going to recognise in a practical way the unspeakable services the Navy has rendered to the nation as an act of gratitude and before we are forced to it by rising trouble before which the scandal of the police strike will pale into insignificance?' Leaders, articles, and letters appeared in the press in profusion, all supporting the cause of *both* officers and men and demanding that the Government do the right thing by them.

There had not been a general review of officers' pay since 1869; even then there had only been some adjustments in the pay scales (1870). Flag officers' rates of pay dated back to 1816; those of captains to 1864; and the maximum rate of a paymaster commander went back to 1854. A lieutenant's starting pay was fixed at 10/- *per diem* in 1854. There it was when the war came,

---

[27] Geddes to Lloyd George, 26 September 1918; Lloyd George MSS. As an illustration of Geddes's last remark, dockyard shipwrights, when working afloat at Scapa, were able to earn from £6 to £7 a week—nearly the pay of a Commander—and skilled labourers from £5 to £6 a week. Additionally, both received the Service ration.

and it was only 12/- when the war ended. Commanders received 20/- a day from 1864, only 23/- when the war ended. Chaplains and naval instructors were receiving the same rates in 1918 as in 1870, except for a few minor improvements in the lower grades in 1917. Other branches (engineer officers, medical officers, and marines) had, by comparison, done somewhat better since 1903. Finally, pension scales were practically the same as in 1870.[28]

The grave post-Armistice reports caused the Admiralty to make a general signal to the Fleet on 27 December that 'the whole question of the pay of both officers and men has been engaging their attention and their recommendations will be placed before H.M. Government at earliest possible moment'. Madden testified at this time to the seriousness of the situation. His inquiries in the 1st Battle Squadron showed that few of the Hostilities officers and men would volunteer to serve on, 'because both officers and men feel that pay and allowances are inadequate to meet the high prices of living now ruling, and they can do far better ashore.'[29] Wemyss singled out the crux of the whole difficulty: 'The fact that they have been living and serving alongside of highly paid Australian and United States ratings has also brought home to them the fact that the British Naval Officers and men are paid considerably below their market value, and now that they have been on leave and realise for themselves how greatly other general wages have risen, and how the price of living has gone up, the discontent is making itself more felt.'[30]

A Committee under Vice-Admiral Sir Martyn Jerram (Naval Personnel Committee), which had been considering proposals for revision of rates of pay and allowances, was reconstituted on 6 January 1919 as the Naval Pay Committee. Its new charge was to inquire into the pay, allowances, and pensions of all ranks and ratings. Working with the Committee were twelve 'advisory representatives' from the lower deck. Subsequently, a separate

---

[28] Admiralty Memorandum for the War Cabinet, 'Naval Officers' Pay' (G.T.-7505), 18 June 1919.

[29] Madden to Beatty, 27 December 1918; Beatty MSS. The Admiralty announcement that Prize money would probably not exceed 30/– a share had disappointed the men, 'and it is very desirable that when this is paid, a clear statement should be published showing the disposal of the whole Prize Fund.' *Ibid.*

[30] Wemyss to Lloyd George, 4 January 1919; Lloyd George MSS. Many of the ratings, when they came home on leave at Christmas, 'rather than burden their wives with the additional expense of their upkeep at home, had returned to the Fleet before the expiration of their leave'. Long, 8 May 1919; W.C. 564.

committee under Rear-Admiral Sir Lionel Halsey was appointed to deal with officers' pay, allowances, and retired pay. On 1 February the Government gave *ad interim* increases recommended by the Jerram Committee, pending the reports of the Committees and a permanent improvement in rates of pay.

The Jerram Committee reported on 27 March. The Admiralty's proposals, based on the Committee's recommendations, were in the hands of the Chancellor of the Exchequer on 11 April. At the War Cabinet of 29 April the First Lord strongly urged the acceptance of the Jerram Report forthwith. 'It was impossible to exaggerate the seriousness of the position. . . . He was strongly of the opinion that the Navy would accept nothing less than the present recommendations.' The War Cabinet balked. The Prime Minister was not converted, and Churchill and Bonar Law favoured a go-slow policy, because of the possible effects the acceptance of the naval pay proposals might have on the Army and the Air Force. The War Cabinet reached no decision but agreed to consider the proposals again after receiving Air Ministry and War Office reports on their probable effects upon the pay rates of their Services.[31] On 6 May the First Lord received serious reports regarding the feelings of the lower deck and a strong note from Wemyss that he would resign if the pay and pension recommendations of the Jerram Committee were not accepted by the War Cabinet the next day. On Thursday, 8 May, Long informed the War Cabinet that 'if this settlement was delayed over the week-end it would be at the gravest possible risk. . . . If, however, an acceptance of the Jerram Committee's Report were announced by the following Saturday he thought affairs would calm down.'[32] The next day the War Cabinet accepted the bulk of the Jerram Report: 42 of the 60 recommendations, with ten others promised for later consideration. Had they not, Wemyss would have resigned: he had gone to the meeting with his resignation in his pocket. The new rates of pay brought the basic rate of an able seaman up to 4/- a day. Long-service pensions were augmented; allowances were raised. The men and indeed the whole Navy and the country expressed their complete satisfaction. 'An old scandal, which lay heavily on the nation, has at last been removed,' declared the *Daily Telegraph* (10 May). For the *Naval and Military Record* (21

[31] W.C. 560.   [32] W.C. 564.

May) 'the liberal way in which the claims of the lower deck have been met is a good omen for the equally just demands of the officers, who are still waiting with exemplary patience to learn their fate'. The Halsey Committee reported on 9 May. Most of its recommendations for increases in pay and allowances were accepted by the Admiralty in June and were announced in July. They, too, were long overdue. As an example of the new pay scales, a lieutenant found himself with 17/- a day (up from 11/-), and there was about the same proportionate increase for the more senior officers.[33]

Not apparent at the time was a grave oversight: the increases in pay, etc. for the officers and men were not linked to the cost of living. This was to create difficulties in a few years, when the Treasury tried to take advantage of the reduced cost of living to scale down the benefits. Marriage allowances were not introduced until the mid-20s for the men, 1938 for the officers.

The settlement of the pay problems accomplished one of the two major post-war tasks that Wemyss had set for himself. The other was a reorganization of the Naval Staff on rational lines. This had been accomplished by August 1919.[34] The Operations Committee, established in September 1917, was now to consist of these members of the Board: the First Lord, First Sea Lord, D.C.N.S., and A.C.N.S. 'It deals with questions of naval strategy and subjects connected with the provision, training, equipment, efficiency, organisation, and utilisation of the Navy as a fighting force, and will meet periodically as necessary.' Working under the Operations Committee was the Naval Staff, which now comprised eight divisions: Intelligence, Plans, Training and Staff Duties, and Trade under the general direction of the D.C.N.S.; Communications, Operations, Local Defence, and Gunnery and Torpedo under the general direction of the A.C.N.S. The duties of each division were carefully described and with a chart in each case to indicate its organization. 'Notes on Procedure' laid down rules of correct procedure with specific examples.

Additionally, war experience had shown the importance of

---

[33] The two Reports and the Government's decisions with respect to them are in Cmd. 149 (Jerram) and Cmd. 270 (Halsey).

[34] 'Instructions for Naval Staff,' Office Memorandum No. 187, 2 August 1919; *Office Memoranda, 1919* (Naval Library). For the major wartime Naval Staff reorganizations, see *From the Dreadnought to Scapa Flow*, iv. 177-8, 218-23, and the chart below.

properly trained officers for Naval Staff work. In 1912 a course of training such officers had been started at the War College. Now, in June 1919, a separate Naval Staff College with a twelve-months course was instituted at Greenwich. The situation looked promising now that the Admiralty were aware of the importance of this kind of training.

EVOLUTION OF THE NAVAL STAFF[35]

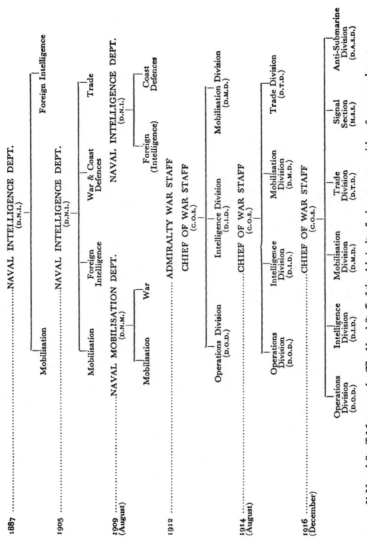

[35] Naval Staff Monograph, *The Naval Staff of the Admiralty*, facing p. 150, with a few amendments.

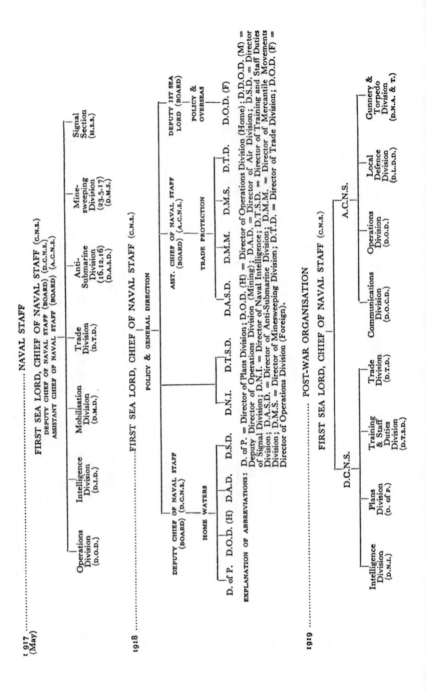

NAVAL STAFF

1917 (May)

FIRST SEA LORD, CHIEF OF NAVAL STAFF (C.N.S.)
DEPUTY CHIEF OF NAVAL STAFF (BOARD) (D.C.N.S.)
ASSISTANT CHIEF OF NAVAL STAFF (BOARD) (A.C.N.S.)

- Operations Division (D.O.D.)
- Intelligence Division (D.I.D.)
- Mobilisation Division (D.M.D.)
- Trade Division (D.T.D.)
- Anti-Submarine Division (16.12.16) (D.A.S.D.)
- Mine-sweeping Division (23.5.17) (D.M.S.)
- Signal Section (H.S.S.)

1918

FIRST SEA LORD, CHIEF OF NAVAL STAFF (C.N.S.)
POLICY & GENERAL DIRECTION

DEPUTY CHIEF OF NAVAL STAFF (BOARD) (D.C.N.S.)
HOME WATERS
D. of P.   D.O.D. (H)   D.A.D.   D.S.D.   D.N.I.

ASST. CHIEF OF NAVAL STAFF (BOARD) (A.C.N.S.)
TRADE PROTECTION
D.T.S.D.   D.A.S.D.   D.M.M.   D.M.S.   D.T.D.

DEPUTY 1ST SEA LORD (BOARD)
POLICY & OVERSEAS
D.O.D. (F)

EXPLANATION OF ABBREVIATIONS: D. of P. = Director of Plans Division; D.O.D. (H) = Director of Operations Division (Home); D.D.O.D. (M) = Director of Operations Division (Mining); D.A.D. = Director of Air Division; D.S.D. = Director of Signal Division; D.N.I. = Director of Naval Intelligence; D.T.S.D. = Director of Training and Staff Duties Division; D.A.S.D. = Director of Anti-Submarine Division; D.M.M. = Director of Mercantile Movements Division; D.M.S. = Director of Minesweeping Division; D.T.D. = Director of Trade Division; D.O.D. (F) = Director of Operations Division (Foreign).

1919

POST-WAR ORGANISATION

FIRST SEA LORD, CHIEF OF NAVAL STAFF (C.N.S.)
D.C.N.S.
A.C.N.S.

- Intelligence Division (D.N.I.)
- Plans Division (D. of P.)
- Training & Staff Duties Division (D.T.S.D.)
- Trade Division (D.T.D.)
- Communications Division (D.O.C.D.)
- Operations Division (D.O.D.)
- Local Defence Division (D.L.D.D.)
- Gunnery & Torpedo Division (D.N.A. & T.)

IX

Naval Policy: Uncertainties and New Rivalries

I am a hopeful and sincere advocate of the League of Nations. . . . But a League of Nations is no substitute for the supremacy of the British Fleet.
WINSTON CHURCHILL at Dundee, 26 November 1918.

The Prime Minister pointed out that the most impressive fact in the War had been the overwhelming superiority of the British Navy. While our Allies recognised its value it also somewhat alarmed them.
LLOYD GEORGE at War Cabinet meeting, 25 October 1918.

. . . she has ever maintained her commercial supremacy by superior naval strength. In turn she has crushed Spain, Holland, and Germany because they threatened her supremacy on the sea. Her objection to our building program, both commercial and naval, is because of a belief that we are now probably threatening that supremacy.
ADMIRAL BENSON to President Wilson, 28 April 1919.

I. THE NAVY ESTIMATES

THE First Lord's speech in the Commons on 12 March 1919 introducing the Navy Estimates for 1919–20 was necessarily of a very general character. It was impossible, he stated, for the Admiralty to present detailed Estimates until the Peace Conference had settled the general scheme of world armaments of the future. He asked for £149,200,000. This compares with the last pre-war Estimates of £51 million and wartime naval expenditure of £205 million in 1915–16, £209 million in 1916–17, £227 million in 1917–18, and £325 million (estimated) for 1918–19. At the time of the Armistice expenditure was actually at the rate of over £350 million a year. The most interesting passage in Long's speech, and the only piece of positive information that he gave, was that the Admiralty were reducing new construction. The long list of ships which had been cancelled since the Armistice included the three battle cruisers *Howe*, *Rodney*, and *Anson*.[1] The only capital ship under construction was the battle cruiser *Hood*, which had been launched in August 1918. Long refused to discuss questions of future naval policy. He excused himself on the grounds that the best brains of the Navy were exhausted by the strain of war and needed a short period of recuperation before they addressed themselves to the post-war problems, and that determination of British naval policy must await the decisions of the Peace Conference.

There was sharp criticism in the Conservative press of Long's failure to explain naval policy, whether past, present, or future. The liberal press was aghast at the 'extravagant' estimates in view of the 'non-existence' of the German Fleet and the fact that all other sizeable fleets were those of Britain's Allies. The *Manchester Guardian* (13 March), for instance, declared:

> On the question of the work which the navy is now doing in the Russian expeditions; on the grave questions raised by the disclosures of Lord Jellicoe [*The Grand Fleet, 1914–16*, published early in 1919] and others with regard to the acute danger of this country in the early stages of the war; on the question of the organisation of the Admiralty for war, past, present, and future; on the question how far our grave deficiencies have been due to a failure to draw on the best brains of the country for the service of the navy, and how far that failure persists or is likely to revive—on these things, which are of great moment and interest to the country, the First Lord preserved a placid reticence, preferring to emit cries of joy over the historic achievements of the navy, which really no one fails to realise.

By July the shape of the 1919–20 Estimates was clearer. The total amount envisaged now was £170,901,500. 'The Board of Admiralty are fully conscious of the fact that the sum asked for

---

1 Some £860,000 had been spent on them. The decision to cancel their construction forthwith had been reached at a Board meeting of 27 February 1919. It was also decided then to reconsider the question of building additional battle cruisers after the peace terms were finally settled, 'as unless further Battle Cruisers are built in the near future we shall before long fall behind the United States Navy in ships of that class.' An important reason for stopping the *Howe* and her sister ships was that, their design being three years old, if completed they would not have been up-to-date vessels.

Ordered and under construction on 11 November 1918 were 1,005 vessels, including the 4 battle cruisers, 21 light cruisers, 11 flotilla leaders, 97 destroyers, 73 submarines, and 2 aircraft carriers. Cancelled in the following twelve months were 611 vessels, including, besides the 3 battle cruisers, 4 each of the light cruisers and flotilla leaders, 40 of the destroyers, and 33 of the submarines.

is a gigantic one, and they profoundly regret the necessity for making this tremendous demand upon the public purse . . .' The £119 million increase over the last pre-war Estimates was due 'practically entirely' to the expenditure, non-recurring, necessitated by war commitments and the recent increases in pay, allowances, and pensions. 'I am of course aware,' ran the First Lord's statement, 'that the question will be asked: Against what possible enemy are you preparing?'[2] The answer to this query, which Long did not give, involves us in a larger discussion of the not clearly defined naval policy of the Armistice period.

There was, to begin with, a momentary uncertainty about the future of the capital ship. Some officers were convinced that the day of the battleship was drawing to a close, and that any future war at sea would be won or lost without the participation of the mastodons, which had become too vulnerable. The next naval contest, this school maintained, would be principally an affair of small and speedy surface ships, submarines, and aircraft—and aircraft (bombing planes) would be the deadliest of all. A correspondent writing in *The Naval and Military Record* (2 April 1919) predicted that the largest dreadnought would have little chance against the super bombing planes of the not distant future. 'They would close it at a speed of four miles a minute, and let go their bombs in such quantities that a big percentage of hits would be assured. A single direct hit from a ½-ton bomb with armour-piercing nose would probably cause more destruction than two torpedoes. . . . Neither high speed nor zigzagging will save a ship from practically certain destruction once she has been sighted by a flight of big bombing planes.' The Third Sea Lord and Controller, Bartolomé, represented a parallel line of thought. His view was that, because the gun had, for the moment anyway, defeated the armour, they should drop the capital ship and develop the submarine and the aeroplane.

Other officers argued that nothing had occurred to diminish the importance of the capital ship, even if she had become more vulnerable. Her justification, as summed up by the D.C.N.S. in simplistic terms, lay in her 'power to overcome smaller surface

---

2 Long's memorandum for the War Cabinet, 'Navy Estimates 1919–1920' (G.T.-7645), 5 July 1919. The final Estimates had been trimmed back to £157,528,800, when presented to the House of Commons on 1 December 1919, or an increase of £8,328,000 over the March forecast.

ships than herself, and consequently her strategical function of supporting them remains. If battleships are used for this function, and this has been the accepted view acted upon during the present war, they must be prepared to fight their equals, and the fact of their having become vulnerable to their equals should have the effect on us that we must endeavour to diminish the effect of such vulnerability by tactical methods, and also by modifications in construction.'[3]

Fremantle's was the policy the Admiralty adopted in the post-war period. It remained an axiom, justified by the results of the war, that the command of the sea would rest with the Fleet strongest in capital ships, and in all fleet comparisons the Admiralty emphasized dreadnought and battle-cruiser strength. There was no great fear of the torpedo: no modern British or German capital ship had been sunk by torpedo in the whole war, and under-water protection was being further developed. The Admiralty scheme of June 1919 for a post-war fleet called for 33 battleships and 8 battle cruisers as well as 60 light cruisers and 352 destroyers.

The more important decisions on post-war naval policy waited on the results of the Paris Peace Conference, and these revolved about a new factor on the international scene, the incipient Anglo-American naval rivalry.

2. THE 'SEA BATTLE OF PARIS'

The Royal Navy had emerged from the war with a measure of supremacy which it had never possessed before in all its history: over 1,300 war vessels of 3,250,000 tons, or nearly the naval tonnage of the rest of the world.[4] The principal units were 42 dreadnoughts and battle cruisers, 109 cruisers, 13 aircraft carriers, 527 destroyers and torpedo boats, and 137 submarines. The British public, to say nothing of the Government and the Admiralty, had just begun to assume that, with this preponderance and the practical disappearance of the Kaiser's Fleet, there would be a general slackening of naval construction in Britain and round the world. Yet, within a month after the Armistice the Admiralty were

---

[3] Fremantle's minute of 24 January 1919 on the Third Sea Lord's position; Fremantle MSS.

[4] For capital ship strength of the naval Powers in the Armistice period, actual and projected, see the tables at the end of the chapter.

concerned that the traditional supremacy of the Navy might be lost. The principal challenger was the United States. When the war ended, the American Navy was equal to the combined navies of France, Italy, and Japan. It had 16 dreadnoughts in commission, none over eight years old, and three nearing completion. Of the 16 capital ships in the 1916 programme (10 dreadnoughts, 6 battle cruisers), four had been laid down. The completion of this programme would in a few years' time give the American Navy 35 modern capital ships and a fleet qualitatively superior to the British Fleet, 13 of whose 42 capital ships were obsolescent. This, from the Admiralty's point of view, was bad enough. But the Navy Department had announced plans in the summer of 1918 for another programme, to be commenced in 1919, a six-year one which included 12 more dreadnoughts and 16 more battle cruisers. The General Board of the Navy (an advisory body composed of senior officers of distinction and concerned with programme planning, etc.) explained (10 September 1918) that the goal of this programme was to give the United States a navy at least equal to any other by 1925. Actually, the Board had the Anglo-Japanese combination in mind, but was using numerical equality to this Alliance 'only as a crude index. Its intent was to prepare America for a spectacular future as the world's dominant mercantile power, a destiny dimly visualized except that it was not expected to be fulfilled without a navy powerful enough to command the distant seas.'[5] The Administration had cut the dreadnoughts to 10 and the battle cruisers to 6, so duplicating the 1916 programme, and, like it, it was to be a three-year programme. In October 1918 the Navy Department asked Congress to authorize this programme. The prospect was of an American battle fleet of 39 dreadnoughts and 12 battle cruisers, all modern ships, a force that dwarfed even the Grand Fleet in its prime.

One authoritative study claims that the objective of the Administration's naval policy was 'to force Great Britain to support the league-of-nations project and then to collaborate in a general reduction of armaments on the basis of naval equality with the United States.'[6] The American big-navy programme was, as

---

[5] Warner R. Schilling, *Admirals and Foreign Policy, 1913–1919* (unpublished Yale University Ph.D. dissertation, 1953), pp. 231–2.

[6] Harold and Margaret Sprout, *Toward a New Order of Sea Power: American Naval Policy and the World Scene, 1918–1922* (Princeton, N.J., 1946, 2nd ed.), p. 66.

Professor Schilling has persuasively shown, a good deal more than a bargaining device, a club held over the British at the Peace Conference. The United States meant business. On 23 October 1918 Admiral Benson, the Chief of Naval Operations (equivalent to First Sea Lord), told the Naval Affairs Committee of the House of Representatives that the second programme would 'put our Navy on an equality with any in the world, so far as we can see in the future.' Immediately after the Armistice, Secretary of the Navy Daniels urged Congress to complete the 1916 programme, which, as regards big ships, had been interrupted by the need to utilize the shipyards for the construction of A/S craft. In his annual message to Congress on 2 December Wilson stated that he took it for granted that this programme would be continued, and that the 1918 programme was 'not new but a continuation of the policy entered upon in 1916.' On 30 December Daniels told the House Naval Affairs Committee that, failing the adoption of a disarmament programme by the Peace Conference, the United States would need a Navy 'bigger than any other in the world'. Benson (to say nothing of the London Planning Section, which he had set up in December 1917 as part of Admiral Sims's staff) was, to quote Colonel House, 'obsessed with this idea' of Anglo-American equality. Although he knew that the completion of the 1916 programme would achieve this goal, since the American ships would overall be more modern, he wanted *numerical* equality as well, that is, American *superiority*. The 1918 programme would secure this *summum bonum*. There were, however, such powerful objections to the new programme in Congress that its prospects for passage were poor.[7]

In analysing the drives behind the formidable American plans, the starting point is the general fear in the U.S. Navy of a war that would arise out of trade rivalry with Great Britain. As the London Planning Section declared: 'Four great Powers have arisen in the world to compete with Great Britain for commercial supremacy on the seas—Spain, Holland, France, Germany. Each of these

---

[7] Schilling says that the British had anticipated this eventuality, which was 'no doubt responsible for the fact that during the Peace conference British naval diplomacy ignored the 1918 program and instead concentrated its energy on attempts to get the United States to abandon its 1915 [1916] building program.' *Admirals and Foreign Policy*, pp. 258–9. I am not so certain. Lloyd George harped on the 1916 programme, but the Admiralty records would indicate that the Navy was exercised over *both* programmes.

Powers in succession have been defeated by Great Britain and her fugitive Allies. A fifth commercial Power, the greatest one yet, is now arising to compete for at least commercial equality with Great Britain. Already the signs of jealousy are visible. Historical precedent warns us to watch closely the moves we make or permit to be made.' Again, more bluntly: 'Successful trade rivalry strikes at the very root of British interest and British prosperity, and may even threaten the existence of the British Empire. If British trade is seriously threatened, her people may feel that war is justified—as a measure of self preservation.'[8] Let it be stated here before moving on that neither the British Government nor the British Navy ever had any intention of going to war with the United States over the issue of trade rivalry.

The London Planning Section memorandum of 23 November 1918 cited British maritime practice in time of war as a second possible cause of war. A Navy 'as powerful as any other Navy' was therefore needed to further the growth of 'American ideals of justice and fair dealing.' One hears less and less of this argument as the controversy over the 'Freedom of the Seas' (see below) faded away. In any case, this issue was not one which would seriously exacerbate Anglo-American relations and possibly lead to war unless Britain were already at war with a third Power.

Then there was the League argument. No one Power should be able to dominate it because of overwhelming military or naval strength. Daniels maintained it would be 'improper' for the United States to contribute any less than the 'greatest other power' to a League of Nations naval force, but that if the Peace Conference failed, the United States would need the greatest navy in the world.[9] This was also Benson's position, though there are those

---

[8] Memoranda of 4 and 23 November 1918; *ibid.*, pp. 230, 242–3. Benson reorganized the London Planning Section in December 1918 into his own Naval Advisory Staff in Paris: two Admirals (including himself) and two Captains. Its job was to advise the American Peace Commissioners on naval matters. The Naval Advisory Staff advanced the trade-rivalry argument in a 7 April 1919 memorandum. Schilling cites others as believing that trade competition was the 'key determinant' in post-war relations with Great Britain: Commander W. S. Pye, Fleet Intelligence Officer of the Atlantic Fleet, Admiral Mayo, C.-in-C., Atlantic Fleet, and Admiral McKean, Assistant Chief of Naval Operations. There were critics—less influential officers, including Sims (Wilson considered him hopelessly Anglophile)—of the 1918 building programme who deplored its effect on Anglo-American relations. *Ibid*, pp. 248–57.

[9] Daniels to Wilson, 4 January 1919; Seth P. Tillman, *Anglo-American Relations at the Paris Peace Conference of 1919* (Princeton, N.J., 1961), p. 288.

scholars who have questioned his sincerity. 'In order,' he asserted, 'to stabilize the League of Nations and have it develop into what we intend it to be, the U.S. must increase her naval strength to such a force as will be able to prevent Great Britain at least from dominating and dictating to other powers within the League.'[10]

Despite the Japanese sabre-rattling in the Far East, most American naval planners did not at this time regard the Japanese Fleet as an independent threat. Rather was it the possibility of the co-operation of the Japanese and British Fleets that they felt they had to bear in mind. This was an additional reason for building a Navy at least equal to the Royal Navy.

However they appraised American motives, both Liberal and Conservative press opinion in Great Britain took a generally sympathetic view of American naval ambitions, refusing to see in them a threat to British security. The two Navies, it was felt, would be found working together to keep the peace, whether or not under League auspices, and therefore Britain should welcome an America that was strong at sea. Thus, the Liberal *Westminster Gazette* (4 January 1919): 'We have no jealousy in the matter, for we do not look upon America as a possible enemy, but rather as a powerful colleague in keeping the peace at sea.' Likewise the Conservative *Daily Telegraph* (2 May 1919): As the two Fleets had co-operated so closely to win the peace, 'so they must continue in future years to work in cordial fellowship to maintain that Peace against disturbances from whatever quarter it may come.' Service opinion took the same level-headed approach, holding that the American naval authorities had in view co-operation with Britain in the future policing of the seas rather than a serious rivalry in the matter of naval supremacy. Indeed, there seem to have been more American observers who regarded British naval power as a serious threat to American security than the other way round.

The Admiralty were in this instance not in tune with public opinion. They were suspicious of American plans to have a Navy second to none, and at a time when Britain had virtually ceased the construction of capital ships. The Americans had 21 dreadnoughts and 5 battle cruisers built and building, to say nothing of the considerable number projected. 'The magnitude of this fleet,' warned the D.C.N.S., 'now the only fleet which is a potential

---

[10] Benson to Wilson, 5 May 1919; Daniels, *The Wilson Era*, pp. 369–70.

rival, and consequently menace, to ours, must be a matter of great concern to us, as it must govern our future building programmes.'[11] The Admiralty were puzzled to find that the American President, the chief promoter of the League of Nations, had selected this time to press upon Congress a naval programme which even the Admiralty at the height of the naval rivalry with Germany would have thought large. 'The idea of the League of Nations,' Geddes observed (24 October 1918), 'does not comprise increased armament but decreased armament.' At his request the Plans Division produced a paper showing the effect of the execution of the second building programme:

	Building or Projected	Increase	Total
Dreadnoughts	13	10	23
Battle Cruisers	6	6	12
Light Cruisers	10 ⎫ 258	140	398
Destroyers	248 ⎭		

The Plans Division offered these as probably the two ideas behind the proposed expansion of the U.S. Navy: (1) To protect American interests against Japanese aggression. The naval expansion was 'probably aimed at Japan, for belief in an eventual struggle with that country is deeply rooted in the minds of many Americans and their interests are certainly liable to clash at several points.' America's 'open door' policy in East Asia v. Japan's direct opposite policy, the Philippines, the immigration question in California, and Japan's aggressive policy towards 'China or Siberia': these were possible sources of an American-Japanese war in the future. By the end of 1924 the Japanese Fleet might consist of 8 dreadnoughts, 8 battle cruisers, 7 modern light cruisers, and an indeterminate number of destroyers. (2) The desire for a strong Navy to assist in supporting a League of Nations. '. . . it is generally agreed that any practical plan for a League of Nations and the abolition of war are dependent on a supernational force consisting of the armies and navies of the contracting Powers. A desire to possess a voice in such a League commensurate with her size and wealth may account for the proposed expansion of the U.S.A. Navy.'[12]

The reasons for American naval expansion were of less interest to the Admiralty than the hard fact of the expansion itself. It was,

11 Fremantle's minute of 12 November 1918 on the paper cited in the following note.
12 'Remarks on U.S.A. Building Programme,' 11 November 1918; Admiralty MSS. It was the League factor that the D.N.I. offered as the key to American naval policy:

Geddes deemed, 'the aim and purpose of the President to reduce comparatively the preponderance in sea-power of the British Empire': by naval building, by the allocation of the ships of the High Seas Fleet that Germany would lose under the peace treaty, and by combination with other naval powers jealous of British sea power.[13] The various strands in the deep concern of the Admiralty over the naval situation are brought out in this letter from the new First Lord to the Prime Minister:

I do not want to get into competition with the United States for many reasons:—first, because I believe that if they chose to put all their resources into the provision of a larger Navy the competition between us would be impossible, and we should in the end be beaten from the point of view merely of finance; second, because I naturally do not wish to assume that they will be hostile to us.

The best citizens of the United States, especially the Republicans, are friendly to us, but our secret intelligence makes it perfectly clear that a vigorous campaign is again on foot to promote hostility to England . . . and I am sure you will realise that we might find ourselves in a position in which the U.S.A. were antagonistic, even threateningly so, to us. The Navy, as you have made it quite clear at the Peace Conference, is the very foundation of our existence as a free people, and we cannot afford to trifle with our Naval strength. It may be that the U.S.A. are bluffing, but we cannot, I submit, presume that this is the case, and therefore I recommend diplomatic action which would, I think, result in putting an end to a policy wholly inconsistent with the League of Nations and very dangerous both for us and for the U.S.A.[14]

What the First Lord did not say was that tradition and pride—the 'Britannia rules the waves' outlook, or what Daniels sarcastically called 'their national religion—domination of the seven seas'— constituted an extremely important facet of the British sensitivity to, and annoyance over, American naval plans and prospects.

The threatening Anglo-American naval rivalry was a *leitmotiv* at the Paris peace negotiations and the subject of considerable private negotiation between the two delegations in March and

---

'. . . it is a reasonable surmise that Wilson would push his proposals as to the League of Nations with more confidence if he knew that U.S. preparations would prevent the Naval executive of that League from falling automatically into the hands of Great Britain.' Sinclair's minute, 16 April 1919; Admiralty MSS.

[13] Admiralty memorandum for the War Cabinet (over Geddes's signature), 'United States Naval Policy,' 7 November 1918; Geddes MSS.

[14] Long to Lloyd George, 16 February 1919; Lloyd George MSS.

April 1919. The 'Sea Battle of Paris,' as Daniels called it, began a
climactic phase on a morning late in March, soon after Daniels's
arrival in Paris, when Wemyss, hustled over from London by
Lloyd George, made an unannounced call on the Navy Secretary.
Benson, hearing of this visit, rushed over to defend the pass. He
arrived as Wemyss was bluntly asking Daniels to explain the
purpose of the projected American warships. Benson interjected
that the question was impertinent and the Secretary should not
reply. On this chilly note the meeting adjourned till the afternoon.[15] The afternoon conference was held in an explosive atmosphere. Daniels

never saw two men of their high standing so infuriated as Admiral
Benson and Admiral Wemyss in that conversation. They exchanged
such bitter comments that at one time I feared they would pass the
bounds and have an altercation. But happily nothing worse occurred
than very violent expressions and violent words, and I think this was
partly due to my seeking to calm them down, though doubtless they
would have restrained themselves. The British Admiral thought that
his country ought to have the right to build the biggest navy in the
world and we ought to agree to it. To Benson that would have been
treason to his own country. So you can see how far apart they were.[16]

Benson's prejudices and character had done nothing to lower the
flash point at this famous meeting. He was strongly anti-British
(Lloyd George said he had 'a double dose of Anglo-phobia') and
antagonistic to the Admiralty. Long described him as 'a man of
mulish character and not very quick at grasping any ideas other
than his own.' Yet the vast difference exposed was no personal
difference. The two positions could not be, and obviously were
not going to be, reconciled by the professional heads of the two
Navies.

The politicians now took over. Referring to his conversations
with Long, Daniels writes of 'the battle royal that lasted several
weeks.' In one of their talks, on 29 March, Long received the
impression from Daniels that the United States would be prepared
for an accommodation on their building programme if the Peace
Treaty were satisfactory to the United States. Benson, who had

[15] Schilling, *Admirals and Foreign Policy*, pp. 279–80. He gives the date as 29 March on
the basis of evidence in the Daniels Papers, although elsewhere Daniels, as well as
Benson, has dated this conversation on the 26th, and Wemyss, on the 27th.
[16] Daniels to Captain Dudley W. Knox, U.S.N., 29 January 1937; Benson Correspondence, U.S. Navy Department MSS.

accompanied Daniels, dashed Long's hopes with some frank talk on U.S. naval policy: he was recommending a 'fifty to fifty' Navy, that is, one equal to the Royal Navy. 'I told him,' Long confided in a memorandum, 'that if this was his official and considered advice that he was creating a difficulty which it would be almost impossible to overcome since the British idea, held not only by those responsible for advice but also by the House of Commons and by the Nation, was that in the future the supremacy of the British Navy was an absolute necessity, not only for the very existence of the British Empire but even of the peace of the world.' Benson was not impressed with this line and asserted that the *amour propre* of the American people demanded that the burden of responsibility for the safety of civilization should rest equally with the American Navy. Neither side could understand the point of view of the other. Long remarked that he 'did not believe that Great Britain would sign any League of Nations which did not leave her in a satisfactory position as regards her Navy.'[17] This statement cost Daniels much sleep that night, since he knew how close the League was to the President's heart. Long, in turn, was badly shaken up by Benson's retort, during a conference on 31 March, in response to his assertion that Britain would maintain her supremacy 'at all hazards': 'Well, Mr. Long, if you and the other members of your Government continue to act along the lines you are traveling this morning, I can assure you that it will mean but one thing, and that is war between Great Britain and the United States.'[18]

Dismayed by the Long–Daniels deadlock, on the heels of the Wemyss–Benson impasse, Wilson had Daniels consult with Lloyd George. At a breakfast meeting between the two on 1 April Daniels found the British leader 'quite as vigorous and determined as Walter Long or Admiral Wemyss.'[19] Lloyd George asked, 'What's the use of organizing the world for peace if the United States, the propounder of the League of Nations, insists upon going on with the construction of a big program of capital ships?' Convinced that the completion of the 1916 programme would make the American Navy superior, he wanted the United States to agree to stop that programme. Daniels 'pointed out that he

17 Long's memorandum of 29 March 1919; Lloyd George MSS.
18 Schilling, *Admirals and Foreign Policy*, pp. 281–2.
19 Daniels, *The Wilson Era*, p. 376. The account that follows is based on *ibid.*, pp. 376–8.

would find the United States quite ready to lead in reduction of armament when the League was in action . . . but until permanent peace was assured the United States could not stop its construction program.'

'Why does Britain need a bigger Navy than the United States?' Lloyd George inquired, and answered his own question by saying that the British Empire reached into all continents and that it must have a greater Navy to protect its far-flung empire. 'The United States,' he continued, 'between two oceans has no empire to protect and therefore it ought to be satisfied with a smaller Naval force.' When he stressed the fact that the United States had less need for a Navy because it lacked colonies, I was ready for him.

Daniels had with him two maps which had been prepared by the Naval Advisory Staff. One showed the sea lanes the Royal Navy had to defend; the other, the sea lanes protected by the U.S. Navy.[20] From the latter map it appeared that the United States had the longer sea lanes. Daniels pointed out that

we had to protect the sea lanes from the northern coast of Maine all the way down the Atlantic Coast to and including Patagonia, and then up the western coast of South America, Central America, and North America to Puget Sound; then, skipping Canada, the great territory of Alaska. Besides those, I said we had to protect Hawaii, Guam, Samoa, and the Philippine Islands, not to speak of Cuba, Puerto Rico, San Domingo, Haiti, and the Virgin Islands. To fulfill this obligation it was essential that we have a Navy second to none.

Lloyd George went up in the air. He asked, 'Do you mean to say that your country dominates Mexico, Central America, and all South America?' I replied in the negative . . . but that the Monroe Doctrine in which Britain had acquiesced . . . required that we protect those countries against any attempt to invade their sovereignty or acquisition by a foreign country.

Again, impasse.

The naval battle of Paris may be said to have ended on 10 April, when informal agreements of a general nature were reached through memoranda exchanged between two men of good will, Lord Robert Cecil, acting for Lloyd George, and Colonel House, acting for Wilson. The understanding was that the United States

---

20 *Ibid.*, p. 379, reproduces the maps. The lines were drawn very cleverly. Whereas the American *encircled* the Western Hemisphere, with an attached line extending to the Philippines, the British lines only *touched* Africa, India, and Australia.

would consider postponing work on ships authorized under the 1916 programme but not yet laid down until after the Peace Treaty, so that, in Cecil's words, 'we might have time to discuss and consider the matter together'; that the United States was ready to 'abandon or modify' its 'new naval programme' (House interpreted this to mean the 1918 programme) once the treaty was signed and a League of Nations was in being; that 'some arrangement as to the relative strengths of the fleets ought to be arrived at'; and that the two countries would consult from year to year on their naval programmes. There was also a reaffirmation by House of Wilson's statement of 21 December 1918 in *The Times*, that he fully understood 'the special international questions which arise from the fact of your peculiar position as an Island Empire.'[21] This arrangement did not give Lloyd George what he most wanted, a specific promise to reduce the 1916 programme: House refused to include such a reference in the understanding. The Americans, for their part, got something tangible from the agreement. It was understood that the British would give up their opposition to a Monroe Doctrine amendment to the Covenant of the League of Nations, and this they did. Schilling makes a convincing analysis of these negotiations:

Instead of stopping the construction of 16 American capital ships, Lloyd George had secured an American commitment to discuss future naval programs with the British Government (which was little more than British diplomacy would have achieved in any event); a reaffirmation of an earlier statement by the President (which could or could not imply that Britain had a right to naval superiority); and a promise that the 1918 program would be abandoned or modified (which was a hollow gesture in view of Congress' own endeavor toward this end). Lloyd George's failure was the result of his inferior bargaining position. In the final analysis, he could not afford to be responsible for the defeat of the Monroe Doctrine amendment, even if he had not secured a naval agreement; such a move would have gained Britain nothing except American ill-will, which would hardly be a desirable catalytic for future negotiations. Wilson's success, on the other hand, was assured once he had determined, by refusing to compromise the 1915 [1916] program, to call the Prime Minister's bluff.[22]

[21] Seymour, *The Intimate Papers of Colonel House*, iv. 418–23.
[22] *Admirals and Foreign Policy*, p. 291. He takes issue with the Sprouts' interpretation in *Toward a New Order of Sea Power*, which maintains that the agreement was a compromise by which Lloyd George secured an end to the 1918 programme and Wilson won acceptance of the Monroe Doctrine amendment. 'The fact is,' says Schilling

The agreement may have represented a great American victory, yet it did calm the atmosphere, as the British evidently thought they had got something from it.

The incipient Anglo-American naval rivalry was further defused by Daniels when he visited London (30 April–4 May). His luncheon speech at the Carlton Hotel on 1 May did much to dispel the misgivings of those who had visions of a gigantic navy-building competition. The Secretary of the Navy deprecated as unthinkable the idea of any such competition. 'Whether the navies of America and Great Britain are large or small, the spirit that will animate them is a spirit not of competition but of co-operation.' The First Lord was prepared to accept this assurance at face value.

... on the point of competition he [Daniels] was emphatic and appeared to mean what he said. But of course it is possible that when he talks of no competition, he may mean that he is to build as much as he likes, and that we are not to build in response—though this would be a very unfortunate interpretation of his language. Others besides myself who saw him in Paris, confirm my view that he is very much altered in his tone and manner now; and some of those who have been with him in his tours through the country here, both members of his Staff or of the British Admiralty, hold the view that he has been greatly impressed by all he has seen and heard, and that his mind has been changed as to any attempt to enter into competition with the British Navy.[23]

Any doubts about American intentions were removed with Daniels's statement to a Congressional Committee on 27 May that ships already authorized were to be completed, but after that there was to be no increase in the Navy. This sounded the death knell for the supplementary three-year programme, which had been before Congress since the autumn of 1918. But as events were to demonstrate, there was a naval truce only; the Anglo-American naval rivalry had not been eliminated as a crucial factor in British naval policy and the Anglo-American relationship.

As matters stood, neither Power got a recognition from the

(p. 292 n.), 'that the introduction of the 1918 program into the negotiations was a last minute diplomatic trick; the Advisory Staff did not know about it, and Lloyd George didn't want it.'

Contracts for the last four battleships of the 1916 programme were awarded on 15 May 1919; 1 July was the deadline under the terms of the 1916 navy bill.

[23] Long to Lloyd George, 2 May 1919; Lloyd George MSS.

other of what it wanted most: naval primacy for the British, naval equality for the Americans. The pity is that there were no conflicting strategic interests—only conflicting national egos and pride.

The 'naval battle of Paris' [fairly concludes one scholar] was based on false premises on both sides. On the British side, it rested on unwarrantable fears that American parity or superiority on the seas would pose a threat to the security of the British Empire, and even more, perhaps, on chauvinistic pride in the supremacy of the Grand Fleet as the key symbol of imperial grandeur. On the American side, the naval issue rested on an equally unwarrantable fear that British mastery of the seas posed a threat to American security, when in fact for a hundred years British maritime power had posed little or no danger to the United States and perhaps even served as a protective barrier between the United States and the power struggles of Europe.[24]

The larger significance of the whole naval imbroglio is that it obscured the identity of interests shared by the two great Anglo-Saxon Powers—their common interest in a world order under the rule of law guaranteed by a League of Nations whose ultimate sanction would have been the overwhelming naval and economic might of the two super-Powers.

At no time in the Armistice period and beyond did the Admiralty regard war between the British Empire and the United States as in the least likely. 'The possibility of war with the United States in the near future,' thought the First Sea Lord, 'need not be seriously considered.'[25] Also representative of Admiralty thinking was this Plans Division statement: 'The chances of such a war are remote and so opposed to the fundamental interests of both parties that the wisdom of constructing naval bases merely with that end in view is open to doubt.'[26] When in August 1919 the Admiralty asked the War Cabinet what standard would govern

24 Tillman, *Anglo-American Relations at the Peace Conference of 1919*, pp. 293–4.
25 Wemyss's memorandum for the First Lord, 25 February 1919; Wemyss MSS.
26 Plans Division paper, 'British Imperial Bases in the Pacific,' 28 April 1919; Admiralty MSS. In making out a case for the revised 1919–20 Navy Estimates, Long used the argument that 'if trouble arises in Ireland—and this seems almost inevitable—it is at least within the bounds of possibility that the United States of America may be forced by political exigencies of their own to assume hostile action towards ourselves; I do not mean, to make war—but to attempt to dictate. So long as we possess the command of the sea . . . we can ignore any action of this kind. But once we lose this supremacy we should undoubtedly find ourselves in a very unpleasant and unsatisfactory position.' Long's memorandum for the War Cabinet, 'Navy Estimates 1919–1920' (G.T.-7645), 5 July 1919.

the size of the Navy *vis-à-vis* the United States and 'any probable combination,' it received the Delphic reply: 'No alteration should be made without Cabinet authority in the pre-war standard governing the size of the Navy.'[27] This decision was 'intended to prevent the inclusion of comparisons with the United States, the Prime Minister having stated that the United States had always been omitted in Pre-War Estimates.'[28] Contingency planning there was, though apparently not before June 1919.

It was actually the Japanese Navy that loomed up as a more likely opponent in any naval war of the years ahead. Japan's notorious '21 Demands' on China (18 January 1915) had revealed her extravagant territorial ambitions on the Asian mainland. As far back as 1916 the Admiralty had found Japan's attitude not 'entirely satisfactory. . . . There is no doubt but that they have ideas of a greater Japan which will probably comprise parts of China and the Gateway to the East, the Dutch East Indies, Singapore and the Malay States. At present this is a dream of certain politicians.'[29] Japan's ambitions in Asia, which posed a threat to the safety of British trade and territorial interests in the Far East, the uncertainty about the future of the Anglo-Japanese Alliance, and the powerful Fleet the Japanese were building (8 dreadnoughts and 8 battle cruisers by 1923, none older than nine years) led the Admiralty to maintain a strong naval force in Eastern waters after the war. The plan was for a fleet composed of a battle cruiser, 5 light cruisers, 8 flotilla leaders, 18 destroyers, and 12 submarines. There would also be the Royal Australian Navy of one battle cruiser, 4 light cruisers, a flotilla leader, 11 destroyers, and 6 submarines.

A full discussion of the strategy of a war with Japan revealed the expectation that the British Imperial fleet, inferior to the Japanese in the Pacific (temporarily only, it was hoped), would be forced to adopt a more or less defensive policy, especially in the opening stages. An expedition against Hong Kong seemed probable. For this reason, and because Hong Kong would be the most suitable base from which to conduct an economic blockade of Japan, the decision (10 June 1919) was to strengthen the island's defences 'to

---

[27] Admiralty memorandum for the War Cabinet (over Long's signature), 'Post-War Naval Policy' (G.T.-7975), 12 August 1919, and W.C. 616A, 15 August 1919.
[28] Board Minute 924, 18 August 1919; Admiralty MSS.
[29] Admiralty War Staff, 'Neutral Powers,' 30 December 1916; Beatty MSS.

a pitch suitable for resisting battleship attack,' station a strong submarine flotilla there, and make Hong Kong their primary naval base in Asian waters. Three days later the Director of Plans, Captain Fuller, proposed 'to consider the naval policy to be followed by the Empire in the event of wars with Japan and the U.S.A., with a view to preparing a basis for the issue of instructions to the various Commanders-in-Chief, etc.'[30] Some months later the Deputy Director of Plans stated that 'the most probable opponent is assumed, unofficially, to be Japan rather than the U.S., with whom it is our policy to keep on good terms at all costs, on account of their strong strategic and financial position. A clash of interests with the Japanese is always possible, in view of their aggressive tendencies in the Pacific.'[31]

The Anglo-American naval differences coloured the discussions on many of the important questions that came up prior to and during the Peace Conference. It began with a heated dispute over the 'Freedom of the Seas.'

3. THE 'FREEDOM OF THE SEAS'

Point 2 of President Wilson's Fourteen Points (8 January 1918) —he had never consulted the Allies about them—read: 'Absolute freedom of navigation upon the seas, outside territorial waters, alike in peace and in war, except as the seas may be closed in whole or in part by international action for the enforcement of international covenants.' It was on the strength of the Fourteen Points that Germany had agreed (12 October 1918) to negotiate terms of Armistice. It was not until then that the British gave the Fourteen Points a close scrutiny. On Point 2 the positions of the British and Americans proved irreconcilable.

What did the United States mean by the term 'Freedom of the Seas'? The President had discussed it with Geddes during the latter's visit to Washington in October 1918. Geddes reported these as Wilson's views: 'Many nations, great and small, chafed under the feeling that their sea-borne trade and maritime development proceeded only with the permission and under the shadow

---

[30] Plans Division, 'British Imperial Bases in the Pacific,' 28 April 1919, and Board and Staff minutes of May and June; Admiralty MSS.
[31] Captain Barry Domvile's minute, 6 November 1919 (on Madden to Admiralty, 17 October); Admiralty MSS.

of the British Navy. He had always felt that the deepest-rooted cause of the present war was this feeling in Germany—an unjust fear and jealousy of the British Navy, but a feeling none the less real.'[32] What the President seemed to be saying was that it was the historical American position that belligerents must not interfere with neutral vessels on the high seas—that is, complete freedom of passage for neutral trade in time of war, which had been repeatedly violated by the Royal Navy when it stopped neutral merchantmen and shepherded to a British port for search those suspected of carrying goods helpful to the enemy's war effort.

The Admiralty's conclusions on the issue were presented to the War Cabinet on 17 October 1918:

(i) Acceptance of the proposal would result in making sea-power of little value to a nation *dependent upon it* for existence whilst providing a military Power with free lines of oversea communication.

(ii) The right to decide for ourselves questions which concern such vital interests, could not be surrendered to any League or combination of nations for by assenting to the proposal we should give up by a stroke of the pen the sea-power we have for centuries maintained and have never yet misused. On this basis the British Empire has been founded, and on no other can it be upheld.[33]

Balfour supported the Admiralty case with the argument that 'only militarism would be the gainer,' if the principle were adopted, because, until the League of Nations was strong enough to preserve the peace, 'every attempt to limit the use of sea power merely added to the relative strength of land power.'[34]

The Admiralty spelled out their stand to the Imperial War Cabinet at the request of that body (20 November) by drafting a memorandum and through an oral statement by Lord Lytton, Additional Parliamentary Secretary to the Admiralty, on 24 December. In the former the nub of the argument is contained in this paragraph: '*The foregoing examination may be summarised by saying that the restriction of an enemy's maritime commerce is the most vital operation in maritime war; that the continuance of belligerent trade in neutral ships*

---

[32] Geddes, 'Notes of an Interview with the President at the White House, Wednesday, October 16th, 1918'; Geddes MSS.

[33] Admiralty memorandum for the War Cabinet (signed by Wemyss), 'An Inquiry into the Meaning and Effect of the Demand for "Freedom of the Seas" '; Geddes MSS.

[34] Balfour's memorandum of 23 October 1918; Roskill, *Naval Policy between the Wars*, i. 82.

or through neutral ports may completely outflank naval power; and that, therefore, rules designed to protect a neutral assisting a belligerent by these means must inevitably break down when vital issues are at stake and the opposing navy is in a position to dispute them.'[35] Lytton's presentation stressed that

much depended on the precise meaning of the phrase 'Freedom of the Seas.' If it meant complete freedom of neutral trade from capture or search in war time, which in fact also meant freedom for belligerent trade, that would mean paralysing our sea power. It was unthinkable that we should assent to such a conclusion, and if it were forced on us it would become a dead letter in time of war. In a life-and-death struggle we should inevitably use any means consistent with the dictates of humanity. It was, therefore, to some modified interpretation of the phrase that we should have to look for any basis of profitable discussion. He thought that such discussion would most probably develop into an attempt to create a Code of Regulations of Maritime Warfare in the direction of extending the Regulations of the Paris Convention [1856] and the London Declaration [1909] in the interest of neutrals. There were grave naval objections to any such code, more particularly owing to the fact that it would rapidly become obsolete owing to the continuous change in the methods and conditions of war. If, however, we were forced to discuss any such code, we should have to decide whether we would take our stand on our interest as neutrals or on our interest as belligerents. The Admiralty considered that we should take our stand on our belligerent interest. In any future naval war we could probably protect our interest as neutrals by exercising pressure on the belligerents, just as the United States had put pressure on us while they were a neutral Power, and in the last resort it might even be the lesser of two evils to become a belligerent ourselves. On the other hand if we accepted a position which hampered our sea power in war we should have no remedy.[36]

There was no chance of British acceptance of a principle which would have nullified the advantages of sea power and the historical role of the British Navy by depriving the Navy of the long-sanctioned belligerent right of search and seizure of contraband. Lloyd George was so adamant on the point that he was prepared

---

[35] 'The Freedom of the Seas,' 21 December 1918, *Admiralty Policy in Relation to the Peace Settlement*, January 1919, pp. 77–83, for the entire memorandum; Naval Library. It is a revision (mainly stylistic) of a Plans Division paper of 4 December 1918 prepared in consultation with Dr. Pearce Higgins, an authority in international law; Admiralty MSS.

[36] I.W.C.-46.

(as was Clemenceau) to continue the war without the United States rather than give up the right of naval blockade which he believed Point 2 to require.[37] With the Prime Minister taking the lead, the War Cabinet decided on 26 October: 'The Prime Minister and Mr. Balfour should make it perfectly clear to the Conference that we do not accept the doctrine of the Freedom of the Seas, and that a notification to this effect must be made in some form to Germany before we entered into peace negotiations.'[38] The strategy was to avoid the subject coming up for discussion in the Peace Conference by making the unacceptability of the doctrine clear at the outset. This position, which was accepted by the European Allies, was conveyed to Wilson: the Allies reserved 'complete freedom' on the question, if it came up at the Peace Conference. Lloyd George left no doubt that the British people would not tolerate the acceptance of Point 2—he would be out as Prime Minister if he did. It is true that British press opinion was almost violently opposed to the acceptance of a principle which would, they claimed, stultify British naval power in war time, the essence of which was a blockade or threat of blockade (in the non-technical sense).

Wilson at first held out for the acceptance of Point 2, threatening 'to build up the strongest navy that our resources permit,' if it were not.[39] That is to say, the United States would do this in order to protect its commerce. There were sharp discussions between the two Governments. The upshot was a compromise that Lloyd George had suggested: the principle of the Freedom of the Seas and its application would be discussed at the Peace Conference. Wilson's dispatch of 5 November to the German Government, his last before the Armistice, observed that the Allied Governments 'must point out, however, that Clause Two, relating to what is usually described as the "freedom of the seas," is open to various interpretations, some of which they could not accept. They must, therefore, reserve to themselves complete freedom on this subject when they enter the Peace Conference.' It was, then, the British

---

[37] Lloyd George, *The Truth about the Peace Treaties* (London, 1938, 2 vols.), ii. 81.

[38] W.C. 491B.

[39] Wilson's cable to House, 4 November 1918; Seymour, *The Intimate Papers of Colonel House*, iv. 179. House talked just as tough, threatening that America would make a separate peace, warning that she would always be ready for war to protect her maritime rights, and even predicting that she might be on the opposite side in Britain's next war.

understanding that they were not bound at the Peace Conference by Article 2; they were committed only to *discussing* the question there.

The whole issue of the Freedom of the Seas, which poisoned relations between the two Navies, more especially on the American side, was shelved at Paris. By the end of April it was apparent that the question would not even come up for discussion. President Wilson afterwards, in a speech in San Diego, California, 19 September 1919, explained why:

> One of the principles I went to Paris most insisting on was the freedom of the seas. Now, the freedom of the seas means the definition of the right of neutrals to use the seas when other nations are at war, but under the League of Nations there are no neutrals, and, therefore, what I have called the practical joke on myself was that by the very thing that I was advocating it became unnecessary to define freedom of the seas. All nations . . . being comrades and partners in a common cause, we all have an equal right to use the seas.[40]

In other words, the concept of the League of Nations had made the concept of neutrality and neutral rights obsolete.

The Freedom of the Seas controversy revealed to the British as in a flash the apparent American ambition to achieve naval supremacy. The discussions over the League of Nations seemed to point in the same direction.

4. THE LEAGUE OF NATIONS AND ARMAMENTS LIMITATION

A League of Nations was the last of Wilson's Fourteen Points. Geddes believed that the President had 'an idea that the great power of the British Navy might in some way be used in connection with the League of Nations and thereby cease to be a cause of jealousy and irritation.'[41] Although American naval opinion was divided on the feasibility and value of a League, an influential segment was ready to accept the idea of a permanent international fleet under the League *if* this force were not dominated by one Power, meaning Great Britain. Captain Roskill asserts that without doubt 'senior US naval officers saw in the proposal for a League Navy both a weapon to further their claim for "a navy

---

[40] Tillman, *Anglo-American Relations at the Paris Peace Conference of 1919*, p. 289.
[41] Geddes, 'Notes of an Interview with the President at the White House, Wednesday, October 16th, 1918.'

second to none" and a means of putting a term to British preponderance at sea.'[42] The U.S. Navy later dropped the whole idea as impracticable: a League Navy would result in 'natural temperamental frictions,' its commanders would direct operations in line with their national interests, and, anyway, Britain would never confide her security to a League navy. They advocated instead that an international fleet be organized by international agreement on an *ad hoc* basis.

The Admiralty—Wemyss, least of all—had no faith in a League of Nations. Without an effective force to uphold its decisions, it would never rise above the level of a debating society. Wemyss saw no hope of establishing a truly effective international navy. 'The difficulties and disabilities of an international fleet, hastily collected on the outbreak of war, might well be such as to lead to its defeat by a single well-directed navy of half its size . . .' The co-ordination of naval action would be simplified if the fleets concerned were able to work together. This was another way of saying that Great Britain and the United States should furnish the bulk of the naval forces of the League and arrange the supreme command between themselves. But, *au fond*, Wemyss had no use for a League of Nations or an international naval force. The security of the British Empire could not safely be left to an international organization and an international fleet. They must rely upon a Fleet strong enough to ensure the Empire's oversea communications in time of war.[43] At about this time the Admiralty were damning the League on the higher ground that

the Admiralty cannot ignore the possibility that the success of a League of Nations in diminishing armaments (which is presumed to be one of its objects equally with the prevention of war) may be delayed rather than advanced by the immediate adoption of these binding covenants. In their view the existence of a state of mutual confidence among the Powers is a condition precedent to effective organisation for peace, and covenants entered into before that confidence has had time to develop may impair its growth. The Admiralty have a definite responsibility for the defence of the sea communications of the Empire and of its territories from oversea attack. It appears to them that (until in course of time the international intercourse of the League creates a new atmos-

---

[42] Roskill, *Naval Policy between the Wars*, i. 85.
[43] Wemyss, 'The Naval Aspects of a League of Nations,' 18 December 1918; Admiralty MSS.

phere) that responsibility is in no way diminished. If, in addition, H.M. Government are under covenant to go to war in certain circumstance[s] from motives other than those of self-protection, and cannot put complete confidence in the effective naval co-operation of other members of the League, the responsibility of the Admiralty is actually increased, and the estimate of the required strength of the Navy may also have to be increased. As the strongest naval Power Great Britain may be in a somewhat exceptional position in this respect; but, in so far as similar considerations operate universally, a scheme of binding covenants may defeat its own object.[44]

Wilson's Point 4 stipulated that 'Adequate guarantees [should be] given and taken that national armaments will be reduced to the lowest point consistent with domestic safety.' Wilson had never advanced any specific proposals to implement this Point. Within two months of the Armistice he had decided it would not be feasible to reach an agreement on general disarmament at the Peace Conference. He anticipated that the League would work out a scheme. The American naval authorities all along regarded disarmament as unrealistic, and this, too, was the feeling in the Royal Navy. The Admiralty were obdurately opposed to limitation on principle. Their position paper emphasized:

(1) The maintenance of a powerful British Navy is a purely defensive policy. For this reason it has never been a menace to the peace of the world. . . . The British Navy exists for purely protective purposes and is no stronger than such purposes require. The geographical situation of the British Empire renders its very existence dependent upon the maintenance of its sea communications and the power to defend them against oversea aggression. . . .

(2) The situation and circumstances of the British Empire are unique . . . of no nation can it be said, as it can be of the British Empire, that sea power is necessary to its very existence, and that the loss of its navy would mean the extinction of its national life. . . .

. . . the Admiralty cannot agree to any proposals for the reduction of armaments the effect of which would be to take away from them and to place in the hands of some international tribunal the responsibility of determining what naval force is required for the protection of the Empire. . . .

At the same time the Admiralty are in entire sympathy with the desire to reduce the total naval armaments of the world. The predominance they desire to assure for the British Navy is purely an

---

[44] *Admiralty Policy in Relation to the Peace Settlement*, pp. 13–14.

adequate superiority for reasonably possible contingencies and in no sense an excessive superabundance of strength.[45]

The Admiralty had, accordingly, considered four possible principles by which navies might be limited and standards of relative strength fixed: by value of oversea trade, tonnage of mercantile marine, pre-war or existing strength, and length of coast line. Although any of these proposals would safeguard British maritime predominance, the Admiralty found all four 'illogical or full of difficulties and impracticabilities' and concluded that 'any attempt to set up arbitrary and artificial standards of relative strength or to limit the natural expression of a nation's instinctive and reasonable determination to judge how best to protect its own interests is foredoomed to failure.'[46]

In the event, the Admiralty both won and lost. Disregarding the misgivings of their naval advisers, the Government accepted the idea of a League of Nations, whose Covenant, or constitution (adopted on 28 April 1919), became Part I of the Peace Treaty with Germany. But there was no provision in it for an international force of any kind. Although Articles 10, 11, and 16 envisaged concerted action by the League in case of aggression or threat of aggression against a Member, 'any war or threat of war,' or 'should any Member of the League resort to war in disregard of its covenants under Articles 12, 13 or 15' (the arbitration clauses), there was no provision even for a League Military or Naval Staff.

The attitude of the Admiralty towards armaments limitation did not discourage the Prime Minister from continuing to stress the need for an understanding on armaments among the victor Powers. The British delegation was ready to discuss even the limitation of navies. At a meeting with Clemenceau and Colonel House on 10 March 1919 Lloyd George spoke of the necessity for an Anglo-American naval agreement to head off a rivalry in building programmes. The best the Powers could do was, first, to state in the preamble to the Military, Naval, and Air clauses of the Versailles Treaty (Part V): 'In order to render possible the initiation of a general limitation of the armaments of all nations, Germany undertakes strictly to observe the military, naval and

---

[45] Admiralty memorandum for the War Cabinet, 'Limitation of Armaments,' December 1918; *ibid.*, pp. 14–15.
[46] *Ibid.*, pp. 15–17.

air clauses which follow.' In the Allied reply to the German observations of 16 June 1919 on the peace terms, it was stated that the military, naval, and air clauses were 'the first steps toward that general reduction and limitation of armaments which they seek to bring about as one of the most fruitful preventives of war, and which it will be one of the first duties of the League of Nations to promote.' The duties of the League in this sphere were defined in Article 8 of the Covenant, which expressed the pious hope that armaments would be reduced 'to the lowest point consistent with national safety and the enforcement by common action of international obligations. The Council, taking account of the geographical situation and circumstances of each state, shall formulate plans for such reduction for the consideration and action of the several Governments.' This article (the second sentence in slightly different phraseology) had first appeared in a draft of 14 February 1919. The Admiralty had joined the other fighting Services in demanding further and fuller consideration of Article 8 because its adoption 'involves consequences of so grave a nature and so prejudicial to the interests of this and other countries.' They felt

bound to point out that the introduction at the present stage of proposals for the limitation of armaments, before the League of Nations has established its power to afford security to its members, may delay rather than advance the reduction of armaments, since many intricate and delicate questions, the solution of which should preferably await an atmosphere of security, will be involved.

Further, the acceptance of the proposal for limitation of armaments entails a serious constitutional consequence which the Admiralty, Army Council, and Air Council cannot accept without the strongest protest: namely, the abrogation of their constitutional duty of advising their Government as to the strength of their Naval, Military and Air Forces.[47]

It was clear by the spring that international disarmament, which had been almost taken for granted in high governmental quarters in the month or two after the Armistice, was as remote as ever. Everywhere the problem was seen to be an insoluble one, at least before the League was in being. The millennium receded and the Admiralty could rest easy.

[47] David Hunter Miller, *The Drafting of the Covenant* (New York, 1928, 2 vols.), i. 286–7. The memorandum was addressed to Lord Robert Cecil, one of the British representatives on the League of Nations Drafting Committee.

As prominently as the American and Japanese Navies bulked in Admiralty calculations, and as disturbing as were the implications of possible Peace Treaty provisions on the Freedom of the Seas, an international naval force, and naval disarmament, the overriding concern of the Royal Navy during the Armistice period was to secure a Peace Treaty that would drastically reduce German sea power. This is the subject of the next chapter. The principal obstacle was the policy of Wilson's naval advisers. Benson, the leading spokesman of their point of view, was opposed to a practical liquidation of German naval power, ostensibly because this was such a serious derogation of German sovereignty as to provoke Germany to go to war sometime in the future. In truth, Benson wanted to leave Germany as a naval Power of some strength in order for her to serve as a balance to, and restraining influence on, the British Navy. Conversely, any strengthening of British sea power at Germany's expense was detrimental to American naval interests. Benson did not press his case too hard, probably because he knew that Wilson and the American Peace Commissioners were not sympathetic to his position. Chapter X brings out the lesson, always forgotten by idealists, that every nation puts its own interests first and the devil take the hindmost.

A NOTE ON RELATIVE STRENGTH OF NAVIES[48]

If vessels of the pre-'Orion' classes [1909-10 programme, completed in 1912] and equivalent ships in other Navies are omitted the relative estimated strength of the various Navies in capital ships in 1923-24 will be as follows:

Estimated strength by 1923-24:

	Dreadnoughts	Battle Cruisers	Total
Great Britain	24	6	30
United States	21	6	27
France	12	–	12
Italy, 1921	4	–	4
Japan	8	8	16

This Estimate includes the United States Programme which has actually been approved but not the further Programme now under

[48] Admiralty memorandum for the War Cabinet (G.T.-7229), 7 May 1919. Reproduced verbatim with a few editorial changes.

consideration in America which, if adopted, would render the position even more unsatisfactory.

Comparative Force List in January 1919

	Dreadnoughts	Battle Cruisers	Total
Great Britain	33	9	42
United States	16	–	16
France	7	–	7
Italy	5	–	5
Japan	7(a)	7(b)	14

(a) Includes 'Satsuma' class: 4–12″; 12–10″.
(b) Three of these are really powerfully armed cruisers, with 4–12″ and 8–8″ guns.

Estimated Comparative Force List 1923–24
showing ships laid down and projected

	Dreadnoughts	Battle Cruisers	Total
Great Britain	33	10	43
United States	29	6	35
France	16	–	16
Italy	6	–	6
Japan	11(a)	11(b)	22

(a) }
(b) } as above.

X

The Naval Settlement with Germany

What I would like to see would be to tow all these German ships at Scapa Flow into the middle of the Atlantic and to surround them with ships of all the Allied countries, and to the music of all our national airs sink them ostentatiously.

LLOYD GEORGE in a conversation with Jonathan Daniels, early April 1919.

1. COLONIES, KIEL CANAL, HELIGOLAND, BALTIC, AND SUBMARINES

THE Allied Naval Council had come to an end with the settlement of the naval Armistice terms. A Committee of Allied Naval Advisers, the Naval Peace Terms Committee, which included Wemyss, Benson, and others of the old Naval Council, had the task of drafting the naval provisions of the Peace Treaty.

The problem of the German Fleet apart, the Admiralty were mainly concerned with the disposal of the German colonies and the status of the Kiel Canal and Heligoland. The Admiralty drew up recommendations for the Government on these issues in January 1919 after intensive discussions and memorandizing with which Beatty was directly associated. The disposal of the colonies was a matter of absorbing interest to the Admiralty. The first set of 'possible terms of peace' the Admiralty had set forth during the war provided for the cession to the Allies of all German oversea possessions, primarily as 'a selfish precaution on our part for reducing the number of possible hostile naval bases abroad which could shelter submarines, etc., to prey on our commerce.'[1] There

---

[1] 'Notes on the Possible Terms of Peace by the First Sea Lord of the Admiralty,' Jackson (P.-8), 12 October 1916. (Referred to below as 'Possible Terms of Peace.') They were concurred in by the Board of Admiralty. The 'etc.' in the quotation referred primarily to surface raiders. In 1918 the threat to commerce of aircraft operating from the German bases in a future war was added to the Admiralty brief.

was never any wavering on this point, and public opinion would have violently opposed anything less. The Admiralty statement of policy in January 1919 made out a strong case for not returning the colonies. On it very largely depended the future security of the world's trade routes. Enemy surface raiders, operating for the most part from German home bases, had destroyed over 600,000 tons of shipping. Had these raiders been able to operate from German oversea bases like Rabaul (New Guinea), Dar-es-Salaam (German East Africa), and Duala (Cameroons), their campaign would have been even more successful. Fortunately for the Allies, the British and Japanese had been able to seize and occupy Germany's colonies early in the war. They could not count on such good fortune in a war of the future.

If then Germany's colonies should be returned to her, we should be faced with the problem, not only of maintaining naval forces in home waters on a scale of which this war has given us the measure, but also squadrons to deal with surface raiders and a great anti-submarine organisation of patrol craft, submarine chasers, aircraft, mines, nets, etc., in every large colonial port. The expense of this, added to that of storing the country with a three to six months' supply of food and raw material, necessary to provide time to get anti-submarine measures into working order and despatch expeditions, would be an unbearable strain upon the country's resources.[2]

There were, of course, economic and other non-strategic considerations that influenced the British Government.

There were few difficulties in Paris over the principle of non-restoration. The troubles that arose pertained to the division of the colonial spoils. Under Article 119 of the Peace Treaty Germany renounced her colonies in favour of the big Powers. A Council of Four[3] decision on 7 May made a rough allocation to mandatories for administration under the terms of the mandates charter (Article 22 of the League Covenant). German East Africa and German South West Africa went to Great Britain and the Union

2 *Admiralty Policy in Relation to the Peace Settlement*, p. 9.
3 The Heads of the five principal delegations (Great Britain, the United States, France, Italy, Japan) and their Foreign Ministers constituted the Supreme Council, popularly known as the Council of Ten. It met infrequently after 24 March, from which date the Council of Four, which consisted of the Heads of the principal delegations, less Japan, made the definitive decisions until the signing of the Treaty of Versailles. (It was a Council of Five when Japan was represented.)

of South Africa, respectively, as class 'B' mandates (Ruanda–Urundi, detached from the former German East Africa, later went to Belgium as a 'B' mandate), and Togoland and the Cameroons were left to a joint recommendation by France and Britain, which Powers afterwards partitioned the two colonies as 'B' mandates. The German islands in the Pacific were awarded as 'C' mandates, Japan receiving those north of the Equator; New Zealand, the German Samoan Islands; the British Empire, Nauru (later assigned to Australia); Australia, all other German possessions south of the Equator. For all practical purposes both classes of mandate, as distinct from the class 'A' mandates of the Middle East, whose eventual independence was envisaged, were colonial possessions.

The Kiel Canal in German hands was a strategic menace: it enabled the High Seas Fleet at one and the same time to threaten in the North Sea and the Baltic. The war-time solution favoured by the Admiralty was internationalization, on the lines of the Suez Canal, with all the North Sea states sharing in the control. Demolition, which was regarded as the perfect solution, was not practicable, as 'the demolition of a canal of appreciable commercial value might savour of barbarism; the United States would possibly enter a strong protest, and our Allies might be impressed by it.'[4]

After the war the Admiralty looked at the problem afresh. Nobody could suggest any practical method of mulcting Germany of this valuable asset. It could be turned over to Denmark, which would have involved an extension of Danish territory as far south as the Canal; but the Danes laid no claim to this territory. Moreover, Germany would quickly recover it in the event of war. The complete destruction of the Canal was mooted, only to be rejected quickly in view of its commercial utility to all nations. The Admiralty considered other possibilities: to internationalize it; to leave it free but undefended. It was realized that if Germany were deprived of her Navy and kept impotent navally, the strategic importance of the Canal to her would disappear. This was the key to the line finally adopted by the Admiralty. 'The Kiel Canal should in future be open at all times to the commerce and war vessels of all nations on equal terms.'[5] This became, with slight

4 'Notes on the Possible Terms of Peace.'
5 *Admiralty Policy in Relation to the Peace Settlement*, p. 9.

changes, Part II, Clause 4, of the 'Preliminary Terms' of the naval settlement discussed by the Council of Ten on 6 March. Admiral Benson would not agree to it on the ground that it could only be justified as a punitive measure. Balfour defended the clause on strategic grounds. If the Germans retained the Canal under existing conditions, 'the strength of the German Fleet would be doubled, the Baltic would be a German lake, the freedom of Sweden and Denmark, Finland, Latvia and Esthonia, and even of Russia, would be jeopardised, if the last ever again became a maritime power. Consequently, from an international point of view, the question was of extreme importance. The use of the Canal for purely strategic reasons must be restricted as had been done in the case of the Panama Canal and the Suez Canal, where the provisions now suggested were already in operation.' Lansing, the American Secretary of State, conceded the great strategic advantage of the Canal to Germany, but the Allied purpose would be served by destroying the fortifications and preventing their reconstruction. 'Furthermore, he failed to see why all commercial ships of other countries passing through the Kiel Canal should be given special privileges. The same privileges might be asked in the case of the Cape Cod Canal, in the United States of America.' Clearly, it was the possible precedent that disturbed the Americans. Lloyd George could see no injustice in applying to the Kiel Canal the system in force at the Panama and Suez Canals. 'Far from being a disadvantage or injustice to Germany, the traffic so created would be of great benefit to her ports.' The French supported him; but it was agreed, on Colonel House's motion, that the question be referred to the International Ports, Waterways and Railways Commission.[6] In the end, the British accepted more moderate, if somewhat ambiguous, terms (Council of Four, 25 April), which became Article 380 of the Versailles Treaty: 'The Kiel Canal and its approaches shall be maintained

6 *Papers Relating to the Foreign Relations of the United States. The Paris Peace Conference, 1919* (Washington, D.C., 1942–7, 13 vols.), iv. 225–6. Vols. iii–vi are the minutes of the Council of Ten and Council of Four. The I.C. Series papers at the P.R.O. (Cab. 28) and the C.F. series (Cab. 29) have the same material. However, the Council of Four minutes are not complete in either source. One must go to Paul Joseph Mantoux, *Les Délibérations du Conseil des Quatre (24 Mars–28 Juin 1919)* (Paris, 1955, 2 vols.), for the minutes of a number of the early meetings. The only naval material of importance not to be found in the American and British sources cited above are the minutes of the 15 April meeting on the Heligoland question in Mantoux, i. 251–5. See below, p. 255.

free and open to the vessels of commerce and of war of all nations at peace with Germany on terms of entire equality.'

As regards Heligoland, whose possession had enabled Germany to maintain an efficient patrol of the Bight and to deny freedom of movement to British surface craft penetrating the Bight, the Admiralty were undecided while the war was on what should be done about it. On the one hand, in 1916 the Third Sea Lord (Tudor), the Fourth Sea Lord (Lambert), and the Commander of the Battle Cruiser Fleet (Beatty) had strongly recommended that Heligoland should pass into British possession at the peace. For Tudor, 'One of our greatest troubles has been that we have had so little to attack, but with Heligoland in our possession, and fortified, Germany would either have to leave it unmolested—a valuable outpost for us—or she would be presenting us with constant objects for attack, and would undoubtedly sustain considerable losses.' Beatty wanted Heligoland for the Fleet, 'not merely for purposes of naval strategy, but more particularly where we look to the requirements of air strategy in the immediate future.' On the other hand, the First Sea Lord (Jackson), Second Sea Lord (Gough-Calthorpe), Chief of the Admiralty War Staff (Oliver), and the C.-in-C., Grand Fleet (Jellicoe) considered that, on balance, the disadvantages of taking possession of Heligoland clearly outweighed the advantages. Thus, Jackson, though admitting that Heligoland in British hands 'would bring our base of observation 300 miles nearer the German coast' and be 'a thorn in the side of the enemy,' saw that Heligoland would at the same time be 'a very great anxiety to us,' in that it would be extremely difficult to hold it. Jellicoe emphasized that a British-occupied Heligoland 'would be to us a great incubus and drag on the fleet, exposing the fleet to great risks [from mines and submarines] with no commensurate advantage, unless the fortified Heligoland is entirely self-supporting and in no way dependent on the fleet'— that is, for protecting supply ships.[7]

With the war over, the Admiralty made a more detailed study of the Heligoland problem. They considered five alternatives:

(1) Cession to the League of Nations, with Holland or Denmark

---

[7] These opinions of the Admiralty and the Grand Fleet Command were given to the First Lord (Balfour) in October 1916, in response to his request for comment on whether the German possession of Heligoland helped their Fleet and whether its possession by Britain would help the British Fleet. 'Heligoland' (G.-142), April 1917.

as the mandatory Power, after the destruction of all defence works. This was supported only by the Deputy First Sea Lord, and he preferred to have the island ceded outright to Denmark. The objection of the Admiralty was that Germany would probably seize the island if she went to war.

(2) Heligoland to be occupied by Great Britain. This had no support, because the supply and defence of the island would be too difficult unless they were prepared to make it impregnable and maintain a strong garrison.

(3) Germany to retain Heligoland, but with all its defences destroyed. This would nullify the island's military value, which lay mainly in its impregnable gun defences. With these destroyed the harbour works would be relatively unimportant.

(4) Germany to retain Heligoland, the harbour as well as all defences being destroyed. Fortifications could be extemporized at comparatively short notice; if the harbour works were destroyed, the difficulty of landing guns would be greatly increased.

(5) Germany to retain Heligoland, but with the island razed to high-water mark. This levelling would be the only certain way of preventing its being used in the future for military purposes. This was the solution preferred by Beatty, the D.C.N.S., and the A.C.N.S.

The return of Heligoland to Britain (from whom Germany had received it in 1890 in exchange for Zanzibar) had the backing of the Service. 'The key of the mad dog's kennel must be in our pocket,' urged one ancient mariner, 'for there is no knowing when the evil beast will get another attack of hydrophobia . . .'[8] The Board preferred a variation of (4) above: destruction of the fortifications and harbour works by German labour and at German expense, with the ownership of the island to be determined by the peace negotiators. This view was concurred in by the Allied Admirals at the end of February—the island of Dune to be treated in identical fashion—except for Benson, who was opposed to the destruction of the harbours. Heligoland came before the Council of Ten on 6 March in the British-sponsored form: 'The fortifications, military establishments, and harbours of the Islands of Heligoland and Dune shall be destroyed under the supervision of Allied Commissioners, by German labour and at the expense of

8 Admiral C. C. Penrose Fitzgerald, 'Sea Power Wins,' *Contemporary Review*, June 1919.

Germany, within a period to be determined by the Commissioners, which shall not exceed one year from the date of this Convention. . . . The disposal of the Islands will be decided by the final Treaty of Peace.'[9] Lloyd George and Wemyss stated their opposition to a return of the islands to Germany, and Benson entered the reservation he had made earlier. It was agreed to hold over the Heligoland clause for further consideration.

The Admiralty did not swerve from their declared position, and they had the firm support of Balfour. 'To sum up, the significance of the harbour lies in the protection which is afforded to it by the fortifications on the Island; and, unless the Island is reduced to such a condition that it is impossible to erect fortifications upon it, the harbour should be destroyed so as to render it no longer an object of temptation to an aggressive Germany.'[10] It was Balfour who persuasively argued the Admiralty case for destruction at the Council of Four meeting on 15 April. 'It is evident that we cannot leave Heligoland as it was before the war. It constituted a menace . . . for all the Powers with North Sea interests. During the war it was a formidable base for submarines and minelayers,' etc. Wilson, though not convinced of the necessity of destruction, would not oppose it 'if it was absolutely necessary.' Though no formal decision was actually taken that day, perhaps because no secretary had been present, it was afterwards declared (Council of Four, 29 April) that one had been taken on 15 April. As stated in Article 115 of the Peace Treaty, it registered another victory for the British position, being very similar to the clause that had been discussed on 6 March: 'The fortifications, military establishments, and harbours of the Islands of Heligoland and Dune shall be destroyed under the supervision of the Principal Allied Governments by German labour and at the expense of Germany within a period to be determined by the said Governments. . . . These fortifications, military establishments and harbours shall not be reconstructed, nor shall any similar works be constructed in future.' Germany was permitted to retain the islands.

American opposition to the British position stiffened when the problem of Germany's coast defences came up for settlement. The provision which was submitted to the Council of Ten on 6 March

---

[9] *Foreign Relations of the United States. The Paris Peace Conference, 1919*, iv. 248.
[10] Admiralty memorandum by Long for the War Cabinet, 'Heligoland' (G.T.-7004), 18 March 1919.

was what the Admiralty wanted (Benson and the Japanese naval representative entered reservations): 'All fortified works and fortifications within 50 kilometres of the German coast or on German islands off that coast shall be disarmed and dismantled. The construction of any new fortifications within the same limits is forbidden.' The U.S. Naval Advisory Staff questioned the desirability of leaving Germany's sea frontier in so defenceless a state, and Secretary of State Lansing argued their case at this meeting. '. . . the Conference was going beyond reason. . . . Germany should be permitted to defend herself.' He was challenged by Balfour, who held that the fortifications in question were 'centres from which offensive naval operations could be undertaken.' The best the United States could get was a Council decision on 17 March (Lloyd George had suggested it) that made a specious distinction between offensive and defensive fortifications: 'All fortified works and fortifications, other than those mentioned in Articles 35 and 36 [Articles 115, 195 of the Peace Treaty—respectively, the destruction of the fortifications, etc. of Heligoland and Dune and the prohibition of fortifications between latitudes 55° 27 'N. and 54° 00 'N. and longitudes 9° 00 'E. (about 10 miles east of Cuxhaven) and 16° 00 'E. and the installation of guns commanding the maritime routes between the North Sea and the Baltic], now established within fifty kilometres of the German coast or on German islands off that coast shall be considered as of a defensive nature and may remain in their existing condition. No new fortifications shall be constructed within these limits.'[11] The decision, which became Article 196 of the Peace Treaty, amounted to this: all fortifications in the North Sea, except Heligoland and Dune, would be considered defensive and be allowed to remain as constituted. However, German fortifications in the Baltic would be destroyed. Benson acquiesced with reluctance in a provision whose effect would be to deprive the German Fleet of a safe refuge in the Baltic and force it to be based in time of war in the North Sea, that is, where the British Navy could most easily contain it. Moreover, the German Baltic coast would be vulnerable to a first-class naval Power like Great Britain, which

---

11 *Foreign Relations of the United States. The Paris Peace Conference*, iv. 224–5, 249 (6 March), 296–7 (17 March). Latitude 55° 27' N. was the existing frontier between Denmark and Germany. The Peace Treaty through a 1920 plebiscite in North Schleswig brought it 32 miles to the southward.

could operate in the North Sea and Baltic at the same time. The Admiralty had done very well indeed.

Article XXII of the Armistice, which called for the surrender of all the German submarines, led to a bitter inter-Allied controversy: the British and Americans *v.* the French and Italians. The first two Powers took the view that submarines had best be entirely abolished by international decree, a course to which the Latin Powers objected. British reasoning was that submarine warfare was aimed at them in particular. Great Britain had suffered more than all the other nations, Allied and neutral combined, to the point where she had been within measurable distance of defeat. There was a general feeling, in and outside official quarters, that the submarine had not been defeated out-and-out, that it remained a possible source of danger, and that, in Beatty's words, 'its use in war tends to outrage the laws of civilisation and humanity when in the hands of a weaker power . . .'[12] In January 1919 the Board decided to work for 'a universal prohibition against the building of submarines in the future, together with a general destruction of existing submarines, under effective guarantees of International Law and a League of Nations.' If this were not possible, 'their employment against Merchant Shipping should be governed by the general principles applicable also to surface ships.'[13] The Admiralty had solid American backing. Daniels expressed his antipathy to submarines as forcibly as did any British Admiral: 'I believe all submarines should be sunk and no more should be built by any nation, if and when the League of Nations becomes a fact. At the best they are stilettos and, like poison gas, should be put beyond the pale.'[14]

By this date, however, majority opinion among the department heads at the Admiralty was no longer in favour of prohibition of

---

12 *Admiralty Policy in Relation to the Peace Settlement*, p. 19.

13 *Ibid.*, p. 21.

14 Daniels to Wilson, 4 March 1919; Daniels, *The Wilson Era*, p. 374. The official American position had the support of Admiral Benson and the Naval Advisory Staff, who, among other arguments, advanced the proposition that the abolition of submarines would facilitate disarmament by making unneeded a host of A/S vessels. The London Planning Section used the argument of the 'moral and material interests of humanity.' On the other hand, the General Board, believing that the Peace Conference, composed as it was of big and small Powers, would never outlaw the submarine, strongly opposed abolition and urged that the United States work for civilized rules of submarine warfare. The Washington Planning Committee thought submarines would be useful to defend the American coasts. Schilling, *Admirals and Foreign Policy*, pp. 153–60.

submarines. One factor in the change of policy was the arguments of the Department of Naval Construction about the 'impracticability' of such a ban (it would be extremely difficult to detect the building of small submarines, and in time of war one or more combatant states would build submarines anyway) and the advantage of permitting the type (the submarine would help to prevent wars by making them more risky).[15] The other, and probably more important, factor in the British attitude was the strong French opposition to the abolition of submarines.

On 1 May 1919 there was a long discussion by the Allied Admirals on the problem of the suppression of submarine warfare. De Bon pointed out the submarine was the weapon of the weaker powers and its suppression was desired by the nations to whose advantage it would be: those with powerful navies which were rich enough to build and maintain war fleets. Furthermore, he said, the fact that a nation had used the submarine in an inhumane way was no argument for suppressing a weapon whose use everyone had considered perfectly legitimate prior to the war. Finally, French public opinion showed itself to be hostile to all this breaking up of *matériel* after such a destructive war and at the very moment when its Parliament was voting credits for rebuilding the French Fleet, which had been so diminished without replacements. The French Minister of Marine declared: 'There is no treacherous weapon, there can only be treachery in the way the weapon is used.' The long and short of the matter was that the minor Powers would not part with a weapon which, comparatively cheap as it was to produce, had shown itself on occasion to be a match for the largest and costliest armourclad.

Whatever the precise reasons, the Admiralty were not by the spring of 1919 working for prohibition of the submarine. There was no British indecision as regards the fate of the German submarines.

It was not possible to separate the problem of the future of the submarine from that of the disposition of the U-boats, the surrender of which was called for under Article XXII of the Armistice. Eventually, the Germans surrendered 176 U-boats. The operation began on 19 November 1918, the boats coming to Harwich in

15 The Admiralty materials are to be found in the U.S. naval archives. See Warner R. Schilling, 'Weapons, Doctrine, and Arms Control: a Case from the Good Old Days,' *Journal of Conflict Resolution*, September 1963.

batches, the crews returning to Germany. Tyrwhitt, anxious that there be no demonstration suggesting any crowing over a beaten enemy, ordered the Harwich Force to maintain a strict silence when passing or being passed by German submarines. By the New Year 114 of the submarines had been delivered. The Allied Naval Armistice Commission discovered during an inspection tour of German ports in December that 64 submarines could put to sea or be towed and 125 others were building. This suggested that the Germans retained a considerable potential for U-boat warfare. At the renewal of the Armistice on 16 January, Germany was required immediately to send to Allied ports all boats which could put to sea or be towed. All others, including those under construction, were to be destroyed and all submarine building was to cease forthwith.

As part of its scheme of a universal ban upon the use of this underhand weapon, the Admiralty wanted the Peace Treaty to order the destruction within three months of the signing of all U-boats surrendered, building, unfit for sea, or interned in neutral countries. This action would 'prevent the Central Powers commencing another submarine campaign in the near future; and while removing the possibility of any disagreement among the Allied and Associated Powers as to the distribution of the submarines, it will be a judgment on the enemy for the outrages committed by his submarines during the war.'[16]

Previous to the discussion of the Admirals on 5 February, about 40 of the surrendered boats had been allotted to America, France, Italy, and Japan for propaganda purposes, and on 21 January, in order to relieve the congestion at Harwich, the authority of the Supreme War Council had been obtained for the sale of all surrendered U-boats in excess of 80, on condition that they were broken up, the proceeds of the sale to be divided among the Allies on a scale to be subsequently settled. This authority was subsequently suspended in deference to Clemenceau's wishes when he discovered what was going on (Council of Ten, 6 February). However, 55 had already been sold. By April the remainder of the submarines had been surrendered, and in March the French undertook to accommodate a certain number.

At the first meeting of the Naval Peace Terms Committee, 5

16 *Admiralty Policy in Relation to the Peace Settlement*, pp. 4–5.

February, none of the Admirals suggested that any of the German submarines should be added to the active fleets of the Allies. It was agreed instead that these vessels should be 'destroyed or broken up'—a victory for the Anglo-American position. Benson stressed that 'the total and immediate destruction of the submarines would produce a moral and psychological effect on the whole world that would be very valuable.'[17] The 'destroyed *or* broken up' was intended as a sop to the French and Italians, who were looking at the practical side of the question. The breaking-up of the submarines would make a nice profit and would create employment, a point of special importance for Italy. In the form in which the clause appeared in the preliminary peace terms (Part I, Clause 3) for Council of Ten discussion on 6 March it read:

(a) All German submarines, without exception, submarine salvage vessels, and docks for submarines (including the tubular dock), are to be surrendered to the Allies and the United States of America. Those which can proceed under their own power, or which can be towed, shall be taken by the Germans into Allied ports, to be there destroyed* or broken up.

Germany shall inform the neutral Powers concerned that she authorises the delivery to the Allies and the United States of America of all German submarines in neutral ports.

(b) The German submarines which cannot be delivered in Allied ports, as well as those which are in course of construction, shall be completely broken up by the Germans, under the supervision of Allied and United States Commissioners.

The breaking-up of these submarines shall be completed within a maximum period of three months after the signature of the present Convention.

(c) The Naval Commission appointed by the Allies and the United States of America to supervise the execution of the terms of the Armistice has decided as to which submarines are to proceed or are to be towed to Allied ports and which are to be broken up by the Germans. The decisions of this Commission shall be strictly carried out.

By this date, however, the French had had second thoughts, and de Bon, in reference to the asterisk in the clause, 'makes reservations on this point' (footnote in the original). As a consequence the Council of Ten reserved Clause 3(a), the manner of disposal of the

17 'Extract from minutes of the First Meeting of the Naval Peace Terms Committee . . .'; Wemyss MSS.

submarines to be surrendered, for further consideration. Part I Clause 9, however, which prohibited the construction of submarines in Germany or the acquisition of submarines by Germany, was accepted. At a meeting of the Council of Four on 25 April Wilson expressed his opposition 'to submarines altogether, and hoped the time would come when they would be regarded as contrary to International Law. In his view, they should be regarded as outlaws.' Lloyd George 'did not think that Navies ought to be strengthened by submarines . . . he would like to destroy all the German submarines.' De Bon, however, with Clemenceau's backing, wanted to keep permanently as additions to the French Fleet the approximately 50 German boats that had been placed in the care of France. In view of this demurrer, the Council agreed that the words in the second sentence of the submarine article, 'to be there destroyed or broken up,' should be struck out, and the Admirals were to consider further the question of the disposal of the submarines.[18] The report of the Admirals on 7 May, with de Bon dissenting, stated: 'Whatever be the future as regards submarine warfare, they see no necessity for increasing submarine armaments by distributing the German submarines at a moment when the menace of the German fleet has been removed and a general reduction of armaments is desired.'[19] The issue had not been resolved when the final peace terms were drawn up.

Article 188 of the Versailles Treaty called for the surrender to the Allies within one month of the Treaty coming into force of all submarines that could proceed under their own power or be towed. The rest, and those building, were to be broken up by Germany within three months under Allied supervision. Article 191 forbade the construction or acquisition of submarines by Germany. The problem remained of what to do with the surrendered boats. Only the French insisted that they be permitted to incorporate some of them in their Fleet. The question was not finally settled until 2 December 1919, when at a meeting of the Council of Heads of Delegations (the principal governing body after the signing of the Peace Treaty with Germany: the five Great Powers), the French obtained a decision that, to compensate them for the stoppage of submarine building during the war, they were to receive 10 submarines in good condition; all other

---

[18] *Foreign Relations of the United States. Paris Peace Conference, 1919*, v. 240–1.
[19] *Ibid.*, vii. 366.

German submarines (including the 43 already distributed for propaganda purposes) were to be broken up within one year under the supervision of an Inter-Allied Naval Commission. The basis for the distribution of the boats that had not already been distributed was reserved.

2. DISPOSAL OF THE HIGH SEAS FLEET

The great problem to be decided in the interval between the Armistice and the Peace was the fate of the surface warships still in German hands as well as of the interned ships at Scapa Flow. In January 1919 the Admiralty made up their mind: the annihilation of Germany as a serious naval power required that all the interned vessels and the nine remaining dreadnoughts (eight, really) be surrendered to the Allies and sunk in deep water within three months after the signing of the Peace Treaty. The warships interned in neutral ports were to be dealt with similarly. Also to be surrendered as soon as possible after the signing of the treaty and sunk were vessels building which were in a sufficiently advanced state to be launched; those not were to be broken up under Allied supervision within three months of the signing. The remaining vessels, mostly obsolete and obsolescent, would remain with Germany for self-protection and police duties, while not giving her naval predominance in the Baltic. The reasons which dictated this policy were stated: '(i) To reduce the Naval power of the enemy. (ii) To prevent the enemy again acquiring the ships. (iii) To avoid disagreement among the Allies and Associated Powers as regards the distribution of the Ships.'[20]

The Allied Admirals bought the British package in its essentials. Of the ships still in German hands they would, besides the remaining 8 dreadnoughts, also sink 8 light cruisers, 42 modern destroyers, 50 modern torpedo boats, and limit the future German seagoing fleet to 6 pre-dreadnoughts, 6 light cruisers, 12 destroyers, 12 torpedo boats, and *no* submarines, with German construction limited to the replacement of these units on their attaining a specified age (20 years for capital ships and light cruisers, 15 for destroyers and torpedo boats). Replacement tonnage was limited to 10,000 for armoured ships, 6,000 for light cruisers, 800 for

[20] *Admiralty Policy in Relation to the Peace Settlement*, pp. 5–6.

destroyers, and 200 for torpedo boats. Total personnel was not to exceed 15,000. A note was attached to these naval conditions: 'Admiral Benson does not agree to the limitation of the German Fleet after the final Treaty of Peace, except as imposed by the League of Nations.'[21]

The Council of Ten approved these naval clauses on 6 March: the limitation of the future German Navy as above (eventually, Article 181 of the Versailles Treaty); the destruction of warships building (eventually, Article 186); and the surrender to the Allies of the ships recommended for destruction, but reserving 'the manner of disposal' for later decision (eventually, Articles 184, 185, which make no mention of the actual disposal); the replacement provisions as above (Article 190); the total personnel of the German Navy as above (Article 183).

The French, with Italian support, advocated the partition of the German Fleet among the Allies and contended with some show of reason that France should be allowed a generous share—the distribution to be on the basis of war losses and the fact of retardation of French building owing to concentration on their military commitments. Each Power could dispose of its share as it saw fit. The French hoped to recoup their losses by incorporating some of the German ships into their Fleet and by breaking up the remainder and utilising the material. Initially, the French had evinced no interest in division, but in February 1919 Clemenceau and Leygues, the Minister of Marine, decided to work for this and carried a somewhat reluctant C.O.S., de Bon, with them. At the Council of Ten meeting of 6 March Leygues had expressed deep concern over the clause recommending the destruction of the surrendered ships and proposed that a decision on what was to be done with them be reached separately at a later date. Since the Italians advanced claims for similar rights (they had demolition rather than incorporation in mind), the Council postponed a decision.

To get the United States to agree to reduce her building programme Lloyd George now attempted to exploit Benson's fear that the Royal Navy would incorporate the major portion of the German surface fleet. At a private meeting between Lloyd George, House, and Clemenceau on 7 March, Lloyd George indicated his

---

[21] 'Preliminary Terms of Peace with Germany. Naval Conditions,' 25 February 1919, signed by the five Allied Admirals; Admiralty MSS.

willingness to accept the French demand for distribution. House, as he cabled the President, 'told George that we would never consent to the British augmenting their navy so largely; if this were done it would surely lead to American and British rivalry in this direction.'[22] A compromise was arrived at: 'The ships should be partitioned but that Great Britain, the United States, and Japan should sink those coming to them.'[23] Lloyd George had agreed to the sinking of the American and British shares on the understanding that the two Powers would not in the future build against each other. 'Since Lloyd George had threatened to keep Britain's share of the German ships unless the United States reduced its naval building and House had threatened that American building would increase unless Britain sank her share of the ships, it is clear that their informal agreement would remain mutually acceptable only as long as each believed that the other had been successfully threatened.'[24] The agreement solved nothing.

Daniels, when he arrived in Paris (25 March), let it be known that the United States Navy had no desire to share in any division of the German ships but had no objections to the other naval Powers dividing them as they pleased. 'This surprised our Allies and they thought I was being generous.' It was nothing of the kind. Daniels was 'sure that none of these German ships would fit into the organization of our Navy, and it was not generosity at all but a recognition of a situation. . . . The German ships were not built on the same pattern as the American ships and would be as much of a liability as an asset.'[25] He soon had a change of heart after Benson and the Naval Advisory Staff had forcibly made their position known to him. The Secretary now wanted all the German ships to be sunk, not divided in any way. As he wrote the President, 'The most tangible evidence of faith in reduction of armament would be the impressive act of eliminating this great fleet as one whole.' Again, sinking the lot would be a 'moral lesson . . . of tremendous significance to the whole world.'[26] Left unsaid was the all-important consideration that if the warships were not destroyed, the British would acquire the lion's share and thereby augment

[22] Schilling, *Admirals and Foreign Policy*, p. 269.
[23] House's cable to Wilson (then in the United States), 7 March 1919; Seymour, *The Intimate Papers of Colonel House*, iv. 358.
[24] Schilling, *Admirals and Foreign Policy*, pp. 270–1.
[25] Daniels, *The Wilson Era*, p. 373.
[26] 30 March, 14 April 1919; *ibid.*, pp. 373, 382.

PLATE V

ACTING VICE-ADMIRAL SIR ROGER KEYES

Commanding Dover Patrol, 1918

Portrait by Glyn Philpot : Imperial War Museum

PLATE VI

VICE-ADMIRAL THE HON. SIR SOMERSET
GOUGH-CALTHORPE
Commander-in-Chief, Mediterranean, 1917–19

Portrait by Philip Connard: Imperial War Museum

ADMIRAL SIR LEWIS BAYLY
Commanding Coast of Ireland Station, 1915–19

Photograph: Lafayette Ltd.

their naval superiority. The estimate of the Naval Advisory Staff was that Britain would receive between 10 and 20 of the German capital ships, with the United States probably getting none in any distribution based on naval war losses or effort. The actual Admiralty capital-ship distribution figures, on the basis of war-time losses, were: Britain, 13 dreadnoughts, 4 battle cruisers; France, 4 dreadnoughts; Italy, 3 dreadnoughts; Japan, a dreadnought and a battle cruiser; United States, none.[27]

Wemyss had summed up the British position this way: 'There are obvious and weighty objections to such a division of the spoils, which would be directly opposed to the generally accepted principle of reduction of armaments, having anything but a good moral effect on the world, and might well even give rise to disagreement among the Allies as to the basis of distribution. . . . British and American Naval opinion is in favour of sinking as being by far the most satisfactory solution; the moral effect on Germany and the whole world would be good, and all possibility of disagreement among the Allies would be avoided.'[28] Lloyd George was in principle wholeheartedly with his naval advisers on this issue.

As with the Americans, there was much more to the British position than moral considerations. The Admiralty did not want the German warships for themselves—they did not need them, and the costs of adapting them to British requirements were considered prohibitive—but they had no desire to see the Fleet of a major naval Power strengthened. As Long pointed out to Admiral de Bon and Leygues: 'If the United States were determined to proceed with their huge programme, we should have to reconsider our position, and might ourselves be obliged to utilise our share for the purpose for which they were built. In fact the whole situation rests upon the action taken by the Americans.'[29] Moreover, figures worked out by the Plans Division of the Naval Staff highlighted the difficulties inherent in any distribution scheme. As between a distribution on the basis of wartime naval losses and one in accordance with the French proposals that those countries

---

[27] Plans Division figures attached to an undated (March? 1919) memorandum, probably by Long; Lloyd George MSS. On 2 May Fuller, the D. of P., gave the Naval Advisory Staff a copy of this distribution scheme at their request.

[28] 'Naval Conditions for Peace with Germany,' 28 February 1919; Admiralty MSS.

[29] Undated memorandum; see above, note 27.

which had been prevented from adding to their naval strength during the war should have ships allocated to them to make up for this (specifically, that distribution be based on losses during the war *plus* the addition of ships that would have been built if projected peace building programmes had been carried out)—as between the two, the figures showed that the first method was decidedly more favourable to Britain.[30] The French naturally preferred *their* way. Wemyss's patience was sorely tried by the French attitude. 'Personally, I am very fond of the French, but they are a terrible people to deal with—dreadfully grasping and suspicious always . . .'[31]

The Admiralty had to fight not only the French but a powerful segment of the Royal Navy which opposed destruction. Madden (Second-in-Command of the Grand Fleet, and from April 1919, C.-in-C. of the new main fleet, the Atlantic Fleet) spearheaded a campaign within the Navy for the allocation of the German warships on the basis of war losses, a distribution that would give the lion's share to Great Britain.[32] If the interned capital ships were fitted with modified bulges for torpedo protection and fitted with the British director system of firing, they would remain first-class ships for some years, and, with the light cruisers and the best of the destroyers and submarines, would obviate the need to build against the projected ambitious American programme and enable Britain to maintain her sea supremacy over all nations at a modest outlay. Madden had another reason for wanting these ships: they could test their protection and the new British shell ('Dreyer's

---

30 Their table (24 April 1919, Admiralty MSS.) showed the approximate forces in 1923-4, if the German ships were distributed on the basis of naval losses during the war (column A), if on the basis of the French proposals (column B), and if the German ships were sunk (column C).

	Dreadnoughts			Battle Cruisers			Cruisers and Light Cruisers			Leaders and Destroyers		
	A	B	C	A	B	C	A	B	C	A	B	C
G.B.	46	42	33	14	14	10	94	93	75	499	495	418
France	20	22	16	—	—	—	4	4	—	46	45	32
Italy	12	12	9	—	—	—	11	12	9	66	67	56
Japan	10	11	9	10	10	9	17	17	15	46	45	43
U.S.	29	30	29	6	6	6	14	14	13	342	345	339

Since the capital ships of the U.S. projected programme, which had not yet been approved, could not be laid down till 1921, they were not included.

31 Wemyss to Gough-Calthorpe, 18 March 1919; Wemyss MSS.

32 Wemyss's memorandum of 28 February gave these as the respective percentages of warship tonnage lost: Britain, 74; France, 13; Italy, 7½; Japan, 4; United States, 1½.

pills') by commissioning the best vessel in each class and firing at it at battle ranges; a vessel of each German class should fire at a similar type British ship to test their shell and British protection. These experiments would be costly but would save the Navy millions in the future and give them information on which to build when the *matériel* and tactical lessons of the war had been digested. The United States, Madden held (28 March), favoured destruction because it would assist them 'to become the premier Naval Power with the least possible delay.' He was prepared to concede the sinking or breaking up of the German surface vessels only if the United States agreed to cancel or modify their new programme and cease competing with Britain for sea supremacy.[33]

Beatty expressed his 'complete concurrence' with the naval-supremacy facet of Madden's views. 'If we in the immediate future are to avoid a large building programme, and at the same time counter the American effort, it is necessary to press for the division of German vessels on the basis of Naval losses sustained by the Allies. Such a division should enable us to tide over the next few years, whilst concentrating thought on the training of personnel and the development of new types.'[34] Madden also had powerful support on the Board and the Naval Staff (D.C.N.S., D. of P., and D.O.D. (Home), Fergusson, Fuller, and Pound, respectively), to say nothing of the Conservative press and the iron and steel trades. The *Daily Mail* suggested (1 March) that, following a division according to the ratio of Allied war losses, Britain could, if she wished, sink her share. It would be wiser, though, to break up the ships: this would employ labour and not sacrifice the steel in them. The influential *Naval and Military Record* expressed this opinion (13 March): 'But the fact that we do not want these ships ourselves is no reason why we should deny them to our friends.'

The Admiralty had a measure of support in the Service and in the country. Beresford, for example, held the strong opinion that the battleships should have their valuable metals stripped from them, then be sunk in the middle of the Atlantic. 'If they are divided among the Allies, they will always create a fester and irritating sore in Germany, the same as the loss of Alsace–Lorraine

---

[33] Madden to Beatty, 26 November 1918, Beatty MSS., and to Admiralty, 20, 28 March 1919, Beatty, Admiralty MSS., respectively.
[34] Beatty to Admiralty, 4 April 1919; Admiralty MSS.

created in France.'[35] The Liberal press also preferred sinking the German ships to dividing them among the Allies, whose 'only result would be,' said the *Daily News* (26 February), 'to saddle the taxpayers of the countries concerned with the maintenance of proportionately larger navies with no visible advantage on the credit side whatever; and this as a preliminary measure to the disarmament of which we are all talking. . . . Let the ships be broken up and their commercial value realised and divided.' The truth, the *Manchester Guardian* imagined (10 March), was that 'the Admiralty would like, by eliminating the German navy altogether, to lower the whole level of naval armaments throughout the world, and thinks sinking the surest mode of elimination. That is a very proper aim . . .'

The Board wavered when it appeared that the United States had no intention of giving up its plans to build a 'fifty to fifty' Navy, that is, one equal to the British Navy. The Admiralty were prepared to reconsider their position if the United States proceeded with its huge programme. Ultimately, political considerations— the necessity for Anglo-American harmony and the profound reluctance to do anything to stimulate a naval competition with the United States which the British could not win—determined that the Admiralty would not depart from their declared policy of favouring the sinking of the ships. The American decision to scrap their second (1918) programme was probably a contributing factor.

Meanwhile, there was the problem of the French, who simply were not to be put off. At a meeting of the Council of Four on 25 April Admiral Benson pressed for a definite settlement of the disposition issue to avoid misunderstandings when the Peace Treaty was signed. His own position was plain: 'any decision, except to sink the ships, meant an increase of armaments.' Lloyd George again played on American fears that the British Navy would not sink their share of the capital ships. Since the discussion of the disposition problem could go on for a day or two, he suggested that the Treaty need only state that the ships were to be surrendered. Admiral de Bon reviewed the French case, his essential point being, 'For no aggressive desires of any kind, France did not want to lose this opportunity for repairing her losses.' Lloyd George

---

[35] Beresford to Lord Stamfordham (the King's Private Secretary), 14 March 1919; Windsor MSS.

expressed sympathy with the French position. He thought that France 'should have some of these ships, and sink a corresponding number of old ships, or if unwilling to sink them, she might break them up . . .' The best that Wilson could manage was an agreement that if Germany raised the disposal question, they would promise her that it would be settled for the signing of the Peace Treaty.[36]

And there the matter lay. Neither the Admirals nor the politicians could reach agreement. The deadlock continued into June, to the point where the 'Four' were even reluctant to discuss the question any further. Wemyss expressed himself frankly to the Deputy First Sea Lord: 'You and I know what an embarrassment it would be to us to have any of these German ships, and you and I know that we should like to see them sunk, but I do see that they are a pawn in the game.'[37] No decision as to final disposal had been reached when the peace terms were signed at Versailles on 28 June. But already the situation had undergone a sensationally dramatic change.

[36] *Foreign Relations of the United States. The Paris Peace Conference, 1919*, v. 238–9.
[37] Wemyss to Hope, 6 June 1919; Wemyss MSS.

XI

Götterdämmerung

(21 June 1919)

(*Plan B, p. 276*)

I rejoice over the sinking of the German Fleet in Scapa Flow. . . . the stain of surrender has been wiped out from the escutcheon of the German Fleet. The sinking of the ships has proved that the spirit of the Fleet is not dead. This last act is true of the best traditions of the German Navy.

ADMIRAL SCHEER, in an American newspaper interview, as reported in *The Times*, 1 July 1919.

. . . this deed of stupid cunning and impotent arrogance . . .

THE TIMES, 23 June 1919.

True to their motto of 'Safety first', the German seamen did not scuttle their dishonoured fleet until they could do so with the minimum of personal risk. . . . If intelligent Germans can discover any cause for pride in the end of their fleet, as a people they must be even more degenerate than we think them.

NAVAL AND MILITARY RECORD, 2 July 1919.

I. INTERNMENT

ON 22 November 1918 there had begun the inspection of the interned ships in the Firth of Forth to make certain there was no ammunition on board. The ships were then moved in batches to Scapa Flow, arriving between 25 and 27 November and anchoring at their appointed positions. The destroyers and other small craft were moored in pairs in Gutter Sound, between the islands of Hoy and Fara; the battleships and cruisers, to the north and west of Cava. Interned were 11 battleships, 5 battle cruisers, 8 light cruisers, and 50 destroyers. The first order of business at Scapa was the removal of the wireless apparatus on board and the immobilization of the guns by the removal of the breech blocks. Next, the crews, which had arrived about 400 strong in the battleships, the other ships in proportion, for a total of about 4,700 officers and men, were gradually reduced to maintenance size: 175–200 officers and men for the capital ships down to about 20 in each destroyer. After a final reduction on 17 June 1919 of 2,200 at the request of the German Commander, Rear-Admiral von Reuter, the crews were brought down to 140 for each capital ship and the others in proportion, with a total of 1,800 officers and men.

The state of affairs in the German Fleet was one of complete demoralization, a mood that had set in on 21 November. A blue-jacket in the dreadnought *Nassau* expressed it succinctly: 'That day hid within its bosom the most shameful deed in all the history of the sea. The voluntary surrender of the German Fleet.'[1] Four acute internment problems intensified the demoralization. (1) *Discipline.* There was a minimum of discipline, the officers having practically no authority. 'All proposed orders are considered and countersigned by the men's committee before they are executed and then they are carried out as convenient.'[2] The men lounged about, smoked cigarettes in the presence of their officers, turned out late, etc. A British officer who had business in the German fleet in its first days of internment returned extremely depressed by 'the sight of discipline and efficiency gone to pot. The mess decks were in an appalling condition of dirt and the officers were dumb with shame when our men came on board.'[3] (2) *Food.* Supplies arrived from Germany twice a month. There was sufficient food, but it was monotonous and not of good quality. (Included was a good deal of brandy.) Given conditions at home, this was to be expected, yet it made the food situation no more bearable. Catching fish and seagulls furnished a dietary supplement. Sometimes fights took place over the distribution of stores, so that the British had to supervise the operation. (3) *Recreation.* The men had a great deal of time, but could do little with it except fish. Though permission was often asked, the British authorities would not permit the crews to go ashore, not even on the small rocky islands inside the Flow, or even to visit or communicate in any way with sister ships. Nor were British seamen

---

1 Ludwig Freiwald, *Last Days of the German Fleet* (London, 1932), p. 281.
2 Madden to Jellicoe, 29 November 1918; Jellicoe MSS.
3 Midshipman Ian Sanderson to his father, 1 December 1918, reporting the impressions of the Gunnery Officer of the *Malaya*, Lieutenant-Commander Andrew B. Downes.

and officers (except as noted below) allowed to go on board a German ship. 'We allow no communication whatsoever with the ships,' Sanderson wrote home (26 January 1919). 'It is as well to treat them as lepers after the way in which they have conducted the war for which they longed so much.' The main reason for the rigid non-fraternization policy may have been the fear of contamination by the subversive tendencies rampant in the German fleet. The British authorities could not prevent all contact between the two sides. There was barter between the men, the Germans exchanging liquor (Scapa was 'dry'), personal possessions like cameras and binoculars, and souvenirs, including Iron Crosses and bits of their ships, for food and everyday necessities like cigarettes and soap. (4) The slow postal service and the indescribable filth in some of the ships did nothing to raise morale.

'The men in the big ships have not a kick left in them', wrote Sub-Lieutenant Andrew Yates on 11 May. 'They are the most beaten lot I ever saw and I don't think will do anything. The destroyers are however quite aggressive still and the officers very Prussian.' Yates, with a display of the leg-pulling humour for which he is well known, asked a band on the dreadnought *Kaiser*'s quarter-deck to play for him 'The Hymn of Hate'. 'They told me', he related, 'they never played "Gott strafe England" now, as they had been too much "strafed" themselves by both Gott and England.'

Control of the interned ships was exercised through von Reuter, who flew his flag in the dreadnought *Friedrich der Grosse*. (He had commanded the 4th Scouting Group at Jutland.) He was responsible for complying with the naval terms of the Armistice and the orders laid down by Beatty and by Madden after him. He was permitted to visit his ships or to issue any correspondence only on necessary and urgent business, and then only through a British drifter that was at his service; occasional visits of his staff officers were allowed to arrange for the repatriation of officers and men. Communication between the German ships was ordinarily by visual means, not through personal contacts. Senior officers of German ships could take passage in one of the three British 'communication drifters' from one ship to another only in exceptional circumstances and provided they had previously obtained permission from the British Senior Officer Afloat. The only regular communication between the guardships and the Germans was a daily visit to the Admiral by a staff officer from the British flagship to learn if he had requests or complaints. Otherwise, excepting a few conferences between senior officers and visits of a medical officer or chaplain as needed, or by British navigation officers to shift German ships that had dragged their anchors, no communication took place between the British and German authorities other than in writing. Any communication necessary between von Reuter and the British Admiral was carried on through the drifter that lay alongside the former's ship. The same drifter collected and distributed the mails.

At first the Battle Cruiser Force constituted the guardships to the interned fleet, with Admiral Pakenham in command. Oliver relieved him in December and was relieved by Keyes on 21 March 1919. By then the Battle Cruiser Force was the Battle Cruiser Squadron—reduced to one squadron: the *Lion*, *Renown*, *Princess Royal*, and *Tiger*. On 1 May Sir Arthur Leveson, Vice-Admiral Commanding 2nd Battle Squadron, Atlantic Fleet, took over the supervision of the German ships, and on 18 May Sir Sydney Fremantle, Vice-Admiral Commanding 1st Battle Squadron, Atlantic Fleet (*Revenge*, flag). Armed trawlers and drifters patrolled the anchorage; their orders were to watch for and report at once if the German ships appeared to be settling down or sinking. The British were, then, alert to the possibility that the ships might be scuttled. The likelihood seemed remote.

Von Reuter was an ideal prisoner—straightforward, co-operative in every way, and punctually carrying out the orders transmitted to him. Fremantle has written: 'One could not help feeling a considerable sympathy with von Reuter in the very unenjoyable position of being in nominal command of ships manned by mutinous crews.[4] Our restrictions gave him little opportunity to exercise command of his ships, and requests for any assistance from us had to be made through him. He was an easy and reasonable man to deal with, and a man of his word who was never, except in one momentous instance, consciously disloyal to the terms of the Armistice.' The Admiral was so co-operative that his gaolers seemingly had nothing to fear. The only exception to the correct conduct of the German officers and men was on 31

---

[4] Reuter, whose health was poor, asked and received permission to transfer his flag to the light cruiser *Emden* (25 March) after his men had shown their 'insolent' feelings by stomping over his head and preventing him from sleeping!

May, the third anniversary of Jutland, when, partly, no doubt, to annoy the British, some of the German ships (from their position presumably battle cruisers) fired off red and white Very lights, and the *Seydlitz*, *Moltke*, and most of the destroyers arranged decorations with German ensigns and red flags. Fremantle ordered that none of these was to be in sight from outboard and decreed that no dressing ships was permissible. The Germans carried out these orders after a brief display of force. 'Generally speaking, however,' Fremantle says, 'they appeared to be accepting their lot with submissive equanimity, but towards the end in some spirit of discontent.'

There was no danger of the German ships weighing anchor and taking off for home, since they lacked the fuel to steam very far into the North Sea. The one possible danger was a scuttling in violation of Article XXXI of the Armistice: 'No destruction of ships . . . to be permitted . . .' What could be done to prevent this? The British had no authority to place guards in the ships so long as the Germans complied with the Armistice terms. Oliver, when in command of the guardships, was convinced that the Germans would be up to some tricks. He drew up a plan to send armed parties in trawlers alongside the German ships at daybreak, take off all the crews, and transfer them to an empty military camp at Nigg on the north shore of Cromarty Firth. On succeeding Beatty as C.-in-C. in April, Madden approved the plan, but the Admiralty evinced no interest. Oliver's successor, Keyes, had a scheme to seize the ships by a *coup de main* as soon as he was ordered, under the expected terms of the Peace Treaty, to demand their immediate surrender. Leveson, when he succeeded Keyes, recommended a *coup* before a peace treaty was imminent and the removal of all the men to Nigg. Again, the Admiralty paid no heed —possibly because nobody was minding the shop. Wemyss and Hope were often away in Paris on naval peace terms business.

I had no anxiety [wrote Fremantle] that any gross breach of the armistice would be committed until possibly the last moments before the German representatives were required to sign the Treaty.

I had, however, considerable anxiety as to the possibility of damage being done to the German ships either—

(i) In the event of the Treaty being signed, during the interval between the signing of the Treaty and the repatriation of the German officers and men; or

(ii) In the event of the Treaty not being signed, before I was able to assure the surrender of the ships.[5]

To his surprise, Fremantle had received no instructions from Madden or the Admiralty on the disposition of the interned ships and their crews at the termination of the Armistice, scheduled for noon on 21 June, simultaneously with the time fixed for signing the peace terms.[6] Expecting that these would require the surrender of the interned ships, and aware of the distinct possibility that von Reuter would scuttle them first, Fremantle submitted a scheme to Madden on 16 June for a surprise seizure of the interned ships at midnight of 21–22 June with large forces from the battleships. The boarding parties were, Fremantle tells us, 'to confine all officers and men, to search the ships for indications of preparations for sinking, and as far as possible, to keep the ships afloat.' Madden approved the plan on the 19th.

2. THE SCUTTLING

Madden had been anxious for some time to get the whole of the Atlantic Fleet (two battle squadrons and the battle cruiser squadron) together for a cruise as soon as the political situation would permit. Since there would be few opportunities on this cruise for carrying out certain minor practices and exercises which

---

[5] Fremantle to Madden, 24 June 1919; 'Scuttling of the German Ships at Scapa Flow' (G.T.-7674), 10 July 1919. Wemyss's opinion was that if the Germans did not sign, they ought at once to seize the ships, 'for this perpetual hanging on and waiting is getting well nigh unbearable.' Wemyss to Hope, 6 June 1919; Wemyss MSS.

[6] Madden was not to blame. He had on 22 April requested the Admiralty to keep him informed of the political situation, so that he might put into operation, if necessary, orders for seizure which he had drawn up for the eventuality of a German refusal to sign the peace terms, and before the ships' companies had received news of the refusal, in order to prevent their sinking or damaging the ships. 'I indicated the duties to be performed, e.g., engine-room parties to secure all engine-room and boiler inlets, torpedo parties to secure tube doors and sluices, carpenters to secure the sea cocks, etc. The Rear-Admiral, First Battle Squadron [the Hon. Victor Stanley], prepared good orders on these lines, and the parties were exercised for rapid action.' On 13 June, during a visit to the Admiralty, he had asked the D.C.N.S. for a daily appreciation of the political situation beginning on 17 June, so as to be prepared to take action. 'The Admiralty were, however, not able to give me any useful intelligence, and on Saturday, 21st June, they had no reliable indication of the German attitude towards the peace terms.' Madden to Beatty, 24 June 1919; Beatty MSS. Madden did regret that he had not repeated to Fremantle the announcement in an Admiralty telegram of 17 June that the period required for signing the peace terms had been extended from 21 to 23 June.

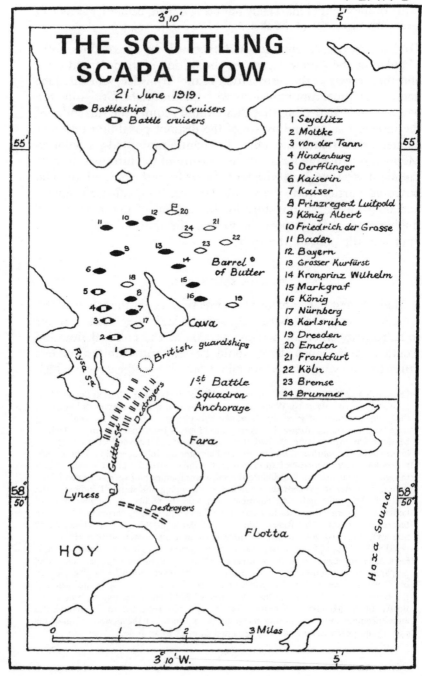

PLAN B

THE SCUTTLING
SCAPA FLOW

21 June 1919.

● Battleships   ◇ Cruisers
◐ Battle cruisers

1	Seydlitz
2	Moltke
3	von der Tann
4	Hindenburg
5	Derfflinger
6	Kaiserin
7	Kaiser
8	Prinzregent Luitpold
9	König Albert
10	Friedrich der Grosse
11	Baden
12	Bayern
13	Grosser Kurfürst
14	Kronprinz Wilhelm
15	Markgraf
16	König
17	Nürnberg
18	Karlsruhe
19	Dresden
20	Emden
21	Frankfurt
22	Köln
23	Bremse
24	Brummer

Barrel of Butter

Cava

British guardships

1st Battle Squadron Anchorage

Rysa S^{d.}

Gutter S^{d.}   Destroyers

Fara

Lyness   Destroyers

Flotta

HOY

Haxa Sound

0   1   2   3 Miles

3° 10' W.   5'

were necessary to full efficiency, Fremantle proceeded to run off these practices and exercises. He had completed all but one, the exercise of a massed daylight destroyer attack against a battle squadron in formation. Good weather was necessary, as it would be difficult in a seaway to recover the torpedoes. Bad weather had twice deferred this exercise. On the night of 20 June, the weather prospects being favourable, Fremantle ordered the squadron to sea the next morning. His mind was not at ease, however. He had seen a press statement the preceding evening announcing that the Armistice expiration had been extended to 10 a.m. on the 23rd. (Actually, at 5 p.m., 20 June, the Council of Four, in Paris, had authorized the seizure of the German ships on the expiration of the Armistice, now set for 7 p.m. on 23 June.) Fremantle received no official confirmation from the Admiralty, but he assumed the story to be true. He planned to return to the Flow on the 23rd and carry out the seizure plans that night.

Before sailing, Fremantle informed von Reuter unofficially of the extension of the Armistice. Von Reuter afterwards claimed that he had not received this news until the evening of the 21st. This was a quibble, since he had given his order for scuttling at 10 a.m. on the 21st, and the Armistice was originally set to terminate at noon that day. According to his statement to Fremantle while a prisoner in the *Revenge*, he had read in an English newspaper, on that fateful Saturday morning, 21 June, that the original naval terms were unchanged. Therefore, not having been informed of the extension of the period for signing the peace terms, and believing that the Armistice would terminate at noon that day, and that the Allies would then resume hostilities and move to seize the interned fleet, he had given the order to sink the ships in order to prevent their falling into the hands of the Allies. He would, he stated, have given the order even if the British squadron had been in harbour.

This is not the whole truth. As early as January von Reuter had mentioned the idea of sinking the fleet to his C.O.S.[7] However, it was only after he had learned through the newspapers on 11 May of the Allied peace conditions which had been presented to the Germans at Versailles on 7 May that he started to think seriously about the naval implications of the peace terms and prepared

[7] Von Reuter, *Scapa Flow: the Account of the Greatest Scuttling of All Time* (London, 1940), p. 79.

detailed plans to scuttle his ships.[8] Was he inspired, encouraged, or commanded by his Government or by naval authorities to execute the scuttling? Yes and No. We have it on Admiral Raeder's authority that the Chief of the *Admiralstab*, von Trotha, 'privately impressed upon Junior Captain [Commander] Oldekop, Admiral von Reuter's Chief of Staff, that the ships must be scuttled at all costs. This important message was sent through Junior Captain Quaet-Faslem, the commander of the dispatch boat which maintained communications between Admiral von Reuter and Germany.'[9] We also know of a letter of 9 May from von Trotha to von Reuter which contains a veiled invitation to scuttle.

From press news and utterances in the British House of Lords, it appears that our opponents are considering the idea of depriving us of the Interned Ships on the conclusion of peace; they waver between the destruction or the distribution among themselves of these ships. . . . These hostile intentions are in opposition to the hitherto unquestioned German right of ownership of the vessels . . . you may rest assured that it will be no more than the plain duty of our Naval Delegates at Versailles to safeguard the fate of our interned ships in every way, and to arrive at a solution which is in accordance with our traditions and our unequivocal German rights. In this connection, the first condition will be that the ships remain German . . . their surrender to the enemy remains out of the question.[10]

Von Reuter willingly took the responsibility after the event, and I would not challenge his veracity. The initiative, I believe, was his. The idea that the High Seas Fleet was rather to be scuttled than handed over to Germany's adversaries was so common among Imperial German naval officers that von Reuter scarcely needed any encouragement, let alone an order. Being convinced that no German Government would sign the Versailles treaty, he had

---

8 See Vice-Admiral Friedrich Ruge, *Scapa Flow 1919: Das Ende der deutschen Flotte* (Oldenburg, 1969), pp. 130–3.

9 Grand-Admiral Erich Raeder, *My Life* (Annapolis, 1960), p. 105. Raeder gives no date for the message. He himself was then employed in the *Admiralstab*.

10 'Scuttling of the German Ships at Scapa Flow.' Admiral Ruge writes of this letter: 'On 9 May, that is, two days after the presentation of the Peace terms, there had been no sort of negotiations whatsoever; no one in Germany had any idea what was to be achieved. Admiral von Trotha obviously still knew nothing of the text when he wrote his letter. It was grotesque that anyone should read out of this the order to scuttle the ships.' Ruge, *Scapa Flow 1919*, p. 191.

made up his mind to scuttle at the date provided for the signature, as the refusal to sign would restore the state of war.

The order to scuttle was executed in accordance with a carefully prepared plan. Von Reuter had no difficulty in making his preparations, since British orders did not permit any boarding of the German ships. He managed to get his orders through to the commanding officers of his ships. Plans had been ready for a month. In his order of 17 June, the Admiral made certain that as soon as the reduction in personnel had taken place, every possible measure would be taken to ensure an immediate scuttling whenever he gave the executive signal. All internal watertight doors, hatchway covers, ventilation openings, port-holes, were to be kept open at all times. Individual commanding officers were left to decide whether to take additional measures such as: to clear away underwater torpedo-tube doors, leaving only one fastening bolt, open up a condensor, open all except one valve in the sea-water flooding system—in short, to make each ship as un-watertight as possible. There were plans, too, for a speedy evacuation of the ships after the sinkings had begun, and for transmitting the Admiral's message to the ships. The scheme was developed with skill and secrecy. The reduction of the crews in June simplified von Reuter's problems, since he had been able to include among the repatriated those considered to be unreliable and who might have obstructed the scuttling plan.

Paragraph 5 of von Reuter's orders of 17 June stated: 'Sinking is only to take place (a) in the case of forcible intervention on the part of the English. (b) On the receipt of special orders from me.' Paragraph 11 read: 'It is my intention to sink the ships only if the enemy should attempt to obtain possession of them without the assent of our Government. Should our Government agree in the peace terms to the surrender of the ships, then the ships will be handed over, to the lasting disgrace of those who have placed us in this position.'[11]

On 18 June Reuter sent written orders to his commanding officers (via the British mail drifter!) to make all preparations for sinking their ships when he signalled the order. This occurred at about 11.20 a.m. on 21 June. (It followed a signal of about 10 a.m. to stand by for the signal to scuttle.) It was an apparently innocent

---

[11] 'Scuttling of the German Ships at Scapa Flow.'

flag signal, which had been prearranged in von Reuter's orders of 17 June: 'To all Commanding Officers and the Leader of the Torpedo Boats [Destroyers]. Paragraph Eleven of to-day's date. Acknowledge. Chief of the Interned Squadron.' This called for the immediate commencement of scuttling operations. Since the German Admiral had the privilege of making signals to his ships, this aroused no interest. Nor was the unusual signal activity, as von Reuter's orders were passed along, the occasion for comment. The crews opened the sea-cocks, the watertight doors, etc. Nothing out of the ordinary was noticed until about noon, when it was observed that the *Friedrich der Grosse* had taken a heavy list to starboard (she was the first to sink—at 12.16 p.m.). At the stroke of noon the German ships hoisted the German ensign on the mainmast. The cat was out of the bag; it was obvious that something unusual was happening.

Where was Fremantle? At 9 that morning the First Battle Squadron (5 battleships, 9 destroyers) had weighed and proceeded out of harbour into the Pentland Firth, some eight miles from the harbour. Left behind as the sole guard over the Germans were two destroyers (one of them defective), a destroyer depot ship, and several trawlers and drifters. After the squadron sailed, Fremantle read the translation of a message from von Reuter which had arrived in the *Revenge* while she was weighing. Von Reuter requested the immediate forwarding of this message to the naval authorities in Germany: 'In the English papers I have to-day perceived that in the German counter-proposal the Government intended to use the interned ships as an object of trade. Even if economical distress is so great as this, my feelings of patriotism and honour cannot accommodate themselves to such a treatment of the interned German Fleet. In this view of the matter I am assured of the support of all the Officers of the Squadron. Accordingly I request that a new adjustment of the Peace Terms may be caused or, if this is not attainable, that we Officers and officials may be definitely relieved before the surrender.'[12] One might have thought that this important communication would have caused Fremantle to cancel the exercise and speed back; but no, he decided not to deal with it until he had completed the scheduled exercise and returned to harbour. He saw no cause for anxiety. Von Reuter would not violate the Armistice terms: he

12 In Fremantle to Madden, 24 June 1919; *ibid.*

PLATE VII

BRITISH SEAMEN WATCHING THE SURRENDER

Photograph : The Sphere

ADMIRAL SIR DAVID BEATTY

at the surrender of the High Seas Fleet, 21 November 1918

Photograph : Graphic Photo Union

PLATE VIII

SCUTTLED GERMAN BATTLESHIP, 'BAYERN' AT SCAPA FLOW
Photograph : Imperial War Museum

GERMAN DESTROYER SINKING AT SCAPA FLOW
One of the 'G 101–104' Series, still moored to her buoy
Photograph : by permission of V.-Adm. Friedrich Ruge

H.M. WHALER 'RAMNA'
Perched on the armoured belt of the scuttled battle cruiser *Moltke* at
Scapa Flow
Photograph : Imperial War Museum

had been so co-operative. Madden afterwards cleared Fremantle. 'I do not consider that the signal from Admiral von Reuter . . . need have aroused any suspicion in the mind of the Vice Admiral Commanding First Battle Squadron, or necessitated the putting off of the exercise.'[13]

The first destroyer attack had taken place in the exercise, and the destroyers were recovering the torpedoes, when Fremantle received an urgent W/T signal at 12.20 p.m. from one of the guard destroyers, 'German battleship sinking,' soon followed by a message from the officer commanding the naval base at Scapa: 'German ships sinking; some already sunk.' Fremantle immediately cancelled the exercise (12.35) and proceeded at full speed to Scapa Flow, the first division anchoring in the Flow at 2.30 p.m., and the second division at 4 p.m. En route the Admiral gave instructions to his ships to do all they could to prevent the ships from sinking and if possible to beach those still afloat.

The guardships and other small craft rushed in from the base were, despite their best efforts, unable to prevent or delay the ships from sinking. By the time Fremantle was on the scene (2.30), only the larger ships were left afloat. It was an awesome and fantastic sight that greeted them—of vessels, small and large, in various stages of sinking, some with their sterns almost vertical above the water. A German destroyer officer who witnessed the spectacle writes: 'It was a marvellous sight. All over the vast bay ships were in various stages of sinking . . . Everywhere cutters, whalers, and rafts were being manned or were already pulling or drifting away, and British guard destroyers and drifters were hurrying to and fro, giving the general alarm with their sirens. In the intervals, sounds of firings were to be heard.'[14] Add to the picture the explosive water spouts and gigantic upsurges of oil as the big ships went down. There were some amusing incidents, like the German officer who insisted on handing over his sword with appropriate ceremony.

---

[13] Madden to Admiralty, 27 June 1919; *ibid.* He added, 'My view of the situation during this week was, that, the ships being interned, there was no authority to place armed guards on board or to seize them, unless there was reason to doubt the honour of Rear Admiral von Reuter or to believe that he had lost control of his ships' companies. Events proved that he had full control of his men and I had no reason to doubt his good faith.'

[14] Vice-Admiral Friedrich Ruge, 'Scapa Flow,' *United States Naval Institute Proceedings*, December 1959.

As noted, the desperate and sustained attempts of the British ships to forestall the inevitable were doomed to failure. The bulk of the German fleet went down. It was all over by 5 p.m.: 400,000 tons of metal and machinery worth £70 million had been sent to the bottom of the Flow. Fifteen of the 16 German capital ships were sunk. The *Baden*, Germany's latest battleship, obstinately refused to sink: she was beached in a waterlogged condition and was later raised. Of the 8 light cruisers, 4 went down; the *Emden*, *Frankfurt*, *Bremse*, and *Nürnberg* were beached in a sinking condition. Of the 50 destroyers, 32 were sunk, 14 were beached, and 4 were kept afloat in a partly flooded condition. The Germans had suffered 10 men killed and about 16 wounded—all incurred when the British fired at German ships to prevent men still on board from lowering their boats, the idea being to encourage them to undo their work. One of the dead men was the captain of the dreadnought *Markgraf*, Commander Schumann, shot by boarders when he failed to carry out an order.[15] The British picked up and held as prisoners all Germans in lifeboats or in the water; none was fired upon. 'The Germans,' an officer recorded at the time, 'all came aboard with a very truculent air, particularly the officers, who had their hands in their pockets and slouched along in a most insolent manner. This could not be allowed, so Lieutenant-Commander (T) and I stationed ourselves in a suitable position and corrected their lack of manners before allowing them to proceed further.'

At about 4 p.m. von Reuter was brought on board the *Revenge*.

15 A macabre incident, not without its humorous side, on the morning following the scuttling is worth relating. The officer who had the morning watch in the *Ramillies* tells it. 'It was one of those utterly calm mornings one sometimes experienced at Scapa Flow in summer; the surface of the sea like glass and not a breath stirring. About 5.30 a.m. I was on the quarterdeck, taking a look round, when Horne, one of our Sub-Lieutenants, arrived in high indignation. He occupied one of the cabins right aft on the middle deck; and as the "R" class, as completed, drew rather more water than originally had been contemplated, the scuttles of those cabins were rather close to the water. Waking early, Horne had looked out of his scuttle to see what the weather was like; and had found himself gazing at short range into the face of a dead German officer. Which was no small shock to him! And so he came to complain to me as Officer of the Watch. What had happened was that the body of the dead Captain Schumann had been left overnight in the cabin of the motor boat in which it had been brought to us—I surmise until our "chippy chaps" had had time to make a coffin for it. In the prevailing calm the boat, which had been secured to what we called the stern boom, had swung round until she was lying close under our counter, with her cabin windows abreast and close up to the scuttle of poor Horne's cabin.' Commander W. M. Phipps Hornby's letter to the author, 16 September 1968.

'I received him personally in the normal manner,' Fremantle relates, 'but without any of the usual honours to which a foreign Admiral is entitled, and informed him that I considered his order for the sinkings, which had been given two hours before the original termination of the Armistice and in all probability 48 hours before what was eventually the terminal date of which he had been officially informed, was a breach of the Armistice orders which had been signed by his Government,[16] and that I considered him guilty of treacherous conduct. I could not resist feeling some sympathy with von Reuter who had preserved his dignity when placed, against his will, in a highly unpleasant and invidious position.' In the late afternoon, shortly before sailing for Invergordon, whose nearby military prisoner-of-war camps at Nigg were prepared to receive the German crews (approximately 1,800, distributed among the five battleships), Fremantle let it be known through a general order that the Germans, having broken the Armistice, would be treated as prisoners of war. He brushed aside the German Admiral's protest. On the morning of the 22nd Fremantle turned his prisoners over to the military authorities at Invergordon, but not before a dramatic scene was staged on the quarter-deck of the flagship. Fremantle achieved some relief of his indignation by addressing von Reuter and his staff (his German interpreter translated), a scornful expression on his face:

Admiral von Reuter: I cannot permit you and your officers to leave naval custody without expressing to you my sense of the manner in which you have violated common honour and the honourable traditions of seamen of all nations.

With an armistice in full operation you recommenced hostilities without notice by hoisting the German flag in the interned ships and proceeding to sink and destroy them.

You have informed my interpreter that you considered the Armistice had terminated.

You had no justification whatever for that assumption.

You would have been informed by me of the termination of the Armistice and whether the representatives of your nation had or had not signed the Treaty of Peace.

Indeed, letters in readiness to send to you to that effect as soon as I had received official intimation from my Government were written and signed.

[16] Articles XXIII and especially XXXI. See above, p. 183.

Further, can you possibly suppose that my Squadron would have been out of harbour at the moment of the termination of the Armistice?

By your conduct you have added one more to the breaches of faith and honour of which Germany has been guilty in this war.

Begun with a breach of military honour in the invasion of Belgium, it bids fair to terminate with a breach of naval honour.

You have proved to the few who doubted it that the word of the New Germany is no more to be trusted than that of the old.

What opinion your country will form of your action I do not know.

I can only express what I believe to be the opinion of the British Navy, and indeed of all seamen except those of your Nation.

I now transfer you to the custody of the British military authorities as prisoners of war guilty of a flagrant violation of Armistice.

'They stood with expressionless faces,' Fremantle recalls, 'and when the short address was over, clicked their heels and descended the accommodation ladder without a word.'[17]

For a while the Admiralty contemplated trying von Reuter by naval court-martial under the Defence of the Realm Act. When the Judge Advocate of the Fleet ruled that they could not do so, the Admiralty considered the possibility of trying the Admiral in a civil court under a charge of barratry. The Law Officers apparently ruled against this, too.

Let us back up. Fremantle was a flag officer of no extraordinary abilities upon whom Fortune smiled beyond his deserts. Another Admiral, Alexander-Sinclair, for example, might have found reason for remaining in harbour at that particular juncture (21 June). Yet even if Fremantle's squadron were in harbour, it would not have exercised any deterrent effect on von Reuter or the German crews. And once the Germans set about scuttling their ships, it is difficult to see what could have been done to stop von Reuter and prevent the sinkings. The preparations for scuttling were most thorough and the British were denied the right to board the ships for periodical inspection. So even had they been in a position to send boarding parties the moment it became apparent that the German ships were beginning to sink, I doubt whether

---

[17] According to von Reuter, he made this answer in German, facing the interpreter: 'Tell your Admiral that I am unable to agree with the purport of his speech and that our comprehension of the subject differs. I alone carry the responsibility. I am convinced that any English naval officer, placed as I was, would have acted in the same way.' Von Reuter, *Scapa Flow*, p. 118.

they would have been in time to save, at any rate, many of them. They would have been trying to save ships about whose internal arrangements they knew virtually nothing. Before valves opened to admit sea water could be closed, their whereabouts would first have to be discovered! Even had the boarding parties 'acted tough' and driven the German crews below at pistol point, I doubt whether in the time available to them the Germans themselves could have undone their handiwork quickly enough. For example, in some at least of the few ships saved it had been found that important watertight doors had been securely lashed open. The fact is that the deed was as good as done once the German crews began to carry out their Admiral's orders to open the sea-cocks, on account of the short time necessary to sink a ship. It was estimated that a 'Queen Elizabeth,' for example, could be sunk in from 25 minutes to one hour from the time of receipt of the orders; the *Friedrich der Grosse* sank within 50 minutes of von Reuter's order. 'A ship could be too far gone to admit of her being saved when half the periods of time mentioned above had elapsed.' At best, had he remained in harbour, Fremantle might have been able to beach a larger number of ships.

Madden was 'convinced that no step short of seizing the ships and removing the crews would have insured their safety and being wise now after the event this should have been done; as soon as von Reuter became aware that whether the Germans signed or not the Fleet was lost to them, it was then (Tuesday, 17th) that he decided to act or received orders to do so.'[18] The fatal error was obviously the Armistice provision that the German ships should be interned with their own crews on board, instead of surrendered outright as was done with the submarines. Madden and Fremantle had taken all the precautions they could think of to safeguard the interned ships, short of placing guards on board or periodically examining the ships. But the placing of guards permanently on board would have been equivalent to seizure: according to international law, 'internment' meant that the ships were to be disposed of in such a way as to prevent them from taking any kind of hostile action, but otherwise their liberty of action must not be interfered with. In other words, internment carried with it the German right to look after their own ships and made it illegal for the British to

18 Madden to Beatty, 24 June 1919.

place armed guards on board. Periodical examination would not have prevented the ships being sunk.

Fremantle never received any comment, approval, or censure from either his Commander-in-Chief or the Admiralty, though the Admiralty were 'quite convinced that nothing we could have done would have prevented the Germans from sinking their ships if they had determined to do so.'[19] Fremantle was in due course promoted and continued to serve in important appointments.

We must return to the narrative. A furious Madden telegraphed the Admiralty on the 23rd that Germany be punished by being allowed to retain only 2 light cruisers, 6 destroyers, and 6 torpedo boats; that von Reuter and the ships' companies remain prisoners of war until the Scapa anchorage was cleared by junior German officers and men; and if it developed that von Reuter had acted on orders from Authority, there must be further punishments in the shape of occupation of Heligoland and Borkum. The latter might eventually be ceded to Holland.

That morning the Council of Four discussed the scuttling. It was decided that the legal experts should prepare a text that day 'stating the theory of jurisprudence on which action could be taken,' and directing the Admirals to report what ships remained to Germany, with a view to demanding the surrender of some or all in place of those sunk. The text prepared by the legal advisers later in the day minced no words: the destruction of the German ships was a clear breach of Article XXIII of the Armistice and gave the Allies the right to reparation and to prosecute those responsible before military tribunals. A meeting of Admirals at the French Ministry of Marine the same afternoon submitted the required list and pointed out that except for the 5 modern light cruisers and 14 destroyers of the 1908–9 programme, and 8 torpedo boats, the ships on the list (including 21 pre-dreadnoughts, 15 light cruisers, 3 cruisers, 59 destroyers, 64 torpedo boats, and 8 coast defence ships) were of small or no military value and suitable only for breaking-up purposes. The Admirals recommended that 'if a measure of punishment is required,' all the ships on the list be surrendered. Even they 'would be totally inadequate as compensation for the ships which have been sunk.'[20] On 25 June, in a

[19] Long to Lloyd George, 1 July 1919; Lloyd George MSS.
[20] 'Scuttling of German Warships at Scapa Flow,' a report of the meeting; *Foreign Relations of the United States. Paris Peace Conference, 1919*, vi. 664–5.

letter to the German peace delegation, the Allies cited Articles XXIII and XXXI of the Armistice, severely condemned the violation, and warned the Germans that 'when the investigations have been completed into all the circumstances, they will exact the necessary reparation.'[21] The German Government stated on the 27th they had not ordered the sinking and had had no advance knowledge of it.

The United States' reaction to the scuttling was generally one of 'a good riddance.' In Britain the Conservative press was wrathful. The scuttling was a 'vile,' 'despicable,' and 'dishonourable' act, but one in character—a proof of the low and treacherous character of the Germans. 'There is only seen in this deliberate contempt for a solemn bond of honour that unchangeable spirit of the "scrap of paper" which for ever stamps the Hun' (*Daily Express*, 23 June). 'The Germans have a genius for reminding us at opportune moments of the ineradicable treachery of their character' (*Pall Mall Gazette*, 23 June). The same newspaper shrilly called for a penalty, an indemnity equivalent to the value of the ships, that would 'leave no German in doubt whether treachery pays.' The *Daily Mail* (23 June) was of the same opinion. *Punch* (2 July), in a cartoon titled 'The End of a Perfect "Tag," ' depicts the ships sinking, with the flagship flying this signal: 'Germany expects that every man this day will do the dirty.' *The Morning Post* (24 June) and *Saturday Review* (28 June) struck different notes. The former took those responsible for the naval terms of the Armistice to task for having failed in 'the elementary quality of commonsense. Anyone not a fool would have seen the danger of leaving these German ships in German hands.' The *Saturday Review* agreed, but went a step further: 'The scuttling . . . so indignantly denounced, strikes us as the only plucky and justifiable thing the Germans have done in the war. It is exactly what British sailors would have done had their ships been interned in German ports.' Anyhow, little had been lost: 'The ships were of no use to us; and the authorities were at their wits' end to know what to do with them.' This is a fair reflection of British naval opinion, too, though there were those officers who, like Richmond, turned their anger against the Navy itself. 'The wheel has come full circle; the Navy has ended as it began with unpreparedness. Under our noses the

21 *Ibid.*, vi. 695–6.

Germans were able to sink their ships simply because of a total lack of imagination and of any precautions to prevent them from doing so.'[22]

On the Liberal side, the *Daily Chronicle* (23 June) spoke of a 'gross outrage' and declared they would be well within their rights to hold the scuttlers to long-term penal servitude. For the *New Statesman* (28 June) the sinking was a 'palpable breach of faith.' Other Liberal journals, however, regarded the suicide of the German Fleet as a good thing: the idea had always been to sink these ships, and a major bone of contention had been removed.

On 24 June, in reply to questions in the House of Commons, Long differentiated clearly between internment and surrender. The decision of the Allied Governments in favour of internment had rendered the prevention of scuttling impossible. 'Had they been surrendered they would have passed into the control of the country in whose port they were interned, and that country would have been responsible, through its officers, for their safety, but, being only interned, it was the right of the Germans to have their own guards. . . . His Majesty's Admiralty had no right whatever, even of access to the ships, except in a formal way, and no right to place guards upon them. The act of sinking is a very simple one in itself, involving only the opening of the sea cocks, and it could have been performed at any time.' Long refused to be drawn on whether the Government had pleaded for the surrender of the ships and had been overruled by Wilson. The First Lord's emphatic statement vindicated the Admiralty and calmed tempers. The attacks in the press and Parliament now came to an end.

Excitement was initially as great on the other side of the Channel—for a different reason. The French, led by Clemenceau, were angered by the alleged laxity of the British security arrangements. There were unpleasant suggestions in the French and Italian press that the British Government might have been privy to the sinking as a subtle policy to obviate a distribution that would have reduced British naval supremacy somewhat. Is there any substance in the hints—or charge? Lieutenant-Commander Kenworthy (an untrustworthy source at best) thought so. He later wrote:

[22] Richmond to Commander Carlyon Bellairs, 23 June 1919; *Portrait of an Admiral,* p. 349.

When it was known that the French and Italians would insist on a present of German warships . . . and that the Americans would support this demand in order to lessen British preponderance at sea, and thus weaken us diplomatically, it is common knowledge that the Admiralty let the state of affairs be known to the German Navy Office in Berlin and to the German Admiral nominally in command of the High Sea Fleet at Scapa. And hints were dropped to the effect that we would sympathize with a gallant enemy who preferred naval *hara-kiri* to the humiliation of being surrendered as prize to the two Latin Navies whom they had never met in battle. Still worse, that the formerly landlocked Poles and Serbs should get some of these proud battle-scarred vessels of war.[23]

He cites no evidence for this blatant assertion, and indeed there is none. Geoffrey Cousins lists these

pertinent questions which have never been satisfactorily answered:

[1] Why did all the available warships put to sea, leaving the Flow without 'caretakers'?

[2] Why did Fremantle go out of the Flow for torpedo exercises instead of conducting them in the anchorage, where recovery of these valuable missiles was much easier?

[3] Why did his ships steam so far into the North Sea before starting the practice?

[4] Why was there no *official* intimation to von Reuter that the Armistice had been extended?

[5] Why, if Fremantle suspected an attempt at scuttling, was there no provision for a closer watch on the German ships and plans for a quick recall in the event of trouble?[24]

The answers to these queries are as follows:

1. This is the principal proof adduced then and since of British 'perfidy.' It did 'look like a case of a sentry deserting his post,' Madden confessed. But Cousins's statement is not strictly factual. One destroyer was left behind, and she was supported by a number of trawlers and drifters.

2. Granted that Scapa Flow afforded an extensive expanse of

<hr>

23 J. M. Kenworthy (Lord Strabolgi), *Sailors, Statesmen—and Others: an Autobiography* (London, 1933), pp. 146–7.

24 Cousins, *The Story of Scapa Flow* (London, 1965), pp. 26–7. For the rebuttal that follows I owe much to Commander W. M. Phipps Hornby (letter of 24 October 1966), who has studied the whole scuttling episode with care. He was himself, as noted, an officer in the *Ramillies*, 1st Battle Squadron.

water, the exercise was of a kind that required more sea room than the Flow could afford.

3. One can only guess at the answer. It may be related to No. 2 above: that is, that the Admiral wanted to ensure that there was adequate sea room for the exercise, so that nobody would be, even unconsciously, influenced in the handling of his formation by considerations of the need to keep adequately clear of the land.

4. This is a puzzler. It could be that the Admiralty relied on the German naval authorities to notify von Reuter through the 'proper Service channels.'

5. The last part of the question is answered under No. 1, above. There was a destroyer left on guard. Once the scuttling began, events happened with considerable rapidity. When the Captain of the guard destroyer 'tumbled to' what was afoot, he lost no time in getting through an appropriate signal to the Admiral at sea. It is pertinent to note that not very long before the 21st ships of the 1st Battle Squadron were instructed to detail boarding parties, to be ready to go away at short notice.

Cousins's queries will not sustain an indictment of Fremantle, Madden, or the Admiralty. Madden and Fremantle were genuinely furious over the 'outrage.' Wemyss, who would have been the key figure in any connivance with the Germans, was not the sort of person who would knowingly have lent himself to anything so shady and conniving as the scuttling of the German ships. Admittedly, he was delighted at the turn of events; but his letter to the Deputy First Sea Lord, then in Paris, has no intimation that the Admiralty had practised perfidy:

I look upon the sinking of the German Fleet as a real blessing. It disposes once for all of the thorny question of the distribution of these ships and eases us of an enormous amount of difficulties.

It appears that the German Admiral thought that the Armistice expired at noon on Saturday, and consequently believed he was not breaking the terms of Armistice. There was not a moment during which they could not have done this, though I must confess that I was beginning to think that they never would do it. We were all prepared to seize the ships as arranged, but they forestalled us by forty-eight hours.

I do not know what the opinion in Paris will be; probably they will be rather sick; but as I said before, it is a happy conclusion. . . . I suppose there will be an outcry at the beginning, but when the facts of the case become known, I think that everybody will probably think like me, 'Thank the Lord'.[25]

It was the very fact that the scuttling solved a grave rift among the Allies—the disposition of the spoils was causing a great deal of friction and bitter argument—that put it into some people's minds that the deed had been connived at. My own feeling is that, while undoubtedly the sinking got the British into bad odour with many (the Latins especially), by solving a dangerous and knotty problem it probably averted still greater and more lasting unpleasantness. And as a secondary benefit, it prevented what could easily have boiled up into a schism in the Royal Navy itself.

There can be no question where the ultimate responsibility for 21 June lay. As Lloyd George told a Council of Four meeting on 24 June:

The case for the British Admiralty was that, at the time of the Armistice, the French and British naval representatives had pressed for the surrender of the German Fleet. Admiral Benson, however, had urged very strongly that surrender should not be demanded and that the Armistice should not be risked for this purpose. Marshal Foch had supported Admiral Benson very strongly. He had said that he did not wish to risk the lives of good soldiers for bad ships which had never fought a decisive battle. The Supreme War Council, consisting of the Prime Ministers and of Colonel House, had over-ruled the French and British Admiralties and unanimously agreed to ask only for the internment of the German [surface] ships . . . The British Admiralty had come to the conclusion that none but German crews could be put on board, as the removal of the German personnel would have been a breach of the Armistice. All that could be done was to exercise general surveillance over the fleet.

The French and American Admirals could see no reason for there not having been an armed British guard on board every one of the interned ships.[26]

<hr>

[25] Wemyss to Hope, 22 June 1919; *Wester Wemyss*, p. 432. Or, as Fremantle put it years later: 'Their sinking relieved the tired negotiators of Armistice and Peace terms from many international discussions which might have proved acrimonious, and there can be little doubt that the cause of International Peace and goodwill was best served by the ships being at the bottom of the sea, or their relegation to the shipbreakers' yard.'

[26] *Foreign Relations of the United States. Paris Peace Conference, 1919*, vi. 649–50, 653–4.

The Admiralty were furious.[27] 'When we remember,' Long protested to Lloyd George, 'that it was mainly due to Admiral Benson that our advice was not taken it seems rather an outrage that his successor should now seek to blame us.' Attached was a Wemyss memorandum which spelled out the essentials for the Prime Minister's benefit:

A study of the reports of the proceedings of the Allied Naval Council will show that Admiral Benson's whole desire was internment in neutral ports, which precluded the presence of armed guards.

A mixture of Allies and Germans locked up together would have been an impossible situation, and the only way to have ensured against sabotage would have been the entire removal of the Germans, which would have been surrender, and would have been contrary to the terms of Armistice. . . .

It is worth while to again point out the following facts:—

(a) That the original intention was that these ships should be interned in a neutral port, under which circumstances it would have been out of the question for British guards to have been on board. The fact that Scapa Flow was only accepted as a place of internment because it was found impracticable to find a neutral port in which to intern these ships is no reason why their status as German property should have been altered.

(b) To have placed a British guard on board these ships whilst the German crew remained would have created an obviously impossible situation. Their presence would have 'ipso facto' taken the command out of German hands and placed it in that of the British. Considering that these ships were interned, and were, therefore, still of German nationality, this would have been obviously wrong, and a breach of Armistice.

(c) The presence of such a guard would not have rendered impossible the sinking of the ships, unless, indeed, there had been a sentry permanently over each valve: an impossible state of affairs, surrounded as they would have been by enemy personnel.

From what we know it is a legitimate deduction that any attempt to place an armed guard on board any of these ships at any time would have immediately produced the very result that it was intended to prevent, and had Admiral von Reuter thought that such would occur

---

27 Beatty was included in their explosive wrath, since he had expressed the view that they ought to have put guards on board the ships. 'It does not seem quite fair to his late colleagues, either ashore or afloat, inasmuch as he has never hinted at the subject on any of the occasions when he has been talking matters over with us.' Long to Lloyd George, 1 July 1919; Lloyd George MSS.

on arrival in British ports, he would probably have sunk his ships on the way over here.[28]

Wemyss's otherwise faultless statement puts too much of the blame on Benson and overlooks the fact that Lloyd George, albeit reluctantly and under pressure from Foch and Benson, had joined House, Clemenceau, and Orlando (the Italian Prime Minister) in holding out against the surrender of the German ships and insisting on the wisdom of internment.

I fear that the British Government and the Admiralty, for all that they were in a most difficult position, will never be wholly clear of the charge of connivance, however unjustly imputed. It is a good illustration of the old adage about the near impossibility of catching up with a lie.

3. EPILOGUE

Four major units were salvaged from the scuttled tonnage at Scapa: the *Baden*, which was handed over to Great Britain and was sunk in 1921 after being utilised for various trials; the light cruiser *Emden*, which was given to France and was used as a target ship before being sunk in 1921; the light cruiser *Nürnberg*, which was allotted to Britain and was eventually broken up; and the light cruiser *Frankfurt*, which went to the United States and was sunk by a bomb in deep water. The other ships sunk were subsequently salvaged and broken up—that is, all but the seven ships still in Scapa Flow, lying in too deep water: 3 dreadnoughts and 4 light cruisers (*König, Markgraf, Kronprinz Wilhelm; Köln, Brummer, Dresden, Karlsruhe*). The bells of the *Friedrich der Grosse* and *Derfflinger*, which had lain in a Clydeside shipbreaker's yard, were ceremoniously returned to the German Navy at a Clydeside ceremony on 30 August 1965. A cable from German Naval Headquarters in Bonn was read at the ceremony: 'We consider it a happy development that the bitter past has been overcome and the German Navy, together with the Royal Navy, are united in NATO to protect peace.' The bells are kept in places of honour in Germany: one at the Headquarters of the Navy, the other in the Naval Academy at Flensburg.

The Peace Treaty with Germany, whose terms had been accepted

28 Long to Lloyd George, 30 June, and Wemyss's memorandum of 30 June 1919; Lloyd George MSS.

by the Germans on 23 June, was signed on 28 June. Article 184 declared that the interned ships should now be considered as finally surrendered; the scuttling had obviously complicated the execution of this provision. Article 185 stipulated that Germany was to surrender to the Allies her remaining 8 dreadnoughts and 8 light cruisers which had not been part of the interned fleet, with the addition of 42 more destroyers and 50 torpedo boats. All these ships became the property of the Allies, who were to decide on the disposition. The future German Navy was limited to a maximum of 6 pre-dreadnoughts, 6 light cruisers, 12 destroyers, 12 torpedo boats, and no submarines (Article 181). All ships building were to be broken up (Article 186). The naval terms of the peace treaty with Austria (St. Germain, 10 September 1919) followed similar lines.

The difficult problem remained of the disposition of the surrendered German ships, including those that had not sunk on 21 June. The French were still determined to get some of the German ships—specifically, 5 capital ships, 6 light cruisers, and 32 destroyers. If the French were allotted any ships, the Italians demanded equal treatment, and the Japanese were interested in a share if there was to be a division. To pacify the French and Italians, and perhaps to make amends for British responsibility, nominal, anyway, for the scuttling, Lloyd George was ready to meet them part of the way. He proposed (14 November) that all the German ships which were to be surrendered, including those at the bottom of Scapa Flow, be divided on the basis of war losses, with the tonnage lost at Scapa to be deducted from the British share. The Americans, their position unchanged, resisted. They would still have all the ships destroyed, whether through sinking or breaking up. Following extended and laborious discussions, the Heads of Delegations of the five Great Powers reached agreement on 9 December 1919.

The final settlement called for a distribution of the German surface warships in accordance with war losses: Great Britain, 70 per cent (less the scuttled tonnage); France and Italy, each 10 per cent; Japan, 8 per cent; United States, 2 per cent, to which she later waived claim because the proportion was insufficient. The allocated tonnage was to be sunk or rendered incapable of service as war vessels under the supervision of the Inter-Allied Naval Commission within an 18-month time limit, and to be completely broken up within five years.[29] Exceptions were the 5 light cruisers and 10 destroyers each that France and Italy were to receive for incorporation in their Fleets, or for any other use. In addition, each of the five principal Allies was to receive on loan one capital ship, one light cruiser, and, in the case of Britain, the United States, and Japan, three destroyers as well for experimental or propaganda purposes. (Britain received the *Baden* under this provision.) Finally, as a penalty for the serious violations of the Armistice—the scuttling at Scapa Flow, the destruction of *UC-48* off Ferrol, and of certain submarines en route to England for surrender—Germany undertook, under a protocol signed at Paris on 10 January 1920, to hand over as reparation five light cruisers and 400,000 tons of floating docks, floating cranes, tugs, and dredgers.

The 1920–21 *Brassey's Naval and Shipping Annual* contains a useful résumé of the ultimate disposition of the German surface fleet:

	Sunk at Scapa Flow*	Great Britain	France	Italy	Japan	U.S.	Other	Total
Battleships	10	5	1	—	2	1	—	19
Battle cruisers	5	—	—	—	—	—	—	5
Light cruisers	5	6	5	3	1	1	—	21
Leaders and destroyers	—	39	12	3	4	3	—	61
Torpedo boats	—	38	—	—	—	—	12	50

* Salvaged ships are included in the other columns.

* * *

The Admiralty and the Navy had every right to be pleased with the Treaty of Versailles. Britain's larger naval interests had been well secured. There was no mention of the Freedom of the Seas or of an international naval force under the League, and only a couple of innocuous references to naval disarmament. Germany lost her colonies and the possibility of using Heligoland and the

---

[29] Under this provision the eight remaining dreadnoughts, among other vessels, were handed over in 1920 and disposed of as follows: Britain—*Westfalen, Posen, Rheinland, Helgoland*, all scrapped in 1921–4; United States—*Ostfriesland*, sunk in bombing tests, 1921; France—*Thüringen*, scrapped in 1923; Japan—*Nassau* and *Oldenburg*, sold to a British firm and scrapped in 1921.

Kiel Canal for aggressive purposes. She had been deprived of her submarines and of all but a few of her major surface craft, so reducing her to third-rank naval status for the indefinite future. The tricky problem of distribution was handled so skilfully that it was obvious in June 1919 that, whatever the final solution, it would not impair British naval supremacy. The scuttling was, so to speak, the icing on the cake. Well might the First Lord tell the King that the peace terms were 'absolutely satisfactory.' Fresh naval rivalries were brewing, with the United States and Japan. But they were not immediate and pressing threats to British maritime supremacy. The former was in a quiescent stage at the moment and, in any case, American naval expansion was not ever likely to threaten British security in the way German naval ambitions had. The Japanese cloud was, in 1919, no more than that. The all-important fact for the moment was that the scuttling and the peace terms had ended the existence of the greatest fleet that Germany had ever possessed, the embodiment of her will, or so it had always appeared in British eyes, to achieve world domination. And once again in their history the British could proudly declaim:

> The fleet of the foemen of England
> hath found not one but a thousand graves;
> And he that shall number and name them
> shall number by name and tale the waves.

XII

Reflections on an Era

Education ought to receive prodigious attention after the war, for our failures have been largely due directly to our lack of education. I don't think, however, this is yet realised.

RICHMOND in a paper of March 1917.

As regards the question of preparedness of the Fleet, it is undoubtedly the case that in many directions the actual experience of War very quickly modified pre-existing views as to essential requirements. This, however, was true not only of us but of our enemy also, and no good purpose is served by suggesting that he showed greater foresight than we, in cases where this cannot be substantiated.

WEMYSS in a memorandum of early 1919.

Yet, in spite of its mistakes, in gallantry and in fighting efficiency [the Fleet] was probably far ahead of its standard at any previous period of history, and, moreover, it most assuredly had achieved its purpose.

VICE-ADMIRAL C. V. USBORNE, *Blast and Counterblast.*

I. THE PERFORMANCE OF THE NAVY, 1914–18

NOBODY was ever able to convince Marshal Foch of how essential sea power was to the Allied cause in 1914–18. Lloyd George tried hard and often. 'He thought the allocation to the sea services of so many fit men who could have been sent to the Army was sheer waste, and the traditional obsession of a great sea power. He always asked: "What have the Navy done? Have they done any fighting?" Our own generals, too, in their various memoranda, almost completely ignored the call of the sea on our manhood. And yet they could have had no armies on any battlefield, had it not been for the complete command of the sea which our sailors and their auxiliary helpers on shore succeeded in maintaining, and the British people would have been driven to make peace in order to avert famine.'[1] Asquith, the former Liberal Prime Minister, erred in the opposite direction to the generals

---

[1] *War Memoirs of David Lloyd George* (London, 1933–6, 6 vols.), v. 2607–8.

when he declared in an election speech, 9 December 1918: 'With all deference to our soldiers this war had been won by sea power. It was by the constant, unrelaxing, ever tightening efforts of the Fleet, nobly and efficiently supported by the mercantile marine, that we had step by step drained away from the enemy forces their resources.' Beatty's encomium on British sea power (before the officers and men of the 1st Battle Cruiser Squadron in the *Lion*, 24 November 1918) gave the Army some credit. He claimed that 'the war . . . has been won by sea-power. . . . Military successes have been great. . . . But all that would have been of no value without the sea-power of England.' It seems to me that Richmond's assessment of the role of sea power comes nearest the truth:'. . . sea-power would have been impotent to defend the liberties of Europe unsustained by land-power. Nothing is clearer than the interdependence of the two, nothing more misleading or objectionable than the attribution of success to one or the other separately.'[2]

The 'ultimate objects' of British naval policy were set forth by the Admiralty as

firstly, to bring pressure to bear on the enemy people so as to compel their Government to come to terms, and secondly, to resist the pressure applied by them so that we may carry on the war undisturbed. In order to achieve these objects, British naval power must be directed into the following channels:—

    (A) The protection of the Sea Communications of the Allied armies, more particularly in France, where the main offensive lies.

    (B) Prevention of enemy trade as a means of handicapping his military operations and exerting pressure on the mass of his people.

    (C) Protection of British and Allied Trade, on which depends the supply of munitions and food to the Allied armies and people.

    (D) Resistance to Invasion and Raids.[3]

In short, it was the function of British sea power to ensure the use of the sea for Allied purposes and to deprive the enemy of its use. This sea power had four major components—the Fleet, bases, the merchant navy, and the shipbuilding industry. All played their

---

[2] Richmond, *National Policy and Strength and Other Essays* (London, 1928), p. 77.
[3] Operations Division, Naval Staff, 'Present Naval Policy,' 17 September 1917; Admiralty MSS.

part—to say nothing of the tremendous natural advantage of Britain lying like a breakwater across the exits from the North Sea—but it was above all the Grand Fleet, taking full advantage of this favourable geographical position and constantly holding the High Seas Fleet in check, that underpinned the entire Allied war effort.

The Navy had been completely successful in performing its four main tasks. Its basic strategy of a distant blockade—the close blockade of an enemy fleet, eighteenth-century style, was no longer possible in an age of torpedoes, mines, and long-range coastal artillery—had done its work. Whereas at no time in the war was there any widespread privation in Britain, though there were shortages and queues in 1917–18, it was quite different in Germany. There the growing demoralization of the home front in 1918 caused by the blockade, and which culminated in a revolutionary outbreak, had given the *coup de grâce* to the German military effort. The cumulative effects of food and clothing shortages (the former was the result mainly of the cutting off of imported fodder and fertilisers), and the absence of any hope of real improvement, had proved too much for the German people. We should add the run-down transport system and the closing of factories or the reduction in their working hours on account of the lack of raw materials or replacement machinery.

Judged by the ultimate and decisive results, the Royal Navy had performed its job superbly. There were, nevertheless, many critics, mostly in the Service—the 'Young Turks' (Richmond and his followers) in the lead—who during the war and for much of the interwar period wrote and spoke as if the conduct of the war at sea had, by and large, been a failure.[4] This disappointment, and

---

4 In quoting Richmond, Dewar & Co. as extensively as I do, I do not wish to credit these 'professional agitators' with an importance of which as a group they were quite devoid, both during the war and afterwards. Richmond and Dewar were their own worst enemies. They contrived to put people's backs up by their conviction of the absolute correctness of the positions they espoused (one officer who knew Richmond states that it was quite impossible to *discuss* anything with him: he merely wanted to lay down the law) and their ill-concealed contempt of their intellectual inferiors, especially those who did not share their enthusiasm for the study of, and practical benefits to be derived from, naval history. An excess of intellectual arrogance is no way to win friends and influence people. But it was these Young Turks who had the most to say about the failures and larger lessons of the war, during and for long after hostilities, and, allowing for an overstatement of their case and for hindsight, it still strikes me that many of the points they made have substance.

indeed anger and resentment, had three foci: the alleged (1) passive strategy of the Fleet and the resultant failure, Jutland apart, to meet the High Seas Fleet in a pitched battle; (2) unpreparedness for war; and (3) series of blunders.

The more aggressive spirits in the Navy regarded the cautious British strategy, with its dependence on a distant blockade to control Germany's sea communications, and the refusal to incur unacceptable risks, as a huge mistake. They maintained that the Admiralty and the Grand Fleet should not have been satisfied to contain the High Seas Fleet but should have been prepared to take risks to bring on a fleet action. The doctrine of 'passage and communication' was condemned by the many proponents of a 'decisive victory,' who never tired of charging that the Navy's leaders, with few exceptions, were negating the 'Nelson spirit' by their conservative strategy and tactics. There can be no question about the tremendous benefits that would have followed the destruction of the High Seas Fleet. This *might* have made possible the entry of the Navy into the Baltic in force and opened up the possibility of joint operations directed against the German coast. I stress *'might,'* since the U-boats and mines might have rendered such a strategy impracticable. Certainly a decisive victory over the German Fleet would have quickly brought the unrestricted submarine campaign under control, for it would have been followed by a reduction in the strength of the Grand Fleet and a concentration of naval resources on the A/S campaign. This would have released a large trained personnel for the A/S war and a large proportion of the *matériel* which was required for the upkeep of the Grand Fleet. Also, the Fleet would have been able to operate in the Heligoland Bight and put a stranglehold on the sailing and return of the U-boats. Finally, the defeat of the German Fleet could well have had such a crushing effect on German morale as to have got their leaders thinking about working for a negotiated peace. The argument, in brief, was that because a decisive victory over the High Seas Fleet would have shortened the war, greater risks should have been taken with the Grand Fleet.

Such a policy never commended itself either to the Admiralty or to the C.-in-C., Grand Fleet. The submarine and mine threats had a cramping influence on Grand Fleet strategy, the former by generally restricting the operations of the battle fleet to open waters in the northern half of the North Sea (particularly after the August

1916 sortie of the High Seas Fleet) and by forcing the capital ships and cruisers to proceed to sea screened by a host of destroyers. The latter was an obsession. Few subjects figure so prominently in the correspondence of the Cs.-in-C. with the Admiralty as the plea for more destroyers or that the destroyer complement not be reduced. If there was the standard screen—at least 40 for the battle fleet alone was Jellicoe's requirement—the ships were safe; otherwise, they were almost bound to be sunk. And this at a time when the destroyers had no detecting devices (or, in some cases, only ineffective hydrophones) and only depth charges for attacking submarines. There were times when some of the big ships were left behind rather than take the battle fleet to sea without full destroyer protection. The fuelling requirements of the destroyers—they could remain out for about three days—placed a definite limit on the length of time the battle fleet could remain at sea, unless, as happened in the early days, the heavy ships remained at sea without their screen. In heavy weather the battle fleet had the choice of remaining in harbour, since the destroyers could not keep up with the fleet, or proceeding at reduced speed with their destroyer screen. This is not to suggest that destroyers were not very useful vessels in screening the battle fleet against submarine attack.[5] Additionally, they were extremely important in an action, whether for attacking the enemy battle fleet with torpedoes or defending their own fleet from destroyer attacks with gunfire and torpedoes. But the thought does occur that the Grand Fleet could have managed very well with fewer

[5] I do not know on how many occasions during four years of war a U-boat was in a position to attack a capital ship and in how many such cases an attack was attempted and was frustrated by the action taken by one or more destroyers. I suspect it is impossible to arrive at precise answers; but it is my impression that there were few such occasions, other than for a while in 1916. Tactically, U-boats seemed deadly, but strategically they never got at the Grand Fleet successfully except for the light cruisers *Nottingham* and *Falmouth* in the High Seas Fleet sortie of August 1916. On the other hand, the old battleships *Triumph*, *Majestic* (at anchor, to be sure), *Cornwallis*, and *Britannia*, despite destroyer protection (1, 6, 1, and 2 destroyers, respectively), were torpedoed, the first two in May 1915 (Dardanelles), the third in January 1917, and the last-named two days before the Armistice. I can find no instance of a U-boat shying off because of the presence of destroyers. The U-boat commanders often tried to let the destroyer screen pass over the boat and attacked the formation (or convoy) from within. When submarine attacks on battleships under destroyer cover failed, this was generally reported as due to actions taken by destroyers (e.g. attack frustrated by a ramming destroyer—periscope broken—or attack frustrated by being forced to go deep by an approaching destroyer). Sometimes a submarine was forced by the mere presence of destroyers to fire her torpedoes at a great distance, which would enable the attacked vessel to take

destroyers and not have allowed its strategy to be so heavily conditioned by the destroyer factor. The war was nearly lost by assuming that because of Grand Fleet needs there could not possibly be enough destroyers to guard mercantile convoys.

In the case of German mines, in some ways their *psychological* effect far outstripped their danger to warships. The loss of the dreadnought *Audacious*, one of the newest dreadnoughts, on 27 October 1914 off the north of Ireland after striking only one mine of a line laid by a German auxiliary cruiser may have had a traumatic effect on the Navy, which thereafter was as mine-conscious as it was torpedo- and submarine-conscious. This is less understandable after the whole Fleet had been equipped with paravanes (used to cut channels through minefields at high speed) in 1917. It was, however, not until after their effectiveness was proved when the battle cruisers went through mines off the Firth of Forth early in 1918, cutting several with their paravanes, that the Grand Fleet had sufficient confidence to operate freely in waters where there were no *known* minefields. P.V.s would not, of course, have justified deliberately manœuvring in waters known to be mine-studded, particularly at high speed and under full helm, for under those conditions the P.V. on the outside of the turn came in much closer to the ship and the stern swept quite a broad path of water, half sideways, which suited a mine perfectly.

The conservatism in strategy was paralleled by a conservatism in tactics. Conspicuous was the high degree of centralization in command: the C.-in-C. manœuvred his big fleet in battle, allowing only a strictly limited scope to individual initiative. As a corollary, there was the tendency, at Jutland and in other actions, to do nothing without an order from the C.-in-C. The value of initiative in battle was a facet of tactics in which the German Navy excelled

---

avoiding measures. However, in the reports of most of the U-boat commanders as well as of the High Seas Fleet Command, failures in 1916 were more frequently attributed to insufficient speed of the submarine, too high speed of the enemy vessel, slowness of the U-boat in diving, and (High Seas Fleet) difficulties in transmitting W/T instructions or information to U-boats than to the presence of destroyers. See *Der Krieg in der Nordsee*, vi, Chapter 3, especially pp. 19–29, 60–7. I have singled out 1916 because for about five months (May–October) the High Seas Fleet boats were employed mainly against enemy naval forces in the North Sea. This was a period when, as a political gesture after the *Sussex* incident, the Germans conducted their U-boat war in strict accordance with Prize Law, so to all intents and purposes bringing to a standstill this war as hitherto conducted.

and whose value was belatedly, and then only partially, recognized in the Royal Navy. The rigid single-line-ahead formation of 1914–16 was modified in 1917–18 to permit divided tactics 'when the defeat of the enemy has been ensured.' Underlying both the centralization in command and the unwieldy long rigid line was the fear of losing cohesion and giving the enemy a chance to concentrate on a portion of the fleet. The dangers, in other words, bulked larger than the opportunities that more aggressive tactics might open up. This, at any rate, is how the critics of these tactics have viewed the matter. Although I find myself generally in sympathy with this position, it is not clear in examining the experience of Jutland where greater decentralization would have made much difference.[6]

A more rapid development of maritime air power in 1914–18, especially as regards aircraft carriers and torpedo-carrying planes, would have opened up interesting opportunities for a more offensive strategy and tactics. Was there a failure to develop naval aviation as speedily as possible? When the war came, the members of the Board of Admiralty were fully occupied with the Fleet and other ship matters, and it would have been unreasonable to expect them to learn in detail about aircraft—a very recent invention—and to study how they might be used. Certainly there was nothing to lead them to think that here was a means of influencing effectively the war at sea. The main reason was the limitations of the aircraft then available. It is true that aeroplanes were playing a useful part in the war in France, but the naval problem was different. Seaplanes had not only to fly long distances, but to carry the heavy weight of floats. This involved seriously taxing their under-powered and unreliable engines, and limiting bomb loads to a minimum. Also, rising and landing required a smooth sea.

It was clear by the end of the first year of the war that the future of naval aviation lay in the replacement of seaplanes by aeroplanes —this was generally accomplished in the Grand Fleet in 1917–18 —and the provision of efficient aircraft carriers, ships able to carry aircraft and to keep station with the Grand Fleet. A fine opportunity was missed in the summer of 1915. Flight-Commander H. A. Williamson gave the Admiralty the 'island-type' design for an aircraft carrier (the design to which all carriers were subse-

---

[6] See *From the Dreadnought to Scapa Flow*, iii. 183–4.

quently built). His idea was that they should take an ocean liner and convert her to his design as rapidly as possible. Had this been done, Group Captain Williamson believes, and the job handed over to a live wire of the type of Beaverbrook (Minister of Aircraft Production in World War II), the Royal Navy would have had an effective fleet aircraft carrier in time for Jutland. Instead, Williamson's design was turned down and not adopted until too late in the war (*Hermes*).[7] Similarly, there was no energetic development of torpedo-carrying aircraft while the war was on. The difficulties of weight-lifting in a seaplane applied still more when the weight of the torpedo—apart from its warhead, comparable to a bomb—had to be added. In theory numbers of efficient torpedo-carrying planes might have accomplished much in the last year of the war: they might have done valuable service in a fleet action or conceivably (as Beatty proposed) in attacks on enemy ships at anchor in their bases—if they were operated from suitable fleet carriers. But there was no genuine fleet action after Jutland; the essential carriers were not available; and there was no hope of having efficient torpedo planes during the war. To sum up, the status of naval aviation in 1914–18 was not such as to encourage a more aggressive fleet strategy or tactics with existing *matériel*.

Returning to our main theme, can we justify a bolder strategy and tactics in view of the submarine and mine dangers *as evaluated by the highest naval authorities*, and in view of these two overriding considerations: (1) the utterly disastrous effects that a serious weakening of the Grand Fleet would have had on the whole Allied position—it would have enabled the Germans to raise the so-called blockade of Germany, clear the oceans of Allied transports and supply ships, cut the communications of British armies overseas, and starve out Great Britain; (2) the fact that the blockade was achieving the same goal as a great naval victory, though much more slowly? The governing authorities of the Navy, including the successive Cs.-in-C., Grand Fleet, never felt that the game was worth the candle, a decision whose wisdom was not doubted by Scheer. 'In itself,' he remarked after the war, 'Admiral Jellicoe's slow blockade strategy was correct and accomplished its purpose. No fault can be found with it, provided his confining the

---

7 See *From the Dreadnought to Scapa Flow*, iv. 15 n.

Fleet to a blockade can be reconciled with the traditions of the British Navy.'[8] The proviso was founded on a misreading of the British tradition.

Considering how naval history had always been taught and written, it was natural that the public at large had expected a succession of pitched battles and smashing victories. In the Navy training and long tradition had focused naval thought too exclusively on the idea of battle and too little on the control of communications or the protection of merchant shipping. 'The tendency,' one Admiral has pointed out, 'was to view maritime war merely as a kind of gladiatorial contest between two opposing fleets without ultimate aim or purpose, whereas its real object—control of passage by sea—was ignored.' The Nelson Tradition, or what it was supposed to be, is an important facet of the 'tendency.'

The Navy was hypnotised by its past. In the pre-war years there was much talk about the 'Nelson Touch' and the 'Nelson Tradition.' The practical consequence was to think that the essence of naval war was the battle—that the Navy's principal *raison d'être* was to meet and annihilate the High Seas Fleet in a second Trafalgar. There was an impression that the officers commanding British squadrons in Nelson's day, and in the age of sail generally, brooked no denial by the enemy of their demand for action; if he would not come out to fight, then they went in and annihilated him. The simple fact is that the admirals of the past, including Nelson, did not act in the hot-headed and rash manner suggested, and did not achieve the results—'not victory, but annihilation,' in Nelson's words—which were attributed to them. The pioneer naval historian John Knox Laughton stated the case accurately: 'The more closely Nelson's actions and letters are studied, the more clearly will it be seen that the point on which his thoughts continually dwell was not the mere "going at 'em," but the most advantageous way to "go at 'em"; and that, in every instance, the dash and impetuosity which caught the popular fancy were guided by genius, and controlled by prudence and foresight.'[9]

---

8 Scheer's interview in the *New York World*, as reported in *The Times*, 1 July 1919. Tirpitz was writing at this time: 'At the beginning of the war the fact had not emerged so clearly as it did later that the British fleet fulfilled its *raison d'être* simply by lying quietly at Scapa Flow.' Grand-Admiral Alfred von Tirpitz, *My Memoirs* (London, 1919, 2 vols.), ii. 366.
9 Laughton, *Nelson* (London, 1895), pp. 123–4.

There were times—long periods—when Britain's fighting admirals were engaged in watching and waiting for the enemy's fleet to put to sea. Indeed, there has never been in the history of the Royal Navy a decisive battle at sea—a final action ending a war. A misreading of history was responsible for a misapprehension as to the way in which sea power influenced the result even before the advent of the mine and the submarine, which revolutionized naval warfare.

The primacy-of-battle fetish in the Navy had other sources. It was partly a reflection of the uncertainties of naval warfare in the twentieth century. In these circumstances many officers believed it was 'better to get it over with.' Then, too, the boredom in the Grand Fleet naturally generated a desire for battle at any cost. There was also the feeling that, compared with the activity and sacrifices on the Western Front, the Fleet was not doing enough. There were many instances of naval officers resigning their commissions and joining the Army! Then there was Mahan's teaching (stressed in his *Naval Strategy* and implied in his other writings) that a navy's principal function was battle. The contrary teaching in Corbett's *England in the Seven Years' War* and *Some Principles of Maritime Strategy* had little influence; indeed, he was heavily attacked for it by the 'battleship Admirals'. Corbett had written in the former: '. . . it must not be forgotten that convenient opportunities of winning a battle do not always occur when they are wanted. The dramatic moments of naval strategy have to be worked for, and the first preoccupation of the fleet will almost always be to bring them about by interference with the enemy's military and diplomatic arrangements.'[10]

It must also be borne in mind that it takes two navies to make a fight. The High Seas Fleet adopted a defensive strategy from the start. This was natural and to be expected. As Admiral Duff remarked, 'It has always been a mystery to me how anyone in possession of the full situation could expect the High Sea Fleet to come out and fight. We piled up a Fleet against them that gave them no possible chance even under the command of a Nelson.'[11]

A greater number of British officers than those in the battle *à outrance* school, including these officers but also brainier officers of the Richmond–Dewar–Drax type, the Young Turks proper,

10 Julian S. Corbett, *England in the Seven Years' War* (London, 1907, 2 vols.), i. 3–4.
11 Duff to Admiral the Hon. Sir Alexander Bethell, 21 December 1918; Duff MSS.

were critical of the 'passive strategy'. It is difficult to see where the Fleet could have done more, *within the confines of the accepted strategy*, except perhaps, as the Young Turks had continually urged, in a more aggressive and imaginative use of aircraft and in amphibious operations in the Mediterranean theatre. The perspective of time profoundly modified the views of at least one of their number, Drax, a Richmond disciple. Contrast his wartime castigation of 'the criminal folly of passive defence' with the following re-evaluation a generation later:

> I think it entirely incorrect to suggest that our Naval strategy from 1914 to 1918 lacked initiative or aggressiveness. The Grand Fleet was the main cover for all our operations in the outer seas against submarines, raiders, enemy cruisers, etc. These operations were always conducted with great aggressiveness and much initiative. . . .
>
> The Grand Fleet contained a large number of Flag and other Officers who were conspicuous for their offensive spirit: for example, Beatty, Tyrwhitt, Sturdee, Brock, Pakenham, Alexander Sinclair, Cowan, Browning, and a number of others. . . .
>
> On one occasion Jellicoe took the Grand Fleet out of the North Sea and moved it to the West Coast of Scotland, due to the increasing submarine risk. Several Grand Fleet officers thought that this was unduly cautious and Jellicoe was persuaded to bring the Fleet back a few days later. Thereafter, it continually cruised in the North Sea in all weathers and under all conditions, ready to engage any enemy that could be found there.
>
> Nothing could have been more aggressive than Beatty's actions at Heligoland and the Dogger Bank, or his dashing pursuit of enemy forces, sometimes superior in strength, on other occasions.
>
> Nothing could have been more aggressive than Tyrwhitt's splendid handling of the Harwich Force, which was frequently in action at a short distance from the enemy's main base. One of his rules for his Captains was 'Remember that having been launched to an attack, you can attack as you please, but you never turn back.'[12]

The publication of Jellicoe's *The Grand Fleet* early in 1919 gave the nation a shock with its disclosure that the Navy, Nelson's heirs, had been woefully unprepared for war in 1914. The nation learned for the first time, *inter alia*, of the inferior projectiles,

---

[12] Admiral Sir Reginald Drax's letter to the author, 27 March 1946. 'Ginger' Boyle (Lord Cork and Orrery) and Keyes certainly must be included in Drax's 'and a number of others.'

searchlights, mines, and torpedoes, and the lack of submarine defences at the northern bases and of docks suitable for large ships on the East Coast. These serious disclosures by the former C.-in-C. constituted a terrible indictment of the Admiralty and of a Service which was generally regarded as *sans peur et sans reproche*. The question of the hour was: Why were not the war-revealed deficiencies foreseen? There were many calls in Parliament and the press for an inquiry, which was not granted, and a thankfulness that the Germans had not fought a general action in the early stages of the war.

There are many reasons for the unsatisfactory *matériel* position. One must begin with the pre-war Cabinets, enemies of 'bloated' naval armaments and devoted to the principle of social reform before guns. Thus, because money was lacking to provide big docks, British naval constructors had to design capital ships which would go into smaller docks. Larger docks would, as with the German Navy, have made possible broader-beamed capital ships and consequently ships less liable to destruction by mine or torpedo. But docks made no appeal to the imagination of the country, as did dreadnoughts, say, and cost a great deal of money. The want of financial provision does not explain all the forms of unpreparedness. The Royal Navy had behind it centuries of honoured traditions, and such traditions tended to conservatism and a suspicion of basic change. The slow pre-war development of mines can be put under this head. British naval officers did not hold mines in high regard: they were the weapons of a weak Power on the defensive. There was provision for sweeping up enemy mines, but little interest in providing the Navy with effective mines for its own use. There was less excuse for the ineffective mines of 1914–16, after war experience had quickly proven the value of underwater weapons.

Much of the unpreparedness can be accounted for by the needs of the Navy in the changed conditions of modern sea warfare being largely an unknown factor and the people in responsible positions only human. The Second Sea Lord, Sir Frederick Hamilton, wrote, 'Simply because officials are not omniscient, and prophecy is a difficult art, even for men of Ld Fisher's capacity and experience.'[13] As an illustration, the British Fleet was without doubt short

13 Diary, 21 April 1916; Hamilton MSS.

of destroyers. Admiral Bacon offers a rational explanation. 'What led to this shortage was the impossibility of forecasting the trend that the war would take, unless human beings had been endowed with the spirit of inspired prophecy. It was thoroughly appreciated that the Grand Fleet would require destroyers; but the occupation of the Belgian coast, and the consequences which followed from that occupation, were never anticipated.'[14] One should also recall that unrestricted submarine warfare made further and unexpected demands on Britain's shipbuilding resources.

Take the undefended state of Scapa Flow at the outbreak of the war, which could so easily have led to irretrievable disaster. In 1914 the majority of senior officers still looked upon the submarine as too slow, unreliable, and vulnerable to be regarded as a threat to the Fleet. The Germans themselves had no idea that these craft, which were then usually accompanied by 'mother ships,' could proceed on long cruises unattended. The possibility, therefore, of submarines operating in the way they actually did during the war, and the consequent need for anti-submarine defences of the kind established at Scapa Flow from the autumn of 1914, had not been foreseen by naval authorities before the war. Only the question of land defences to repel a raid by surface craft in the absence of the Grand Fleet had been raised and was outstanding when the war began.

It may help to place things in proper perspective if I cite from a scholarly study of the American naval administration in the Second World War. When the United States found itself at war after Pearl Harbor, 'Deficiencies were marked in antisubmarine and antiaircraft defenses. Many of the larger ships lacked modern sound gear and had no real protection against submarines unless accompanied by destroyers. The Navy still had no program for small vessels for convoy duty. There were not nearly enough aircraft carriers or planes to protect the Fleet from air attack. Not only was antiaircraft ordnance lacking but the quantity needed had been gravely underestimated. Even when the American submarines got into action, many of their torpedoes were faulty.'[15] Where the Royal Navy in 1914–18 was grievously at fault was in taking an unconscionable time to remedy some of the more glaring

---

[14] Bacon, *The Dover Patrol, 1915–17* (London, 1919, 2 vols.), ii. 17.
[15] Robert G. Albion and Robert H. Connery, *Forrestal and the Navy* (New York, 1962), pp. 86–7.

weaknesses. It needed the jolt of Jutland to arouse the Fleet and the Admiralty to doing something about the shell, the searchlights, etc.

On another level there was the disposition, especially after the war, to make invidious and on the whole accurate comparisons between German and British *matériel*. The fact is that the highly developed German metallurgical, shipbuilding, engineering, and chemical industries were well ahead of the British for various reasons, among others the relative neglect of British science and of scientific training and technical education. Another explanation of the overall German superiority in *matériel* is their remarkable foresight and attention to detail. As an illustration, when the *Blücher* finally sank in the Dogger Bank action (24 January 1915) and 400 or 500 men were thrown into the water, every man was wearing an efficient lifebelt which kept him upright in the water. It was only some time after the *Blücher* sinking that the Admiralty provided lifebelts (cork) for the sailors, and then only for special duties such as buoy jumpers. Inflatable waistcoats made by Gieves were purchased by some officers; they were issued by the Admiralty only to Fleet Air Arm pilots. (These waistcoats had flasks for brandy which some servants were suspected of emptying!) The story goes that when trying out an inflatable rubber collar lifebelt devised by the Admiralty, a man jumped from the deck and broke his neck! To show what the British were up against, I will cite another example of the German mind compared with the British, quoting the recollections of a flag officer:

Some months before the War, the *Breslau* and my ship, a very old cruiser, were lying off Alexandretta and I became very friendly with their navigator, von Muntz, a very fine type of officer. One day we decided to go for a walk and climb the snow-capped mountains behind the town. I landed in ordinary clothes with a walking stick and a packet of sandwiches. Muntz arrived looking exactly like a Christmas tree with a large and heavy ruck sack packed with ample provisions, a waterproof, a woollen sweater, spare stockings, a box of chocolates, and a torch. He was also carrying a hunting knife and a small rifle in case we were attacked by the dangerous dogs in the villages. He explained to me that the woollen sweater was for use when we reached the snow line and that the chocolates and the torch were to be used to amuse the children!! Though we saw none, we saw some fierce dogs who rushed at us and I just stopped him in time from shooting, for, as in Greece, if you shoot a dog, his owner is entitled to shoot you.[16]

16 Vice-Admiral B. C. Watson's letter to the author, 2 March 1966.

The Germans were ahead of the British in shell, fuses, searchlights, mines, torpedoes, etc. The British failed to see clearly enough the effects of plunging fire and the futility of testing shell and armour plates with 'normal' impact. On the whole, German ships were better and more stoutly built than the British, just as the French ships were better in the days of Nelson. The weaker protection of British capital ships was a calculated risk to ensure greater striking power. Moreover, whereas the British ships were designed for worldwide operations, and also as a home for sailors, the German ships were designed for short-range operations, and the comfort of the sailors was a factor of no importance.[17] This saved the German constructors many tons to put into armour and made possible the subdivision of the ship into many small watertight compartments. The Germans produced as nearly as possible an unsinkable ship. It strikes me, however, that British self-depreciation went too far. Their battleships gave an excellent account of themselves at Jutland, even if nobody knows how well they would have stood up to prolonged punishment in close action.[18] But the denigration of British capital-ship designs long ago assumed the status of an article of faith.

If the Service had a pet target, it was the battle cruisers. A host

[17] One hoary legend needs to be killed off—that, in contrast to the British officers and men, who were getting the opportunity to learn to be seamen *at sea*, the Germans courted a deterioration by having their ships' companies live ashore in barracks when the ships were in port. The fact is that barracks were never officially provided for the crews, though during the war in some bases outside Germany land billets were requisitioned and furnished for better relief of the crews of destroyers and submarines on the initiative of the flotilla captains. This was the case in Flanders, to mention one well-known example. Kapitän zur See Gerhard Bidlingmaier's carefully researched letters to the author, 19, 29 January 1969. The wartime diary of seaman Stumpf, of the dreadnought *Helgoland* (Daniel Horn (ed.), *War, Mutiny and Revolution in the German Navy: the World War I Diary of Seaman Richard Stumpf* (Brunswick, New Jersey, 1967)), confirms Bidlingmaier's finding that the crews of the High Seas Fleet ships always lived on board.

[18] The D.N.C. and other Admiralty experts, having made a careful examination of the raised *Baden*, concluded (1921) that in the principal features of design they had little to learn from their late enemy. This was going a mite too far. Commander W. M. Phipps Hornby, who lived on board the *Baden* for weeks, employed on salving her, got to know her internal arrangements as well as those of his own ship, the *Ramillies*. It is his 'considered opinion—which I know coincided with that of others engaged on the same job—that, *considered as a fighting machine*, anyhow on balance the *Baden* was markedly in advance of any comparable ship of the Royal Navy.' Perhaps, as he suggests, the D.N.C. and others unconsciously were loath to concede that the young German Navy had much to teach them. Commander Phipps Hornby's memorandum for the author, June 1969.

of critics maligned Fisher for having introduced the type, pointing to their vulnerability at Jutland. The loss of these battle cruisers was due to the fact that they were engaged with capital ships, which they were *never* intended for. Originally called 'armoured cruisers,' *not* 'battle cruisers,' their primary duty was to act as super scouting cruisers, ships fast and powerful enough to push home a reconnaissance in the face of an enemy's big armoured cruisers. It does not seem to have occurred to Fisher that Britain's potential enemies might evolve ships of comparable type, in which case the British battle cruisers might find themselves engaged, not with vessels of inferior force, but with their like. His failure to foresee that conditions could arise when his battle cruisers would be called upon to withstand heavy punishment is a mark against him. The 'Invincible' and succeeding classes were very vulnerable and quite unequal to receiving heavy-shell projectiles. Even so, the losses on 31 May 1916 were in all probability due to the magazines not being flash-tight rather than to weakness in armour protection.[19]

It was not only a case of the unpreparedness of the Fleet in numerous *matériel* respects. There were many naval mistakes, the details of which became generally known only after the war. Of course, the Navy had been aware of them all along: they constituted a main reason for the threnody of criticism during the hostilities. The more notorious of the distressing errors of commission included the circumstances in which the battle cruiser *Goeben* was suffered to pass from Messina to the Dardanelles without being engaged, the loss of the old cruisers *Cressy*, *Hogue*, and *Aboukir*, the episode of Cradock's tragic end at Coronel, the bungle made of the Scarborough Raid operation, the haste with which the Admiralty plunged into the Dardanelles adventure, the unexplained desistance from the pursuit of Hipper in the Dogger Bank action, the limitations of British gunnery (and, many added, the tactics) at Jutland, the shortcomings of the campaign in the Narrow Seas, which included the bold enemy destroyer raids into the Channel, the policy of 'hunting' all over the ocean for U-boats and surface raiders, instead of relying on the convoy system, and the failure to destroy the *Goeben* during her sortie in January 1918.

I hold it to be an axiom that the normal foulups of any war are regularly interpreted as military blunders. A number of them, to

19 See *From the Dreadnought to Scapa Flow*, iii. 174–5.

be sure, are. But as Clausewitz said, 'Everything is very simple in War, but the simplest thing is difficult.' The critics rarely made allowance for 'the play of the contingent and the unforeseen' (H. A. L. Fisher's phrase), which is rarely absent from a sea action. And how could anyone expect perfection in the amazingly difficult business of war after a century of peace? Many of the difficulties, uncertainties, and mistakes were unavoidable through the lack of modern experience. The gruelling test of battle naturally had brought to the fore a host of defects—in the *matériel*, in tactical doctrine, and in the system of command. One of the sharpest critics of the naval side of the war wrote, when the war could be examined dispassionately, 'Apart from the shock and disappointment of Jutland, I think the Navy felt [after the war] that we had much to be proud of. I defy anyone to prove that any other Navy, after 100 years of peace at sea, would have done better in the same circumstances.'[20] Nonetheless, when every allowance has been made, there were underlying weaknesses in the administration and outlook of the Navy which seriously hampered the efficient prosecution of the war and maximized the blundering.

2. FUNDAMENTAL WEAKNESSES

The Royal Navy possessed a qualitative superiority in personnel (see below) and a quantitative superiority in *matériel*—ships, anyway. Lacking were two vital elements, a well-organized and competent Naval Staff at the Admiralty and an officer corps thoroughly trained in the more sublime aspects of their profession, namely, strategy and tactics. I shall examine these deficiencies in turn.

Until 1912 N.I.D. was, practically speaking, the Naval Staff, but it had no representation on the Board and lacked trained officers. The few officers who urged the necessity for special staff training and the formation of a true Staff were strongly opposed on the grounds that the conduct of and preparation for war was the special preserve of senior officers and that officers below flag

[20] Admiral Drax's letter to the author, 15 July 1964. 'Mistakes were of course made,' writes Admiral James, 'and an "authority" whose name I cannot give once said, "He who makes the fewest mistakes emerges victorious." We embarked on a full dress war after 100 years of peace and after a dynamic revolution in weapons. Only a superman could have handled these weapons without making any mistakes.' James to Chatfield, 17 January 1938; Chatfield MSS.

rank should confine themselves to technical and routine duties. After the Agadir Crisis of 1911 had revealed the bankruptcy of the no-staff system, the Government decided to establish a War Staff and begin training staff officers. However, the new Staff, inaugurated by Churchill in 1912 in the teeth of considerable resistance in the Service, was for years of little value. The Chief of the Admiralty War Staff had no executive power, the Operations Division had little or nothing to do with the conduct of operations and was confined to routine administrative work, and there was no Naval Staff College where officers could be trained in staff duties. 'The old dog had merely been provided with a War Staff collar,' one critic observed.

The lack of any organization for covering the transport of the Army to France (the passage was made in security only because no attempt was made by the Germans to attack), the mix-up at Heligoland Bight on 28 August 1914 (when 'the orders were drafted so badly that certain important latitudes and longitudes were put down wrong and a collision between our submarines and B.C.s was only avoided by a stroke of luck'[21]), the Coronel disaster, the Dardanelles muddle, the lack of any sound principles of trade defence until late in the war, the initial neglect of mining, wrong tactical ideas concerning destroyers—these are examples of dangers incurred through the lack of a properly constituted and efficient Staff. There was, in other words, nobody in Whitehall with sufficient authority and organization to survey and work out the naval problem as a whole and to secure the minute and all-round correlation of means to ends.

It was not until May 1917 that the Naval Staff began to be put on a proper footing. The First Sea Lord became Chief of the Naval Staff. Even then, and till the end of the war, despite further reforms like the formation in September 1917 of a Plans Division to deal with the consideration and preparation of strategic plans, there was no proper Naval Staff. Nor was there while the war lasted a supply of trained officers competent to perform Naval Staff duties, or, until after the war, an efficient system for training such officers. The Staff was, if we exclude a number of bright younger officers who joined the Staff in responsible positions towards war's end (Reginald Henderson, W. W. Fisher, Dreyer, James, and others whom Jellicoe brought in from the Grand Fleet

21 Diary, 11 July 1915; Dewar MSS.

when he went to the Admiralty, and Richmond and Fuller, who joined the Staff in 1918), merely a nondescript collection of officers. Many of them were retired officers who had been recalled in the war and who were as ignorant of the principles of staff work as they were of strategy and operations. In the words of a British naval officer (1951): '. . . officers who made any real study of war from the point of view of Staff work were regarded as cranks or lunatics, hunters of soft jobs; and the gin-and-bitters school were quite content to be left to the guidance of their splendid but not always highly trained instincts.'[22] For such reasons, apart from its newness, the Naval Staff had neither the prestige nor the influence commensurate with the importance of its functions.

Dewar had been on the Staff only a few weeks when he put his finger on a sore weakness in procedures. 'The more I see of the present organization the more certain I am that no good will ever come of it. Round and round go the dockets solemn slow stately and sure and meanwhile the ships are being sent rapidly to the bottom.'[23] Years afterwards he spelled out this shortcoming:

Prior to the first war, few naval officers realised the necessity for or objects of a Naval Staff and its administration was absorbed into the existing system of administration without opposition. The Secretary's department marked incoming papers and telegrams to every division or department which might be directly or indirectly concerned with their contents. A single docket might have as many as ten or so markings. The various authorities wrote their minutes independently of each other, without any preliminary discussion. It was nobody's business to co-ordinate these disconnected and frequently conflicting opinions or to clarify contradictory statements by discussion between the parties concerned. The docket eventually returned, perhaps after several months, to the permanent official who usually wrote the final minute which was supposed to convey the general sense of the other minutes and suggest a course of action on a subject of which he might know little or nothing. It was then referred to the V.C.N.S. [D.C.N.S.] or C.N.S. for decision.

The multiplicity of references to different authorities and failure to place the responsibility for advising the Board on a definite individual meant that months and even years were wasted on questions which could have been settled in a few days or weeks.[24]

The Naval Staff suffered from other handicaps, as witness these

22 Quoted in Godfrey, *Naval Memoirs*, i. 85.
23 Dewar to Richmond, 20 June 1917; Dewar MSS.
24 'The Problem of Naval Command' (1946?); Dewar MSS.

two situations, the first revealing the poor intra-Staff co-operation. The D.A.S.D. prepared a paper on A/S policy in March 1918 at about the same time as the Plans Division, but with absolutely no co-operation from, or any advice sought from, Plans. Beatty was 'simply astonished that such a procedure should be possible.'[25] The second instance pertains to the work of Plans in the last year of the war. This division of the Staff repeatedly submitted proposals in papers entitled 'The Anti-Submarine Campaign in 1918,' 'Deep Minefields in the Kattegat,' 'Raids in the Downs, Dover Straits, etc.', 'Holland and the War,' 'Scandinavian Convoys and Covering Force', and so on. Too often Authority reached no decisions on the points raised in them or arrived at decisions without reference to the recommendations made by Plans. The D.T.S.D., Richmond, examined 64 such papers and discovered that in 24 cases the schemes were approved or subsequently carried out, 8 schemes were disapproved of, in 28 cases no intimation was given to Plans whether the schemes were approved or not, and in 4 cases the papers were still in circulation. 'I have now finished examining the papers of Plans Division. They reveal a state of things almost incomprehensible. The attitude of Duff, Fremantle & Hope towards proposals made by Plans is invariably one of self-defence or of opposition to suggestions—a sort of resentment that anyone should suggest that there remained any way of improving upon the current measures. There is no attempt whatever to examine the proposals, to seek in every quarter for help which will further our ends in this war. The spirit is a petty, departmental, jealous one.'[26] Richmond's recommendation that Plans come directly under the First Sea Lord was not accepted.

Finally, there is what Dewar called 'pseudo-disciplinary inhibitions,' which blocked 'the advisory channels of communication between the First Sea Lord and members of the War Staff.' This opens up the larger question of an officer's education and general outlook in our period, together with certain related matters.

It was a tenaciously held theory of Richmond's that the many naval failures had a common cause, which was to be found in Whitehall's long neglect of naval education and of the training of officers for the higher duties of their profession. They had been brought to 'a state of intellectual bankruptcy' by the 'deplorable'

---

[25] Bellairs to Dewar, 2 April 1918; Dewar MSS.
[26] Diary, 3 July 1918; *Portrait of an Admiral*, p. 312.

methods of officer education. Captain Drax echoed that conviction in a private memorandum of 1917: 'The number of errors that badly trained people can make and do make in war is simply amazing.'

No basic changes were made while the war lasted, despite various committees that considered the problem. Richmond hoped to reform officers' training when he became D.T.S.D. early in 1918 with the duty of advising the First Sea Lord on the principles of education and training. He had thought about the subject for many years. Wanting to place education on firmer and wider foundations, he pushed for a widening of the system of special entry from public schools (1913–) at the expense of early entry, which had been of great service during the war. He also wanted to do away with the system which tried, after the midshipmen went to sea, to carry on general education simultaneously with the performance of duty as an officer—a system which had survived despite repeated condemnations by committees which sat on the subject. He would give the public-school entrants a nine-months' course in gunnery, engineering, and navigation. 'Then come to sea as *officers*, able to do their work in the ship, not under continual instruction but learning their duties by doing them.' He also advocated a definite scheme for the promotion of ratings to midshipmen, and he protested against the belief in examinations as the best test of an officer. As a member of the teaching profession, I find myself in complete sympathy with Richmond's view that examinations are not a reliable criterion of an officer's (or any student's) capacity: 'A meeting in 2 S.L.'s room to-day on the subject of the post-war training of the young Lieutenants. . . . [Heath asked] Wouldn't I give a 5 first [-class certificate] man an advantage over a 5 3rd-classes man? No, I said. One man is not necessarily a better officer. I have since looked up the records of Beatty, Keyes & Tyrwhitt, the 3 outstanding naval Commanders of the war. They muster *one* first class between them! The war might never have occurred for all that men like Heath have learned from it.'[27] Not only are examinations an unreliable

---

[27] Diary, 20 November 1918; *Portrait of an Admiral*, pp. 325–6. Five firsts (Seamanship, the preliminary theoretical course at Greenwich, Gunnery, Torpedo, and Navigation) was the top notch in pre-Selborne Scheme (1902) days. There were three classes in each subject and the certificates given to the Sub-Lieutenants affected their dates of promotion to Lieutenant. The Selborne Scheme (until 1913) did away with all the courses at the schools and the exams were done at sea.

indicator of future professional success; they lead to cramming, and knowledge acquired in this fashion will usually not endure long. More reprehensibly, cramming for regurgitation purposes does not teach anyone to *think*, to use his reasoning powers. I do not propose to suggest alternatives to examinations; they do exist, however.

Richmond was frustrated on all fronts, his ideas being too far ahead of his time. Thus, Board resistance effectively blocked any settled policy for promotion from the lower deck until 1929. A long post-war memorandum best sums up Richmond's views and pinpoints the failures of the system of naval education. Excerpts follow.

Enough attention is not paid to the need for general education, with the result that the naval officer is circumscribed in his views & unfitted, very often, to deal with problems involving abstract thought and reasoning. There is no attempt to develop the reasoning faculties.

Technical education is begun too young, and at the same time an attempt is made to teach too much. . . .

On coming to sea the boys' scholastic education is still incomplete and naval instructors have to be carried in all ships bearing midshipmen. . . . incompatibility of the position of an officer and a schoolboy. . . .

The training at sea is further vitiated by a rigorous examination system. The examinations are so extensive that instructing officers are obliged to devote their whole attention to training the boys to pass them, and small time, if any, is left to train the boys to become efficient officers, seamen, and fighting men. . . .

After passing these examinations, education (except in so far as experience is education) ceases. No further mental effort is called for unless the officers become specialists; & these form a proportion only [of] the whole, and their work is of a purely technical character. . . .

Thus, while in the early stages the instruction fails to establish a habit of thinking—substituting for it a process of memorising—in the later stages the reasoning powers are neither exercised nor developed.

Warlike matters remain untaught until an officer goes to a Staff College (soon to be established) or a War College. This teaching does not take place in most cases until an officer reaches Post Captain's, or even Admiral's, rank. The mind has then to grapple with a set of wholly new problems, of an order different from any it has hitherto dealt with. Many Captains & Admirals never go there at all—and considering their age it is not to be said that they miss very much. But it is a serious matter that the principles of strategy & tactics are not taught to younger officers at an age when their minds are flexible & inquisitive.

The result is the Doctrine of NO Doctrine; so many officers, so many ideas, is the present Service rule. Hence, lack of preparation for war, as no one had clear & agreed upon views as to how war would be conducted. This applied both to strategy & tactics; it was the direct outcome of the educational system. Although, for example, young officers would, in war, have the duties of boarding and examining ships imposed upon them, they [knew] nothing about merchant ships, their cargoes or their papers, nor how to examine them; and again, the tactical principles of the defence of a convoy should be known to the Commander of the escort force; this had not been indoctrinated; but it was learned by such expensive experiences as the losses of the *Mary Rose* and *Strongbow* [October 1917]. . . .

A lack of thoroughness pervades the whole system of training except in the specialist branches. Seamanship, the most practical of all arts, is largely taught out of books; and in spite of the attention paid to gunnery & torpedo, no complaint is more common than the ignorance of the younger officers concerning these matters. This is largely on account of the desultory nature of the instruction, the lack of good groundwork & general education, & the paralysing effects of an exaggerated examination system.

No encouragement has been given to officers to commit their thoughts to paper. On the contrary, every discouragement to the discussion of problems of the naval Service has been imposed, partly by Regulations, partly by consequences. This has had the direct effect of stifling thought & the power of discussion. Unaccustomed to reason or to write, uninstructed in the principles of naval war & policy, naval officers of high standing not infrequently find themselves in difficulty when they reach the responsible offices in administration in which they have to explain the reasons for the views they hold.[28]

Without disputing a single one of Richmond's statements, I would point out that, as in any system of education, however faulty, the exceptional person will rise above it and prosper. *Vide* Richmond himself, to take one example!

The sad part was that so many senior officers had good brains, which they never had been asked to use. And was it any wonder that not many officers took a serious interest in the higher side of their profession, for instance, by attending lectures or reading naval history and using it in an intelligent manner? Richmond put the average officer's knowledge of naval history at about 'the level of little Arthur's history of England. Worse than that. They

[28] Enclosure in Richmond to Lord Haldane, 15 February 1919; *ibid.*, pp. 333–7.

read without understanding, without analysing or trying to draw any lessons from the past. They do not know that the value of history lies in the study of cause and effect. So our "practical" friends will repeat like parrots that invasion is impossible: but not one will be able to say why he holds that view, or be prepared to support it in argument.'[29] It was not only that their naval education had never taught officers to value naval history for the lessons they could extract; the close study of naval history had no appeal for many of them because, to quote one senior officer (1951), 'they felt that steam and science had so revolutionized naval warfare that there was nothing to be learnt from a dead past.' The attitude of many senior officers towards the study of naval history did nothing to encourage an interest in it. Officers steeped in naval history, officers who studied war, were labelled as cranks. Dewar records these revealing episodes:

A Lieut. called Cooper won the history prize with a very good essay on the life of Samuel Hood. Corbett was most eulogistic about it. Jellicoe told R. [Richmond] with great glee that he had looked up his past records and found that he had been badly reported on by his Captain. The inference being that only Bl——y fools are good at history!! When Richmond wrote and asked [Commodore] S. Hall to join the N.S. [the Naval Society, which published the *Naval Review*] Hall replied that he would but hoped that R. was not taking up writing as it would do him no good. Also remember [Vice-Admiral] Gamble's remark after [W. W.] Fisher's lecture. 'V. G. lecture but I am sure he can be no use in a ship.'[30]

There is no doubt that officers gain wisdom from the study of naval history, even if Richmond and his disciples sometimes disregarded the golden rule of the historian—that history never repeats itself exactly and, therefore, historical analogies have definite limits. As Arnold Toynbee says, historians are 'never in a position to guarantee that the entities which we are bringing into comparison are properly comparable for the purpose of our investigation.' We can make generalizations about the past and derive principles and broad lessons, no more, but this is quite ample justification for the study of naval history, or any history for that matter.

The study of strategy, tactics, and command suffered from

29 Richmond to Dewar, 8 April 1917; Dewar MSS.
30 Diary, 27 June 1915; Dewar MSS.

reasons that had nothing to do with the faults of the system of naval education. The dynamic years when the old Victorian 'show-the-flag' and 'police-the-seas' Navy was being transformed at great speed into the majestic fleet which assembled at Scapa Flow and in the Forth when war was imminent was a period when nearly all the officers were absorbed in progressing towards gunnery and torpedo efficiency—a full-time job—or organizing and directing the work of the large ships' companies in the capital ships. Richmond, the Dewar brothers, Drax, H. G. Thursfield, Webb, and a handful of other younger officers, as well as a few more senior ones like Slade, struck a line of their own; but in those hectic days few officers, however gifted, could do what they were doing and also find time to study war. Anyway, strategy and tactics were supposed to be solely the concern of admirals! The trouble was that these worthies were themselves immersed in *matériel* concerns. To help correct this condition a 'War Course' for senior officers (the ancestor of the Naval War College of today) was started in 1900 whose basic syllabus included naval history, strategy, and tactics. With all its weaknesses (for one, the inculcation of the accepted tactics: students were not encouraged to apply their critical faculties), it was a step in the right direction. But it came too late to affect the situation in 1914. When war came, in Churchill's well-known words, 'We had competent administrators, brilliant experts of every description, unequalled navigators, good disciplinarians, fine sea-officers, brave and devoted hearts: but at the outset of the conflict we had more captains of ships than captains of war. . . . At least fifteen years of consistent policy were required to give the Royal Navy that widely extended outlook upon war problems and of war situations without which seamanship, gunnery, instrumentalisms of every kind, devotion of the highest order, could not achieve their due reward.'[31]

The number of officers of flag rank who failed in some respect during the war was high: Sturdee, Oliver, Christian, Milne, Moore, Jackson, Jellicoe, Beatty, Duff, Leveson, Jerram, Battenberg, Troubridge, Warrender, Goodenough, and—but why go on. Not unusual, perhaps, considering the magnitude and duration of the war and the new factors in naval warfare. In any case, this is far from asserting that there were no competent senior

[31] Churchill, *The World Crisis* (London, 1923–31, 5 vols. in 6), i. 93.

officers. Jellicoe, whatever his failings—and they include his tendency to be absorbed in details and to attempt to do too much himself—and his mistakes, had that 'Mahanesque' 'intuitive ability which practice gives to size up a situation,' which is the mark of a great fleet commander. The French call this invaluable asset in a commander *coup d'œil*, 'at a glance.' (More on this below.) Beatty was one of those people in connection with whom there seems to have been no *via media*. Either he was greatly admired, or the reverse. My own estimate is that the passage of time has not increased his stature as the Battle Cruiser Fleet Commander of 1914–16: a grand leader in many ways but not really at the top of the tree. But he had what Marshal of the R.A.F. Sir John Slessor (writing of the American Air Force General 'Hap' Arnold, of World War II fame) calls 'the big man's flair for putting his finger on the really important point.' This tremendous asset, together with his unusually broad mind and sympathy for the views of talented younger officers, made him a huge success as C.-in-C., Grand Fleet, in which position these formidable assets were of the greatest value. Beatty's most important achievement as C.-in-C. has gone unnoticed: it was to a large degree his doing that Grand Fleet morale remained remarkably high till the end of the war. Tyrwhitt, I am inclined to think, was in many ways the outstanding British sea officer of the war, as Hipper was on the German side. Wemyss, that 'broad-minded, shrewd man of the world,' fitted the office of First Sea Lord with distinction. The last member of my 'Big Five' is 'Reggie' Hall, a 'genius in his own sphere,' to quote Richmond, and brilliantly successful. On another level I would single out Keyes and Duff. Of the former, Churchill, in unveiling the tablet to Keyes's memory in St. Paul's, said: 'In many ways his spirit and example seemed to revive in our stern and tragic age the vivid personality and unconquerable dauntless soul of Nelson himself.' As for Duff, there is not a shadow of a doubt that convoy saved Great Britain and the Allies from disaster and enabled them to win the naval war. Duff was, with Jellicoe and the rest of the Admiralty High Command, slow to appreciate the value and feasibility of convoy; nevertheless, he deserves the highest credit for the work he did in organizing and extending the convoy system, above all through his staunch support of the real brain behind it, Commander R. G. H. Henderson, his Naval Assistant.

There were other senior officers who knew their business—O. de B. Brock and Goodenough, to mention two. Many of the more important appointments, however, left something to be desired.

Admiral Dewar never uttered wiser words than these: 'The right man in the right place is one of the secrets of success in every form of human endeavour, but the difficulty is not only to find him, but to get him there.' This should have been obvious. Yet the weaknesses in the officer selection process cost the Navy and Britain dearly in the First War. Why were so many poor appointments made to important jobs? How did that pleasant Yorkshire squire, Bridgeman, ever become First Sea Lord (1911–12)? Why Carden as Commander of the Eastern Mediterranean Squadron in the early months of the war? Why Moore as Beatty's Second-in-Command at the time of the Dogger Bank? Why Burney as Jellicoe's Second-in-Command? Why Hayes-Sadler as Commander of the Aegean Squadron in 1918? Why was the overall quality of the Sea Lords no higher? And so forth and so on almost *ad infinitum*. Before examining this problem I must outline the selection machinery. The constitutional position was that the appointment of admirals and captains was the prerogative of the First Lord, who had a Naval Secretary who kept all the records of service and advised him. In practice, the First Sea Lord had a big hand in the appointments. Much, of course, depended on the personalities of the First Lord, First Sea Lord, and Naval Secretary. A strong, wilful First Lord like Churchill might override the First Sea Lord and the Board, as Churchill did when he appointed Beatty his Naval Secretary in 1911. In wartime the concurrence of a C.-in-C. to the appointment of an admiral in his command was a practical necessity: it would never have done if an admiral distrusted or disliked by a C.-in-C. were appointed to one of his squadrons. The Naval Secretary usually would correspond with a C.-in-C. about a new captain for a battleship, but not always.

Why were there so many square pegs in round holes? For one thing, there was no system of weeding out unfit Admirals. Then there was the 'Buggins's turn' tradition, against which Fisher had fought hard but which operated again when he left the Admiralty. 'And just as Lord Spencer put Nelson over the heads of scores of Admirals [actually, two] to go and win the Battle of the Nile so ought not we ever to hesitate to put the right man in the right place absolutely regardless of all considerations. . . . *There is only one rule in War. "The fittest man without any regard to seniority."* [32] This 'rule' was not followed. To take one example, when the First Lord, Carson, wanted to promote Tyrwhitt from Commodore to Rear-Admiral in 1917, he found 'a rooted objection to promote any man out of his turn.' [33] His exceptional war record notwithstanding, Tyrwhitt had to wait until 1918.

There was an extreme reluctance to remove men who had failed, whether from considerations of friendship, the natural distaste for sacking or transferring such an officer, or the fear that this would hurt fleet morale. Thus, Jellicoe and Beatty were, I think, inexcusably lenient with officers who had let them down or had performed with no particular distinction. The names of Warrender and Burney readily come to mind in the case of Jellicoe, and Seymour in the case of Beatty. This disposition to keep on officers who had been proven unfit for their particular job was not confined to the Navy. On the other hand, Fisher erred in the opposite direction: he was all for getting rid of an officer after a single failure and had to be restrained by Churchill.

Another difficulty was the general assumption that because an officer had demonstrated ability in a particular sphere of work, he would be great in something quite different, and, conversely, that because he had not shone, say, as executive officer of a ship, he could not be a success in a different and wider field of responsibility. Little attempt was made to discover the aptitudes of officers and put them to the best use. A pre-war illustration is Admiral Sir Charles Briggs, a fine officer of unimpeachable character who had the esteem of the Service, but who was not a conspicuous success as Controller, 1910–12. Administration was simply not his *métier.*

The senior officers serving at the Admiralty in the war were, as a lot, mediocrities. There is an extenuating circumstance: the distaste of many of the older officers for wartime service at Whitehall in the face of the attractions of a seagoing appointment. The latter offered the possibilities of adventure, excitement, and glory; the former stood for humdrum work and difficult relations with the despised politicians. Tyrwhitt is one example of a senior officer who hated the thought of duty at the Admiralty and

---

[32] Fisher to Jellicoe, 7 February 1915; Jellicoe MSS.
[33] Diary, 15 June 1917; Lieutenant-Colonel à Court Repington, *The First World War* (London, 1920, 2 vols.), i. 579.

becoming one of the 'Admiralty Warriors.' In his case, however, an officer was perfectly positioned.

Another obstacle to getting the best qualified officer into a particular job was the prejudice in the Navy generally and certainly at the Admiralty against independent thought. It was heresy for a younger officer especially—the sin against the Holy Ghost— to question a decision of a Sea Lord or of the Board, or to differ from his seniors, and it took high moral courage, as it could involve the risk of professional ruin. Officers who expressed independent or unorthodox opinions were viewed with suspicion by Authority. One example follows. In 1911 a gunnery officer in the Home Fleet reported to his Captain that a changing gunnery technique rendered certain gunnery practices obsolete and wasteful of time and ammunition. He therefore suggested the introduction of more realistic firings, including divisional practices in unfavourable conditions of wind and weather such as would probably occur in battle. The C.-in-C., Home Fleet, Sir William May, expressed general agreement with these proposals but personally informed the officer that the First Sea Lord (A. K. Wilson) favoured the retention of these obsolete firings and if the paper were forwarded, its implied criticism of Admiralty policy might prejudice his chances of promotion to commander. He advised him to withdraw his paper.[34] The practical consequence of this outlook was that the Admiralty refused to make the best use of the few officers whose independent thought and power of analytical criticism marked them as 'impractical visionaries.'

Indeed, intellect itself was suspect, and 'character' and gallantry were valued far above it. Character, leadership, and unlimited physical and moral courage are the vital personal requirements in senior officers, and all these the Navy of the Fisher Era had in fair measure. Right behind these qualities in importance, but the one in which the Navy was most bitterly short at all levels, was brilliance of intellect. As Drax lamented in 1917, 'Masterly strategy, deep knowledge of the Art of War, keen and rapid brain-work—these were pitiably absent.' Where intellect did exist it was not very often fully appreciated by senior officers.

The best case history of the dominant attitudes regarding independent thought and superior intellect is Herbert Richmond, the

---

[34] Richmond, 'The Service Mind,' *Nineteenth Century and After*, January 1933.

brainiest officer of his generation. By nature a mutineer, he wrecked his prospects for an appointment commensurate with his abilities in 1914–18, and for the highest appointments after the war, by his forthright ideas on naval problems. And so, for instance, when Leveson, the D.O.D., left the Admiralty in January 1915, Richmond, as A.D.O.D. and beautifully equipped for the post, was the logical successor. He was not appointed D.O.D., despite Beatty's support, and four months later was shipped off to Italy as liaison officer with the Italian Fleet—a perfect waste of his talents. Who had succeeded Leveson as D.O.D.? Captain Thomas Jackson, an utter disaster, as events proved. Wemyss told Richmond when he came to the Admiralty in 1918 that he was 'looked on as "dangerous," full of "wild-cat" schemes.' At the end of the year Richmond noted in his diary: 'Geddes is very angry with me & it's already decided to get rid of me. . . . He said [to another officer] I had annoyed everybody —true enough, I don't doubt, for that is a way with people whose opinions differ fundamentally from those of their surroundings.' And a few days later:

> Wemyss sent for [me] yesterday afternoon to tell me that I was to be relieved. . . . he said the reason was that I was unsuitable . . . I replied that it was evident that I was—that I held very strong views, which were the result of 25 years' thought and study. 'Yes,' said he, 'that's just it. *That's* your fault. You're a specialist. All you specialists are the same.' I asked in what I was a 'specialist.' He didn't reply, but went on inveighing against them. . . . This was extraordinarily funny . . . The drawback to my being Director of Training & Staff Duties is that I have spent several years studying those matters. How we worship the amateur in this country![35]

K. G. B. Dewar was another officer of high intellectual attainments and independent views who spent the war in a backwater (command of an old battleship and of the Devonport Gunnery School, etc.) until his appointment as Assistant Director of Plans in 1918. There were exceptions—brainy, intellectual younger officers like O. de B. Brock, who held important appointments during the war and got to the top of their profession afterwards.

Although Dewar and some others of his pattern were not successful executive officers—organizing and managing a ship's

---

[35] Diary, 15 April, 17, 20 December 1918; *Portrait of an Admiral*, pp. 310, 327, 328–9.

company and drawing loyal, wholehearted service from their officers and men—there is no doubt that they had brains and gave far more thought to war than their contemporaries. Richmond was the exception—a first-rate commander and a captain for whom officers would do their best.

One of the curses of the Service with deep roots was 'senior officer veneration': that is, blind obedience to, and blind confidence in, a superior. This 'Senior Officer is always right' syndrome was hardly conducive to the development of independence of thought. One Admiral traces this outlook to general Victorian attitudes. '. . . the divine wisdom attributed to senior officers just because they were senior, and the dread by these officers of allowing anyone junior to Post Captain to think, at any rate aloud. The attitude was not confined to the Navy, but applied to families, where the father was never questioned to his face, to the Army and to business and industry.'[36] It also arose from the early entry of officers. The young men learned to treat everything said by their superior officers as the gospel truth. The classic example of senior officer veneration was the *Victoria* disaster of 1893. In the course of manœuvres off Tripoli 'Sir George Tryon evidently in a moment of aberration mistook the distance of columns apart. The naval mind was so spell bound with the cult of the "humble salute" that as the signal went up and death stepped upon the bridge not one single officer of a venturous brave and independent race, dared to spring forward and whisper or shout or yell "Sir, you can't do it; we're only six cables apart." So H.M.S. *Victoria* and the Admiral and his flag went to the bottom.'[37] Beatty knew the harm this attitude did to the Service. 'We must destroy the fetish that exists that an officer with four stripes on his arm must be a better man than he with three.'[38]

The over-centralized administration at the Admiralty made it extremely difficult for the directing authorities to concentrate on the larger questions of policy. We read, to take one example, that when a cruiser was having some alterations made to her which involved the cutting through of some decks, the D.C.N.S., Oliver, most closely went into all this.[39] Every paper, no matter how large

[36] Sir Angus Cunninghame Graham's letter to the author, 16 November 1966.
[37] Captain A. C. Dewar to Vice-Admiral K. G. B. Dewar, 28 February 1957; Dewar MSS.
[38] Beatty to Carson, 30 April 1917; Chalmers, *Beatty*, p. 448.
[39] For other examples, see *From the Dreadnought to Scapa Flow*, iv. 57.

or small the matter, went to the First Sea Lord or the D.C.N.S. Immersion in the flood of 'paperasserie' seriously hampered the work of the Naval Staff.

It was [Admiral Dewar wrote from personal experience] nobody's business in Operations or any other division to plan or think ahead or to investigate such questions as the relative merits or demerits of patrolling and convoy. That kind of work was not done because the higher ranks did not delegate authority to do it. Instead of confining their attention to important questions of policy and the general direction of affairs, they immersed themselves in a flood of routine and current business, much of which could have been decided without reference to the Admiralty. The human mind can only work efficiently on one thing at a time but they had to switch continually from one subject to another in order to keep pace with the flow of telegrams and papers. Hence, matters requiring thought and discussion had to be evaded or decided with insufficient knowledge of the facts or issues involved.

The same feature of excessive centralization characterized naval methods of command. If war experience pointed to one overriding lesson it was, as Drax expressed it: 'Trust the man on the spot. *Don't* treat him as a senseless automaton who can only be moved intelligently by detailed directions from headquarters.' Two million operational telegrams passed through the Admiralty War Registry during the war. The Admiralty frequently issued detailed orders to squadrons and fleets over the heads of the responsible commanders, who were naturally in a better position to judge what ought to be done. Recall, for example, Cradock and the events prior to Coronel and Milne and the events preceding the escape of the *Goeben*. The Admiralty even issued detailed orders to individual destroyers and submarines, and, as a general rule, exercised direct command of operations in the North Sea. In the Scarborough Raid (17 December 1914), if it had been left to the C.-in-C., the whole Grand Fleet probably would have been concentrated between Scarborough and Heligoland, so as to bring the slower and weaker German forces to action in daylight. He would certainly not have risked defeat in detail by sending his four battle cruisers and a single squadron of battleships (six dreadnoughts) to face probably the whole High Seas Fleet. Yet that is precisely what the Admiralty told Jellicoe to do. The Grand Fleet narrowly escaped heavy losses which might have altered the whole course of the war in Germany's favour. The two forces were closing and the destroyers were in contact when the German C.-in-C., imagining himself in contact with the entire Grand Fleet, turned about and made for home.

The Germans employed a different system. Their Naval High Command defined the strategical policy for each command in brief War Orders; beyond intelligence reports and occasional directives, they did not issue operational orders. The initiation and execution of operations were the responsibility of the executant authorities. There can be no argument about the relative efficiency of the British and German systems.

To recapitulate some of the things I have been saying, I would set down four 'laws' or principles of human relations whose wisdom is fully attested by the experience of the Navy in the Fisher Era. (1) *The principle of selection*, which calls for putting in the best man available for a particular appointment without regard to favouritism or seniority. This must be qualified by the principle of harmony (see below). (2) *The principle of decentralization*, in order to give those in the more responsible positions the time and the energy to think about and to deal with the larger aspects of war preparation or war. (3) *The principle of encouragement* of juniors who possess ideas and vision. (4) *The principle of harmony*, to which I have not alluded: the crucial importance of choosing First Lords and First Sea Lords who would be temperamentally compatible and who would complement and supplement each other. Granted that it is sometimes difficult or impossible to foretell whether people will harmonize well. When this principle was adhered to, the results were excellent, as in the successful McKenna–Fisher combination (1908–10) and the Geddes–Wemyss partnership. When this principle was disregarded or not taken fully into account, as in the Churchill–Bridgeman, Churchill–Fisher, Balfour–Jackson, and Geddes–Jellicoe tandems, the results were dismal. Of course, the principle of harmony applies equally right down the scale. A moderate dose of common sense applied to all four areas would have worked wonders in our period. That it was not, in any consistent way, merely emphasizes that man is not primarily a rational being. Rather is he, in the words of the historian Allan Nevins, 'primarily an emotional being, and even when he is most rational his thinking processes are insensibly coloured by subjective feeling.'

3. THE HUMAN FACTOR

Those who used the many instances of naval unpreparedness and the horrendous catalogue of mistakes and shortcomings with which to belabour the politicians and the Naval High Command during and after the war were faced at the outset with the embarrassing fact that Britain actually had won the war and that the victory of the Navy had been extraordinarily complete even without any striking success. Those who pointed to the last scene, the High Seas Fleet taken into custody, had the better of the argument. How is this victory to be explained? Obviously, some things must have been right with the Navy! The explanation favoured by the Young Turks is summed up in this extract from Richmond's diary (3 November 1918): 'Dined last night with Lord Haldane. . . . He recognises fully how greatly the High Command of the Navy has failed in this war, & that our victory at sea is due solely to crushing superiority & not at all to skill.'[40] This contains more than a grain of truth, since the crushing numerical superiority of the Navy in most categories of ships had intimidated the German Navy. A much larger grain is contained in a *Daily Telegraph* leader (12 February 1919) which drew this moral from Jellicoe's book: 'The main advantage which we possessed over the Germans lay in the character, the seamanship, and the courage of our seamen.'

The personnel factor in the British naval triumph needs to be stressed. That blunderer, General Kuropatkin, C.-in-C. of the Russian Army in the Japanese War, was capable of this insight: 'Mere ships do not make a fleet, nor do they form the strong right arm of an empire, for the strength of a nation does not lie in armour, guns, and torpedoes, but in the souls of the men behind these things.' It is, indeed, a truism that naval battles are won by men, not by ships. Mahan had written that it was by its men, rather than its *matériel*, that the British Navy of the eighteenth century had triumphed. And so in the twentieth. The Captain of the *Vindictive*, which had played so gallant a part at Zeebrugge on St. George's Day, 1918, offered this tribute: 'Those who worship *matériel* have followed a false god. The crux of all fighting lies with the personnel—a fact borne out again and again on this particular

---

[40] *Portrait of an Admiral*, p. 325.

night just as throughout past history.'[41] The main conclusion to be drawn from Jellicoe's *The Grand Fleet* is that the British Navy won, not because it was better prepared than the German Navy, or had better and more *matériel*, but because its spirit gave it the priceless power of initiative, improvisation, and, above all, *confidence*. The really great strength of the Royal Navy ever since the Elizabethan sea dogs has been its supreme self-confidence—its innate conviction of invincibility, which in 1914–18 rested on heavy material resources as well as on the tradition of great commanders and resounding victories—and its *esprit de corps* and strong sense of professional pride. Emblazoned at one end of the main hall at Osborne was the legend: 'There is nothing the Navy cannot do,' which was a quotation from some admiral. The officers may have been, as Drax insisted, the victims 'of that deplorable defect in the English temperament, hereditary lack of imagination,' but there is no denying their technical competence and their energy, courage, determination, perseverance, and unwavering confidence. These formidable assets were the product of a fabulous maritime tradition centuries old and superior seamanship and discipline.[42]

Officers and men were equally superb. Of the men Admiral Sir William James writes:

A boy who wished to join the Navy had to have good references. He was joining a long-service Service with the opportunity of signing on for pension after 12 years man's service. The Petty Officers and Chief Petty Officers, the majority of whom had signed on for pension, were the salt of the earth. The Royal Marines, the only long-service regiment in this country and I think in the world, have always been famous for their morale. The stokers, who in these coal-burning ships were a large part of the ship's company, were not recruited from such a good source as the seamen and Marines, and in peacetime there were very occasionally minor troubles with them, but the same good discipline prevailed once war broke out. I was Commander of the *Queen Mary* during the first two years of the war and I very seldom had to deal with a 'defaulter.' Everyone from Captain to youngest boy were imbued with a spirit of determination to see the thing through. Everything possible

---

[41] Captain A. F. B. Carpenter, *The Blocking of Zeebrugge* (London, 1922), p. 193.
[42] I cannot resist quoting what one officer of the First War told another in 1966: 'I have come to the conclusion that you and I were born about the right time. We should have been too frightened to climb up and down masts and yards and too bloody stupid to deal with the modern gadgets'!

was done to prevent boredom. There is no doubt that the discipline throughout the war was excellent.[43]

The courage, skill, and devotion of the merchant seamen and fishermen were just as high. They had 'sea-instinct.'

Look at the way our fisher-folk crowded to our fleets to do the hard sea work to which their lives at sea had inured them, and for which our Navy had neither the vessels nor the men. As the crews of the old Cinque Port vessels and the volunteer fleet crowded to the flag when invasion by Frenchman or Spaniard was threatened; so our fisher-folk and officers and men of the Merchant Navy, Royal Naval Reserve, and Royal Naval Volunteer Reserve rallied, unarmed, to do our auxiliary work in the Great War. Nothing but heredity could have inspired the men of the Merchant Navy to sail, continuously and calmly, when at any moment an unseen mine or torpedo might have sealed their fate in an open sea, where all possible succour was rendered practically impossible.[44]

The German Navy collapsed in part because it overlooked the fundamental truth that the human factor is always the decisive

---

43 Admiral James's letter to the author, 24 June 1964. The reference to 'man's service' in the second sentence may need a word of explanation. A boy became a man (ordinary seaman) at the age of 18. He was then bound to serve 12 years. Then, at 30, he could volunteer to serve for a further 10 years at the end of which he was given a pension.

44 Bacon, *The Concise Story of the Dover Patrol*, p. 298. I cannot accept Corelli Barnett's thesis that the officers of the Fisher Era showed a decadence stemming from a narrow class outlook. 'Drawing most of its officers from 1 per cent of the nation, the Royal Navy never tapped that great reservoir of urban middle-class talent that made Scheer's fleet so well-educated and so intelligent. . . . its background was still that of gentlefolk . . .' Barnett, *The Swordbearers* (London, 1963), pp. 185–6. Without attempting to argue the effect of an officer's social background on his outlook, I would point out that the middle class, however one defines it, was well represented in the officers corps. Officers ranged from aristocratic down to middle class; few were from the working class. In the Executive Branch there was a sprinkling of aristocrats and a certain number of country gentlemen; but the upper ranks of the professions and of commerce were represented and many were the sons of officers in the Army and Navy. In the case of the non-Executive branches, the 'social mean' tended to be lower—middle to upper middle class. As a group, lowest down the scale of all, were the officers of the Engineering Branch. An officer of those days says: 'What so many people do not realize is that the Royal Navy was a poor man's service; the Naval Officer with private means was a very rare bird.' Captain C. R. O, Burge's letter to the author, 21 October 1966. More pertinent to Barnett's argument. I do not see any evidence of decadence stemming from a supposedly narrow social outlook in 1914–18. And how was it that the officers of 1939–45, with practically the same social background, had not decayed further? One can hardly think of decadence in connection with Cunningham's Mediterranean Fleet or those who fought the Battle of the Atlantic.

one. That their lower-deck personnel proved unequal to the strain of war is obvious. The real weakness of the German naval system lay in the gulf that divided officer from rating. Thus, when the crews of the High Seas Fleet went ashore at Wilhelmshaven, their officers did not take all the trouble the British did to give them opportunities for recreation and give them outside interests. And they maintained an aloof attitude towards the men. A British officer of the First War compares the attitudes of the two Services:

The German officer was much too serious in his dealings with his men. To him 'war was war,' and nothing more. No cricket, no boxing, no football, no concerts, etc., to take the men's minds off their plight— no sympathy between officers and men—just the war.

Contrast this with the British naval officers' ideas of discipline. Men and officers played together, boxed each other, ran races, pulled in boats, got up concerts and otherwise amused themselves—even though there was 'a war on.' 'All work and no play makes Jack a dull boy.' That was the difference—the vital difference—between the two navies.[45]

The indifference to the human factor is also seen in the harsh discipline, bad food, and general disregard for the sensibilities of the men. Is it any wonder that by 1917 the men utterly mistrusted the officers, bitterly resented their living in high style, and yearned for peace? We must add the monotony induced by the stultifying routine and the inactivity of the Fleet to complete the picture of the sharp decline in the morale of the German lower deck in the latter part of the war. But the decline did not extend to the submarine crews, who were kept very active and lived cheek by jowl with their officers.

Basically, though, what ailed the German Navy was the absence of a maritime tradition. Admiral Chatfield analysed it this way: 'The Germans have never been a sea nation; efficient as they are they have not the real seaman's spirit or character. Great as was the navy Kaiser Wilhelm and von Tirpitz created, skilful as had been their preparations, the design of their ships, the experimental work which they must have carried out, and the skill of the German industrialist, there was something lacking. Was it tradition, character, or something deeper, that caused their first action on contact invariably to be to turn for home?'[46] Admiral Tirpitz

---

[45] Captain J. D. Munro, *Scapa Flow: a Naval Retrospect* (London, 1932), p. 225.
[46] Chatfield, *The Navy and Defence*, p. 150.

admitted, 'The German people did not understand the sea. In the hour of its destiny it did not use its fleet.' 'We were defeated by the old traditional English naval prestige . . . This prestige made our governors fear to send our fleet to battle while there was still time.'[47]

Lacking sea instincts and overawed by the prestige and over-whelming strength of the Royal Navy, the Germans did not handle their surface fleet with enterprise or spirit at any time in the war. They had no confidence in victory and they were afraid to sustain ship losses. (Admiral Bacon suggests the latter was 'due to the military instinct of hating to lose *matériel*. "Saving the guns" has always been a tradition among armies.') They abandoned the tip-and-run raids on the East Coast for fifteen months after losing one ship, the pseudo-battle cruiser *Blücher*, in the Dogger Bank operation. They did not press the destroyer raids into the Dover Straits with full energy. Not once did they knowingly risk a major fleet action with the Grand Fleet. Indeed, no one except Tirpitz would ever voluntarily have risked the test of battle. The business of the High Seas Fleet was to avoid such confrontations. Their tactics were those of the guerrilla, depending on surprise and speed. The outbreak of hostilities found Britain with a considerable but by no means overwhelming superiority in capital ships. Had the Germans elected to strike at once with all the force at their disposal, they probably would have gained a larger measure of success than attended their waiting, attritional, *guerre de course* strategy. In the early spring of 1918 the Germans had another excellent chance to influence the course of events, perhaps decisively, through a bold use of their Fleet to disrupt the flow of British military reinforce-ments to France. Again the hesitation to incur risks cost them a wonderful opportunity to achieve a knock-out blow on the Western Front. They never made full use of their chief advantage. Whereas the British Fleet had always to be ready, which put a great strain on the personnel, the German Fleet held the initiative: it could choose the right moment to seek battle, and till then could relax, train and refit, though it was inevitable that long spells in harbour would affect morale.

This is not to suggest that the High Seas Fleet was useless to the Germans. Far from it. Even as a 'fleet in being,' it made an indis-

<hr />

[47] Tirpitz, *My Memoirs*, ii. 445, 312.

pensable contribution to the total German war effort, protecting the coast against invasion, keeping the Baltic a German lake—thereby protecting the supplies of important war material from the Scandinavian states—and, in 1917–18, serving as the shield for the minesweeping operations in the North Sea that kept the exit and homeward routes open for the submarines. I should add, not as an afterthought, that the Germans fought their ships with exemplary bravery, as, for instance, at the Falklands and the *Blücher* at the Dogger Bank.

To ruminate for a moment on the pre-war years, I wonder how wise the Germans were in deciding to rival Britain on the seas. As I summed up the larger consequence in Volume i: 'The naval rivalry did not cause the war, but it ensured that when the war did break out, Great Britain would be on the side of Germany's enemies.' This was foreseen as early as November 1906 by Friedrich von Holstein, who until his retirement in April 1906 had for many years been the powerful Head of the Political Section of the German Foreign Office. In an extraordinarily prescient letter he pointed out the damaging consequences of Germany's ill-conceived naval ambitions:

(1) The more we arm at sea, the more we push England into the arms of France;

(2) we cannot, even if we treble our taxes, build a fleet to match the Anglo-French fleet, or even the English fleet alone;

(3) in a war against France alone, as that of '70 showed, the fleet plays an insignificant role.

(4) it is a threat and a challenge to England to say openly—as the Navy League has for years, each time it makes new demands for the navy—that the armaments are directed *against* England. . . .

Marschall [Marschall von Bieberstein, German Ambassador at Constantinople] said to me last summer, after we had discussed all problems of foreign policy for an entire day: 'Yes, the fleet, there is the greatest danger.' The danger is increased by the fact that in ship building (armour plate, etc.) there is a profit of countless millions, far greater than in the colonies. Not everyone who clamours for ships is a selfless patriot.

Germany stands or falls with her army, and for that every sacrifice must be made. The fleet increases the number of our enemies, but will never be strong enough to vanquish them. We cannot hope, now or later, for an equal fight at sea. The land army must—as in '70—equalize the inequality of the naval forces.

335

It is *not* economic rivalry alone that has made England our enemy. This exists in her relations with America and Japan. What is frightening the English is our accelerated fleet building and the anti-English motivation behind it. We have actually stated, not once but several times—and by no means always by non-official authorities—that our naval armament is directed against England and that we should be mistress of the seas. By making statements of this kind, Germany is left to stand alone. We cannot complain if the English finally begin to take us seriously.[48]

It is a thousand pities that the governing authorities displayed no such wisdom. Tirpitz failed to understand that English opinion was so fully aware of the country's dependence on naval supremacy that it would never tolerate a hostile naval challenge in Europe, especially one coming from a nation already distinguished for its declared hostility to Britain's world position. What for Tirpitz was a deterrent was to Britain a provocation which led her in exactly the opposite direction to that desired by him.

Behind the naval rivalry lay the true cause of British Teutophobia and suspicion of the German Navy—what a top Foreign Office official once called 'the generally restless, explosive, and disconcerting activity of Germany in relation to all other States,' that is, the belief that Germany aimed at Continental, then world, hegemony. The rapid expansion of the German Navy was proof of what Grey called Germany's 'itch to dominate'. How else could one account for the creation of a great Fleet *in addition to* a formidable Army? To judge by Germany's extravagant war aims of 1914–18, the British had justifiable concern over Germany's prewar aspirations to world-power status.

The British were not without blame for the exacerbation of the naval rivalry. I have special reference to the shrill anti-German tone of the press, which embittered the Emperor, Tirpitz, and other high German authorities with their harping, if sometimes with good cause, on the aggressive purposes behind the German naval expansion. One can sympathize with Tirpitz when he plaintively confided to the British Naval Attaché that he 'thought Anglo-German relations would undoubtedly be sweetened if the

---

48 Holstein to Maximilian von Brandt, 20 November 1906; Norman Rich and M. H. Fisher (eds.), *The Holstein Papers* (Cambridge, 1955–63, 4 vols.), iv. 449–50.

British Press would leave Germany alone for a bit.'[49] The Admiralty and their supporters exaggerated, subconsciously, I think, the German naval threat at a time when the Liberal commitment to social reform made it increasingly difficult for the Navy to secure the kind of estimates it believed essential for national and imperial security.

The crux of the Anglo-German problem came to be that neither Power was prepared to concede that which the other most desired: Germany wanted a political agreement which would guarantee British neutrality in the event of a Continental war; Britain, a naval agreement that would ensure British naval supremacy. Each was prepared to *discuss* what the other wanted— as the *second* order of business. Even then it was unlikely that the British would have been willing to disrupt their diplomatic combinations and risk isolation against Germany, and that the Germans would have accepted any naval agreement that would have hampered their freedom in the matter of armaments. Unable to reach an accommodation in either the naval or the political sphere, both Powers heeded the dictates of *Realpolitik* and continued their competition in naval armaments.

It has never been clear to me what the Germans hoped to gain, since they lacked the resources and the will to achieve preponderance on both land and sea. Certainly, one of the motives behind the 1898 and 1900 navy laws, that a powerful battle fleet would enhance Germany's alliance value, had no point after the Triple Entente had come into existence. As for the British, they acted on the classical slogan, '*Si vis pacem, para bellum.*' This made sense if an overwhelming naval superiority could be achieved—it would act as a deterrent to attack. Unhappily, steps in that direction (the great dreadnought programme of 1909–10) only confirmed the whole experience of modern history by intensifying fear, and consequently naval building, in Germany, with the predictable result in Britain. No policy-maker in either country had the imagination, wisdom, and moral courage to break the vicious circle; but, then, no policy-maker anywhere since that time has done any better.

---

[49] Report of the Attaché (Captain Hugh Watson), 21 March 1914; *Pre-War Despatches from Naval Attaché, Berlin (1903–1914)*, a bound collection in the Naval Library. Tirpitz revealed his ignorance of the workings of the British press on this occasion when he asserted, not for the first time: 'It is the best handled Press in the world.' This, too, was the Emperor's warped view.

And so the naval rivalry continued, adding little to the security of the two Powers, yet poisoning relations between the two Governments and between their peoples and driving Britain into ever closer political and military and naval relations with the French that had practically destroyed her freedom of action by August 1914.

* * *

Leadership is a most difficult art to define. Captain Roskill has made a valiant try in his *The Art of Leadership*. He makes small allowance for charismatic qualities, yet these can be very important where they exist. Consider Beatty, for example. And Roskill would have us believe that an officer can make himself a leader. I hold that leadership traits (on the highest level, at any rate) are innate and cannot be learned, although the Services (in the United States as well as in Britain) stress the attainability of this *summum bonum* through education, training, and experience. These can *develop* leadership qualities *where they already exist*. This is not to deny that a *measure* of leadership can be developed in some officers at all levels with no natural aptitude for it.

Certainly great leaders appear in different forms. St. Vincent and Nelson were in different moulds, and so were the outstanding leaders of 1914–18. Thus, Jellicoe and Beatty were contrasts in physical appearance, mannerisms, temperament, and character, yet both were equally good leaders, inspiring loyalty and affection throughout the Grand Fleet when each was C.-in-C.

It is not a simple matter to analyse precisely why this officer or that officer was a fine leader. It is, as I have suggested, a gift, a sort of magic. Elsewhere, in an article on Nelson as a leader, I have set down twelve leadership traits that recur most often in studies of the careers of outstanding naval and military officers, viz. (1) humanity and a sense of identification, which stem from a sincere love of one's fellows; two forms of close identification between leader and led: (2) thoughtfulness and (3) the leader as external group representative, that is, as the official spokesman for the group; (4) loyalty, that is, standing by one's officers and men under all circumstances; (5) tact; (6) the leader as arbitrator and mediator of conflict and dissension among his officers; (7) satisfaction of the need for recognition: giving credit where credit is due, etc.; (8) selflessness; (9) the leader as exemplar—a model of behaviour admired by a group; (10) personality—the sort that inspires great personal loyalty: showmanship, panache may be elements in the leader's personality;[50] (11) professional expertise: the leader must be an expert in his field, a source of information, skills, and group confidence; (12) confidence in one's subordinates. I would now add (13), moral courage, to the attributes of a great leader and would put special stress on (12). A fundamental difference between the leaders and others is this. The real leader assumes that all his officers and men are going to do their best and is surprised and grieved if he finds that some are not playing. The others assume nothing and wait for proof that their officers and men are doing their best. The sailors are very quick to detect when they are trusted. When they are, they respond to every demand.

If an officer has, in earlier years, won a reputation for gallantry, officers and men are glad to be serving under him, as they feel he will not lose any opportunity of attacking. Cowan, for instance, was a menace as a captain in peacetime: he more than once nearly had a mutiny. But officers and men were glad to be with him in wartime. Of course, the successful commander must have the ability to make the correct decisions in the heat of battle as well as being a good leader of men. The two are separate, yet closely related: an unsuccessful leader does not remain a leader for long.

Leadership in war seems to be a very different matter from leadership in peacetime in another sense. 'In peace,' Chatfield writes, 'intellect pulls its full weight, in thinking out plans for war like the chess-player, in devising, or making others devise, new material with which to fight; in laboriously working at the office or school in administering or teaching. For this work, which is irksome and requires patience, persistence and attention to small detail, the mere man of character, the war leader, has often neither aptitude nor inclination.'[51]

The experience of 1914–18 would indicate that specialist officers do not as a rule make good leaders. Too much attention to detail tends to obscure their horizon. All the important naval commands towards the end of the war were held by 'salt horses': Wemyss at

---

[50] I have often wondered why the individual eccentricity one finds in so many of the naval leaders of the Fisher Era—Fisher himself, A. K. Wilson, Beresford, Beatty, Cowan, Keyes, Tyrwhitt, Pakenham, Browning, *et. al.*—has become such a rare commodity in the Royal Navy! The answer could be as simple as this—that we live in an age of conformity.

[51] Chatfield, *The Navy and Defence*, p. 168.

the Admiralty; Beatty, Grand Fleet; Tyrwhitt, Harwich; Keyes, Dover; Gough-Calthorpe, Mediterranean.

Richmond made fun of Jellicoe for not having read Mahan until 1917, right in the middle of a war. I cannot detect anything approaching an absolute correlation between outstanding intellect, including an expert knowledge of naval history, and leadership in time of war. Mahan makes this perceptive comment on the value of practical experience and a knowledge of history:

The situation at Copenhagen, wrote Nelson at a certain moment, looks to the novice in war more formidable than it is. That is the statement, and the illustration, of personal experience applied to a present condition and problem. It is a statement, general in character, of the intuitive ability which practice gives to size up a situation. The French call it *coup d'œil*—at a glance. Napoleon has said: On the field of battle the happiest inspiration—again *coup d'œil*—is often only a recollection. This is a testimony to the value of historical illustration, which is simply recorded experience; for, *whether the recollection be of what some other man did, or whether it be of some incident one's self has seen and recalls, it draws upon the past*; and that, too, not in a general way, but by specific application to an instant emergency, comprehended at a glance, just because it is familiar.

The two sayings complement each other. Nelson affirms the value of experience—which is History in the making—to develop the faculty of quickly and accurately estimating a situation. Napoleon states the value of History—which is experience recorded—in supplying precedents, available for particular use in a particular emergency.[52]

Practical experience and history indeed complement each other. It was Corbett's opinion that the 'theoretical study of strategy' must not be regarded as 'a substitute for judgment and experience, but as a means of fertilising both . . .'[53] If I read these dicta of Mahan and Corbett correctly, naval history is only one of the two principal forms of 'historical illustration'; experience and history do not *have to* go together; and, in any case (Corbett is clearer on this), the prime factor in a war leader is the former.[54] In other words, a commander like a Jellicoe or Beatty can possess *coup*

---

52 Captain A. T. Mahan, *Naval Strategy* (London, 1911), pp. 9–10. The italics are mine.
53 Julian S. Corbett, *Some Principles of Maritime Strategy* (London, 1911), p. 8.
54 Richmond would have agreed. 'It is idle to depend upon happy inspirations on the spur of the moment. The man who has the best chance of getting such happy inspirations is he whose mind is stored with previous experience; his own experience, preferably; otherwise, someone else's.' *National Policy and Naval Strength*, p. 289.

d'œil founded on personal experience and the ability to recall its lessons instantly and almost instinctively as the occasion arises.

*   *   *

A calamitous weakness in the British direction of the war was the want of mutual trust between the seamen, on the one side, and the military leaders and politicians on the other. It is a sad fact of life, often remarked on by commanders-in-chief, that in war one spends a large part of one's time fighting one's own people.

Although on the whole the relations, professional and social, between the officers of the two Services and the co-operation between the fighting formations were excellent (in the one important combined operation, at the Dardanelles), Admiralty–War Office relations left much to be desired. There was little community of thought on major strategy, as seen, for instance, in their disagreement on the correct strategy *vis-à-vis* a German invasion attempt. A partial cause of this state of affairs was the absence before and during the war of any regular inter-Service organization for the discussion and formulation of strategy. Fremantle writes of the Admiralty's 'relations with the War Office, which held scarcely any communication with us except on the highest level in the War Cabinet.'

Far more serious and harmful was the intense mistrust and dislike the Admirals felt for the politicians—the 'frocks,' in General Sir Henry Wilson's coinage. Examples dot the records liberally. Here are a few. Wemyss: 'Damn all these politicians to Hell. It is time we had an N.O. [naval officer] as Dictator!' 'I am under the impression that I have got on fairly good terms with the Prime Minister, but with these slippery gentlemen you never can tell what their real opinions are.' 'I hate Lloyd George, but I think the remainder of the Cabinet are far worse than him.'[55] Beatty: 'These politicians are all alike, a disgusting breed without real patriotism.'[56] Sir Henry Jackson, on leaving the Admiralty: 'My greatest relief is that I shall be clear of the politicians. If we win the war, it will be in spite of them, not because of them.'[57] Admiral

---

[55] Wemyss to Keyes, 8 December 1916, to Beatty, 7, 18 February 1918; Keyes, Wemyss, and Beatty MSS., respectively.

[56] Beatty to Lady Beatty, 31 May 1917; Beatty MSS.

[57] Jackson to Sturdee, 26 November 1916; Sturdee MSS.

Sir Stanley Colville (C.-in-C., Portsmouth, 1916–19): 'O, how I hate and loathe these politicians. Patriotism and the war they don't care about in reality. All they care for is votes and office.'[58] And so forth and so on. It would be a simple matter to compile an anthology of such critical remarks. The root causes of these feelings of antipathy and distrust lie in the unhappiness of the sailors with the 'farce' of the 'so-called blockade' which permitted Germany to receive vital supplies by sea through neutral countries, the politicians' 'weak-kneed pandering' to the trade unions, the belief that the politicians (Balfour was acknowledged as an exception) lacked a sound grasp of naval strategy and the art of naval warfare, and, finally, the extreme annoyance over Churchill's meddling in strategy and operations, the contempt for Asquith's weakness as a war leader, and the distrust of Lloyd George's devious methods. The politicians insisted on having the last word in the larger matters, regarding the Admirals as advisers only, particularly where political considerations came into the picture.

The solution to the chronic differences lay, as the Navy was apt to see it, in the politicians deferring to the seamen in matters of grand strategy, or, what came to the same thing, having a seaman as First Lord in time of war. The politicians, on their part, were disposed to agree with the French statesman Briand's dictum that 'war is much too serious a matter to be left to soldiers and sailors.' Lloyd George had the commonsensical solution—'that no great national enterprise can be carried through successfully in peace or in war except by a trustful co-operation between expert and layman—tendered freely by both, welcomed cordially by both.'[59]

* * *

An era came to an end on 21 June 1919. Never again was the Royal Navy to possess such overwhelming might as it had enjoyed

---

[58] Colville to Vice-Admiral Sir Frederick Hamilton (Second Sea Lord), 24 February 1917; Hamilton MSS.

[59] Lloyd George, *War Memoirs*, iii. 1169. Or, as Lord Ismay once put it: 'A country may have powerful armed forces, led by brilliant commanders; it may have statesmen of great competence; it may have a civil population which is disciplined and resolute; it may have immense wealth; it may have industries which are most efficiently organised; but unless the statesmen and the soldiers at the summit work together in a spirit of mutual esteem, the essential co-ordination between all these diverse elements of strength will be lacking, and there is bound to be a deadly waste of blood and treasure.' *The Memoirs of General the Lord Ismay* (London, 1960), p. 50.

in war and peace for nearly two decades. It was, in a sense, appropriate that the symbol of this era of supremacy himself survived but another year. I can most fittingly conclude this study of the Royal Navy in the Fisher Era with a few thoughts on the redoubtable and irrepressible 'Jacky' himself. He had what one writer calls the 'six essentials of a great military leader': 'guts, charm, ruthlessness, vision, strength, and brains.' He gave the Navy a considerable shake-up when it needed it badly. Certainly only a genius like Lord Fisher could have transformed the complacent, somnolent, late Victorian Navy into the Grand Fleet of 1914. He is open to criticism, mainly for his stubborn refusal to create a naval staff and his contribution, through his combative personality, inability to compromise, and questionable methods, to the most serious schism the Navy had known up to that time. There are extenuating circumstances for his disruption of the Nelsonian 'band of brothers' tradition. One is the powerful aid of that stormy petrel Beresford. 'Charlie B.' was a born rebel to whom fighting constituted authority, especially the Admiralty (in the name of causes, to be sure, some of which were excellent), came naturally. Of greater significance is the fact that the Navy was not what I would call an adaptive society. Accommodation to change was not its forte. The practical consequence was, as Beresford once said, the lot of the reformer in the Navy was much like that of the early Christian. In a Service as conservative and tradition-bound as was the pre-war Navy moderate methods to introduce radical changes would not have succeeded. Time was short and there was a tremendous amount to do. It is worth remarking that Fisher's methods, whatever may be said against them, were not so completely alien to the temper of the age as is often claimed. We have only to recall the direct methods, often degenerating into violence, employed by the trade unions, the suffragettes, and the contending forces in Ireland in the last years before the war, to which we could add the increasingly strident tones of Parliamentary debates.

An all too common criticism of Fisher is that he did so much to set the materialist tone of the Navy during his years of power. It is true that the pre-war Admiralty had concentrated their attention on the problem of 'hardware,' and had paid little regard to the problem of how the Fleet was to be used and how new or improved weapons such as the torpedo and the mine would affect tactics. Earlier in this chapter I tried to show that the obsession with *matériel* was a perfectly natural development. Here I would add that the great achievement of these *matériel*-minded officers of the early twentieth century was that, besides giving the Navy a preponderant advantage in numbers of ships, they strengthened the Nelsonian tradition of invincibility by instilling into the minds of officers and men confidence in themselves, in their leaders, and in their weapons. None of them doubted, even when the war at sea took disastrous turns, that they would beat the enemy.

The efficiency of the Navy was Fisher's monomania. The Fleet that fought and, despite all deficiencies and errors, defeated the High Seas Fleet was largely his creation. 'Where should we all be to-day, were it not for your foresight, your bold determination?' Lord Esher wrote to the Admiral in the last year of the war.[60] Similarly, the great editor, J. L. Garvin: 'Had he not had the force and courage to revolutionise a conservative service and make the Dreadnought navy to meet Germany on the sea, it would have been God help us when war broke out.'[61] Admiral Bacon's verdict is a just one: '. . . if it had not been for Lord Fisher we might not improbably have lost the War. He did not win it, but most certainly paved the way for our doing so by the wholehearted services he rendered in reorganizing the British Navy.'[62] His major war-time contribution, after being recalled by Churchill, was the construction programme he commenced, but for which the A/S campaign of 1917–18 might not have succeeded.

One cannot leave Fisher without recalling his remarkable vision. Esher told him in 1908, 'the prophets are not in it with you,' and Sir Frederick Treves, the distinguished surgeon, said in 1919, 'As a prophet you have advantages over Jeremiah. You have lived to see your prophecies come true. He, poor man, did not.' Fisher foretold in 1911 the date of the First War as the autumn of 1914; prophesied, when flying was in its infancy, the revolution that maritime aircraft would achieve; predicted years before the war the unrestricted submarine campaign on shipping (but not the antidote); and had a vision of an amphibious landing craft ('amphibious hippopotami crawling up the beaches') thirty years before 'D' Day in World War II. He was also ahead of his

60 21 July 1918; M. V. Brett and Oliver, Viscount Esher (eds.), *Journals and Letters of Reginald, Viscount Esher* (London, 1934–8, 4 vols.), iv. 208.
61 Garvin to Carson, 24 January 1917; Carson MSS.
62 Bacon, *From 1900 Onward*, p. 366.

time in his appreciation of the immense advantages to a maritime Power of an amphibious strategy, with the Army employed as 'a projectile fired by the Navy' at points unexpected by the enemy. To the end the old sea dog lost none of his uncanny prophetic instinct. It was on a visit to the aircraft carrier *Furious* at Rosyth on 31 December 1918 that he made one of his amazing forecasts. Pointing to some small torpedoes secured to the side walls in the hangar, the Admiral asked, 'What are these?' The Commander of the ship, H. C. Buckle, replied, 'Torpedoes, Sir, for the torpedo bombers.' Fisher: 'Scrap the lot, or put them away in cotton wool till the next war!' Buckle: 'When will that be, Sir?' Fisher: '20 years' time!'

I have said it before and I now repeat: the name of 'Fisher' will forever be connected with the Royal Navy at the apex of its power, and the historian can safely accept the judgement of *The Times* in the last paragraph of its eloquent tribute (14 July 1920) after the Admiral's death: 'Let the schoolmen say what they will . . . this man's fame is safe with history. The people knew him and loved him. His body is buried in peace, but his name liveth for evermore.'

Bibliography*

i. UNPUBLISHED PAPERS

The most important materials consulted by the author in the preparation of the five volumes were collections of unpublished papers, viz. (the present location is indicated in parentheses):

Admiralty Record Office MSS. (Public Record Office.) These are, naturally, of the highest value. Although successive First Lords and First Sea Lords carted off much of their own records, more than enough remains to keep a scholar very happy. Under a Parliament Act of 1958, records 50 years old were opened to scholars. In 1966 documents of the First World War and post-war period through 1922 were opened for public inspection 'in a single operation instead of being released a year at a time,' as would normally have happened under the 50-year rule. Under an Act of Parliament of 1967 a 30-year rule became operative in 1968. Still withheld for reasons of 'public policy' are unnamed categories of documents. These include court-martial proceedings, which are subject to a 100-year rule. The P.R.O. Admiralty papers are staggering in quantity and are not made manageable by the haphazard way in which the Admiralty arranged them.

Especially important are these classes: Adm. 1 (*Papers*), containing the registered files of the Admiralty Secretary's Department which were selected for permanent preservation; Adm. 116 (*Cases*), containing registered files which were detached by the Admiralty registry from the main series of registered files and put into cases, simply on account of their larger size; Adm. 137 (*1914–1918 War Histories*), containing registered and unregistered papers and various operational papers which passed through the hands of the Naval Historical Section; Adm. 167 (*Board minutes and memoranda*); and the Station Records (correspondence), which include Adm. 121 (Mediterranean), Adm. 125 (China), Adm. 128 (North American and West Indies), Adm. 144

---

* The reader is referred to my bibliographical essay, 'The First World War at Sea', Chapter XIV, Robin Higham (ed.), *A Nation at War: a Guide to the Bibliography of British Military History* (to be published in 1971 (?) by the University of California Press). An asterisk against the collections of papers in the first section of the bibliography indicates that this material was not available in time to be of use or is still restricted. I include these references for completeness sake. Addresses of individuals are given where they may not be readily available.

(Channel Fleet), and Adm. 145 (Atlantic Fleet). There are reference volumes with a breakdown of these classes on the search room shelves. Some of the more important specific references are these:

PRE-WAR

Miscellaneous memoranda from D.N.I.
  and others from 1889 onwards: Adm. 116/866B
Anglo-German naval relations, 1902–14: Adm. 116/940B
Imperial Conference on the Defence of
  the Empire, 1909: Adm. 116/1100B

THE WAR

28 August 1914 action in the Bight: Adm. 137/1943, 1949,
  2139

Escape of *Goeben*, August 1914: Adm. 137/2165
Scarborough Raid, 16 December 1914: Adm. 137/1943, 2084
Coronel, 1 November 1914: Adm. 137/1022
The Falklands, 8 December 1914: Adm. 137/1906, 1950,
  1989
The Dogger Bank, 24 January 1915: Adm. 137/1943, 1949,
  1989, 2134, 2135,
  2138, 2139

The Dardanelles, 1915—Proceedings of
  the Dardanelles Commission: Cab. 19/33
Lowestoft Raid, 25 April 1916: Adm. 137/1944, 2088
Jutland, 31 May–1 June 1916: Adm. 137/1906, 1945,
  1946, 1988, 2089,
  2134, 2137, 2139,
  2141, 2142, 2151

High Seas Fleet Sortie, 19 August 1916: Adm. 137/1947, 2089
Mary Rose convoy incident,
  17 October 1917: Adm. 116/1599A
Heligoland Bight, 17 November 1917: Adm. 137/583, 585
  (signal logs), 586
  (track charts)

The second convoy incident,
  12 December 1917: Adm. 137/625
Goeben sortie, 20 January 1918: Adm. 116/1807, Adm.
  137/630, 2182
Zeebrugge–Ostend, 22–23 April 1918: Adm. 137/1950, 1990,
  2090, 2151, 2276,
  2760, 2707, 2708
High Seas Fleet sortie, 23–25 April 1918: Adm. 137/1988

Grand Fleet Battle Orders:

Adm. 116/1341
(1914–16)
Adm. 116/1342
(1916–18)
Adm. 116/1343
(in force at Jutland)
Also: Adm. 137/288, 289
(1914–15)
Adm. 137/1965
(alterations,
1916–18)
Adm. 137/341
(G.F.B.I.s—Grand
Fleet Battle
Instructions—and
Manœuvring
Orders)*

Minutes of the Operations Committee,
Board of Admiralty: Adm. 1/8564
Work of the Plans Division, 1917–18:   Adm. 1/8524
War Operations and Policy, 1914–1918, a
mine of interesting but unrelated
matters: Adm. 116/1348–1351

POST-WAR

The Scuttling: G.T.–7674
(Cab. 24/83)

Asquith MSS. (Department of Western MSS., Bodleian Library).
Endless quantities of material left by H. H. Asquith (afterwards first
Earl of Oxford and Asquith), Liberal Prime Minister, 1908–16. The
naval material consists mainly of some correspondence with First Lords
and a large number of Cabinet papers, the latter now available in the
Cabinet Office records at the P.R.O.

Balfour MSS. (British Museum Add. MSS. 49683–49962). The
personal and official correspondence of A. J. (afterwards first Earl of)
Balfour, as Prime Minister, 1902–05, Member of the War Council in
World War I, 1914–15, and First Lord of the Admiralty, 1915–16.
Particularly valuable are his correspondence when First Lord with the
First Sea Lord (Jackson) and the C.-in-C. (Jellicoe) in 49714 and the

* The two classes for the Battle Orders are, with certain minor modifications—Staff
minutes, letters excluded in the Adm. 116 volumes—duplicated. The Adm. 116
materials are better arranged.

correspondence with Churchill (First Lord), 1912–15, in 49694. Correspondence pertaining to Jellicoe's dismissal as First Sea Lord will be found in 49709.

Barley–Waters MSS. (Naval Historical Branch, Ministry of Defence). A mass of valuable papers and raw material on trade defence in the First War, by Lieutenant-Commander D. W. Waters and the late Commander F. Barley. There is a duplicate set (not quite complete) in the Naval Library, Ministry of Defence.

*Battenberg MSS.** (in the custody of Lord Brabourne, senior trustee of the Broadlands Archives Trust). Discovered only a few years ago. With few exceptions, the records are of the pre-war years. The papers will not be available to scholars at least until the authorized biographer of Prince Louis, John Terraine, is finished with them.

Beatty MSS. (2nd Earl Beatty). The Admiral's personal and official correspondence, also a goodly collection of valuable wartime naval memoranda. One of the most important unpublished collections of papers. See under *Barnes, John*, below, p. 366.

*Bellairs MSS.** (McGill University Library). A sizeable collection of the papers, including correspondence, of Commander Carlyon Bellairs, a leading Fisher critic. Useful for the whole Fisher Era.

Bellairs MSS. (Naval Library, Ministry of Defence). Grand Fleet papers, 1917–18, of Rear-Admiral Roger M. Bellairs, who was Beatty's War Staff Officer. Unaccountably missing (lost or misplaced?) at this writing.

Bethell MSS. (Mrs. Agatha Marsden-Smedley, 31 Draycott Place, London, S.W.3). Important for the Duff and Jellicoe letters, 1917–18, to Admiral the Hon. Sir Alexander Bethell.

Bradford MSS. (arrange for examination through the National Maritime Museum Library). Include 45 letters from Jellicoe to Admiral Sir Edward Bradford.

Cabinet Office Records (Public Record Office). Important for the study of many naval topics; most of these series of papers have indexes. Especially valuable are the minutes of the Committee of Imperial Defence (C.I.D.), 1902–39 (Cab. 2), the War Council (Nov. 1914–May 1915), Dardanelles Committee (June–Oct. 1915), and War Committee (Nov. 1915–Nov. 1916) (Cab. 22), and the War Cabinet and Imperial War Cabinet (Dec. 1916–Oct. 1919) (Cab. 23); the 'I.C.' series of wartime conferences, including the minutes of the Allied Naval Council, and of the Council of Ten at the Peace Conference (Cab. 28); the

'C.F.' series, including the minutes of the Council of Four at the Peace Conference (Cab. 29); the Cabinet letters in the Royal Archives, 1868–1916 (Cab. 41); the papers of the C.I.D. (Cab. 3 to 6, especially Cab. 3, 'Home Defence' series), the War Council, Dardanelles Committee, and War Committee (Cab. 24); and the papers of the Dardanelles Commission (Cab. 19). Indispensable aids to the efficient use of the Cabinet Office materials are: *List of Cabinet Papers, 1880–1914* (P.R.O. Handbook No. 4), *List of Papers of the Committee of Imperial Defence to 1914* (P.R.O. Handbook No. 6), *List of Cabinet Papers, 1915 and 1916* (P.R.O. Handbook No. 9), and *The Records of the Cabinet Office to 1922* (P.R.O. Handbook No. 11), all skilfully prepared by Mr. A. W. Mabbs and colleagues.

Carson MSS. (the Hon. Edward Carson). However, the great bulk of Carson's Admiralty papers which are extant, some 200 items, are in the Public Record Office of Northern Ireland (Law Courts Building, May Street, Belfast), catalogued under D.1507/4. Material on Jellicoe's dismissal (December 1917) is in D.1506/1/2. The Belfast material includes a number of interesting items, but the cream of Carson's naval papers appear to have been destroyed in the Blitz. They had, fortunately, been seen by the authorized biographer, Ian Colvin.

*Churchill MSS.** (the Chartwell Trust). They are expected to be made available (in the Churchill College Library, Cambridge?) after the completion of the authorized biography.

*Corbett MSS.** (Mr. W. C. B. Tunstall, Coaters, Bignor, Sussex). The papers of Sir Julian Corbett constitute an important source for the study of British naval policy between 1900 and 1918, more particularly with respect to Fisher and the dreadnought policy.

Crease MSS. (Naval Library, Ministry of Defence). The records of Captain T. E. Crease, Naval Secretary to Lord Fisher during much of his two appointments as First Sea Lord and in the first year of his chairmanship of the Board of Invention and Research (1915–16). One stout volume includes the inside story of Fisher's resignation in May 1915; another volume consists of the proceedings of the Beresford Inquiry of 1909.

*De Robeck MSS.** (Churchill College, Cambridge). The papers of Admiral of the Fleet Sir John de Robeck. Of special interest for the Dardanelles. Application to see papers at Churchill College should be made in advance to the Librarian.

Dewar MSS. (National Maritime Museum). The valuable diary and correspondence of Vice-Admiral K. G. B. Dewar.

Domvile MSS. (Admiral Sir Barry Domvile). Diaries extending over seventy years; of special value for the Harwich Force. Destined for the National Maritime Museum, Greenwich.

Drax MSS. (Churchill College, Cambridge). Contain a plethora of source material on Grand Fleet tactics.

Duff MSS. (Lieutenant-Commander Peter Dolphin, R.N. (ret.), Road Farm Cottage, Churt, Surrey). Admiral Sir Alexander Duff's important Grand Fleet diary, 1914–16, and some material on the introduction of the convoy system. The main collection (papers and correspondence regarding the introduction of convoy) is at the National Maritime Museum.

*Dumas MSS.** (Mrs. Dumas, Woodpeckers, Snakey Lane, Preston Park, Brighton, Sussex). Diaries of Admiral P. H. Dumas, 1905–14; 90 per cent domestic but with entries on the pre-war Fisher régime at the Admiralty and the German Navy (Dumas was Naval Attaché in Berlin, 1906–8).

Esher MSS. (4th Viscount Esher). The correspondence of the extremely influential second Viscount Esher, a member of King Edward's entourage and of the pre-war Committee of Imperial Defence. Since Esher was wrapped up in purely military concerns during the war, this collection loses much of its value to the naval historian for the war years. A selection from these papers was published in the four-volume *Journals and Letters of Reginald, Viscount Esher*, edited by M. V. Brett and Oliver, Viscount Esher.

Evan-Thomas MSS. (British Museum Add. MSS. 52504–52506). Correspondence and papers of Admiral Sir Hugh Evan-Thomas, Rear-Admiral Commanding 5th Battle Squadron at Jutland. The wartime letters are of some interest. Most valuable is the post-war correspondence (including Jellicoe letters) pertaining to Jutland.

Fisher MSS. at Kilverstone Hall (3rd Baron Fisher) has mostly press cuttings and family correspondence. The far more valuable collection is at Lennoxlove (14th Duke of Hamilton). Copies of its excellent catalogue are to be found in a number of leading universities in Britain and the United States as well as at Lennoxlove.

Foreign Office MSS. (Public Record Office). In addition to the 'General Correspondence' through 1905 (Germany, F.O. 30, France, F.O. 27, etc.), continued in 'General Correspondence, Political' (F.O. 371), and more valuable in many ways, are the Foreign Office Private Collections (F.O. 800 series), notably the Balfour, Grey, Hardinge, Lansdowne,

Lascelles, and Nicolson Papers. Of use mainly for the naval rivalry with Germany. For the Grey Papers, which are easily the most important, see the separate entry below, *Grey MSS*. A helpful aid is P.R.O. Handbook No. 13, *The Records of the Foreign Office, 1782–1939*, prepared by Mr. M. Roper.

Fremantle MSS. (National Maritime Museum). The Naval Staff papers and minutes of 1918, when Admiral Sir Sydney Fremantle was D.C.N.S.

Frewen MSS. (Mrs. Lena Frewen, Sheephouse, Brede, Sussex). The beautifully written 55 volumes of diaries (1903–57) of Captain Oswald M. Frewen, of which the first 44 are indexed; also a few important post-war letters from Jellicoe dealing with Jutland (British Museum, Add. MSS. 53738).

Geddes MSS. (Public Record Office, Adm. 116/1804–1810, the first volume of which has an excellent index to all the papers). First Lord correspondence, 1917–18, of Sir Eric Geddes.

German Ministry of Marine MSS. (Bundesarchiv–Militärarchiv, 7800 Freiburg im Breisgau, Wiesentalstrasse 10). Among the more valuable of these records are the 'Akten des kaiserlichen Marine-Kabinetts', 1890–1918 (the office headed by Admiral Georg von Müller), the voluminous papers of Rear-Admiral Magnus von Levetzow (Chief of the Operations Section of Scheer's staff, and, from August 1918, Chief of Staff of the Operations Department of the *Admiralstab*), and the folders on the major naval actions which were prepared by the German Office of Naval History in the interwar period and consist of the War Diary of the Kommando der Hochseestreitkräfte, letters, and action reports. The National Archives, Washington, have microfilm copies of all the Ministry of Marine records; the Naval Library, Ministry of Defence, has microfilm copies of selected 'Akten', all the Levetzow material, and the K.d.H. War Diary.

Godfrey MSS. (Naval Library, Ministry of Defence). Admiral John H. Godfrey's Naval Staff College Jutland lectures and papers supplementing the lectures; also a collection of Mediterranean papers of 1917–18.

Grey MSS.* (Public Record Office, F.O. 800/61, 62: Germany, 1906–9, 1910–14; F.O. 800/87, 88: Admiralty, 1905–13, 1914–16). The Foreign Office correspondence of Sir Edward Grey. Volumes 61 and especially 87 and 88 (until Churchill's resignation as First Lord) are particularly valuable; volume 62 has little of consequence not to be found in Gooch and Temperley (see below, p. 362).

Hall MSS.* (Commander Richard A. Hall, R.N. (ret.), 18 Rivermead Court, London, S.W.6). The papers of Rear-Admiral Sir Reginald Hall are few and of value only for some five typescript chapters (of which Admiral James made full use) for an autobiography which was to run to fifteen or twenty chapters. But Commander Hall's memory (he is 'Blinker' Hall's son) might be helpful to a scholar.

Hamilton MSS. (National Maritime Museum). The private and official correspondence and a valuable diary for October 1915–June 1916 of the Second Sea Lord, Sir Frederick Hamilton.

Hankey MSS.* (2nd Baron Hankey). A formidable mass featuring the wartime diaries of Sir Maurice (afterwards 1st Baron) Hankey (a number of interesting and even significant bits were not used in his *The Supreme Command*), family correspondence, copies of his letters to prominent people, and the more important letters he received. The papers may be made available in the Churchill College Library when the authorized biographer, Captain Stephen Roskill, is finished with them. I was privileged to examine only the diaries of 1917–18.

Harper MSS. (British Museum, Add. MSS. 54477–54480). Consist of the correspondence of Vice-Admiral J. E. T. Harper at the time (1919–20) he was preparing the official Admiralty account of Jutland, the original *Harper Record* (typescript and unpublished set of proofs), and a Harper memorandum of extraordinary interest, 'Facts Dealing with the Official Record of the Battle of Jutland and the Reason It Was Not Published.' It has been reproduced as an appendix to the *Jellicoe Papers* (ed. A. Temple Patterson), Vol. ii. The complementary document, the minutes of the Beatty Board, will appear in the *Beatty Papers* (ed. John Barnes). See Captain Geoffrey Bennett, 'The Harper Papers,' *Quarterly Review*, January 1965 (pp. 16–25), for an analysis of the papers, less the memorandum, not then available.

Jackson MSS. (Naval Library, Ministry of Defence). The First Sea Lord papers (1915–16) of Admiral of the Fleet Sir Henry Jackson: letters from Jellicoe, Beatty, and other officers.

Jellicoe MSS. (British Museum, Add. MSS. 48989–49057). This is a most important primary source, covering all phases of the Admiral's career. The volumes of special interest include 48990–48992 (correspondence with the Admiralty when C.-in-C., Grand Fleet), 49006–49009 (letters from Fisher, Madden, Beatty, Jackson), 49014, 49027–49028, 49040–49042 (Jutland material), and 49038 (autobiographical notes). The second Earl Jellicoe has a small collection of his father's personal correspondence (the great bulk of which, alas, has been lost over the years), and Jellicoe's marginal comments on Churchill's *The World Crisis*, Vols. i, ii. See under *Patterson*, below, p. 390.

Kelly MSS. (National Maritime Museum). The papers of Admiral Sir Howard Kelly, good on the Mediterranean in 1914 and the Adriatic in 1917–18.

Keyes MSS. (on loan to the Churchill College Library, Cambridge). The extensive and valuable papers, mainly correspondence, of Admiral of the Fleet Lord Keyes.

Kitchener MSS. (Public Record Office). Include some interesting correspondence on invasion prospects early in the war and the naval aspects of the Dardanelles–Gallipoli operation.

Lansdowne MSS. (8th Marquess of Lansdowne). Contain the correspondence of the 5th Marquess of Lansdowne, Foreign Secretary, 1902–5, with the Admiralty. They are of value for the light thrown on the initial stages of the Anglo-German naval rivalry. There are a number of interesting letters on Anglo-German naval affairs in 1902–4 among the Lansdowne MSS. at the P.R.O.: F.O. 800/129.

Lloyd George MSS. (The Beaverbrook Library, 33 St. Bride Street, London, E.C.4). Contain a scattering of material pertaining to naval affairs—mostly in 1917–19 correspondence. Apply to the Librarian at least one week in advance, indicating preference in dates.

McKenna MSS. (Churchill College Library, Cambridge). Contain the personal and official correspondence of Reginald McKenna, First Lord of the Admiralty, 1908–11. This is not a large collection, but it is a choice one.

National Maritime Museum Library (Greenwich, London, S.E.10). In addition to the more important collections noted elsewhere in this section, it contains the papers of Sir W. Graham Greene, Secretary of the Admiralty, 1911–17 (miscellaneous memoranda), Sir James Thursfield (a leader-writer on *The Times*, 1880–1923, and its Naval Correspondent from 1887), his son Rear-Admiral H. G. Thursfield, and of other officers of the Fisher Era, notably Sir Louis Hamilton (war diary), Sir Charles Madden (a war diary of the Grand Fleet, useful for movements and activities but not for policy), Sir Martyn Jerram (most interesting are the China Papers; some Jutland material), Sir W. W. Fisher (wartime plans for attacking the German coast, a paper on repelling destroyer attacks, and 1917–18 papers on A/S warfare), Sir William Tennant (war diary, post-war Jutland lectures), Sir Gerard Noel, Sir William May, Sir Berkeley Milne (material on the *Goeben* episode of 1914), Sir Walter Cowan, and Admiral Sir Edmond Slade (1908 diary when D.N.I.).

Naval Library, Ministry of Defence (Empress State Building, Earls Court, London, S.W.7). Contains much wealth in addition to the more important collections noted in this section: the Newbolt Papers (correspondence and minutes pertaining to the Admiralty vetting of Sir Henry Newbolt's *Naval Operations*, Vols. iv, v), a few *Corbett Papers*, the *Tweedmouth* (9 vols.), *Selborne* (2 vols.), *Cawdor* (1 vol.), and *Robinson* (2 vols.) MSS.: largely printed Admiralty papers of the Fisher reform era, with quite a bit of duplication, though Vol. ii of the Robinson MSS. includes Fisher correspondence (Robinson, who changed his name to Geoffrey Dawson in 1917, was the Editor of *The Times*, 1912–19, 1923–41), and there are three cases of Tweedmouth correspondence in addition to the prints. The Naval Library has four volumes of Fisher's *Naval Necessities* (papers on his projects and reforms) and Jellicoe's full notes on the Admiralty *Narrative* (below, p. 361).

Oliver MSS. (National Maritime Museum). Admiral of the Fleet Sir Henry Oliver's staff minutes and correspondence on the naval bombardment of the Dardanelles and valuable, detailed 'recollections' in two typescript volumes which cover 1880–1939.

Richmond MSS. (National Maritime Museum). The extensive diaries and correspondence of Admiral Sir Herbert Richmond.

Roskill MSS. (Captain S. W. Roskill, R.N. (ret.)). Important unpublished papers and correspondence on Jutland and miscellaneous correspondence and papers on the war.

Royal Archives (Windsor Castle). The beautifully indexed correspondence of King Edward VII and King George V with high political and naval personages. This is an important source, even if much of King Edward's files were burned after his death.

Sturdee MSS. (Captain W. D. M. Staveley, R.N.). A miscellany, important for a number of letters from Jellicoe and Beresford, and for material on Grand Fleet tactics.

Sydenham MSS. (British Museum, especially Add. MSS. 50836). Contain memoranda by Lord Sydenham (then Sir George Clarke) as Secretary of the Committee of Imperial Defence, 1904–7. Only a few bear on naval affairs.

*Troubridge MSS.** (Lieutenant-Commander Sir Peter Troubridge, Bt., R.N. (ret.)). A few score letters from well-known people of the period, but almost entirely social, and a notebook in which the Admiral had drafted some reminiscences, including a *pièce justificative* on the *Goeben* affair.

Tyrwhitt MSS. (Lady Agnew, Pinehurst, South Ascot, Berkshire). Contain several interesting letters from Beatty. They are especially valuable for Tyrwhitt's frank commentary in his hundreds of wartime letters to members of his family.

United States Navy Department Records (National Archives, Washington, D.C.). Chiefly valuable for Admiral Sims's reports from London, 1917–18, in Record Group 45, Admiral Benson's personal papers and correspondence as Chief of Naval Operations, also in Record Group 45, and assorted materials for 1917–18 in the Records of the Chief of Naval Operations in Record Group 38. See Warner R. Schilling, *Admirals and Foreign Policy, 1913–1919* (unpublished Yale University Ph.D. dissertation, 1953), pp. 345–8, for a discussion of the arrangement and content of the U.S. Naval records.

Wester Wemyss MSS. (the Hon. Mrs. Frances Cunnack, Saint-Suliac, Ille-et-Vilaine, France). Most valuable for the First Sea Lord papers (1918–19) of Admiral of the Fleet Sir Rosslyn Wemyss. They feature a voluminous correspondence with the C.-in-C., Grand Fleet (Beatty), much of which is duplicated in the Beatty Papers, and Wemyss's unpublished memoirs for 1917–19 ('Admiralty I' and 'Admiralty II'). The University of California, Irvine, Library has a microfilm copy of the 1918–19 correspondence and the memoirs.

Williamson MSS.* (Churchill College Library, Cambridge). The papers of Group Captain H. A. Williamson, a pioneer of maritime air power.

Yexley MSS.* (Commander H. Pursey, R.N., 43 Farnaby Road, Bromley, Kent). The papers of the Editor of the lower-deck organ, *The Fleet*. Important for lower-deck matters. Includes Fisher correspondence.

ii. BRITISH OFFICIAL WORKS—UNPUBLISHED

(All, except as noted, are available in the Naval Library, Ministry of Defence.†)

† In addition to what follows, the Naval Library has such valuable unpublished Admiralty records of the pre-war and war periods as *Pre-War Dispatches from Naval Attaché, Berlin (1903–1914)*, Naval Attaché Reports, 1904–1914, in printed bound annual volumes under the title *Reports on Naval Affairs*, and a miscellany of N.I.D. material of formidable proportions. The Library of the University of California, Irvine, has a copy of the first named.

Board of Invention and Research (B.I.R.), reports and minutes of meetings, 1915-17 (6 vols.). (Also in the Lennoxlove MSS.)

'Chronological List of German U-Boats Sunk in First World War, 1914-1918,' n.d. This is the final approved list, differing in some cases from the printed 'Final Return' in C.B. 1292.

D.N.C. Department, Admiralty, *Records of Warship Construction during the War, 1914-1918* (1919).

Director of Statistics, Admiralty, 'Statistical Review of the War against Shipping' (December 1918).

D.T.M. Department, Admiralty, *Mining Manual* (1922-4, 3 vols.).

Ministry of Shipping, *The System of Convoys for Merchant Shipping in 1917 and 1918* (n.d.; post-war). There is a copy with Lord Salter's papers. Excellent on the organization and workings of the convoy system.

——, *A Report of Shipping Control during the War. The Work of the Transport Department and Ministry of Shipping up to the Armistice, 11th November, 1918* (n.d.). Copy in Lord Salter's possession. A valuable summary of all aspects of convoy.

Technical History Section, Admiralty: fifty monographs (1919-20), collectively known as *The Technical History*, and whose most useful volumes for my purposes were:

TH 1 *Submarine v. Submarine*
TH 4 *Aircraft v. Submarine. Submarine Campaign, 1918*
TH 7 *The Anti-Submarine Division of the Naval Staff. December 1916–November 1918*
TH 8 *Scandinavian and East Coast Convoy Systems, 1917–1918*
TH 13 *Defensive Arming of Merchant Ships*
TH 14 *The Atlantic Convoy System, 1917–1918*
TH 15 *Convoy Statistics and Diagrams*
TH 21 *Submarine Administration, Training, and Construction*
TH 23 *Fire Control in H.M. Ships*
TH 24 *Storage and Handling of Explosives in Warships*
TH 28 *Guns and Gun Mountings*
TH 29 *Ammunition for Naval Guns*
TH 30 *Control of Mercantile Movements. Part I. Text*
TH 31 *Control of Mercantile Movements. Part II. Appendices*
TH 32 *Control of Mercantile Movements. Part III. Plans*
TH 37 *Inception and Development of the Northern Base* (Scapa Flow)
TH 39 *Miscellaneous Convoys*
TH 40 *Anti-Submarine Development and Experiments Prior to December 1916*
TH 51 *Development of the Paravane*

The others are on more or less esoteric subjects, such as *Naval Medical Transport during the War* (TH 3), *The Development of the Gyro-Compass Prior to and during the War* (TH 20), *Admiralty Airship Sheds* (TH 43), etc. TH 38 was not issued.

Naval Staff Studies

Anti-Submarine Division, *Monthly Reports* (May 1917–November 1918).

——, *R.N.A.S. Anti-Submarine Reports* (monthly, June 1917–March 1918). Continued in:

Air Division, *Naval Air Operations* (monthly reports, April–October 1918).

Gunnery Division, *Grand Fleet Gunnery and Torpedo Memoranda on Naval Actions, 1914–1918* (1922).

——, *Report of the Committee Appointed to Investigate the Attacks Delivered on and the Enemy Defences of the Dardanelles Straits. 1919* (1921). The 'Mitchell Committee' Report.

Historical Section, *History of the Second World War. Defeat of the Enemy Attack on Shipping, 1939–1945* (1957, 2 vols.). The first chapter of Vol. 1A is 'Some Lessons from the First World War,' and there are excellent plans and tables in Vol. 1B. *A restricted publication.*

Lieutenant-Commander D. W. Waters, 'Notes on the Convoy System of Naval Warfare, Thirteenth to Twentieth Centuries.' Part II. 'First World War, 1914–18' (1960). (Part I, covering the earlier period, was issued in 1957.)

Intelligence Division, *German Navy Tactical Orders* (1920). 'Translation of orders recovered from various ships sunk at Scapa.'

Leith, Captain Lockhart, *The History of British Minefields* (1920, 2 vols.).

Operations off the East Coast of Great Britain, 1914–1918 (1940).

Review of German Cruiser Warfare, 1914–1918 (1940).

Torpedo Division, *Remarks of the Naval Staff on Anti-Submarine Operations* (1927).

Training and Staff Duties Division, *Addendum No. 1 to Naval Tactical Notes, Vol. i, 1929* (1931).

——, *History of British Minesweeping in the War* (1920). Captain Lionel L. Preston, Director of Minesweeping at the Admiralty, 1917–19, was the author.

——, 'Monographs (Historical)' on the war*: thirty-nine (including

* The principal writers of the Naval Staff Histories, work on which commenced in 1919, were Captain A. C. Dewar, succeeded by Instructor-Captain Oswald Tuck in 1920, assisted by Lieutenant-Commander J. H. Lloyd-Owen. 'As you know well heavy gun fire is not allowed, only short guns with rabbits for targets. . . . Behind the lack of really critical staff histories is the attitude of most officers. They don't want to study. They have certain preconceptions and don't want to hear what the

one that was later withdrawn), the most important of which for the purposes of this study were:

Monograph No.	Title	Year of Publication
8	*Naval Operations Connected with the Raid on the North-East Coast, December 16th, 1914*	1921
11	*The Battle of Heligoland Bight, August 28th, 1914*	1921
12	*The Action off Dogger Bank, January 24th, 1915*	1921
13	*Summary of the Operations of the Grand Fleet, August 1914 to November 1916*	1921
18	*The Dover Command,* Vol. i. (No Vol. ii was produced, as the subject was considered to be adequately covered in the Official History, *Naval Operations.*)	1922
19	*Tenth Cruiser Squadron,* Vol. i (covered 1914–Feb. 1916; no Vol. ii was issued).	1922
21	*The Mediterranean, 1914–1915* (superseded No. 4, *Goeben and Breslau,* of 1920).	1923
23	*Home Waters—Part I. From the Outbreak of the War to 27 August 1914*	1924
24	*Home Waters—Part II. September and October 1914*	1924
27	*Battles of Coronel and Falkland Islands* (superseded No. 1, *Coronel,* of 1920, and No. 3, *Falklands,* of 1920).	1922
28	*Home Waters—Part III. From November 1914 to the End of January 1915* (includes a revised No. 8).	1925
29	*Home Waters—Part IV. From February to July 1915*	1925

---

historian has to say.' Captain A. C. Dewar to Vice-Admiral K. G. B. Dewar, 1 March 1952; Dewar MSS. The uncritical tone of the staff monographs on the Second War, to which Dewar was referring, applies equally well to those of the First War, including the 'T.H.' series, which were as much Staff histories as the Historical Section products. 'The idea,' Admiral Dewar wrote later, 'was that, eventually, these monographs would provide the material for a proper Staff history of the war.'

Monograph No.	Title	Year of Publication
30	*Home Waters—Part V. From July to October 1915*	1926
31	*Home Waters—Part VI. From October 1915 to May 1916*	1926
32	*Lowestoft Raid, 24th–25th April 1916*	1927
33	*Home Waters—Part VII. From June 1916 to November 1916*	1927
34	*Home Waters—Part VIII. From December 1916 to April 1917*	1933
35	*Home Waters—Part IX. 1st May, 1917, to 31st July, 1917* (No monographs were issued for Home Waters between August 1917 and November 1918.)	1939
—	*Mediterranean Staff Papers relating to Naval Operations from August 1917 to December 1918.* (No monographs were issued for the Mediterranean between 1916 and July 1917.)	1920
—	*The Naval Staff of the Admiralty. Its Work and Development*	1929
—	*Naval Staff Appreciation of Jutland* (Withdrawn in about 1928 and most copies destroyed. See *From the Dreadnought to Scapa Flow*, Vol. iii, pp. viii–ix.) The Naval Library does not have a copy. There is one with the Harper MSS. at the British Museum, the Roskill MSS., and in the Library of the University of California at Irvine.	1922

The other monographs are concerned with the German Cruiser Squadron in the Pacific, 1914 (No. 2), Cameroons, 1914 (No. 5), passage of the British Expeditionary Force, August 1914 (No. 6), the Patrol Flotillas at the start of the war (No. 7), the White Sea Station (No. 9), East Africa, 1914–15 (No. 10), the first Australian convoy, 1914 (No. 14), operations in Mesopotamia and the Persian Gulf, 1914–16 (No. 15), the China Squadron, 1914 (No. 16), the East Indies Squadron, 1914 (No. 17), the Cape of Good Hope Station, 1914 (No. 20), the Atlantic Ocean, 1914 (No. 22), the Baltic, 1914 (No. 25), the Atlantic, from the Falklands to May 1915 (No. 26), the Archangel River Flotilla, 1919 (un-numbered).

Naval Staff College (Greenwich) *Lectures.* By Commander John Creswell
(on the directing staff of the College, 1931–2):
'Mediterranean, 1914' (three lectures, 1932)
'The Battle of Heligoland Bight, 28th August, 1914' (1932)
'The Scarborough Raid, 16th December, 1914' (1932)
'The Dogger Bank Action, 24th January, 1915' (1932)
'The Operations of 19th August, 1916' (1931)
'The Grand Fleet, 1917–1918' (1931)
All these lectures are in Captain Creswell's possession (Ellerslie,
Cattistock, Dorchester, Dorset).

Captain J. H. Godfrey (Deputy-Director of the Naval Staff College,
1928–30), 'Jutland' (seven lectures, 1929–30, a revision of
Ramsay's, below; with the Godfrey MSS. in the Naval Library).
Admiral Godfrey's set has, in addition, important supplementary 'Papers for reference purposes by lecturer'.

Commander W. G. Tennant (on the directing staff of the College,
1931–2), 'Jutland' (seven lectures, 1932, a revision of Godfrey's;
with the Tennant MSS. at the National Maritime Museum).

Naval War College (Greenwich) *Lectures.* Captain B. H. Ramsay
(Instructor in the Senior Officers' War Course, 1927–9),
'Jutland' (five lectures, 1929; with the Jellicoe MSS. in the
British Museum).

iii. OFFICIAL WORKS—PUBLISHED

British

Admiralty, *Narrative of the Battle of Jutland* (London, H.M.S.O., 1924).
Essentially the *Naval Staff Appreciation of Jutland* without the
judgements and criticisms. (See also below, p. 363, Cmd. 1068,
Battle of Jutland.)

Aspinall-Oglander, Brigadier-General C. F., *History of the Great War.
Military Operations. Gallipoli* (London, Heinemann, 1929–32, 2
vols.).

Bell, A. C., *A History of the Blockade of Germany and of the Countries
Associated with Her in the Great War, Austria-Hungary, Bulgaria, and
Turkey, 1914–1918* (London, H.M.S.O., 1961). The author, a
member of the Historical Section, C.I.D., prepared this printed
official history in 1931. It was originally intended to be included
in the Corbett and Newbolt *Naval Operations.*

Corbett, Sir Julian S., and Newbolt, Sir Henry, *History of the Great War.*

Naval Operations (London, Longmans, 1920–31, 5 vols.; rev. ed. of i, the events of 1914, 1938, of iii, which includes Jutland, 1940). Corbett was the author of i–iii, Newbolt of iv–v, and Lieutenant-Colonel E. Y. Daniel, R.M., was responsible for the revised editions. There are also map volumes for each volume but ii, which has its own maps in a pocket. Map volumes i and iii are in revised editions. Detailed, authoritative; restrained judgements. *Naval Operations*, which was part of the 'Official History of the War', was prepared in the Historical Section of the C.I.D. under the direction of Corbett, then Newbolt after Corbett's death. It was intended to be an interim semi-popular treatment of the subject for the public, as opposed to the Staff History which was being written by the Historical Section of the Naval Staff.

Edmonds, Brigadier-General Sir James E., *History of the Great War. Military Operations. France and Belgium, 1917*, Vol. ii (London, H.M.S.O., 1948).

Fayle, C. Ernest, *History of the Great War. Seaborne Trade* (London, Murray, 1920–4, 3 vols.). Indispensable for trade warfare and defence.

Gooch, G. P., and Temperley, Harold (eds.), *British Documents on the Origins of the War, 1898–1914* (London, H.M.S.O., 1926–38, 11 vols. in 13), Vols. iii, vi, vii, x (Part 2). Especially important for Anglo-German naval relations.

Hurd, Sir Archibald, *History of the Great War. The Merchant Navy* (London, Murray, 1921–9, 3 vols.). An inspiring story told in an unemotional style.

Raleigh, Sir Walter, and Jones, H. A., *History of the Great War. The War in the Air* (Oxford, Clarendon Press, 1922–37, 6 vols.). Raleigh wrote i, Jones, the other five. There are, in addition, map volumes for i and iii, and a volume of Appendices. Not always reliable in its treatment of the R.N.A.S.

Salter, J. A., *Allied Shipping Control: an Experiment in International Administration* (Oxford, Clarendon Press, 1921).

Command and Parliamentary Papers (published by H.M.S.O.)

256 (1909). *Report of the Sub-Committee of the Committee of Imperial Defence appointed to inquire into certain questions of Naval Policy raised by Lord Charles Beresford, 12 August 1909.*

Cd. 8490 (1917). *Dardanelles Commission. First Report*, 12 February 1917.

Cmd. 371 (1919). *Dardanelles Commission. Final Report*, 4 December 1917.

Cd. 9221 (1918). *Mercantile Losses.* Abbreviated title.

199 (1919). *Merchant Shipping. War Losses.*

200 (1919). *Navy. War Losses.*

Cmd. 1068 (1920). *Battle of Jutland, 30th May to 1st June, 1916. Official Despatches, with Appendices.*

Cmd. 2870 (1927). *Reproduction of the Record of the Battle of Jutland,* by Captain J. E. T. Harper and others. Substantially the unpublished and disputed *Harper Record* of 1919 but without the diagrams.

Cmd. 270 (1919). *Navy. Pay, Half Pay, Retired Pay, and Allowances of Officers* (recommendations of committees). Abbreviated title.

Cmd. 149 (1919). *Navy. Pay, Allowances, and Pensions of the Royal Navy and Royal Marines* (recommendations of Admiral Jerram's Committee). Abbreviated title.

German

Lepsius, Johannes, Mendelssohn-Bartholdy, Albrecht, and Thimme, Friedrich (eds.), *Die Grosse Politik der europäischen Kabinette, 1871–1914* (Berlin, Deutsche Verlagsgesellschaft für Politik und Geschichte, 1922–7, 40 vols. in 54). Vols. xx ff. cover the pre-war decade and are important for the Anglo-German naval rivalry.

Germany, Ministry of Marine, *Der Krieg zur See, 1914–1918,* a series of seven sets (Berlin, Mittler), of which the first three were the more useful for my purposes:

Der Krieg in der Nordsee (1920–65, 7 vols.). Vols. i–v, by Captain Otto Groos, vi and vii, by Admiral Walther Gladisch. There is a supplementary volume of Jutland maps for Vol. v.

Der Handelskrieg mit U-Booten (1932–66, 5 vols.), by Rear-Admiral Arno Spindler. Vol. i covers the war through January 1915; ii, February–September 1915; iii, October 1915–January 1917; iv, February–December 1917; v, 1918.

Der Krieg in den türkischen Gewässern (1928, 1938, 2 vols.), by Rear-Admiral Hermann Lorey. Vol. i, *Die Mittelmeer-Division*; Vol. ii, *Der Kampf um die Meerengen.*

Der Kreuzerkrieg in den ausländischen Gewässern (1922–37, 3 vols., rev. ed. of i, 1927). Vols. i and ii by Captain Erich Raeder, iii, by Vice-Admiral Eberhard von Mantey.

Der Krieg in der Ostsee (1922–64, 3 vols.). Vol. i by Captain Rudolph Firle, ii, by Lieutenant Heinrich Rollmann, and iii, by Admiral Ernst von Gagern.

Die Kämpfe der kaiserlichen Marine in den deutschen Kolonien (1935), Vice-Admiral Kurt Assmann, ed.

Die Überwasserstreitkräfte und ihre Technik (1930), by Captain Paul Köppen.*

American

United States Department of the Navy. Office of Naval Records, *The Northern Barrage and Other Mining Activities* (1920).

United States Department of State, *Papers Relating to the Foreign Relations of the United States. The Paris Peace Conference, 1919* (Washington, United States Government Printing Office, 1942–47, 13 vols.), Vols. iii–vi for the minutes of the Council of Ten and Council of Four at the Paris Peace Conference (12 January–28 June 1919), Vols. vii–ix for the minutes of the Council of Heads of Delegations (1 July 1919–10 January 1920). And see the Mantoux volume, below, p. 387.

iv. PUBLISHED WORKS

Where there is more than one publisher, the British is the one ordinarily cited. The list includes volumes whose publication came too late to be useful and others which had not yet been published when this list was prepared.

Aberdeen, Countess of, *Edward Marjoribanks, Lord Tweedmouth, Kt., 1849–1909: Notes and Recollections* (London, Constable, 1909). Brief biographical notes. Tweedmouth's tenure as First Lord of the Admiralty (1905–8) is treated in a few unsatisfactory pages.

Agar, Captain Augustus, *Footprints in the Sea* (London, Evans, 1959). An autobiography with a few bits of interest on the early days of naval aviation and the post-war Baltic operations.

Alboldt, E., *Die Tragödie der alten deutschen Marine* (Berlin, Deutsche Verlagsgesellschaft für Politik und Geschichte, 1928). See *Das Werk*, etc., below, pp. 399–400.

Altham, Captain Edward, *Jellicoe* (London, Blackie, 1938). A good short biography.

Appleyard, Rollo, *Charles Parsons: His Life and Work* (London, Constable, 1933). The inventor of the steam turbine for the propulsion of ships played a not insignificant role in the early twentieth-century *matériel* revolution in the Navy.

---

* See further, Gert Sandhofer, 'The Compiling of the Official History of the German Navy to 1945,' in Robin Higham (ed.), *Official Histories* (Kansas State University Press, 1970), for other official German works on the war, in particular the fifteen specialized papers listed under 'Collections of Official Papers.' Not mentioned is an unpublished official work by Admiral Hermann Jacobsen, *Die Entwicklung der Schiesskunst in der kaiserlich deutschen Marine* (a 'Service Monograph,' Berlin, 1928).

Arthur, Sir George, *Life of Lord Kitchener* (London, Macmillan, 1920, 3 vols.), Vol. iii. Material on Kitchener and the naval aspects of Dardanelles–Gallipoli. Superseded by Magnus and James.

Ashmead-Bartlett, Ellis, *The Uncensored Dardanelles* (London, Hutchinson, 1928). A brilliant war correspondent 'describes those stirring events and sombre scenes [April–September 1915] just as they appeared to me at the time, and I endeavour to throw what light I can on the characters of the leading actors in the drama, and to discover the underlying motives of their actions.'

Aspinall-Oglander, Brigadier-General Cecil F., *Roger Keyes* (London, Hogarth Press, 1951). The authorized biography by the official historian of the Gallipoli campaign. Uncritical—ludicrously so on the Zeebrugge operation of 1918.

Aston, Major-General Sir George, *Secret Service* (London, Faber, 1930). Chapters illustrating the work of the Secret Services during the war, written by a marine officer. Here and there one finds a point worthy of note.

Bacon, Admiral Sir Reginald, *The Dover Patrol, 1915–1917* (London, Hutchinson, 1919, 2 vols.). A persuasive, highly detailed account of his command of the Dover Patrol. A note of self-justification runs through the volumes. Keyes's *Naval Memoirs*, Vol. ii, is a necessary corrective.

——, *The Jutland Scandal* (2nd ed., London, Hutchinson, 1925). A blast at the Admiralty *Narrative* and other Jellicoe denigrators, 'dedicated to those two neglected goddesses Justice and Truth now worshipped in an obscure corner of the British Pantheon.' The pro-Jellicoe bias is patent in this and all the other of Bacon's writings. But they should not on that account be dismissed as rubbish: they are far from that.

—— *et al.*, *The World Crisis by Winston Churchill: a Criticism* (London, Hutchinson, 1927). Chapters I and V (by Lord Sydenham of Combe and Bacon, respectively), the latter especially, are devastating critiques of Churchill's version of Jutland.

——, *The Life of Lord Fisher of Kilverstone* (London, Hodder & Stoughton, 1929, 2 vols.). The first authorized biography: sympathetic to its subject but not slavishly so. Outdated in important respects, yet still very useful. Bacon was intimately involved in the 'Fisher Revolution.'

——, *The Concise Story of the Dover Patrol* (London, Hutchinson, 1932). A condensation of the two-volume *The Dover Patrol* (above).

——, *The Life of John Rushworth, Earl Jellicoe* (London, Cassell, 1936). The authorized biography and a good one, though Bacon did not have access to *all* the Jellicoe Papers. (He refused to allow his manuscript to be 'vetted' by Jellicoe's Literary Executors.)

Bacon, *From 1900 Onward* (London, Hutchinson, 1940). A volume of reminiscences which, because of the author's important jobs, is well above the usual volume of memoirs for historical interest. There are shrewd vignettes of Fisher, Churchill, Jellicoe, and A. K. Wilson.

—— and McMurtrie, Francis E., *Modern Naval Strategy* (London, Muller, 1940). The larger problems of naval warfare—command of the sea, amphibious warfare, convoys, etc.—persuasively argued with abundant illustrations from the First War. Many of the statements could be challenged.

'Barfleur' (Admiral Sir Reginald Custance), *Naval Policy : a Plea for the Study of War* (London, Blackwood, 1907). Articles which had appeared in print in the preceding two years. A blast against the '*matériel* school'.

Barnes, John (ed.), *The Beatty Papers*, Vol. i (1908–1919) (London, Navy Records Society, 1970). (Barnes is also preparing a new authorized biography of the Admiral.)

Barnes, Eleanor C. (Lady Yarrow), *Alfred Yarrow : His Life and Work* (London, Arnold, 1923). Sir Alfred Yarrow, Bt., was the great marine engineer and shipbuilder, whose chief work was done in the improvement of small vessels, especially destroyers and gunboats. The latter chapters, on the war period, have some value.

Barnett, Correlli, *The Swordbearers : Studies in Supreme Command in the First World War* (London, Eyre & Spottiswoode, 1963). The Jellicoe chapter, the only one on a naval figure, is written from the standard published sources; a bit far-fetched in attributing the unsatisfactory aspects of Jutland to the 'decadent and uncreative' pre-war social system.

Bauer, Admiral Hermann, *Reichsleitung und U-Bootseinsatz, 1914–1918* (Lippoldsberg, Klosterhaus, 1956). Bauer's writings, of which this and the next title are the most important, are key works on the U-boat campaign, along with those by Michelsen and Gayer. Bauer was Senior Officer, U-boats, from the beginning until June 1917.

——, *Als Führer der U-boote im Weltkriege, 1914–1918* (2nd ed., Leipzig, Koehler & Amelang, 1943).

Bayly, Admiral Sir Lewis, *Pull Together! The Memoirs of Admiral Sir Lewis Bayly* (London, Harrap, 1939). Straightforward autobiography, best on his command of the Western Approaches, 1915–18.

Beaverbrook, Lord, *Politicians and the War, 1914–1916* (London,

Butterworth, 1928). A book, like its more valuable sequel, 'designed to emphasise the immense importance of what may be called the civilian aspect of war direction—a thing which war-books tend to neglect.' Material on the May 1915 crisis and the Dardanelles operation.

——, *Men and Power, 1917–1918* (London, Hutchinson, 1956).

Bellairs, Commander Carlyon, *The Battle of Jutland* (2nd ed., London, Hodder & Stoughton, 1920). The anti-Jellicoe bias and patent inaccuracies of this first detailed study of the battle seriously detract from its value.

Beloff, Max, *Imperial Sunset: Britain's Liberal Empire, 1897–1921* (London, Methuen, 1969). Contains good, pithy discussions of naval defence problems in both British and Imperial contexts, based on the most recent scholarship and some original archival research.

Benn, Captain Wedgwood, *In the Side Shows* (London, Hodder & Stoughton, 1919). Material on the wartime exercise of naval air power in the Adriatic and Near East.

Bennett, Captain Geoffrey, *Coronel and the Falklands* (London, Batsford, 1962). The standard work on the two battles from the British angle.

——, *Cowan's War: the Story of British Naval Operations in the Baltic, 1919–1920* (London, Collins, 1964). A detailed account, based on the Cowan and Admiralty Papers; not always easy to see the forest for the wood, but the fault is as much that of the confused events themselves, to say nothing of the frightfully complex historical background.

——, *The Battle of Jutland* (London, Batsford, 1964). A straightforward, highly vivid narrative which eschews controversy; makes use of some fresh material.

——, *'Charlie B.': the Life of Admiral Lord Charles Beresford* (London, Peter Dawnay, 1968). The first full-length biography; a competent and reasonably impartial work, based on the rediscovered Beresford Papers (few of interest for the Fisher Era).

——, *Naval Battles of the First World War* (London, Batsford, 1968). The first satisfactory survey of the naval side of the war.

Beresford, Admiral Lord Charles, *The Betrayal* (London, P. S. King, 1912). 'This book is a statement of facts . . . the truth concerning the naval administration and the naval policy in force during the years from 1902 . . .' A sharp and not unbiased critique of major aspects of the Fisher Revolution.

——, *The Memoirs of Admiral Lord Charles Beresford* (2nd ed., London, Methuen, 1914, 2 vols.), Vol. ii. A record of his life in the Navy,

1859–1909. Chapters on his two last appointments, the Mediterranean and Channel Fleets, 1905–9. There is only one brief reference to his great enemy, Fisher—a generous tribute to his work as Mediterranean C.-in-C. (1899–1902)!

Bingham, Commander the Hon. Barry, *Falklands, Jutland, and the Bight* (London, Murray, 1919). A personal account by a gallant officer who took part in the first and third actions as a gunnery officer in the battle cruiser *Invincible*, and at Jutland as commander of a destroyer division.

Birnbaum, Karl E., *Peace Moves and U-boat Warfare: a Study of Imperial Germany's Policy towards the United States, April 18, 1916–January 9, 1917* (Stockholm, Almqvist & Wiksell, 1958). Some useful detail on the evolution of German submarine policy in the nine months preceding, and including, the fateful decision to commence unrestricted U-boat warfare on trade. Based mainly on unpublished German official sources, including the German Ministry of Marine records.

Blake, Robert (ed.), *The Private Papers of Douglas Haig, 1914–1919* (London, Eyre & Spottiswoode, 1952). The many references to Jellicoe are the volume's chief value for the naval historian.

——, *The Unknown Prime Minister: the Life and Times of Andrew Bonar Law, 1858–1923* (London, Eyre & Spottiswoode, 1955). Of use only for the May 1915 crisis.

Bone, David W., *Merchantmen-at-Arms: the British Merchant Service in the War* (London, Chatto & Windus, 1919). A sympathetic and charming account, illustrated by the superb drawings of Muirhead Bone, the Official War Artist.

Bonham-Carter, Victor, *Soldier True: the Life and Times of Field-Marshal Sir William Robertson* (London, Muller, 1963). American edition: *The Strategy of Victory, 1914–1918: the Life and Times of the Master Strategist of World War I, Field-Marshal Sir William Robertson* (New York, Holt, 1964). A solid and reliable study, but of interest only for the passing references to the Navy and the sailors.

Bonham-Carter, Lady Violet, *Winston Churchill As I Knew Him* (London, Collins, Eyre & Spottiswoode, 1965). Does not go far beyond the published record, but does add a number of interesting Fisher and Churchill sidelights.

Bowman, Gerald, *The Man Who Bought a Navy: the Story of the World's Greatest Salvage Achievement at Scapa Flow* (London, Harrap, 1964). The circumstances of the scuttling of the High Seas Fleet and, in greater detail and of more interest, the story of the salving of the sunken ships. 'The man who bought a navy' was the engineer Ernest Cox.

Boyle, Andrew, *Trenchard* (London, Collins, 1962). The eminently readable biography of a fascinating character, with some material, not all of it accurate, on naval air power in the First War and the amalgamation of the R.N.A.S. and R.F.C. to form the R.A.F. in 1918.

Bradford, Vice-Admiral Sir Edward E., *Life of Admiral of the Fleet Sir Arthur Knyvet Wilson* (London, Murray, 1923). This great strategist and seaman of the early twentieth century deserves a fuller and more scholarly treatment. Since he left few papers, this may be asking too much.

Brett, Maurice V., and Esher, Oliver, Viscount, *Journals and Letters of Reginald, Viscount Esher* (London, Nicholson & Watson, 1934–8, 4 vols.), Vols. ii–iv. Many references to naval events and personalities in the whole Fisher Era.

Bridge, Admiral Sir Cyprian, *The Art of Naval Warfare* (London, Smith, Elder, 1907). 'The main object is to show the value—indeed, the necessity—of a knowledge of naval history . . .' A splendid little book on strategy and tactics by one of the few senior officers of the time who was much concerned with the more sublime aspects of the naval profession.

——, *Sea-Power and Other Studies* (London, Smith, Elder, 1910). A collection of his essays printed in 1898–1908, mostly on naval strategy, past and present.

Brodie, Bernard, *Sea Power in the Machine Age* (rev. ed., London, Oxford, 1943). A standard work of outstanding merit on the evolution of naval *matériel* in the nineteenth and twentieth centuries, and of its impact on strategy and tactics. But Chapter XVI, 'The Undersea Arm in the World War', should be used with reserve, the discussion on the convoy system being inaccurate in important essentials.

Brodie, C. G., *Forlorn Hope 1915: the Submarine Passage of the Dardanelles* (London, W. J. Bryce, 1956). The sub-title indicates the contents of this readable little volume. All about the heroic exploits of the British 'E' boats in the spring of 1915.

Brownrigg, Rear-Admiral Sir Douglas, *Indiscretions of the Naval Censor* (London, Cassell, 1920). The author was the Naval Censor in question. Interesting footnotes to the war at sea.

Bruce, J. M., *British Aeroplanes, 1914–18* (London, Putnam, 1957). With Thetford, the standard work in the field; concise text, detailed specifications, good illustrations.

Bywater, Hector C., *Cruisers in Battle: Naval 'Light Cavalry' Under Fire, 1914–1918* (London, Constable, 1939). A detailed record of the actions in which the light cruisers, British and German, played a prominent role. Based on correspondence with officers who took part in these actions, as well as on the British and German official histories.

Bywater and Ferraby, H. C., *Strange Intelligence: Memoirs of Naval Secret Service* (London, Constable, 1931). An entertaining volume by two naval journalists without benefit of access to Admiralty records.

Callwell, Major-General Sir Charles E., *Experiences of a Dug-Out, 1914–1918* (London, Constable, 1920). Callwell was Director of Military Operations at the War Office in the first year of the war. Of some value for the Dardanelles.

Campbell, Rear-Admiral Gordon, *My Mystery Ships* (London, Hodder & Stoughton, 1928). The fascinating story of the experiences of the most famous of the Q-ship commanders.

Carpenter, Captain A. F. B., *The Blocking of Zeebrugge* (London, Herbert Jenkins, 1922). The Captain of the *Vindictive* tells in detail the story of the action.

Carr, Lieutenant William G., *By Guess and By God: the Story of the British Submarines in the War* (London, Hutchinson [1930]). A charming little book on many of the principal submarine exploits.

——, *Brass Hats and Bell-Bottomed Trousers: Unforgettable and Splendid Feats of the Harwich Patrol* (London, Hutchinson, 1939). The subtitle describes the contents accurately. Carr is incapable of writing a dull book, but he only emphasizes the need for a more authoritative work on the Harwich Force.

——, *Good Hunting* (London, Hutchinson, 1940). Anecdotes on the A/S campaign of the latter part of the war by this master storyteller.

Chalmers, Rear-Admiral William S., *The Life and Letters of David, Earl Beatty* (London, Hodder & Stoughton, 1951). The authorized life, and a good one (like its successors), by an officer who served on Beatty's staff from August 1915 until the end of the war. Sympathetic, as one would expect, yet judicious at the same time.

——, *Max Horton and the Western Approaches* (London, Hodder & Stoughton, 1954). The biography of the great submariner of the Second War, whose Baltic exploits in the First War had already made him a legendary figure. Little on Horton the man.

——, *Full Cycle: the Biography of Admiral Sir Bertram Ramsay* (London, Hodder & Stoughton, 1959). The authorized life of an officer who is best remembered for his command of the Home Fleet in World War II; but there is some material of interest on the First War. Full use of Ramsay's diary and correspondence.

Chaput, Rolland A., *Disarmament in British Foreign Policy* (London, Allen & Unwin, 1935). The useful material is the excellent treatment, based on the then available sources, of the post-war naval disarmament of Germany and of the naval disarmament problem at the Paris Peace Conference.

Chatfield, Admiral of the Fleet Lord, *The Navy and Defence* (London, Heinemann, 1942). The first volume of a two-volume auto-biography of one of Britain's greatest twentieth-century admirals, covering his naval career from 1886 to 1932. Generally avoids controversial matters but contributes some new material and interesting observations to the story of the Navy through the war and beyond.

Chatterton, E. Keble, *Q-Ships and Their Story* (London, Sidgwick & Jackson, 1922). Like all the subsequent books of this most prolific of writers on sea subjects, eminently readable and interesting narratives based on eye-witness accounts.

——, *The Auxiliary Patrol* (London, Sidgwick & Jackson, 1923).

——, *Gallant Gentlemen* (London, Hurst & Blackett, 1931). A miscellany of naval actions, including the *Goeben* episode, Coronel, and the Falklands.

——, *The Sea-Raiders* (London, Hurst & Blackett, 1931). The operations of the German surface raiders.

——, *The Big Blockade* (London, Hurst & Blackett, 1932). The story of the 10th Cruiser Squadron, 'an attempt to give an authentic account from first-hand information of the greatest and most devastatingly effective blockade since ships first sailed the seas.'

——, *Danger Zone : the Story of the Queenstown Command* (London, Rich & Cowan, 1934).

——, *Dardanelles Dilemma : the Story of the Naval Operations* (London, Rich & Cowan, 1935). Best on the purely naval operations that preceded the combined operations.

——, *Seas of Adventures : the Story of the Naval Operations in the Mediterranean, Adriatic, and Aegean* (London, Hurst & Blackett, 1936).

——, *Fighting the U-Boats* (London, Hurst & Blackett, 1942). 'The detailed story of the period covering the years 1914–16, examining one by one how, where, and why each enemy submarine was sunk.'

——, *Beating the U-Boats* (London, Hurst & Blackett, 1943). Completes the story begun in *Fighting the U-Boats*, showing the 'means and methods' by which the U-boats were defeated in 1917–18.

Childers, Erskine, *The Riddle of the Sands* (London, Smith, Elder, 1903; other editions and publishers, 1905, 1908, 1910). An imaginary story of secret German preparations for a sudden descent on

England while the Channel Fleet was decoyed away. Influential in its time.

Chivers, T. A., *The Anglo-Japanese Alliance, 1902–1911, with particular reference to British Naval and Military Opinion* (unpublished M.A. thesis, University of Wales, 1961).

Chrisman, Herman Henry, *Naval Operations in the Mediterranean during the Great War, 1914–1918* (unpublished Stanford University Ph.D. dissertation, 1931).

Churchill, Randolph S., *Winston Churchill* (London, Heinemann, 1966–67, 2 vols.). Vol. ii, with three 'companion' volumes of source materials (1969), covers the 1900–14 period. Martin Gilbert is writing Vol. iii, the war through 1916 (publication in 1971; two companion volumes, 1972), with iv to follow: 1917–22 (1973; three companion volumes, 1974). Randolph Churchill pretty much allowed the sources to speak for themselves; Gilbert will combine this approach with the more traditional professional one of commenting on and interpreting the sources.

Churchill, Winston S., *The World Crisis* (London, Butterworth, 1923–31, 5 vols. in 6), Vols. i–iii. Vol. i covers 1911 through 1914; ii, 1915; iii (in two parts), 1916–18. A skilful *apologia*, not always reliable, yet an absolutely indispensable source on the Navy during Churchill's time as First Lord, 1911–15. Vol. iii contains his account of Jutland, which was strongly influenced by the anti-Jellicoe bias of Vice-Admiral K. G. B. Dewar, who served as his consultant.

——, *Thoughts and Adventures* (London, Butterworth, 1932). Chapters on the U-boat war and the Dover barrage.

——, *Great Contemporaries* (London, Butterworth, 1937). Includes brief essays on Balfour and Fisher, the latter especially good.

'Civis' (Sir William White), *The State of the Navy in 1907: a Plea for Inquiry* (London, Smith, Elder, 1907). One of the most publicized broadsides against the Fisher reforms, by the onetime Director of Naval Construction. Most of the chapters had already appeared as letters in the *Spectator*.

Cobden Club, The, *The Burden of Armaments: a Plea for Retrenchment* (London, Unwin, 1905). A representative little-navy tract of the times.

Colvin, Ian, *The Life of Lord Carson* (London, Gollancz, 1932–6, 3 vols., Vol. i by Edward Majoribanks), Vol. iii. The authorized biography. Several chapters on Carson's period as First Lord of the Admiralty (December 1916–July 1917), which, though not extraordinary, take on special meaning because Colvin was able to see all of Carson's Admiralty papers. See *Carson MSS.*, above.

Corbett, Julian S., *Some Principles of Maritime Strategy* (London, Longmans, 1911). The major theoretical work of this prolific and highly talented naval historian. 'It represented Corbett's strategic ideas codified.' Not nearly as influential as Corbett would have liked.

Cork and Orrery, Admiral of the Fleet the Earl of, *My Naval Life, 1886–1941* (London, Hutchinson, 1942). Well described as 'a straightforward story, told with many touches of humour, of a straightforward naval life.'

Cousins, Geoffrey, *The Story of Scapa Flow* (London, Muller, 1965). A popular account.

Cowie, Captain J. S., *Mines, Minelayers and Minelaying* (London, Oxford, 1949). A very useful, not too technical, illustrated history of the subject by an officer with minelaying experience in both world wars.

Creswell, Commander John, *Naval Warfare: an Introductory Study* (2nd ed., London, Sampson, Low, 1942). A sound and thoughtful statement of the principles of naval warfare viewed in the light of historical experience.

Cronon, E. David (ed.), *The Cabinet Diaries of Josephus Daniels, 1913–1921* (Lincoln, Nebraska, University of Nebraska Press, 1963). Scattered laconic references to the Royal Navy by the wartime American Secretary of the Navy.

Cunningham of Hyndhope, Admiral of the Fleet Viscount, *A Sailor's Odyssey* (London, Hutchinson, 1951). Britain's number one sailor of the Second War joined the Navy in 1897. The pages on the Dardanelles operations in 1915, in which Cunningham took part with the destroyers, were of greatest interest for the purposes of the present work.

Custance, Admiral Sir Reginald, *The Ship of the Line in Battle* (London, Blackwood, 1912). A series of papers read at the Royal Naval War College, Portsmouth, 1910–12: an examination of the capital ship in action from Trafalgar to Tsushima, intended to 'disclose some military principles which should tend to focus thought, steady opinion, and even guide the naval architect in his designs.' Much of the point was to discredit the dreadnought type.

—— See 'Barfleur,' above.

Daniels, Josephus, *The Wilson Era: Years of War and After* (Chapel Hill, University of North Carolina Press, 1946). The memoirs of the U.S. Secretary of the Navy. Good for Anglo-American naval relations in 1917–18, the introduction of convoy, and the naval aspects of the Paris peace negotiations.

Davies, Vice-Admiral Richard Bell, *Sailor in the Air* (London, Peter

Davies, 1967). A very readable account of the formative years (and beyond) of British naval aviation by one of its pioneers.

Dawson, Captain Lionel, *Flotillas: a Hard-Lying Story* (London, Rich & Cowan, 1933). The interesting reminiscences (mainly 1900–18) of an officer much of whose career was spent in command of torpedo craft. The author is a raconteur *par excellence*. ('Hard Lying' is the term for the special allowance granted to men serving in destroyers, trawlers, and other small uncomfortable craft.)

——, *Gone for a Sailor* (London, Rich & Cowan, 1936). Another entertaining and informative volume of autobiography, this one on his early years in the Service, 1900–14.

——, *Sound of the Guns: Being an Account of the Wars and Service of Admiral Sir Walter Cowan* (Oxford, Pen-in-Hand, 1949). The well-written Service story of one of the most offensively-minded of naval officers, whose career spanned the period 1884–1945; best on Cowan in the Baltic hostilities after the First War.

De Chair, Admiral Sir Dudley, *The Sea is Strong* (ed. Somerset de Chair, London, Harrap, 1961). Except perhaps for the story of Jellicoe's dismissal in December 1917, this autobiography of an admiral who made his mark as Commander of the Northern Patrol in 1914–16 is not very revealing or interesting.

Dewar, Vice-Admiral K. G. B., *The Navy from Within* (London, Gollancz, 1939). This is an extremely important book on the Royal Navy in the first three decades of the twentieth century—chock full of information and insights, though excessively critical of the Establishment.

Doenitz, Admiral Karl, *Memoirs: Ten Years and Twenty Days* (London, Weidenfeld & Nicolson, 1959). A little on the U-boat campaign.

d'Ombrain, Nicholas, *The Military Departments and the Committee of Imperial Defence, 1902–1914: a Study of the Structural Problems of Defence Organisation* (unpublished Oxford D.Phil. dissertation, 1969). Of outstanding merit; based on a wealth of unpublished material. A revised version is being prepared for publication.

Domvile, Admiral Sir Barry, *By and Large* (London, Hutchinson, 1936). A book of reminiscences, best on the activities of the Harwich Force, in which the author, a gunnery officer, served during the entire war.

Domville-Fife, Charles W. (ed.), *Evolution of Sea Power* (London, Rich & Cowan, 1939). Chapters by various contributors on such large topics as anti-submarine warfare, the capital ship, etc., with many references to the experience of the First War.

Dorling, Captain Taprell, *Men O'War* (London, P. Allan, 1929). Five naval biographies, including two seamen of modern times, Fisher and Beresford.

——, See 'Taffrail,' below.

Dreyer, Admiral Sir Frederic, *The Sea Heritage: a Study of Maritime Warfare* (London, Museum Press, 1955). A wordy, badly organized study by Jellicoe's Flag-Captain in the First War—yet a valuable book for its interesting material on the pre-war and war periods. The Jutland material is the highlight.

Dugdale, Blanche E. C., *Arthur James Balfour, First Earl Balfour* (London, Hutchinson, 1936, 2 vols.). The authorized and still standard biography by his niece, though rather sketchy on Balfour's time as First Lord of the Admiralty.

Edwards, Lieutenant-Commander Kenneth, *We Dive at Dawn* (London, Rich & Cowan, 1939). A highly readable account of British submarine development before, and exploits during, the war.

Ehrman, John, *Cabinet Government and War, 1890-1940* (Cambridge, The University Press, 1958). The Lees-Knowles lectures delivered at Cambridge in 1957. A succinct and commendable account of the development of the higher organization for war, beginning with the antecedents of the C.I.D. in the 1890s. The first three of the four chapters carry the story through the First War.

Everitt, Don, *The K Boats* (London, Harrap, 1963). A harshly critical account of this class of British wartime (and early post-war) submarine. Contains much information but lacks balance.

Ewing, Alfred W., *The Man of Room 40: the Life of Sir Alfred Ewing* (London, Hutchinson, 1939). Chapters 8 and 9 concern his Admiralty work, 1902–14, as Director of Naval Education, and 1914–17, as the Head of the famed 'Room 40', the Navy's secret intelligence branch.

Fawcett, Lieutenant-Commander H. W., and Hooper, Lieutenant G. W. W. (eds.), *The Fighting at Jutland* (London, Macmillan, 1921). There is also an abridged edition (1921). Vivid personal narratives of the action by officers and men who were there, arranged chronologically. An invaluable record.

Fisher, Admiral of the Fleet Lord, *Memories* (London, Hodder & Stoughton, 1919). With the following title, the Admiral's explosive, disorganized memoirs: incidents, observations, anecdotes. Includes a chapter on the Dardanelles and another giving his views on a Naval War Staff.

——, *Records* (London, Hodder & Stoughton, 1919). The more valuable of the two volumes, dealing mostly with his policies.

Fraser, W. Lionel, *All to the Good* (London, Heinemann, 1963). Chapter

5, by this well-known London banker, contains memories of his service in Room 40.

Freiwald, Ludwig, *Last Days of the German Fleet* (London, Constable, 1932). A little book mainly on the collapse of discipline in the High Seas Fleet in the last days of the war; includes a description of the surrender of the flower of the Fleet and of the scuttling. The author was a seaman in the battleship *Nassau*.

Fremantle, Admiral Sir Sydney R., *My Naval Career, 1880–1928* (London, Hutchinson, 1949). One of the more informative of naval autobiographies, with excellent descriptions of leading personalities.

Frewen, Oswald, *Sailor's Soliloquy* (ed. G. P. Griggs, London, Hutchinson, 1961). Frewen's memoir of his early years in the Navy, 1887–1910, based on his diaries. A valuable and entertaining picture of the Navy in the era of the Fisher Revolution by a talented young officer.

Frost, Commander Holloway H., *The Battle of Jutland* (London, B. F. Stevens & Brown, 1936). Still the most complete secondary work on the battle, but hypercritical of British strategy and tactics and with a tendency to be wise after the event.

Gamble, C. F. Snowden, *The Air Weapon* (London, Oxford, 1931). The growth of British military aviation down to the outbreak of war. An excellent source on the beginnings of British naval (as well as military) aviation in Britain. (This was supposedly Vol. i; it was to have been followed by two others, carrying the story through 1929; they never appeared.)

Gaunt, Admiral Sir Guy, *The Yield of the Years: a Story of Adventure, Afloat and Ashore* (London, Hutchinson, 1940). A rambling account by the Naval Attaché in Washington, 1914–18; of only slight value.

Gayer, Lieutenant-Commander Albert, *Die deutschen U-Boote in ihrer Kriegführung, 1914–1918* (Berlin, Mittler, 1930). Four pamphlets; a primary source on the U-boats, by a U-boat flotilla commander, afterwards (1918) a department head in the U-boat Office of the Ministry of Marine.

Geddes, Baron, *The Forging of a Family* (London, Faber, 1952). Chapter XVI, 'Eric's Record'—Sir Eric Geddes, Controller, then First Lord of the Admiralty, 1917–18—includes a few pages on his Admiralty experience and a number of insights on the manner of man he was.

Gibson, Langhorne, and Harper, Vice-Admiral J. E. T., *The Riddle of Jutland* (London, Cassell, 1934). Intended for the general reading public; not free from bias.

Gibson, R. H., and Prendergast, Maurice, *The German Submarine War, 1914–1918* (2nd ed., London, Constable, 1931). The first full account, still standard, based on the latest sources then available. The tables in the appendices are especially useful.

Godfrey, Admiral John H., *The Naval Memoirs of Admiral J. H. Godfrey* (privately printed, 1964–6, 7 vols. in 10, copy in the Naval Library). His career in the Service spanned 1903–45. Several cuts above the usual naval reminiscences. Vols. i and ii carry the story into 1919. Particularly good on the Dardanelles in 1915 and the Mediterranean in 1917–18.

Gollin, Alfred M., *The Observer and J. L. Garvin, 1908–1914* (London, Oxford, 1960). Important for Fisher's relations with, and use of, the press, specifically, *The Observer*, through its Fisher-like Editor, Garvin.

——, *Proconsul in Politics: a Study of Lord Milner in Opposition and in Power* (London, Blond, 1964). Marginal; some material on Jellicoe and the introduction of convoy: the orthodox interpretation.

Goodenough, Admiral Sir William, *A Rough Record* (London, Hutchinson, 1943). The thoughts and reflections, as well as the autobiography, of the great cruiser commander of the First War.

Gordon, Donald C., *The Dominion Partnership in Imperial Defense, 1870–1914* (Baltimore, Johns Hopkins, and London, Oxford, 1965). The naval aspects of the partnership receive their due in this fine work based on a wealth of archival material, British, Canadian, and Australian.

Görlitz, Walter (ed.), *The Kaiser and His Court: the Diaries, Note Books and Letters of Admiral Georg Alexander von Müller, Chief of the Naval Cabinet, 1914–1918* (London, Macdonald, 1961). Valuable for the outlook of the German Naval High Command.

Graham, Gerald S., *The Politics of Naval Supremacy* (London, Oxford, 1966). The Wiles Lectures delivered at the University of Belfast by the Rhodes Professor of Imperial History at King's College, London. Chapter IV, on the 'Pax Britannica' of the nineteenth century, constitutes a superb background for a study of the Fisher Era.

Grant, Robert M., *U-Boats Destroyed* (London, Putnam, 1964). Essentially a succinct examination of the circumstances under which each of the 178 submarines was lost. Based on the German records, as is the sequel:

——, *U-Boat Intelligence, 1914–1918* (London, Putnam, 1969). Emphasizes the work of N.I.D. in defeating the U-boats, with a revised, more accurate table of 'U-boats sunk'.

Grenfell, Commander Russell, *The Art of the Admiral* (London, Faber,

1937). On principles of strategy and high command, with many references to the First War.

Grenfell, see 'T 124', below.

Gretton, Vice-Admiral Sir Peter, *Former Naval Person: Winston Churchill and the Royal Navy* (London, Cassell, 1968). An excellent study with fresh insights and some new material.

Grey, C. G., *Sea-Flyers* (London, Faber, 1942). An informal, disjointed, not always reliable book on naval aviation, with stress on the British experience, from pre-war years into the Second War, by an early and influential aviation journalist.

Grey of Fallodon, Viscount, *Twenty-Five Years, 1892–1916* (London, Hodder & Stoughton, 1925, 2 vols.). Includes material on pre-war Anglo-German relations, as viewed by the onetime Foreign Secretary (1905–16).

Gröner, Erich, *Die deutschen Kriegsschiffe, 1815–1945* (Munich, Lehmanns, 1966–7, 2 vols.), Vol. i. Vol. ii is on special ships, auxiliaries, etc. Authoritative compilation of statistics on German warships, liberally illustrated with sketches.

Guichard, Lieutenant Louis, *The Naval Blockade, 1914–1918* (London, Philip Allan, 1930). A simple and clear account of the Allied blockade by an officer in the Historical Section of the French Ministry of Marine.

Guinn, Paul, *British Strategy and Politics, 1914–1918* (London, Oxford, 1965). A scholarly examination of the politico-military factors which influenced British strategy and of the ideas and role played by the leading politicians, soldiers, and seamen. Much fuller on the military side.

Haldane, Viscount, *Before the War* (London, Cassell, 1920). The War Secretary of 1905–12. Includes his famous mission to Berlin in 1912.

——, *Richard Burdon Haldane: an Autobiography* (London, Hodder & Stoughton, 1929). Important references to naval matters in 1911–12: the naval staff problem, the Haldane Mission, though much of the latter had appeared in his earlier book.

Hale, Oron J., *Publicity and Diplomacy, with Special Reference to England and Germany, 1890–1914* (New York, Appleton–Century, 1940). A scholarly, still useful volume on Anglo-German relations.

Halpern, Paul G., *The Mediterranean Naval Situation, 1908–1914* (Cambridge, Mass., Harvard University Press, 1970). Examines the Mediterranean naval policies of all the Mediterranean Powers. Based on the British, French, German, Italian, and Austro-Hungarian archives.

——, (ed.), *The Keyes Papers*, Vol. i (to 1928) (London, Navy Records Society, 1972?).

Hamilton, General Sir Ian, *Gallipoli Diary* (London, Arnold, 1920, 2 vols.). The diary of the commander (until mid-October 1915) of the Allied forces on Gallipoli; a great deal on the British senior officers on the spot and on the Navy's role in the operations.

Hammond, J. L., *C. P. Scott of the Manchester Guardian* (rev. ed., London, Bell, 1934). The famous Editor was a Fisher partisan who worked hard during 1916 to get the Admiral back to the Admiralty. The story is outlined here.

Hampshire, A. Cecil, *The Phantom Fleet* (London, Kimber, 1960). These dummies—mocked-up merchant ships representing modern capital ships—make for an interesting story of maritime deception in both World Wars.

Hankey, Lord, *Government Control in War* (Cambridge, The University Press, 1945). The Lees-Knowles lectures of 1945, by one who knew better than anyone the inside working of the machinery for the higher direction of the First War. A small but valuable book. Chapters II and III concern the Fisher era.

——, *The Supreme Command* (London, Allen & Unwin, 1961, 2 vols.). Assistant Secretary of the C.I.D. (1908–12), then Secretary, and subsequently Secretary of the War Council and its wartime successors culminating in the War Cabinet, Hankey was in possession of every defence secret throughout this period (and indeed well beyond). These volumes, based on his wartime diaries and recollections, are far more valuable on the grand strategy and military sides, yet have many important references to naval matters.

——, *The Supreme Control at the Paris Peace Conference 1919* (London, Allen & Unwin, 1963). A sequel to the preceding title. The naval references are not as numerous as one could wish.

Hargreaves, Reginald, *The Narrow Seas* (London, Sidgwick and Jackson, 1959). A skilfully told story of the influence of the English Channel on British history.

Harper, Rear-Admiral J. E. T., *The Truth about Jutland* (London, Murray, 1927). A popular volume marred by excessive pro-Jellicoe bias.

Harris, Wilson, *J. A. Spender* (London, Cassell, 1946). The famed Editor of the *Westminster Gazette* was in frequent touch with Lord Fisher from 1904, and there are many references to him.

Hase, Commander Georg von, *Kiel and Jutland* (London, Skeffington, 1921). Jutland as seen through the eyes of the gunnery officer of the battle cruiser *Derfflinger*. A standard source.

Hashagen, Commander Ernst, *The Log of a U-Boat Commander* (London,

Putnam, 1931). One of the better 'inside' accounts of U-boat operations: tactics, problems, etc.

Hassall, Christopher, *Edward Marsh, Patron of the Arts: a Biography* (London, Longmans, 1959). Marsh was Churchill's Private Secretary, 1905–15. The volume contains a few glimpses of Churchill as First Lord.

Hezlet, Vice-Admiral Sir Arthur, *The Submarine and Sea Power* (London, Peter Davies, 1967). A thoughtful survey by a former Flag Officer (Submarines).

Hickling, Vice-Admiral Harold, *Sailor at Sea* (London, Kimber, 1965). An entertaining autobiography, featuring a valuable first-hand account of Coronel and the Falklands.

Higham, Robin, *The British Rigid Airship, 1908–1921* (London, Foulis, 1961). The best volume on the subject.

——, *Armed Forces in Peacetime: Britain, 1918–1940, a Case Study* (London, Foulis, 1962). 'One of the purposes of this book is to show that military history is not merely a study of battles, but that it is involved in and reflects . . . the whole fabric and life of the nation.' Chapter I is an interesting discussion of the transition from the Armistice to the peace settlement.

Hilbert, Lothar W., *The Role of Military and Naval Attachés in the British and German Service, with Particular Reference to Those at Berlin and London and Their Effect on Anglo-German Relations, 1871–1914* (unpublished Ph.D. dissertation, Cambridge University, 1954).

Hirst, Paymaster Commander Lloyd, *Coronel and After* (London, Peter Davies, 1934). An excellent source on Coronel and the Falklands; the author took part in both actions in the *Glasgow*.

Hislam, Percival A., *The North Sea Problem* (London, Holden & Hardingham, 1914). A little book that got much publicity: on 'the menace embodied in the extraordinary growth of German naval power' and the declining strength of the British Navy *vis-à-vis* the German. The author was a well-known naval journalist.

Horn, Daniel (ed.), *War, Mutiny and the Revolution in the German Navy: the World War I Diary of Seaman Richard Stumpf* (Brunswick, New Jersey, Rutgers University Press, 1967). A unique document, especially valuable for the vivid picture of the increasing boredom and demoralization, and the reasons thereof, in the High Seas Fleet in 1917–18.

Hough, Richard, *Dreadnought: a History of the Modern Battleship* (London, Michael Joseph, 1965). Illustrations, profiles, technical data, and running commentary. A useful supplement to Parkes.

——, *The Big Battleship: the Curious Career of H.M.S. Agincourt* (London,

Michael Joseph, 1966). American edition: *The Great Dreadnought : the Strange Story of H.M.S. Agincourt* (New York, Harper & Row, 1967). The well-told story of the fabulous onetime Brazilian, and then Turkish, dreadnought, taken over for the Royal Navy early in the war—the ship with the heaviest armament afloat in the war.

——, *The Pursuit of Admiral von Spee: a Study in Loneliness and Bravery* (London, Allen & Unwin, 1969). A well-balanced, dramatically told account of Coronel and the Falklands, mainly written from the German angle and with new material.

——, *First Sea Lord: an Authorised Biography of Admiral Lord Fisher* (London, Allen & Unwin, 1969). The Admiral is brought back to life in vivid fashion. Some new material on Fisher's personal life.

Hovgaard, William, *Modern History of Warships* (London, Spon, 1920). Not dated despite its age. All types of warships in all the navies of any consequence in the ironclad age; also, chapters on design and construction of hull, machinery, ordnance, mines and torpedoes, and protection. The author was Professor of Naval Design and Construction, Massachusetts Institute of Technology.

Hoy, H. C., *40 O.B.* (London, Hutchinson, 1932). Anecdotal. Hoy was private secretary to Admiral Hall, the D.N.I., but was not himself a worker in Room 40.

Hubatsch, Walther, *Die Åra Tirpitz: Studien zur deutschen Marinepolitik, 1890–1918* (Göttingen, Musterschmidt, 1955). Indispensable to an understanding of the German Navy in the Fisher Era. Professor Hubatsch is undoubtedly Germany's leading authority on German naval history.

——, *Der Admiralstab und die obersten Marinebehörden in Deutschland, 1848–1945* (Frankfurt-on-Main, Bernard & Graefe, 1958). The evolution and role of the German Admiralty Staff.

Hughes, E. A., *The Royal Naval College, Dartmouth* (London, Winchester Publications, 1950). The history of the Navy's public school since its inception as part of the Selborne–Fisher Scheme, sympathetically told by a long-time member of the staff.

Hurd, Sir Archibald, *Who Goes There?* (London, Hutchinson, 1942). Mostly about some of the First Lords and leading Admirals of the Fisher Era, above all, McKenna, Churchill, Fisher, and Jellicoe. The author was a top-flight naval journalist of the time who afterwards became the Official Historian of the merchant navy in the war.

Hyde, H. Montgomery, *Carson* (London, Heinemann, 1953). Carson's time at the Admiralty in 1917 is ably summarized; some new material.

Irving, Lieutenant-Commander John, *Coronel and the Falklands* (London, Philpot, 1927). The first, and still useful, full account in English of the two actions.

——, *Jutland* (Kimber, 1966). Graphic account, based on the standard sources, of the narrative of the battle by one who was there.

James, David, *Lord Roberts* (London, Hollis & Carter, 1954). There are passing references to pre-war naval affairs in this fine book.

James, Robert Rhodes, *Gallipoli* (London, Batsford, 1965). The outstanding work on the campaign—beautifully written, perceptive, though better on the operation itself (more particularly the military side) than on its genesis.

James, Admiral Sir William, *Blue Water and Green Fields* (London, Methuen, 1940). Previously published attractive sketches and essays in naval history, including the Heligoland Bight action of 1914, the escape of the *Goeben*, and Jutland.

——, *Admiral Sir William Fisher* (London, Macmillan, 1943). The authorized, if rather thin, biography (the subject left few papers) of 'W.W.,' one of the outstanding officers of the inter-war period, whose reputation was firmly established as Director of the Anti-Submarine Division at the Admiralty, 1917–18.

——, *The Sky Was Always Blue* (London, Methuen, 1951). The memoirs of a senior naval officer, 'a refreshing oasis amid the arid desert of most admirals' memoirs.' The author joined the Service in 1895 and held a wide variety of interesting appointments, not least of them the headship of 'Room 40' in 1917–18.

——, *The Eyes of the Navy: a Biographical Study of Admiral Sir Reginald Hall* (London, Methuen, 1955). American edition: *The Code Breakers of Room 40: the Story of Admiral Sir Reginald Hall* (New York, St. Martin's Press, 1956). A most readable authorized account of the career of Hall, focusing, naturally, on his remarkable performance as D.N.I. in 1914–18.

——, *A Great Seaman: the Life of Admiral of the Fleet Sir Henry F. Oliver* (London, Witherby, 1956). A short authorized biography of an almost legendary character whose Service career spanned the years 1878–1927. Based on the Admiral's post-war recollections (typescript).

Jameson, Rear-Admiral Sir William, *The Fleet that Jack Built: Nine Men Who Made a Modern Navy* (London, Hart-Davis, 1962). A. K. Wilson, Beresford, Fisher, Scott, Jellicoe, Beatty, Tyrwhitt, Keyes, and an earlier admiral, Keppel, are treated sympathetically in a series of essays on their professional careers intended for the general reader. Fisher, the 'Jack' in the title, receives the most attention.

——, *The Most Formidable Thing* (London, Hart-Davis, 1965). A splendid account of the submarine from its earliest days to the end of World War I, thoroughly researched and clearly written. The author was himself a submariner. Particularly good on the U-boat campaign of the First War.

——, *Submariners V. C.* (London, Hart-Davis, 1962). On the pioneers of submarine warfare in 1914–18; particularly interesting for the exploits of Holbrook, Boyle, and Nasmith in navigating the Dardanelles in 1915.

Jane, Fred T., *Heresies of Sea Power* (London, Longmans, 1906). The principles of sea power as viewed in the light of naval history. The book was widely read and discussed in the Service when it first appeared—the 'Guerre de Course' and 'The Invasion of England' chapters, in particular,

——, *The British Battle Fleet* (2nd ed., London, Library Press, 1915, 2 vols.), particularly Vol. ii. Presents 'the exact state of our Navy when the fighting began.' *Matériel* mainly.

Jellicoe, Admiral of the Fleet Earl, *The Grand Fleet, 1914–16: Its Creation, Development and Work* (London, Cassell, 1919). Not a literary masterpiece, yet a most important primary source. 'The narrative necessarily includes an account of the organisation and development of the Grand Fleet, and its bases . . . and the manner in which the changing conditions of naval warfare were met . . .' Jutland receives full attention.

——, *The Crisis of the Naval War* (London, Cassell, 1920). The U-boat threat of 1917 and how it was met during Jellicoe's year as First Sea Lord. 'At that time, however,' Jellicoe wrote in the introduction to the following title, 'it was not desirable to give full details of our methods, and all the information which we now [1934] possess on the subject was not then available.'

——, *The Submarine Peril* (London, Cassell, 1934). An authoritative story of the anti-submarine campaign in the critical year 1917, including a consideration of why the introduction of convoy was delayed so long. Written in part as a reply to Lloyd George's charges (*War Memoirs*, Vol. iii) that the Admiralty had dragged their feet and had to be pushed into convoy—by the Prime Minister.

Jenkins, Roy, *Asquith* (London, Collins, 1964). An outstanding life, based on the Asquith Papers, and containing many references to naval matters. Asquith's weaknesses as a war leader are not fully brought out.

Jerrold, Douglas, *The Royal Naval Division* (London, Hutchinson, 1923). A chronicle of the splendid work done by the 'Naval Division.'

Johnson, Franklyn A., *Defence by Committee: the British Committee of Imperial Defence, 1885–1959* (London, Oxford, 1960). The first detailed study of the C.I.D. A splendid work, even though most of the pertinent records were not available and the author tends to magnify the pre-war role of the C.I.D.

Kahn, David, *The Codebreakers* (New York, Macmillan, 1967). Chapter 9, on Room 40, has made a skilful use of the published sources.

Kemp, Lieutenant-Commander P. K., *H.M. Submarines* (London, Jenkins, 1952). A pithy, well-written history. The best sections are devoted to the deeds of British submarines in the two World Wars. The destroyers are treated similarly in:

——, *H.M. Destroyers* (1956). The origins, development, and role of the destroyer through the Second War. Includes three good chapters on the destroyers at Jutland.

——, *Fleet Air Arm* (London, Jenkins, 1954). A clearly told, if brief, history of naval aviation from its beginnings in 1911 through World War II.

—— (ed.), *The Papers of Admiral Sir John Fisher* (London, Navy Records Society, 1960–4, 2 vols.). The principal papers documenting the Fisher Revolution of 1904–6.

Kenworthy, Lieutenant-Commander J. M. (Lord Strabolgi), *Sailors, Statesmen—and Others: an Autobiography* (London, Rich & Cowan, 1933). A wealth of information on the Navy of 1901–19, when the author, who was one of the 'Young Turks' during the war, served; strongly biased and must be used with care.

——, *The Real Navy* (London, Hutchinson, 1932). All about the Navy —discipline, the daily round, bases, etc.; some naval reminiscences; and two chapters on lessons of the war.

Kerr, Admiral Mark, *Land, Sea, and Air: Reminiscences of Mark Kerr* (London, Longmans, 1927). A chatty mixture of reminiscences and observations. Best on his experiences as commander of the British squadron in the Adriatic, 1916–17. The author was in the Navy from 1877 till 1918.

——, *The Navy in My Time* (London, Rich & Cowan, 1933). A potpourri of his wartime experiences—again, best on the Adriatic —and of the changes that had taken place in the Navy since he joined.

——, *Prince Louis of Battenberg, Admiral of the Fleet* (London, Longmans, 1934). 'This book does not profess to be a complete life of Prince Louis, but only a series of sketches . . .' The author was severely handicapped by the apparent paucity of papers left by Prince Louis. See *Battenberg MSS.*, above, p. 349.

Keyes, Admiral Sir Roger, *The Naval Memoirs of Admiral of the Fleet Sir*

Roger Keyes (London, Butterworth, 1934–5, 2 vols.). Vol. i deals with 1910–15: its underlying theme, it has been well said, is 'If only de Robeck had taken my advice'; ii, with 1916–18. Based on his letters to his wife. Full of interesting material and strong opinions. A useful corrective to Bacon's *Dover Patrol*.

——, *Adventures Ashore and Afloat* (London, Harrap, 1939). Memoirs dealing with the earlier part of his career, ending in 1905.

—— (Admiral of the Fleet Lord Keyes), *Amphibious Warfare and Combined Operations* (Cambridge, The University Press, 1943). The Lees-Knowles lectures of 1943. Two of the chapters are on the Dardanelles and Zeebrugge operations.

King-Hall, Admiral Sir Herbert, *Naval Memories and Traditions* (London, Hutchinson, 1926). His naval service spanned the years 1874–1919. Oddments of interest, especially for 1906–12.

King-Hall, Louise (ed.), *Sea Saga: Being the Naval Diaries of Four Generations of the King-Hall Family* (London, Gollancz, 1935). Selections from the diaries of four naval members of her family covering the period from Trafalgar through World War I. The last segment, the diary and letters of Commander Stephen King-Hall, 1906–19, is the one most germane to the Royal Navy in the Fisher Era.

King-Hall, Commander Stephen, *A North Sea Diary, 1914–1918* (London, Newnes, 1936). Originally published under the title *A Naval Lieutenant, 1914–1918*, by 'Étienne' (London, Methuen, 1919). This and the following title are most interesting for the accounts of the main North Sea actions of the war, in all of which the author's ship, the light cruiser *Southampton*, was present.

——, *My Naval Life, 1906–1929* (London, Faber, 1952).

Langmaid, Captain Kenneth, *The Sea Raiders* (London, Jarrolds, 1963). A condensed account of the operations of the German surface raiders in both wars.

——, *The Approaches Are Mined!* (London, Jarrolds, 1965). The development of sea-mining and the role played by this weapon in the two World Wars.

Laurens, Commander Adolphe, *Histoire de la guerre sous-marine allemande (1914–1918)* (Paris, Société d'Éditions Géographiques, Maritimes et Coloniales, 1930). This vintage account retains some value.

Le Fleming, H. M., *Warships of World War I* (London, Ian Allan [1962?]). A reference volume: the basic data on all the British and German ships; illustrated.

Legg, Stuart, *Jutland* (London, Hart-Davis, 1966). Well-edited eyewitness accounts, British and German.

Le Queux, William, *The Invasion of 1910: With a Full Account of the Siege of London* (London, Eveleigh Nash, 1906). An imaginary story of a German invasion intended to focus national attention on 'England's grave peril,' her 'utter unpreparedness for war.' Created quite a stir.

Leslie, Sir Shane, *Long Shadows* (London, Murray, 1966). These memoirs contain a perceptive sketch of Beatty and of his reactions to Jutland.

Lewis, Michael, *England's Sea-Officers: the Story of the Naval Profession* (London, Allen & Unwin, 1939). Useful for 'background' and for the discussion of the Fisher–Selborne reform of naval education.

——, *The Navy of Britain* (London, Allen & Unwin, 1948). The main thrust of this classic work (a history of the Royal Navy rather than a naval history of Britain) is pre-twentieth century; a useful 'background' volume for the twentieth century, though it touches on the Fisher Era in many places.

Lloyd George, David, *War Memoirs of David Lloyd George* (London, Nicholson & Watson, 1933–6, 6 vols.). Most of the naval references are in Vols. iii and iv, the former especially: introduction of the convoy system.

——, *The Truth About the Peace Treaties* (London, Gollancz, 1938, 2 vols.). American edition: *Memoirs of the Peace Conference* (New Haven, Conn., Yale University Press, 1939, 2 vols.). Not much on the naval side.

Long, Viscount, *Memories* (London, Hutchinson, 1923). Chapter XVII, on Long as First Lord of the Admiralty (1918–21), does not say much.

Longmore, Air Chief Marshal Sir Arthur, *From Sea to Sky, 1910–1945* (London, Geoffrey Bles, 1946). The memoirs of a pioneer of naval aviation: a valuable source for the first years of the R.N.A.S.

Low, Archibald M., *Mine and Countermine* (London, Hutchinson, 1940). A popular history of the mine by a scientist.

Lowe, Peter, *Great Britain and Japan, 1911–1915: A Study of British Far Eastern Policy* (London, Macmillan, 1969). A thoroughly researched monograph with some discussion of the naval side of the alliance, mainly in the context of Imperial relations and the outbreak of the war.

Lowis, Commander Geoffrey L., *Fabulous Admirals and Some Naval Fragments* (London, Putnam, 1957). A treasure trove of yarns about colourful naval personalities of the first decades of the century.

Lumby, E. W. R. (ed.), *Papers Relating to Naval Policy and Operations in the Mediterranean, 1911–1915* (London, Navy Records Society, 1971?).

Macintyre, Captain Donald, *Jutland* (London, Evans, 1957). A lucid popular work, based on standard sources. Likewise for the following titles.

——, *The Thunder of the Guns: a Century of Battleships* (London, Muller, 1959). A general account of the modern battleship in action: American Civil War through the Second War.

——, *Wings of Neptune: the Story of Naval Aviation* (London, Peter Davies, 1963). A general history which includes a concise summary of the pioneer days of the R.N.A.S. prior to and during the First War.

Mackay, Ruddock F., *Fisher of Kilverstone* (Oxford, Clarendon Press, 1971?).

McKenna, Stephen, *Reginald McKenna, 1863–1943* (London, Eyre & Spottiswoode, 1948). The authorized life of the First Lord of the Admiralty of 1908–11. Satisfactory, no more, on naval affairs.

Magnus, Philip, *Kitchener: Portrait of an Imperialist* (London, Murray, 1958). An excellent biography of the formidable Field Marshal whose relations with the sailors in 1914–16 were generally not happy.

Manning, Frederic, *The Life of Sir William White* (London, Murray, 1923). The penultimate chapter in this biography of the Director of Naval Construction, 1885–1902, is on the dreadnought controversy of 1906 ff.

Manning, Captain T. D., *The British Destroyer* (London, Putnam, 1961). The reference book on the subject for those who cannot afford, or do not have ready access to, the much more detailed work by March, below.

Mantoux, Paul Joseph, *Les Délibérations du Conseil des Quatre (24 Mars–28 Juin 1919)* (Paris, Éditions du Centre National de la Recherche Scientifique, 1955, 2 vols.). The only source for the minutes of a number of the Council of Four meetings.

March, Edgar J., *British Destroyers, 1892–1953* (London, Seeley Service, 1966). A veritable encyclopedia and the classic work on the subject.

Marder, Arthur J., *British Naval Policy, 1880–1905: the Anatomy of British Sea Power* (London, Putnam, 1941). American edition: *The Anatomy of British Sea Power: a History of British Naval Policy in the Pre-Dreadnought Era, 1880–1905* (New York, Knopf, 1940).

——, *Portrait of an Admiral: the Life and Papers of Sir Herbert Richmond* (London, Cape, 1952). The papers of the brilliant, acerbic

Richmond—diary entries mainly, but also some correspondence and memoranda which are woven into the diary—cover the years 1909–20.

Marder, *Fear God and Dread Nought : the Correspondence of Admiral of the Fleet Lord Fisher of Kilverstone* (London, Cape, 1952–9, 3 vols.). The selected and annotated correspondence with biographical essays prefacing each section.

——, *From the Dreadnought to Scapa Flow : the Royal Navy in the Fisher Era, 1904–1919* (London, Oxford, 1961–70, 5 vols.). Vol. i, 1904–14; ii, the war to eve of Jutland; iii, Jutland to end of 1916; iv, 1917; v (the present volume), 1918–19.

Maurice, Major-General Sir Frederick, *Haldane* (London, Faber, 1937–39, 2 vols.). An uneven biography of the great War Secretary whose concerns, as in the 'Haldane Mission' of 1912, touched on naval problems in the pre-war years.

——, *Lessons of Allied Co-Operation : Naval, Military and Air, 1914–1918* (London, Oxford, 1942). A valuable study of the co-ordination, or lack of co-ordination, in the Allied war effort.

Michelsen, Vice-Admiral Andreas, *Der U-Bootskrieg, 1914–1918* (Leipzig, Koehler, 1925). The author was Senior Officer, U-boats, June 1917 till the end of the war, in succession to Bauer.

Middlemas, Keith, *Command the Far Seas : a Naval Campaign of the First World War* (London, Hutchinson, 1961). The dramatic story of the German surface raiders of 1914–15 and how they were disposed of. The *Goeben*, Coronel, and the Falklands are spotlighted. The story is well told, but with a number of errors in technical matters and without much new material.

Milne, Admiral Sir A. Berkeley, *The Flight of the 'Goeben' and the 'Breslau'* (London, Eveleigh Nash, 1921). Milne's unconvincing *apologia*.

Monger, George, *The End of Isolation : British Foreign Policy, 1900–1907* (London, Nelson, 1963). Draws on considerable new unpublished sources; naval problems enter the story, but, principally, this volume is of value for the diplomatic background.

Moon, Howard, *The Invasion of the United Kingdom : Public Controversy and Official Planning, 1888–1918* (unpublished University of London Ph.D. dissertation, 1968).

Moore, E. Marjorie, *Adventure in the Royal Navy : the Life and Letters of Admiral Sir Arthur William Moore* (published privately, Liverpool, 1964). The life of her uncle, Admiral Sir Arthur Moore (1847–1934), who entered the Royal Navy in 1860 and retired in 1912. Moore's own account, written in 1932, supplemented by some of his correspondence and by stories and other material he gave to the author at various times.

Moore, Major W. Geoffrey, *Early Bird* (London, Putnam, 1963). The absorbing recollections of a R.N.A.S. flight-commander in the First War; especially interesting for the development of flying in aircraft carriers.

Moorehead, Alan, *Gallipoli* (Hamish Hamilton, 1956). Many (on the whole minor) inaccuracies and superseded by James as *the* volume on the whole campaign, but remains a standard work if only for the extraordinary skill with which the story is told.

Morison, Elting E., *Admiral Sims and the Modern American Navy* (Boston, Mass., Houghton Mifflin, 1942). Authorized scholarly biography, important for 1917–18.

——, *Men, Machines, and Modern Times* (Cambridge, Mass., M.I.T. Press, 1966). Chapter 2, 'Gunfire at Sea: a Case Study of Innovation,' though concerned with the United States Navy in the early twentieth century, contributes importantly to an understanding of the opposition to the Fisher revolution.

Mountevans, Admiral Lord, *Adventurous Life* (London, Hutchinson, 1946). The breezy autobiography of a rather flamboyant officer —'Evans of the *Broke*'; best on the Dover Patrol and the unforgettable *Broke* action.

Munro, Captain D. J., *Scapa Flow : a Naval Retrospect* (London, Sampson Low, 1932). Dull reminiscences of a King's Harbour Master who had much to do with improving Scapa Flow's wartime defences. More interesting is the sequel:

——, *Convoys, Blockades and Mystery Towers* (London, Sampson Low [1932?]). War reminiscences, 1917–18, largely concerned with his experiences as a Commodore of Convoy.

Murray, Lady (Oswyn), *The Making of a Civil Servant: Sir Oswyn Murray, G.C.B., Secretary of the Admiralty, 1917–1936* (London, Methuen, 1940). A not entirely satisfactory life of probably the most brilliant of the Permanent Secretaries of the Admiralty in modern times. Weak on the workings and organization of the Admiralty.

Nicolson, Harold, *King George the Fifth: His Life and Reign* (London, Constable, 1952). The authorized life: a number of interesting references from the Royal Archives to naval personalities and events, pre-war and wartime.

Nish, Ian H., *The Anglo-Japanese Alliance: the Diplomacy of Two Island Empires, 1894–1907* (London, The Athlone Press, 1966). Good on the naval facets of the Alliance and its 1905 renewal.

North, John, *Gallipoli: the Fading Vision* (London, Faber, 1936). The first of the more detailed accounts; well-written, highly critical;

primarily concerned with the purely military operations. Superseded by James.

Olson, Mancur, Jr., *The Economics of Wartime Shortage: a History of British Food Supplies in the Napoleonic War and in World Wars I and II* (Durham, North Carolina, Duke University Press, 1963). Chapter 4 deals effectively with the successful British attempts to circumvent the U-boat blockade.

Owen, Frank, *Tempestuous Journey: Lloyd George, His Life and Times* (London, Hutchinson, 1954). A thoroughly unsatisfactory life, though the author had access to the Lloyd George Papers.

Oxford and Asquith, Earl of, *Memories and Reflections, 1852–1927* (London, Cassell, 1928, 2 vols.). Vol. ii. Most of the useful material is indexed under 'Fisher' and 'Churchill.'

Padfield, Peter, *Aim Straight: a Biography of Admiral Sir Percy Scott* (London, Hodder & Stoughton, 1966). The only full-length study of the officer who, with Fisher, was primarily responsible for the pre-war gunnery revolution. Much new material.

Papers Relating to the Foreign Relations of the United States. The Paris Peace Conference, 1919. (Washington, D.C., United States Government Printing Office, 1942–7, 13 vols.) See above, p. 364, for a note on contents.

Parkes, Oscar, *British Battleships* (rev. ed., London, Seeley Service, 1966). The monumental and classic work on the subject with a vast array of plans, diagrams, photographs, and an excellent text.

Pastfield, Rev. John L., *New Light on Jutland* (London, Heinemann, 1933). A valuable little booklet concerned mainly with the technical aspects of the battle: armour, gunnery, etc.

Patterson, A. Temple (ed.), *The Jellicoe Papers* (London, Navy Records Society, 1966–8, 2 vols.). An ably edited selection of the Admiral's correspondence, mainly from the Beatty Papers and his papers in the British Museum and the Admiralty records in the P.R.O. Vol. i carries through Jutland.

——, *Jellicoe: a Biography* (London, Macmillan, 1969). A very competent study that makes good use of primary sources.

Pears, Commander Randolph, *British Battleships, 1892–1957* (London, Putnam, 1957). An illustrated popular history of the capital ship. Inferior in every way to Oscar Parkes.

Pelly, Admiral Sir Henry, *300,000 Sea Miles: an Autobiography* (London, Chatto & Windus, 1938). Most valuable for the material on the battle cruiser *Tiger* in the First War (through Jutland), whose captain Pelly was.

Penn, Commander Geoffrey, *'Up Funnel, Down Screw!' The Story of the*

Naval Engineer (London, Hollis & Carter, 1955). A carefully researched and exceptionally well-written volume on the engineering branch, the engineer's role and status, from the 1820s till recent years.

——, *Snotty : the Story of the Midshipman* (London, Hollis & Carter, 1957). Particularly good on the Selborne–Fisher Scheme and subsequent developments.

Petrie, Sir Charles, *Walter Long and His Times* (London, Hutchinson, 1936). The penultimate chapter is concerned with Long's time as First Lord of the Admiralty (January 1919–February 1921). Not very revealing.

Pitt, Barrie, *Zeebrugge* (London, Cassell, 1958). A lively popular work (as is the following title), written from a decidedly pro-Keyes point of view and claiming more from the results of the Zeebrugge raid than the facts warrant.

——, *Coronel and Falkland* (London, Cassell, 1960). American edition: *Revenge at Sea* (Stein & Day, 1964). Thorough use of the standard printed sources.

Pochhammer, Captain Hans, *Before Jutland: Admiral von Spee's Last Voyage* (London, Jarrolds, 1931). The Coronel and Falklands actions as described by the First Officer of the *Gneisenau*, who was one of the few German survivors at the Falklands.

Pohl, Admiral Hugo von, *Aus Aufzeichnungen und Briefen während der Kriegzeit* (Berlin, Karl Siegismund, 1920). A slight volume of wartime letters of the second of the four Cs.-in-C. of the wartime High Seas Fleet.

Pollen, Arthur Hungerford, *The Navy in Battle* (London, Chatto & Windus, 1918). American edition: *The British Navy in Battle* (New York, Doubleday, Page, 1918). Pollen was a well-known naval journalist, and this narrative of the Royal Navy in action (through the Zeebrugge operation of 1918), following introductory chapters on principles of sea power, naval *matériel*, etc., is of interest as revealing how much, or how little, was known about the principal actions in 1918. Should be used with extreme caution, particularly for Jutland.

Potter, E. B., and Nimitz, Fleet Admiral Chester W. (eds.), *Sea Power: a Naval History* (New York, Prentice-Hall, 1960). A conventional but useful narrative of the naval actions in World War I.

Pound, Reginald, *Evans of the Broke* (London, Oxford, 1963). A first-class biography of the adventurous and rather flamboyant Admiral Lord Mountevans. The famed destroyer clash in April 1917, from which Evans got his popular sobriquet, is a highlight of the volume.

Pound and Harmsworth, Geoffrey, *Northcliffe* (London, Cassell, 1959). Thin on naval references, which is a pity: Northcliffe's newspapers played a considerable role in various naval agitations.

Preston, Richard A., *Canada and 'Imperial Defense': a Study of the Origins of the British Commonwealth's Defense Organization, 1867–1919* (Durham, North Carolina, Duke University Press, 1967). An exhaustive analysis of the evolution of Dominion (and later, Commonwealth) co-operation in defence, stressing Canada and including a perceptive treatment of the naval facets.

Puleston, Captain William D. (U.S.N.), *High Command in the World War* (London, Scribner's, 1934). 'My effort has been to reveal the methods employed by the High Command to carry out the policies of the statesmen of the countries concerned. That is, to develop first the policies of the statesmen and second the strategy and grand tactics of the admirals and generals.' Not very revealing on the naval side.

Raeder, Grand-Admiral Erich, *My Life* (Annapolis, Maryland, U.S. Naval Institute, 1960). Condensed from Raeder's *Mein Leben* (Tübingen, Schlichtenmayer, 1956–7, 2 vols.). Good on naval personalities, the German side of the main actions in the North Sea, and unrestricted submarine warfare.

Ranft, Bryan (ed.), *Defence of Trade, 1914–18* (London, Navy Records Society, no date fixed).

Rayleigh. Lord, *The Life of Sir J. J. Thomson* (Cambridge, The University Press, 1942). Thomson, the distinguished scientist, was a member of the main committee of the Board of Invention and Research, whose Chairman was Lord Fisher. A few bits on Fisher and the B.I.R.

Repington, Lieutenant-Colonel Charles à Court, *Vestigia* (London, Constable, 1919). The last three chapters ('Blue Water and Invasion,' 'The Kaiser's Letter to Lord Tweedmouth,' 'Storm Warnings') contain naval material on the pre-war years.

——, *The First World War, 1914–18* (London, Constable, 1920, 2 vols.). The wartime experiences and reflections of *The Times* Military Correspondent, as seen through his diaries. Many references to naval affairs.

Reuter, Vice-Admiral Ludwig von, *Scapa Flow: the Account of the Greatest Scuttling of All Time* (London, Hurst & Blackett, 1940). The thought-provoking story of an unrepentant sinner, the commander of the interned fleet who gave the order to scuttle.

Richmond, Admiral Sir Herbert W., *National Policy and Naval Strength and Other Essays* (London, Longmans, 1928). This and the following volume include thoughtful observations on various aspects of the war at sea, 1914–18.

——, *Sea Power in the Modern World* (London, Bell, 1934).

——, *Statesmen and Sea Power* (London, Oxford, 1946). The author's aim was to indicate 'the manner in which the statesmen of this country have dealt with this matter of sea power during the last three and a half to four centuries.' A cogent, if necessarily brief, treatment of the pre-war and First War period: continental warfare *v.* the full use of sea power, etc.

Riddell, Lord, *Lord Riddell's War Diary, 1914–1918* (London, Nicholson & Watson, 1933). This and the following title contain many references to naval affairs and personalities. Riddell was a press lord close to Lloyd George.

——, *More Pages from My Diary, 1908–1914* (London, Country Life, 1934).

——, *Lord Riddell's Intimate Diary of the Peace Conference and After, 1918–1923* (London, Gollancz, 1933). Just a few naval references, mostly on the war at sea.

Robertson, Field-Marshal Sir William, *Soldiers and Statesmen, 1914–1918* (London, Cassell, 1926, 2 vols.). A few bits and pieces on the naval side of the war.

Robertz, Heinrich H., *Die deutsch-englischen Flottenbesprechungen im Sommer 1908* (Bonn, Dümmlers, 1939). A detailed study written entirely from printed sources.

Robinson, Douglas H., *The Zeppelin in Combat: a History of the German Naval Airship Division, 1912–1918* (rev. ed., London, Foulis, 1966). The standard work on the subject, which makes full use of German sources.

Rodman, Admiral Hugh, *Yarns of a Kentucky Admiral* (Indianapolis, Indiana, Bobbs-Merrill, 1928). The light memoirs of the Commander of the American battle squadron attached to the Grand Fleet.

Roskill, Captain S. W., *Naval Policy between the Wars* (London, Collins, 1968), Vol. i. Badly organized and something of a jungle of facts in places, yet an indispensable work for its extensive use of British and American source material and its shrewd judgements. The Armistice period is dealt with in the first seven chapters, *passim.*

——, *H.M.S. Warspite* (London, Collins, 1957). A model ship biography —of all seven 'Warspites' (1596–1947), the last of which, especially her service at Jutland, is featured.

——, *The Strategy of Sea Power* (London, Collins, 1962). Based on the Lees-Knowles Lectures (1961), this little volume on the development and application of the principles of sea power is a classic. The summing up of the naval aspects of the First War is done particularly well.

Roskill, (ed.), *Papers relating to the Naval Air Service, 1908–1918* (London, Navy Records Society, 1969). A second volume (no date fixed) will have the papers to 1939.

——, *Hankey: Man of Secrets* (London, Collins, 1970), Vol. i. Carries through the war. The authorized biography of the Secretary of the War Cabinet.

Ruge, Vice-Admiral Friedrich, *Scapa Flow 1919: Das Ende der deutschen Flotte* (Oldenburg, Stalling, 1969). The author, a junior destroyer officer in the interned fleet, tells a most interesting story, even if there is little that is new.

Rutter, Owen, *Red Ensign: a History of Convoy* (London, Robert Hale, 1942). Exactly what the title indicates; well done.

Salter, Lord, *Memoirs of a Public Servant* (London, Faber, 1961). Includes chapters on the 1917–18 experiences of the Director of Ship Requisitioning, touching on the introduction of convoy and related matters.

Samson, Air Commodore Charles R., *Fights and Flights* (London, Benn, 1930). The wartime memoirs of a naval aviation pioneer. Particularly good for the Dardanelles in 1915.

Scheer, Admiral Reinhard, *Germany's High Sea Fleet in the World War* (London, Cassell, 1920). The informative complement to Jellicoe's *The Grand Fleet*.

Schilling, Warner R., *Admirals and Foreign Policy, 1913–1919* (unpublished Yale University Ph.D. dissertation, 1953). A superior dissertation, based on such unpublished materials as the American naval records and the Benson, Daniels, and Woodrow Wilson Papers. The last five chapters (VI–IX) are concerned with the Armistice period and feature the Anglo-American naval confrontation in relation to the German peace settlement. A revised and expanded study making use of much new archival material is nearing completion. Tentative title: *Admirals and Foreign Policy, 1913–1921* (New York, Columbia University Press, 1971?).

Schofield, Vice-Admiral B. B., *British Sea Power in the Twentieth Century* (London, Batsford, 1967). Includes a résumé of 1914–18 strategy.

Schoultz, Commodore G. von, *With the British Battle Fleet: War Recollections of a Russian Naval Officer* (London, Hutchinson, 1925). Gossipy recollections of the Russian Attaché to the Grand Fleet, 1915–18. A valuable source, if used with some caution.

Schubert, Paul, and Gibson, Langhorne, *Death of a Fleet, 1917–1919* (London, Hutchinson, 1933). A good popular account of the High Seas Fleet, from the decline in discipline in the latter part of the war to the scuttling at Scapa.

Schurman, D. M., *The Education of a Navy: the Development of British Naval Strategic Thought, 1867–1914* (London, Cassell, 1965). Excellent, analytical chapters on the Colomb brothers (Captain Sir John, R.M.A., and Vice-Admiral Philip), Mahan, Laughton, Richmond, and Corbett, with an assessment of their contributions to naval history and British strategy.

——, *Sir Julian Corbett and the Royal Navy* (1970?). An authorized biography, based on the Corbett papers.

Scott, J. D., *Vickers: a History* (London, Weidenfeld & Nicolson, 1962). An interesting volume on the operations of the mammoth armament manufacturers, making use of new and authoritative material. Many references to naval design and construction before and during the First War.

Seymour, Charles (ed.), *The Intimate Papers of Colonel House* (Boston, Mass., Houghton Mifflin, 1928, 4 vols.), Vol. iv. Good for naval material in the Armistice period.

Seymour, Lady, *Commander Ralph Seymour, R.N.* (Glasgow, The University Press, 1926). A memoir of her son, Beatty's ill-starred Signal Officer during the war. Contains a number of Seymour's wartime letters.

Shankland, Peter, *The Phantom Flotilla* (London, Collins, 1968). A colourful account of 'the Great War's strangest naval battle', the defeat of the German Navy on Lake Tanganyika.

—— and Hunter, Anthony, *Dardanelles Patrol* (London, Collins, 1964). The fabulous exploits of the British submarines which penetrated the Sea of Marmara in the spring of 1915. Some of the material has been drawn from 'the memory and records' of the leader of that gallant lot, the late Admiral Sir Martin Dunbar-Nasmith, V.C.

Sims, Rear-Admiral William S., *The Victory at Sea* (London, Murray, 1920). Indispensable for Anglo-American naval relations, 1917–18, and for the origins and development of the convoy system. Sims was the Commander of the American naval forces in European waters.

Siney, Marion C., *The Allied Blockade of Germany, 1914–1916* (Ann Arbor, Michigan, The University of Michigan Press, 1957). A scholarly treatment of the subject.

Smith, Vice-Admiral Humphrey H., *A Yellow Admiral Remembers* (London, Arnold, 1932). This and the title that follows are highly humorous, anecdotal reminiscences of the author's thirty-seven years in the Navy, 1889–1926. Of particular interest are the two chapters in the first book on the Northern Patrol.

Smith, *An Admiral Never Forgets* (London, Seeley Service [1938?]).

Snowden, Philip, 'Dreadnoughts and Dividends' (World Peace Foundation Pamphlet Series, Vol. iv, No. 5, Boston, Mass., 1914). An interesting little pamphlet whose views were widespread in radical and socialist circles.

Sommer, Dudley, *Haldane of Cloan: His Life and Times, 1856–1928* (London, Allen & Unwin, 1960). Makes full use of the Haldane Papers. Useful mainly for the War Secretary's mission to Berlin in 1912.

Spender, J. A., *The Life of the Right Hon. Sir Henry Campbell-Bannerman* (London, Hodder & Stoughton, 1923, 2 vols.), Vol. ii. The authorized biography of the Liberal Prime Minister contains a number of references to the German naval rivalry and the British navy estimates.

——, *Life, Journalism and Politics* (London, Cassell, 1927, 2 vols.). Good mainly for the references to Lord Fisher.

——, and Asquith, Cyril, *Life of Herbert Henry Asquith, Lord Oxford and Asquith* (London, Hutchinson, 1932, 2 vols.). A miscellany of naval references for the period of Asquith's prime-ministership.

Sprout, Harold, and Sprout, Margaret, *Toward a New Order of Sea Power: American Naval Policy and the World Scene, 1918–1922* (2nd ed., Princeton, New Jersey, The University Press, 1943). Long the standard work and still useful.

Stanford, Peter Marsh, *Corbett's Work with Fisher at the Admiralty, 1904–1910* (unpublished MS.; copy in Naval Library). Has used some of the Corbett papers. Superseded by Schurman's biography.

Steinberg, Jonathan (ed.), *The de Robeck Papers* (London, Navy Records Society, no date fixed).

Sueter, Rear-Admiral Murray F., *Airmen or Noahs* (London, Pitman, 1928). The first chapters constitute an important source on the early years of naval aviation, by one of its pioneers.

Sydenham of Combe, Colonel Lord, *My Working Life* (London, Murray, 1927). The author was (as Lieutenant-Colonel Sir George Clarke) the first Secretary of the C.I.D., 1904–7. Chapter XIV, on this period, includes some naval material.

Sykes, Major-General Sir Frederick, *From Many Angles: an Autobiography* (London, Harrap, 1942). Sykes was one of the founders of the R.F.C. and the second Chief of the Air Staff (1918–19). A number of references to the R.N.A.S. in the war, especially its role in the Gallipoli campaign.

T 124 (Captain Russell Grenfell), *Sea Power* (rev. ed., London, Cape, 1941). A highly controversial discussion of larger problems of naval strategy, with many examples drawn from the First War.

Taffrail (Captain Taprell Dorling), *Swept Channels: Being an Account of the Work of the Minesweepers in the Great War* (London, Hodder & Stoughton, 1935). Not so much a history of minesweeping as an attempt, very successful, to capture the atmosphere of the work of this force.

——, *Endless Story: Being an Account of the Work of the Destroyers, Flotilla-Leaders, Torpedo-Boats and Patrol Boats in the Great War* (London, Hodder & Stoughton, 1931). An authoritative and vividly written account of the work of the light craft. The destroyer actions at Jutland are particularly well done.

Temperley, H. W. V. (ed.), *A History of the Peace Conference of Paris* (London, Oxford, and Hodder & Stoughton, 1920–4, 6 vols.), Vol. ii. The naval chapter was written by Captain A. C. Dewar, R.N., of the Historical Section, Admiralty.

Tennyson d'Eyncourt, Sir Eustace H. W., *A Shipbuilder's Yarn* (London, Hutchinson, 1948). The autobiography of the Director of Naval Construction, 1912–24. Not especially revealing.

Terraine, John, *Douglas Haig: the Educated Soldier* (London, Hutchinson, 1963). Material on Haig's relations with the sailors, in 1917 particularly, in this, the authorized biography.

Terry, C. Sanford (ed.), *Ostend and Zeebrugge, April 23: May 10, 1918: the Dispatches of Vice-Admiral Sir Roger Keyes and Other Narratives of the Operations* (London, Oxford, 1919). Keyes's dispatches of 9 May and 15 June 1918, the narratives issued through the Press Bureau on 26 April and 15 May 1918, and the German Admiralty's accounts.

Thetford, Owen, *British Naval Aircraft Since 1912* (2nd ed., London, Putnam, 1962). A standard reference work on the subject.

Thomson, Sir J. J., *Recollections and Reflections* (London, Bell, 1936). Useful for his work as a member of the Board of Invention and Research, of which he was a member, and for some Fisher sidelights.

Tillman, Seth P., *Anglo-American Relations at the Paris Peace Conference of 1919* (Princeton, New Jersey, The University Press, 1961). Important monograph, but unable to use unpublished British documents on naval matters. The naval clauses *re* Germany, the scuttling, and the Anglo-American naval rivalry are all discussed.

The Times Book of the Navy (London, The Times, 1914). Describes the Fleet at the beginning of the war: *matériel*, personnel, the organization of the Admiralty, etc.

Tirpitz, Grand-Admiral Alfred von, *My Memoirs* (London, Hurst & Blackett, 1919, 2 vols.). Revealing reminiscences and strategic ideas of the longtime (1897–1916) Secretary of State for the Imperial German Navy.

——, *Politische Dokumente der Aufbau der deutschen Weltmacht* (Berlin, Cotta, 1924–6, 2 vols.). Invaluable collection of correspondence and other papers covering German naval policy from 1905 to 1918.

Toye, Francis, *For What We Have Received: an Autobiography* (New York, Knopf, 1948). Brief sketches of 'Room 40' and its personnel, 'Blinker' Hall, the D.N.I., and the High Seas Fleet at Scapa Flow, by a young naval officer who later became a well-known music critic.

Trevelyan, George Macaulay, *Grey of Fallodon: the Life and Letters of Sir Edward Grey* (London, Longmans, 1937). An appealing biography, based on the Grey Papers, treating, *inter alia*, Anglo-German relations in the pre-war decade.

Troubridge, Laura, *Memories and Reflections* (London, Heinemann, 1925). Chapter IX has a few notes on the escape of the *Goeben* and the Troubridge court martial, by his sister-in-law, reflecting the family interpretation of the whole incident.

Tupper, Admiral Sir Reginald, *Reminiscences* (London, Jarrolds, 1929). His service career spanned 1873–1921. Of interest for the story of the work of the 10th Cruiser Squadron, which he commanded in 1916–17.

Turner, E. S., *Gallant Gentlemen: a Portrait of the British Officer, 1600–1956* (London, Michael Joseph, 1956). A general work of charm, if not very much depth, on the character and outlook of military and naval officers. The twentieth-century age of specialization is handled well.

Tweedie, Admiral Sir Hugh, *The Story of a Naval Life* (London, Rich & Cowan, 1939). His naval life, 1890–1935, included war service in monitors on the Belgian coast and in the eastern Mediterranean, and in Grand Fleet destroyers. Not a classic autobiography.

Tyler, J. E., *The British Army and the Continent, 1904–1914* (London, Arnold, 1938). An older account, not without value, of the pre-war military conversations with France and Belgium.

United States Air Force Academy, *Command and Commanders in Modern Warfare* (ed. Lieut.-Col. William Geffen, U.S. Air Force Academy, Colorado, 1969). Part II: papers by Arthur J. Marder, *et al.* on 'British Naval Leaders in World War I.'

Upplegger, Fritz, *Die englische Flottenpolitik vor dem Weltkrieg, 1904–*

1909 (Stuttgart, Kohlhammer, 1930). A pioneering study, but wholly dependent upon published material. Outdated.

Usborne, Vice-Admiral C. V., *Smoke on the Horizon: Mediterranean Fighting, 1914-1918* (London, Hodder & Stoughton, 1933). Detailed examination of selected operations: the Dardanelles (half the book), anti-submarine warfare, the sortie of the *Goeben* and *Breslau*, and one or two others.

——, *Blast and Counterblast: a Naval Impression of the War* (London, Murray, 1935). Experiences and reflections, mainly on the pre-war drive for gunnery efficiency, Grand Fleet activity in the early part of the war, the advent of the paravane, and, most valuable, the Eastern Mediterranean naval scene in the latter part of the war.

Waldeyer-Hartz, Captain Hugo von (Imperial German Navy), *Admiral von Hipper* (London, Rich & Cowan, 1933). The German side of the war as seen through this able biography; mostly on the First War and of some value for Jutland especially.

Walker, Sir Charles, *Thirty-Six Years at the Admiralty* (London, Lincoln Williams, 1934). The reminiscences of an Admiralty civil servant (1895-1931), who ultimately became Deputy Secretary of the Admiralty. Some interesting sidelights but of peripheral value to the naval historian.

Walker, Lieutenant-Commander Charles F., *Young Gentlemen: the Story of Midshipmen from the XVIIth Century to the Present Day* (London, Longmans, 1938). A highly entertaining account of midshipmen through the centuries written for the general reader.

Waters, Lieutenant-Commander D. W., 'The Philosophy and Conduct of Maritime War,' Part I, 1815-1918 (*Journal of the Royal Naval Scientific Service*, May 1958). *Restricted.*

Weldon, Captain L. B., '*Hard Lying*': *Eastern Mediterranean, 1914-1919* (London, Herbert Jenkins, 1925). Essentially a diary kept by the author. Includes chapters on Dardanelles–Gallipoli, 1915.

Das Werk des Untersuchungsausschusses der Verfassungsgebenden deutschen Nationalversammlung und des deutschen Reichstages 1919-1930. Vol. X/i of 4th series, *Die Ursachen des deutschen Zusammenbruches im Jahre 1918* (Berlin, Deutsche Verlagsgesellschaft für Politik und Geschichte, 1928). The naval proceedings of the Reichstag Committee of Inquiry which debated the causes of Germany's defeat in the war and subsequent collapse are extremely important for the German side of the war, above all the testimony of Vice-Admiral Adolf von Trotha (Scheer's Chief of Staff). The highly critical testimony of Alboldt, a pre-war warrant officer and wartime subordinate dockyard official, who was appointed by the Reichstag Committee in 1926 as its special authority for the naval proceedings, must be used with extreme caution. Alboldt's evidence and other material were published separately by him. See *Alboldt*, above, p. 364.

Wester Wemyss, Admiral of the Fleet Lord, *The Navy in the Dardanelles Campaign* (London, Hodder & Stoughton, 1924). Making use of his letters and diaries, the Second-in-Command of the naval squadron at the Dardanelles wrote this vivid and highly critical account.

Wester Wemyss, Lady, *The Life and Letters of Lord Wester Wemyss* (London, Eyre & Spottiswoode, 1935). Extracts from the letters and diaries of the First Sea Lord (1917–19), with connecting passages and commentary by his wife. A valuable source.

Widenmann, Wilhelm, *Marine-Attaché an der kaiserlich-deutschen Botschaft in London, 1907–1912* (Göttingen, Musterschmidt, 1952). The pre-war German Naval Attaché adds a little to our knowledge of Anglo-German naval relations.

Williamson, Samuel R., Jr., *The Politics of Grand Strategy: Britain and France Prepare for War, 1904–1914* (Cambridge, Mass., Harvard University Press, 1969). A badly needed study, featuring the military and naval conversations. Clearly written and based on a wide range of published and unpublished British and French source materials.

Woodward, E. L., *Great Britain and the German Navy* (London, Oxford, 1935). The first detailed study of the pre-war Anglo-German naval rivalry; the Admiralty records were not available, yet this pioneer work is still of value.

——, *Great Britain and the War of 1914–1918* (London, Methuen, 1967). Makes no pretence to original scholarship; an excellent general treatment of the British war effort on land and sea, as well as of the home front.

Woollard, Commander Claude L. A., *With the Harwich Naval Forces, 1914–1918* (privately printed, Antwerp, 1931). Personal experiences, supplemented by those of brother officers.

Wyatt, H. F., and Horton-Smith, L. Graham H., *Britain's Imminent Danger* (2nd ed., London, Imperial Maritime League, 1912). A shrill plea by the joint founders of the Imperial Maritime League for restoring the naval supremacy of Britain, in view of 'the vast decline of its relative naval strength.'

Yexley, Lionel, *The Inner Life of the Navy* (London, Pitman, 1908). An excellent account of the 'inner social life' of the lower deck by their unofficial spokesman. Deals with such topics as joining the Navy, victualling, uniforms, home service, foreign service.

Young, Desmond, *Rutland of Jutland* (London, Cassell, 1963). The first half of this volume deals with highlights of the naval career (1901–23) of one of the pioneers of naval aviation; the rest, of little naval interest, with his post-war civilian career.

Young, Filson, *With the Battle Cruisers* (London, Cassell, 1921). A popular account of the Battle Cruiser Fleet in 1914–15 by a Lieutenant, R.N.V.R., who served in the *Lion*.

Young, Kenneth, *Arthur James Balfour* (London, Bell, 1963). Very disappointing on the naval facets of Balfour's career, especially in his time as First Lord of the Admiralty (1915–16).

V. NEWSPAPERS AND PERIODICALS

(Consulted for naval leaders, naval articles, and miscellaneous information on naval affairs.)

A. *Newspapers* (all published in London except the *Manchester Guardian*)

> *Daily Chronicle*
> *Daily Express*
> *Daily Mail*
> *Daily News* (became the *Daily News and Leader* in May 1912)
> *Daily Telegraph*
> *Globe*
> *Manchester Guardian*
> *Morning Post*
> *The Observer* (Sundays)
> *Pall Mall Gazette*
> *Standard* (discontinued in March 1916)
> *The Times*
> *Westminster Gazette*

B. *Periodicals*

> *Blackwood's Magazine*
> *Contemporary Review*
> *Economist*
> *Edinburgh Review*
> *Fortnightly Review*
> *John Bull*
> *London Magazine*
> *Nation* (*1907–*)
> *National Review*
> *New Statesman* (*1913–*)
> *Nineteenth Century and After*

Punch
Saturday Review
Spectator

C. *Professional Periodicals**

Army and Navy Gazette
Broad Arrow (merged with *Army and Navy Gazette* in April 1917)
Journal of the Royal Naval Scientific Service (1945–   )† (restricted)
Journal of the Royal United Service Institution†
Land and Water**
Marine Rundschau †(suspended August 1914–20)
Mariner's Mirror (1911–   )†
Naval and Military Record
The Naval Review (restricted) †***
The Navy League Journal (title changed to *The Navy* in 1909)
United Service Magazine
United States Naval Institute Proceedings†

vi. MISCELLANEOUS

Brassey's Annual: the Armed Forces Year-Book (the present title; *The Naval Annual* in the Fisher period except for 1915–16: *Brassey's Naval Annual*).

British Broadcasting Corporation, Sound Archives: broadcasts on Jutland by Admirals Sir William Goodenough (13 January 1938, No. 719/22), Sir Ernle Chatfield (14 March 1941, No. 3789/92), and Sir Frederick Dreyer (3 August 1955, No. SLP 22872). The Goodenough is particularly good!

Dictionary of National Biography, twentieth-century supplements (Oxford, Clarendon Press, 1912–70).

General Index to Parliamentary Papers, 1900–1949 (London, H.M.S.O., 1960). Abbreviated title. Pages 504–13 list the naval reports and papers.

Hansard Parliamentary Debates.

* Those marked with a dagger were checked up to the present day, the others only until the summer of 1919.

** A sportsmen's weekly until the outbreak of the war; it then devoted itself entirely to the war.

*** Founded in 1912 (first issue, 1913) for the study of the 'higher' aspects of the naval profession; more or less authoritative articles by R.N. officers on all facets of British naval history; circulates only among the members, but its files may be consulted in the Naval Library (Ministry of Defence), National Maritime Museum Library, and Royal United Service Institution; has been thoroughly checked for material, which, however, may not be attributed to the *Naval Review*.

BIBLIOGRAPHY

Jane's Fighting Ships (title since 1916; *All the World's Fighting Ships*, 1898–1904, *Fighting Ships*, 1905–15).
The Navy League Annual (1907–8 through 1915–16).
The Navy List (published by H.M.S.O. monthly for the Admiralty). Rank, seniority, and appointment of all serving officers. The Naval Library has a complete set; the University of California, Irvine, Library, a fairly complete one for 1904–19.

vii. ADDENDA

Berghahn, Volker R.: This young scholar has been exploiting the pre-war German naval archives with great success. His University of Mannheim *Habilitation: Deutsche Rüstungspolitik, 1897–1908*, is being prepared for publication (1972?). And see his 'Zu den Zielen des deutschen Flottenbaus unter Wilhelm II', *Historische Zeitschrift*, December 1969, and, with W. Deist, 'Kaiserliche Marine und Kriegsausbruch 1914. Neue Dokumente zur Juli-Krise', *Militärgeschichtliche Mitteilungen*, 1/1970.
Chatfield MSS. (2nd Baron Chatfield). Contains some interesting post-war Jutland material, which I have consulted for an eventual second edition of Volume iii.
History of the First World War (London, Purnell, 1969–). An imaginative popular weekly which includes illustrated essays on many naval aspects of the war. The charts, photographs, and text are generally of high quality.
Patterson, A. Temple: Professor Patterson is writing the authorized lives of Admirals Chatfield and Tyrwhitt.
Ranft, Bryan, *The Naval Defence of British Sea-Borne Trade, 1860–1905* (unpublished Oxford D.Phil. dissertation, 1967). This fine study, which has fully exploited the British archival resources, deserves to be noted, even though its terminal date barely penetrates the Fisher Era.
Röhl, J. C. G., 'Admiral von Müller and the Approach of War, 1911–1914', *Historical Journal*, December 1969. A stimulating comparison of the pre-war diaries of the Kaiser's Chief of the Naval Cabinet as edited by Müller after the war* with the original manuscript diaries in the Bundesarchiv–Militärarchiv. Röhl says there is reason to believe that the printed text of the 1914–18 diaries (see above, p. 377) is as unreliable as that of the pre-war diaries.

---

* Walter Görlitz (ed.), *Der Kaiser . . . : Aufzeichnungen des Chefs des Marinekabinetts Admiral Georg Alexander v. Müller über die Ära Wilhelms II* (Göttingen, 1965).

Index

All officers and titled people are indexed under the highest rank and title attained. Ships are indexed under 'Warships', British and German.

Admiralty: reorganization of Board functions (January 1918), 6, 11n.; alterations in Naval Staff organization, 7–8, 9, 11, 217–20; clarification of Board responsibility for operations, 8–9; development, weaknesses of Naval Staff, 313–16; over-centralized administration, methods of command, 327–9; relations with War Office, 341

Aircraft, British: 160, 162; and *Goeben* sortie, 16–17, A/S campaign, 32, 33, 34, 64–5, 87, 104; results of formation of R.A.F., 64n.; and convoy system, 85, 91–5, 105, offensive schemes, 141–2; in a future war, 223; and potential for strategy, tactics, 303–4

Alexander-Sinclair, Adm. Sir Edwyn Sinclair (1865–1945): 284; offensive spirit, 307

Allen, Capt. Charles Henry (1890–1962): and High Seas Fleet sortie, 154

Allied Naval Council: 12, 25, 30; creation, constitution, 20; meetings, 20, 20–1n., 21, 23, 27, 32, 35; relationship to Supreme War Council, 24n.; and Dutch neutrality, 163n., Naval Armistice terms, 176, 177, 180, 181–2, 183, 186n., 292; comes to end, 249

Anderson, Sir Alan Garrett (1877–1952): 6n.; leaves Board, 6

Anglo-American Naval Rivalry (post-war): 222n., 224–5, 228, 296; U.S. building programmes, purposes, 225–8; British public opinion and U.S. naval ambitions, 228; the Admiralty are suspicious, 228–30; 'Sea Battle of Paris', 230–5; the rivalry is defused, 235; significance of 'Sea Battle of Paris', 235–6; Admiralty and likelihood of war with U.S., 236–7; tables of relative strength, 247–8; *and see* Versailles Treaty

Anglo-German Naval Rivalry (pre-war): 335–8

Appleyard, Acting Cdr. (R.N.V.R.) Rollo (1867–1943): and 'the law of convoy size', 100n.

Asquith, H.H.: *see* Oxford and Asquith

Austrian Navy: and Allied Mediterranean strategy, 12, 21, 22, 23, 24, 28, 38, 141, Naval Armistice terms, 184n., naval peace terms, 294

Bacon, Adm. Sir Reginald Hugh Spencer (1863–1946): superseded by Keyes at Dover, 39; attributes, 40; and German destroyer raid, 42, 44n., Zeebrugge operation, 46, 47, 48–50, 51, 52, 57–8; on destroyer shortage, 309, the merchant seamen and fishermen, 332, German naval strategy, 334, Fisher's work, 344

Balfour, 1st Earl of (Arthur James Balfour, 1848–1930): and Northern Barrage, 69, 71–2, problem of Russian Baltic Fleet, 139; on Naval Armistice terms, 181; and 'Freedom of the Seas', 239, 241, Heligoland problem, 253, 255, Germany's coast defences, 256; relations with H. B. Jackson, 329; respected by Navy, 342

Baltic Operations (post-war): 194–5

Bartolomé, Adm. Sir Charles Martin de (1871–1941): appointed Controller and Third Sea Lord, 6; stays on, postwar, 201; on the capital ship, 223

Battenberg, Prince Louis of: *see* Milford Haven

Bayly, Adm. Sir Lewis (1857–1938): suggests Zeebrugge blocking operation, 46; attributes, 121–2; relations with U.S. Navy, 121–3

Beatty, Countess (Ethel Field, m. 1st Earl, ? –1932): at surrender of High Seas Fleet, 191; and Beatty's ambition to be First Sea Lord, 210

Beatty, Adm. of the Fleet, 1st Earl (David Beatty, 1871–1936): 4, 140, 340; strategic views, 3, 131–8, 159–60; on Wemyss as First Sea Lord, 4; relations with Wemyss, 10–11, 186n., 187, 203–211 (post-war), with Jellicoe, 10, 203; and Grand Fleet needs, 11; reaction to escape of *Goeben*, 19; supports Zeebrugge operation, 47; and Northern Barrage, 67–72, *passim*, 73; and A/S campaign, 97n., 98; on U.S. 6th B.S., 125; relations with Rodman, 126; on Sturdee, 128; irked at German refusal

Beatty, Adm.—*cont.*
to fight, 129; is important factor in fleet morale, 129–30, 131; supports Richmond's strategic ideas, 141; urges naval air offensive, 141–2; and problem of a German move, 144, 145; and High Seas Fleet sortie, 145–56, *passim*, Channel ports crisis, 158; thinks invasion risk small, 161; views on Naval Armistice terms, 165, 176–80, *passim*, 182, 185–7; sizes up situation, July 1918, 165–6; on possibilities of a German move in last months, 167–8; is warned of possible German move, 171; intentions if the High Seas Fleet moved, 172n.; and reception of Armistice, 187, 188; makes internment arrangements, 189–90, 272; and surrender of High Seas Fleet, 191–3; hauls down flag, 199, 202; on Long as First Lord, 200, Fergusson as D.C.N.S., 201; promoted Admiral of the Fleet, 202; attributes, 210–11; raised to peerage and given money grant, 211; appointed First Sea Lord, 212; and lower-deck grievances, 212, Heligoland problem, 253, 254, disposal of High Seas Fleet, 267; on the scuttling, 292n., role of sea power, 298; offensive spirit, 307; on Naval Staff inefficiency, 316; record in examinations, 317; evaluation, 321, 322; appointed Naval Secretary, 323; reluctance to remove officers, 324; supports Richmond for D.O.D., 326; on 'senior officer veneration', 327; as a leader, 338, 340–1; individuality, 339n.; attitude toward politicians, 341

Bellairs, R.-Adm. Roger Mowbray (1884–1959): on night attacks by surfaced U-boats, 94, possibility of High Seas Fleet sortie, 145

Benson, Adm. William Shepherd (1855–1932): critical of Royal Navy, 126; wants softening of Naval Armistice terms, 182, 183, 184–5; on British determination to keep naval supremacy, 221, U.S. 1918 building programme, 226; and U.S. naval expansion, 226, 227–8; organizes London Planning Section, 226, and Naval Advisory Staff, 227n.; and 'Sea Battle of Paris', 231–2; Anglophobia, 231; and German Navy, 247; member of Naval Peace Terms Committee, 249; and Heligoland problem, 254, 255, Germany's coast defences, 256–7; favours abolition of submarines, 257n.; and disposal of U-boats, 260, disposal of High Seas Fleet, 263, 264, 268, internment of High Seas Fleet, 291, 292, 293

Bentinck, Adm. Sir Rudolf Walter (1869–1947): on Richmond, 9–10; appointed Naval Secretary, 200

Beresford, Adm., 1st Baron (Charles William de la Poer Beresford, 1846–1919): 209; and disposal of High Seas Fleet, 267–8; individuality, 339n.; and 'band of brothers' tradition, 343; on lot of reformer, 343

Bernard, Capt. Montague Robert (1884–1952): and German destroyer raid, 43, 44n.

Blackett, Baron (life peer) (Patrick Maynard Stuart Blackett, 1897–   ): and ocean convoy statistics, 91

Bonham-Carter, Lieut.-Cdr. Philip Herman (1891–1934): and *Goeben* sortie, 17, 18

Boyle, Adm. the Hon. Sir Algernon Douglas Edward Harry (1871–1949): and Zeebrugge operation, 40

Boyle, Adm. Sir W. H. D.: *see* Cork and Orrery

Brand, Adm. the Hon. Sir Hubert George (1870–1955): on Richmond, 9–10

Bridgeman, Adm. Sir Francis Charles Bridgeman-(1848–1929): as First Sea Lord, 323; relations with Churchill, 329

Briggs, Adm. Sir Charles John (1858–1951): as Controller, 324

Brock, Wing-Cdr. Frank Arthur (? –1918): illuminates Channel barrage, 41; and Zeebrugge operation, 53

Brock, Adm. of the Fleet Sir Osmond de Beauvoir (1869–1947): 189; appointed D.C.N.S., 201; offensive spirit, 307; evaluation, 323, 326

Browning, Adm. Sir Montague Edward (1863–1947): 128; head of Allied Naval Armistice Commission, 184; appointed Second Sea Lord, 201, 204n.; attributes, 201, 307; individuality, 339n.

Burney, Adm. of the Fleet Sir Cecil, 1st Bt. (1858–1929): evaluation, 323, 324

Capelle, Adm. Eduard von (1855–1931): and submarine output, 81, 105

Capital Ship, the: post-war debate over, 223–4

Carden, Adm. Sir Sackville Hamilton (1857–1930): as Commander, Eastern Mediterranean Squadron, 323

Carpenter, V.-Adm. Alfred Francis Blakeney (1881–1955): and Zeebrugge operation, 40, 51, 54; on the personnel factor in war, 330–1

Carson, Baron (life peer) (Edward Henry Carson, 1854–1935): wants to promote Tyrwhitt, 324
Cecil, Lord Robert: see Cecil of Chelwood
Cecil of Chelwood, 1st Viscount (Edgar Algernon Robert Gascoyne-Cecil, 1864–1958): 246n.; and 'Sea Battle of Paris', 233–4
Chalmers, R.-Adm. William Scott (1888–): on theatrical entertainments in Grand Fleet, 130–1
Chatfield, Adm. of the Fleet, 1st Baron (Alfred Ernle Montacute Chatfield, 1873–1967): on U.S. 6th B.S.–Grand Fleet relations, 125, expectation of battle, 128, Beatty as a leader, 129–30, surrender of German Fleet, 165; appointed Fourth Sea Lord, 201; on what ailed German Navy, 333, leadership, 339
Christian, Adm. Arthur Henry (1863–1926): 321
Churchill, Sir Winston Leonard Spencer (1874–1965): 344; on Zeebrugge operation, 58; almost succeeds Geddes as First Lord, 200; opposes Wemyss's appointment to Malta Governorship, 205n.; and lower-deck pay, 216; on League of Nations, 221; inaugurates Naval Staff, 314; on naval officers in 1914, 321, Keyes, 322; and naval appointments, 323; relations with Bridgeman, Fisher, 329, with naval officers, 342
Clemenceau, Georges (1841–1929): 26, 245; and 'Freedom of the Seas', 241, disposal of U-boats, 259, 261, disposal of High Seas Fleet, 263; and the scuttling, 288, internment of High Seas Fleet, 293
Colville, Adm. the Hon. Sir Stanley Cecil James (1861–1939): attitude toward politicians, 342
Commerce Protection, British: U-boats destroyed, 35, 36, 41, 42, 73, 81–2, 106; mercantile shipping construction, 79–80, 83, 106, 108; increasing official optimism re A/S campaign, 105–7; the public is allergic to this optimism, 106–7; Admiralty concern over the U-boats in autumn, 107, 108–9; and see Commerce Warfare, German, Convoy System, Dover Straits, Mediterranean Sea, Northern Barrage
Commerce Warfare, German: shipping destroyed, February 1917–January 1918, 77; shipping destroyed in 1918, 77–8, 104; world's daily average loss, 1917–18, 79; losses due to enemy

minelaying, 79; new mercantile construction exceeds war losses, 80; repair of damaged ships, 80; decline in daily shipping destruction per U-boat commander, 80–1; German post-mortems, 96; statistics of shipping losses, 110–12; losses and shipbuilding output compared, 113; and see Commerce Protection, British, Convoy System, Submarines, German
Convoy System: opposition to, 30, 30–1n., 99–101; in Mediterranean, 36, 37, 86–7, 92; a complete antidote to German mining, 79; development, effectiveness, 85–7; final statistics, 87; analysis of strength of system, 88–91; role of aircraft, 91–5; causes alteration in U-boats' strategy, 96; and the one German attempt to disrupt system, 96–7; evaluations, 97–103, 108; the weak link, 104; handicaps, 104–5; statistics, 114–17; and Scandinavian convoys, 131, 132, 133, 136, 137, 145–9, 152, 153, 154, 156, 167, 168n.
Coode, R.-Adm. Charles Penrose Rushton (1870–1939): 7
Corbett, Sir Julian Stafford (1854–1922): on naval strategy, 306, study of naval strategy, 340
Cork and Orrery, Adm. of the Fleet, 12th Earl of (William Henry Dudley Boyle, 1873–1967): offensive spirit, 307n.
Cowan, Adm. Sir Walter Henry, 1st Bt. (1871–1956): on Zeebrugge operation, 58; surrender of High Seas Fleet, 193–4, Baltic situation, post-war, 195; offensive spirit, 307, 339; individuality, 339n.
Cradock, R.-Adm. Sir Christopher George Francis Maurice (1862–1914): 312, 328
Cresswell, Capt. John (1895–): on submarines and Goeben sortie, 18, High Seas Fleet sortie, 150, 153
Cromie, Cdr. Francis Newton Allen (1882–1918): and plans to destroy Russian Baltic Fleet, 139–40
Crooke, Adm. Sir Henry Ralph (1875–1952): 8n.
Cunningham of Hyndhope, Adm. of the Fleet, 1st Viscount (Andrew Browne Cunningham, 1883–1963): 4
Cunninghame Graham of Gartmore, Adm. Sir Angus Edward Malise Bontine (1893–): on 'senior officer veneration', 327

Daniels, Josephus (1862–1948): on effectiveness of Northern Barrage, 73;

Daniels, Josephus—*cont.*
and British mission to discuss intensified A/S measures, 109; rejects British invitation to make Sims honorary member of Board, 124n.; critical of Royal Navy, 126–7, 230; and U.S. naval expansion, 226, 227, 'Sea Battle of Paris', 231–3; defuses Anglo-American naval rivalry, 235; favours abolition of submarines, 257; and disposal of High Seas Fleet, 264

Dawson, Geoffrey (1874–1944): announces Beatty's appointment as First Sea Lord, 205

De Bon, V.-Adm. Ferdinand-Jean-Jacques (1861– ?) : 28; and Channel ports crisis, 158, Naval Armistice terms, 182; favours retention of the submarine, 258; and disposal of U-boats, 260, 261, disposal of High Seas Fleet, 263, 265, 268

De Robeck, Adm. of the Fleet Sir John Michael, 1st Bt. (1863–1928) : post-war honours, 211

Dewar, Capt. Alfred Charles (1875–1969): on Keyes, 40; studies war, 321; on *Victoria* disaster, 327

Dewar, V.-Adm. Kenneth Gilbert Balmain (1879–1964): appointed Assistant Director of Plans, 7; and problem of a High Seas Fleet sortie, 146, 147, 148n.; attributes, 299n.; strategic ideas, 306–7; on Heligoland Bight action (1914), 314, shortcomings of Naval Staff, 315, 316, 328, Service attitude toward naval history, 320; studies war, 321; war-time appointments, 326; evaluation, 326–7

Dickens, Adm. Sir Gerald Charles (1879–1962): on Mediterranean naval problems, 12, Otranto Straits Barrage, 36n., French naval effort, 37, Italian contribution to A/S campaign, 37, neglect of Mediterranean, 38

Doenitz, Adm. of the Fleet (Grossadm.) Karl (1892–): 86; on convoy system, 77, 89, U-boat tactics, 95n.

Domvile, Adm. Sir Barry Edward (1878–): on Japan as potential enemy, 238

Dover Straits: and A/S campaign, 35, 40–2, 64–6, 84, 85, 104, 108, 134, 136; German destroyer raid of 14–15 February, 42–5; *and see* Zeebrugge Operation

Drax, Adm. the Hon. Sir Reginald Aylmer Ranfurly Plunkett-Ernle-Erle- (1880–1967): strategic ideas, 306–7; on the Navy's performance, 1914–18, 313, naval education, 317; studies war,

321; on intellect in Navy, 325, excessive centralization of command, 328, lack of imagination in Navy, 331

Dreyer, Adm. Sir Frederic Charles (1878–1956): 266–7; appointed Director of Naval Artillery and Torpedo, 8; first joins Naval Staff, 314

Drury-Lowe, V.-Adm. Sidney Robert (1871–1945): and surrender of High Seas Fleet, 191

Duff, Adm. Sir Alexander Ludovic (1862–1933): 127n.; as A.C.N.S., 6; opinion of Allied Naval Council, 20; on A/S measures, 77, convoy system, 97, 101; and Washington mission to discuss A/S measures, 109; on a naval air offensive, 142; and problem of a High Seas Fleet sortie, 147n.; stays on as A.C.N.S., post-war, 200–1; and Heligoland problem, 254; on German naval strategy, 306; attitude towards Plans Division, 316; evaluation, 321, 322

Esher, 2nd Viscount (Reginald Baliol Brett, 1852–1930): evaluation of Fisher's work, 344

Evan-Thomas, Adm. Sir Hugh (1862–1928): on Richmond, 9–10

Everett, Adm. Sir Allan Frederic (1868–1938): 127n.; on Richmond, 9; steps down as Naval Secretary, 200

Ferguson, Cdr. Adam (1891–1949): and German destroyer raid, 44

Fergusson, Adm. Sir James Andrew (1871–1942): appointed D.C.N.S., 201; attributes, 201; appointed A.C.N.S., 201n.; and disposal of High Seas Fleet, 267; and interned fleet, 275n.

Fisher, Adm. of the Fleet, 1st Baron (John Arbuthnot Fisher, 1841–1920): 209, 308); predicts German invasion attempt, 159; and surrender of High Seas Fleet, 192, battle-cruiser type, 312; on naval appointments, 323–4; too ready to remove officers, 324; relations with McKenna, Churchill, 329; individuality, 339n.; reflections on 'Jacky', 343–5

Fisher, Adm. Sir William Wordsworth (1875–1937): on defeat of U-boats, 82; joins Naval Staff, 314

Foch, Marshal Ferdinand (1851–1929): 29; and Channel ports crisis, 158; opposes harsh Naval Armistice terms, 180, 181, 184–5; and internment of

High Seas Fleet, 291, 293; on sea power in the war, 297

Fremantle, Adm. Sir Sydney Robert (1867–1958): appointed D.C.N.S., 6; attributes, 6–7; as Wemyss-Beatty buffer, 11; lists objectives of a *Goeben* sortie, 12–13; his orders for a *Goeben* sortie, 14; on the Zeebrugge operation, 59; and Northern Barrage, 69–70; on effectiveness of Northern Barrage, 73; and A/S campaign, 98; on naval offensive schemes, 142–3; and problem of High Seas Fleet sortie, 146, 147n., and other German moves, 156–7; invasion bogy, 163–4, Dutch problem, 163n., imminence of a High Seas Fleet move, 171–2; on German Naval Armistice, 176–7; leaves Admiralty, 201; on the capital ship, 223–4; concerned over U.S. naval expansion, 228–9; and Heligoland problem, 254, interned fleet, 273–5, scuttling, 277, 280–1, 283–4, 285, 286, 289, 290, 291n.; attitude towards Plans Division, 316; on Admiralty-War Office relations, 341

French Navy: and Mediterranean strategy, 12, 20, 21–9, 38, A/S campaign in Mediterranean, 32, 34, 36, 37; post-war strength, 247–8; *and see* Versailles Treaty

Frewen, Capt. Oswald Moreton (1887–1958): war-weariness, 129

Fuller, Adm. Sir Cyril Thomas Moulden (1874–1942): appointed Director of Plans, 7, 315; attributes, 7; and problem of a High Seas Fleet sortie, 147, war plans *re* U.S., Japan, 238, disposal of High Seas Fleet, 265n., 267

Gamble, Adm. Sir Douglas Austin (1856–1934): underrates intellect, 320

Garvin, James Louis (1868–1947): evaluation of Fisher's work, 344

Gauchet, V.-Adm. Dominique-Marie (1857–1931): 20, 28

Geddes, Sir Eric Campbell (1875–1937): 6n.; relations with Wemyss, 3, 10, 329; clarifies Board responsibility for operations, 8–9; on improved efficiency of Navy, 11, Italian Navy, 20–1n., 22, 28; and Admiralissimo question, 29, 30; on convoy system in Mediterranean, 30–2n.; Zeebrugge operation, 59n.; and Northern Barrage, 69–70; shipbuilding rate, 80; optimistic over A/S campaign, 106; and Washington mission to discuss A/S measures, 109;

criticizes U.S. share in naval war, 127; on Beatty's strategic views, 132; and problem of Russian Baltic Fleet, 139; on a naval air offensive, 142; and Naval Armistice terms, 180, 181, 182, 185, 186, declaration of Armistice, 187; retires from Admiralty, 199; relations with Jellicoe, 199, 329; and Grand Fleet appointments, 204; offers to appoint Beatty First Sea Lord, 206–7, 208, 209; and lower-deck grievances, 213, 214, U.S. naval expansion, 229, 230, 'Freedom of the Seas', 238–9, League of Nations, 242; angry with Richmond, 326

George V, King (1865–1936): 5; on Wemyss as First Sea Lord, 3, surrender of High Seas Fleet, 192

German Destroyer Raid (February 1918): *see* Dover Straits

Godfrey, Adm. John Henry (1888–   ): on Otranto Straits Barrage, 36, Gough-Calthorpe as negotiator of Turkish Armistice, 169

Goeben Sortie: 12–19; British reaction, 19–20

Goodenough, Adm. Sir William Edmund (1867–1945): on Richmond, 9–10; evaluation, 321, 323

Gough-Calthorpe, Adm. of the Fleet the Hon. Sir Somerset Arthur (1864–1937): 340; on Hayes-Sadler, 13, French Navy, 37; and *Goeben* sortie, 14, 15, 18, 19, Mediterranean problems, 21–2; on convoy system, 30, 86; and Straits of Otranto offensive, 32, 36; signs Allied armistice with Turkey, 169, and leads Allied fleet up to Constantinople, 169–70; opposes British possession of Heligoland, 253

Grand Fleet: 98–9, 143, 307; relations with U.S. 6th B.S., 124–6; morale, 128–31; main fleet moves to Rosyth, 130, 144; numerical strength compared with High Seas Fleet, 133–4, 137, 138; the battle-cruiser position, 140; and High Seas Fleet sortie, 152–3, 154, reception of Armistice, 187–8, surrender of High Seas Fleet, 190–4, role in winning the war, 199, 299; ceases to exist, 202–3; *matériel* shortcomings, 307–13; and Scarborough Raid, 328–9; *and see* Beatty, Jellicoe, Strategy, British Naval, Tactics, British Naval

Grant, Adm. Sir Heathcote Salusbury (1864–1938): 126

Grey of Fallodon, 1st Viscount (Edward Grey, 1862–1933): on German naval expansion, 336

Haig, Field-Marshal, 1st Earl (Douglas Haig, 1861–1928): disgusted with Italian attitude, 26; and Third Ypres, 47, Navy's aircraft needs, 65; prepares to abandon Channel ports, 157; opposes Navy's Armistice terms, 179; created Earl, 211

Haldane, 1st Viscount (Richard Burdon Haldane, 1856–1928): on the reason for victory at sea, 330

Hall, Adm. Sir William Reginald (1870–1943): and problem of a High Seas Fleet sortie, 146; expects German attack on Rosyth, 172n; relieved as D.N.I., 201; evaluation, 322

Halsey, Adm. Sir Lionel (1872–1949): leaves Board, 6; and work of officers' pay committee, 216, 217

Hamilton, Adm. Sir Frederick Tower (1856–1917): on Navy's unpreparedness, 308

Harwich Force: 143, 144, 259, 307

Hayes-Sadler, Adm. Arthur (1863–1952): and Goeben sortie, 13–14, 16, 17, 18, 19; evaluation, 323

Heath, Adm. Sir Herbert Leopold (1861–1954): continues as Second Sea Lord, 5–6; leaves Admiralty, 201; on examinations, 317

Henderson, Adm. Sir Reginald Guy Hannam (1881–1939): joins Naval Staff, 314; evaluation, 322

High Seas Fleet, German: sortie, background, in Britain, 145–8, in Germany, 148–9, the operation, 149–55, aftermath, 155–6; and plans for action against Grand Fleet, 170–1; mutiny, 172–5, 184–5, 333; surrender, 165, 188–94; and Versailles Treaty, 230, 262–9, 293–5; internment, 270–5; scuttling, 275–84, aftermath, reflections, 284–93, 296; defensive strategy, 306, 334; superiority in matériel 310–11; and legend of ships' companies living ashore, 311n.; and system of command, 329, the human factor, 332–3, absence of a maritime tradition, 333–4; contribution to war effort, 334–5

Hipper, Adm. Franz von (1863–1922): 312; and High Seas Fleet sortie, 149, 151–2, 153; appointed C.-in-C., High Seas Fleet, 166; plans for action against Grand Fleet, 171, 172; calls off operation, 174; evaluation, 322

Holland: see Northern Neutrals

Holstein, Baron Friedrich von (1837–1909): on Germany's naval ambitions, 335–6

Holtzendorff, Adm. of the Fleet (Grossadm.) Henning von (1853–1919): strategic ideas, 149, 166

Hope, Adm. Sir George Price Webley (1869–1959): appointed Deputy First Sea Lord, 6; attributes, 6n.; and Naval Armistice terms, 176, 183; stays on as Deputy First Sea Lord, post-war, 201; and Heligoland problem, 254, interned fleet, 274; attitude toward Plans Division, 316

House, Edward Mandell ('Colonel House') (1858–1938): 180n., 245; and 'Sea Battle of Paris', 233–4, 'Freedom of the Seas', 241n., Kiel Canal settlement, 252, disposal of High Seas Fleet, 263–4, internment of High Seas Fleet, 291, 293

Imperial Naval Problems: 195–6

Imperial War Cabinet: and Northern Barrage, 70, 'Freedom of the Seas', 239

Italian Navy: and Mediterranean strategy, 12, 20, 20–1n., 21–9, 38; British opinion of, 22; and A/S campaign in Mediterranean, 32, 34, 36, 37–8; post-war strength, 247–8; and see Versailles Treaty

Jackson, Adm. of the Fleet Sir Henry Bradwardine (1855–1929): opposes British possession of Heligoland, 253, 321; relations with Balfour, 329; attitude toward politicians, 341

Jackson, Adm. Sir Thomas (1868–1945): as D.O.D., 326

James, Adm. Sir William Milbourne (1881–): on the Zeebrugge operation, 60, 63–4; and High Seas Fleet sortie, 155–6; on mistakes in the war, 313n.; joins Naval Staff, 314; on the men, 331–2

Japanese Navy: and A/S campaign in Mediterranean, 36–7, post-war U.S. naval policy, 225, 228, 229, British naval policy, 237–8, 296; post-war strength, 247–8; and see Versailles Treaty

Jellicoe, Adm. of the Fleet, 1st Earl (John Rushworth Jellicoe, 1859–1935): 132, 199; superseded by Wemyss as First Sea Lord, 3–4; on Wemyss as First Sea Lord, 4n.; attributes, 5; relations with Beatty, 10. 203; and Admiralissimo question, 26, 29, 30; on naval strategy in 1918, 39, German destroyer raid, 44n.; and Zeebrugge operation, 46, 47,

49, 50, formation of R.A.F., 64n.; on Bayly's rudeness, 122, U.S. Navy-Royal Navy co-operation, 124, 126; criticizes the 'new' strategy, 128, 136–7; comparison of his and Beatty's strategy, 138; and invasion bogy, 161–2, surrender of High Seas Fleet, 192, Empire Mission, 195; relations with Geddes, 199, 329; promoted Admiral of the Fleet, 202; voted money grant by Parliament, 211; disclosures in his *The Grand Fleet*, 222, 307–8, 331; opposes British possession of Heligoland, 253; and Grand Fleet destroyer requirement, 301, Grand Fleet strategy, 304–5, 307, 328; brings new blood to Admiralty, 314–15; evaluation, 321, 322; reluctance to remove officers, 324; as a leader, 338, 341; and naval history, 340

Jerram, Adm. Sir Thomas Henry Martyn (1858–1933): 321; and work of Naval Pay Committee, 215–216

Jutland, Battle of: 300, 302, 303, 304, 310, 311, 312, 313

Kelly, Adm. Sir William Archibald Howard (1873–1952): Commanding British Adriatic Force, 33

Kenworthy, Lieut.-Cdr. J. M.: *see* Strabolgi

Kerr, Adm. Mark Edward Frederic (1864–1944): 64n.

Keyes, Adm. of the Fleet, 1st Baron (Roger John Brownlow Keyes, 1872–1945): 7, 340; appointed to Dover command, 39; and Zeebrugge operation, 39, 47–8, 50–60, 62, 63–4, 143; attributes, 39–40, 307n.; reinvigorates Dover command, 40; and A/S campaign in Dover Straits, 40–2, 64–5, German destroyer raid, 42, 43, 44–5, crisis over Channel ports, 157–8; on Naval Armistice terms, 177; appointed to command of B.C. Squadron, 204, 206, 207; post-war honours, 211; and interned fleet, 273, 274; record in examinations, 317; evaluation, 322; individuality, 339n.

Lambe, Air V.-Marshal Sir Charles Laverock (1875–1953): and the Zeebrugge operation, 62, a naval air offensive, 142

Lambert, Adm. Sir Cecil Foley (1864–1928): appointed Commander, Aegean Squadron, 19; dislikes new command

arrangement, 26–7; favours British possession of Heligoland, 253

Lansing, Robert (1864–1928): on Kiel Canal settlement, 252, Germany's coast defences, 256

Law, Andrew Bonar (1858–1923): and lower-deck pay, 216

Leveson, Adm. Sir Arthur Cavenagh (1868–1929): 321, 326; and interned fleet, 273, 274

Levetzow, R.-Adm. Magnus von (1871–1939): and plans for action against Grand Fleet, 171

Ley, Adm. James Clement (1869–1946): 7

Leygues, Georges (1857–1933): and disposal of High Seas Fleet, 263, 265

Lloyd-George of Dwyfor, 1st Earl (David Lloyd George, 1863–1945): on the Zeebrugge operation, 39, 58, mastery of the submarine, 106; sends Northcliffe to U.S., 127; and problem of Russian Baltic Fleet, 139; favours merchant shipbuilding over battle cruisers, 140; and Naval Armistice terms, 178, 179, 180, 181, 183, 185, 186n.; tries to persuade Geddes to stay on, 199; asks Churchill to succeed Geddes, 200; appoints Long First Lord, 200n.; and Wemyss's ambition to be Governor of Malta, 205n., succession to Wemyss, 208; and peerage for Beatty, 211, lower-deck pay, 216; on role of British Navy, 221; and 'Sea Battle of Paris', 231, 232–4, 234–5n.; on Benson, 231, standard of naval strength, 237; and 'Freedom of the Seas', 240–1, armaments limitation, 245, disposal of German Fleet, 249, 263–4, 265, 268–9, 294, Kiel Canal settlement, 252, Heligoland problem, 255, Germany's coast defences, 256, disposal of U-boats, 261; on the scuttling, 291; and internment of High Seas Fleet, 293; on role of sea power, 297; attitude of Navy toward him, 341, 342; on expert-layman co-operation, 342

Lockhart, Sir Robert Hamilton Bruce (1887–): and destruction of Russian Fleet, 138

Long, 1st Viscount (Walter Hume Long, 1854–1924): appointed First Lord, 199; attributes, 200; reception of appointment, 200; and Beatty-Wemyss row, 205–10, *passim*; on Wemyss as First Sea Lord, 210; refuses to accept Wemyss's resignation, 211; and lower-deck, officers' grievances, 215n., 216; on 1919–20 Navy Estimates, 221–3, U.S. naval expansion, 230; and 'Sea

Long, Viscount—*cont.*
Battle of Paris', 231–2; on Benson, 231; accepts Daniels's assurance, 235; on possible trouble with U.S., 236n.; and disposal of High Seas Fleet, 265; on the scuttling, 288, 292, peace terms, 296
Longmore, Air Chief Marshal Sir Arthur Murray (1885–   ): and A/S campaign in Adriatic, 33
Lynes, R.-Adm. Hubert (1874–1942): and Zeebrugge operation, 52–3n.
Lytton, 2nd Earl of (Victor Alexander George Robert Bulwer-Lytton, 1876–1947): on 'Freedom of the Seas', 239–40

McKenna, Reginald (1863–1943): relations with Fisher, 329
Madden, Adm. of the Fleet Sir Charles Edward, 1st Bt. (1862–1935): 136; on Beatty as C.-in-C., 3, the 'new' strategy, 137–8, the internment negotiations, 189, Wemyss as First Sea Lord, 208; post-war honours, 211; and lower-deck, officers' grievances, 215, disposal of High Seas Fleet, 266–7; and interned fleet, 272, 274, 275; takes precautions against scuttling, 275n.; and the scuttling, 281, 285, 286, 289, 290
Mahan, R.-Adm. Alfred Thayer (1840–1914): on naval strategy, 306, the personnel factor in war, 330, experience and knowledge, 340
May, Adm. of the Fleet Sir William Henry (1849–1930): discourages criticism, 325
Mediterranean Sea: command and strategic problems in, 20–30; A/S offensive in Adriatic (Otranto Straits Barrage), 30–5, its effectiveness, 35–6, 76, 87; Allied contributions to A/S campaign, 36–8; convoy system, 36, 37, 86–7, 92; *and see Goeben* Sortie
Meurer, R.-Adm. Hugo (1869–1943): makes internment arrangements, 189–190
Michelsen, V.-Adm. Andreas (1869–1932): and U-boat routes, 42; on effectiveness of Northern Barrage, 74, attacks on convoys, 89–90
Milford Haven, Adm. of the Fleet, 1st Marquess of (Louis Alexander Mountbatten, Prince Louis of Battenberg, 1854–1921): 4, 321
Milne, Adm. Sir Archibald Berkeley, 2nd Bt. (1855–1938): 321, 328
Milner, 1st Viscount (Alfred Milner, 1854–1925): 25n.; on the Zeebrugge operation, 58

Mines, British: 168; and *Goeben* sortie, 15–16, 18, Mediterranean strategy, 26, 26–7n; Heligoland Bight barrage, 75–6, 104, 134, 135, 136, 160; quality, 308; *and see* Dover Straits, Northern Barrage
Mines, German: 166, 167, 168, 300, 304; and shipping destroyed, 79; convoy a complete antidote to, 79; psychological effect of, 302
Minesweeping, British: 79, 308; introduction of paravane, 302
Minesweeping, German: 147
Moore, Adm. Sir Archibald Gordon Henry Wilson (1862–1934): evaluation, 321, 323
Murray, Sir Oswyn Alexander Ruthven (1873–1936): on Richmond, 9; against proposal to merge offices of C.-in-C. and First Sea Lord, 206n.

Napier, V.-Adm. Sir Trevylyan Dacres Willes (1867–1920): on Richmond, 9–10
Napoleon I, Emperor (1769–1821): 38, 145, 340
Naval Armistice, German: early Admiralty views, 175–6; draft Allied Armistice conditions, 176; British views, 176–80; views of Allied Naval Council, Supreme War Council, 180–3; internment of High Seas Fleet, 183, 285–6, 288, 291–3; other naval terms, 183–4; and the German naval mutiny, 184–5; Beatty's unhappiness over terms, 185–6; reception of declaration at Admiralty and in Grand Fleet, 187–8
Navy Estimates of 1919–20: 221–3, 263n.
Nelson, V.-Adm., 1st Viscount (Horatio Nelson, 1758–1805): 53, 191, 300, 305, 323, 338, 340, 343, 344
Newbolt, Sir Henry John (1862–1938): on Fremantle's orders *re Goeben* sortie, 14, German destroyer raid, 44n., the Zeebrugge operation, 63, effectiveness of Northern Barrage, 73, Heligoland Bight barrage, 75, defeat of U-boat campaign, 80, German failure to disrupt convoy system, 96, High Seas Fleet sortie, 149, 154–5, imminent High Seas Fleet move in October, 172
Northcliffe, 1st Viscount (Alfred Charles William Harmsworth, 1865–1922): reports U.S. criticism of British naval strategy, 126–7
Northern Barrage: 39, 147; establishment, 66–7, 136; problems, 67–72;

effectiveness, 73–5, 84, 108; and convoy system, 76; possibility of a raid on, 167, 168n.

Northern Neutrals: in British naval strategy, 69–72 (Norway), 163 (Holland)

Norway: *see* Northern Neutrals

Oliver, Adm. of the Fleet Sir Henry Francis (1865–1965): 321; leaves Board, 6; and Zeebrugge operation, 46, 49n., 50; concurs in Beatty's strategic views, 135; opposes British possession of Heligoland, 253; and interned fleet, 273, 274, over-centralized administration at Admiralty, 327

Orlando, Vittorio Emanuele (1860–1952): and naval redistribution in Mediterranean, 24, internment of High Seas Fleet, 293

Oxford and Asquith, 1st Earl of (Herbert Henry Asquith, 1852–1928): on role of sea power, 297–8; attitude of Navy toward him, 342

Paine, R.-Adm. Sir Godfrey Marshall (1871–1932): 64n.

Pakenham, Adm. Sir William Christopher (1861–1933): 207; and interned fleet, 273; offensive spirit, 307; individuality, 339n.

Personnel, British Naval: problems of pay, etc., 177, 212–15; settlement of pay problems, 215–17; education of officers, 316–20; officers' immersion in *matériel* concerns, 321; evaluation of senior officers, 321–3; poor appointments and reasons thereof, 323–6; 'senior officer veneration', 327; four 'laws' of human relations, 329; the personnel factor in the victory at sea, 330–2, 344; social background of officers, 332n.; and art of leadership, 338–41; relations with the military, 341; officers' distrust of politicians, 341–2; conservatism of officers, 343

Pipon, V.-Adm. Sir James Murray (1882–): on Japanese Mediterranean flotilla, 37

Pirrie, 1st Viscount (William James Pirrie, 1847–1924): appointed Controller-General of Merchant Shipbuilding, 6n.; favours merchant shipbuilding over battle cruisers, 140

Pound, Adm. of the Fleet Sir Alfred Dudley Pickman Rogers (1877–1943):

7; and Zeebrugge operation, 47, disposal of High Seas Fleet, 267

Pringle, V.–Adm. Joel Roberts Poinsett (1873–1932): relations with Bayly, 123

Rebeur-Paschwitz, V.-Adm. Hubert von (1863–1933): and *Goeben* sortie, 14, 15, 16

Reuter, V.-Adm. Ludwig von (1862–1943): and surrender of High Seas Fleet, 190; and interned fleet, 271, 272, 273, the scuttling, 275, 277–86, *passim*, 289, 290, 292–3

Richmond, Adm. Sir Herbert William (1871–1946): on Hope, 6n., Fremantle, 7n.; appointed D.T.S.D., 9–10, 315; ideas on naval education, 9, 297, 316–20; on German destroyer raids, 44, convoy escorts, 101, Duff, 101; strategic ideas, 141, 306–7; on Browning as Second Sea Lord, 201, Fergusson as D.C.N.S., 201, the scuttling, 287–8, role of sea power, 298; leader of 'Young Turks', 299; attributes, 299n.; on work of Plans Division, 316; studies war, 321; a case history of attitudes *re* independent thought, 325–6; evaluation, 327; on the reason for victory at sea, 330, Jellicoe, 340, 'happy inspirations', 340n.

Robertson, Field-Marshal Sir William Robert, 1st Bt. (1860–1933): and invasion bogy, 162, 164

Rodman, Adm. Hugh (1859–1940): relations with Grand Fleet, 124, 125–6

'Room 40': and High Seas Fleet sortie, 147, 148, 153, 155–6, 167–8

Roosevelt, Franklin Delano (1882–1945): critical of British naval strategy, 127

Roskill, Capt. Stephen Wentworth (1903–): on convoy system, 76, U.S. proposal for a League of Nations Navy, 242–3; leadership, 338

Russian Navy: Black Sea Fleet and Allied strategy, 20–5, *passim*, 28, 29n., 30; Baltic Fleet and British strategy, 138–40

Sandford, Lieut. Richard Douglas (1891–1918): and the Zeebrugge operation, 56

Scarlett, Air V.-Marshal Francis Rowland (1875–1934): appointed Director of Air Division, 7–8

Scheer, Adm. Reinhard (1863–1928): on factors in U-boats' decline, 83–4; and High Seas Fleet sortie, 148–9, 150, 151, 153, 154; becomes Chief of

Scheer, Adm.—*cont.*
Admiralstab, 166; plans action against Grand Fleet, 170-4, *passim*; on the scuttling, 270, Jellicoe's Grand Fleet strategy, 304-5
Schröder, Adm. Ludwig von (1854-1933): on the Zeebrugge operation, 39, 61
Sea Power, British: role of, 1914-18, 297-9
Seymour, V.-Adm. Sir Michael Culme-, 4th Bt. (1867-1925): 19
Seymour, Cdr. Ralph Frederick (1886-1922): 190n,; on internment negotiations, 189, surrender of High Seas Fleet, 191, 193; Beatty's reluctance to remove him, 324
Sims, R.-Adm. William Sowden (1858-1936): 28; and Northern Barrage, 67; on effectiveness of Northern Barrage, 73, 74, and convoy system, 90, 99, 101; and relations with Royal Navy, 122-4, Daniels, 124n.; criticizes U.S. 1918 naval programme, 227n.
Sinclair, Adm. Sir Hugh Francis Paget (1873-1939): on Richmond, 9-10; succeeds Hall as D.N.I., 201; attributes, 201-2; on U.S. naval policy, 229-30n.
Slade, Adm. Sir Edmond John Warre (1859-1928): studies war, 321
Spindler, R.-Adm. Arno Spindler (1880-1967): 90n.; on reasons for U-boats' decline, 84; post-mortem on submarine campaign, 96
Stanley, Adm. the Hon. Sir Victor Albert (1867-1934): and interned fleet, 275n.
Strabolgi, Lieut.-Cdr., 10th Baron (Joseph Montague Kenworthy, 1886-1953): charges British complicity in scuttling, 288-9
Strategy, British Naval: 343; the 'new' strategy, 128, 131-8; offensive schemes mooted, 141-3; and possible German moves, 143-8, 156-8, 166-9, invasion bogy, 158-64; conservatism of, 300-5; primacy-of-battle fetish, 305-6; 'passive strategy', 306-7; *and see* Beatty, Grand Fleet, Jellicoe
Sturdee, Adm. of the Fleet Sir Frederick Charles Doveton, 1st Bt. (1859-1925): 321; leaves Grand Fleet, 128; voted money grant by Parliament, 211; offensive spirit, 307
Submarines, British: 147, 160, 162, 167, 168; and *Goeben* sortie, 17-18
Submarines, German: 300, 304, 307, 309, 344; losses, 35, 36, 41, 42, 73, 82-3; sinkings of merchant tonnage:

comparison of High Seas Fleet and Flanders flotillas, 46n.; statistics of boats available for operations, operational boats at sea, output, 81; war loss figures for 1918, 81-2; falling off in morale, 82-3, 104; reasons for decline in U-boat successes, 83-5; influence of convoy air escorts, 92-5; altered strategy of U-boat campaign, 96; the one attempt to disrupt convoy system, 96-7; reasons for increased U-boat losses, 104; Scheer proposes a 'great U-boat programme', 107-8; U-boat statistics, 118-20; and High Seas Fleet sortie, 149; recall of boats on anti-commerce operations, 170; in Hipper's plan for action against Grand Fleet, 171; and mutiny of High Seas Fleet, 174-5; attacks on capital ships, 301-2n; *and see* Commerce Protection, British, Commerce Warfare, German, Convoy System, Dover Straits, Mediterranean Sea, Mines, British, Naval Armistice, German, Northern Barrage, Versailles Treaty, Zeebrugge Operation
Supreme War Council, Allied: 25; and Mediterranean naval command situation, 24; establishment, functions, 24n.; and Admiralissimo question, 26, 29, Channel ports crisis, 158; draws up Turkish Armistice terms, 169; and German Naval Armistice terms, 176, 180-1, 183, surrendered U-boats, 259

Tactics, British Naval: 343; conservatism of, 302-3
Tennyson-d'Eyncourt, Sir Eustace Henry William, 1st Bt. (1868-1951) (D.N.C.): on German warship designs, 311n.
Thaon di Revel, Adm. of the Fleet (Grande Ammiraglio) Paolo, Duke (1859-1948): and Mediterranean strategy, 24, 25, 26, 29
Thursfield, R.-Adm. Henry George (1882-1964): studies war, 321
Tirpitz, Adm. of the Fleet (Grossadm.) Alfred von (1849-1930): on British naval strategy, 305n., what ailed the German Navy, 333-4, German naval strategy, 334; and Anglo-German naval rivalry, 336-7
Titterton, Cdr. George Arthur (1890-   ): and the Zeebrugge operation, 62-3
Tomkinson, V.-Adm. Wilfred (1877-   ): and the Zeebrugge operation, 40

Tothill, Adm. Sir Hugh Henry Darby (1865–1927): stays on as Fourth Sea Lord, 6; leaves Admiralty, 201

Triangi di Maderno, V.-Adm. Arturo, Count (1864–1935): and Italian obstructionism, 27

Trotha, V.-Adm. Adolf von (1868–1940); on reasons for High Seas Fleet mutiny, 174–5; and the scuttling, 278

Trotsky, Leon (Lev Davydovich Trotski) (1879–1940): and problem of Russian Fleet, 138, 139, 140

Troubridge, Adm. Sir Ernest Charles Thomas (1862–1926): 321

Tryon, V.-Adm. Sir George (1832–1893): 327

Tudor, Adm. Sir Frederick Charles Tudor (1863–1946): favours British possession of Heligoland, 253

Tupper, Adm. Sir Reginald Godfrey Otway (1859–1945): 72

Tyrwhitt, Adm. of the Fleet Sir Reginald Yorke, 1st Bt. (1870–1951): 189, 340; suggests Zeebrugge operation, 46–7; and internment of U-boats, 190; post-war honours, 211; and surrender of U-boats, 259; offensive spirit, 307; record in examinations, 317; evaluation, 322; promotion delayed, 324; attitude toward Admiralty duty, 324–325; individuality, 339n.

United States Navy: 144; relations with Royal Navy, 25, 121–7; and A/S campaign, 33, 35, 37, Northern Barrage, 66–8, 70, 73; on convoy system, 98, 99; 6th Battle Squadron–Grand Fleet relations, 124–6; and precaution against battle-cruiser raid, 168n.; in World War II, 309; and see Anglo-American Naval Rivalry, Versailles Treaty

Usborne, V.-Adm. Cecil Vivian (1880–1951): on Otranto Straits Barrage, 34–5, 36n., Fleet efficiency, 297

Vanselow, Capt. Ernest (1876– ?): and Armistice negotiations at Compiègne, 184

Versailles Treaty (naval terms): 247; 'Freedom of the Seas', 227, 238–42; League of Nations, 227–34, passim, 239, 242–6; disposal of High Seas Fleet, 230, 262–9, 293–5; armaments limitation, 244–6; disposal of German colonies, 249–51; Kiel Canal settlement, 251–3; Heligoland settlement, 252n., 253–5, 256; Germany's coast defences, 255–7; question of abolition of submarines, 257–8; disposal of the U-boats, 258–62; evaluation re Britain, 295–6

Walwyn, V.-Adm. Sir Humphrey Thomas (1879–1957): 72

Warburton, Cdr. Geoffrey (1897–1953): and High Seas Fleet sortie, 150–1, 153–4

War Cabinet: and Mediterranean strategy, 25–6, 28; on British naval failures, 45; approves the 'new' strategy, 128, 136; and problem of Russian Baltic Fleet, 138–40; defers battle-cruiser construction, 140; and invasion bogy, 158, 161, 162, Dutch problem, 163n., Naval Armistice terms, 179, lower-deck pay, 216, standard of naval strength, 236–7, 'Freedom of the Seas', 241

Warrender, V.-Adm. Sir George John Scott, 7th Bt. (1860–1917): evaluation, 321, 324

Warships, British[1]: Aboukir (Cr.), 312; Agamemnon (B.), 13, 14, 22, 169; Amazon (T.B.D.), 43, 44; Anson (B.C.), 222; Ark Royal (S.C.), 17; Audacious (D.), 302; Brilliant (Cr.), 56; Britannia (B.), 301n.; C-3 (S.M.), 56; Caledon (L.C.), 194n.; Cardiff (L.C.), 190–1; Cornwallis (B.), 301n.; Cressy (Cr.), 312; Dreadnought (D.), 144; E-2 (S.M.), 17–18; E-12 (S.M.), 17, 18; E-14 (S.M.), 17–18; E-42 (S.M.), 150, 154; Empress (S.C.), 17, 170; Falmouth (L.C.), 301n.; Furious (A.C.), 345; H-2 (S.M.), 34; H-4 (S.M.), 36; Hermes (A.C.), 304; Hogue (Cr.), 312; Hood (B.C.), 140, 222; Howe (B.C.), 222; Intrepid (Cr.), 52, 55–6; Iphigenia (Cr.), 52, 55–6; Invincible (B.C.), 133, 312; J-4 (S.M.), 150; J-6 (S.M.), 150–1, 153–4; King Edward VII (B.), 144; Leven (T.B.D.), 41; Lion (B.C.), 133, 273; Lizard (T.B.D.), 15, 16; Lord Nelson (B.), 13, 14, 22, 169; Majestic (B.), 301n.; Manxman (S.C.), 17; Mary Rose (T.B.D.), 319; Melpomene (T.B.D.), 43; New Zealand (B.C.), 133; Nottingham (L.C.), 301n.; Princess Royal (B.C.), 133, 273; Queen Elizabeth (D.), 131, 153, 154, 189, 191, 202; Ramillies (D.),

---

[1] Abbreviations: A.C.: aircraft carrier; B.: pre-dreadnought battleship; B.C.: battle cruiser; Cr.: armoured cruiser; D.: dreadnought; L.C.: light cruiser; S.C.: seaplane carrier; S.M.: submarine; T.B.D.: destroyer.

Warships, British—cont.
311n.; Renown (B.C.), 133, 273; Rodney (B.C.), 222; Sappho (Cr.), 56; Sirius (Cr.), 56; Strongbow (T.B.D.), 319; Superb (D.), 29n., 144, 169; Temeraire (D.), 29n., 169; Termagant (T.B.D.), 43; Thetis (Cr.), 52, 55–6; Tiger (B.C.), 133, 273; Tigris (T.B.D.), 15, 16; Triumph (B.), 301n.; V-4 (S.M.), 150; Victoria (B.), 327; Vindictive (Cr.), 51, 55, 56, 57, 59; Warspite (D.), 131; Warwick (T.B.D.), 55, 59; Zubian (T.B.D.), 43

Warships, German: Baden (D.), 173, 177, 184, 282, 293, 295, 311n.; Blücher (B.C.), 310, 335; Bremse (L.C.), 168, 282; Breslau (L.C.), 12, 13, 14, 15, 16, 310; Brummer (L.C.), 168, 293; Derfflinger (B.C.), 133, 172, 293; Dresden (L.C.), 190, 293; Emden (L.C.), 282, 293; Frankfurt (L.C.), 282, 293; Friedrich der Grosse (D.), 190, 272, 280, 285, 293; Goeben (B.C.), 12–20, 22, 23, 29n., 30, 169, 312, 328; Helgoland (D.), 173, 295n.; Hindenburg (B.C.), 133, 137; Kaiserin (D.), 173; Karlsruhe (L.C.), 293; Köln (L.C.), 293; König (D.), 190, 293; Königsberg (L.C.), 189; Kronprinz Wilhelm (D.), 173, 293; Mackensen (B.C.), 133, 137, 177, 184; Markgraf (D.), 149, 173, 293; Moltke (B.C.), 133, 151–5, passim, 274; Nassau (D.), 295n.; Nürnberg (L.C.), 282, 293; Oldenburg (D.), 151, 154, 295n.; Ostfriesland (D.), 295n.; Posen (D.), 295n.; Regensburg (L.C.), 173; Rheinland (D.), 295n.; Seydlitz (B.C.), 133, 191, 274; Stralsund (L.C.), 149; Thüringen (D.), 173, 295n.; submarines: U-54, 89, U-55, 42, U-92, 73, U-102, 73, U-103, 82, 83, U-109, 42, U-110, 82, U-156, 73, UB-16, 61, 83, UB-22, 75, UB-35, 41, UB-52, 36, UB-53, 35, UB-55, 82, UB-56, 41, UB-59, 66, UB-64, 89, UB-86, 75, UB-104, 73, UB-123, 73, UB-127, 73, UC-48, 295, UC-71, 66; Von der Tann (B.C.), 133, 172; Westfalen (D.), 295n.

Watson, V.-Adm. Bertram Chalmers (1887–   ): on the German naval officer, 310

Webb, Adm. Sir Richard (1870–1950): studies war, 321

Wemyss, Adm. Sir Rosslyn: see Wester Wemyss

Wester Wemyss, Adm. of the Fleet, 1st Baron (Rosslyn Erskine Wemyss, 1864–1933): 339–40; relations with Geddes, 3, 10, 329; appointed First Sea Lord, 3–4; on superseding

Jellicoe, 3–4; attributes, methods, 4–5; and Admiralty reorganization of January 1918, 6; on Fremantle, 7n., Dreyer, 8n.; clarifies Board responsibility for operations, 8–9; brings Richmond to Admiralty, 9–10, 326; on Beatty-Jellicoe relations, 10; relations with Beatty, 10–11, 186n., 187, 203–11 (post-war); and Mediterranean strategy, 12, 23, 24–5, 27, 28, 30; reaction to escape of Goeben, 19; appoints Keyes to Dover command, 39; and Zeebrugge operation, 50, 54, 59, Northern Barrage, 39, 67, 68–9, 74; on convoy system, 97; pays tribute to Sims, 124; concurs in Beatty's strategic views, 135, 144; and problem of High Seas Fleet sortie, 146; takes charge during sortie, 152; and crisis over Channel ports, 157–8, invasion bogy, 161, 162; on naval views on the German Armistice, 165, possibilities of a German move in the last months, 166–9; mood of Navy and Admiralty toward end of war, 176; against prolongation of war, 177; and Naval Armistice terms, 177–87, passim; and reception of Armistice at Admiralty, 188, internment of German surface ships, 189; acts for First Lord, 199; on Churchill as First Lord, 200; stays on as First Sea Lord, post-war, 200–1; plans to leave Admiralty, 204–5; helps Beatty to get earldom, 211; resigns as First Sea Lord, 211–12; promoted Admiral of the Fleet and accepts peerage, 212; and lower-deck, officers' grievances, 215, 216, post-war reorganization of Naval Staff, 217–18, 'Sea Battle of Paris', 231; on likelihood of war with U.S., 236; and a League of Nations, 243; member of Naval Peace Terms Committee, 249; and Heligoland problem, 255, disposal of High Seas Fleet, 265, 266, 269, interned fleet, 274, 275n.; on the scuttling, 290–1, 292–3, Fleet preparedness, 297; evaluation, 322; and relief of Richmond as D.T.S.D., 326; attitude toward politicians, 341

White, Lieut.-Cdr. Geoffrey Saxton (1886–1918): and Goeben sortie, 17, 18

Whitehead, V.-Adm. Frederic Aubrey (1874–1958): on Mediterranean convoy system, 86

William II, Emperor (1859–1941): 168; on British press, 337n.

Williams-Freeman, Cdr. Frederick Arthur Peere (1889–1939): and Goeben sortie, 17

Williamson, Group Capt. Hugh Alexander (1885–): and development of aircraft carrier, 303–4

Wilson, Adm. of the Fleet Sir Arthur Knyvet, 3rd Bt. (1842–1921): and criticism of Admiralty policy, 325; individuality, 339n.

Wilson, Field-Marshal Sir Henry Hughes, 1st Bt. (1864–1922): supports Navy on Armistice terms, 178

Wilson, Thomas Woodrow (1856–1924): rejects British invitation to make Sims honorary member of Board, 124n.; critical of Royal Navy, 126; and pre-Armistice negotiations with Germany, 170; opposes excessive naval terms, 179; and U.S. naval building programmes, 226, 229, 230n.; on Sims, 227n.; and 'Sea Battle of Paris', 232, 234, 'Freedom of the Seas', 238–9, 241–2, League of Nations, 242, armaments limitation, 244, German Navy, 247, Heligoland problem, 255; favours outlawing submarines, 261; and disposal of High Seas Fleet, 269

Yexley, Lionel (1861–1933): and lower-deck grievances, 213–14

'Young Turks': membership, criticisms, 299–300; strategic ideas, 306–7; and the reason for victory at sea, 330

Zeebrugge (and Ostend) Operation: 39, 40, 152; early schemes, genesis, 45–50; Keyes's plan, 50–3; false starts, 53–4; the operation, 54–6; criticisms, 57–8; results, moral and material, 58–64, 143

THE MAPS

Large-scale versions of the maps that follow
may be seen and downloaded from the book's page
on the publishers' websites.

CHART 1

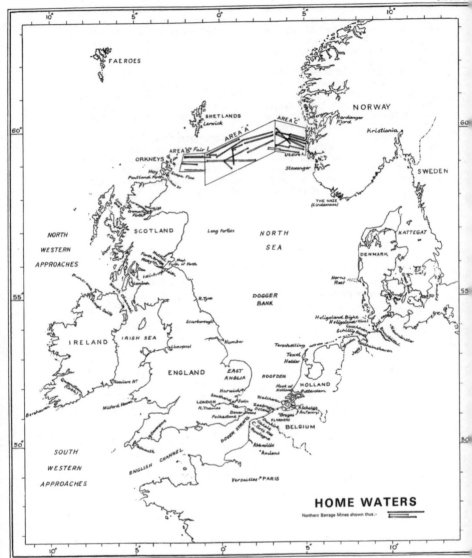

HOME WATERS

Northern Barrage Mines shown thus :-

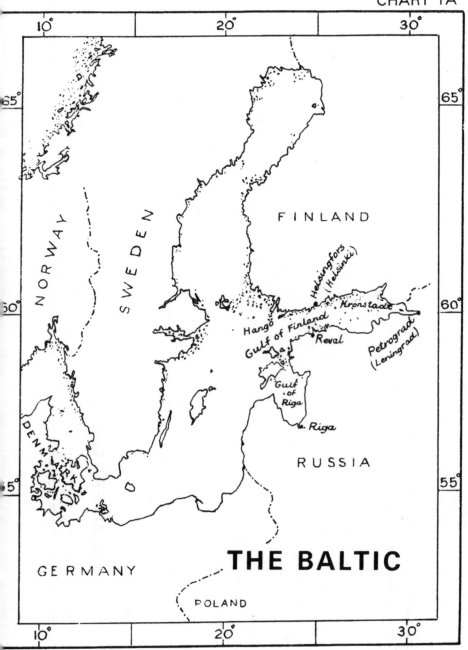

THE BALTIC

CHART 2

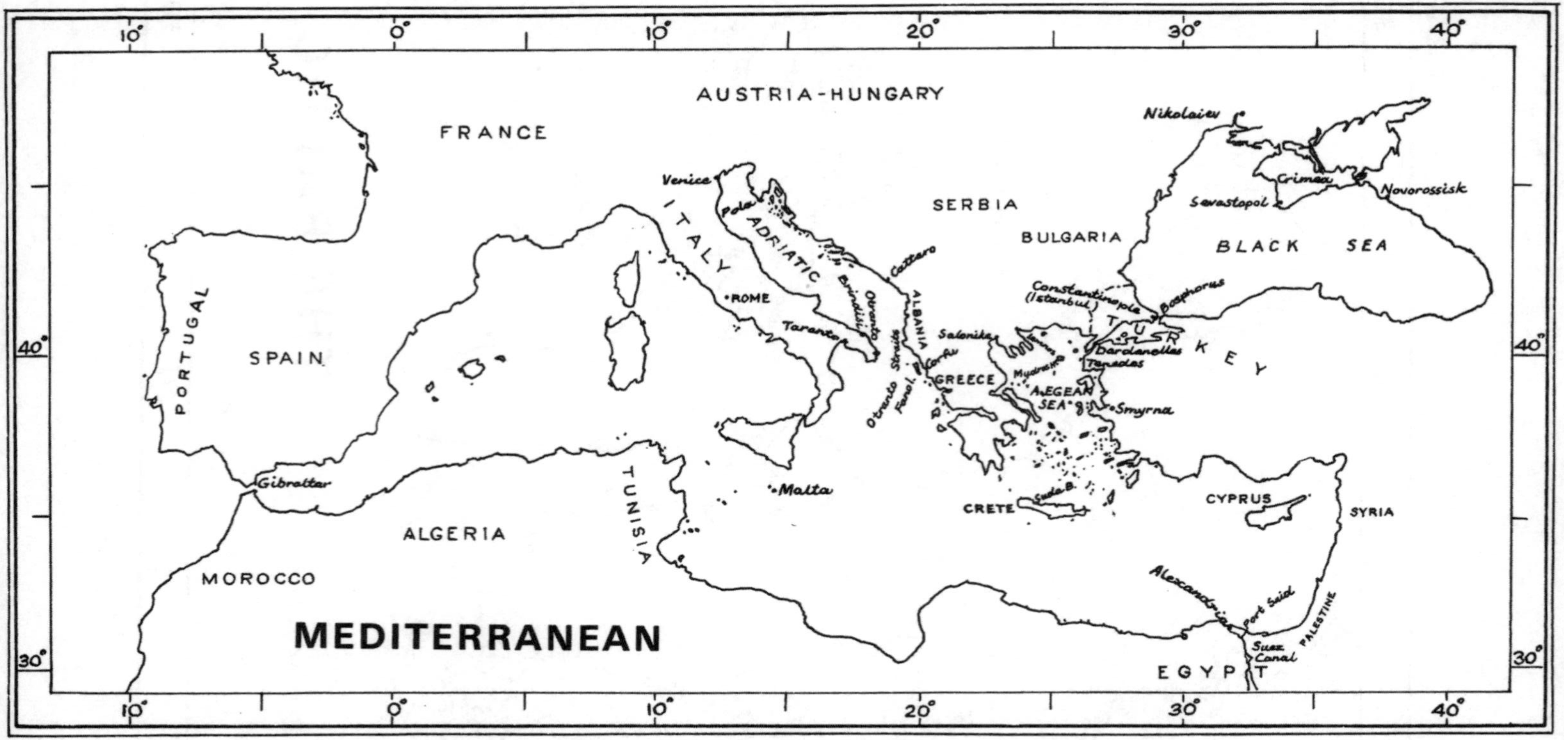
MEDITERRANEAN
FRANCE
AUSTRIA-HUNGARY
SERBIA
BULGARIA
BLACK SEA
Nikolaiev
Crimea
Sevastopol
Novorossisk
Venice
Pola
ADRIATIC
ITALY
ROME
Taranto
Brindisi
Otranto
Cattaro
ALBANIA
Otranto Straits
Fano I.
Corfu
Salonika
GREECE
Mudros
AEGEAN SEA
Constantinople (Istanbul)
Bosphorus
TURKEY
Dardanelles
Tenedos
Smyrna
CRETE
Suda B.
CYPRUS
SYRIA
PALESTINE
Alexandria
Port Said
Suez Canal
EGYPT
Malta
TUNISIA
ALGERIA
MOROCCO
Gibraltar
SPAIN
PORTUGAL
10°
0°
20°
30°
40°

CHART 3

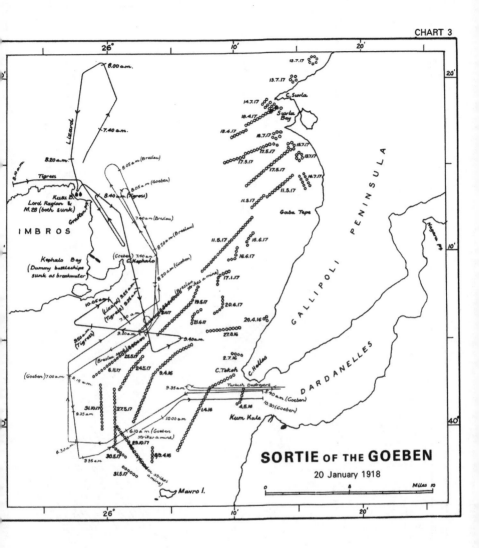

SORTIE OF THE **GOEBEN**

20 January 1918

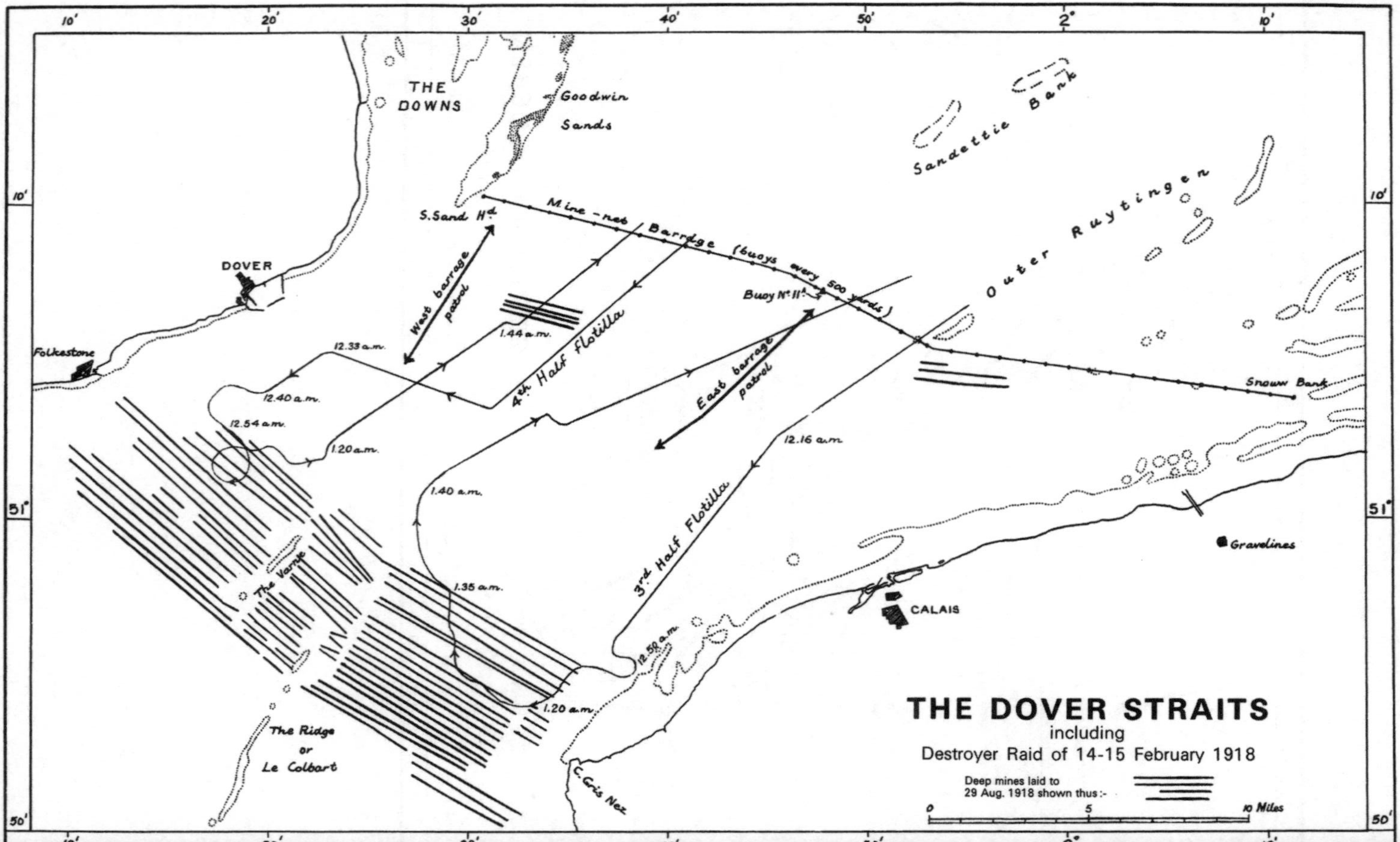

CHART 4

THE DOVER STRAITS

including

Destroyer Raid of 14-15 February 1918

Deep mines laid to
29 Aug. 1918 shown thus:-

Gravelines

CALAIS

C. Gris Nez

The Ridge
or Le Colbart

Varne

S. Sand H⁵

THE DOWNS

Goodwin Sands

DOVER

Folkestone

Snow Bank

Sandettie Bank

Outer Ruytingen

Mine-net Barrage (buoys every 500 yards)

Buoy N° 11

East Barrage patrol

West barrage patrol

3rd Half Flotilla

4th Half Flotilla

12.16 a.m.
12.28 a.m.
1.20 a.m.
1.35 a.m.
1.40 a.m.
1.44 a.m.
12.33 a.m.
12.40 a.m.
12.54 a.m.
1.20 a.m.

0   5   10 Miles

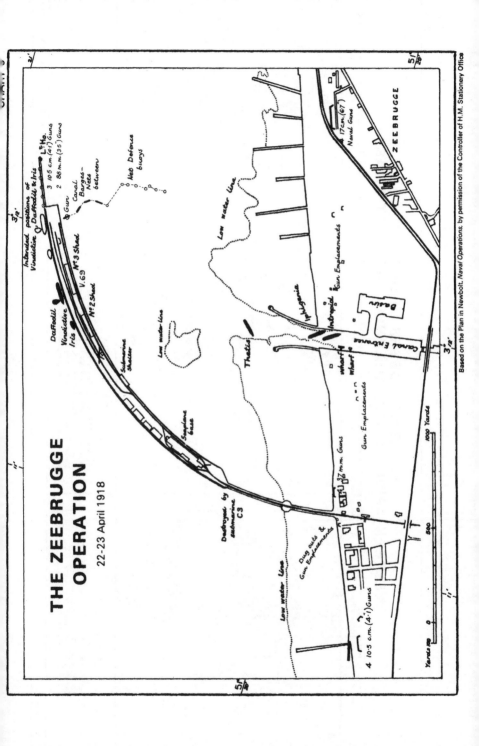

THE ZEEBRUGGE OPERATION

22-23 April 1918

Intended positions of Vindictive, Daffodil & Iris

L.te Ho.
3 10·5 c.m. (4·1") Guns
2 88 m.m. (3·5") Guns

Canal Barges – Nets between

Gun

Net Defence buoys

Daffodil
Vindictive
Iris

N.º 3 Shed
V. 69
N.º 2 Shed

Submarine Shelter

Low water line

Seaplane base

Destroyed by submarine C3

Low water line

Dug outs & Gun Emplacements

4 10·5 c.m. (4·1") Guns

Thetis

Intrepid

Iphigenia

Gun Emplacements

Basin

Canal Entrance

Wharf

Wharf

Gun Emplacements

32 m.m. Guns

Low water line

17 c.m. (6·7") Naval Guns

ZEEBRUGGE

3/2'

3/2'

Yards 100   0   500   1000 Yards

Based on the Plan in Newbolt. *Naval Operations*. by permission of the Controller of H.M. Stationery Office

CHART 6

SHIPPING LOSSES IN 1918
WESTERN APPROACHES, CHANNEL, AND EAST COAST

• - - - - - Ship sunk by U-Boat
✦ - - Ocean Convoy Assembly Point

Plan (i) 5th Quarter of Unrestricted S/M Warfare
Feb.-April 1918

Plan (ii) 6th Quarter of Unrestricted S/M Warfare
May-July 1918

Plan (iii) 7th Quarter of Unrestricted S/M Warfare
Aug.-Oct. 1918

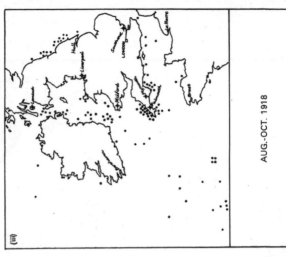

AUG.-OCT. 1918

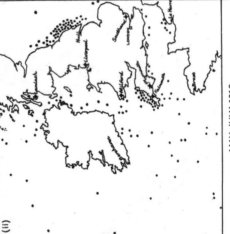

MAY-JULY 1918

By May 1918: Dover Straits Barrage fully effective:
Passage abandoned by U-Boats.
June 1918: Special Inshore Track, Downs to Portland,
started. By end of July 1918, nearly all E. Coast shipping
put into convoy and escorts strengthened from patrols.

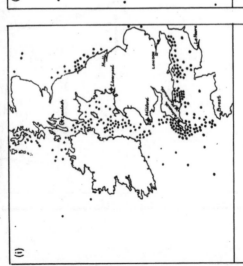

FEB.-APR. 1918

End of March 1918: Liverpool made
additional Convoy Assembly Port.
End of April 1918: New York to Bay of
Biscay Convoys started.